A Critical Edition of

An Apology for the Life of Mr. Colley Cibber, Comedian

Summary

Only the first two editions of the *Apology* are relevant to the establishment of a text, and of these the second, though it contains some corrections probably by Cibber, is in other ways inferior. The first edition has been used, therefore, as a copy text, the corrections of the second having been inserted into it.

In the Introduction I have attempted to show that Cibber, as a result of the publication of his *Apology*, became a symbol for what the Opposition saw as the degeneration of English culture under the reign of the Hanoverians and the domination of Walpole. He had become, as a result of his own failures of character and of accidents of history, a ludicrous figure in the 1730's. But after 1740, when the *Apology* appeared, he acquired a larger and more tangible significance; for his enemies he became at once cause, victim, and emblem of the decay of morals and taste in his own age. Pope fully exploited this symbolic potential in the *Dunciad* (B).

The notes of the text itself serve primarily to permit the book to fulfill adequately its promise of being a history of the stage in Cibber's time. Many corrections and amplifications have been necessary, and certain episodes are given a fuller explanation than would have been necessary for a contemporary of Cibber's. The Appendices serve merely to provide information considered too minor for the notes themselves. The work of R. W. Lowe, in his edition of the *Apology* in 1889, provided a foundation for the present work, but much new material was available for the present edition.

TABLE OF CONTENTS

SATIRE & SENSE

Important texts,
for the most part dramatic,
from the Restoration
and Eighteenth Century

Edited by
STEPHEN ORGEL
Stanford University

A GARLAND SERIES

A Critical Edition of
AN APOLOGY FOR THE LIFE OF
MR. COLLEY CIBBER, COMEDIAN

JOHN MAURICE EVANS

GARLAND PUBLISHING, INC.
NEW YORK & LONDON • 1987

Library of Congress Cataloging-in-Publication Data
Cibber, Colley, 1671–1757.
A critical edition of An apology for the life of
Mr. Colley Cibber, comedian.

(Satire & sense)
Original text of C. Cibber's an apology for
the life of Mr. Colley Cibber with corrections
inserted from the second edition.
Bibliography: p.
1. Cibber, Colley, 1671–1757—Biography.
2. Dramatists, English—18th century—Biography.
3. Theatrical managers—Great Britain—Biography.
4. Actors—Great Britain—Biography.
5. Theater—Great Britain—History—18th century.
I. Evans, John Maurice. II. Title. III. Series.
PR3347.A8 1987   828'.509 [B]   87-8749
ISBN 0-8240-6013-X (alk. paper)

The volumes in this series are printed on
acid-free, 250-year-life paper.

Printed in the United States of America

PREFACE

1

The present text of *An Apology for the Life of Mr. Colley Cibber, Comedian* follows faithfully that of the first edition which was published on 7 April 1740 in quarto and sold for one guinea—a price which drew derisive comment from Cibber's enemies. The second edition, issued soon after on 14 May 1740 was a less expensive octavo, printed probably to reap profit from the popularity of the first. Another edition, erroneously called "the fourth edition" on its title page, was printed by George Faulkner in Dublin in 1740; its precise date is unknown. From Faulkner comes one of the strongest testimonies of the *Apology*'s interest to contemporaries. According to Thomas Davies:

> As soon as Cibber's Apology [sic] reached Dublin, Falkner [sic], the printer, sent it to the Dean of St. Patrick's, who told him, next day, that Cibber's book had captivated him; he sat up all night to read it through. When Falkner [sic] gave information of this to Cibber, he shed tears of joy.[1]

From these evidences we may conclude that Cibber was closely associated with the three earliest editions of his Apology. It remains for the editor to justify his selection of the first as a copy text.

2

Eighty-eight textual variants distinguish the first and second editions, apart from variants of punctuation which I have not noted. Only a very few of these represent changes significant enough to suggest that the author himself was responsible for them. Probably no more than four can be safely attributed to Cibber. It is now impossible to determine with certainty, as will appear below, which of the remaining minor verbal changes or corrections of spelling belong to the compositor and which to Cibber.

---

[1] Thomas Davies, *Dramatic Miscellanies* (London, 1785), III, 508.

The first of Cibber's four significant revisions appears on page 44.[2] The first edition had read "From Nottingham I again return'd to my Father at *Chattsworth*, where I staid till my Lord came down, with the new Honours of Duke of *Devonshire*, Lord Stewart of his Majesty's Houshold, and Knight of the Garter!" One must suppose that the error in dating the occasion when the Earl of Devonshire was created Duke had been brought to Cibber's attention, for the second edition reads simply "till my Lord came down, with the new Honours of Lord Stewart . . ." In the first edition there had also been a slip in his placing the union of the theaters in 1708 (p. 173); in the second edition he corrected this to 1707. In the first edition the statement (p. 226) that "Mrs. Tofts was but an Adept" had been meant, presumably, to convey the meaning that she was but a novice; if this was not the fault of a compositor and, therefore, certain to be corrected in any case, the sport it provided journalists, notably Fielding in *The Champion*, caused it to be changed to "was not an Adept." Finally, Cibber improved his French at one point (p. 341) from "Place a Dame!" To "Place a la Dame."

Other changes exist, but are in most cases of a sort at least as justifiably assigned to a compositor as to Cibber. Typical is the change on p. 11 from "he can't" to "he cannot"; on p. 20 from "among'em" to "among them"; on p. 157 from "further" to "farther"; on p. 309 from "it seems amazing" to "it is amazing." Variants somewhat more difficult to assign are the second edition's "Mr. Wilks" for the first edition's "Wilks" (p. 179); "which is a Quality" for "Quality" (p. 19); and "the Conductor" for "the chief Conductor" (p. 282). These may have been Cibber's revisions, but it would be impossible to prove it. There is also a great deal of simple deterioration, and this in fact constitutes the great majority of the eighty-eight variants. Thus, on p. 61, "be so often tempted" becomes "be also tempted"; on p. 102, "may we not venture" becomes "may we may not venture"; on p. 147 "best They [sic] had done" becomes "best they done," etc.

The Dublin edition, the only other which might be considered relevant to the establishment of a text of the *Apology*, follows the readings of the first on all of the major points of variance

---

[2]Subsequent page numbers, unless otherwise indicated, refer to the present edition.

between the two London editions of 1740. Sample collations throughout show it to have no independent authority. We may suppose from Davies's anecdote, cited above, that a copy of the uncorrected first edition was sent to Faulkner in Dublin to be reset and printed there, evidently with Cibber's authorization.

Two other editions of the *Apology* appeared in Cibber's lifetime, one in 1750 and one in 1756. Both were the work of Robert Dodsley, to whom Cibber had sold his copyright for fifty guineas on 24 March 1749/50. Neither has any textual authority. To the text of the second edition of 1740, Dodsley freely added his own collection of historical and antiquarian materials on old plays and the rise of the English theater, but these lie outside our purposes here.

I have used as copy-text in this edition the 1740 London quarto. Into this I have inserted the alterations that I believe required Cibber's intervention and certain others which constitute an improvement of the original, always with indication of the original reading in the textual notes. Other changes in the second edition are always with indication of the original reading in the textual notes. Other changes in the second edition are recorded in the textual notes, but not incorporated in the text.

3

Anyone attempting to prepare a critical edition of Cibber's *Apology* owes an immense debt of gratitude to Robert W. Lowe, whose edition, published in 1889, has until now remained standard.[3] His knowledge of the theater and actors of the Restoration and early eighteenth century, and especially his important research in theatrical bibliography, have enormously benefited students of that period. His familiarity with contemporary materials is amply documented.

Lowe's information is not, however, systematically presented, nor is it really, by present standards, either very exact or very full. Later scholars like William Van Lennep, Leslie Hotson,

---

[3]*An Apology For the Life of Mr. Colley Cibber*, 2 vols. (London, 1889). Subsequent citations of Lowe's work are to this edition. I should note that Bellchambers' edition (London, 1822), upon which Lowe sometimes depends, has proved almost useless to me.

Allardyce Nicoll,[4] Emmett Avery, Arthur Scouten, John Loftis, and Richard Hindry Barker have made it possible today to test nearly every assertion Cibber makes by documents quite independent of the *Apology*. I have enjoyed, therefore, a considerable advantage over Lowe, as will be clearly seen on comparing (for example) the notes on Chapters XIV-XV in this edition with Lowe, II, 97-116, 120-49.

Throughout Cibber's age and the period following, his work, with all its rambling irregularities, remained the basic history of the English theater between 1600 and the 1730's. For this reason, modern accounts which seem to corroborate the *Apology* must be skeptically inspected to make sure that their authority derives from elsewhere. I have taken care to draw on the work of the scholars just cited only where they indicate a source of information independent of the *Apology*, and I have sought to supplement them from documents, diaries, letters, or histories that are also independent of Cibber. It is agreeable to admit that Cibber proves more often than not to have been a good historian. Where his account is accurate, I have set beside it the documentation that confirms it.

Wherever possible, I have used only documents or reprints of these. If I have often been compelled to cite the same materials as Lowe, it has been after examining the primary materials at first hand. Where Lowe directed me to materials which otherwise I might not have seen, I have given him general credit by noting that he has cited them; but only where I specifically depend upon his work, as in the quotation of Cibber's baptismal record (p. 5) have I systematically given him as a source with page references.[5] Where I have used the same materials as Lowe, I have done my best to bring others to bear as well.

Lowe's textual procedure is far from being that of a modern editor. "I have reprinted the text of the second [edition]," he states, "because it was certainly revised by the author, and many

---

[4]The works of Nicoll and Hotson are cited especially frequently in my notes to Cibber's text, and in the great majority of cases I am referring to documents which they print in part or in full rather than their summaries.

[5]Robert W. Lowe, ed., *An Apology For the Life of Mr. Colley Cibber* (London, 1889), I, 4 n. Lowe notes that he had seen the bill of sale.

corrections made. But I have carefully compared my text with that of the first edition, and, wherever the correction is more than merely verbal, I have indicated the fact in a note . . ." (I, ix). As he acknowledges, the second edition was marred by an "avalanche of commas" (I, ix) supposedly inserted by Cibber's printer; Lowe removes these, and corrects "obvious errors" (I, ix), preferring to make an emended but inferior text acceptable by his correcting rather than bring a superior text into line with its author's intentions by inserting later changes. Moreover, he forgets to state sometimes that he has gone back to the language of the quarto—e.g. at p. 109, 11. 14 and 27; p. 121, 1. 2; p. 141, 1. 15; and p. 147, 1. 24. These liberties, though minor, should be remarked, if only to correct the misleading impression which Lowe conveys, that Cibber's second edition, published five weeks after the first, contained major revisions making it more authoritative than the first. Precisely the opposite is the case.

Since a great deal of the material of the *Apology* is personal and rambling—predominantly so in the opening chapters and frequently so throughout—the choice of passages to annotate can be debated. How much expansion and background are required for Cibber's moralizing and political apologetics is a question that can be argued indefinitely. When he plays literary historian, the editor's task becomes more concrete, and editorial needs can be more surely defined. Occasionally whole chapters tended to require mainly one form of annotation, like Chapter IV, which deals largely with history (see notes on pp. 55 and 56); Chapter V, on the other hand, deals primarily with gossip about actors and actresses, causing the documentation to be largely illustrative rather than corrective and factual.

I have included in appendices a number of interesting or historically useful passages too substantial to incorporate into my notes. Also included is a Biographical Appendix, which supplies birth and death dates for the theatrical personages of the *Apology*. Of many of the actors mentioned little is known beyond what Cibber tells; others, like Betterton, are important in their own right, and are treated somewhat more fully by Cibber. In both cases, therefore, it has not seemed unjust to provide simply a brief identification. Cibber frequently deals later on more completely with a figure whom he first introduces in a list; if neither Cibber nor the editor appear on the first occasion to have done justice to a performer, the reader is advised to read on. Less prominent historical figures are accounted for systematically in the notes themselves, for they most often figure in the narrative in an incidental way rather than as recurrent *personae*.

4

To Professor Maynard Mack, who first showed me the splendors of Pope, and afterwards directed my work on the King of the Dunces, my greatest thanks are due. His kindness has been very great, both in directing my work on Cibber, and in providing encouragement in other ways. I should also like to express my gratitude to Professor Eugene Waith, who, in a seminar which began with Shakespeare and ended with the likes of Rowe and Cibber, showed me how a theatrical literature of less than the highest artistic worth could be used as the key to the significance of an era. Mr. Steven Klass, my colleague in graduate school, was most generous in allowing me to profit from his study of Cibber's relations with Pope, and Mr. Herman Taylor of Washington and Lee University has been extremely helpful in tracking down the sources of some of Cibber's Latin Tags. My thanks also extend to the staffs of the Sterling Memorial Library and the Beinecke Rare Book and Manuscript Library of Yale University, the British Museum, the Victoria and Albert Museum, The Public Record Office, and the McCormick Library of Washington and Lee University for their assistance in locating the diverse materials needed for this edition. I wish to express gratitude also for the funds supplied by Yale University Graduate School for the xeroxing of the first edition of Cibber's *Apology*, and to the John Glenn Committee of Washington and Lee University for its grant which enabled me to complete my work of tracking down materials on Cibber in London.[6] Thanks are due also Mrs. Mary Hartless for her care in preparing the final typescript. To my wife more thanks and apologies are due than can be expressed, for her support,

---

[6]I was able there to examine the few Cibber MSS. which remain, and to make use of the especially rich collections of contemporary materials available in the BM.

for her brave endurance of a long exposure to Cibber, and for her many services in the preparation of this edition.

KEY TO ABBREVIATIONS

Apology: The text of the present edition.

Apology, 2nd ed.: *An Apology for the Life of Mr. Colley Cibber, Comedian* Written by Himself. The Second Edition (London, Printed by John Watts for the Author, 1740).

Ault: Ault, Norman, *New Light on Pope* (London, 1949).

Avery: *The London Stage: 1660-1800, A Calendar of Plays, Entertainments and Afterpieces etc. . . .*, Part 2: 1700-1729, ed. Emmett L. Avery, 2 vols. (Carbondale, Ill., 1960).

Baker: Baker, David Erskine, *Biographia Dramatica, or, A Companion to the Playhouse*, 2 vols. (London, Printed for Mess. Rivingtons . . . , 1728).

Barker: Barker, Richard Hindry, *Mr. Cibber of Drury Lane* (New York, 1939).

Bellchambers: Cibber, Colley, *An Apology for the Life of Mr. Colley Cibber*, a new ed. by Edmund Bellchambers (London, 1822).

Betterton: Betterton, Thomas, *A History of the English Stage* (London, 1741).

Blast: A Blast upon Bays; or, *A New Lick at the Laureat*, 2nd ed. (London, Printed for T. Robbins, 1742).

BM: British Museum.

Boswell: *The Life of Samuel Johnson*, ed. Arnold Glover (London, 1925), 3 vols.

Burnet: Gilbert Burnet, *The History of His Own Time*, 2 vols. (London, 1724-34).

The Champion: a journal written by Henry Fielding and James Ralph, 1739-44.

Chetwood: Chetwood, William Rufus, *A General History of the Stage* (London, Printed for W. Owen, 1749).

Chetwood, *Lives*: [Chetwood, William Rufus], *The British Theatre*, containing *The Lives of the English Dramatic Poets* . . . to which is prefixed A Short View of the Rise . . . of the English Stage (Dublin, Printed for Peter Wilson, 1750).

Cibber, *Dram. Works: The Dramatic Works of Colley Cibber, Esq.*, 5 vols. (London, Printed for W. Feales, 1736).

Cibber, *Letter: A Letter from Mr. Cibber to Mr. Pope, Inquiring into the Motives that Might Induce Him in His Satyrical Works, to be so frequently Fond of Mr. Cibber's Name* (London, 1740).

Cibber, *Second Letter: A Second Letter from Mr. Cibber to Mr. Pope* (London, Printed for A. Dodd, 1743).

Comparison, ed. Wells: *A Comparison Between The Two Stages: A Late Restoration Book of The Theatre,* ed. Staring B. Wells (Princeton, 1942).

Davies, *Dram. Misc.*: Davies, Thomas, *Dramatic Miscellanies* consisting of Critical Observations of Several Plays of Shakespeare: with a Review of his Principal Characters, and Those of Various Eminent Writers . . . with Anecdotes of Dramatic Poets, Actors etc. A New Edition, 3 vols. (London, Printed for the Author [etc.], 1785).

Davies, *Garrick* (1784): Davies, Thomas, *Memoirs of the Life of David Garrick, Esq.*, 4th ed., 2 vols. (London, Printed for the Author, 1784).

DNB: *Dictionary of National Biography.*

Downes, *Roscius* (1789): *Roscius Anglicanus,* or an *Historical Review of the Stage,* with additions by the late Mr. Thomas Davies (London, Printed for the editor, 1789 [ENTERED AT STATIONERS HALL]).

Downes, *Roscius,* ed. Summers: Downes, John, *Roscius Anglicanus,* ed. Montague Summers (London, n.d.).

Dudden: Dudden, F. Homes, *Henry Fielding: His Life, Works, and Times,* 2 vols. (Oxford, 1952).

Egoist: The Egoist: or *Colley upon Cibber* (London, Printed and sold by W. Lewis, 1743).

Faber: Faber, Harold, *Caius Gabriel Cibber* (Oxford, 1926).

Genest: Genest, John, *Some Account of the English Stage, from 1660-1830,* 10 vols. (Bath, 1832).

Hotson: Hotson, Leslie, *The Commonwealth and Restoration Stage* (Cambridge, Mass., 1928).

Langbaine: *The Lives and Characters of the English Dramatic Poets.* Also An Exact Account of all the Plays that were ever yet printed in the English Tongue . . . First begun by Mr. Langbaine and continued down to this Time, by a Careful Hand [Charles Gildon] (London, Printed for Tho. Leigh [1699]).

Laureat: *The Laureat;* or, *The Right Side of Colley Cibber, Esq. . . .* to which is added, *The History of the Life of Aesopus the Tragedian* (London, Printed for J. Roberts, 1740).

Life of Betterton: [Gildon, Charles], *The Life of Mr. Thomas Betterton* (London, Printed for Robert Gosling, 1710).

Loftis, *Politics:* Loftis, John, *The Politics of Drama in Augustan England* (Oxford, 1963).

Loftis, *Steele:* Loftis, John, *Steele at Drury Lane* (Berkeley, 1952).

L.C.: Lord Chamberlain's Records.

Lowe: Cibber, Colley, *An Apology for the Life of Mr. Colley Cibber*, ed. Robert W. Lowe, 2 vols. (London, 1889).

Lowe, *Betterton*: Lowe, Robert W., *Thomas Betterton* (London, 1891).

Luttrell: Luttrell, Narcissus, *A Brief Historical Relation of State Affairs*, 6 vols. (Oxford, 1857).

Nicoll: Nicoll, Allardyce, *History of English Drama: 1660-1800*, Vol. I, Restoration, 1660-1700; Vol. II, Early Eighteenth Century.

OED: Oxford English Dictionary.

Plumb, I: Plumb, J. H., *Sir Robert Walpole: The Making of a Statesman* (London, 1956).

Plumb, II: Plumb, J. H., *Sir Robert Walpole: The King's Minister* (London, 1960).

Pope, *Correspondence: The Correspondence of Alexander Pope*, ed. George Sherburn, 5 vols. (Oxford, 1956).

Pope, *Poems: The Twickenham Edition of the Poems of Alexander Pope*, Gen. Ed. John Butt, 6 vols. (New Haven, [1951-62]).

PRO: Public Record Office.

Scouten: *The London Stage 1660-1800*, Part 3, 1729-1747, ed. Arthur Scouten, 2 vols. (Carbondale, Ill., 1961).

Senior: Senior, Dorothy, *The Life and Times of Colley Cibber* (London, 1928).

Smithers, *Addison*: Smithers, Peter, *The Life of Joseph Addison* (Oxford, 1954).

Spectator: The Spectator, ed. Gregory Smith, 4 vols. (London, n.d.).

Steele, *Theatre: Richard Steele's The Theatre: 1720*, ed. John Loftis (Oxford, 1962).

Tatler: The Tatler, ed. George Aitken, 4 vols. (London, 1898).

TC: An Apology for the Life of Mr. T... C..., being a Proper Sequel to the Apology for the Life of Mr. Colley Cibber ... (London, Printed for J. Mechell, 1740).

T. Cibber, *Lives*: Cibber, Theophilus, *The Lives and Characters of the most Eminent Actors and Actresses of Great Britain and Ireland*, Part I (London, Printed for R. Griffiths, 1753).

Van Lennep: *The London Stage: 1660-1800*, Part 1, 1660-1700, ed. William Van Lennep (Carbondale, Ill., 1965).

Victor, *London*: Victor, Benjamin, *The History of the Theatres of London and Dublin*, 2 vols. (London, Printed for T. Davies, 1761).

Victor: Victor, Benjamin, Vol. III, *The History of the Theatres of London* (London, Printed for T. Becket, 1771).

INTRODUCTION

1

By 7 April 1740, when the *Apology for the Life of Mr. Colley Cibber, Comedian* was published, Cibber had passed through a distinguished, if controversial, career as the leading actor-dramatist of his generation and had reached old age—he was in his late sixties—bearing the burden of an honor which rendered him absurd. Since his appointment in 1730 as Poet Laureate, a position which placed upon him the duty of praising a Hanoverian king, and indirectly, the increasingly resented Walpole ministry, the opposition had tended to focus some of its impotent anger upon the ludicrous verses and inept person of Cibber. Because in his years of power Walpole had gradually driven a larger number of the abler men of England into opposition and had moved repeatedly to stifle their criticism, attacks on Cibber as desecrator of the Muse, violator of language, and prostitute of wit, had acquired a more ominous character than the intrinsic absurdity of his works or his person seemingly justified. As the enemies of Walpole saw it, Cibber's coxcombry threatened to become a national disease, possibly fatal to the genius of English culture. It was Pope, finally, whose imagination gave Cibber his most important place in English literature; as Pope interpreted the evolution of politics, the intellectual and moral decay which had been permitted to spread over England since the death of Queen Anne had become triumphant in the 1730's. This vision was climaxed by a new version of the *Dunciad* in 1743 in which Cibber replaced Theobald as King of the Dunces. In order to understand how Colley Cibber evolved into this symbolic and mythic figure, and to understand what part the *Apology* had in confirming his last and permanent role, it is necessary to examine the man's own character, and his historical place in the life—and death—of the theater.

An Apology for the Life of Mr. Colley Cibber contains only a part of the truth about the life of the actor-dramatist-laureate, because it is not likely that he knew the truth about himself. The author of *The Laureat: or, The Right Side of Colley Cibber, Esq.*, a parody of the *Apology*, came close to the center of the issue when he observed,

> Now, I think, the World would not have been inflamed with any violent Curiosity to have seen him abroad, nor did they much desire it. I think too that the Motives which have prompted him thus to strip himself and dance naked before the People, were the same that incited him to act upon the Stage, *Interest* and *Vanity*. I must go farther yet, and say, that in my opinion his very Nakedness is a Disguise, and that *Colley Cibber* is not the Character he pretends to be in this Book, but a mere Charletan, a *Persona Dramatis*, a *Mountebank*, a counterfeit *Colley* . . . (p. 15)

Incisive though this may be, one must examine Cibber's life in more detail to understand the meaning of "Interest," "Vanity," "Nakedness," and "Disguise" in his *Apology*.

Throughout his career Cibber's driving force had been the desire for fame at whatever cost. It is not clear, however, that he supposed that he would pay so high a price in popular contempt and resentment. The fact that he had arrived so solidly—at least he possessed the credentials of success—enabled him to look backward from his advanced age in 1740 on the experiences of his childhood with a sense of tolerance and amusement which the reader cannot share. The earliest anecdotes of the *Apology*, which tell of his experiences in Grantham School, foreshadow a lifetime pattern of Cibber's relations with his masters and his colleagues. In 1685, when news arrived that Charles II had died, the boys at the school were assigned to write a funeral oration:

> This Oration, such as it was, I produc'd the next Morning: All the other Boys pleaded their Inability, which the Master taking rather as a mark of their Modesty than their Idleness, only seem'd to punish, by setting me at the Head of the Form: A Preferment dearly bought! Much happier had I been to have sunk my Performance in the general Modesty of declining it. A most uncomfortable Life I led among 'em, for many a Day after! I was so jeer'd, laugh'd at, and hated as a pragmatical Bastard (School-boys Language) who had betray'd the whole Form, that scarce any of 'em would keep me company; and tho' it so far advanc'd me into the Master's Favour, that he wou'd often take me from the School, to give me an Airing with him on Horseback, while they were left to their Lessons; you may be sure, such envy'd Happiness did not encrease their Good-will to me:

> Notwithstanding which, my Stupidity cou'd take no warning from their Treatment.[1]

Instead, he alone produced an ode for the coronation of James II, as he relates in the subsequent passage, an act which led to further ostracism.

Difficult to explain as the result of indifference or stupidity, these acts reveal a capacity visible all through his life to ignore the feelings and judgments of those who, properly speaking, should have been his peers and colleagues. Instead, Cibber seeks the approval of his superiors, or those in authority. As a boy of fourteen he cannot have been unaware of how offensive his actions would be to his fellow students; he must have elected consciously to seek approval from above despite certainty that this meant envy from below. "Happiness" to Colley was coterminous with escape from the ranks of ordinary men; the penalty was "envy," but envy itself became the proof of his escape.

Because he needed to be reassured from above and to be set off from the crowd, it was natural that he should choose the stage as his career when, as he relates, the refusal of Winchester College to admit him cut him off from what he assumed was the avenue to higher rank.[2] Although the stage satisfied his need to be set apart from ordinary men, the low standing of the profession in his time apparently troubled him considerably, for he devotes much attention in the *Apology* to arguing the injustice of this. He devotes considerably more to making it clear—as in the Dedication—that he had achieved social acceptance among men of high rank.[3]

Cibber's characterization of himself in the Dedication—it constitutes a frame for the chronological narrative—portrays him as a veteran of battle, at rest, laden with hard-won honors. Unfortunately, his emotional rank remained that of a private for whom the society of generals was exciting but not easy. Thus, in his Dedication "To a Certain Gentleman" (never identified) he toadies:

---

[1]*Apology*, p. 20; subsequent quotations are from the present text.
[2]*Apology*, pp. 34-35.
[3]Cf. *Apology*, pp. 45 ff.

> Let me talk never so idly to you, this way; you are, at least, under no necessity of taking it to yourself: Nor when I boast of your Favours, need you blush to have bestow'd them. Or I may now give you all the Attributes, that raise a wise, and good-natur'd Man, to Esteem, and Happiness, and not be censured as a Flatterer by my own, or your Enemies . . . (pp. *D*1-*D*2)

As it progresses, the address becomes still more fulsome:

> Nor is my *Vanity* half so much gratified, in the Honour, as my Sense is in the *Delight* of your Society! When I see you lay aside the Advantages of Superiority, and by your own Chearfulness of Spirits, call out all that Nature has given me to meet them; then 'tis I taste you! then Life runs high! I desire! I possess you! (p. *D*7)

To which the author of *The Laureat*, with perfect aptness, replied,

> Fye, *Colley*, Fye; have some small Regard to Decency; you cou'd go no higher than this if your *Patron* were of the *Feminine Gender*. (p. 7)

Cibber's embarrassing adjectness joined with his rapturous, unconscious suggestion of sexual union illustrates, as strongly as possible, how little capacity he possessed for controlling the figure he presented. This obtuseness, a disadvantage for anyone, would seem in an actor and dramatist grounds for certain failure. Though the author never permits his reader to forget his successes, contempt for the man, even before he came Poet Laureat, was widespread.

Indeed, he seized any occasion to proclaim his importance. In recalling how the Earl of Chesterfield (whom he coyly leaves nameless, but does not fail to identify as a *Lord*) teased his friends without giving offense, Cibber remarks,

> Having often had the Honour to be my self the Butt of his Raillery, I must own I have receiv'd more Pleasure from his lively manner of raising the Laugh against me, than I could have felt from the smoothest flattery of a serious Civility. Tho' Wit flows from him with as much ease as common Sense from another, he is so little elated with the Advantage he may have over you, that whenever your good Fortune gives it against him, he seems more pleas'd with it on your side than his own. The only advantage he makes of his Superiority of Rank is, that by always waving [sic] it himself, his inferior finds he is under the greater Obligation not to forget it. (p. 10)

All this his eminence as an actor had opened for him. It is evident that Cibber believed that he had

the approval of men of rank. His professional life had served as a means to achieve a social end,

and in itself did not confirm his sense of his own worth. What really counted for him was the

illusion that his achievement had placed him on an equal footing with the highest ranks of society.

He goes on with serene arrogance to remark, later in the same chapter,

> When I look into my present Self, and afterwards cast my Eye round all my Hopes,
> I don't see any one Pursuit of them that shou'd so reasonably rouze me out of a
> Nod in my Great Chair, as a call to those agreeable Parties I have sometimes the
> Happiness to mix with, where I always assert the equal Liberty of leaving them,
> when my Spirits have done their best with them. (p. 12)

No doubt Cibber's success in society was real, for he "performed" to the best of his

powers for the "great," the only audience he ever really cared for. Nevertheless, one suspects that

Chesterfield's "raillery" may not have been quite so benign and lacking in irony as Cibber, in his

uncritical bliss, supposed. On the stage Cibber's only claim to greatness as an actor was in the role

of coxcomb.[4] It is not difficult to imagine that in his social life he unintentionally played the same

role as a subtle flattery to the powerful men he wished to please.

> As for his conversation in the company of men of wit, Dr. Johnson remarked that,
> taking from [it] all that he ought not to have said, he was a poor creature ... It is
> wonderful that a man, who for forty years had lived with the great and witty,
> should have acquired so ill the talents of conversation: and he had but half to
> furnish; for one half of what he said was oaths.[5]

3

The image of Cibber swearing and strutting calls to mind Sir Plume in *The Rape of the

Lock*, in whom also fear led to bluster.[6] It also led in Cibber's case to a love for roles in the grand

style. The author of a parody of the *Apology* remarks,

---

[4]Cf. Barker, pp. 32-33. See Also Appendix F.
[5]Boswell, II, 127.
[6]E.g., Canto IV, 127-30.

... how odd it is, that he should take so much Pains, that he should labour so hard to be thought to be (what he himself owns he cou'd not by Nature be) a good Tragedian; every Body owns him excellent in Comedy ... [7]

His failure in heroic parts was absolute. Nevertheless, he could not bring himself to accept his limitations. Instead he resorted to sophisticated defenses, both claiming and disavowing greatness in tragedy:

I have elsewhere allow'd, that my want of a strong and full Voice, soon cut short my Hopes of making any valuable Figure, in Tragedy; and I have been many Years since, convinced, that whatever Opinion I might have of my own Judgement, or Capacity to amend the palpable Errors, that I saw our Tragedians, most in favour, commit; yet the Auditors, who would have been sensible of any such Amendments (could I have made them) were so very few, that my best Endeavor would have been but an unavailing Labour, or, what is yet worse might have appeared both to our Actors, and to many Auditors, the vain mistake of my own Self-Conceit.[8]

In his early career after the turn of the century, as he edged nearer the center of power, that is, out of the rank of common actors, he toadied to his master, John Rich, a fact he admits in a manner somewhat shamefaced and disguised. On the other hand, as he acquired power himself and became a manager of the Drury Lane Theater, his insecurity betrayed him into precisely the patterns of bluster and deception which had made him despise Rich. His need for approbation led him, neurotically, to behave in a way that produced its opposite. Inwardly irresolute, he bullied; inwardly unsure of his worth, he proclaimed it. Though he achieved a measure of unquestionable success as a theater manager, it was at the cost of almost total alienation from fellow actors, from fellow managers—his jealousy of Booth and Wilks is apparent throughout the *Apology*—and from playwrights whom he took perverse pleasure in humiliating before the company, an act which he joyfully termed "*Choaking* of *Singing*-Birds."[9] His relations with actors were notorious; Davies remarks that "his treatment of the actors has been generally condemned as unfriendly, if not tyrannical."[10]

---

[7]*Laureat*, p. 41; Cf. Appendix F.
[8]*Apology*, p. 128.
[9]*Laureat*, p. 121; cf. *TC*, p. 71, and Davies, *Dram. Misc.*, III, 473-76.
[10]Davies, *Dram. Misc.*, III, 504; See also pp. 486-91.

As he represents his relations with these men in the *Apology*, hostilities arose because they failed to recognize his good will. His colleagues, like his fellows in school, were unimportant to him, but because they were nearer to him as he wrote his memoirs, he represents their motives far less charitably. He sees their opposition to his climb toward success as motivated by deep corruption of character. Even his closest associates, like Booth and Wilks, as they appear in the *Apology*, balance precariously on the knife-edge of wickedness. An avowed enemy, Christopher Rich, falls immediately into the pattern of the clever tempter, unrelenting and subtle. Relating how Wilks, early in his acting career, strengthened his own position to a point where he could make demands of Rich, Cibber remarks:

> Not but our good Master, was as sly a Tyrant, as ever was at the Head of a Theatre; for he gave the Actors more Liberty and fewer Days Pay, than any of his Predecessors: He would laugh with them over a Bottle, and bite them, in their Bargains: He kept them poor, that they might not be able to rebel; and sometimes merry, that they might not think of it . . . (p. 146)

When Wilks pressed for payment of his overdue salary, Cibber reveals himself to have been Rich's confidant, but in the role of arbitrator, selflessly advancing the proud and ungrateful Wilks' cause:

> How far soever my Advice might have contributed to our Master's settling his Affairs upon this Foot [to Wilks' advantage], I never durst make the least Merit of it to Wilks, well knowing that his great Heart would have taken it as a mortal Affront had I (tho' never so distantly) hinted, that his Demands had needed any Assistance, but the Justice of them. (p. 149)

Unlike the hated John Rich, Cibber never lost control of the theater. With his fellow managers, he succeeded in meeting the formidable challenge presented by Italian opera, pantomime, and even ballad-opera, though in every case, even when he sustained himself against the innovators by copying them, he hated having to adjust. Probably his only real innovation in theatrical taste came at the beginning of his career (1696), when he wrote what is often termed the first sentimental comedy, *Love's Last Shift*. [11]   As for the rest, his own plays exploited fashions

which others originated or opportunities others had the integrity to resist. The most notorious

instances were *The Non-Juror* and *Love in a Riddle*. *The Non-Juror* (1717) shamelessly took

advantage of anti-Catholic sentiments lingering from the Stuart uprising of 1715, and won him the

enduring hatred of Tories, Jacobites, and Catholics. Because the Ideology of the play fitted so

perfectly the needs of George I's ministry, the king gave Cibber a purse of 200 pounds as a

reward.[12] Much later (1728), having refused Gay's *Beggar's Opera* and thereby missed the

greatest theatrical success of the age, he attempted to imitate it the following season with his insipid

Love in a Riddle.

> After the vast Success of that new Species of Dramatick Poetry, the *Beggars Opera*:
> The Year following, I was so stupid, as to attempt something of the same Kind,
> upon a quite different Foundation, that of recommending Virtue, and Innocence;
> which I ignorantly thought, might not have a less Pretence to favour, than setting
> Greatness, and Authority, in a contemptible, and the most vulgar Vice, and
> Wickedness, in an amiable Light. (p. 141)

Gay meanwhile had written *Polly*; for unexplained reasons it was forbidden by the Lord

Chamberlain, though this probably constituted an act of revenge for the injuries sustained by Sir

Robert Walpole in *The Beggar's Opera*. *The Craftsman*, a Tory journal edited by Pulteny and

Bolingbroke, insinuated in a manner typical of opposition newspapers, that Cibber was personally

responsible for the interdiction of *Polly*.[13]

> What an involuntary Compliment did the Reporters of this Falshood [sic] make me?
> to suppose me of Consideration enough, to influence a great Officer of State, to
> gratify the Spleen, or Envy, of a Comedian, so far, as to rob the Publick of an
> innocent Diversion (if it were such) that none, but that cunning Comedian, might be
> suffered to give it them. This is so very gross a Supposition, that it needs only its
> own senseless Face, to confound it; let that alone, then, be my Defence against it.
> (p. 143)

---

[11]E.G., Ernest Bernbaum, *The Drama of Sensibility* (Cambridge, Mass., 1915), pp. 1-2,
72-77.

[12]Cibber, *Letter,* p. 24.

[13]*The Craftsman*, 14 December 1728.

Nonetheless, the result was that the opposition saw to it that Cibber's play, a dreary affair of innocent shepherds and oracles, met a swifter death than its defects would have led to.

Despite ever-present elements of farce in his career as actor, manager, and author, Cibber contributed significantly to keeping legitimate theater alive during a difficult time, when the audience of courtiers who had supported the Restoration theater turned in dangerous numbers to the novelty of Italian opera, and when the new middle-class audiences were bemused by flashy pantomimes and the extravagant shows to be found in the rival theaters. But by the late 1720's, he was established as a partisan figure, unhonored by those whose liberty to satirize the government was in part due to him,[14] and wearied by the responsibilities which he held.

4

On 27 September 1730, Laurence Eusden, the Poet Laureate, died; and for the post, which would be filled from the threadbare ranks of poets whose political opinions or loyalties did not render them unacceptable, three moved to the fore: Lewis Theobald, Pope's old rival as editor of Shakespeare and reigning King of Dulness; Stephen Duck, the "thresher poet," who was enjoying a moment of fashion at court; and Colley Cibber, whose claims to the office were weakest, since he had no reputation at all as a poet. The strong contender appeared to be Duck.[15] It is probable that Pope wrote the following epigram which appeared in the *Grub-Street Journal*, 2 November 1730:

> Shall Royal praise be rhym'd by such a ribald,
> As fopling C[ibbe]r, or Attorney T[heobal]d?
> Let's rather wait one year for better luck;
> One year may make a singing Swan of *Duck.*
> Great G—! such servants since thou well can'st lack,

---

[14]Cf. Introduction below, pp. lv ff.

[15]Barker, pp. 154-64, provides a detailed account of the struggle. Ault, pp. 315-24, supplements Barker.

Oh! save the Salary, and drink the Sack![16]

He followed this on 19 November 1730 in *The Guardian* with a discussion of the election noting,

> ... a *canticle* must be composed and sung in laud and praise of the new poet. If Mr. CIBBER be laureated, it is my opinion no man can *write* this but himself: And no man, I am sure, can *sing* it so affectingly.[17]

For whatever reasons, and none can satisfactorily explain the choice, the Duke of Grafton, as Lord Chamberlain, officially named Cibber, 3 December 1730. His action annoyed and surprised nearly everyone.

The reaction was at first satire focusing upon the absurdity of the choice; Pope, in the 1735 edition of his *Works*, closed a note to the first *Dunciad* with the following biting couplets:

> In merry old England it once was a rule,
> The King had his Poet, and also his Fool:
> But now we're so frugal, I'd have you to know it,
> That C[ibbe]r can serve both for Fool and for Poet.[18]

Cibber's official verse soon vindicated all those who had ridiculed his appointment. From the moment his first *New Year's Ode* appeared without his consent in the *Gentleman's Magazine* (January, 1731),[19] his productions were occasions for gleeful parody. It is clear that Cibber did not value his official poems very highly, but he was not without a certain pride in them. In 1743, he complained that his poems, "constantly creep into papers without my consent or knowledge. How they come there I do not give myself the trouble to inquire. Probably some poor spy of the press may filch them out of the several parts of the voices at a practice."[20] Pride in his work also appears in Dr. Johnson's anecdote:

---

[16]Pope, *Poems*, VI, 327, 330.

[17]Reprinted in Pope, *Poems*, V, 415-16.

[18]*Dunciad* (a), line 319; Pope, *Poems*, V, 186-87.

[19]Barker, p. 161, notes that the *Grub-Street Journal* devoted a full page to it, and that other newspapers continued the assault long afterwards.

[20]*Egoist*, p. 50.

Colley Cibber once consulted me as to one of his birth-day Odes, a long time before it was wanted. I objected very freely to several passages. Cibber lost patience, and would not read his Ode to an end . . . [21]

We do not know the ode Johnson was referring to, but the sort of thing that drew his objections

may perhaps be inferred from the following:

> The Sun, we saw precede,
> Those mighty Joys restor'd,
> Gave to our future Need,
> From great Plantagenet a Lord.
>
> From whose high Veins this greater Day arose,
> A second GEORGE, to fix our World's Repose,
> From CHARLES restor'd, short was our term of Bliss,
> But GEORGE from GEORGE entails our Happiness.
>
> *From a Heart, that abhors the Abuse of High Pow'r*
> *Are our Liberties duly defended;*
> *From a Courage, inflam'd by the Terrors of War,*
> *With his fame, is our Commerce extended.*
>
> *Let our publick high Spirits be rais'd, to their Height*
> *Yet our Prince, in that Virtue, will lead 'em.*
> *From our Welfare, he knows that his Glory's more bright;*
> *As Obedience enlarges our Freedom.*[22]

Cibber, however unable he might be to improve on them, was too intelligent a man not to

realize how pitiful such efforts were. He could only be embarrassedly aware that he stood, at least

in title, at the head of the ranks of living English poets, while below him in the official hierarchy

stretched Pope, Swift, Gay, Thomson, Dyer, etc. In the *Apology*, for instance, his account of his

appointment reveals a curious attitude, both defensive and humble:

In the Year 1730, there were many Authors, whose Merit wanted nothing but Interest to recommend them to the vacant *Laurel,* and who took it ill, to see it at last conferr'd upon a Comedian; . . (p. 28)

---

[21]Boswell, II, 356.

[22]Quoted in Kenneth Hopkins, *The Poets Laureate* (New York, 1955), pp. 225-26.

He goes on to sneer at the deluge of "Epigrams, and satyrical Flirts" set going by his enemies, and to recount how his friends cruelly made sure that he saw them all. His mention of Pope as "our most celebrated living Author" has a pathetic ring to it. He turns about, nonetheless, and insists that Pope's attacks on him were inspired by need to boost the sale of his poems:

> He considers that my Face and Name are more known than those of many thousands of more consequence in the Kingdom: That therefore, right or wrong, a Lick at the *Laureat* will always be a sure Bait, *ad captandum vulgus*, to catch him little Readers! . . (p. 22)

Cibber continually hovered at the threshold of self-recognition. "His very Nakedness is a Disguise," the author of *The Laureat* had maintained, and we may understand this to mean a disguise which protected Colley himself from the unendurable recognition of his own triviality and his failure to achieve greatness. The jauntiness and friskiness of his exposures disclose the pitiable half-light in which he saw himself.

Cibber's genuine social success followed his being appointed Laureate. The office gave him social prestige; he became "a person of some standing in the world—he was indeed almost respectable. He could go to court, he could discuss the plans for the royal birthday, . . . he could mingle familiarly with the fine gentlemen at White's . . . . The doors of the beau monde were at last open to him and he took full advantage of his opportunities."[23] Not long after his entry into society began the disintegration of the old triumvirate of managers of the Drury Lane Theater: Cibber, Wilks, and Booth (their patent had been renewed on 3 July 1732). Booth retired in July 1732; Wilks died 27 September 1733; and Cibber, having temporarily assigned his share and authority to his son Theophilus, abruptly sold it for a large profit a few months later and withdrew altogether from the management of the theater.[24] He moved completely into the world of society

---

23Barker, p. 162.
24Barker, p. 167.

which he was enjoying fully for the first time. After this he made appearances as a hired actor, frequently in the 30's, less commonly in the 40's.[25]

5

It is not surprising that Cibber's name appears in Pope's *Imitations of Horace* published during the 1730's. Personal hostilities between the two, begun by the *Non-Juror*[26] and revived by Cibber's supposed part in the suppression of *Polly*, no doubt lay behind Pope's readiness to satirize Cibber. Yet in the *Imitations*, Pope increasingly dramatized himself as the scourge of a society gradually shifting off its center. The many figures who appear in those poems acquire symbolic values that often seem to distort historical fact and the ambivalences of personality in order to express the meaning of his own time in its widest perspective. (An obvious instance of this is the treatment of Lord Hervey in the *Epistle to Dr. Arbuthnot*, where he becomes the Tempter "at the ear of Eve," Queen Caroline.)[27]

What is really surprising is the infrequency of Cibber's name in the *Imitations*. Except for, "And has not Colly [sic] still his Lord, and Whore?" (l. 97) in the *Epistle to Dr. Arbuthnot,* the dozen or so references to Cibber in Pope's acknowledged poems or in their critical paraphernalia during this period rarely represent him in an entirely negative way. Indeed, in the *First Epistle of the Second Book of Horace, Imitated* (1737), Pope went out of his way to praise Cibber's best play:

> . . . the People's Voice is odd,
> It is, and it is not, the voice of God.
> To Gammer Gurton if it give the bays,
> And yet deny the Careless Husband praise,
> Or say our fathers never broke a rule;
> Why then I say, the Publick is a fool.
> (89-94)

---

[25]As full a listing of casts during this period was possible is provided by Scouten; q.v. I, lxxxix-xc.

[26]Ault, pp. 298-311, provides a detailed account of these beginnings.

[27]Pope, *Poems*, IV, 118, line 319.

Later Cibber maintained, in speaking of these lines, "The late General *Dormer* intimated to me, that he believed Mr. *Pope* intended them as a Compliment to *The Careless Husband*; but if it be a Compliment, I rather believe it was a compliment to that Gentleman's Good-nature, who told me a little before this Epistle was publish'd that he had been making Interest for a little Mercy to his Friend *Colley* in it."[28] However that may be, the lines stand. It is clear that Pope knew Cibber's limitations, but their essential differences, as recently as 1738, when the *First Epistle of the First Book of Horace, Imitated*, appeared, had not led to open hostility. In that poem Pope merely complains that he is,

> Now sick alike of Envy and of Praise.
> Publick too long, ah let me hide my Age!
> See modest Cibber now has left the Stage: . . . (4-6)

Whatever ironies gleam in it, this statement should not in itself have made Cibber unhappy. If he had any grounds during this period for feeling that Pope persecuted him, the justification lay in a number of devastatingly witty occasional poems which Pope circulated, mainly anonymously.[29]

It is necessary, therefore, to look beyond personal hostilities between Pope and the Laureate if Pope's recasting of the revised version of the *Dunciad* is to be understood. By 1742 Pope appears to have had little if anything against Cibber, but he had everything against what Cibber espoused, profited from, and symbolized.

6

Because resentment against Walpole had grown more vehement during the 1730's, parody of Cibber's official Birthday and New Year odes and mockery of his role as Poet Laureate had become commonplace practices of opposition wits. These became still more frequent in the latter years of the decade. In the pages of *Common Sense*, an anti-government newspaper patronized by

---

[28]Cibber, *Letter*, p. 52.
[29]Cf. Pope, *Poems*, VI, 302, 305, 327, 360.

Chesterfield, Lyttleton, and other friends of Pope,[30] he was identified with the Goddess of Nonsense or Dullness. His laureateship was made increasingly a symbol of the political and literary state and his poetry an epitome of the taste of the age. On Saturday, 16 December 1737, *Common Sense* printed the following speech:

> I am Nonsense, Terrestrial Goddess, your [Common Sense's] avow'd and irreconciliable Foe; who finding no Adoration in *White-Fryers*, have fix'd my Shrine in *Bartholomew Close* . . . My Power is too universally known and acknowledg'd, not to be dreaded by all those who dare oppose me. I have the Ladies, the Poetasters, and the M[inister] on my Side . . .
> The present glorious *Laureat* is a poet after my own Heart . . .

Admitting that Cibber had fallen once from her favor when he wrote *The Careless Husband*, Nonsense ends by claiming "but he is now all, and forever, my own; and I can boast of no greater Work, even among the most happy Labours of my most laborious Bards, than the last *incomprehensible Ode* upon the 30th of *October* [the kind's birthday]."

This passage shows how general was the acceptance of the mythic frame which the Scriblerians had imposed on contemporary history. What is more surprising is how perfectly Cibber's characterization of himself in the earlier chapters of the *Apology* accords ironically with observations published in *Common Sense*, 8 March 1740, the month before the appearance of the *Apology*. The author of the article was distressed by his profound intuition that his civilization was being undermined, not by aggressive or external evil, but by dry rot. Outwardly this decay was visible only in irresponsible use of language. But where words are misused, meaning and action no longer seem necessarily linked, and reform becomes impossible.

> When A Vice or a Folly grows prevalent and fashionable, it changes its Name at its Confirmation, assumes a softer, if not a meritorious one, and under this Protection it becomes invidious at least, if not dangerous to attack and expose it. In this Confusion and Misapplication of Denominations, Vice exults in its Exemption from Infamy its greatest Check, and Virtue mourns the Loss of those honorary Distinctions so justly due to her, and but too often her only Reward; while the Unwary mistaking the Signs, frequently set up to their Cost at the wrong House . .
>
> [One] would not at first imagine, that a Man of nice and jealous Honour, only meant a deliberate Murtherer; a careful Man, a Thief; an honest Gentleman, only a

---

[30]George Sherburn, ed., *Pope*, Correspondence, IV, 209, n.

> Whig or Tory, according as the person is who gives him the character; or that a very honest Fellow, meant nothing but a very drunken one; and a very good Sort of Man, or a very good-natur'd Man, meant either nothing at all, or meant a Fool. Yet this is the true State of the Case, as daily Experience shows us . . .

Good nature, or good humor, a traditional virtue, in its new form merely serves to justify those who wish to take advantage of a general inability to discriminate between decent amiability and moral turpitude.

> But there is a much worse, and more numerous Sort of Fools; which are the crafty, subtle designing Fools; who rise just enough out of the Fool, to get a little into the Knave, and who have just Sense enough to know, that they have not Sense enough to recommend them, and therefore have Recourse to the Appearances of great good Nature, which they produce upon all Occasions like Bills of Health, to get Admittance. These people have reduc'd good Nature to a Science, and proceed systematically. They have the word always in their Mouths, and declare it to be the Rule by which they guide themselves, and judge of others.

After passing over fools genuinely without the power of judgment, the author proceeds to discuss those who exploit the tolerance of others:

> These Fools are the implacable Enemies of Men of Parts; they hint and lament their ill Nature; wish they would employ their Wit better, and even thank God that they have none themselves, since they find it is always to be exercised at the expense of good Nature. Thus endeavouring (as indeed it is their Interest) to confound Wit and ill Nature together, and make them seem inseparable. With these the numerous Body of abler knaves combines, though from different Motives, and between them both, under the false and interested Pretense of good Nature, they have almost establish'd a general amnesty for Vice and Folly.

The shift and disintegration of moral values in the period, as the opposition viewed it, were perfectly represented in Cibber's explanations of himself. To be sure, he expected sympathy for the folly he confessed: "But why make my Follies publick? Why not? I have passed my Time very pleasantly with them."[31] When viewed from the perspective of the *Common Sense* writer, Cibber's indulgence made him the perfect man of the times. His moralizing self-justification in the opening chapter of the *Apology* fitted the needs of the opposition satirist like a glove:

> Even admitting they [Cibber's follies] were injudiciously chosen, would it not be Vanity in me to take Shame to myself for not being found a Wise Man? Really, Sir, my Appetites were in too much haste to be happy, to throw away my Time in pursuit of a Name I was sure I could never arrive at. (p. 2)

---

[31]*Apology*, p. 2.

Later in the same chapter, his new morality is even more explicit:

> Now, as among the better sort, a readiness of Wit is not always a Sign of intrinsick Merit; so the want of that readiness is no Reproach to a Man of plain Sense and Civility, who therefore (methinks) should never have these lengths of Liberty taken with him. Wit there becomes absurd, if not insolent; ill-natur'd I am sure it is, which Imputation a generous spirit will always avoid, for the same Reason that a Man of real Honour will never send a Challenge to a Cripple. (pp. 7-8)

Though Cibber presents his exaltation of happiness and good nature as a defense of his own life, by extension he is defending—at least as his enemies saw it—the new order. This line of argument had already been anticipated and rejected by the opposition in the article from *Common Sense* quoted above.

Cibber's easy tolerance of his own failings was firmly associated with the politically expedient conduct by which, notoriously, Walpole had rescued from retribution the ministers regarded as responsible for the South Sea Bubble, and by which he had risen to leadership in Parliament during the years 1721-22, earning for himself the title of Skreen-Master General.[32]

> The protecting and skreening of Iniquity and Guilt, especially with Relation to the Publick, is most unjustly term'd good Nature: Though it can only proceed from a Participation of the Crime, a Willingness to commit it, or a Consciousness of equal Guilt. Virtue knows no Indulgence to Crimes, it punishes the Offence, though it pities the Offender. The avow'd Patron and *Skreen* of all Corruption and publick Guilt, has wisely and *for good Reasons* propagated, and establish'd this Doctrine; and branded with the want of *good Nature* and *Candour* those who, from a real Benevolence to Mankind, endeavor to detect and punish such Crimes, as necessarily tend to the Subversion of all Government and the Ruin of all Society.[33]

Thus, moral laxity joined with sentimental tolerance were for the opposition the identifying characteristics of the Walpole era.

Among the opposition, therefore, may be seen a tendency in the months following the publication of the *Apology* to satirize Walpole through the figure of Cibber.

> The Person who at present happens to be the Object of publick Hatred, has been made to pass in Review before the People several Times, within these few Years:—He has been dress'd up as a *Sejanus*, as a *Pallas*, the Freedman,—as a *Gaviston* [sic], a *Spenser* [sic], and a *Woolsey* [sic]; But, as if too much Honour had been done him, even by satyrizing him under those Names, a facetious Author

---

[32]Plumb, I, 283-328, 329-58, and 359-80.

[33]*Common Sense*, 8 March 1740.

has now degraded him into a Player, and attacked him at once in the Character of *Colley Cibber*, Comedian, and of Aesopus the Tragedian.[34]

The article continues, speaking of the book-length parody and attack on Cibber's *Apology, The Laureat: Or, The Right Side of Colley Cibber*, which had printed with it a second attack called the *Life of Aesopus the Tragedian*::

> ... diverted with the Author's pleasant and genteel Raillery, before I suspected that any Thing farther was intended than to make the Publick merry at the Expence of an absurd, wrong-headed Character, who contrived to become as odious in his Mock-Ministry, as it was possible for ᵔ Man in his low Station of Life to make himself,—by Degrees the Lineam' ʌts of another Person began to appear, at last his whole Figure, so plain, that I forgot *Cibber* and *Aesopus*.

It becomes clear, therefore, that an attack on Cibber could be expected to be understood as an indirect—and safe—assault on the King's Minister:

> ... I made an End of my Pamphlet, and met with the description of another Actor, (I am afraid a much worse Actor than *Cibber*) one who has play'd his Part upon a very large Stage, and had the greatest part of *Europe* for Spectators; his Fate has indeed been different from that of *Cibber, Cibber* has met with various Success, sometimes applauded, tho' oftner rebuked; but this other Actor has been hiss'd from his first Appearance upon the Stage, to this very Day ...

Furthermore, the poets and journalists who were believed by the opposition to be in the hire of Walpole were not infrequently referred to as "Sons of Dullness" who "eat the Bread of Flattery."[35]

That poets might praise the ministry was explained by the hypothesis that they were hired.

> That Legion of Duncers which our Great Man, to shew his excellent Judgment and fine Taste, hath listed into his service, have tired all the Excisement and Custom-House Offices, from the Orchades to the Land's End of the County of *Cornwall*, with stupid Encomiums On the Advantages of Bribery, Corruption, and all the Tricks and Rogueries necessary for supporting an arbitrary and blundering Minister; but they have not (that I can recollect) made their Addresses in form to that Goddess under whose auspicious Influence they live and write.[36]

---

[34]*Common Sense*, 13 December 1740.
[35]*Common Sense*, 23 August 1740.
[36]*Common Sense*, 23 August 1741.

In the "Panegyrick upon DULNESS" which follows, the condition of Britain is ironically praised in a lengthy—and dull—catalogue of ills; it is worthy of note primarily as evidence of the use made of the mythology of the 1728 *Dunciad*.

7

By the end of the 1730's Cibber was becoming, willy-nilly, a symbol. His pathetic efforts to provide an *Apology* which would somehow show the world that the public figure was a caricature of a wise man who could recognize his own vanity—and that of the world—and still laugh, seemed to have come to nothing. Instead of being accepted by his deprecators as a gesture of reconciliation, the *Apology* had provided them with ammunition to use against him. The full powers of Cibber's imagination had been employed in the only half-intentional structuring of his book as a struggle of order, represented by the Whig-Walpole Party, against disorder, represented by Tories, Catholics, Jacobites, opera, pantomimes, and rival playhouses.

As the drama unfolds in the *Apology*, the representative of order, who is Cibber himself, moves onto the historical scene with the Glorious Revolution, and onto the stage shortly after.[37] His efforts first to find a place for himself in the theater, and then to dominate it are worked out so that the passage of the Stage Licensing Act of 1737 stands as a triumph, a death blow both to irresponsible Tory counter-revolutionary propaganda and to the debilitating struggle to keep competing theaters alive. The Licensing Act symbolized, for a Walpolean, the death blow to the forces of disharmony. But for a man committed to the social, moral, and religious, of not necessarily to the political order of the past, it symbolized a final disaster to humane letters (and civilization), the culminating victory in a campaign which had begun with the accession of George I. Fortunately, Cibber's basic *intention* to be truthful—allowing for considerable warping of facts

---

[37]In the *Apology*, p. 37, Cibber remarks of the Revolution of 1688, ". . . you cannot but observe, that the Fate of King *James,* and of the Prince of *Orange*, and of so minute a Being as my self, were at once upon the Anvil . . ."

to make his part seem consistent—producted a rich dialectical narrative, with the eternal battle to maintain order against chaos sounding through historical and personal events. The book enabled Cibber to be seen as a partisan of the Whig-Hanoverian version of the New Jerusalem, or as a prince and general of Triumphant Dulness.

It is not surprising that in his references to his political loyalties during the era of the Tory ministry, from 1710 until the death of Anne, Cibber implies that he was a dedicated Whig; Loftis, however, cites a suggestion by John Dennis in 1720, that Cibber's Whig loyalty began in 1715: "I would fain hear of some Proof that he gave his Zeal for the Protestant Succession, before the King's Accession to the Crown."[38] It is impossible now to judge whether the memory of an elderly man had deceived him into believing in the role he constructed, or whether this distortion of fact represents conscious disingenuousness. Whatever the truth may be, the effect of his self-dramatization was to make identical his own, the theater's, and the nation's well-being. His version of history suggests that after the accession of George I, which was also the period of the ascendancy of Wilks, Booth, and Cibber, the only disorders resulted from the lingering powers of Tory malevolence. The earlier importation and rise of opera and the development of pantomime are conceived (as by Pope and others) to be a betrayal of national culture:

> Although the Opera is not a Plant of our Native Growth, nor what our plainer Appetites are fond of, and is of so delicate a Nature, that without excessive Charge, it cannot live long among us; especially while the nicest *Connoisseurs* in Musick fall into such various Heresies in Taste, every Sect pretending to be the true one: Yet, as it is call'd a Theatrical Entertainment, and by its Alliance, or Neutrality, has more, or less affected our Domestick Theatre, a short View of its Progress may be allow'd a Place in our History. (p. 224)

Throughout he implies that opera is decadent and that the taste for it is effete, a source of division:

> But what is still more ridiculous, these costly Canary-birds [Italian singers] have sometimes infested the whole Body of our dignified Lovers of Musick, with . . . childish Animosities: Ladies have been known to decline their Visits, upon Account of their being of a different musical Party. *Caesar* and *Pompey* made not a warner Division, in the *Roman* Republick, than those Heroines, their Country

---

[38]From the "Advertisement" prefixed to Dennis' *The Invader of His Country*, quoted by Loftis, *Politics*, pp. 56-57. See *Apology*, p. 208 and n.

Women, the *Faustina* and *Cuzzoni* blew up in our Common-wealth, of Academical Musick, by their implacable Pretensions to Superiority! (p. 243)

Disagreement in the arts and more particularly competition among theaters, no matter how trivial, is seen to undermine the nation, and to result from a failure of reason. In this respect Pope and Cibber stand remarkably close: as in Book IV of the *Dunciad*, the voice of Italian opera ironically says,

'O *Cara! Cara!* silence all that train [the Muses]:
Joy to great Chaos! let Division reign:
Chromatic tortures soon shall drive them hence,
Break all their nerves, and fritter all their sense:
One Trill shall harmonize joy, grief, and rage,
Wake the dull Church, and lull the ranting Stage;
To the same notes thy sons shall hum, or snore,
And all thy yawning daughters cry, *encore.* (53-60)

Cibber's detestation of Italian opera lacked Pope's detachment. At every reference, it is clear that his main objection to it lay in its success in attracting audiences which he thought properly belonged to him and Drury Lane.

The theme of money stands as a touchstone of Cibber's value system. The *Apology*'s continual discussion of financial negotiations reveals how profoundly its author embraced a commercial interpretation of social health. For Cibber the only reliable index by which to evaluate the theater, a play, or an actor—not to mention a government—was its capacity to enhance and increase prosperity. Although as a manager his duty was to draw audiences (and one must sympathize with him in this) the degree to which he was willing to swallow his pride for success shocked his own age. As Fielding remarked,

. . . How completely doth he arm us against so uneasy, so wretched a passion as the fear of shame! how clearly doth he expose the emptiness and vanity of that phantom, reputation![39]

In all these ways the *Apology* embodies doctrine which a man of Pope's cast of mind would abominate. Before its publication, Cibber was to Pope merely a contemptible fool, a hired poetaster serving a government of scoundrels who were plundering the country. After its

---

[39]*Joseph Andrews*, Book I, Ch. 1.

publication, the canker of politics, Walpole, appeared to be balanced by a precisely equivalent literary and cultural canker. As has been shown, satirists had tended to conflate the images of stage-manager, laureate, goddess of dullness, and minister, but after the revelations of the *Apology*, Colley Cibber became for Pope all these at once. And yet it was not Cibber the man Pope wished to expose. When in March 1742 the *New Dunciad* appeared, Dulness and Cibber were shown together:

> She mounts the Throne: her head a Cloud conceal'd,
> In broad Effulgence all below reveal'd,
> (Tis thus aspiring Dulness ever shines)
> Soft on her lap her Laureat son reclines.
> (Book IV, 17-20)

But Pope's note on the last line shifts its meaning radically:

With great judgment it is imagined by the Poet,

that such a Collegue [sic] as Dulness had

elected, should sleep on the Throne, and have

very little share in the Action of the Poem.

Accordingly he hath done little or nothing from

the day of his Anointing; having past through

the second book without taking part in any thing

that was transacted about him, and thro' the

third in profound Sleep. Nor ought this, well

considered, to seem strange in our days, when

so many King-consorts have done the like.

Clearly Pope is aiming this at George II, a "King-Consort," i.e., a king in name only whose power is exercised by another. Cibber stands as a convenient and inclusive surrogate for a failed king *and* his evil minister. An additional note to the same line takes up Cibber's insulting suggestion, quoted above, that Pope attacked him only to attract readers; after having cited (inaccurately) the

passage from the *Apology* ending "*ad captandum vulgus*," the note states,

> Now if it be certain, that the works of our Poet have owed their success to this ingenious expedient, we hence derive an unanswerable Argument that this Fourth DUNCIAD as well as the former three hath had the Author's last hand, and was by him intended for the Press: Or else to what purpose halth he crowned it, as we see, by this finishing stroke, the profitable *Lick* at the *Laureate*?

The grotesque vanity of Cibber's claim seems to have rankled with Pope. A conciliatory

but tactless gesture which followed, equating Pope's art with the glance of a belle, seems not to

have helped matters.

> But the Pain which the Acrimony of those Verses [the portrait of Atticus] gave me is, in some measure, allay'd, in finding that this inimitable Writer, as he advances in Years, has since had Candour enough to celebrate the same Person for his visible Merit. Happy Genius! whose verse, like the Eye of Beauty, can heal the deepest Wounds with the least Glance of Favour.[40]

The threat contained in the *New Dunciad* brought forth, in July 1742, Cibber's *Letter from*

Mr. Cibber to Mr. Pope, Inquiring into the Motives that Might induce him in his Satyrical Works,

to be so frequently fond of Mr. Cibber's Name. In this Cibber responded to the line, ". . . has not

Colly still his Lord and Whore," by telling the tale of Pope in the bagnio [see Appendix A], a tale

of doubtful veracity but of considerable tastelessness and cruelty.[41] It was at once immensely

popular.[42] Cibber tried to repeat his success in another pamphlet, *The Egoist, or Colley upon*

Cibber, a rehashing of the first letter, in which he attempted to assert his dignity. Pope had made

no answer to the first letter, but to this he, or a friend, sent Cibber a spruious proof-sheet of the

first page of the forthcoming poem,[43] to which Cibber replied with *A Second Letter from Mr.*

Cibber to Mr. Pope. In Reply to Some Additional Verses in His Dunciad Which He Has not yet

---

[40]*Apology*, p. 24.

[41]Ault, pp. 300-304, provides considerable evidence to show that the tale, as Cibber tells it, is a lie.

[42]Baker, pp. 204-20, and Ault, pp. 298-324, give full accounts of the pamphlet wars that grew out of these letters.

[43]James Sutherland, ed., Pope, *Poems*, V, xxxiv.

Published (15 February 1743); here he mainly concerned himself with the inaccuracy of Pope's saying that Caius Gabriel Cibber's statues of two lunatics, "Great Cibber's brazen, brainless brothers stand,"[44] when in fact they

> do not *stand* but *lye*. Do you observe, *Sir*? I say they are no more upright than you are when you *stand*, or write; nay they *lye* as flat, as you sometimes do when you *write* . . . You see, *Sir*, how low I am forced to sink, that I may be upon a Par with your Satire, by not seeming to undeserve it . . . Dear Mr. *Pope*, not to be too serious with you, are you sure that any Man's calling me stupid is a Proof of my being so? (p. 2)

This was followed by some pages of purposeless and jejune abuse, revealing how much Cibber dreaded Pope's revenge. And they seem to have daunted Pope somewhat, though they did not succeed in shaking his purpose. Cibber had shown that a fool could be destructive and vicious when cornered, and Pope wrote to Warburton, 24 March 1742/43, "I begin to be more scrupulous of hurting [Cibber], & wish him more Conscientiously impudent."[45]

Earlier in January, he had written to Lord Orrery in a tone that anticipated the tone of the revised *Dunciad*:

> I have lost all Ardor and Appetite, even to Satyr, for nobody has Shame enough left to be afraid of Reproach, or punish't by it. And Cibber himself is the honestest Man I know, who has writ a book of his *Confessions*, not so much to his Credit as St. Augustine's, but full as true, & as open. Never had Impudence and Vanity so faithful a Professor. I honour him next to my Lord _____.[46]

When the newly formed poem appeared 29 October 1743, Theobald was no longer King of the Dunces: the rightful claimant to the throne had replaced him. Cibber must have been surprised to find, instead of lashing abuse and personal vindictiveness, a deeper and more poignant tone, pervaded by a sense of resignation. That it should be Cibber who presided over the most brilliant poem of its age seems paradoxical; but it must be remembered that for his mock celebration of the final destruction of English civilization Pope could find no figure who gathered into himself more intelligibly all the substantial and accidental causes leading to that eclipse. The *Apology*, therefore,

---

[44]*Dunciad* (B), I, 32.
[45]Pope, *Correspondence*, IV, 448-49.
[46]14 January 1742, *Correspondence*, IV, 437-38.

with its disclosure of a character formed by the new age and embracing its values with enthusiasm had provided the *Dunciad* with a representative hero.

8

In addition to the possibilities it offered to satirists, the book did offer a reasonably accurate history—at least in general outline—of one of the great eras of English theater, from 1660 to 1737. Its errors of fact—noted in the text—do not detract seriously from the value of an account written from first or second-hand experiences. In characterizing the acting style of Betterton, for instance, as in the character of Hamlet he confronted the ghost of his father, Cibber manages to be both respectful and detached, enabling a modern reader to guess, at least dimly, what was valued in the Restoration tradition by the early eighteenth century:

> . . . you may observe that in this beautiful Speech, the Passion never rises beyond an almost breathless Astonishment, or an Impatience, limited by filial Reverence, to enquire into the suspected Wrongs that may have rais'd him from his peaceful Tomb! and a Desire to know what a Spirit so seemingly distrest, might wish or enjoin a sorrowful Son to execute towards his future Quiet in the Grave? This was the Light into which *Betterton* threw this Scene; which he open'd with a Pause of mute Amazement! then rising slowly, to a solemn, trembling Voice, he made the Ghost equally terrible to the Spectator, as to himself! and in the descriptive Part of the natural Emotions which the ghastly Vision gave him, the boldness of his Expostulation was still govern'd by Decency, manly, but not braving; his Voice never rising into that seeming Outrage, or wild Defiance of what he naturally rever'd. (pp. 60-61)

The strengths of the *Apology* as history are substantial throughout. One suspects, however, that Cibber's interest declined during the composition of the book; for though the material becomes denser and historically more useful in the later chapters, despite the author's eagerness to hurry through the entangled financial and contractual squabbles that burdened the actor-managers during the decade of 1710-20, the sharp portraits and anecdotes that enlivened the earlier sections grow infrequent. Cibber seems to have had neither the will nor the energy to render these complex times accurately, and the work falls apart as it attempts, half-heartedly, to deal with the 1720's:

A quiet Time, in History, like a Calm, in a Voyage, leave us, but in an indolent Station: To talk of our Affairs, when they were no longer ruffled, by Misfortunes, would be a Picture without Shade, a flat Performance, at best. As I might, therefore, throw all that tedious Time of our Tranquility, into one Chasm, in my History, and cut my Way short, at once, to my last Exit, from the Stage, I shall, at least, fill it up with such Matter only, as I have a Mind should be known, how few soever may have Patience to read it... (p. 306)

In part, the difficulty of describing this period is due to the growth of the London theatrical world caused, first, by the Opera's reaching a maturity where it could exist independently of legitimate theater, and, then, after the death of Anne had given the younger Rich a free hand, the emergence of pantomime as a rival form of entertainment. Competing theaters, always distressing to Cibber, created too difficult a pattern of events for him to bring into focus.

With a complex world of political and commercial entanglements to deal with, Cibber the historian was defeated. He could only look back nostalgically to the simplicity of the earlier period, and rejoice at the restoration of monopoly by the Stage Licensing Act. Paradoxically, it had been Cibber's and his partners' financial success which had destroyed the old simplicity, by attracting rivals into the field when the royal patents had become no longer effectual as a means of limiting theatrical performances. Many of these rivals, acting as instruments of the opposition, Cibber himself had prepared for, having fought between 1710-20 for the right to present plays without prior approval by the Lord Chamberlain. As the numbers and varieties of theaters had multiplied during these years, the exercise of control had become relatively lax. Yet the *Apology*, as has been noted, tends to conceal Cibber's effectiveness here, in order to make his role consistent. But because he must play the hero, he does reveal his triumphant dealings with Lord Chamberlain.

Although it had been necessary, even in 1737, for Walpole to use highly questionable tactics—the invention of an obscene play, *The Golden Rump*, which was purportedly disrespectful of the monarchy—to persuade Parliament to pass the Licensing Act, which restrained unauthorized performances,[47] the opposition's unrelenting use of theaters as political weapons had finally

---

[47]Loftis, *Politics*, pp. 128-53, especially pp. 138-42.

permitted the Great Man, in response to continually sharper thrusts, to force the issue. Cibber defends Walpole's ruinous measures because they appeared necessary for political and cultural unity. The text of the *Apology* shows that he never realized that his own dislike of rival playwrights had in part accounted for the proliferation of theaters in much the same way that Walpole had nourished the opposition by alienating so many men of talent in the kingdom. Thus both had the effect of perpetuating the disunity they wished to end, and Cibber's book, intended to celebrate a triumph of English culture, ironically celebrates a conclusion.

The *Apology*, seen from whatever perspective, as theatrical or personal history, or as a document in the history of sensibility and culture, can hardly be called with justice a dull book. Nor can it ever again be, as it was in its earlier years, a widely popular book. Except for specialists in the history of the theater or, ironically, for critics of the Dunciad, Pope's epigram has proved to be true:

> Quoth *Cibber* to *Pope*, tho' in Verse you foreclose,
> I'll have the last Word, for by G-d I'll write prose.
> Poor *Colley*, thy Reas'ning is none of the strongest,
> For know, the last Word is the Word that lasts longest.[48]

---

[48]Pope, *Poems,* VI, 397.

A N

A P O L O G Y

FOR THE

L I F E

O F

Mr. Colley Cibber, Comedian,

A N D

Late P A T E N T E E of the *Theatre-Royal.*

With an Historical View of the STAGE *during his* OWN TIME.

W RITTEN BY H IMSELF.

---------------- *Hoc est*
Vivere bis, vitâ posse priore frui.   Mart. lib. 2

When Years no more of active Life retain,
'Tis Youth renew'd, to laugh 'em o'er again.   Anonym.

* *

L O N D O N :

Printed by John Watts for the A U T H O R.

M DCC XL.

TO A

CERTAIN GENTLEMAN.

SIR,

BECAUSE I know it would give you
less Concern, to find your Name in
an impertinent Satyr, than before the
daintiest Dedication of a modern Author, I conceal it.

Let me talk never so idly to you, this
way; you are, at least, under no necessity of
taking it to yourself: Nor when I boast of your
Favours, need you blush to have bestow'd them.
Or I may now give you all the Attributes, that

DEDICATION.

raise a wife, and good-natur'd Man, to Esteem, and Happiness, and not be censured as a Flaterer by my own, or your Enemies. — I place my own first; because as they are the greater Number, I am afraid of not paying the greater Respect to them. Yours, if such there are, I imagine are too well-bred to declare themselves: But as there is no Hazard, or visible Terror, in an Attack, upon my defenceless Station, my Censurers have generally been persons of an intrepid Sincerity. Having therefore shut the Door against them, while I am thus privately addressing you, I have little to apprehend, from either of them.

Under this Shelter, then, I may safely tell you, That the greatest Encouragement, I have had to publish this Work, has risen from the several Hours of Patience you have lent me, at the Reading it. It is true, I took the Advantage of your Leisure, in the Country, where moderate Matters serve for Amusement; and there indeed, how far your Good-nature, for an old Acquaintance, or your Reluctance to put the

DEDICATION.

Vanity of an Author out of countenance, may
have carried you, I cannot be sure; and yet Appearances give me stronger Hopes: For was not
the Complaisance of a whole Evening's Attention, as much as an Author of more Importance
ought to have expected? Why then was I desired the next Day, to give you a second Lec-
ture? Or why was I kept a third Day, with
you, to tell you more of the same Story? If
these Circumstance have made me vain, shall
I say, Sir, you are accountable for them? No,
Sir, I will rather so far flatter myself, as to suppose it possible, That your having been a Lover
of the Stage (and one of those few good Judges,
who know the Use, and Value of it, under a
right Regulation) might incline you to think
so copious an Account of it a less tedious Amusement, than it may naturally be, to others of different good Sense, who may have less Concern,
or Taste for it. But be all this as it may; the
Brat is now born, and rather, than see it starve,
upon the Bare Parish Provision, I chuse thus
clandestinely, to drop it at your Door, that it

DEDICATION.

may exercise One of your Many Virtues, your
Charity, in supporting it.

If the World were to know, into whose
Hands I have thrown it, their Regard to its
Patron might incline them, to treat it as One
of his Family: But in the Consciousness of what
I *am,* I chuse not, Sir, to say who You *are.*
If your Equal, in Rank, were to do publick
Justice to your Character, then indeed, the Concealment of your Name might be an unnecessary Diffidence: But am I, Sir, of Consequence
enough, in any Guise, to do Honour to Mr.——?
were I to set him, in the most laudable Lights,
that Truth, and good Sense could give him, or
his own Likeness would require; my officious
Mite would be lost in that general Esteem,
and Regard, which People of the first Consequence, even of different Parties, have a Pleasure, in paying him. Encomiums to Superiors,
from Authors of lower Life, as they are naturally liable to Suspicion, can add very little
Lustre, to what before was visible to the public Eye: Such Offerings (to use the Style they

DEDICATION.

are generally dress'd in) like *Pagan* Incense,
evaporate, on the Altar, and rather gratify the
Priest, than the Deity.

But you, Sir, are to be approach'd in Terms,
within the Reach of common Sense: The honest Oblation of a chearful Heart, is as much
as you desire, or I am able to bring you: A
Heart, that has just Sense enough, to mix Respect, with Intimacy, and is never more delighted, than when your rural Hours of Leisure admit me, with all my laughing Spirits,
to be my idle self, and in the whole Day's
Possession of you! Then, indeed, I have Reason to be vain; I am, then, distinguish'd, by a
Pleasure too great, to be conceal'd, and could
almost pity the Man of graver Merit, that dares
not receive it, with the same unguarded Transport! This Nakedness of Temper the World
may place, in what Rank of Folly, or Weakness they please; but till Wisdom, can give
me something, that will make me more
heartily happy, I am content, to be gaz'd at,
as I am, without lessening my Respect, for

those, whose Passions may be more soberly cover'd.

Yet, Sir, will I not deceive you; 'tis not the
Lustre of your publick Merit, the Affluence of
your Fortune, your high Figure in Life, nor
those honourable Distinctions, which you had
rather deserve than be told of, that have so
many Years made my plain Heart hang after
you: These are but incidental Ornaments, that,
'tis true, may be of Service to you, in the
World's Opinion; and though, as one among
the Crowd, I may rejoice, that Providence has
so deservedly bestow'd them; yet my particular
Attachment has risen from a meer natural, and
more engaging Charm, The Agreeable Companion! Nor is my Vanity half so much grati-
fied, in the *Honour,* as my Sense is in the *Delight* of your Society! When I see you lay aside
the Advantages of Superiority, and by your own
Chearfulness of Spirits, call out all that Nature
has given me to meet them; then 'tis I taste
you! then Life runs high! I desire! I possess
you!

DEDICATION.

Yet, Sir, in this distinguish'd Happiness, I give
not up my farther Share of that Pleasure, or of
that Right I have to look upon you, with the
publick Eye, and to join in the general Regard
so unanimously pay'd to that uncommon Virtue, your *Integrity!* This, Sir, the World allows
so conspicuous a Part of your Character, that,
however invidious the Merit, neither the rude
License of Detraction, nor the Prejudice of
Party, has ever, once, thrown on it the least
Impeachment, or Reproach. This is that commanding Power, that in publick Speaking, makes
you heard with such Attention! This it is, that
discourages, and keeps silent the Insinuations of
Prejudice, and Suspicion; and almost renders
your Eloquence an unnecessary Aid, to your
Assertions: Even your Opponents, conscious of
your *Integrity,* hear you rather as a Witness, than
an Orator—— But this, Sir, is drawing you too
near the Light, *Integrity* is too particular a Virtue to be cover'd with a general Application.
Let me therefore only talk to you, as at *Tuscu-
lum* (for so I will call that sweet Retreat, which

12. *simplex Munditiis*] Horace, *Odes*, I, v, 5: "Plain in thy neatness" (Milton's translation).

DEDICATION.

your own Hands have rais'd) where like the
fam'd Orator of old, when publick Cares permit, you pass so many rational, unbending
Hours: There! and at such Times, to have been
admitted, still plays in my Memory, more like
a fictitious, than a real Enjoyment! How many
golden Evenings, in that Theatrical Paradise of
water'd Lawns, and hanging Groves, have I
walk'd, and prated down the Sun, in social
Happiness! Whether the Retreat of *Cicero,* in
Cost, Magnificence, or curious Luxury of Antiquities, might not out-blaze the *simplex Munditiis,* the modest Ornaments of your *Villa,* is not
within my reading to determine: But that the
united Power of Nature, Art, or Elegance of
Taste, could have thrown so many varied Objects, into a more delightful Harmony, is beyond my Conception.

When I consider you, in this View, and as
the Gentleman of Eminence, surrounded with
the general Benevolence of Mankind; I rejoice,
Sir, for you, and for myself; to see *You,* in this
particular Light of Merit, and myself, some-

DEDICATION.

times, admitted to my more than equal Share of you.

If this *Apology* for my past Life discourages you not, from holding me, in your usual Favour, let me quit this greater Stage, the World, whenever I may, I shall think This the best-acted Part of any I have undertaken, since you first condescended to laugh with,

S I R,

Your most obedient,

most oblig'd, and

most humble Servant,

Novemb. 6.
1739.

COLLEY CIBBER.

THE

CONTENTS

CHAP. I.

THE Introduction. The Author's Birth. Various Fortune at School. Not likd' by those he lov'd there. Why. A Digression upon Raillery. The Use and Abuse of it. The Comforts of Folly. Vanity of Greatness. Laughing, no bad Philosophy.   page I.

CHAP. II.

He that writes of himself, not easily tir'd. Boys may give Men Lessons. The Author's Preferment at School attended with Misfortunes. The Danger of Merit among Equals. Of Satyrists and Backbiters. What effect they have had upon the Author. Stanzas publish'd by himself against himself.   p. 18

CHAP. III.

The Author's several Chances for the Church, the Court, and the Army. Going to the University. Met the Revolution at Nottingham. Took Arms on that Side. What he saw of it. A few Political Thoughts. Fortune willing to do for him. His neglect of her. The Stage preferr'd to all her Favours. The Profession of an Actor consider'd. The Misfortunes and Advantages of it.   p. 34.

CHAP. IV.

A short View of the Stage, from the Year 1660 to the Revolution. The King's and Duke's Company united, composed the best Set of English Actors yet known. Their several Theatrical Characters.   p. 53.

CHAP. V.

CHAP. VI.

CHAP. VII.

CHAP. VIII.

CHAP. IX.

CHAP. X.

CHAP. XI.

CHAP. XII.

CHAP. XIII.

C H A P. XIV.

C H A P. XV.

C H A P. XVI.

A N

A P O L O G Y

F O R   T H E

LIFE *of Mr.* COLLEY CIBBER, & *c.*

C H A P. I.

The Introduction. The Author's Birth. Various Fortune at School. Not lik'd by those he lov'd there. Why. A Digression upon Raillery. The Use and Abuse of it. The Comforts of Folly. Vanity of Greatness. Laughing, no bad Philosophy.

You know, Sir, I have often told you, that one time or other I should give the Public some Memoirs of my own Life; at which you have never fail'd to laugh, like a Friend, without saying a word to dissuade me from it; concluding, I suppose, that such a wild Thought could not possibly require a serious Answer. But you see I was in earnest. And now you will say, the World will find me, under my own Hand, a weaker Man than perhaps I may have pass'd for, even among my Enemies.————With

all my Heart! my Enemies will then read me with Pleasure,
and you, perhaps, with Envy, when you find that Follies,
without the Reproach of Guilt upon them, are not inconsistent with Happiness. ----- But why make my Follies pub-
lik? Why not? I have pass'd my Time very pleasantly with
them, and I don't recollect that they have ever been hurtful to any other Man living. Even admitting they were
injudiciously chosen, would it not be Vanity in me to take
Shame to myself for not being found a Wife Man? Really, Sir,
10   my Appetites were in too much haste to be happy, to throw
away my Time in pursuit of a Name I was sure I could never
arrive at.

Now the Follies I frankly confess, I look upon as, in some
measure, discharged; while those I conceal are still keeping the
Account open between me and my Conscience. To me the
Fatigue of being upon a continual Guard to hide them, is
more than the Reputation of being without them can repay.
If this be Weakness, *defendit numerus*, I have such comfortable Numbers on my side, that were all Men to blush, that are
20   not Wise, I am afraid, in Ten, Nine Parts of the World ought
to be out of Countenance: But since that sort of Modesty is
what they don't care to come into, why should I be afraid of
being star'd at, for not being particular? Or if the Particularity
lies in owning my Weakness, will my wisest Reader be so inhu-
man as not to pardon it? But if there should be such a one,
let me, at least, beg him to shew me that strange Man, who is
perfect! Is any one more unhappy, more riduculous, than he
who is always labouring to be thought so, or that is impatient,
when he is not thought so? Having brought myself to be easy,
30   under whatever the World may say of my Undertaking, you
may still ask me, why I give myself all this trouble? Is it for
Fame, or Profit to myself, or Use or Delight to others? For all
these Considerations I have neither Fondness nor Indifference: If
I obtain none of them, the Amusement, at worst, will be a Re-

CHAPTER I

17.   Oldfield, Wilks, and Booth] Mrs. Anne Oldfield (1683-1730), Robert Wilks

(1681-1733), and Barton Booth (1681-1733). *Lives* or *Memoirs* of these famous

actors appeared very shortly after their deaths, and these appear to have sold well.

The Authentick Memoirs of the Life of Mrs. Anne Oldfield (1730) had six

editions; Edmund Curll, the publisher, probably wrote *The Faithful Memoirs of*

Mrs. Anne Oldfield (1730), signed by 'William Egerton.' *The Memoirs of the*

Life of Robert Wilks, Esq. (1732) had three editions; again, Edmund Curll

probably wrote *The Life of that Eminent Comedian, Robert Wilks, Esq.* (1733).

The Memoirs of the Life of Barton Booth: To which are added several poetical

pieces, written by himself appeared in the year of his death.

ward that must constantly go along with the Labour. But behind all this, there is something inwardly inciting, which I can
not express in few Words; I must therefore a little make bold
with your Patience.

A Man who has pass'd above Forty Years of his Life upon a
Theatre, where he has never appear'd to be Himself, may have
naturally excited the Curiosity of his Spectators to know what
he really was, when in no body's Shape but his own; and whether he, who by his Profession had so long been ridiculing his
10 Benefactors, might not, when the Coat of his Profession was
off, deserve to be laugh'd at himself; or from his being often
seen in, the most flagrant, and immoral Characters; whether he
might not see as great a Rogue, when he look'd into the Glass
himself, as when he held it to others.

It was, doubtless, from a Supposition that this sort of Curiosity wou'd compensate their Labours, that so many hasty Writers
have been encourag'd to publish the Lives of the late Mrs. *Oldfield*, Mr. *Wilks*, and Mr. *Booth*, in less time after their Deaths
than one cou'd suppose it cost to transcribe them.

20 Now, Sir, when my Time comes, lest they shou'd think it
worth while to handle my Memory with the same Freedom, I
am willing to prevent its being so odly besmear'd (or at best but
flatly white-wash'd) by taking upon me to give the Publick
This, as true a Picture of myself as natural Vanity will permit
me to draw: For, to promise you that I shall never be vain,
were a Promise that, like a Looking-glass too large, might break
itself in the making: Nor am I sure I ought wholly to avoid
that Imputation, because if Vanity be one of my natural Features, the Portrait wou'd not be like me without it. In a Word,
30 I may palliate, and soften, as much as I please; but, upon an
honest Examination of my Heart, I am afraid the same Vanity
which makes even homely People employ Painters to preserve a
flattering Record of their Persons, has seduced me to print off
this *Chiaro Oscuro* of my Mind.

16.   *Louis the Fourteenth . . .* Old Age] I am unable to confirm this; it is known,
      however, that Louis XIV had a large collection of medals and curios, having in
      his youth acquired a taste for collecting from Mazarin (*Louis XIV: an Informal
      Portrait,* by W. H. Lewis [London, 1959], p. 126). These are now housed in the
      Biblioth'eque Nationale.

19.   first Appearance . . . last Exit] Cibber's first documented appearance on the stage
      was as a servant in Richard Southerne's *Sir Anthony Love* on 17 September 1690
      (Van Lennep, p. 388; cf. Davies, *Dram. Misc.*, III, 446), his last on 15 February
      1745 in his own adaptation of Shakespeare's *King John,* called *Papal Tyranny in
      the Reign of King John.* His rare appearances in the years after his retirement in
      1733 were well attended; contemporary comments indicate that this was partly a
      result of interest in his highly mannered style of acting, which Garrick had begun
      to displace. See Lily B. Campbell, "The Rise of a Theory of Stage Presentation
      in England during the Eighteenth Century" (*PMLA*, XXXII, 1917, 163-200);
      Earl R. Wassermann, "The Sympathetic Imagination in Eighteenth-Century
      Acting" (*Journal of English and Germanic Philology,* xlvi, 1947), 264-72), and
      Alan S. Downer, "Nature to Advantage Dressed: Eighteenth-Century Acting"
      (*PMLA*, LVIII, 1943, 1002-37). Horace Walpole, in a letter to Mann (3
      December 1741 OS) remarks, "old Cibber plays to night [Sir John Bruce in *The
      Provoked Wife*] and all the world will be there."

30.   the *Rehearsal*] By George Villiers, Duke of Buckingham (first performed in
      1675, later revised). Cibber alters the speech slightly, in the play, Act III, scene
      iv; Prince Pretty-man discovers that he is not the fisherman's son as he had
      thought and shows alarm. Bayes, the author of the heroic play, defends this
      reaction by saying, "Phoo, that is not because he [Prince Pretty-man] has a mind
      to be his son, but for fear he should be thought to be nobody's son at all."

4

And when I have done it, you may reasonably ask me, of
what Importance can the History of my private Life be to the
Publick? To this, indeed, I can only make you a ludicrous
Answer, which is, That the Publick very well knows, my Life
has not been a private one; that I have been employ'd in their
Service, ever since many of their Grandfathers were young Men;
And tho' I have voluntarily laid down my Post, they have a sort
of Right to enquire into my Conduct, (for which they have so
well paid me) and to call for the Account of it, during my
10   Share of Administration in the State of the Theatre. This Work,
therefore, which, I hope, they will not expect a Man of my
hasty Head shou'd confine to any regular Method: (For I shall
make no scruple of leaving my History, when I think a Digression may make it lighter, for my Reader's Digestion.) This
Work, I say, shall not only contain the various Impressions of
my Mind, (as in *Louis the Fourteenth* his Cabinet you have seen
the growing Medals of his Person from Infancy to Old Age,)
but shall likewise include with them the *Theatrical History of my*
Own Time, from my first Appearance on the Stage to my last
20   *Exit.*

If then what I shall advance on that Head, may any ways contribute to the Prosperity or Improvement of the Stage in being,
the Publick must of consequence have a Share in its Utility.

This, sir, is the best Apology I can make for being my own
Biographer. Give me leave therefore to open the first Scence of
my Life, from the very Day I came into it; and tho' (considering my Profession) I have no reason to be asham'd of my Original; yet I am afraid a plain dry Account of it, will scarce
admit of a better Excuse than what my Brother *Bays* makes for
30   Prince *Prettyman* in the *Rehearsal,* viz. *I only do it, for fear I*
should be thought to be no body's Son at all; for if I have led a
worthless Life, the Weight of my Pedigree will not add an
Ounce to my intrinsic Value. But be the Inference what it will,
the simple Truth is this.

11.   11-12 Man of my hasty Head] Man of hasty Head 2nd ed.

his 'Colly' ancestors had been considerable landowners and that during the reign of Charles I, possibly in his service, large amounts of property had been sold.

21. Free-School of *Grantham*] This school is presumably the one founded under Edward VI and attended by Sir Isaac Newton.

1.   born in London] "The christening of Colley Cibber is recorded in the Baptismal

Register of the Church of St. Giles-in-the-Fields. The entry reads:

> November 1671   Christenings
> 20. Colly sonne of Caius Gabriel Sibber and Jane ux."
> (Lowe, I, 7 n.)

3.   *Caius Gabriel Cibber*] See Biographical Appendix; for a complete account of his

life and works, see Harold Faber, *Caius Gabriel Cibber* (Oxford, 1926); see also

Margaret Whinney, *Sculpture in Britain: 1530-1830* (Penguin, 1964), pp. 48-50,

plates 36-38.

8-9.   no ill Monuments of his Fame] The column Cibber speaks of is commonly

known as the 'Monument,' a commemorative market at the place where the great

fire started. The statues, formerly much admired, are now in the possession of

the Corporation of London at the Guildhall; their former position and Cibber's

curiously worded description of them served in Book I of the *Dunciad* (B) for a

witty point:

> Where o'er the gates [of Bedlam], by his fam'd father's hand
> Great Cibber's brazen, brainless, brothers stand . . .
> (31-32)

Harold Faber (p. 43) says that they represent "in all their gruesome and stern

reality two of the patients at the time, of which one is said to have been a servant

of Oliver Cromwell. They recline on mattresses of rushes, naked, closely

shaven. One is imbecile rather than melancholy, the other, in irons, is raving.

The position and whole arrangement remind one of the figures by Michael Angelo

on the tombs of the Medicis, but the treatment is sufficiently original to protect

Cibber from a charge of plagiarism." Faber provides photographs between pp.

42 and 43.

14.   Wright's History of *Rutlandshire*] James Wright, The History and Antiquities of

the County of Rutland (1684), pp. 64-65. Wright confirms Cibber's claim that

I was born in *London,* on the 6th of *November* 1671, in
Southampton-Street, facing *Southampton-House.* My Father,
Caius Gabriel Cibber, was a Native of *Holstein,* who came into
England some time before the Restoration of King *Charles* II.
to follow his Profession, which was that of a Statuary, & c.
The *Basso Relievo* on the Pedestal of the Great Column in the
City, and the two Figures of the *Lunaticks,* the *Raving* and
the *Melancholy,* over the Gates of *Bethlehem-Hospital,* are no ill
Monuments of his Fame as an Artist. My Mother was the
10 Daughter of *William Colley,* Esq; of a very ancient Family of
Glaiston in *Rutlandshire,* where she was born. My Mother's
Brother, *Edward Colley,* Esq; (who gave me my Christian Name)
being the last Heir Male of it, the Family is now extinct. I
shall only add, that in *Wright's* History of *Rutlandshire,* publish'd in 1684, the *Colley's* are recorded as Sheriffs and Members of Parliament from the Reign of *Henry* VII. to the latter
end of *Charles* I. in whose Cause chiefly Sir *Antony Colley,* my
Mother's Grandfather, sunk his Estate from Three Thousand to
about Three Hundred *per Annum.*
20 In the Year 1682, at little more than ten Years of Age, I
was sent to the Free-School of *Grantham* in *Lincolnshire,* where
I staid till I got through it, from the lowest Form to the upper-
most. And such Learning as that School could give me, is the
most I pretend to (which, tho' I have not utterly forgot, I can
not say I have much improv'd by Study) but even there I remember I was the same inconsistent Creature I have been ever
since! always in full Spirits, in some small Capacity to do right,
but in a more frequent Alacrity to do wrong; and consequently often under a worse Character than I wholly deserv'd : A
30 giddy Negligence always posses'd me, and so much, that I remember I was once whip'd for my *Theme,* tho' my Master told
me, at the same time, what was good of it was better than any
Boy's in the Form. And (whatever Shame it may be to own it)
I have observ'd the same odd Fate has frequently attended the

7.   Envy, Malice or Ingratitude] Fielding, in *Joseph Andrews*, Book I, Chapter III,

       says of Parson Adams, ". . . he did, no more than Mr. Colley Cibber, apprehend

       any such Passions as Malice and Envy to exist in Mankind; which was indeed less

       remarkable in a Country Parson than in a gentleman who hath passed his Life

       behind the Scenes, —a Place which hath been seldom thought the School of

       Innocence, and where a little Observation would have convinced the great

       Apologist that those Passions have a real existence in the human Mind" [Lowe].

20.   glouting] *OED*: "glout: to look sullen, frown, scorn" [Lowe].

6

course of my later Conduct in Life. The unskilful openness, or
in plain Terms, the Indiscretion I have always acted with from
my Youth, has drawn more ill-will towards me, than Men of
worse Morals and more Wit might have met with. My Ignorance, and want of Jealousy of Mankind has been so strong, that
it is with Reluctance I even yet believe any Person, I am acquainted with, can be capable of Envy, Malice, or Ingratitude: And
to shew you what a Mortification it was to me, in my very boyish
Days, to find my self mistaken, give me leave to tell you a
10 School Story.

   A great Boy, near the Head taller than my self, in some wran-
gle at play had insulted me; upon which I was fool-hardy enough
to give him a Box on the Ear; the Blow was soon return'd with
another, that brought me under him, and at his Mercy. Another Lad, whom I really lov'd, and thought a good-natur'd one,
cry'd out with some warmth, to my Antagonist (while I was
down) Beat him, beat him soundly! This so amaz'd me, that I
lost all my Spirits to resist, and burst into Tears! When the Fray
was over I took my Friend aside, and ask'd him, How he came
20 to be so earnestly against me? To which, with some glouting
Confusion, he reply'd, Because you are always jeering, and making a Jest of me to every Boy in the School. Many a Mischief
have I brought upon my self by the same Folly in riper Life.
Whatever Reason I had to reproach my Companion's declaring
against me, I had none to wonder at it, while I was so often hurting him: Thus I deserv'd his Enmity, by my not having Sense
enough to know I *had* hurt him; and he hated me, because he
had not Sense enough to know, that I never *intended* to hurt
him.

30   As this is the first remarkable Error of my Life I can reccol-
lect, I cannot pass it by without throwing out some farther Reflections upon it; whether flat or spirited, new or common, and consequently like me; I will therefore boldly go on; for I am only

oblig'd to give you my *own,* and not a *good* Picture, to shew as
well the Weakness, as the Strength of my Understanding. It is
not on what I write, but on my Reader's Curiosity I relie to be
read through: At worst, tho' the Impartial may be tir'd, the Ill-
natur'd (no small number) I know will see the bottom of me.

     What I observ'd then, upon my having undesignedly provok'd
my School-Friend into an Enemy, is a common Case in society;
Errors of this kind often sour the Blood of Acquaintance into an
inconceivable Aversion, where it is little suspected. It is not
enough to say of your Raillery, that you intended no Offence;
if the Person you offer it to has either a wrong head, or wants
a Capacity to make that distinction, it may have the same effect as the Intention of the grossest Injury: And in reality, if you
know his Parts are too slow to return it in kind, it is a vain and
idle Inhumanity, and sometimes draws the Aggressor into difficulties not easily got out of: Or to give the Case more scope,
suppose your Friend may have a passive Indulgence for your
Mirth, if you find him silent at it; tho' you were as intrepid as
Caesar, there can be no Excuse for your not leaving it off. When
you are conscious that your Antagonist can give as well as take,
then indeed the smarter the Hit the more agreeable the Party:
A Man of chearful Sense, among Friends will never be grave
upon an Attack of this kind, but rather thank you that you have
given him a Right to be even with you: There are few Men
(tho' they may be Masters of both) that on such occasions had
not rather shew their Parts than their Courage, and the Preference is just; a Bull-Dog may have one, and only a Man can
have the other. Thus it happens, that in the coarse Merriment
of common People, when the Jest begins to swell into earnest; for
want of this Election you may observe, he that has least Wit generally gives the first Blow. Now, as among the better sort, a
readiness of Wit is not always a Sign of intrinsick Merit; so the
want of that readiness is no Reproach to a Man of plain Sense
and Civility, who therefore (methinks) should never have these

20.   two Persons] Lowe (I, 14) identifies the first of these characters as the Earl of

Chesterfield and cites the *Laureat's* (p. 18) identification of the second as "Mr.

E_____e"; Lowe completes this as Erskine. But the circumstances of this

character seem exactly to fit Giles Earle. See *Notes and Queries*, 11th Series, IV

(July-December, 1911), 382, 475.

8

lengths of Liberty taken with him. Wit there becomes absurd,
if not insolent; ill-natur'd I am sure it is, which Imputation a
generous Spirit will always avoid, for the same Reason that a Man
of real Honour will never send a Challenge to a Cripple. The
inward Wounds that are given by the inconsiderate Insults of
Wit, to those that want it, are as dangerous as those given by
Oppression to Inferiors; as long in healing, and perhaps never
forgiven. There is besides (and little worse than this) a mutual
Grossness in Raillery, that sometimes is more painful to the
10   Hearers that are not concern'd in it, than to the Persons engag'd. I
have seen a couple of these clumsy Combatants drub one another
with as little Manners or Mercy as if they had two Flails in their
Hands; Children at play with Case-knives could not give you
more Apprehension of their doing one another a Mischief. And
yet when the Contest has been over, the Boobys have look'd round
them for Approbation, and upon being told they were admirably
well match'd, have sat down (bedawb'd as they were) contented,
at making it a drawn Battle. After all that I have said, there
is no clearer way of giving Rules for Raillery than by Example.
20   There are two Persons now living, who tho' very different in
their manner, are, as far as my Judgment reaches, complete Masters of it; the one of a more polite and extensive Imagination,
the other of a Knowledge more closely useful to the Business of
Life: The one gives you perpetual Pleasure, and seems always to
be taking it; the other seems to take none, till his Business is
over, and then gives you as much as if Pleasure were his only
Business. The one enjoys his Fortune, the other thinks it first
necessary to make it; though that he will enjoy it then, I cannot
be positive, because when a Man has once pick'd up more than
30   he wants, he is apt to think it a Weakness to suppose he has
enough. But as I don't remember ever to have seen these Gentlemen in the same Company, you must give me leave to take them
separately.

1.   22 the one]   one   2nd ed.

29.   *ex pede Herculem*] I.E. "as we know a Hercules by the size of his foot."

The first of them, then, has a Title, and--- no matter what;
I am not to speak of the great, but the happy part of his Character, and in this one single light; not of his being an illustrious, but a delightful Companion.

In Conversation he is seldom silent but when he is attentive,
nor ever speaks without exciting the Attention of others; and
tho' no Man might with less displeasure to his Hearers, engross
the Talk of the Company, he has a Patience in his Vivacity that
chuses to divide it, and rather gives more Freedom than he takes;
10   his sharpest Replies having a mixture of Politeness that few have
the command of; his Expression is easy, short, and clear; a stiff
or study'd Word never comes from him; it is in a simplicity of
Style that he gives the highest Surprize, and his Ideas are always
adapted to the Capacity and Taste of the Person he speaks to:
Perhaps you will understand me better if I give you a particular
Instance of it. A Person at the University, who from being a
Man of Wit, easily became one of his Acquaintance there, from
that Acquaintance found no difficulty in being made one of his
Chaplains: This Person afterwards leading a Life that did no
20   great Honour to his Cloth, oblig'd his Patron to take some gentle
notice of it; but as his Patron kenw the Patient was squeamish,
he was induc'd to sweeten the Medicine to his Taste, and therefore with a smile of good-humour told him, that if to the many
Vices he had already, he would give himself the trouble to add
one more, he did not doubt but his Reputation might still be set
up again. Sir *Crape*, who could have no Aversion to so pleasant
a Dose, desiring to know what it might be, was answered, *Hy-*
pocrisy, Doctor, only a little Hypocrisy!   This plain Reply can
need no Comment; but *ex pede Herculem*, he is every where pro-
30   portionable. I think I have heard him since say, the Doctor
thought Hypocrisy so detestable a Sin that he dy'd without committing it. In a word, this Gentleman gives Spirit to Society the
Moment he comes into it, and whenever he leaves it, they who
have Business have then leisure to go about it.

C

1. 17 easily became one of his Acquaintance] easily became
his acquaintance 2nd ed.

15. *set the table in a roar*] "Where be your gibes now? your gambols? your songs? your flashes of merriment, that were wont to set the table on a roar?" Hamlet, V, i, speaking of Yorick [Lowe].

    Having often had the Honour to be my self the Butt of his
Raillery, I must own I have receiv'd more Pleasure from his lively
manner of raising the Laugh against me, than I could have felt
from the smoothest flattery of a serious Civility. Tho' Wit flows
from him with as much ease as common Sense from another, he
is so little elated with the Advantage he may have over you, that
whenever your good Fortune gives it against him, he seems more
pleas'd with it on your side than his own. The only advantage
he makes of his Superiority of Rank is, that by always waving

10   it himself, his inferior finds he is under the greater Obligation
not to forget it.

    When the Conduct of social Wit is under such Regulations,
how delightful must those *Convivia,* those Meals of Conversation
be, where such a Member presides; who can with so much ease
(as *Shakespear* phrases it) *set the Table in a roar.* I am in no pain
that these imperfect Out-lines will be apply'd to the Person I
mean, because every one that has the Happiness to know him,
must know how much more in this particular Attitude is wanting to be like him.

20   The other Gentleman, whose bare Interjections of Laughter
have Humour in them, is so far from having a Title, that he
has lost his real name, which some Years ago he suffer'd his
Friends to railly him out of; in lieu of which they have equipp'd
him with one they thought had a better sound in good Company.
He is the first Man of so sociable a Spirit, that I ever knew capable of quitting the Allurements of Wit and Pleasure, for a
strong application to Business; in his Youth (for there was a
Time when he was young) he set out in all the hey-day Expences
of a modish Man of Fortune; but finding himself over-weighted

30   with Appetites, he grew restiff, kick'd up in the middle of the
Course, and turn'd his Back upon his Frolicks abroad, to think
of improving his Estate at home: In order to which he clapt
Collars upon his Coach-horses, and that their Mettle might not
run over other Poeple, he ty'd a Plough to their Tails, which

---

1. 1 the Butt] the But 2nd ed.

Tho' it might give them a more slovenly Air, would enable him
to keep them fatter in a foot pace, with a whistling Peasant beside them, than in a full trot, with a hot-headed Coachman behind them.   In these unpolite Amusements he has laugh'd like a
Rake, and look'd about him like a Farmer for many Years.   As
his Rank and Station often find him in the best Company, his
easy Humour, whenever he is called to it, can still make himself
the Fiddle of it.

     And tho' some say, he looks upon the follies of the World like
10 too severe a Philosopher, yet he rather chuses to laugh, than to
grieve at them; to pass his time therefore more easily in it, he
often endeavours to conceal himself, by assuming the Air and
Taste of a Man in fashion; so that his only Uneasiness seems to
be, that he can't quite prevail with his Friends to think him a
worse Manager, than he really is; for they carry their Raillery to
such a height, that it sometimes rises to a Charge of downright
Avarice against him.   Upon which head it is no easy matter to
be more merry upon him, than he will be upon himself.   Thus
while he sets that Infirmity in a pleasant Light, he so disarms your
20 Prejudice that, if he has it not, you can't find in your Heart to
wish he were without it.   Whenever he is attack'd where he
seems to lie so open, if his Wit happens not to be ready for you,
he receives you with an assenting Laugh, till he has gain'd time
to what it sharp enough for a Reply, which seldom turns out to
his disadvantage.   If you are too strong for him (which may possibly happen from his being oblig'd to defend the weak side of
the Question) his last Resource is to join in the Laugh, till he has
got himself off by an ironical Applause of your Superiority.

     If I were capable of Envy, what I have observ'd of this Gen-
30 tleman would certainly incline me to it; for sure to get through
the necessary Cares of Life, with a Train of Pleasures at our
Heels, in vain calling after us, to give a constant Preference to
the Business of the Day, and yet be able to laugh while we are
about it, to make even Society the subservient Reward of it, is a

1.   14 he can't] he cannot 2nd ed.

8.   *Cum ratione insanire*] Terence, *The Eunuch I*, line 18: "to be mad with method."

25.   *Servetur . . . processerit*] Horace, *Ars Poetica*, 126-27: "Let it be preserved to the last such as it set out from the beginning."

12

State of Happiness which the gravest Precepts of moral Wisdom
will not easily teach us to exceed. When I speak of Happiness,
I go no higher than that which is contain'd in the World we
now tread upon; and when I speak of Laughter, I don't simply mean that which every Oaf is capable of, but that which
has its sensible Motive and proper Season, which is not more limited than recommended by that indulgent Philosophy,

Cum ratione insanire.

When I look into my present Self, and afterwards cast my Eye
10   round all my Hopes, I don't see any one Pursuit of them that
shou'd so reasonably rouze me out of a Nod in my Great Chair,
as a call to those agreeable Parties I have sometimes the Happiness to mix with, where I always assert the equal Liberty of
leaving them, when my Spirits have done their best with them.

    Now, Sir, as I have been making my way for above Forty
Years through a Crowd of Cares, (all which, by the Favour of
Providence, I have honesly got rid of) is it a time of Day for
me to leave off these Fooleries, and to set up a new Character?
Can it be worth my while to waste my Spirits, to bake my
20   Blood, with serious Contemplations, and perhaps impair my
Health, in the fruitless Study of advancing myself into the better Opinion of those very --- very few Wise Men that are as old
as I am? No, the Part I have acted in real Life, shall be all of
a piece.

      ------ *Servetur ad imum,*

  Qualis ab incepto processerit.   Hor.

I will not go out of my Character, by straining to be wiser than
I *can* be, or by being more affectedly pensive than I *need* be;
whatever I am, Men of Sense will know me to be, put on what
30   Disguise I will; I can no more put off my Follies, than my Skin;
I have often try'd, but they stick too close to me; nor am I sure
my Friends are displeas'd with them; for, besides that in this
Light I afford them frequent matter of Mirth, they may possibly
be less uneasy at their *own* Foilbles, when they have so old a Pre-

distasteful pretence to knowledge which he did not possess (e.g., see Fielding,

The Champion, December 25, 1739; April 15, 1740; April 22, 1740).

12. *Socrates . . . Even* or *Odd*] Valerius Maximus, 1.8.8: "Socrates non erubuit tunc, cum interpoista harundine cruribus suis cum parvulis filiolis ludens ab Alcibiade visus est": "Socrates did not blush when he was seen by Alcibiades playing with his small children with a reed between his legs." This anecdote appears in early commentaries on Horace, *Sat.*, II, iii, 248: "Ludere par impar, equitare in harundine longa": "To play odd and even and to ride on a long reed." It is almost certain, therefore, that Cibber confused text and commentary, especially since Horace mentions both 'even and odd' and Agesilaus' game (see note following).

13. *Agesilaus . . .* Hobby-horse] Cf. Plutarch, Agesilaus and Pompey, section XXV; also Aelian, *Var. Hist.*, 1, 12, 15.

15. Emperor *Adrian . . . Animula*] Referring to Hadrian's poem beginning: "Animula vagula blandula": "Dear little fleeting soul . . ."; cf. Pope's translation "Ah Fleeting Spirit! wand'ring Fire,/ That long hast warmed my tender Breast . . ." (*Poems*, VI, 93).

24. *My Mind . . . to me*] Cibber either misquotes, or refers to an unidentified song which resembles Sir Edward Dyer's "My mind to me a kingdom is" (1588).

31. Imitator of *Horace . . .* reading them] Cibber's representation of himself as untouched by Pope's mentions of him in *Imitations of Horace* (published at intervals from 1733-38) is disingenuous; this passage itself is an instance of Cibber's concern for his reputation, as is the entire *Apology* and the series of letters to Pope which followed it (cf. Introduction, p. xxviii).

33. find myself . . . *dispraisingly* spoken of] There are numerous mentions of Cibber in the *Imitations* (see Introduction, pp. xviii ff.). For 'dispraisingly' see *Othello*, III, iii, 71-74: "What! Michael Cassio,/ That came a-wooing with you, and so many a time/ When I have spoke of you dispraisingly/ Hath ta'en your part . . ." Cibber's habit of giving snatches of quotations, sometimes, as in this instance, in grotesquely inappropriate contexts, appeared to his contemporaries to be a

cedent to keep them in countenance: Nay, there are some frank
enough to confess, they envy what they laught at; and when I
have seen others, whose Rank and fortune have laid a sort of Restraint upon their Liberty of pleasing their Company, by pleasing themselves, I have said softly to myself, ------ Well, there is
some Advantage in having neither Rank nor Fortune! Not but
there are among them a third Sort, who have the particular Happiness of unbending into the very Wantonness of Good-humour,
without depreciating their Dignity: He that is not Master of that

10   Freedom, let his Condition be never so exalted, must still want
someting to come up to the Happiness of his Inferiors who enjoy it. If *Socrates* cou'd take pleasure in playing at *Even or Odd*
with his Children, or *Agesilaus* divert himself in riding the
Hobby-horse with them, am I oblig'd to be as eminent as either
of them before I am as frolicksome? If the Emperor *Adrian*,
near his death, cou'd play with his very Soul, his *Animula, &c.*
and regret that it cou'd be no longer companionable; if Greatness, at the same time, was not the Delight he was so loth to
part with, sure then these chearful Amusements I am contending

20   for, must have no inconsiderable share in our Happiness; he
that does not chuse to live his own way, suffers others to chuse
for him. Give me the Joy I always took in the End of an
old Song,
        My Mind, my Mind is a Kingdom to me!
If I can please myself with my own Follies, have not I a plentiful Provision for Life? If the World thinks me a Trifler, I
don't desire to break in upon their Wisdom; let them call me
any Fool, but an Unchearful one! I live as I write; while my
Way amuses me, it's as well as I wish it; when another writes

30   better, I can like him too, tho' he shou'd not like me. Not
our great Imitator of *Horace* himself can have more Pleasure in
writing his Verses, than I have in reading them, tho' I sometimes find myself there (as *Shakespear* terms it) *dispraisingly* spoken
of: If he is a little free with me, I am generally in good com-

14. *Me . . . my Wants, and grieve*] Horace, *Epistles II*, ii, 126-28. Cibber's version

    should be compared with Pope's:

    > If such the Plague and pains to write by rule
    > Better (say I) be pleas'd, and play the fool;
    > Call, if you will, bad Rhiming a disease,
    > It gives men happiness, or leaves them ease. (180-83)

17. merry Monarch . . . Elopement] Charles II, early in his stay in Scotland (arrived 16

    June 1651), was subjected to much criticism for his and his parents' morals by the

    officials of the Scottish Presbyterian Kirk. His departure for France was brought

    about primarily by his army's destruction at the battle of Worcester on 22 August

    1651 (*DNB*, article Charles II). Burnet's account of this period (I, 51-58) may be

    the source of Cibber's story.

29. Frogs in the Fable . . . King *Log*] The frogs asked Jupiter for a king and were

    given a log; this did not satisfy them so they were given a stork which ate them.

    Cf. the *Dunciad* (A), Book I, 251-60.

pany, he is as blunt with my Betters; so that even here I might
laugh in my turn. My Superiors, perhaps, may be mended by
him; but, for my part, I own myself incorrigible: I look upon
my Follies as the best part of my Fortune, and am more concern'd to be a good Husband of Them, than of That; nor do
I believe I shall ever be rhim'd out of them. And, if I don't
mistake, I am supported in my way of thinking by *Horace* himself, who, in excuse of a loose Writer, says,

> *Praetulerim scriptor delirus, inersque videri,*
10 > *Dum mea delectent, mala me, aut denique fallant,*
> *Quam sapere, et ringi* -----

which, to speak of myself as a loose Philosopher, I have thus
ventur'd to imitate:

> *Me, while my laughing Follies can deceive,*
> *Blest in the dear Delirium let me live,*
> *Rather than wisely know my Wants, and grieve.*

We had once a merry Monarch of our own, who thought chearfulness so valuable a Blessing, that he would have quitted one
of his Kingdoms where he cou'd not enjoy it; where, among
20 many other hard Conditions they had ty'd him to, his sober
Subjects wou'd not suffer him to laugh on a *Sunday*; and tho'
this might not be the avow'd Cause of his Elopement, I am not
sure, had he had no other, that this alone might not have serv'd
his turn; at least, he has my hearty Approbation either way; for
had I been under the same Restriction, tho' my staying were to
have made me his Successor, I shou'd rather have chosen to follow him.

How far his Subjects might be in the right, is not my Affair
to determine; perhaps they were wiser than the Frogs in the Fa-
30 ble, and rather chose to have a Log, than a Stork for their King;
yet I hope it will be no Offence to say, that King *Log* himself
must have made but a very simple Figure in History.

The Man who chuses never to laugh, or whose becalm'd Passions know no Motion, seems to me only in the quiet State of

1.   20   many other hard Conditions] many other Conditions   2nd ed.

a green Tree; he vegetates, 'tis true, but shall we say he lives?
Now, Sir, for Amusement. ---- Reader, take heed! for I find a
strong impulse to talk impertinently; if therefore you are not as
fond of seeing, as I am of shewing myself in all my Lights, you
may turn over two Leaves together, and leave what follows to
those who have more Curiosity, and less to do with their Time,
than you have. ----- As I was saying then, let us, for Amusement, advance this, or any other Prince, to the most glorious
Throne, mark out his Empire in what Clime you please, fix

10   him on the highest Pinnacle of unbounded Power; and in that
State let us enquire into his degree of Happiness; make him at
once the Terror and the Envy of his Neighbours, send his Ambition out to War, and gratify it with extended Fame and Vic-
tories; bring him in triumph home, with great unhappy Cap-
tives behind him, through the Acclamations of his People, to re-
posses his Realms in Peace. Well, when the Dust has been
brusht from his Purple, what will he do next? Why, this envy'd Monarch (who, we will allow to have a more exalted Mind
than to be delighted with the trifling Flatteries of a congratula-

20   ting Circle) will chuse to retire, I presume, to enjoy in private
the Contemplation of his Glory; an Amusement, you will say,
that well becomes his Station! But there, in that pleasing Rumination, when he has made up his new Account of Happiness,
how much, pray, will be added to the Balance more than as it
stood before his last Expedition? From what one Article will
the Improvement of it appear? Will it arise from the conscious
Pride of having done his weaker Enemy an Injury? Are his
Eyes so dazzled with false Glory, that he thinks it a less Crime
in him to break into the Palace of his Princely Neighbour, be-

30   cause he gave him time to defend it, than for a Subject feloniously to plunder the House of a private Man? Or is the Outrage of Hunger and Necessity more enormous than the Ravage
of Ambition? Let us even suppoose the wicked Usage of the
World, as to that Point, may keep his Conscience quiet; still,

30. *dulce . . . loco*] Horace, *Odes*, IV, 12, 28: "It is delightful to indulge in festivity in season."

what is he to do with the infinite Spoil that his imperial Rapine
has brough home? Is he to sit down, and vainly deck himself with the Jewels which he has plunder'd from the Crown of
another, whom Self-defence had compell'd to oppose him? No,
let us not debase his Glory into so low a Weakness. What Appetite, then, are these shining Treasures food for? Is their vast
Value in seeing his vulgar Subjects stare at them, wise Men
smile at them, or his Children play with them? Or can the new
Extent of his Dominions add a Cubit to his Happiness? Was not

10   his Empire wide enough before to do good in? And can it add to
his Delight that now no Monarch has such room to do mischief
in? But farther; if even the great *Augustus,* to whose Reign
such Praises are given, cou'd not enjoy his Days of Peace, free
from the Terrors of repeated Conspiracies, which lost him more
Quiet to suppress, than his Ambition cost him to provoke them.
What human Eminence is secure? In what private Cabinet then
must this wondrous Monarch lock up his Happiness, that common Eyes are never to behold it? Is it, like his Person, a Prisoner to its own Superiority? Or does he at last poorly place it in

20   the Triumph of his injurious Devastations? One Moment's
Search into himself will plainly shew him, that real and reasonable Happiness can have no Existence without Innocence and
Liberty. What a Mockery is Greatness without them? How
lonesome must be the Life of that Monarch, who, while he
governs only be being fear'd, is restrain'd from letting down his
Grandeur sometimes to forget himself, and to humanize him
into the Benevolence and Joy of Society? To throw off his cum-
bersome Robe of Majesty to be a Man without Disguise, to have
a sensible Taste of Life in its Simplicity, till he confess, from the

30   sweet Experience, that *dulce est desipere in loco,* was no Fool's
Philosophy. Or if the gawdy Charms of Pre-eminence are so
strong that they leave him no Sense of a less pompous, tho' a
more rational Enjoyment, none sure can envy him, but those
who are the Dupes of an equally fantastick Ambition.

18.   *Os Sublime*] Ovid, *Metamorphoses*, I, 84-86.

> Pronaque cum spectant animalia cetera terram,
> os homini sublime dedit coelumque videre
> iussit et erectos ad sidera tollere vultus.

"And though all other animals are prone, and fix their gaze upon the earth, he [the

god] gave to man an uplifted face and bade him stand erect and turn his eyes to

heaven."

My Imagination is quite heated and fatigued, in dressing up
this Phantome of Felicity; but I hope it has not made me so
far misunderstood, as not to have allow'd, that in all the Dispen-
sations of Providence, the Exercise of a great and virtuous Mind
is the most elevated State of Happiness: No, Sir, I am not for
setting up Gaiety against Wisdom; nor for preferring the Man of
Pleasure to the Philosopher; but for shewing, that the Wisest, or
Greatest Man, is very near an unhappy Man, if the unbending
Amusements I am contending for, are not sometimes admitted to
10   relieve him.

How far I may have over-rated these Amusements, let graver
Casuists decide; whether they affirm, or reject, what I have as-
serred, hurts not my Purpose; which is not to give Laws to
others; but to shew by what Laws I govern myself: If I am mis-
guided, 'tis Nature's Fault, and I follow her, from this Persuasion; That as Nature has distinguish'd our Species from the mute
Creation, by our Risibility, her Design must have been, by that
Faculty, as evidently to raise our Happiness, as by our *Os Sublime*
(our created Faces) to lift the Dignity of our Form above them.

20   Notwithstanding all I have said, I am afraid there is an absolute Power, in what is simply call'd our Constitution, that will
never admit of other Rules for Happiness, than her own; from
which (be we never so wise or weak) without Divine Assistance,
we only can receive it: So that all this my Parade, and Grimace
of Philosophy, has been only making a might Merit of Following my own Inclination. A very natural Vanity! Though it is
some sort of Satisfaction to know it does not impose upon me.
Vanity again! However, think It what you will that has drawn
me into this copious Digression, 'tis now high time to drop it:
30   I shall therefore in my next Chapter return to my School, from
whence, I fear, I have too long been Traunt.

CHAPTER II

6. Coxcomb] Cibber's combination of vanity and shamelessness, manifested in his application of this word to himself, shocked his contemporaries; see Fielding's comment (*Joseph Andrews*, Book I, Chap. I) in Introduction, p. xxxi.

   In his old age Cibber had free acceptance in the houses of the Whig aristocracy; Horace Walpole remarks to the Hon. Henry Seymour Conway (31 October 1741) "The company was all extremely good [at large assemblies at Sir Thomas Robinson's] there were none but people of the first fashion except Mr. Kent, Mr. Cibber, Mr. Swiney, and the Parson's family, and you know all these have an alloy . . . Cibber and Swiney have long had their freedom given them of this end of the town" (Walpole letters, ed. Toynbee, I, 115).

22. In . . . 1684-5] 6 February 1685.

C H A P. II.

He that writes of himself, not easily tir'd. Boys may give Men Lessons. The Author's Preferment at School attended with Misfortunes. The Danger of Merit among Equals. Of Satyrists and Backbiters. What effect they have had upon the Author. Stanzas publish'd by himself against himself.

It often makes me smile, to think how contentedly I have sate myself down, to write my own Life; nay, and with less Concern for what may be said of it, than I should feel, were I to do the same for a deceas'd Acquaintance. This you will easily account for, when you consider, that nothing gives a Coxcomb more Delight, than when you suffer him to talk of himself; which sweet Liberty I here enjoy for a whole Volume together! A Privilege, which neither cou'd be allow'd me, nor wou'd be-
10 come me to take, in the Company I am generally admitted to; but here, where I have all the Talk to myself, and have no body to interrupt or contradict me, sure, to say whatever I have a mind other People shou'd know of me, is a Pleasure which none but Authors, as vain as myself, can conceive.—But to my History.

However little worth notice the Life of a School-boy may be suppos'd to contain; yet, as the Passions of Men and Children have much the same Motives, and differ very little in their Effects, unless where the elder Experience may be able to conceal them: As therefore what arises from the Boy, may possibly be a
20 Lesson to the Man, I shall venture to relate a Fact, or two, that happen'd while I was still at School.

In *February*, 1684-5, died King *Charles* II. who being the only King I had ever seen, I remember (young as I was) his Death made a strong Impression upon me, as it drew Tears from

1. 11   here, where I have] here, when I have 2nd ed.

17.   Chapel in *Whitehall*] James II, as Duke of York had openly converted to Roman Catholicism in 1669, but continued to receive communion from the Church of England at Christmas and Easter for four years following, and attended its services for seven years after his conversion. He had the sympathy of his brother the King, who converted on his deathbed. (See F. C. Turner, *James II* [London, 1948], pp. 125-27).

the Eyes of Multitudes, who look'd no further into him than I
did: But it was, then, a sort of School-Doctrine to regard our
Monarch as a Deity; as in the former Reign it was to insist he
was accountable to this World, as well as to that above him.
But what, perhaps, gave King *Charles* II. this peculiar Possession of so many Hearts, was his affable and easy manner in conversing; a Quality that goes farther with the greater Part of
Mankind than many higher Virtues, which, in a Prince, might
more immediately regard the publick Prosperity. Even his indo-
10 lent Amusement of playing with his Dogs, and feeding his
Ducks, in St. *James's Park*, (which I have seen him do) made
the common People adore him, and consequently overlook in
him, what, in a Prince of a different Temper, they might have
been out of humour at.

I cannot help remembering one more Particular in those Times,
tho' it be quite foreign to what will follow. I was carry'd by
my Father to the Chapel in *Whitehall*; where I saw the King,
and his royal Brother the then Duke of *York,* with him in the
Closet, and present during the whole Divine Service. Such Dis-
20 pensation, it seems, for his Interest, had that unhappy Prince,
from his real Religion, to assist at another, to which his Heart
was so utterly averse.---- I now proceed to the Facts I promis'd to
speak of.

King *Charles* his Death was judg'd, by our School-master, a
proper Subject to lead the Form I was in, into a higher kind of
Exercise; he therefore enjoin'd us, severally, to make his Funeral Oration: This sort of Task, so entirely new to us all, the
Boys receiv'd with Astonishment, was a Work above their Capacity; and tho' the Master persisted in his Command, they one
30 and all, except myself, resolv'd to decline it. But I, Sir, who
was ever giddily forward, and thoughtless of Consequences, set
myself roundly to work, and got through it as well as I could.
I remember to this Hour, that single Topick of his Affability
(which made me mention it before) was the chief Motive that

1. 7 a Quality] which is a Quality 2nd ed.

4. *Arlington's* . . . Death] Cibber's memory betrays him: Arlington did not die until 28 July 1685. Since he had been of Monmouth's party, his relations with Charles were strained (cf. Turner, *James II*, pp. 163-64).

13. pragmatical] *OED*: "Unduly or improperly busy or forward; officious, meddlesome, interfering, intrusive. b. conceited, self-important, etc."

20

warm'd me into the Undertaking; and to shew how very childish
a Notion I had of his Character at that time, I rais'd his Humanity, and Love of those who serv'd him, to such height, that
I imputed his Death to the Shock he receiv'd from the Lord *Arlington's* being at the point of Death, about a Week before him. This
Oration, such as it was, I produc'd the next Morning: All the
other Boys pleaded their Inability, which the Master taking rather as a mark of their Modesty than their Idleness, only seem'd
to punish, by setting me at the Head of the Form: A Prefer-
10 ment dearly bought! Much happier had I been to have sunk
my Performance in the general Modesty of declining it. A most
uncomfortable Life I led among 'em, for many a Day after! I
was so jeer'd, laugh'd at, and hated as a pragmatical Bastard
(School-boys Language) who had betray'd the whole Form, that
scarce any of 'em wou'd keep me company; and tho' it so far
advanc'd me into the Master's Favour, that he wou'd often take
me from the School, to give me an Airing with him on Horse-
back, while they were left to their Lessons; you may be sure,
such envy'd Happiness did not encrease their Good-will to me:
20 Notwithstanding which, my Stupidity cou'd take no warning
from their Treatment. An Accident of the same nature happen'd soon after, that might have frighten'd a Boy of a meek
Spirit, from attempting any thing above the lowest Capacity. On
the 23d of *April* following, being the Coronation-Day of the
new King, the School petition'd the Master for leave to play;
to which he agreed, provided any of the Boys wou'd produce an
English Ode upon that Occasion.------ The very Word, *Ode,* I
know, makes you smile already; and so it does me; not only
because it still makes so many poor Devils turn Wits upon it,
30 but from a more agreeable Motive; from a Reflexion of how little I then thought that, half a Century afterwards, I shou'd be
call'd upon twice a Year, by my Post, to make the same kind of
Oblations to an *unexceptionable* Prince, the serene Happiness of
whose Reign my halting Rhimes are still so unequal to---This,

1. 12 among 'em] among them 2nd ed.

1. *Haec . . . juvat*] "Forsan et haec olim meminisse juvabit," Virgil, *Aeneid*, I, 207. "Perchance even these [distresses] it will someday be a joy to recall."

7. *Sing! . . . Song*] Perhaps a misquotation of Fielding's parody of Cibber's *Birthday Odes* in *The Historical Register for the Year 1736* (Act I), which begins, "This is a Day, in days of yore/ Our fathers never saw before . . ." and has the chorus, "Then sing the day,/ And sing the song." The formula "Sing the day" appears to have stimulated many parodies, and Cibber's snatch may be a generalized memory; cf. *The Grub Street Journal,* January 1732, 1733, *passim.*

13. Tits] *OED*: "Tit: a small horse, a nag."

18. writing . . . acted] Cibber wrote parts for himself in his own plays throughout his career, and suggests here that this fact has inspired jealousy.

I own, is Vanity without Disguise; but, *Hae olim meminisse juvat:* The remembrance of the miserable Prospect we had then before us, and have since escap'd by a Revolution, is now a Pleasure, which, without that Remembrance, I cou'd not so heartily have enjoy'd. The Ode I was speaking of fell to my Lot, which, in about half an Hour I produc'd. I cannot say it was much above the merry Style of *Sing! Sing the Day, and Sing the Song,* in the Farce: Yet, bad as it was, it serv'd to get the School a Play-day, and to make me not a little vain upon

10   it; which last Effect so disgusted my Play-fellows, that they left me out of the Party I had most mind to be of, in that Day's Recreation. But their Ingratitude serv'd only to increase my Vanity; for I consider'd them as so many beaten Tits, that had just had the Mortification of seeing my Hack of a *Pegasus* come in before them. This low Passion is so rooted in our Nature, that sometimes riper heads cannot govern it. I have met with much the same silly sort of Coldness, even from my Cotempora- ies of the Theatre, from having the superfluous Capacity of wri- ting myself the Characters I have acted.

20   Here, perhaps, I may again seem to be vain; but if all these Facts are true (as true they are) how can I help it? Why am I oblig'd to conceal them? The Merit of the best of them is not so extraordinary as the have warn'd me to be nice upon it; and the Praise due to them is so small a Fish, it was scarce worth while to throw my Line into the Water for it. If I confess my Vanity while a Boy, can it be Vanity, when a Man, to remember it? And if I have a tolerable Feature, will not that as much belong to my Picture, as an Imperfection? In a word, from what I have mentioned, I wou'd observe only this; That when

30   we are conscious of the least comparative Merit in ourselves, we shou'd take as much care to conceal the Value we set upon it, as if it were a real Defect: To be elated, or vain upon it, is shewing your Mony before People in want; ten to one, but some who may think you have too much, may borrow, or pick

11. 17-18 Cotemporaries] Contemporaries 2nd ed.

4.   Caesar . . . Chastity] Suetonius, *Julius Caesar*, section 74.

11.   Nero] Suetonius, *Nero*, section 20 ff.

25.   celebrated living Author] Pope.

31.   *ad captandum vulgus*] "To catch the rabble."

your Pocket before you get home. He who assumes Praise to
himself, the World will think overpays himself. Even the Suspicion of being vain, ought as much to be dreaded as the Guilt
itself. *Caesar* was of the same Opinion, in regard to his Wife's
Chastity. Praise, tho' it may be our due, is not like a *Bank-
Bill,* to be paid upon Demand; to be valuable, it must be voluntary. When we are dun'd for it, we have a Right and Privilege to refuse it. If Compulsion insists upon it, it can only
be paid as Persecution in Points of Faith is, in a counterfeit
10   Coin: And who, ever, believ'd Occasional Conformity to be sincere? *Nero,* the most vain Coxcomb of a Tyrant that ever
breath'd, cou'd not raise an unfeigned Applause to his Harp by
military Execution: Even where Praise is deserv'd, Ill-nature and
Self-conceit (Passions, that poll a majority of Mankind) will
with less reluctance part with their Mony, than their Approbation. Men of the greatest Merit are forc'd to stay 'till they die,
before the World will fairly make up their Account: Then, indeed, you have a Chance for your full Due, because it is less
grudg'd when you are incapable of enjoying it: Then, perhaps,
20   even Malice shall heap Praises upon your Memory; tho' not for
your sake, but that your surviving Competitors may suffer by a
Comparison. 'Tis from the same Principle that *Satyr* shall have
a thousand Readers, where *Panegyric* has one. When I therefore find my Name at length, in the Satyrical Works of our most
celebrated living Author, I never look upon those Lines as Malice meant to me, (for he knows I never provok'd it) but Profit
to himself: One of his Points must be, to have many Readers:
He considers that my Face and Name are more known than those
of many thousands of more consequence in the Kingdom: That
30   therefore, right or wrong, a Lick at the *Laureat* will always be
a sure Bait, *ad captandum vulgus,* to catch him little Readers:
And that to gratify the Unlearned, by now and then intersper-
sing those merry Sacrifices of an old Acquaintance to their Taste,
is a piece of quite right Poetical Craft.

1. 12 to his Harp] of his Harp 2nd ed.

5. Retailers of Politics] Cibber probably alludes, in particular, to satiric political verse

    in *The Craftsman* (1726-50), underwritten by Bolingbroke and Pulteney and

    edited by Nicolas Amhurst with the occasional assistance of Pope, Gay,

    Arbuthnot and others of Bolingbroke's friends, which bitterly pursued the king's

    ministry for ten years with great success.

18. angrily particular] Fielding comments on this in *The Champion* (Tuesday, 29

    April, 1740) as a characteristically Cibberian distortion of syntax. "Thus when he

    says . . . *Satire is angrily particular*, every Dunce of a Reader knows he means

    angry with a particular person . . ."

22. *Atticus*] In the *Epistle to Dr. Arbuthnot*, 11. 193-214.

But as a little bad Poetry, is the greatest Crime he lays to my
charge, I am willing to subscribe to his opinion of *it*. That this
sort of Wit is one of the easiest ways too, of pleasing the generality of Readers, is evident from the comfortable Subsistance
which our weekly Retailers of Politicks have been known to
pick up, merely by making bold with a Government that had
unfortunately neglected to find their Genius a better Employment.

Hence too arises all that flat Poverty of Censure and Invective,
10   that so often has a Run in our publick Papers, upon the Success
of a new Author; when, God knows, there is seldom above
one Writer among hundreds in being at the same time, whose
Satyr a Man of common Sense ought to be mov'd at. When a
Master in the Art is angry, then, indeed, we ought to be alarm'd!
How terrible a Weapon is Satyr in the Hand of a great Genius?
Yet even there, how liable is Prejudice to misuse it? How far,
when general, it may reform our Morals, or what Cruelties it
may inflict by being angrily particular, is perhaps above my
reach to determine. I shall therefore only beg leave to interpose
20   what I feel for others, whom it may personally have fallen upon.
When I read those mortifying Lines of our most eminent Author,
in his Character of *Atticus (Atticus,* whose Genius in Verse, and
whose Morality in Prose, has been so justly admir'd) though I am
charm'd with the Poetry, my Imagination is hurt at the Severity
of it; and tho' I allow the Satyrist to have had personal Provocation, yet, methinks, for that very Reason, he ought not to
have troubled the Publick with it: For, as it is observ'd in the
242d *Tattler,* "In all Terms of Reproof, where the Sentence
"appears to arise from Personal Hatred, or Passion, it is not then
30   "made the Cause of Mankind, but a Misunderstanding between
"two Persons." But if such kind of Satyr has its incontestable
Greatness; if its exemplary Brightness may not mislead inferior
Wits into a barbarous Imitation of its Severity, then I have only admir'd the Verses, and expos'd myself, by bringing them un-

3.   Writer . . . Merit] Pope, *Imitations of Horace*, Epistles II, i (1737):

> . . . . In all Charles's days,
> Roscommon only boasts unspotted Bays;
> And in our own (excuse some Courtly stains)
> No whiter page than Addison remains.
>
>   (213-16)

20.   Modern Liberties] Cibber alludes (perhaps ironically) to the opposition's free use of the word 'liberty' in their fight against the Licensing Act and in other legislative battles.

20.   *Facit . . . versum*] Juvenal, *Satire I*, 79-80: Si natura negat, facit indignatio versum. "Though nature say me nay, indignation will prompt my verse."

27.   *circum praecordia ludit*] Persius, *Satire I*, 117: "plays about the innermost feelings."

der so scrupulous a Reflexion: But the Pain which the Acrimony
of those Verses gave me, is, in some measure, allay'd, in finding
that this inimitable Writer, as he advances in Years, has since
had Candour enough to celebrate the same Person for his visible
Merit. Happy Genius! whose Verse, like the Eye of Beauty, can
heal the deepest Wounds with the least Glance of Favour.

    Since I am got so far into this Subject, you must give me
leave to go thro' all I have a mind to say upon it; because I
am not sure, that in a more proper Place, my memory may be
so full of it. I cannot find, therefore, from what Reason, Satyr
is allow'd more Licence than Comedy, or why either of them
(to be admir'd) ought not to be limited by Decency and Justice.
Let *Juvenal* and *Aristophanes* have taken what Liberties they
please, if the Learned have nothing more than their Antiquity to
justify their laying about them, at that enormous rate, I shall
wish they had a better Excuse for them! The Personal Ridicule
and Scurrility thrown upon *Socrates,* which *Plutarch* too con-
demns; and the Boldness of *Juvenal,* in writing real Names
over guilty Characters, I cannot think are to be pleaded in right
of our modern Liberties of the same kind. *Facit indignatio ver-*
sum, may be a very spirited Expression, and seems to give a
Reader hope of a lively Entertainment: But I am afraid Reproof is in unequal Hands, when Anger is its Executioner; and
tho' an outrageous Invective may carry some Truth in it, yet it
will never have that natural, easy Credit with us, which we give
to the laughing Ironies of a cool Head. The Satyr that can
smile *circum praecordia ludit,* and seldom fails to bring the Reader quite over to his Side, whenever Ridicule and Folly are at
variance. But when a Person satyriz'd is us'd with the extremest
Rigour, he may sometimes meet with Compassion, instead of
Contempt, and throw back the Odium that was design'd for
him, upon the Author. When I would therefore disarm the
Satyrist of this Indignation, I mean little more, than that I wou'd
take from him all private or personal Prejudice, and wou'd still

leave him as much general Vice to scourge as he pleases, and
that with as much Fire and Spirit as Art and Nature demand to
enliven his Work, and keep his Reader awake.

 Against all this it may be objected, That these are Laws
which none but phlegmatick Writers will observe, and only Men
of Eminence should give. I grant it, and therefore only submit them to Writers of better Judgment. I pretend not to restrain others from chusing what I don't like; they are welcome
(if they please too) to think I offer these Rules, more from an Incapacity to break them, than from a moral Humanity. Let it be
so! still, That will not weaken the strength of what I have asserted,
if my Assertion be true. And though I allow, that Provocation is
not apt to weigh out its Resentments by Drachms and Scruples,
I shall still think, that no publick Revenge can be honourable,
where it is not limited by Justice; and, if Honour is insatiable
in its Revenge, it loses what it contends for, and sinks itself, if not
into Cruelty, at least into Vain-glory.

 This so singular Concern which I have shewn for others, may
naturally lead you to ask me, what I feel for myself, when I am
unfavourably treated by the elaborate Authors of our daily Papers. Shall I be sincere? and own my Frailty? Its usual Effect
is to make me vain! For I consider, if I were quite good for nothing, these Pidlers in Wit would not be concern'd to take me to
pieces, or (not to be quite so vain) when they moderately charge
me with only Ignorance, or Dulness, I see nothing in That which
an honest Man need be asham'd of: There is many a good Soul,
who, from those sweet Slumbers of the Brain, are never awa-
ken'd by the least harmful Thought; and I am sometimes tempted to think those Retailers of Wit may be of the same Class;
that what they write proceeds not from Malice, but Industry;
and that I ought no more to reproach them, than I would a Lawyer that pleads against me for his Fee; that their Detraction,
like Dung, thrown upon a Meadow, tho' it may seem at first to

deform the Prospect, in a little time it will disappear of itself,
and leave an involuntary Crop of Praise behind it.

   When they confine themselves to a sober Criticism upon what
I write; if their Censure is just, what Answer can I make to it?
If it is unjust, why should I suppose that a sensible Reader will
not see it, as well as myself? Or, admit I were able to expose
them, by a laughing Reply, will not that Reply beget a Rejoin-
der? And though they might be Gainers, by having the worst
on't, in a Paper War, that is not Temptation for me to come into it. Or (to make both sides less considerable) would not my
bearing Ill-language, from a Chimney-sweeper, do me less harm,
than it would be to box with him, tho' I were sure to beat him?
Nor indeed is the little Reputation I have, as an Author, worth
the trouble of a Defence. Then, as no Criticism can possibly
make me worse than I really am; so nothing I say of myself can
possibly make me better: When therefore a determin'd Critick
comes arm'd with Wit and Outrage, to take from me that small
Pittance I have, I would no more dispute with him, than I
wou'd resist a Gentleman of the Road, to save a little Pocket-
Money. Men that are in want themselves, seldom make a Conscience of taking it from others. Whoever thinks I have too
much, is welcome to what share of it he pleases: Nay, to make
him more merciful (as I partly guess the worst he can say of what
I now write) I will prevent even the Imputation of his doing me
Injustice, and honestly say it myself, *viz.* That of all the As-
surances I was ever guilty of, this, of writing my own Life, is
the most hardy. I beg his Pardon!--- Impudent is what I shou'd
have said! That thro' every Page there runs a Vein of Vanity
and Impertinence, which no *French Ensigns memoires* ever came
up to; but, as this is a common Error, I presume the Terms of
Doating Trifler, Old Fool, or *Conceited Coxcomb,* will carry Contempt enough for an impartial Censor to Bestow on me; that my
Style is unequal, pert, and frothy, patch'd and party-colour'd,

1.   15 nothing I say] nothing I can say 2nd ed.

11. *Cinna ... vult ... et est Pauper*] Martial, *Epigrams* VIII, xix: "Pauper videri Cinna vult, et est pauper."

33. complete Revenge ... less agreeably] With the appearance of the revised *Dunciad*, Cibber's pose of detachment gave way to concern for his reputation, and he made angry counter-attacks in a series of public letters to Pope (see Introduction, pp. xxxi ff).

like the Coat of an *Harlequin;* low and pompous, cramm'd
with Epithets, strew'd with Scraps of second-hand *Latin* from
common Quotations; frequently aiming at Wit, without ever
hitting the Mark; a mere Ragoust, toss'd up from the Offals of
other Authors: My Subject below all Pens buy my own, which,
whenever I keep to, is flatly dawb'd by one eternal Egotism:
That I want nothing but Wit, to be as an accomplish'd a Coxcomb here, as ever I attempted to expose on the Theatre: Nay,
that this very Confession is no more a sign of my Modesty,
10   than it is a Proof of my Judgment; that, in short, you may
roundly tell me, that --- *Cinna (or Cibber) vult videri Pauper, et*
est Pauper.

　　When humble Cinna *cries,* I'm Poor and Low,
　　You may believe him --- he is really so.

　　Well, Sir Critick! and what of all this? Now I have laid
myself at your Feet, what will you do with me? Expose me?
Why, dear Sir, does not every Man that writes, expose himself?
Can you make me more ridiculous than Nature has made me?
You cou'd not sure suppose, that I would lose the Pleasure of
20   Writing, because you might possibly judge me a Blockhead, or
perhaps might pleasantly tell other People they ought to think
me so too. Will not they judge as well from what *I* say, as
from what *You* say? If then you attack me merely to divert
yourself, your Excuse for writing will be no better than mine.
But perhaps you may want Bread: If that be the Case, even go
to Dinner, i' God's name!

　　If our best Authors, when teiz'd by these Triflers, have
not been Masters of this Indifference, I shou'd not wonder if it
were disbeliev'd in me; but when it is consider'd that I have
30   allow'd, my never having been disturb'd into a Reply, has proceeded as much from Vanity as from Philosophy, the Matter
then may not seem so incredible: And, though I confess, the
complete Revenge of making them Immortal Dunces in Immor-

11. 22-23   as from what <u>You</u> say?]   as what <u>You</u> say?   2nd ed.

24.   *Laurel*] See Introduction, pp. xxx ff.; cf. also E. K. Broadus, *The Laureateship*, and Barker, Chapter VIII, "The Contest for the Laurel."

tal Verse, might be glorious; yet, if you will call it Insensibility in me, never to have winc'd at them, even that Inssensibility
has its Happiness, and what could Glory give me more? For
my part, I have always had the Comfort to think, whenever
they design'd me a Disfavour, it generally flew back into their
own Faces, as it happens to Children when they squirt at their
Play-fellows against the Wind. If a Scribbler cannot be easy,
because he fancies I have too good an Opinion of my own Productions, let him write on, and mortify; I owe him not the

10 Charity to be out of temper myself, merely to keep him quiet,
or give him Joy: Nor, in reality, can I see, why any thing mis-
represented, tho' believ'd of me by Persons to whom I am unknown, ought to give me any more Concern, than what may
be thought of me in *Lapland*: 'Tis with those with whom I
am to *live* only, where my Character can affect me; and I will
venture to say, he must find out a new way of Writing that will
make me pass my Time *there* less agreeably.

You see, Sir, how hard it is for a Man that is talking of
himself, to know when to give over; but if you are tired, lay

20 me aside till you have a fresh Appetite; if not, I'll tell you a
Story.

In the Year 1730, there were many Authors, whose Merit
wanted nothing but Interest to recommend them to the vacant
Laurel, and who took it ill, to see it at last conferr'd upon a
Comedian; insomuch, that they were resolv'd, at least, to shew
Specimens of their superior Pretensions, and accordingly enli-
ven'd the publick Papers with ingenious Epigrams, and satyrical
Flirts, at the unworthy Successor: These Papers, my Friends,
with a wicked Smile, would often put into my Hands, and de-

30 sire me to read them fairly in Company: This was a Challenge which I never declin'd, and, to do my doughty Antago-
nists justice, I always read them with as much impartial Spirit,
as if I had writ them myself. While I was thus beset on all
sides, there happen'd to step forth a poetical Knight-Errant to

12. *To the Author*] I have been unable to locate a copy of this issue of the *Whitehall Evening Post* or, indeed, January issues for the years immediately after to check Cibber's claims; however, his letter and poem are very similar in style to others which appeared in opposition newspapers in January during the 1730's, as attacks on his New Year Odes.

my Assistance, who was hardy enough to publish some compassionate Stanzas in my Favour. These, you may be sure, the
Raillery of my Friends could do no less than say, I have written
to myself. To deny it, I knew would but have confirm'd their
pretended Suspicion: I therefore told them, since it gave them
such Joy to believe them my own, I would do my best to make
the whole Town think so too. As the Oddness of this Reply
was, I knew, what would not be easily comprehended, I desired
them to have a Day's Patience, and I would print an Explanation to it: To conclude, in two Days after I sent this Letter, with
some doggerel Rhimes at the Bottom,

To the Author of the Whitchall Evening-Post.

SIR,

THE Verses to the Laureat, in yours of Saturday *last, have*
occasion'd the following Reply, which I hope you'll give a
place in your next, to shew that we can be quick, as well as smart,
upon a proper Occasion: And, as I think it the lowest Mark of a
Scoundrel to make bold with any Man's Character in Print, with-
out subscribing the true Name of the Author; I therefore desire,
if the Laureat is concern'd enough, to ask the Question, that you
will tell him my Name, and where I live; till then, I beg leave
to be known by no other than that of,

Your Servant,

Monday, Jan. 11, 1730.

FRANCIS FAIRPLAY.

These were the Verses.

I.

Ah, hah! Sir Coll, *is that thy Way,*
Thy own dull Praise to write?
And wou'd'st thou stand so sure a Lay?
No, that's too stale a Bite.

II.

Nature, and Art, in thee combine,
       Thy Talents here excel:
All shining Brass thou dost outshine,
       To play the Cheat so well.

III.

Who sees thee in Iago's *Part,*
       But thinks thee such a Rogue?
And is not glad, with all his Heart,
       To hang so sad a Dog?

IV.

When Bays *thou play'st, Thyself thou art;*
10   *For that by Nature fit,*
No Blockhead better suits the Part,
       Than such a Coxcomb Wit.

V.

In Wronghead *too, thy Brains we see,*
       Who might do well at Plough;
As fit for Parliament was he,
       As for the Laurel, Thou.

VI.

Bring thy protected Verse from Court,
       And try it on the Stage;
There it will make much better Sport,
20   *And set the Town in Rage.*

VII.

There Beaux, and Wits, and Cits, and Smarts,
       Where Hissing's not uncivil,
Will show their Parts, to thy Deserts,
       And send it to the Devil.

4.   *For* . . . Blood! thou'lt stand it all] As Cibber notes below, this line is from the
Epilogue to *The Non-Juror* (1. 10): The Epilogue, *"spoken by Mrs. Oldfield,"*
ironically remonstrates with Cibber for having dared to write a play on
contemporary politics:

> Wasn't not enough the Criticks might pursue him!
> But must he rouse a Party to undo him!
> These Blows I told him on his Play would fall,
> But he unmoved, cry'd — Blood, we'll Stand it all,
> (7-10)

VIII.

But, ah! in vain, 'gainst Thee we write,
In vain thy Verse we maul!
Our sharpest Satyr's thy Delight,
For—Blood! thou'lt stand it all.

*

IX.

Thunder, 'tis said, the Laurel spares;
Nought but thy Brows could blast it:
And yet—O curst, provoking Stars!
Thy Comfort is, thou hast *it.*

This, Sir, I offer as a Proof, that I was seven Years ago the
same cold Candidate for Fame, which I would still be thought;
you will not easily suppose I could have much Concern about
it, while, to gratify the merry Pique of my Friends, I was capable of seeming to head the Poetical Cry then against me, and
at the same time of never letting the Public know, 'till this
Hour, that these Verses were written by myself: Nor do I give
them you as an Entertainment, but merely to shew you this particular Cast of my Temper.

When I have said this, I would not have it thought Affecta-
tion in me, when I grant, that no Man worthy the Name of an
Author, is a more faulty Writer than myself; that I am not
Master of my own Language, I too often feel, when I am at a
Loss for Expression: I know too that I have too bold a Disregard
for that Correctness, which others set so just a Value upon: This
I ought to be asham'd of, when I find that Persons, of perhaps
colder Imaginations, are allow'd to write better than myself.
Whenever I speak of any thing that highly delights me, I find
it very difficult to keep my Words within the Bounds of Common Sense: Even when I write too, the same Failing will sometimes get the better of me; of which I cannot give you a stronger

10

20

---

*A line in the Epilogue to the Nonjuror.

l. 24   of perhaps] perhaps of 2nd ed.

5.   *outdid . . . Outdoing*?] "In later editions the expression was changed to 'She here out-did her usual excellence'" (Lowe, I, 51). The author of *The Laureat* (p. 36) suggests that the phrase comes from Dryden's Preface to *Cleomenes*: "Mrs. Barry always excellent, has in this Tragedy excelled herself" (cf. p. 94).

14.   *Decies repetita placeret*] Horace, *Ars Poetica*, 365: "Though ten times repeated, it will please."

20.   eminent Pleader] Unidentified.

Instance, than in that wild Expression I made use of in the first
Edition of my Preface to the *Provok'd Husband;* where, speaking of Mrs. *Oldfield's* excellent Performance in the Part of Lady
Townly, my Words ran thus, *viz. It is not enough to say, that
here she outdid* her usual *Outdoing.*--- A most vile Jingle, I grant
it! You may well ask me, How could I possibly commit uch a
Wantonness to Paper? And I owe myself the Shame of confessing, I have no Excuse for it, but that, like a Lover in the Fulness of his Content, by endeavouring to be floridly grateful, I
10 talk'd Nonsense. Not but it makes me smile to remember how
many flat Writers have made themselves brisk upon this single
Expression; wherever the Verb, *Outdo,* could come in, the pleasant Accusative, *Outdoing,* was sure to follow it. The provident Wags knew, that *Decies repetita placeret: so* delicious a
Morsel could not be serv'd up too often! After it had held them
nine times told for a Jest, the Publick has been pester'd with a
tenth Skull, thick enough to repeat it. Nay, the very learned
in the Law, have at last facetiously laid hold of it! Ten Years after it first came from me, it serv'd to enliven the Eloquence of
20 an eminent Pleader before a House of Parliament! What Author
would not envy me so frolicksome a Fault, that had such publick
Honours paid to it?

   After this Consciousness of my real Defects, you will easily
judge, Sir, how little I presume that my Poetical Labours may
outlive those of my mortal *Cotemporaries.*

   At the same time that I am so humble in my Pretensions to
Fame, I would not be thought to undervalue it; Nature will
not suffer us to despise it, but she may sometimes make us too
fond of it. I have known more than one good Writer, very near
30 ridiculous, from being in too much Heat about it. Whoever intrinsically deserves it, will always have a proportionable Right to
it. It can neither be resign'd, nor taken from you by Violence.
Truth, which is unalterable, must (however his Fame may be
contested) give every Man his Due: What a Poem weighs, it

---

1. 20 an eminent Pleader] an eloquent Pleader 2nd. ed.

6.   an emminent Author] Probably Pope.

32.   *Time is the Judge . . . stay the slain*] Edward Young (1683-1765), *To Mr. Pope, Concerning the Authors of the Age* (1730), *Epistle II*, 214-19.

will be worth; nor is it in the Power of Human Eloquence,
with Favour or Prejudice, to increase or diminish its Value. Prejudice, 'tis true, may a while discolour it; but it will always have
its Appeal to the Equity of good Sense, which will never fail, in
the end, to reverse all false Judgment against it. Therefore
when I see an eminent Author hurt, and impatient at an impotent Attack upon his Labours, he disturbs my Inclination to admire him; I grow doubtful of the favourable Judgment I have
made of him, and am quite uneasy to see him so tender, in a
10   Point he cannot but know he ought not himself to be judge of;
his Concern indeed, at another's Prejudice, or Disapprobation,
may be natural; but, to own it, seems to me a natural Weakness. When a Work is apparently great, it will go without
Crutches; all your Art and Anxiety to heighten the Fame of it,
then becomes low and little. He that will bear no Censure,
must be often robb'd of his due Praise. Fools have as good a
Right to be Readers, as Men of Sense have, and why not to give
their Judgments too? Methinks it would be a sort of Tyranny
in Wit, for an Author to be publickly putting every Argument
20   to death that appear'd against him; so absolute a Demand for
Approbation, puts us upon our Right to dispute it; Praise is as
much the Reader's Property, as Wit is the Author's; Applause
is not a Tax paid to him as a Prince, but rather a Benevolence
given to him as a Beggar; and we have naturally more Charity
for the dumb Beggar, than the sturdy one. The Merit of a
Writer, and a fine Woman's Face, are never mended by their
talking of them: How amiable is she that seems not to know she
is handsome.

        To conclude; all I have said upon this Subject is much better
30   contained in six Lines of a Reverend Author, which will be an
Answer to all critical Censure for ever.

                Time is the Judge; Time has nor Friend, nor Foe;
                False Fame will wither, and the True will grow:

1857, a great many of his kinsmen took advantage of the privilege. (Appendix A, pp. 167-69, *Winchester College: its history, buildings, and customs*, by the Winchester College Archeological Society, Winchester, 1926.)

22. pompus Pedigree] The claim of kinship with Wykeham is apparently accurate. A genealogy exists (reprinted by Harold Faber, *Caius Gabriel Cibber*, Oxford, 1926, p. 76) showing Jane Colley's descent from William of Wykeham's sister Agnes. He was not, of course, literally William's "descendant."

CHAPTER III

5.   I am now come to that Crisis . . . Under-proper of the State] Fielding in *Joseph
Andrews* (Book I, i) links *Pamela* and Cibber's *Apology*: "But I pass by these
and many others [biographies of great men] to mention two books lately published
which represent an admirable Pattern of the Amiable in either Sex. The former of
these, which deals in Male-Virtue, was written by the great Person himself, who
lived the Life he hath recorded, and is by many thought to have lived such a Life
only in order to write it. The other is communicated to us by an Historian who
borrows his lights, as the common Method is, from authentic Papers and
Records. The Reader, I believe, already conjectures, I mean the Lives of Mr.
Colley Cibber, and of Mrs. Pamela Andrews. How artfully doth the former, by
insinuating that he escaped being promoted to the highest Stations in Church and
State, teach us a contempt of Worldly Grandeur!"

17.   a Descendant of *William* of *Wickam*] Cibber's claim to *descent* from William of
Wykeham drew notice from the author of TC (p. 5); writing as Theophilus
Cibber, he remarks, "for it seems, by my Father's Mother's side, I was
descended from *William* of *Wickham* the Founder [of] Winchester College] . . .
In what *Branch* [of his family], I am ingenious enough to say I know not, yet
from my Soul I contemn that vile Insinuation which *a certain Counsellor*, at a
certain Trial, made, that it was by some collateral Branch, as *William* of *Wickham*
was a *Churchman* at a time when *Matrimony* was not allow'd of . . . The
inference is evident . . . It equally effects all those educated in *Winchester College*
. . . as descendants of the *Founder*." In the statutes of Winchester, the founder
provided that his kinsmen could enter the college between the ages of seven and
twenty-five, and that they should have priority of election. From the end of the
seventeenth century until the University Commission abolished the practice in

Arm'd with this Truth, all Criticks I defy,
For, if I fall, by my own Pen I die.
While Snarlers strive with proud, but fruitless Pain,
To wound Immortals, or to slay the Slain.

C H A P. III.

The Author's several Chances for the Church, the Court, and the
Army. Going to the University. Met the Revolution at Nottingham. *Took Arms on that Side. What he saw of it. A few*
Political Thoughts. Fortune willing to do for him. His neglect
of her. The Stage preferr'd to all her Favours. The Profes-
sion of an Actor consider'd. The Misfortunes and Advantages
of it.

I am now come to that Crisis of my Life, when Fortune seem'd to be at a Loss what she should do with
me. Had she favour'd my Father's first Designation
of me, he might then, perhaps, have had as sanguine hopes of my being a Bishop, as I afterwards
10   conceiv'd of my being a General, when I first took Arms, at the
Revolution. Nay, after that, I had a third Chance too, equally as good, of becoming an Under-proper of the State. How,
at last, I came to be none of all these, the Sequel will inform
you.

About the Year 1687, I was taken from School to stand at the
Election of Children into *Winchester* College; my being, by my
Mother's side, a Descendant of *William* of *Wickam*, the Founder, my Father (who knew little how the World was to be dealt
with) imagined my having that Advantage, would be Security
20   enough for my Success, and so sent me simply down thither,
without the least favourable Recommendation or Interest, but that
of my naked Merit, and a pompous Pedigree in my Pocket.

7.   *Lewis Cibber* . . . Statue of the Founder] This large bronze statue has an inscription in Latin which reads: "Sacred to the memory of William of Wykeham, Bishop of Winchester and founder of this college. Caius Gabriel Cibber, a relation of his by marriage and statuary to the King, had this statue of him cast in bronze and placed here at his own expense in the year 1697" (*Winchester College: history*, p. 167). Lewis Cibber was admitted to Winchester in the same year the statue was presented, was made a Fellow of New College in 1700, took holy orders, and died in 1711 (Faber, p. 74). Wykeham, in a photograph of the statue in Faber's volume (facing p. 72), stands in medieval episcopal garb, with crozier in the left hand, the right raised in a blessing.

21.   to supply . . . his common Necessities] Cibber may be referring to the need to provide for his brother due to his father's death in 1700 (Faber, p. 75), or to his father's general improvidence, attested by his numerous confinements in debtor's prisons (*ibid.*, pp. 17-22).

27.   Dr. *Compton*] Henry Compton (1632-1713), an important churchman who had been responsible for the religious education of Queens Mary and Anne; he was active in the Revolution of 1688.

Had he tack'd a Direction to my Back, and sent me by the Car-
rier to the Mayor of the Town, to be chosen Member of Parliament there, I might have had just as much chance to have succeeded in the one, as the other. But I must not omit in this
place, to let youi know, that the Experience which my Father
then bought, at my Cost, taught him, some Years after, to take
a more judicious care of my younger Brother, *Lewis Cibber,*
whom, with the Present of a Statue of the Founder, of his own
making, he recommended to the same College. This Statue

10 now stands (I think) over the School Door there, and was so well
executed, that it seem'd to speak ----- for its Kinsman. It was
no sooner set up, than the Door of Preferment was open to
him.

Here, one wou'd think, my Brother had the Advantage of
me, in the Favour of Fortune, by this his first laudable Step into
the World. I own, I was so proud of his Success, that I even
valued myself upon it; and yet it is but a melancholy Reflexion
to observe, how unequally his Profession and mine were provided
for; when I, who had been the Outcast of Fortune, could find

20 means, from my Income of the Theatre, before I was my own
Master there, to supply, in his highest Preferment, his common
Necessities. I cannot part with his memory without telling you,
I had as sincere a Concern for this Brother's Well-being, as my
own. He had lively Parts, and more than ordinary Learning,
with a good deal of natural Wit and Humour; but, from too
great a Disregard to his Health, he died a Fellow of *New College*
in *Oxford,* soon after he had been ordain'd by Dr. *Compton,* then
Bishop of *London.* I now return to the State of my own Affair
at *Winchester.*

30 After the Election, the moment I was inform'd that I was one
of the unsuccessful Candidates, I blest myself to think what a
happy Reprieve I had got, from the confin'd Life of a School-
boy! and the same Day took Post back to *London,* that I might
arrive time enough to see a Play (then my darling Delight) be-

of Cambridge, Cambridge, 1886, II, 542, quoted by Faber, pp. 39-40). Faber cites evidence that Cibber executed the works in Cambridge.

4.   why Providence afterwards took more care of me . . .] Possibly an instance of Cibber's rumored impiety. Davies (*Dram. Misc.*, III, 475-76) notes that "His contempt of religion was justly censured by many. Dennis, in a letter to Sir John Edgar, alias Sir Richard Steele, charges him with spitting at a picture of our Saviour at Bath. At Tunbridge, I have been informed by Dr. Johnson, Cibber entered into a conversation with the famous Mr. William Whiston, with a view to insult him; but Whiston cut him short, by telling him, at once, that he could possibly hold no discourse with him; for that he was himself a clergyman; and Cibber was a player, and was besides, as he had heard, a pimp." The issue of Cibber's religious beliefs cannot now be settled, but it is unlikely, as Lowe argues also (I, 58 n.) that Cibber would have dared to be openly antireligious. It is probable that he viewed this statement as an instance of piety.

16.   *Chattsworth* . . . to a *Grecian*, Magnificence] Caius Cibber worked at Chatsworth from December 1687 to December 1690, leaving some of his work to be completed by others (Faber, pp. 49-52). It is probable that the architect for Chatsworth, William Talman, recommended Cibber to the Earl, since they had worked together previously on the building of Thoresby Hall, the seat of the First Duke of Kingston (ibid., pp. 52-55; Caius Cibber's extensive works which are in the classical style he acquired in Italy, are discussed by Faber, who provides photographs of them facing pages 50, 52 and 54).

27.   *Trinity* College New Library] Sir Christopher Wren, who erected the library in 1676, chose Cibber to make four statues for the top of the east wall. "The four statues representing Divinity, Law, Physics and Mathematics, which stand on the central piers subdividing the balustrade on the East side were executed in 1681 . . . Cibber came to Cambridge with his men and personally superintended the placing of them" (from Willis and Clark, *Architectural History of the University*

fore my Mother might demand an Account of my travelling
Charges. When I look back to that time, it almost makes me
tremble to think what Miseries, in fifty Years farther in Life,
such an unthinking Head was liable to! To ask, why Providence afterwards took more care of me, than I did of myself,
might be making too bold an Enquiry into its secret Will and
Pleasure: All I can say to that Point, is, that I am thankful,
and amaz'd at it!

 'Twas about this time I first imbid'd an Inclination, which I
10 durst not reveal, for the Stage; for, besides that I knew it would
disoblige my Father, I had no Conception of any means, practicable, to make my way to it. I therefore suppress'd the bewitch-
ing Ideas of so sublime a Station, and compounded with my Ambition by laying a lower Scheme, of only getting the nearest way
into the immediate Life of a Gentleman-Collegiate. My Father
being at this time employ'd at *Chattsworth* in *Derbyshire,* by the
(then) Earl of *Devonshire,* who was raising that Seat from a
Gothick, to a *Grecian,* Magnificence, I made use of the Leisure
I then had, in *London,* to open to him, by Letter, my Disincli-
20 nation to wait another Year for an uncertain Preferment at *Winchester,* and to entreat him that he would send me, *per saltum,*
by a shorter Cut, to the University. My Father, who was naturally indulgent to me, seem'd to comply with my Request, and
wrote word, that as soon as his Affairs would permit, he would
carry me with him, and settle me in some College, but rather at
Cambridge, where, (during his late Residence at that Place, in
making some Statues that now stand upon *Trinity* College New
Library, he had contracted some Acquaintance with the Heads of
Houses, who might assist his Intentions for me. This I lik'd bet-
30 ter than to go discountenanc'd to *Oxford,* to which it would have
been a sort of Reproach to me, not to have come elected. After
some Months were elaps'd, my Father, not being willing to let
me lie too long idling in *London,* sent for me down to *Chattsworth* to be under his Eye, till he cou'd be at leisure to carry

3.   Prince of *Orange* . . . landed in the *West*] At Torbay on 5 November 1688.

6.   Earl of *Devonshire* had rais'd] The third Earl of Devonshire, and first Duke (12 May 1694), William Cavendish, was one of the Whig lords who signed a cipher letter inviting William of Orange to displace James II (David Ogg, *England in the Reigns of James II and William III*, p. 202).

9.   being . . . too advanc'd in Years] He was fifty-eight at the time.

21.   Fate of King *James* . . . upon the Anvil] Both *T.C.* (pp. 24-25) and *The Laureat* (pp. 25-26) note ironically Cibber's fondness for linking himself with great figures of State.

32.   Annual Odes] I.e., for the King's birthday and the New Year.

me to *Cambridge*. Before I could set out, on my Journey thither, the Nation fell in labour of the Revolution, the News
being then just brought to *London*, That the Prince of *Orange,*
at the Head of an Army was landed in the *West*. When I came to
Nottingham, I found my Father in Arms there, among those
Forces which the Earl of *Devonshire* had rais'd for the Redress
of our violated Laws and Liberties. My Father judg'd this a
proper Season, for a young Stripling to turn himself loose into
the Bustle of the World; and being himself too advanc'd in
10   Years, to endure the Winter Fatigue, which might possibly follow, entreated that noble Lord, that he would be pleas'd to accept of his Son in his room, and that he would give him (my
Father) leave to return, and finish his Works at *Chattsworth.*
This was so well receiv'd by his Lordship, that he not only admitted of my Service, but promis'd my Father, in return, that
when Affairs were settled, he would provide for me. Upon this,
my Father return'd to *Derbyshire,* while I, not a little transported, jump'd into his Saddle. Thus, in one Day, all my Thoughts
of the University were smother'd in Ambition! A flight Commis-
20   sion for a Horse-Officer, was the least View I had before me. At
this Crisis you cannot but observe, that the Fate of King *James,*
and of the Prince of *Orange,* and that of so minute a Being as
my self, were all at once upon the Anvil: In what shape they
wou'd severally come out, tho' a good *Guess* might be made, was
not then *demonstrable* to the deepest Foresight; but as my Fortune seem'd to be of small Importance to the Publick, Providence thought fit to postpone it, 'till that of those great Rulers
of Nations, was justly perfected. Yet, had my Father's Business
permitted him to have carried me, one Month sooner (as he in-
30   tended) to the University, who knows but, by this time, that
purer Fountain might have wash'd my Imperfections into a Capacity of writing (instead of Plays and Annual Odes) Sermons,
and Pastoral Letters. But whatever Care of the Church might,
so, have fallen to my share, as I dare say it may be now, in

11.   19-20 Commission] Cmmission 1st ed.

11. Happy Nation! . . . cannot all govern.] Cibber's Whig loyalties gave rise to this interpretation of both the 1688 Revolution and the state of England when he was writing (c. 1738). The unity in 1688, he implies, grew out of extremes of oppression, whereas the opposition to Walpole's government—which was growing extremely vehement at this time (Plumb, II, 157 ff., and Archibald S. Foord, *His Majesty's Opposition: 1714-1830,* Oxford, 1964, pp. 111-214)—was the result of too many men seeking to have places in the now-admirable government.

17. seeming Patriots] The word 'Patriot' at this period suggested Bolingbroke, his allies in opposition, and his politics.

31. *longest* rail'd at . . . a Proof of Capacity] TC (p. 25) remarks, "If this Circumstance of being long rail'd at is an indubitable Characterstick of a wise and able Minister, the *Right Honourable Gentleman* [Sir Robert Walpole] . . . has been the most able and wise Minister that ever manag'd the Affairs of this Nation [Walpole had been in power since 1722]." *The Laureat* (p. 26) attacks his logic: ". . . one wou'd imagin [sic] that a Minister who has been rail'd at a long Time, may have deserved to have been rail'd at a long Time . . . may it not be a proof, I think it is a very strong one, that the People suspect his Want of Capacity or Integrity, or both." Cibber is of course speaking of Walpole's skillful outmaneuvering of opponents.

better Hands, I ought not to repine at my being otherwise dispos'd of.

   You must, now, consider me as one among those desperate
Thousands, who, after a Patience sorely try'd, took Arms under
the Banner of Necessity, the natural Parent of all Human Laws,
and Government. I question, if in all the Histories of Empire,
there is one Instance of so bloodless a Revolution, as that in *England* in 1688, wherein Whigs, Tories, Princes, Prelates, Nobles,
Clergy, common People, and a standing Army, were unanimous.
10 To have seen all *England* of one Mind, is to have liv'd at a very
particular Juncture. Happy Nation! who are never divided
among themsevles, but when they have least to complain of!
Our greatest Grievance since that time, seems to have been, that
we cannot all govern; and 'till the Number of good Places are
equal to those, who think themselves qualified for them, there
must ever be a Cause of Contention among us. While Great
Men want great Posts, the Nation will never want real or seeming Patriots; and while great posts are fill'd with Persons, whose
Capacities are but Human, such Persons will never be allow'd
20 to be without Errors; not even the Revolution, with all its Advantages, it seems, has been able to furnish us with unexceptionable Statesmen! for, from that time, I don't remember any one
Set of Ministers, that have not been heartily rail'd at; a Period
long enough, one would think, (if all of them have been as bad
as they have been call'd) to make a People despair of ever seeing
a good one: But as it is possible that Envy, Prejudice, or Party,
may sometimes have a share in what is generally thrown upon
'em, it is not easy for a private Man, to know who is absolutely
in the right, from what is said against them, or from what their
30 Friends or Dependants may say in their Favour: Tho' I can hardly forbear thinking, that they who have been *longest* rail'd at,
must, from that Circumstance, shew, in some sort, a Proof of
Capacity. --- But to my History.

12. old Lion to dance] Fielding (*The Champion*, 6 May 1740) notes this and other instances (*Apology*, p. 104) of Cibber's fondness for similes of animals, ". . . this brings to my Mind a Story which I once heard from *Booth*, that our Biographer had, in one of his Plays in a Local Simile, introduced this generous Beast in some Island or Country where Lions did not grow, of which being informed by the learned *Booth*, the Biographer replied, *prithee tell me where there is a Lion, for God's Curse, if there be a Lion* in Europe, Asia, Africa, or America, *I will not lose my Simile.*"

28. *Tantum religio . . . malorum*] Lucretius, *De Rerum Natura*, I, 102: "So potent was religion in persuading to evil deeds."

It were almost incredible to tell you, at the latter end of King *James's* Time (though the Rod of Arbitrary Power was always shaking over us) with what Freedom and Contempt the common People, in the open Streets, talk'd of his wild Measures to make a whole Protestant Nation Papists; and yet, in the height of our secure and wanton Defiance of him, we, of the Vulgar, had no farther Notion of any Rememdy for this Evil, than a satisfy'd Presumption, that our Numbers were too great to be master'd by his mere Will and Pleasure; that though he might be too hard for our Laws, he would never be able to get the better of our Nature; and, that to drive all *England* into Popery and Slavery, he would find, would be teaching an old Lion to dance.

But, happy was it for the Nation, that it had then wiser Heads in it, who knew how to lead a People so dispos'd into Measures for the Publick Preservation.

Here, I cannot help reflecting on the very different Deliverances *England* met with, at this Time, and in the very same Year of the Century before: Then (in 1588) under a glorious Princess, who had, at heart, the Good and Happiness of her People, we scatter'd and destroy'd the most formidable Navy of Invaders, that ever cover'd the Seas: And now (in 1688) under a Prince, who had alienated the Hearts of his People, by his absolute Measures, to oppress them, a foreign Power is receiv'd with open Arms, in defence of our Laws, Liberties, and Religion, which our native Prince had invaded! How widely different were these two Monarchs in their Sentiments of Glory! But, *Tantum religio potuit suadere malorum.*

When we consider, in what height of the Nation's Prosperity, the Successor of Queen *Elizabeth* came to this Throne, it seems amazing, that such a Pile of *English* Fame, and Glory, which her skilful Administration had erected, should, in every following Reign, down to the Revolution, so unhappily moulder away, in one continual Gradation of Political Errors: All which

2.   *That the Love . . . Support of her Throne*] This is possibly a version of Elizabeth's "Golden Speech" to Commons 30 November 1602: "And though God hath raised me high, yet this I account the glory of my crown, that I have reigned with your love" (quoted by J. E. Neale, *Queen Elizabeth*, p. 400).

28.   Revolution . . . perpetually contested Right to] This passage enunciates a popular view of seventeenth-century English history, yet Fielding (*The Champion*, 6 May 1740) reproaches him for saying that Englishmen had only a "*contested Right to any Liberty before the Revolution.* This is a Discovery, which, if it had entered into the Head of the Jacobitical Writers in King *William's* Reign, would have done their business at once; for, if we had no right to Liberty before the Revolution, none but our great Biographer can tell us what right we had to the Revolution. But his political Principles seem everywhere to be the *Babylonish* Dialect in *Hudibras*, are a party-colour'd Mixture of patched and pieballed Principles, from whose jarring and repugnant Atoms is struck out a *Silver* or rather Golden-*toned* Utility . . ." Cf. James Thomson, *Liberty* (1735-36) IV, 746-1191; speaking of 'liberty' in 'Gothic' times, the poem notes that Englishmen had then only "long-contested rights" (1. 783).

must have been avoided, if the plain Rule, which that wise Princess
left behind her, had been observed, *viz. That the Love of her
People was the surest Support of her Throne.* This was the Principle by which she so happily govern'd herself, and those she had
the Care of. In this she found Strength to combat, and struggle
through more Difficuties, and dangerous Conspiracies, than ever
English Monarch had to cope with. At the same time that she
profess'd to *desire* the People's Love, she took care that her Actions shou'd *deserve* it, without the least Abatement of her Pre-
10 rogative; the Terror of which she so artfully covered, that she
sometimes seem'd to flatter those she was determin'd should obey.
If the four following Princes had exercis'd their Regal Authority with so visible a Regard to the Publick Welfare, it were
hard to know, whether the People of *England* might have ever
complain'd of them, or even felt the want of that Liberty they
now so happily enjoy. 'Tis true, that before her Time, our
Ancestors had many successful Contests with their Sovereigns for
their *ancient Right* and *Claim* to it; yet what did those Successes
amount to? little more than a Declaration, that there was such a
20 Right in being; but who ever saw it enjoy'd? Did not the
Actions of almost every succeeding Reign shew, there were still
so many Doors of Oppression left open to the Prerogative, that
(whatever Value our most eloquent Legislators may have set upon
those ancient Liberties) I doubt it will be difficult to fix the Period of their having a real Being, before the Revolution: Or if
there ever was an elder Period of our unmolested enjoying them,
I own, my poor Judgment is at a loss where to place it. I will
boldly say then, it is, to the Revolution only, we owe the full
Possession of what, 'till then, we never had more than a perpe-
30 tually contested Right to: And, from thence, from the Revolution it is, that the Protestant Successors of King *William* have
found their Paternal Care and Maintenance of that Right, has
been the surest Basis of their Glory.

ascendant over her in every thing. She was a woman of little knowledge, but of a clear apprehension, and a true judgement, a warm and hearty friend, violent and sudden in her resolutions, and impetuous in her way of speaking. She was thought proud and insolent on her favour, tho' she used none of the common arts of a Court to maintain it: For she did not beset the Princess, nor flatter her. She staid much at home and looked very carefully after the education of her children."

17.   Prince of *Denmark*] Prince George, brother of King Christian V of Denmark had married Princess Anne, 28 July 1684 (F. C. Turner, *James II*, p. 224); he joined the Duke of Devonshire c. 25 November 1688, who at this time had not explicitly committed himself to the replacement of James by William (David Ogg, *England in the Reigns of James II and William III*, pp. 216-18).

19.   Princess *Anne* . . . withdrawn . . . from *London*] Anne left London 25 November 1688 (F. C. Turner, *James II*, p. 433). Burnet (I, 792) gives the following account: "When the news [of the building up of forces against James II—and of Anne's husband's defection] came to London, the Princess [Anne] was so struck with the apprehensions of the King's displeasure, and of the ill effects that it might have, that she said to the Lady *Churchill*, that she could not bear the thoughts of it, and would leap out at a window rather than venture on it. The Bishop of *London* was then lodged very secretly in *Suffolk* Street. So the Lady *Churchill*, who knew where he was, went to him, and concerted with him the method of the Princess's withdrawing from the Court. The Princess went sooner to bed than ordinary. And about midnight she went down a back stairs from her closet, attended only by the Lady *Churchill*, in such haste that they carried nothing with them. They were waited for by the Bishop of London, who carried them to the Earl of *Dorset*'s, whose Lady furnished them with everything. And so they went Northward, as far as *Northampton*; where the Earl attended on them with all respect, and quickly brought a body of horse to serve for a guard to the Princess."

34.   Lady *Churchill*] Sarah Churchill (nee Jennings), Duchess of Marlborough (1660-1744). See note on Dedication for a possible explanation of Cibber's flattery of her in the pages following; Burnet (I, 765) comments on her character and influence over Anne, "[Lord Churchill] was in high favour with the King [James II]. But his Lady was much more in Princess *Anne*'s favour. She had an

These, Sir, are a few of my political Notions, which I have
ventur'd to expose, that you may see what sort of an *English* Subject I am; how wise, or weak they may have shewn me, is not
my Concern; let the weight of these Matters have drawn me
never so far out of my Depth, I still flatter my self, that I have
kept a simple, honest Head above Water. And it is a solid Comfort to me, to consider that how insignificant soever my Life was
at the Revolution, it had still the good Fortune to make one,
among the many, who brought it about; and that I, now, with

10   my Coaevals, as well as with the Millions, since born, enjoy the
happy Effects of it.

But I must now let you see how my particular Fortune went forward, with this Change in the Government; of which I shall
not pretend to give you any farther Account than what my simple Eyes saw of it.

We had not been many Days at *Nottingham* before we heard,
that the Prince of *Denmark*, with some other great Persons, were
gone off, from the King, to the Prince of *Orange*, and that the
Princess *Anne*, fearing the King her Father's Resentment might

20   fall upon her, for her Consort's Revolt, had withdrawn her self,
in the Night, from *London*, and was then within half a Days
Journey of *Nottingham*; on which very Morning we were suddenly alarm'd with the News, that two thousand of the King's
Dragoons were in close pursuit to bring her back Prisoner to *London*: But this Alarm it seems was all Stratagem, and was but a
part of that general Terror which was thrown into many other
Places about the Kingdom, at the same time, with design to
animate and unite the People in their common Defence; it being then given out, that the *Irish* were every where at our Heels,

30   to cut off all the Protestants within the Reach of their Fury.
In this Alarm our Troops scrambled to Arms in as much Order
as their Consternation would admit of, when having advanc'd
some few Miles on the *London* Road, they met the Princess in a
Coach, attended only by the Lady *Churchill* (now Dutchess

27. Beauty . . . must . . . shine into equal Warmth] TC (p. 28) notes the strangeness
     of grammar. Fielding (*Joseph Andrews*, Book I, Chap. VII) apostrophizing
     Love, says ". . . nor the Great Cibber, who confounds all Number, Gender, and
     breaks through every Rule of Grammar at his Will, hath so distorted the English
     Language as thou dost metamorphose and distort the human Senses." He also
     had commented on the passage in *The Champion* (29 April 1740).

32. four of the loveliest Daughters, . . . nobly married] The first of these daughters
     was Henrietta (1681-1733), who married Francis, second Earl of Godolphin; she
     became Duchess of Marlborough in 1722 at her father's death, since the patent of
     nobility granted to her father permitted the title to pass through the female line.
     She was notorious for her liaison with Congreve, which lasted until his death in
     1729, and later for her possibly deranged conversations with his waxen image
     which she kept. Anne (1682/3? - 1716) married the Earl of Sunderland and
     became famous for her enthusiasm for the Whig cause (see p. 182, n.). Elizabeth
     (1687-1714) married Scrope Egerton, second Earl and later Duke of Bridgewater.
     Mary (1689-1751) married John, second Duke of Montagu. Sarah, in fact,
     quarrelled bitterly with both of the daughers who survived their father. Cibber
     tactfully fails to mention her son John (1690-1703), Marquess of Blandford, who
     was said to have been very promising (William Coxe, *Memoirs of John Duke of
     Marlborough*, London, 1819, I, 161-5, III, 665).

Dowager of *Marlborough*) and the Lady *Fitzharding,* whom they
conducted into *Nottingham,* through the Acclamations of the Peo-
ple: The same Night all the Noblemen, and the other Persons of
Distinction, then in Arms, had the Honour to sup at her Royal
Highness's Table; which was then furnish'd (as all her necessary
Accommodations were) by the Care, and at the Charge of the
Lord *Devonshire.* At this Entertainment, of which I was a
Spectator, something very particular surpriz'd me: The noble
Guests at the Table happening to be more in number, than At-
10   tendants out of Liveries, could be found for, I being well known
in the Lord *Devonshire's* Family, was desir'd by his Lordship's
Maitre d'Hotel to assist at it: The Post assign'd me was to observe what the Lady *Churchill* might call for. Being so near the
Table, you may naturally ask me, what I might have heard to
have pass'd in Conversation at it? which I should certainly tell
you, had I attended to above two Words that were utter'd there,
and those were, *Some Wine and Water.* These, I remember, came
distinguish'd, and observ'd to my Ear, because they came from
the fair Guest, whom I took such pleasure to wait on: Except
20   at that single Sound, all my Senses were collected into my Eyes,
which during the whole Entertainment wanted no better Amusement, than of stealing now and then the delight of gazing on
the fair Object so near me: If so clear an Emanation of Beauty,
such a commanding Grace of Aspect struck me into a Regard
that had something softer than the most profound Respect in it, I
cannot see why I may not, without offence, remember it; since
Beauty, like the Sun, must sometimes lose its Power to chuse,
and shine into equal Warmth, the Peasant and the Courtier.
Now to give you, Sir, a farther Proof of how good a Taste my
30   first hopeful entrance into Manhood set out with, I remember
above twenty Years after, when the same Lady had given the
World four of the loveliest Daughters, that ever were gaz'd on,
even after they were all nobly married, and were become the
reigning Toasts of every Party of Pleasure, their still lovely Mo-

25.   At *Oxford . . . Denmark* met] Late November 1688. James attempted to leave England 11 December (he made good his escape only 22/23 December). The interregnum ended on 12 February 1689 with the accession of William and Mary (David Ogg, *England in the Reigns of James II and William III*, p. 227). It should be noted that this is Cibber's orthodox Whig version of these events, according to which James left the throne vacant.

ther had at the same time her Votaries, and her Health very often took the Lead, in those involuntary Triumphs of Beauty.
However presumptuous, or impertinent these Thoughts might
have appear'd at my first entertaining them, why may I not hope
that my having kept them decently secret, for full fifty Years,
may be now a good round Plea for their Pardon? Were I now
qualify'd to say more of this celebrated Lady, I should conclude
it thus: That she has liv'd (to all Appearance) a peculiar Favourite of Providence; that few Examples can parallel the Profusion
10   of Blessings which have attended so long a Life of Felicity. A
Person so attractive! a Husband so memorably great! an Offspring
so beautiful! a Fortune so immense! and a Title, which (when
royal Favour had no higher to bestow) she only cou'd receive
from the Author of Nature; a great Grandmother without grey
Hairs! These are such consummate Indulgencies, that we might
think Heaven has center'd them all in one Person, to let us see
how far, with a lively Understanding, the full Possession of them
could contribute to human Happiness------ I now return to our
military Affairs.

20   From *Nottingham* our Troops march'd to *Oxford;* through
every Town we pass'd the People came out, in some sort of Order, with such rural, and rusty Weapons as they had, to meet
us, in Acclamations of welcome, and good Wishes. This, I
thought, promis'd a favourable End of our Civil War, when the
Nation seem'd so willing to be all of a Side! At *Oxford* the Prince
and Princess of *Denmark* met, for the first time, after their late
Separation, and had all possible Honours paid them by the University. Here we rested in quiet Quarters for several Weeks, till
the Flight of King *James*, into *France;* when the Nation being
30   left to take care of it self, the only Security that could be found
for it, was to advance the Prince and Princess of *Orange* to the
vacant Throne. The publick Tranquillity being now settled, our
Forces were remanded back to *Nottingham.* Here all our Officers,
who had commanded them from their first rising, receiv'd Com-

15.   till the *February* following] The mention of Shrewsbury as Secretary of State (below) dates this as February 1690.

30.   Lord *Shrewsbury*] Charles Talbot (1660-1718), twelfth Earl and only Duke of Shrewsbury, was Secretary of State at this period from 9 March 1689-3 June 1690.

11.   new Honours of Lord Steward] Cibber was mistaken on several points here (cf. p. 37 n.); in the first edition he stated that William Cavendish, fourth Earl of Devonshire (1640-1707), had been created Duke at this time when in fact this occurred six years later, 12 May 1694; he corrected this error in the second edition. The Earl was made "lord stewart of the household" on 13 February 1689 (Luttrell, I, 502), but was not given the Garter until 14 May 1689 (Luttrell, I, 534).

21.   sudden Blow upon the Spot] According to Luttrell (I, 401) the blow was delivered to Col. Thomas Colepepper (1637-1708) on 26 April 1687. Evelyn's *Diary*, 9 July 1685 (ed. De Beer, p. 814) recounts a similar incident; on this occasion Colepepper called the Earl of Devonshire an "Excluder" [in favor of excluding James II from the succession]: "My Lord told him he Lied; on which [he] struck him a box o'th'Eare, my Lord him another and fell'd him downe; upon which being soone parted: Culpepper [sic] was seiz'd and commanded by his Majestie [James II] (who was all the while in the B: chamber" to be imprisoned. The relations of the King, Colepepper, and the Earl had apparently changed between the two incidents, for at the later one the Earl "meeting col. Culpepper [sic] in the withdraweing room in Whitehall, while the King and Queen were in the presence, challenged him to walk out, which he refusing, his lordship stroke col. Culpepper with a cane he held in his hand . . ." (Luttrell, I, 401). For this the Earl was fined £30,000 and imprisoned. However, Luttrell adds (I, 418, c. 24 October 1687): "The earl of Devon hath made his peace at Court, and hath kist the Kings hand; he hath given his own bond for the fine, and satisfaction is ordered to be acknowledged on the same." Cf. also Luttrell, I, 402-3, 405, 406, and 417. Nothing to support Cibber's "*double* or *quit*" anecdote can be found.

missions to confirm them in their several Posts; and at the same
time, such private Men as chose to return to their proper Busi-
siness or Habitations, were offer'd their Discharges. Among the
small number of those, who receiv'd them, I was one; for not
hearing that my Name was in any of these new Commissions, I
thought it time for me to take my leave of Ambition, as Ambition had before seduc'd me from the imaginary Honours of
the Gown, and therefore resolv'd to hunt my Fortune in some
other Field.

10   From *Nottingham* I again return'd to my father at *Chattsworth,*
where I staid till my Lord came down, with the new Honours
of Lord Steward of his Majesty's Houshold,
and Knight of the Garter! a noble turn of Fortune! and a deep
Stake he had play'd for! which calls to my Memory a Story we
had then in the Family, which though too light for our graver Histo-
rians notice, may be of weight enough for my humble Memoirs.
This noble Lord being in the Presence-Chamber, in King *James's*
time, and known to be no Friend to the Measures of his Administration; a certain Person in favour there, and desirous to be
20   more so, took occasion to tread rudely upon his Lordship's Foot,
which was return'd with a sudden Blow upon the Spot: For this
Misdemeanour his Lordship was fin'd thirty thousand Pounds;
but I think had some time allow'd him for the Payment. In the
Summer preceding the Revolution, when his Lordship was retir'd
to *Chattsworth,* and had been there deeply engag'd with other
Noblemen, in the Measures, which soon after brought it to bear,
King *James* sent a Person down to him, with Offers to mitigate
his Fine, upon Conditions of ready Payment, to which his Lordship reply'd, that if his Majesty pleas'd to allow him a little
30   longer time, he would rather chuse to play *double* or *quit* with
him: The time of the intended Rising being then so near at
hand, the Demand, it seems, came too late for a more serious
Answer.

1.   12 with the new Honours of Lord Steward of his Majesty's Houshold]
         with the new Honours of Duke of <u>Devonshire</u>, Lord Steward . . . 1st ed.

15.   till the *February* following] The mention of Shrewsbury as Secretary of State
       (below) dates this as February 1690.

30.   Lord *Shrewsbury*] Charles Talbot (1660-1718), twelfth Earl and only Duke of
       Shrewsbury, was Secretary of State at this period from 9 March 1689-3 June
       1690.

However low my Pretensions to Preferment were at this time,
my Father thought that a little Court Favour added to them,
might give him a Chance for saving the Expence of maintaining
me, as he had intended at the University: He therefore order'd
me to draw up a Petition to the Duke, and to give it some Air
of Merit, to put it into *Latin*, the Paryer of which was, that
his Grace would be pleas'd to do something (I really forget what)
for me--- However the Duke upon receiving it, was so good as
to desire my Father would send me to *London* in the Winter,
10 where he would consider of some Provision for me. It might,
indeed, well require time to consider it; for I believe it was
then harder to know what I was really fit for, than to have
got me any thing I was not fit for: However, to *London* I came,
where I enter'd into my first State of Attendance and Dependance
for about five Months, till the *February* following. But alas! in
my Intervals of Leisure, by frequently seeing Plays, my wise
Head was turn'd to higher Views, I saw no Joy in any other Life
than that of an Actor, so that (as before, when a Candidate at
Winchester) I was even afraid of succeeding to the Preferment I
20 sought for: 'Twas on the Stage alone I had form'd a Happiness
preferable to all that Camps or Courts could offer me! and there
was I determin'd, let Father and Mother take it as they pleas'd,
to fix my *non ultra*. Here I think my self oblig'd, in respect
to the Honour of that noble Lord, to acknowledge, that I believe his real Intentions to do well for me, were prevented by my
own inconsiderate Folly; so that if my Life did not then take a
more laudable Turn, I have no one but my self to reproach for
it; for I was credibly inform'd by the Gentlemen of his Houshold, that his Grace had, in their hearing, talk'd of recommend-
30 ing me to the Lord *Shrewsbury,* then Secretary of State, for the
first proper Vacancy in that Office. But the distant Hope of a
Reversion was too cold a Temptation for a Spirit impatient as
mine, that wanted immediate Possession of what my Heart was
so differently set upon. The Allurements of a Theatre are still

4.   Disgrace and Prejudice . . . decently unheeded and forgotten.] One must

sympathize with Cibber's protests against the low standing of actors in society; as

his own experience proves, an actor could rise to acceptance in the highest circles,

but in general to become an actor was to lose caste. The lot of actresses was yet

worse. Nicoll points out (I, 71-72) that after the Restoration they were "looked

upon . . . as little better than prostitutes." Although the profession gained

standing during the eighteenth century, Steele in 1720 (*The Theatre*, No. I,

Saturday, 2 January) had been moved to argue, as Sir John Edgar: "I doubt not

but I shall bring the World into my Opinion, that the Profession of an Actor . . .

ought to receive the same kind Treatment and Esteem, which the world is willing

to pay all other Artists . . . I take leave to say, that the World gives the Profession

of an Actor very unjust Discountenance." Cibber here needs to make the same

defense some twenty years later. The author of *TC* speaking as Theophilus

Cibber (p. 29, quoted in Appendix D) also protests against the popular disesteem

and raises the issue of audience behavior in Cibber's next anecdote. See also Sir

Richard Steele's article in *The Theatre* (No. II, 5 January 1720).

29.   Band-box] *OED*: "A slight box of card-board or very thin chip covered with

paper. for collars, caps, hats, and millinery; originally made for the 'bands' or

ruffs of the 17th c."

so strong in my Memory, that perhaps few, except those who
have felt them, can conceive: And I am yet so far willing to excuse my Folly, that I am convinc'd, were it possible to take off
that Disgrace and Prejudice, which Custom has thrown upon
the Profession of an Actor, many a well-born younger Brother,
and Beauty of low Fortune would gladly have adorn'd the Theatre, who by their not being able to brook such Dishonour to
their Birth, have pass'd away their Lives decently unheeded and
forgotten.

10   Many Years ago, when I was first in the Management of the
Theatre, I remember a strong Instance, which will shew you what
degree of Ignominy the Profession of an Actor was then held
at---- A Lady, with a real Title, whose female Indiscretions had
occasion'd her Family to abandon her, being willing, in her distress to make an honest Penny of what Beauty she had left, desir'd to be admitted as an Actress; when before she could receive
our Answer, a Gentleman (probably by her Relation's Permission)
advis'd us not to entertain her, for Reasons easy to be guess'd.
You may imagine we cou'd not be so blind to our Interest as to
20   make an honourable Family our unnecessary Enemies, by not taking his Advice; which the Lady too being sensible of, saw the
Affair had its Difficulties; and therefore pursu'd it no farther.
Now is it not hard that it should be a doubt, whether this Lady's
Condition or ours were the more melancholy? For here, you
find her honest Endeavour, to get Bread from the Stage, was
look'd upon as on Addition of new Scandal to her former Dishonour! so that I am afraid, according to this way of thinking,
had the same Lady stoop'd to have sold Patches and Pomatum,
in a Band-box, from Door to Door, she might, in that Occupa-
30   tion have starv'd, with less Infamy, than had she reliev'd her Necessities by being famous on the Theatre. Whether this Prejudice may have arisen from the Abuses that so often have crept
in upon the Stage, I am not clear in; tho' when that is grossly
the Case, I will allow there ought to be no Limits set to

---

1.   10 Management] Menagement 2nd ed. Because both spellings of this word
were current at the time of the publication of the Apology (cf. OED),
compositors apparently interchange them freely in both the 1st and 2nd
editions.

6.   I shall now . . . Posts of the Government] *The Laureat* (p. 28) identifies the persons in this anecdote as 'Captain *Montague* [sic], Mr. Secretary *Craggs*,' and 'Miss Santloe (afterwards Mrs. *Booth*).' The defender, James Craggs the Younger (1686-1721), who was Secretary of War, succeeded Addison 13 March 1717 as Secretary of State. The victim, Hester Santlow (or Santloe), married the actor Barton Booth in 1719 (Baker, under "Booth, Barton," I, 32). I am unable to identify the "Capt. Montague."

the Contempt of it; yet in its lowest Condition, in my time,
methinks there could have been no great Pretence of preferring
the Band-box to the Buskin. But this severe Opinion, whether
merited, or not, is not the greatest Distress that this Profession is
liable to.

    I shall now give you another Anecdote, quite the Reverse of
what I have instanc'd, wherein you will see an Actress, as hardly
us'd for an Act of Modesty (which without being a Prude, a Woman, even upon the Stage, may sometimes think it necessary not
to throw off.) This too I am forc'd to premise, that the Truth of
what I am going to tell you, may not be sneer'd at before it be
known. About the Year 1717, a young Actress, of a desirable
Person, fitting in an upper Box at the Opera, a military Gentleman thought this a proper Opportunity to secure a little Conversation with her; the Particulars of which were, probably, no
more worth repeating, than it seems the *Damoiselle* then thought
them worth listening to; for, notwithstanding the fine Things
he said to her, she rather chose to give the Musick the Preference of her Attention: This Indifference was so offensive to
his high Heart, that he began to change the Tender, into the
Terrible, and, in short, proceeded at last to treat her in a Style
too grosly insulting, for the meanest Female Ear to endure un-
resented: Upon which, being beaten too far out of her Discretion, she turn'd hastily upon him, with an angry Look, and a
Reply, which seem'd to set his Merit in so low a Regard, that
he thought himself oblig'd, in Honour, to take this time to resent it: This was the full Extent of her Crime, which his Glory
delay'd no longer to punish, than 'till the next time she was to
appear upon the Stage: There, in one of her best Parts, wherein she drew a favourable Regard and Approbation from the Audience, he, dispensing with the Respect which some People
think due to a polite Assembly, began to interrupt her Performance, with such loud and various Notes of Mockery, as other
young Men of Honour, in the same Place, have sometimes

25.   Insulters of Audiences] See note on p. 46; for a thorough discussion, see Avery, I, clx-clxis. Steele, in *The Theatre*, No. VII, 23 January 1720, suggests that Cibber himself had been the victim of especially strong attacks, which Steele attributes to a naive identification of the actor with the unsympathetic roles he customarily played.

32.   Royal Resentment . . . the worse for it] William Smith joined the Duke's Company in 1662, and left the stage, probably after April 1684 (Van Lennep, p. 326); he reappears in the lists in April 1695 when he played the part of *Scandall* in Congreve's *Love for Love* (Lowe, II, 320-22; cf. Van Lennep, pp. xcvi, xcix; Downes, *Roscius*, ed. Summers, p. 44). His return proves that he did not entirely quit the stage as Cibber asserts; he was an important sharer in the company and continued in its management with Betterton until 1688 (Hotson, pp. 286-87). His death in December 1695 (Van Lennep, p. 450) left the Lincoln's Inn Fields company in distress to find a replacement (Nicoll, I, 284).

made themselves undauntedly merry with: Thus, deaf to all
Murmurs or Entreaties of those about him, he pursued his Point,
even to throwing near her such Trash, as no Person can be suppos'd to carry about him, unless to use on so particular an Oc-
cassion.

     A Gentleman, then behind the Scenes, being shock'd at his
unmanly Behaviour, was warm enough to say, That no Man,
but a Fool, or a Bully, cou'd be capable of insulting an Audience, or a Woman, in so monstrous a manner. The former
10   valiant Gentleman, to whose Ear the Words were soon brought,
by his Spies, whom he had plac'd behind the Scenes, to observe
how the Action was taken there, came immediately from the
Pit, in a Heat, and demanded to know of the Author of those
Words, if he was the Person that spoke them? to which he
calmly reply'd, That though he had never seen him before, yet
since he seem'd so earnest to be satisfy'd, he would do him the
favour to own, That, indeed, the Words were his, and that
they would be the last Words he should chuse to deny, whoever
they might fall upon. To conclude, their Dispute was ended
20   the next Morning in *Hyde-Park*, where the determin'd Com-
batant, who first ask'd for Satisfaction, was oblig'd afterwards
to ask his Life too; whether he mended it or not, I have not yet
heard; but his Antagonist, in a few Years after, died in one of
the principal Posts of the Government.

     Now thought I have, sometimes, known these gallant Insulters
of Audiences, draw themselves into Scrapes, which they have
less honourably got out of; yet, alas! what has that avail'd?
This generous public-spirited Method of silencing a few, was
but repelling the Disease, in one Part, to make it break out in
30   another: All Endeavours at Protection are new Provocations, to
those who pride themselves in pushing their Courage to a Defiance of Humanity. Even when a Royal Resentment has shewn
itself, in the behalf of an injur'd Actor, it has been unable to
defend him from farther Insults! an Instance of which happen'd

33.   School of Morality] Cibber played an important part with his successful *Love's Last Shift* (January 1696) in turning the theater from the amorality of Restoration comedy to the sentimental and edifying norm of the eighteenth century (see below).

in the late King *James's* time. Mr. *Smith* (whose Character as
a Gentleman, could have been no way impeach'd, had he not
degraded it, by being a celebrated Actor) had the Misfortune
in a Dispute with a Gentleman behind the Scenes, to receive a
Blow from him: The same Night an Account of this Action
was carry'd to the King, to whom the Gentleman was represented so grosly in the wrong, that, the next Day, his Majesty
sent to forbid him the Court upon it. This Indignity cast upon
a Gentleman, only for having maltreated a Player, was look'd
10 upon as the Concern of every Gentleman; and a Party was soon
form'd to assert, and vindicate their Honour, by humbling this
favour'd Actor, whose slight Injury had been judg'd equal to so
severe a Notice. Accordingly, the next time *Smith* acted, he
was receiv'd with a Chorus of Cat-calls, that soon convinc'd him,
he should not be suffer'd to proceed in his Part; upon which,
without the least Discomposure, he order'd the Curtain to be
dropp'd; and, having a competent Fortune of his own, thought
the Conditions of adding to it, by his remaining upon the Stage,
were too dear, and from that Day entirely quitted it. I shall
20 make no Observation upon the King's Resentment, or on that of
his good Subjects; how far either was, or was not right, is not
the Point I dispute for: Be that as it may, the unhappy Condition of the Actor was so far from being reliev'd by this Royal Interposition in his favour, that it was the worse for it.

While these sort of real Distresses, on the Stage, are so unavoidable, it is no wonder that young People of Sense (though of
low Fortune) should be so rarely found, to supply a Succession
of good Actors. Why then may we not, in some measure, impute the Scarcity of them, to the wanton Inhumanity of those
30 Spectators, who have made it so terribly mean to appear there?
Were there no ground for this Question, where could be the Disgrace of entring into a Society, whose Insitution, when not
abus'd, is a delightful School of Morality; and where to excel,
requires as ample Endowments of Nature, as any one Profession

since the publication of Jeremy Collier's *Short View of the Stage* (1698). Cibber

discusses the Act at length below.

31.   Reformation . . . Matters of more Importance] Possibly Cibber is suggesting here

a sympathy with the opposition to Walpole—though not to the Whig

establishment. His most important friend in this period (c. 1740), the Earl of

Chesterfield (Barker, p. 234), had been a part of the opposition since 1733

(Plumb, II, 272). Cibber, therefore, is attempting to appear a critic without giving

offense. He may possibly mean simply the Protestant Reformation, which

"preserved" Christianity, or, may refer more specifically to the many societies for

the reformation of manners and morals which grew up after 1688 (Burnet, II,

317-18).

3. *Where's that Palace . . . intrude not?*] Iago to Othello, III, iii, 141-42:

> As where's that palace whereinto foul things
> Sometimes intrude not?

5. Look into *St. Peter's*] Cibber's virulent dislike of the Roman Catholic Church
    was in part due to his adherence to the Whig party which represented itself as
    protecting England from the Jacobite threat of counter-revolution and the
    imposition of Roman Catholicism on England. He had used the theme in several
    of his plays; it occurs for instance in *The Non-Juror* (1717) and in *Papal Tyranny
    in the Reign of King John* (1747).

16. Pantomimical Trumpery] Pantomime in English theaters, which provoked much
    resentment and satiric comment, combined four strains: classical myth, the Italian
    commedia dell'arte, previous English farce, and contemporary satire. "The
    novelty of the eighteenth century pantomime consisted in the elaborating of the
    unspoken devices of Harlequin and Columbine into a regular story . . . Most
    commonly . . . these silent antics of the pantomime characters were combined
    with dialogue recited or sung by other figures moving alongside of the dancers
    and acrobats" (Nicoll, II, 253, and in general, 251-58).

27. If People are permitted to buy it] This idea recurs in the *Apology* (cf. Chapter IV).
    Cf. also Dr. Johnson's *Prologue*: at the opening of the Theatre in *Drury-Lane*
    1747 [Lowe].

> Ah! let not Censure term our Fate our Choice,
> The Stage but echoes back the publick Voice,
> The Drama's Laws the Drama's Patrons give,
> For we, that live to please, must please to live.
>   (51-54)

29. that this Evil wants a Remedy] The Stage Licensing Act had been passed the
    previous year, giving the Lord Chamberlain power to censor plays before
    presentation. Cibber either does not think the restrictions sufficiently severe, or, it
    is possible that this passage was written before the law was enacted (see Loftis,
    Politics, pp. 128 ff.). The question of censorship of the stage had been fought

50

(that of holy Institution excepted) whatsoever? But, alas! as
Shakespear says,

> Where's that Palace, whereinto, sometimes
> Fould things intrude not?

Look into St. *Peter's* at *Rome*, and see what a profitable Farce
is made of Religion there! Why then is an Actor more blemish'd
than a Cardinal? While the Excellence of the one arises from
his innocently seeming what he is not, and the Eminence of the
other, from the most impious Fallacies that can be impos'd upon
10 human Understanding? If the best things, therefore, are most liable to Corruption, the Corruption of the Theatre is no Disproof
of its innate and primitive Utility.

In this Light, therefore, all the Abuses of the Stage, all the
low, loose, or immoral Supplements, to wit, whether, in making Virtue ridiculous, or Vice agreeable, or in the decorated
Nonsense and Absurdities of Pantomimical Trumpery, I give up
to the Contempt of every sensible Spectator, as so much rank
Theatrical Popery. But cannot still allow these Enormities to
impeach the Profession, while they are so palpably owing to the
20 deprav'd Taste of the Multitude. While Vice, and Farcical Folly, are the most profitable Commodities, why should we wonder
that, time out of mind, the poor Comedian, when real Wit
would bear no Price, should deal in what would bring him most
ready Money? But this, you will say, is making the Stage a
Nursery of Vice and Folly, or at least keeping an open Shop for
it.---I grant it: But who do you expect should reform it? The
Actors? Why so? If People are permitted to buy it, without
blushing, the Threatrical Merchant seems to have an equal Right
to the Liberty of selling it, without Reproach. That this Evil
30 wants a Remedy, is not to be contested; nor can it be denied,
that the Theatre is as capable of being preserv'd, by a Reformation, as Matters of more Importance; which, for the Honour of our national Taste, I could wish were attempted; and

then, if it could not subsist, under decent Regulations, by not
being permitted to present any thing there, but what were
worthy to be there, it would be time enough to consider, whether it were necessary to let it totally fall, or effectually support it.

Notwithstanding all my best Endeavours, to recommend the
Profession of an Actor, to a more general Favour, I doubt,
while it is liable to such Corruptions, and the Actor himself
to such unlimited Insults, as I have already mention'd, I doubt,
10 I say, we must still leave him a-drift, with his intrinsick Merit,
to ride out the Storm as well as he is able.

However, let us now turn to the other side of this Account,
and see what Advantages stand there, to balance the Misfortunes
I have laid before you. There we shall still find some valuable
Articles of Credit, that, sometimes overpay his incidental Disgraces.

First, if he has Sense, he will consider, that as these Indig-
nities are seldom or never offer'd him by People, that are remarkable for any one good Quality, he ought not to lay them too
20 close to his Heart: He will know too, that when Malice, Evny,
or brutal Nature, can securely hide or fence themselves in a
Multitude, Virtue, Merit, Innocence, and even sovereign Superiority, have been, and must be equally liable to their Insults;
that therefore, when they fall upon him in the same manner,
his intrinsick Value cannot be diminish'd by them: On the contrary, if, with a decent and unruffled Temper, he lets them pass,
the Disgrace will return upon his Agressor, and perhaps warm
the generous Spectator into a Partiality in his Favour.

That while he is conscious, that, as an Actor, he must be al-
30 ways in the Hands of Injustice, it does him at least this involuntary Good, that it keeps him in a settled Resolution to avoid all
Occasions of provoking it, or of even offending the lowest
Enemy, who, at the Expence of a Shilling, may publickly revenge it.

4.   receiv'd among People of condition] Cibber is apparently referring to himself as
     well as to the actors he lists below.

9.   Captain *Griffin*] Griffin was a Restoration actor who spent thirteen years in the
     army and returned to the stage c. 1701; he retired c. 1708 (Lowe, I, 83-84;
     Apology, XII); for the others listed, see the text *passim*, and Biographical
     Appendix.

26. *Carlisle*] James Carlisle is said by Baker (I, 57) to have been an actor, but to have
     left the stage for the army; he was killed at the battle of Aughrim, 11 July 1691.
     Downes notes (*Roscius*, ed. Summers, p. 39) that at the union of the theaters in
     1682 ". . . Mr. Monfort [sic] and Mr. Carlisle were grown to the maturity of good
     Actors" [Lowe].

26. *Wiltshire*] Summers (ed., Downes, *Roscius*, p. 233 n.) states that Wiltshire had
     joined the Theatre Royal in 1676, and left the stage when he was given a
     Captain's commission early in 1685.

27. King *William*'s reduction of Ireland] William landed in Ireland to put down the
     revolution there on 14 June 1690 at Carrickfergus. The war was ended by the
     signing of the Articles of Limerick on 3 October 1691 (David Ogg, *England in the
     Reigns of James II and William III*, pp. 254-59).

28. first War, in *Flanders*] King William's war against France, declared 8 May 1689,
     marked by a series of French victories at Steenkirk in 1692 and Neerwinden in
     1693 (David Ogg, *William III*, New York, n.d., pp. 74-77).

29. *Ben. Johnson*] The notion that Ben Jonson was an inferior actor is repeated in
     Baker, I, 264. See F. T. Bowers, "Ben Jonson the Actor," *SP*, xxiv (1937),
     392-406. Jonson was Poet Laureate only in the sense that he was given a pension
     in 1618, the reversion of the office of Master of the Revels, by James I. The
     pension was not continued under Charles (Felix E. Schelling, ed., *Ben Jonson's
     Plays*, London, n.d., I, xxii-xxvi).

That, if he excells on the Stage, and is irreproachable in his
Personal Morals, and Behaviour, his Profession is so far from being
an Impediment, that it will be oftner a just Reason for his being
receiv'd among People of condition with Favour; and sometimes
with a more social Distinction, than th best, though more
profitable Trade he might have follow'd, could have recommended him to.

That this is a Happiness to which several Actors, within my
Memory, as *Betterton, Smith, Montfort,* Captain *Griffin,* and
10   Mrs. *Bracegirdle* (yet living) have arriv'd at; to which I may
add the late celebrated Mrs. *Oldfield.* Now let us suppose these
Persons, the Men, for example, to have been all eminent Mer-
cers, and the Women as famous Milliners, can we imagine, that
merely as suchf, though endow'd with the same natural Understanding, they could have been call'd into the same honourable
Parties of Conversation? People of Sense and Condition, could
not but know, it was impossible they could have had such various Excellencies on the Stage, without having something naturally valuable in them: And I will take upon me to affirm,
20   who knew them all living, that there was not one of the number, who were not capable of supprting a variety of Spirited
Conversation, tho' the Stage were never to have been the Subject
of it.

That, to have trod the Stage, has not always been thought a
Disqualification from more honourable Employments; several
have had military Commissions; *Carlisle* and *Wiltshire* were
both kill'd Captains; one, in King *William's* Reduction of *Ireland;* and the other, in his first War, in *Flanders;* and the famous *Ben. Johnson,* tho' an unsuccessful Actor, was afterwards
30   made Poet-Laureat.

To these laudable Distinctions, let me add one more; that of
Publick Applause, which, when truly merited, is, perhaps, one
of the most aggreable Gratifications that venial Vanity can feel.
A Happiness, almost peculiar to the Actor, insomuch that the

CHAPTER IV

15.   not above seven Years before my Admission] These events took place in 1682.

22.   *Henry Killigrew*] Sir William D'Avenant already held a patent issue by Charles I

in 1639. He and Thomas Killigrew (incorrectly called Henry by Cibber) were

granted a monopoly on theatrical productions by Charles II on 9 July 1660 and a

new joint patent on 21 August 1660. They formed their companies from groups

of actors who were already performing just before and in the months following

the Restoration. (The two major companies were Mohun's at the Red Bull

theater, and Rhodes' at the Cockpit.) Killigrew was granted a new individual

patent 25 April 1662; D'Avenant received a validation of his patent from Charles I

on 16 May 1661, a warrant for a license on the surrender of his former patent on

14 August 1662, and on 15 January 1663 a patent granting him and Killigrew full

monopoly.

The author of *TC* (pp. 32-33) calls attention to Cibber's inaccuracies in this

section, and cites Downes' rather more dependable version of this history (for a

more complete account of theatrical activities before the establishment of Killigrew

and D'Avenant, see Nicoll, I, Appendix A).

25.   *King's Servants . . . Drury-Lane*] It was Killigrew's company which became the

King's Men: they first played on Monday, 5 November 1660 at the Red Bull

theater, moving to Gibbon's Tennis Court in Vere Street on Thursday, 8

November, of the same week. The Theatre Royal between Bridge Street and

Drury Lane was not opened until 7 May 1663 (Nicoll, I, 295-98).

best Tragick Writer, however numerous his separate Admirers
may be, yet, to unite them into one general Act of Praise, to
receive at once, those thundring Peals of Approbation, which
a crouded Theatre throws out, he must still call in the Assistance of the skilful Actor, to raise and partake of them.

    In a Word, 'twas in this flattering Light only, though not
perhaps so thoroughly consider'd, I look'd upon the Life of an
Actor, when but eighteen Years of Age; nor can you wonder,
if the Temptations were too strong for so warm a Vanity as
mine to resist; but whether excusable, or not, to the Stage, at
length I came, and it is from thence, chicfly, your Curiosity,
if you have any left, is to expect a farther Account of me.

C H A P. IV.

A short view of the Stage, from the Year 1660 to the Revolu-
tion. The King's and Duke's Company united, composed the
best Set of English *Actors yet known. Their several Theatrical*
Characters.

Tho' I have only promis'd you an Account of all
the material Occurrences of the Theatre during my
own Time; yet there was one which happen'd not
above seven Years before my Admission to it, which
may be as well worth notice, as the first great Revolution of it, in which, among numbers, I was involv'd. And
as the one will lead you into a clearer View of the other, it may
therefore be previously necessary to let you know that

    King *Charles* II. at his Restoration, granted two Patents, one
to Sir *William Davenant*, and the other to *Henry Killigrew*, Esq;
and their several Heirs and Assigns, for ever, for the forming of
two distinct Companies of Comedians: The first were call'd the
King's Servants, and acted at the Theatre-Royal in *Drury-Lane*;

1. *Duke's Company*] The Duke's Men, under D'Avenant, began performances at the same time as the King's Men (5 November) in Salisbury Court; the company had Lisle's Tennis Court in Lincoln's Inn Fields reconstructed and it was occupied sometine in June 1661. The Duke's Theatre in Dorset Garden was begun only in 1670 and was not in existence, as Cibber mistakenly believed, from the time of the formation of the company (Nicoll, I, 300-304).

4. Scarlet Cloth . . . quantity of Lace] Warrants were granted to the actors for the issue of "foure yards of Bastard Scarlett for a Cloake and to each of them a quarter of a yard of Crimson Velvett for the Cape of itt being the usuall Allowance of every second yeare to Commence at October last part" (29 July 1661; from L.C. 7/1 and L.C. 5/137, p. 31, reprinted by Nicoll, I, 363).

6. *Gentlemen of the Great Chamber*] The warrant ordered the "Master of the Greate Wardrobe, to provide and deliver unto His Ma[jesty's] Players the velvet and Bastard Scarlett." Cibber misinterpreted the warrant (from L.C. 7/1 and L.C. 5/137, p. 31. Nicoll, I, 363).

11. *Presentations*] The court attended public performances (for which the managers had difficulty collecting their fees from the Treasury) and also commanded private performances in the royal theaters (Nicoll, I, 305).

14. Command or Decision] For instances of the intervention of the king, the Lord Chamberlain and the Duke of York, see Nicoll, I, 284-342 and 360-66; also Hotson, pp. 210 ff.; pp. 254 ff.; pp. 281 ff.

20. Appetites . . . Fast] The playhouses were not entirely idle from 1642-60. There were surreptitious performances and the publishing of plays also flourished, suggesting that audiences returning to the theater in 1660 were familiar with the older plays through reading. (See "The Reading of Plays during the Puritan Revolution," *Huntington Library Bulletin*, No. 6, 1934, pp. 73-108.)

and the other the *Duke's Company,* who acted at the Duke's
Theatre in *Dorset-Garden.* About ten of the King's Company
were on the Royal Houshold-Establishment, having each ten
Yards of Scarlet Cloth, with a proper quantity of Lace allow'd
them for Liveries; and in their Warrants from th Lord Chamberlain, were stiled *Gentlemen of the Great Chamber:* Whether
the like Appointments were extended to the Duke's Company,
I am not certain; but they were both in high Estimation with
the Publick, and so much the Delight and Concern of the
10 Court, that they were not only supported by its being frequently present at their publick *Presentations,* but by its taking cognizance even of their private Government, insomuch, that their
particular Differences, Pretentions, or Complaints, were generally ended by the *King,* or *Duke's* Personal Command or Decision. Besides their being thorough Masters of their Art, these
Actors set forwards with two critical Advantates, which perhaps
may never happen again in many Ages. The one was, their
immediate opening after so long Interdiction of Plays, during
the Civil War, and the Anarchy that follow'd it. What eager
20 Appetites from so long a Fast, must the Guests of those Times
have had, to that high and fresh variety of Etnertainments,
which *Shakespear* had left prepar'd for them? Never was a
Stage so provided! A hundred Years are wasted, and another
silent Century well advnaced, and yet what unborn Age shall
say, *Shakespear* has his Equal! How many shining Actors have
the warm Scenes of his Genius given to Posterity? without being himself, in his Action, equal to his Writing! A strong
Proof that Actors, like Poets, must be born such. Eloquence
and Elocution are quite different Talents: *Shakespear* cou'd write
30 *Hamlet;* but Tradition tells us, That the *Ghost,* in the same
Play, was one of his best Performances as an Actor: Nor is it
within the reach of Rule or Precept to complete either of them.
Instruction, 'tis true, may guard them equally against Faults or
Absurdities, but there it stops; Nature must do the rest: To ex-

24. *Hart . . .* for *Othello*] Of Hart, Downes (*Roscius* (1789), p. 23) says, "I must not omit the Parts in several Plays of some of the Actors; wherein they excelled in the performance of them. First, *Mr. Hart*, in the Part of *Arbaces* in King and no King; *Amintor*, in The Maids Tragedy; *Othello*; . . . Alexander [in Lee's *Rival Queens*]; towards the latter end of his Acting, if he acted in any one of these but once in a fortnight, the house was filled as at a new play, especially Alexander; he acting that with such grandeur and agreeable Majesty, that one of the Court was pleased to honour him with the Commendation; that Hart might teach any King on earth how to comport himself." In a note to Downes' *Roscius*, Davies (who added to Waldron's edition, p. 15) states that "*Mr. Hart* became [soon] so superior to *Burt*, that he took the lead of him in almost all the plays acted at Drury-Lane; *Othello* was one of his master-parts."

24. *Betterton*] See pages following. Also, Tatler No. 167 and Lowe, *Betterton*.

32. Pleasure . . . languide to Satiety?] Fielding (*The Champion*, Tuesday, 29 April 1740, pp. 159-60) quotes this phrase, among others, and states, "Now in all these instances, tho' a boldness of expression is made use of, which none but great Masters dare attempt and which a school boy would run a great hazard by imitating, yet we may with some little difficult, with the least help of grammar, give a guess at his meaning . . ." *The Laureat* (p. 29) likewise derides it as an instance of "the Cibberian style."

34. Management of the Stage] Cibber was an actor-manager from 1709-33 (Barker, pp. 75-98, 165-67).

4.   before the Restoration, no Actresses] Although it is believed that actresses may have appeared in plays during the reign of Charles I (women certainly took parts in Court Masques of the period), the first fully documented appearance of a woman actress was that of Mrs. Coleman in D'Avenant's 'opera,' *The Siege of Rhodes* in 1656. The fact that they were so readily accepted in Restoration theaters suggests that they had been known before (Nicoll, I, 69-73).

8.   ungain Hoydens] *OED: ungain = ungainly.* Earliest use the form 1709.

17.   Cares of Empire] Cibber is here alluding to the fact that two royal mistresses, Nell Gwyn and Moll Davis, were actresses sponsored by the Duke of Buckingham (Burnet, I, 263, 64).

23.   Approbation of the Court, and their own alternate Choice] D'Avenant secured a warrant (12 December 1660) giving him exclusive right to "reform" a group of plays "that were playd at Blackfriers," to make them "fitt for the Company of Actors appointed under his com[m]and." The list is predominantly of Shakespearean plays, among them *The Tempest, Measure for Measure, Much Ado About Nothing, Romeo and Juliet, Twelfth Night, Henry VIII, King Lear, Macbeth,* and *Hamlet.* In a second warrant (20 August 1668) the list is extended. It is probable that Killigrew was granted a similar warrant at the same time, though it no longer exists; however, a later warrant to Killigrew (January 1669) does exist, granting him rights to a great many Jonson and Shakespeare plays (these warrants are reprinted by Nicoll, I, 352-54). Among the Shakespeare plays granted to Killigrew in 1669 are *Julius Caesar, Anthony* [sic] *and Cleopatra, Coriolanus,* [Titus] *Andronicus, The Merchant of Venice, The Moore of Venice* (from L.C. 5/137, p. 343; 5/139, p. 375; 5/12, p. 212; reprinted by Nicoll, I, 353-54). See also William Van Lennep, "Plays on the English Stage, 1669-1672," *Theatre Notebook,* XVI (1961), 12-20.

cel in either Art, is a self-born Happiness, which something more
than good Sense must be the Mother of.

The other Advantage I was speaking of, is, that before the
Restoration, no Actresses had ever been seen upon the *English*
Stage. The Characters of Women, on former Theatres, were
perform'd by Boys, or young Men of the most effeminate Aspect. And what Grace, or Master-strokes of Action can we
conceive such ungain Hoydens to have been capable of? This
Defect was so well consider'd by *Shakespear,* that in few of his
Plays, he has any greater Dependance upon the Ladies, than in
the Innocence and Simplicity of a *Desdemona,* an *Ophelia,* or
in the short Specimen of a fond and virtuous *Portia.* The additional Objects then of real, beautiful Women, could not but
draw a proportion of new Admirers to the Theatre. We may
imagine too, that these Actresses were not ill chosen, when it is
well known, that more than one of them had Charms sufficient
at their leisure Hours, to calm and mollify the Cares of Empire. Besides these peculiar Advantages, they had a private
Rule or Agreement, which both Houses were happily ty'd down
to, which was, that no Play acted at one House, should ever
be attempted at the other. All the capital Plays therefore of
Shakespear, Fletcher, and *Ben. Johnson,* were divided between
them, by the Approbation of the Court, and their own alternate Choice: So that when *Hart* was famous for *Othello, Betterton* had no less a Reputation for *Hamlet.* By this Order the
Stage was supply'd with a greater variety of Plays, than could
possibly have been shewn, had both Companies been employ'd
at the same time, upon the same Play; which Liberty too,
must have occasion'd such frequent Repetitions of 'em, by their
opposite Endeavours to forestall and anticipate one another,
that the best Actors in the World must have grown tedious and
tasteless to the Spectator: For what Pleasure is not languid to
Satiety? It was therefore one of our greatest Happinesses (during my time of being in the Management of the Stage) that

10

20

30

1. 19 Agreement] Argument 2nd ed.
1. 34 Management] Menagement 2nd ed.

7.   four Houses . . . the same pieces] During the seasons of 1735-36 and 1736-37,
the two patent theaters, Covent Garden and Drury Lane were active; in addition to
these, Fielding's company performed at the Haymarket (the Little or French
theater); and, in 1735-36 Gifford's company acted at Goodman's Fields, moving
for the next season to the new theater in Lincoln's Inn Fields (Nicoll, I, 271-73;
Scouten, I, xix-xxxii). Contrary to Cibber, Scouten argues convincingly that
during this period (from 1720-33) the audiences increased, and that the variety of
plays also grew richer, though, as Cibber states, the companies did depend upon a
small number of popular plays which were given repeatedly by all companies
(Scouten, I, cxxxviii-cxlvii).

20.   a civiliz'd People] (See *Apology*, Chap. XV.) Cibber refers to pantomimes and
other forms of entertainment, which Pope and his circle also deplored (cf.
Imitations of Horace, Epistles II, i, 304-37).

29.   two Legs of Mutton] See *The Champion* (Tuesday, 6 May, 1740): "Another
Observation which I have made on our Author's Similes is, that they generally
have an Eye towards the Kitchens . . . . As we cannot draw the Sarcastical
Conclusion which would attend a less rich Author, we must necessarily conclude
that our Biographer is too much inclined to write on a full Stomach." *The Laureat*
(p. 20) likewise ironically notes the metaphor. The author of *TC* remarks (p. 34),
"Though the Simile has been inserted in many a Twopenny Jest Book, yet, as it is
admirably introduced, I have again ventured to quote it . . ."

we had a certain number of select Plays, which no other
Company had the good Fortune to make a tolerable Figure in,
and consequently, could find little or no Account, by acting
them against us. These Plays therefore, for many years, by
not being too often seen, never fail'd to bring us crowded Audiences; and it was to this Conduct we ow'd no little share of
our Prosperity. But when four Houses are at once (as very lately they were) all permitted to act the same Pieces, let three of
them perform never so ill, when Plays come to be so harrass'd
10   and hackney'd out to the common People (half of which too,
perhaps would as lieve see them at one House as another)
the best Actors will soon feel that the Town has enough of
them.

     I know it is the common Opinion, That the more Play-
houses, the more Emulation; I grant it; but what has this
Emulation ended in? Why, a daily Contention which shall
soonest surfeit you with the best Plays; so that when what *ought*
to please, can no *longer* please, your Appetite is again to be
rais'd by such monstrous Presentations, as dishonour the Taste of
20   a civiliz'd People. If, indeed, to our several Theatres, we
could raise a proportionable number of good Authors, to give
them all different Employment, then, perhaps, the Publick
might profit from their Emulation: But while good Writers
are so scarce, and undaunted Criticks so plenty, I am afraid a
good Play, and a blazing Star, will be equal Rarities. This
voluptuous Expedient, therefore, of indulging the Taste with
several Theatres, will amount to much the same variety as that
of a certain Oeconomist, who, to enlarge his Hospitality, would
have two Puddings, and two Legs of Mutton, for the same Din-
30   ner.--- But, to resume the Thread of my History.

     These two excellent Companies were both prosperous for some
few Years, 'till their Variety of Plays began to be exhausted:
Then of course, the better Actors (which the King's seem to have
been allow'd) could not fail of drawing the greater Audiences.

performance failed]. Steele (*The Spectator*, No. 358, April 21, 1712) had cited this passage, complaining in the same way of damage to the legitimate theater.

29.   Not to dwell . . . surviv'd not long after] In this passage Cibber's information on this extremely complex subject is incomplete and misleading (for a more thorough account, see Nicoll, I, 320-36, or Hotson, Chaps. VI-VII). Briefly, the union was necessary because the King's Men were in grave financial difficulties (cf. above); the articles of union between the companies were signed 4 May 1682, and they began acting as one company 16 November 1682. Mohun and Hart were retired, though Mohun unwillingly. Their retirement was mainly due to age and ill health rather than bitterness at the terms of the union. (Mohun petitioned the King to order the company to grant him the same terms of retirement as Hart, which the King did. The documents are reprinted in Nicoll, I, 365-66.)

19. *Laudatur* et *Alget*] Juvenal, *Satires*, i, 74: "Probitas laudatur et alget," "Honesty is praised and freezes [from neglect]."

20. *Soup maigre*] "thin soup"; the comments on "two Legs of Mutton" (p. 56) were applied to this metaphor as well.

20. Taste and Fashion, with us, . . . had Wings] Cf. Pope, *Imitations of Horace, Epistles* II, i: "(For Taste, eternal wanderer, now flies/ From heads to ears, and now from ears to eyes.)" (312-13); also lines 296 ff.

23. Puppet-shew, in *Salisbury* Change] There appears to be no record of the suppression of a puppet show in Salisbury Change; Avery (I, xxxvi-xxxvii) notes that acting at the May Fair was forbidden in 1709 because the legitimate theaters were being forced to close for the Fair; thereafter they played without pause. *The Tatler* (No. 20, 26 May 1709) after passing judgment favorably on Estcourt's performance in *The Recruiting Officer* remarks that ". . . the crowd of the audience are fitter for representations at Mayfair, than a theatre-royal. Yet that fair is now broke, as well as the theatre is breaking . . . Mrs. Sarabrand, so famous for her ingenious puppet-show, has set up shop in the Exchange, where she sells her little troop under the term of 'jointed babies.'" In succeeding years, Martin Powell established a popular puppet show, which *The Tatler* (Nos. 44, 50, 77, 115) and the *Spectator* (No. 14) mention satirically; Cibber's admission below that this anecdote comes from 'oral tradition,' may account for the apparent chronological discrepancy. Puppet theaters and Italian operas were serious competitors for audiences in the earlier eighteenth century.

28. *Funambuli*] Terence, Prologue I to *Hecyra, The Mother-in-Law*: "Ita populos studio stupidus in funambulo/ Animum occuparat"; "In fact the people's thoughts were blindly preoccupied by a rope dancer" [speaking of why the first

beneficial to the Company: yet the *Tempest* got them more money: (*Roscius*, 1789, pp. 45-46). *Circe*, by Charles D'Avenant was presented at Dorset Garden in May of 1677. Downes (*Roscius*, 1789, p. 46) says, "All the Musick was set by Mr. Banister, and being well performed, it answer'd the expectation of the Company." Nicoll (I, 135) confirms Cibber's judgment of their weakness as art.

11.   Change of the publick Taste] This taste for extravagant performances was not new but had been fully developed in the years before the closing of the theaters in 1642. Elaborate and extremely expensive masques were common in the latter years of Charles I's reign. After the completion of the large Duke's Theatre in Dorset Garden (first used 9 November 1671, Hotson, p. 127), the newer pieces presented there tended towards the spectacular and operatic (Nicoll, I, 331; Hotson, pp. 9-13).

13.   greater Excellence in Action] The assumption that Killigrew's company had ever been more prosperous than D'Avenant's has no foundation. On the contrary, from the reopening of the theaters after the plague which had closed both in 1665, the King's Men were beset by difficulties: conflicts between Killigrew and the actors, destruction by fire of the Theatre Royal (January 25, 1672), and mounting debts, which gave rise to additional conflicts. John Dryden, who had contracted in 1668 to supply the King's Men with three plays annually, began in 1678 to give his plays to the rival Duke's Men (Nicoll, I, 328). In any case, Killigrew appears to have been a poor manager (for a full account, see Nicoll, I, 320-30) so that the company's affairs degenerated steadily until April 1682 when the union of the two companies was effected.

14.   several good Prologues] Cf. Dryden, "Prologue and Epilogue Spoken at the opening of the New House," *Poetical Works*, ed. Noyes, pp. 73-74:

> 'T were folly now a stately pile to raise,
> To build a playhouse while you throw down plays,
> Whilst scenes, machines, and empty operas reign,
> And for the pencil you the pen disdain.   (34-37)

1. *Davenant . . .* Master of the Duke's Company] *TC* (pp. 34-35): "I must here observe Mr. *Cibber* says Sir *William* was Master of the *Duke's Company*, though in a Page before [pp. 53-54] he said they were the King's: This Inadvertance arises from his not rightly counting *ONE, TWO . . .*" D'Avenant had been Master of the Duke's Men, but he had died in 1668. Active management was carried on by Betterton and Harris, Lady D'Avenant holding control for her son Charles D'Avenant who assumed control in his own right in 1673 (Nicoll, I, 330-31); Cibber presumably does not distinguish him from his father.

4. Dramatick Opera's . . . *Tempest, Psyche, Circe*] Cibber here seems unaware of D'Avenant's continued involvement in opera since the mid 1650's; there is no evidence of his company's inferiority to Killigrew's at any period when they competed. *The Tempest* was adapted as an opera by Dryden and D'avenant and performed at Lincoln's Inn Fields in November 1667, and is regarded as the "first step towards a fuller development of the English opera" (Nicoll, I, 133-34). Downes remarks (*Roscius*, 1789, p. 44) that it had "all new in it; as Scenes, Machines; particularly, one scene painted with myriads of Ariel Spirits; and another flying away with a table, furnisht out with fruits, sweet-meats, and all sorts of viands, just when Duke *Trinculo* and his companions were going to dinner; all things performed in it so admirably well, that not any succeeding opera got more money." *Psyche*, by Thomas Shadwell, the "first non-Shakespearian opera," was performed at Dorset Garden, February 1675; involving scenery by Stephenson, dances by St. Andre, vocal music by Locke, and instrumental music by Giovanni Battista Draghi (Nicoll, I, 135). Downes said of it, "In February 1673, the long expected Opera of *Psyche* came forth in all her ornaments; new scenes, new machines, new cloaths, new French dances: this Opera was splendidly set out, especially in scenes; the charge of which amounted to above £800. It had continuance of performance about 8 days together; it prov'd very

Sir *William Davenant,* therefore, Master of the Duke's Company,
to make Head against their Success, was forc'd to add Spectacle
and Musick to Action; and to introduce a new Species of Plays,
since call'd Dramatick Opera's, of which kind were the *Tempest,*
Psyche, Circe, and others, all set off with the most expensive Decorations of Scenes and Habits, with the best Voices and Dancers.

This sensual Supply of Sight and Sound, coming in to the Assistance of the weaker Party, it was no Wonder they should
grow too hard for Sense and simple Nature, when it is consider'd

10 how many more People there are, that can see and hear, than
think and judge. So wanton a Change of the publick Taste,
therefore, began to fall as heavy upon the King's Company, as their
greater Excellence in Action, had, before, fallen upon their Competitors: Of which Encroachment upon Wit, several good Prologues in those Days frequently complain'd.

But alas! what can Truth avail, when its Dependance is much
more upon the Ignorant, than the sensible Auditor? a poor Satisfaction, that the due Praise given to it, must at last, sink into the
cold Comfort of--- *Laudatur & Alget.* Unprofitable Praise can

20 hardly give it a *Soup maigre.* Taste and Fashion, with us, have
always had Wings, and fly from one publick Spectacle to another
so wantonly, that I have been inform'd, by those, who remember
it, that a famous Puppet-shew, in *Salisbury* Change (then standing where *Cecil-Street* now is) so far distrest these two celebrated
Comapnies, that they were reduc'd to petition the King for Relief against it: Nor ought we perhaps to think this strange, when
if I mistake not, *Terence* himself reproaches the *Roman* Auditors
of his Time, with the like Fondness for the *Funambuli,* the Rope-
dancers. Not to dwell too long therefore upon that Part of my

30 History, which I have only collected, from oral Tradition, I shall
content my self with telling you, that *Mohun,* and *Hart* now
gorwing old (for, above thirty Years before this Time, they had
severally born the King's Commission of Major and Captain, in
the Civil Wars) and the younger Actors, as *Goodman, Clark,*

5.   Year 1684] Actually 1682; See p. 57, n.

10.   Terms . . . Actors] For a full account see Hotson, Chapter VII. The difficulties under discussion arose because the investors in the Dorset Garden Theatre had to be paid £7 for each performance, even though their theater was seldom used, in addition to £3 for the use of the Drury Lane Theatre; these extra expenses were deducted before the actors were paid. Later, the actor's troubles were increased as the lawyer Christopher Rich (of whom Cibber treats later) gained control of the company and ran it primarily as a business venture. (For his career at this period, see Hotson, pp. 284 ff.)

29.   Assistant-Manager . . . join'd with us] Owen Swiney, William Collier, and Sir Richard Steele, after Cibber, Doggett, Wilks, and later Booth became managers of Drury Lane, functioned partly (and unsatisfactorily) as assistants. Cf. Barker, pp. 79 ff.

34.   King *William*'s License . . . in its Place] See *Apology*, Chapter VI. *TC* (pp. 35-36) notes here, "One theatre was now in Possession of the whole Town, and the united Patentees imposed their own Terms on the Players: the Actors, who have always as quick a Sense of Injuries, and as high and glorious a Love of Freedom as any people whatever, appeal'd for redress to the Lord Chamberlain, who was then my Lord Dorset, who finding their complaints just, procured from King William, in 1695, a separate License for Mr. Congreve, Mr. Betterton, Mrs. Barry, Mrs. Bracegirdle and others, to set up a *New Theatre* in Lincoln's Inn-Fields . . ."

58

and others, being impatient to get into their Parts, and growing
intractable, the Audiences too of both Houses then falling off,
the Patentees of each, by the King's Advice, which perhaps a-
mounted to a Command, united their Interests, and both Companies into one, exclusive of all others, in the Year 1684. This
Union was, however, so much in favour of the Duke's Company,
that *Hart* left the Stage upon it, and *Mohun* surviv'd not long
after.

One only Theatre being now in Possession of the whole Town,
the united Patentees impos'd their own Terms, upon the Actors;
for the Profits of acting were then divided into twenty Shares,
ten of which went to the Proprietors, and the other Moiety to
the principal Actors, in such Sub-divisions as their different Merit might pretend to. These Shares of the Patentees were pro-
miscuously sold out to Mony-making Persons, call'd Adventurers, who, tho' utterly ignorant of Theatrical Affairs, were still
admitted to a proportionate Vote in the Management of them; all
particular Encouragements to Actors were by them, of Consequence, look'd upon as so many Sums deducted from their private Dividends. While therefore the Theatrical Hive had so
many Drones in it, the labouring Actors, sure, were under the
highest Discouragement, if not a direct State of Oppression. Their
Hardship will at least appear in a much stronger Light, when
compar'd to our later Situation, who with scarce half their Merit, succeeded to be Sharers under a Patent upon five time seasier
Conditions: For as they had but half the Profits divided among
ten, or more of them; we had three fourths of the whole Profits, divided only among three of us: And as they might be said
to have ten Task-masters over them, we never had but one Assistant-manager (not an Actor) join'd with us; who, by the Crown's
Indulgence, was sometimes too of our own chusing. Under this
heavy Establishment then groan'd this United Company, when I
was first admitted into the lowest Rank of it. How they came to
be reliev'd by King *William's* Licence in 1695, how they were

11.　　principal Actors then at the Head of it . . .] See pages following and Biographical

Appendix.

again dispers'd, early in Queen *Anne's* Reign; and from what
Accidents Fortune took better care of *Us,* their unequal Successors,
will be told in its Place: But to prepare you for the opening so
large a Scene of their History, methinks I ought, (in Justice to
their Memory too) to give you such particular Characters of their
Theatrical Merit, as in my plain Judgment they seem'd to deserve. Presuming then, that this Attempt may not be disagreeable to the Curious, or the true Lovers of the Theatre, take it
without farther Preface.

10   In the Year 1690, when I first came into this Company, the
principal Actors then at the Head of it were,

Of Men.	Of Women.
Mr. *Betterton,*	Mrs. *Betterton,*
Mr. *Monfort,*	Mrs. *Barry,*
Mr. *Kynaston,*	Mrs. *Leigh,*
Mr. *Sandford,*	Mrs. *Butler,*
Mr. *Nokes,*	Mrs. *Monfort,* and
Mr. *Underhil,* and	Mrs. *Bracegirdle.*
Mr. *Leigh.*	

20   These Actors, whom I have selected from their Cotemporaries,
were all original Masters in their different Stile, not meer auri-
cular Imitators of one another, which commonly is the highest
Merit of the middle Rank; but Self-judges of nature, from whose
various Lights they only took their true Instruction. If in the
following Account of them, I may be oblig'd to hint at the
Faults of others, I never mean such Observations should extend
to those who are now in Possession of the Stage; for as I desing
not my Memoirs shall come down to their Time, I would not
lie under the Imputation of speaking in their Disfavour to the
30 Publick, whose Approbation they must depend upon for Support.
But to my Purpose.

Betterton was an Actor, as *Shakespear* was an Author, both
without Competitors! form'd for the mutual Assistance, and Illu-

1. 16 Mrs. <u>Butler</u>,] Mrs. Buttler 2nd ed.

3.   could . . . how Betterton . . .] On Betterton's acting, see text and notes following
      and Appendix E.

22.   *Hamlet* perhaps] *TC* (p. 30): "And here our *Apologist* talking of this great Actor
      in the part of *Hamlet*, chuses to introduce his *Eulogium* on him, by his first Attack
      on Mr. *Wilks* ... *Wilks* play'd this Part with great Decency and Justice, and
      always with the general Approbation of the Audience. If in some Places he
      wanted that Strength of Voice and Dignity of Aspect, that Mr. *Bayes* has seen in
      Betterton, this is only saying, that he had not his Person and Voice, that he was
      not Betterton" (cf. *Apology*, XVI, 339). The roles Cibber lists (l. 17) were most
      often played during his lifetime by Booth and Wilks; he is, therefore, indirectly
      discrediting his former colleagues, as *TC* notes.

25.   mis-guided Actor was ... tearing a Passion into Rags] "Passion into rags":
      Hamlet to players, III, ii, c. 10. Wilks, who succeeded to many of Betterton's
      parts, appears to have been given to excessive movement when acting; Davies
      (*Dram. Misc.*, III, 32) gives this anecdote: "Wilks was so far mistaken, in this
      treatment of Hamlet's Ghost, that Booth, one day at rehearsal, reproached him for
      it. 'I thought,' said he, 'Bob, that last night you wanted to play at fisty-cuffs with
      me: you bullied that which you ought to have revered. When I acted the Ghost
      with Betterton, instead of my awing him, he terrified me. But divinity hung
      round that man!'"

stration of each others Genius! How *Shakespear* wrote, all Men
who have a Taste for Nature may read, and know--- but with
what higher Rapture would he still be *read,* could they conceive
how *Betterton play'd* him! Then might they know, the one was
born alone to speak what the other only knew, to write! Pity
it is, that the momentary Beauties flowing from an harmonious
Elocution, cannot like those of Poetry, be their own Record!
That the animated Graces of the Player can live no longer than
the instant Breath and Motion that presents them; or at best
10 can but faintly glimmer through the Memory, or imperfect At-
testation of a few surviving Spectators. Could *how Betterton* spoke
be as easily known as *what* he spoke; then might you see the
Muse of *Shakespear* in her Triumph, with all her Beauties in
their best Array, rising into real Life, and charming her Beholders.
But alas! since all this is so far out of the reach of Description,
how shall I shew you *Betterton?* Should I therefore tell you, that
all the *Othellos, Hamlets, Hotspurs, Mackbeths,* and *Brutus's,*
whom you may have seen since his time, have fallen far short of
him; This still would give you no idea of his particular Excel-
20 lence. Let us see then wat a particular Comparison may do!
whether that may yet draw him nearer to you?

You have seen a *Hamlet* perhpas, who, on the first appearance of his Father's Spirit, has thrown himself into all the straining Vociferation requisite to express Rage and Fury, and the House
has thunder'd with Applause; tho' the mis-guided Actor was all
the while (as *Shakespear* terms it) tearing a Passion into Rags----
I am the more bold to offer you this particular Instance, because
the late Mr. *Addison,* while I sate by him, to see this Scene acted,
made the same Observation, asking me with some Surprize, if I
30 thought *Hamlet* should be in so violent a Passion with the Ghost,
which tho' it might have astonish'd, it had not provok'd him?
for you may observe that in this beautiful Speech, the Passion never rises beyond an almost breathless Astonishment, or an Impatience, limited by filial Reverence, to enquire into the suspected

7.   Ghost ... terrible ... Spectator, as to himself] Cf. Appendix E.

34.   *Be not too tame, neither etc.*] *Hamlet*, III, ii, second speech.

Wrongs that may have rais'd him from his peaceful Tomb! and
a Desire to know what a Spirit so seemingly distrest, might wish
or enjoin a sorrowful Son to execute towards his future Quiet in
the Grave? This was the Light into which *Betterton* threw this
Scene; which he open'd with a Pause of mute Amazement!
then rising slowly, to a solemn, trembling Voice, he made the
Ghost equally terrible to the Spectator, as to himself! and in the
descriptive Part of the natural Emotions which the ghastly Vision
gave him, the bodlness of his Expostulation was still govern'd by
Decency, manly, but not braving; his Voice never rising into
that seeming Outrage, or wild Defiance of what he naturally
rever'd. But alas! to preserve this Medium, between mouthing,
and meaning too little, to keep the Attention more pleasingly
awake, by a temper'd Spirit, than by meer Vehemence of Voice,
is of all the Master-strokes of an Actor the most difficult to
reach. In this noen yet have equall'd *Betterton.* But I am
unwilling to shew his Superiority only by recounting the
Errors of those, who now cannot answer to them, let their
farther Failings therefore be forgotten! or rather, shall I in
some measure excuse them? For I am not yet sure, that they
might not be as much owing to the false Judgment of the Spectator, as the Actor. While the Million are so apt to be transported, when the Drum of their Ear is so roundly rattled; while
they take the Life of Elocution to lie in the Strength of the
Lungs, it is no wonder the Actor, whose end is Applause, should
be so often tempted, at this easy rate, to excite it. Shall I go
 alittle farther? and allow that this Extreme is more pardonable
than its opposite Error. I mean that dangerous Affectation of the
Monotone, or solemn Sameness of Pronunciation, which to my
Ear is insupportable; for of all Faults that so frequently pass upon the Vulgar, that of Flatness will have the fewest Admirers.
That this is an Error of ancient standing seems evident by what
Hamlet says, in his Instructions to the Players, *viz.*

> *Be not too tame, neither,* &c.

1. 26 be so often tempted] be also tempted 2nd ed.
1. 29 Pronunciation] Pronounciation 2nd ed.

3. *Si vis ... ipsi tibi*] *Ars Poetica*, 102-103: "If you wish me to weep, first you must weep yourself."

11. dragg'd the Sentiment along ... where to apply it] Cf. *The Laureat* (pp. 30-31): "Your observation upon Mr. *Booth* too, (tho' it should be true) is not quite so tender a one as it ought to have been on a deceas'd Brother."

28. *Must I give way ... Madman stares*] *Julius Caesar*, IV, iii, 39-49.

31. *There is no terror ...*] *Julius Caesar*, IV, iii, 66: "There is no terror, Cassius, in your *threats*."

62

The Actor, doubtless, is as storngly ty'd down to the Rules of
Horace, as the Writer.

> *Si vis me flere, dolendum est*
> *Primum ipsi tibi* -----

He that feels not himself the Passion he would raise, will talk
to a sleeping Audience: But this never was the Fault of *Bet-*
terton; and it has often amaz'd me, to see those who soon
came after him, throw out in some Parts of a Character, a just
and graceful Spirit, which *Betterton* himself could not but have
applauded. And yet in the equally shining Passages of the
same Character, have heavily dragg'd the Sentiment along,
like a dead Weight; with a long-ton'd Voice, and absent Eye,
as if they had fairly forgot what they were about: If you have
never made this Observation, I am contented you should not
know, where to apply it.

A farther Excellence in *Betterton,* was, that he could vary his
Spirit to the different Characters he acted. Those wild impatient Starts, that fierce and flashing Fire, which he threw into
Hotspur, never came from the unruffled Temper of his *Brutus*
(for I have, more than once, seen a *Brutus* as warm as *Hot-*
spur) when the *Betterton Brutus* was provok'd, in his Dispute
with *Cassius,* his Spirit flew only to his Eye; his steady Look
alone supply'd that Terror, which he disdain'd an Intemperance
in his Voice should rise to. Thus, with a settled Dignity of
Contempt, like an unheeding Rock, he repell'd upon himself the
Foam of *Cassius.* Perhaps the very Words of *Shakespear* will better let you into my Meaning:

> *Must I give way, and room, to your rash Choler?*
> *Shall I be frighted when a Madman stares?*

And a litte after,

> *There is no Terror,* Cassius, *in your Looks!* &c.

4.   Hasty Spark of Anger] Julius Caesar, IV, iii, 111.

10.   *Et, si vis similem pingere, pinge sonum*] Ausonius, Book XIX (Epigrams on Various Matters), XXXII, 8: "And if thou wouldst paint my likeness, paint sound" [spoken by Echo].

24.   *Nat. Lee's Alexander the Great*] *The Rival Queens* or *The Death of Alexander the Great*, by Nathaniel Lee, was first acted 17 March 1677 (Nicoll, I, 100-31, 419).

31.   *Can none remember? ... the leading God*] *The Rival Queens*, II, i.

Not but, in some part of this Scene, where he reproaches *Cassius*, his Temper is not under this Suppression, but opens into
that Warmth which becomes a Man of Virtue; yet this is that
Hasty Spark of Anger, which *Brutus* himself endeavours to
excuse.

But with whatever stength of Nature we see the Poet shew,
at once, the Philosopher and the Heroe, yet the Image of the
Actor's Excellence will be still imperfect to you, unless Language
cou'd put Colours in our Words to paint the Voice with.

10   *Et, si vis similem pingere, pinge sonum,* is enjoining an Im-
possibility. The most that a *Vandyke* can arrive at, is to make
his Portraits of great Persons seem to *think;* a *Shakespear* goes
farther yet, and tells you *what* his Pictures thought; a *Betterton* steps beyond 'em both, and calls them from the Grave, to
breathe, and be themselves again, in Feature, Speech, and Motion. When the skilful Actor shews you all these Powers united, and gratifies at once your Eye, your Ear, your Understanding. To conceive the Pleasure rising from such Harmony,
you must have been present at it! 'tis not to be told you!

20   There cannot be a stronger Proof of the Charms of harmonious Elocution, than the many, even unnatural Scenes and
Flights of the false Sublime it has lifted into Applause. In what
Raptures have I seen an Audience, at the furious Fustian and
turgid Rants in *Nat. Lee's Alexander the Great!* For though I
can allow this Play a few great Beauties, yet it is not without
its extravagant Blemishes. Every Play of the same Author has
more or less of them. Let me give you a Sample from this.
Alexander, in a full crowd of Courtiers, without being occasionally call'd or provok'd to it, falls into this Rhapsody of
30 Vain-glory.

             Can none remember? Yes, I know all must!
And therefore they shall know it agen.

1.   16-17 Powers united] Powers at once united 2nd ed.

10. *Italian* opera] Italian opera, with its use of castrati and the baroque conventions of

singing, entered England in 1705 (Nicoll, I, 62-63, 225-37). It was enormously

popular and cut deeply into the income of the legitimate theater, which responded

with satire and with rival musical entertainments. Attempts to supplant it with

adaptations in the English tradition of Purcell, et al. (e.g., Addison's *Rosamunda*,

performed at the Dorset Garden Theatre in March 1707) were failures (Nicoll, II,

228). Cibber in *The Rival Fools*, V, i, has Sir Oliver Outwit refuse to pay the

musician's large demand.

> *Young Outwit.* Death! sir, they are all Italians.

> *Sir Oliver.* Why, what then, sir mayn't an Italian be a Scoundrel, as well as
> an Englishman?

> *Young Outwit.* Lord, sir, I would not have this heard for the universe.
> Does not the whole nation adore 'em, sir? Is any man allowed common sense,
> among the better sort, that is not ravish'd with their music? And is anything a more
> fashionable mark of a gentleman, than to pay an extravagant price for 't?

[Lowe]

18. *Le Brun*] Seventeenth-century French painter (1619-90) of the court of Louis XIV;

his most famous works, the decoration of Versailles, Vaux-le-Vicomte, and the

design of numerous Gobelins tapestries, were characterized by the use of putti,

satyrs, caryatids and various gods in large allegorical scenes.

64

> When Glory, like the dazzling Eagle, stood
> Perch'd on my Beaver, in the Granic Flood,
> When Fortune's Self, my Standard trembling bore,
> And the pale Fates stood frighted on the Shore,
> When the Immortals on the Billows rode,
> And I myself appear'd the leading God.

When these flowing Numbers came from the Mouth of a *Bet-terton,* the Multitude no more desired Sense to them, than our musical *Connoisseurs* think it essential in the celebrate Airs of an
10 *Italian* Opera. Does not this prove, that there is very near as much Enchantment in the well-govern'd Voice of an Actor, as in the sweet Pipe of an Eunuch? If I tell you, there was no one Tragedy, for many Years, more in favour with the Town than *Alexander,* to what must we impute this its command of publick Admiration? Not to its intrinsick Merit, surely, if it swarms with Passages like this I have shewn you! If this Passage has Merit, let us see what Figure it would make upon Canvas, what sort of Picture would rise from it. If *Le Brun,* who was famous for painting the Battles of this Heroe, has seen this lof-
20 ty Description, what one Image could he have possibly taken from it? In what Colours would he have shewn us *Glory perch'd upon a Beaver?* How would he have drawn *Fortune trembling?* Or, indeed, what use could he have made of *pale Fates,* or *Immortals* riding upon *Billows,* with this blustering *God* of his own making at the *head* of 'em? Where, then, must have lain the Charm, that once made the Pubilck so par-tial to this Tragedy? Why plainly, in the Grace and Harmony of the Actor's Utterance. For the Actor himself is not account-able for the false Poetry of his Author; That, the Hearer is to
30 judge of; if it passes upon him, the Actor can have no Qua-rel to it; who, if the Periods given him are round, smooth, spirited, and high-sounding, even in a false Passion, must throw out the same Fire and Grace, as may be required in one justly

---

1. 25 <u>head</u> of 'em?] <u>head</u> of them 2nd ed.

20. *Alexander* ... reviv'd] This play was given in 1694, two years after Mountfort's death in 1692.

33. toilsome Part] Davies, *Dram. Misc.*, III, 288-90, gives account of several performers who succeeded in reviving the role of Alexander, including Mountfort, George Powel, and Booth whose performance was, Davies says, too restrained. The play was revived in 1733 in Dublin by Delane who became famous in the role (Davies, *Dram. Misc.*, III, 290).

rising from Nature; where those his Excellencies will then be only more pleasing, in proportion to the Taste of his Hearer. And I
am of opinion, that to the extraordinary Success of this very Play,
we may impute the Corruption of so many Actors, and Tragick
Writers, as were immediately misled by it. The unskilful Actor, who imagin'd all the Merit of delivering those blazing
Rants, lay only in the Strength, and strain'd Exertion of the
Voice, began to tear his Lungs, upon every false, or slight Occasion, to arrive at the same Applause. And it is from hence I
10 date our having seen the same Reason prevalent, for above fifty
Years. Thus equally misguided too, many a barren-brain'd Author has stream'd into a frothy flowing Style, pompously rol-
ling into sounding Periods, signifying ----- roundly nothing; of
which Number, in some of my former Labours, I am something
more than suspicious, that I may myself have made one. But,
to keep a little closer to *Betterton.*

When this favourite Play I am speaking of, from its being
too frequently acted, was worn out, and came to be deserted
by the Town, upon the sudden Death of *Monfort,* who had
20 play'd *Alexander* with Success, for several Years, the Part was
given to *Betterton,* which, under this great Disadvantage of the
Satiety it had given, he immediately reviv'd, with so new a
Lustre, that for three Days together it fill'd the House; and
had his then declining Strength been equal to the Fatigue the
Action gave him, it probably might have doubled its Success;
an uncommon Instance of the Power and intrinsick Merit of
an Actor. This I mention, not only to prove what irresistable
Pleasure may arise from a judicious Elocution, with scarce Sense
to assist it; but to shew you too, that tho' *Betterton* never wanted
30 Fire, and Force, when his Character demanded it; yet, where
it was not demanded, he never prostituted his Power to the low
Ambition of a false Applause. And further, that when, from
a too advanced Age, he resign'd that toilsome Part of *Alexander,*
the Play, for many Years after, never was able to impose upon

3.   Proof of his Skill] See notes following on acting and Appendix E.

66

the Publick; and I look upon his so particularly supporting
the false Fire and Extravagancies of that Character, to be a
more surprizing Proof of his Skill, than his being eminent in
those of *Shakespear;* because there, Truth and Nature coming
to his Assistance, he had not the same Difficulties to combat,
and consequently, we must be less amaz'd at his Success, where
we are more able to account for it.

    Notwithstanding the extraordinary Power he shew'd in blow-
ing *Alexander* once more into a blaze of Admiration, *Betterton*
10 had so just a Sense of what was true, or false Applause, that I
have heard him say, he never thought any kind of it equal to
an attentive Silence; that there were many ways of deceiving
an Audience into a loud one; but to keep them husht and quiet,
was an Applause which only Truth and Merit could arrive at:
Of which Art, there never was an equal Master to himself.
From these various Excellencies, he had so full a Possession of
the Esteem and Regard of his Auditors, that upon his Entrance
into every Scene, he seem'd to seize upon the Eyes and Ears of
the Giddy and Inadvertent! To have talk'd, or look'd another
20 way, would then have been thought Insensibility, or Ignorance.
In all his Soliloquies of moment, the strong Intelligence of his
Attitude and Aspect, drew you into such an impatient Gaze, and
eager Expectation, that you almost imbib'd the Sentiment with
your Eye, before the Ear could reach it.

    As *Betterton* is the Centre to which all my Observations upon
Action tend, you will give me leave, under his Character, to
enlarge upon that Head. In the just Delivery of Poetical Numbers, particularly where the Sentiments are pathetick, it is scarce
credible, upon how minute an Article of Sound depends their
30 greatest Beauty or Inaffection. The Voice of a Singer is not
more strictly ty'd to Time and Tune, than that of an Actor in
Theatrical Elocution: The least Syllable too long, or too slightly dwelt upon, in a Period, depreciates it to nothing; which
very Syllable, if rightly touch'd, shall, like the heightening

4.	equally say of any one Actor] The author of *TC* (p. 42) questions whether

Betterton was absolutely superior: "As Mr. *Hart* and Mohun's Excellencies were

forgot by Degrees, Mr. Betterton's arose; when his fail'd by his Death, Mr. Booth

was thought to be a very great Successor: In short, they who remember Betterton

shake their heads at Booth; they that are in full Memory of Booth, with pitiful Scorn

see some Modern Performers, who, half a Century hence, may be highly admired

in their Turn, in Prejudice to *New Adepts* [a slur at Cibber's notorious misuse of

the word "Adept"] in the Profession ..."

12.	shook their Plumes] There was a convention that actors playing the parts of heroes

or persons of high rank wore immense plumed headdresses. This custom persisted

until Garrick allowed it to lapse (Davies, *Dram. Misc.*, III, 97). Cf. S. Rosenfeld,

"The Wardrobes of Lincoln's Inn Fields and Covent Garden," *Theatre Notebook*,

V, 1951. *The Spectator* (No. 42, 18 April, 1711): "The ordinary Method of

making a Hero, is to clap a huge Plume of Feathers upon his Head, which rises so

very high, that there is often a greater length from his Chin to the Top of his Head,

than to the Sole of his Foot," Cf. Pope, *Imitations of Horace, Epistles* II, i, 330-

33.

14.	bawl'd and strutted] See Nicoll, II, 40-50. Cf. *The Spectator,* No. 42, 18 April

1711.

Stroke of Light from a Master's Pencil, give Life and Spirit to
the whole. I never heard a Line in Tragedy come from *Bet-*
terton, wherein my Judgment, my Ear, and my Imagination,
were not fully satisfy'd; which, since his Time, I cannot equally say of any one Actor whatsoever: Not but it is possible to
be much his Inferior, with great Excellencies; which Ishall observe in another Place. Had it been practicable to have ty'd
down the clattering Hands of all the ill Judges who were commonly the Majority of an Audience, to what amazing Perfection
might the *English* Theatre have arriv'd, with so just an Actor
as *Betterton* at the Head of it! If what was Truth only, could
have been applauded, how many noisy Actors had shook their
Plumes with Shame, who, from the injudicious Approbation of
the Multitude, have bawl'd and strutted, in the place of Merit?
If therefore the bare speaking Voice has such Allurements in it,
how much less ought we to wonder, however we may lament,
that the sweeter Notes of Vocal Musick should so have captiva-
ted even the politer World, into an Apostacy from Sense, to an
Idolatry of Sound. Let us enquire from whence this Enchantment rises. I am afraid it may be too naturally accounted for:
For when we complain, that the finest Musick, purchas'd at
such vast Expence, is so often thrown away upon the most miserable Poetry, we seem not to consider, that when the Movement of the Air, and Tone of the Voice, are exquisitely harmonious, tho' we regard not one *Word* of what we hear, yet
the Power of the Melody is so busy in the Heart, that we naturally annex Ideas to it of our own Creation, and, in some
sort, become our selves the Poet to the Composer; and what
Poet is so dull as not to be charm'd with the Child of his own
Fancy? So that there is even a kind of Language in agreeable
Sounds, which, like the Aspect of Beauty, without Words,
speaks and plays with the Imagination. While this Taste therefore is so naturally prevalent, I doubt, to propose Remedies for
it, were but giving Laws to the Winds, or Advice to Inamo-

4.   Instruction ... Concern of the Auditor] Cibber subscribed to a version of neo-classical doctrine which taught that the theater should inculcate virtue; addressing King George I in the Dedication to *The Non-Juror*, he says, "Your Comedians, Sir, are an Unhappy Society, whom some Severe Heads think wholly Useless, ... This Comedy is therefore an Attempt to remove that Prejudice and to shew, what Honest and Laudable Uses may be made of the *Theatre*, when its performances keep close to the true Purposes of its Institution." [Published January 2, 1718] This doctrine probably became current as a defense against Jeremy Collier's attacks.

11.   Trash and Fopperies] Cibber is referring to dances, elaborate mechanical effects, pantomimes, operas, and other forms of theater which he views here as illegitimate.

17.   great Writers that cannot read] This statement was widely mocked: Fielding in *The Champion,* 29 April 1740, says, "... I have very often suspected whether Learning be of such Consequence to a Writer as it is imagined. This, however, I have hitherto Kept to myself . . . I might have never ventured publicly to have declared my opinion, had I not found it supported by one of the *Greatest Writers* of our own Age: I mean Mr. *Colley Cibber,* who in the Apology for his Life, tell us, that *We have frequently Great Writers that cannot Read...*" Cf. also *TC*, pp. 41-42.

20.   *Dryden ... Amphytrion*] Dr. Johnson consulted Cibber and Owen Swiney before writing his *Life of Dryden* as the " 'only two persons then alive who had seen him ... Cibber could tell no more but "that he remembered him a decent old man, arbiter of critical disputes at Will's." You are to consider that Cibber was then at a great distance from Dryden, had perhaps one leg only in the room, and durst not draw in the other.' " (Boswell, II, 271) *Amphytrion* was first presented in October 1690 (Nicoll, I, 407).

rato's: And however gravely we may assert, that Profit ought
always to be inseparable from the Delight of the Theatre; nay
admitting that the Pleasure would be heighten'd by the uniting
them; yet, while Instruction is so little the Concern of the
Auditor, how can we hope that so choice a Commodity will
come to a Market where there is so seldom a Demand for it?

It is not to the Actor therefore, but to the vitiated and low
Taste of the Spectator, that the Corruptions of the Stage (of
what kind soever) have been owing. If the Publick, by whom
they must live, had Spirit enough to discountenance, and declare
against all the Trash and Fopperies they have been so frequently
fond of, both the Actors, and the Authors, to the best of their
Power, must naturally have serv'd their daily Table, with sound
and wholesome Diet.--- But I have not yet done with my Article
of Elocution.

As we have sometimes great Composers of Musick, who cannot sing, we have as frequently great Writers that cannot read;
and tho', without the nicest Ear, no Man can be Master of Poetical Numbers, yet the best Ear in the World will not always
enable him to pronounce them. Of this Truth, *Dryden,* our
first great Master of Verse and Harmony, was a strong Instance:
When he brought his Play of *Amphytrion* to the Stage, I heard
him give it his first Reading to the Actors, in which, though it
is true, he deliver'd the plain Sense of every Period, yet the
whole was in so cold, so flat, and unaffecting a manner, that I
am afraid of not being believ'd, when I affirm it.

On the contrary, *Lee,* far his Inferior in Poetry, was so pathetick a Reader of his own Scenes, that I have been inform'd
by an Actor, who was present, that while *Lee* was reading to
Major *Mohun* at a Rehearsal, *Mohun,* in the Warmth of his Admiration, threw down his Part, and said, Unless I were able to
play it, as welll as you *read* it, to what purpose should I undertake it? And yet this very Author, whose Elocution rais'd such
Admiration in so capital an Actor, when he attempted to be

1.   *[Lee]* ... quitted the Stage] Downes (*Roscius*, ed. Summers, p. 34) records that Lee was stricken with stage-fright at his first performance as Duncan in *Macbeth*. Summers (*ibid.*, p. 212) notes that he returned to the stage, playing "the small part of the Captain of the Watch in Nevil Payne's tragedy, *The Fatal Jealousie* ..."

12.   *Estcourt*] Davies (*Dram. Misc.*, III, 311-312) believed Cibber's harshness derived from jealousy. He and Downes (*Roscius*, ed. Summers, p. 51) confirm the view of his ability as a mimic.

an Actor himself, soon quitted the Stage, in an honest Despair
of ever making any profitable Figure there. From all this I
would infer, That let our Conception of what we are to speak,
be ever so just, and the Ear ever so true, yet, when we are to
deliver it to an Audience (I will leave Fear out of the question)
there must go along with the whole, a natural Freedom, and
becoming Grace, which is easier to conceive than to describe:
For without this inexpressible somewhat, the Performance will
come out oddly disguis'd, or somewhere defectively, unsurpriz-
10 ing to the Hearer. Of this Defect too, I will give you yet a
stranger Instance, which you will allow Fear could not be the
Occasion of: If you remember *Estcourt,* you must have known
that he was long enough upon the Stage, not to be under the
least Restraint from Fear, in his Performance: This Man was so
amazing and extraordinary a Mimick, that no Man or Woman,
from the Coquette to the Privy-Counsellor, ever mov'd or spoke
before him, but he could carry their Voice, Look, Mien, and
Motion, instantly into another Company: I have heard him
make long Harangues, and form various Arguments, even in the
20 manner of thinking, of an eminent Pleader at the Bar, with
every the least Article and Singularity of his Utterance so perfectly imitated, that he was the very *alter ipse,* scarce to be dif-
tinguish'd from his Original. Yet more; I have seen, upon the
Margin of the written Part of *Falstaff,* which he acted, his
own Notes and Observations upon almost every Speech of it, describing the true Spirit of the Humour, and with what tone of
Voice, look, and Gesture, each of them ought to be delivered.
Yet in his Execution upon the Stage, he seem'd to have lost all
those just Ideas he had form'd of it, and almost thro' the Cha-
30 racter, labour'd under a heavy Load of Flatness: In a word,
with all his Skill in Mimickry, and Knowledge of what ought
to be done, he never, upon the Stage, could bring it truly into
Practice, but was upon the whole, a languid, unaffecting Actor.
After I have shewn you so many necessayr Qualifications, not one

29.	Kneller] Sir Godfrey Kneller (1646-1723), the most fashionable portrait painter of his day.

31.	said of *Betterton* ... Time of his Strength] From 1701 Betterton's strength appears to have begun to fail. He retired as manager of the Lincoln's Inn Fields company at the end of March 1705, when he was seventy years old, but continued as a hired actor almost until his death. His benefits (cf. *Tatler*, No. 1, 12 April 1709) appear to have been well attended. (See Lowe, *Betterton*, pp. 178-82.)

of which can be spar'd in true Theatrical Elocution, and have
at the same time prov'd, that with the Assistance of them all
united, the whole may still come forth defective; what Talents
shall we say will infallibly form an Actor? This, I confess, is
one of Nature's Secrets, too deep for me to dive into; let us
content our selves therefore with affirming, That *Genius,* which
Nature only gives, only can complete him. This *Genius* then
was so strong in *Betterton*, that it shone out in every Speech and
Motion of him. Yet Voice, and Person, are such necessary
10 Supports to it, that, by the Multitude, they have been preferr'd
to *Genius* itself, or at least often mistaken for it. *Betterton* had
a Voice of that kind, which gave more Spirit to Terror, than
to the softer Passions; of more Strength than Melody. The
Rage and Jealousy of *Othello*, became him better than the Sighs
and Tenderness of *Castalio:* For tho' in *Castalio* he only excell'd others, in *Othello* he excell'd himself; which you will easily believe, when you consider, that in spite of his Complexion,
Othello has more natural Beauties than the best Actor can find in
all the Magazine of Poetry, to animate his Power, and delight
20 his Judgment with.

The Person of this excellent Actor was suitable to his Voice,
more manly than sweet, not exceeding the middle Stature, in-
clining to the corpulent; of a serious and penetrating Aspect;
his Limbs nearer the athletick, than the delicate Proportion; yet
however form'd, there arose from the Harmony of the whole a
commanding Mien of Majesty, which the fairer-fac'd, or (as
Shakespear calls 'em) the *curled* Darlings of his Time, ever wanted something to be equal Masters of. There was some Years ago,
to be had, almost in every Print-shop, a *Metzotinto*, from *Knel-*
30 *ler,* extremely like him.

In all I have said of *Betterton*, I confine my self to the Time
of his Strength, and highest Power in Action, that you may make
Allowances from what he was able to execute at fifty, to what
you might have seen of him at past seventy; for tho' to the last

7. *Ah! ... see what I see!*] *Hamlet*, III, i, 163-64.

17. kill'd him] Betterton died 28 April 1710.

he was without his equal, he might not then be equal to his
former self; yet so far was he from being ever overtaken, that for
many Years after his decease, I seldom saw any of his Parts, in
Shakespear, supply'd by others, but it drew from me the Lamen-
tation of *Ophelia* upon *Hamlet's* being unlike, what she had seen
him.

> -------*Ah! woe is me!*
> *T' have seen, what I have seen, see what I see!*

The last Part this great Master of his Profession acted, was
Melantius in the *Maid's Tragedy,* for his own Benefit; when being suddenly seiz'd by the Gout, he submitted, by extraordinary
Applications, to have his Foot so far reliev'd, that he might be
able to walk on the Stage, in a Slipper, rather than wholly dis-
appoint his Auditors. He was observ'd that Day, to have exerted
a more than ordinary Spirit, and met with suitable Applause; but
the unhappy Consequence of tampering with his Distemper was,
that it flew into his Head, and kill'd him in three Days, (I think)
in the seventy-fourth Year of his Age.

I once thought to have fill'd up my Work with a select Dissertation upon Theatrical Action, but I find, by the Digressions I
have been tempted to make in this Account of *Betterton,* that all
I can say upon that Head, will naturally fall in, and possibly be
less tedious, if dispers'd among the various Characters of the particular Actors, I have promis'd to treat of; I shall therefore
make use of those several Vehicles, which you will find waiting
in the next Chapter, to carry you through the rest of the Journey,
at your Leisure.

CHAPTER V

1.   Women not admitted to the Stage] Cf. Nicoll, I, 69-73; *Apology*, Chap. IV, 55, n.

6.   *Kynaston*] Downes remarks of Kynaston (and he is quoted by the author of *TC*, p. 45), that "he being very Young made a Compleat Female Stage Beauty, performing his Parts so well, especially *Arthiope* [in Sir William D'Avenant's *The Unfortunate Lovers*] and *Aglaura* [in the play of that name by Sir John Suckling], being Parts greatly moving Compassion and Pity; that it has since been Disputable among the Judicious, whether any Woman that succeeded him so Sensibly touch'd the Audience as he" (*Roscius*, ed. Summers, p. 19). Pepys (7 January 1661) remarks that, "Among other things here, Kinaston, the boy, had the good turn to appear in three shapes: first, as a poor woman in ordinary clothes, to please Morose [in *The Silent Woman*]; then in fine clothes as a gallant; and lastly, as a man; and then likewise did appear the handsomest man in the house."

24.   were us'd to begin] In Cibber's day the plays began usually at six o'clock, the doors being unlocked at five, and sometimes as early as two o'clock (Avery, I, xlvi-xlvii).

CHAP. V.

The Theatrical Characters of the Principal Actors, in the Year
1690, continu'd.
A few Words to Critical Auditors.

THO', as I have before observ'd, Women were not
admitted to the Stage, 'till the Return of King
Charles, yet it could not be so suddenly supply'd
with them, but that there was still a Necessity, for
some time, to put the handsomest young Men into
Petticoats; which *Kynaston* was then said to have worn, with
Success; particularly in the Part of *Evadne,* in the *Maid's Tra-*
gedy, which I have heard him speak of; and which calls to my
Mind a ridiculous Distress that arose from these sort of Shifts,
which the Stage was then put to—The King coming a little before his usual time to a Tragedy, found the Actors not ready to
begin, when his Majesty not choosing to have as much Patience
as his good Subjects, sent to them, to know the Meaning of it;
upon which the Master of the Company came to the Box, and
rightly judging, that the best Excuse for their Default, would
be the true one, fairly told his Majesty, that the Queen was not
shav'd yet: The King, whose good Humour lov'd to laugh at a
Jest, as well as to make one, accepted the Excuse, which serv'd
to divert him, till the male Queen cou'd be effeminated. In a
word, *Kynaston,* at that time was so beautiful a Youth, that the
Ladies of Quality prided themselves in taking him with them
in their Coaches to *Hyde-Park,* in his Theatrical Habit, after
the Play; which in those Days, they might have sufficient time
to do, because Plays then, were us'd to begin at four a-Clock;
The Hour that People of the same Rank, are now going to Dinner—Of this Truth, I had the Curiosity to enquire, and had it

con-

18.   Mistake ... the late Mr. *Booth*] The author of *The Laureat* (p. 33) challenges this:
"I am of Opinion, *Booth* was not wrong in this. There are many of the Sentiments
in this Character, where Nature and common Sense are outraged; and an Actor,
who should give the full comic Utterance to them in his Delivery, would raise what
they call a Horse-Laugh, and turn it into Burlesque."

28.   *Cato, Syphax*] *The Laureat* (p. 33) continues, "I have seen the Original Syphax
[Cibber] in *Cato*, use many ridiculous Distortions, crack in his Voice, and wreathe
his Muscles and his Limbs, which created not a Smile of Approbation, but a loud
Laugh of Contempt and Ridicule on the Actor." He goes on to question that
Addison really approved Cibber's interpretation. (See the account of *Cato*,
Apology, Chap. XIV.)

confirm'd from his own Mouth, in his advanc'd Age: And indeed,
to the last of him, his handsomeness was very little abated; ev'n
at past sixty, his Teeth were all sound, white, and even, as one
would wish to see, in a reigning Toast of twenty. He had something of a formal Gravity in his Mien, which was attributed to
the stately Step he had been so early confin'd to, in a female Decency. But ev'n that, in Characters of Superiority had its proper Graces; it misbecame him not in the Part of *Leon,* in *Fletcher's*
Rule a Wife, & *c.* which he executed with a determin'd Manli-
10 ness, and honest Authority, well worth the best Actor's Imitation. He had a piercing Eye, and in Characters of heroick Life,
a quick imperious Vivacity, in his Tone of Voice, that painted
the Tyrant truly terrible. There were two Plays of *Dryden* in
which he shone, with uncommon Lustre; in *Aurenge-Zebe* he
play'd *Morat,* and in *Don Sebastian, Muley Moloch;* in both these
Parts, he had a fierce, Lion-like Majesty in his Port and Utterance, that gave the Spectator a kind of trembling Admiration!
    Here I cannot help observing upon a modest Mistake, which
I thought the late Mr. *Booth* commited in his acting the Part of
20 *Morat*: There are in this fierce Character so many Sentiments
of avow'd Barbarity, Insolence, and Vain-glory, that they blaze
even to a ludicrous Lustre, and doubtless the Poet intended those
to make his Spectators laugh, while they admir'd them; but
Booth thought it depreciated the Dignity of Tragedy to raise a
Smile, in any part of it, and threfore cover'd these kind of Sentiments with a scrupulous Coldness, and unmov'd Delivery, as if
he had fear'd the Audience might take too familiar a Notice of
them. In Mr. *Addison's Cato, Syphax* has some Sentiments of
near the same Nature, which I ventur'd to speak, as I imagin'd
30 *Kynaston* would have done, had he been then living to have
stood in the same Character. Mr. *Addison,* who had something
of Mr. *Booth's* Diffidence, at the Rehearsal of his Play, after it
was acted, came into my Opinion, and own'd, that even Tragedy, on such particular Occasions might admit of a *Laugh* of

2. *Richard* the *Third*] *The Laureat* (pp. 34-35) excoriates Cibber's adaptation of this play: " ... besides mangling and leaving out many beautiful and just Images in the Original, [Cibber] made him full Amends ... by ransacking all his Works, and pillaging almost all the fine Images he could find in this great Poet's Plays, to inrich this One."

5. transported into ... Laughter] Cibber took the part of the King in his version of *Richard III* and "scream'd thro' four Acts without Dignity or Decency ... but in the fifth Act, he degenerated all at once into Sir *Novelty* [Sir Novelty Fashion, in his own play *Love's Last Shift*]; and when in the Heat of the Battle at *Bosworth Field*, the King is dismounted, our Comic-Tragedian came on the Stage, really breathless, and in a seeming Panick, screaming out this Line thus—*A Harse, a Harse, my Kingdom for a Harse*" (*The Laureat*, p. 35). His ability in playing fops was widely recognized (cf. *The Tatler*, No. 182, 8 June 1710). Downes (*Roscius*, ed. Summers, p. 51) states that Cibber " ... has Arriv'd to an exceeding Perfection, in hitting justly the Humour of a starcht Beau, or Fop; equally ... [as Sir Courtly Nice in John Crowne's play of that name] the late Eminent Mr. *Mounfort*, not much inferior in Tragedy, had Nature given him Lungs Strenuous to his finisht Judgement."

9. *feliciter Audet*] Horace, Epistle II, i, 166: "Spirat tragicum statis et feliciter audet": "For he breathes [a spirit] tragic enough, and dares successfully."

22. *'Twill not be safe ... Arbitrary Power*] *Aurenge-Zebe*, Act IV.

25. *Risum teneatis?*] Horace, *Ars Poetica*, l. 50: "Can you forbear to laugh?"

Approbation. In *Shakespear* Instances of them are frequent, as
in *Mackbeth, Hotspur, Richard* the *Third,* and *Harry* the *Eighth,*
all which Characters, tho' of a tragical Cast, have sometimes familiar Strokes in them, so highly natural to each particular Disposition, that it is impossible not to be transported into an hon-
nest Laughter at them: And these are those happy Liberties,
which tho' few Authors are qualify'd to take, yet when justly
taken, may challenge a Place among their greatest Beauties. Now
whether *Dryden* in his *Morat, feliciter Audet*--- or may be allow'd
the Happiness of having hit this Mark, seems not necessary to be
determin'd by the Actor; whose Business, sure, is to make the
best of his Author's Intention, as in this Part *Kynaston* did, doubtless not without *Dryden's* Approbation. For these Reasons then,
I thought my good Friend, Mr. *Booth* (who certainly had many
Excellencies) carry'd his Reverence for the Buskin too far, in not
following the bold Flights of the Author, with that Wantonness
of Spirit which the Nature of those Sentiments demanded: For
Example! *Morat* having a criminal Passion for *Indamora,* pro-
mises, at her Request, for one Day, to spare the Life of her
Lover *Aurenge-Zebe:* But not chusing to make known the real
Motive of his Mercy, when *Nourmahal* says to him,
　　'Twill not be safe to let him live an Hour!
Morat silences her with this heroical *Rhodomontade,*
　　I'll do't, to shew my Arbitrary Power.
Risum teneatis? It was impossible not to laugh, and reasonably
too, when this Line came out of the Mouth of *Kynaston,* with
the stern, and haughty Look, that attended it. But above this
tyrannical, tumid Superiority of Character, there is a grave, and
rational Majesty in *Shakespear's Harry,* the Fourth, which tho'
not so glaring to the vulgar Eye, requires thrice the Skill, and
Grace to become, and support. Of this real Majesty *Kynaston*
was entirely Master; here every Sentiment came from him, as if

12.   *Send us your Prisoners, or you'll hear of it*] *The First Part of King Henry IV*, I,

iii, 124.

it had been his own, as if he had himself, that instant, conceiv'd
it, as if he had lost the Player, and were the real King he personated! a Perfection so rarely found, that very often, in Actors
of good Repute, a certain Vacancy of Look, Inanity of Voice,
or superfluous Gesture, shall unmask the Man, to the judicious
Spectator; who from the least of those Errors plainly sees, the
whole but a Lesson given him, to be got by Heart, from
some great Author, whose Sense is deeper than the Repeater's
Understanding. This true Majesty *Kynaston* had so entire a Com-
10 mand of, that when he whisper'd the following plain Line to
Hotspur,
          Send us your Prisoners, or you'll hear of it!
He convey'd a more terrible Menace in it than the loudest Intemperance of Voice could swell to. But let the bold Imitator
beware, for without the Look, and just Elocution that waited on
it, an Attempt of the same nature may fall to nothing.

But the Dignity of this Character appear'd in *Kynaston* still
more shining, in the private Scene between the King, and Prince
his Son: There you saw Majesty, in that sort of Grief, which
20 only Majesty could feel! there the paternal Concern, for the Errors of the Son, made the Monarch more rever'd, and dreaded:
His Reproaches so just, yet so unmixt with Anger (and therefore
the more piercing) opening as it were the Arms of Nature, with
a secret Wish, that filial Duty, and Penitence awak'd, might fall
into them with Grace and Honour. In this affecting Scene I
thought *Kynaston* shew'd his most masterly Strokes of Nature; expressing all the various Motions of the Heart, with the same Force,
Dignity, and Feeling they are written; adding to the whole, that
peculiar, and becoming Grace, which the best Writer cannot in-
30 spire into any Actor, that is not born with it. What made the
Merit of this Actor, and that of *Betterton* more suprizing, was,
that though they both observ'd the Rules of Truth, and Nature,
they were each as different in their manner of acting, as in their

13. *Like Flakes … as they fell*] *The Spanish Fryar*, or, *The Double Discovery*
(1679/80), II, i.

personal Form, and Features. But *Kynaston* staid too long upon
the Stage, till his Memory and Spirit began to fail him. I shall
not therefore say any thing of his Imperfections, which, at that
time, were visibly not his own, but the Effects of decaying Nature.

   Monfort, a younger Man by twenty Years, and at this time
in his highest Reputation, was an Actor of a very different
Sytle: Of Person he was tall, well made, fair, and of an agreeable Aspect: His Voice clear, full, and melodious: In Tragedy
10 he was the most affecting Lover within my Memory. His Ad-
dresses had a resistless Recommendation from the very Tone of his
Voice, which gave his Words such Softness, that, as *Dryden* says,
   ----- *Like Flakes of feather'd Snow,*
   They melted as they fell! ----
All this he particularly verify'd in that Scene of *Alexander,*
where the Heroe throws himself at the Feet of *Statira* for Pardon of his past Infidelities. There we saw the Great, the Tender, the Penitent, the Despairing, the Transported, and the
Amiable, in the highest Perfection. In Comedy, he gave the
20 truest Life to what we call the *Fine Gentleman;* his Spirit shone
the brighter for being polish'd with Decency: In Scenes of
Gaiety, he never broke into the Regard, that was due to the
Presence of equal, or superior Characters, tho' inferior Actors
play'd them; he fill'd the Stage, not by elbowing, and corssing it
before others, or disconcerting their Action, but by surpassing them,
in true and masterly Touches of Nature. He never laugh'd at
his own Jest, unless the Point ofhis Raillery upon another requir'd it--- He had a particular Talent, in giving Life to *bons*
Mots and *Repartees:* The Wit of the Poet seem'd always to come
30 from him *extempore,* and sharpen'd into more Wit, from his bril-
lant manner of delivering it; he had himself a good Share of
it, or what is equal to it, so lively a Pleasantness of Humour, that
when either of these fell into his Hands upon the Stage, he

3. character of the *Rover*] Willmore in Mrs. Aphra Behn's *The Rover, or, The Banish't Cavaliers* (1676/77).

8. King *William*'s Queen *Mary*.] This cannot be confirmed, but there is a record of an order to pay William "Monfort" £10 for "Edward ye Third acted before Her Ma^{te}," 10 October 1691 (from L.C. 5/150, p. 306, printed by Nicoll, I, 357).

18. Sir *Courtly Nice*] In *Sir Courtly Nice, or, It Cannot Be* (1685) by John Crowne.

wantoned with them, to the highest delight of his Auditors.
The *agreeable* was so natural to him, that ev'en in that dissolute
Character of the *Rover* he seem'd to wash off the guilt from Vice,
and gave it Charms and Merit. For tho' it may be a Reproach
to the Poet, to draw such Characters, not only unpunish'd, but
rewarded; the Actor may still be allow'd his due Praise in his
excellent Performance. And this is a Distinction which, when
this Comedy was acted at *Whitehall,* King *William's* Queen
Mary was pleas'd to make in favour of *Monfort,* notwithstand-
10 ing her Disapprobation of the Play.

He had besides all this, a Variety in his Genius, which few
capital Actors have shewn, or perhaps have thought it any Addition to their Merit to arrive at; he could entirely change himself; could at once throw off the Man of Sense, for the brisk,
vain, rude, and lively Coxcomb, the false, flashy Pretender to
Wit, and the Dupe of his own Sufficiency: Of this he gave a
delightful Instance in the Character of *Sparkish* in *Wycherly's
Country Wife.* In that of Sir *Courtly Nice* his Excellence was
still greater: There his whole Man, Voice, Mien, and Gesture,
20 was no longer *Monfort,* but another Person. There, the insipid,
soft Civility, the elegant, and formal Mien; the drawling Delicacy of Voice, the stately Flatness of his Address, and the empty
Eminence of his Attitudes were so nicely observ'd and guarded
by him, that he had not been an entire Master of Nature, had
he not kept his Judgment, as it were, a Centinel upon himself,
not to admit the least Likeness of what he us'd to be, to enter
into any Part of his Performance, he could not possibly have so
completely finish'd it. If, some Years after the Death of *Monfort,* I my self had any Success, in either of these Characters, I
30 must pay the Debt, I owe to his Memory, in confessing the Advantages I receiv'd from the just Idea, and strong Impression he
had given me, from his acting them. Had he been remember'd,
when I first attempted them, my Defects would have been more
easily discover'd, and consequently my favourable Reception in

12. tragical Death] Baker, (I, 330-33) gives an account of Mountfort's murder by a Captain Hill and Lord Mohun; Hill, believing or pretending to believe that Mountfort prevented his success with Mrs. Bracegirdle, arranged to abduct her, and failing that murdered Mountfort in cold blood. Hill escaped and Mohun was acquitted by the House of Lords. (Lowe cites *Their Majesties' Servants* [1888], I, 169-72, to suggest that they fought a duel, but this is incorrect.)

17. S*pagnolet*] Lo Spagnaletto, Josef de Ribera (1588-1652), Spanish painter.

21. *Creon*] In *Oedipus* (1678) by John Dryden and Nathaniel Lee.

21. *Maligni*] In *The Villain* (1662) by Thomas Porter.

21. *Machiavil*] In *Caesar Borgia: The son of Pope Alexander the Sixth* (1679) by Nathaniel Lee.

them, must have been very much, and justly abated. If it
could be remembred how much he had the Advantage of me,
in Voice and Person, I could not, here, be suspected of an affected Modesty, or of over-valuing his Excellence: For he sung
a clear Counter-tenour, and had a melodious, warbling Throat,
which could not but set off the last Scene of Sir *Courtly* with an
uncommon Happiness; which I, alas! could only struggle thro',
with the faint Excuses, and real Confidence of a fine Singer, under the Imperfection of a feign'd, and screaming Trebble, which
10   at best could only shew you what I would have done, had Nature
been more favourable to me.

   This excellent Actor was cut off by a tragical Death, in the
33d Year of his Age, generally lamented by his Friends, and
all Lovers of the Theatre. The particular Accidents that attended
his Fall, are to be found at large in the Trial of the Lord *Mohun,*
printed among those of the State, in *Folio.*

   Sandford might properly be term'd the *Spagnolet* of the Theatre, an excellent Actor in disagreeable Characters: For as the
chief Pieces of that famous Painter were of Human Nature in
20   Pain and Agony; so *Sandford,* upon the Stage, was generally as
flagitious as a *Creon,* a *Maligni,* an *Iago,* or a *Machiavil,* could
make him. The Painter, 'tis true, from the Fire of his Genius
might think the quiet Objects of Nature too tame for his Pencil, and therefore chose to indulge it in its full Power, upon those
of Violence and Horror: But poor *Sandford* was not the Stage-
Villain by Choice, but from Necessity; for having a low and
crooked Person, such bodily Defects were too strong to be admitted into great, or amiable Characters; so that whenever, in
any new or revived Play, there was a hateful or mischievous Per-
30   son, *Sandford* was sure to have no Competitor for it: Nor indeed
(as we are not to suppose a Villain, or Traitor can be shewn for
our Imitation, or not for our Abhorrence) can it be doubted, but
the less comely the Actor's Person, the fitter he may be to perform them. The Spectator too, by not being misled by a tempt-

11. prais'd him by their Prejudice] Steele in *The Tatler*, No. 134, 16 February 1710, after commenting on the violence depicted on the English stage, continues, "When poor Sandford was upon the stage, I have seen him groaning upon a wheel, stuck with daggers, impaled alive, calling his executioners, with a dying voice, cruel dogs and villains."

27. … incredible Absurdity] This account of Sandford parallels closely the description Steele had given in *The Theatre*, No. VII, 23 January 1720, of Cibber's experience in attempting to play dignified parts.

ing Form, may be less inclind'd to excuse the wicked or immoral
Views or Sentiments of them. And though the hard Fate of an
Oedipus, might naturally give the Humanity of an Audience
thrice the Pleasure that could arise from the wilful Wickedness
of the best acted *Creon;* yet who could say that *Sandford,* in
such a Part, was not Master of as true and just Action, as the
best Tragedian could be, whose happier Person had recommended him to the virtuous Heroe, or any other more pleasing Favourite of the Imagination? In this disadvantageous Light,
then, stood *Sandford,* as an Actor; admir'd by the Judicious,
while the Crowd only prais'd him by their Prejudice. And so
unusual had it been to see *Sandford* an innocent Man in a Play,
that whenever he was so, the Spectators would hardly give him
Credit in so gross an Improbability. Let me give you an odd
Instance of it, which I heard *Monfort* say was a real Fact. A
new Play (the Name of it I have forgot) was brought upon the
Stage, wherein *Sandford* happen'd to perform the Part of an
honest Statesman: The Pit, after they had sate three or four
Acts, in a quiet Expectation, that the well-dissembled Honesty
of *Sandford* (for such of course they concluded it) would
soon be discover'd, or at least, from its Security, involve the Actors in the Play, in some surprizing Distress or Confusion, which
might raise, and animate the Scenes to come; when, at last, finding no such matter, but that the Catastrophe had taken quite
another Turn, and that *Sandford* was really an honest Man
to the end of the Play, they fairly damn'd it, as if the Author had impos'd upon them the most frontless or incredible Absurdity.

It is not improbable, but that from *Sandford's* so masterly
personating Characters of Guilt, the inferior Actors might think
his Success chiefly owing to the Defects of his Person; and from
thence might take occasion, whenever they appear'd as Bravo's,
or Murtherers, to make themselves as frightful and as inhumna
Figures, as possible. In King *Charles's* time, this low Skill was

12. Complexion of his Ministers] Lowe (I, 134 n.) suggests that this refers to Anthony

Ashley Cooper (1621-1683), first Earl of Shaftesbury.

carry'd to such an Extravagance, that the King himself, who
was black-brow'd, and of a swarthy Complexion, pass'd a pleasant Remark, upon his observing the grim Looks of the Murtherers in *Macbeth;* when, turning to his People, in the Box
about him, *Pray, what is the Meaning,* said he, *that we never
see a Rogue in a Play, but,* Godsfish! *they always clap him on a
black Perriwig? when, it is well known, one of the greatest
Rogues in* England *always wears a fair one?* Now, whether or
no Dr. *Oates,* at that time, wore his own Hair, I cannot be positive: Or, if his Majesty pointed at some greater Man, then
out of Power, I leave those to guess at him, who, may yet, remember the changing Complexion of his Ministers. This Story
I had from *Betterton,* who was a Man of Veracity: And, I confess, I should have thought the King's Observation a very just
one, though he himself had been fair as *Adonis.* Nor can I, in
this Question, help voting with the Court; for were it not too
gross a Weakness to employ, in wicked Purposes, Men, whose
very suspected Looks might be enough to betray them? Or
are we to suppose it unnatural, that a Murther should be thoroughly committed out of an old red Coat, and a black Perriwig?

 For my own part, I profess myself to have been an Admirer
of *Sandford,* and have often lamented, that his masterly Performance could not be rewarded with that Applause, which I saw
much inferior Actors met with, merely because they stood in
more laudable Characters. For, tho' it may be a Merit in an
Audience, to applaud Sentiments of Virtue and Honour; yet
there seems to be an equal Justice, that no Distinction should be
made, as to the Excellence of an Actor, whether in a good or
evil Character; since neither the Vice, nor the Virtue of it, is
his own, but given him by the Poet: Therefore, why is not
the Actor who shines in either, equally commendable?----- No,
Sir; this may be Reason, but that is not always a Rule with us;
the Spectator will tell you, that when Virtue is applauded, he

26.   *Study to live the Character I play*] This actress was Jane Rogers and the line quoted

is from the Epilogue of the anonymous *The Triumphs of Virtue*, performed at

Drury Lane c. 1696. She later lived with Wilks as his mistress (Nicoll, I, 445;

Baker, II, 380).

gives part of it to himself; because his Applause, at the same time,
lets others about him see, that he himself admires it. But when
a wicked Action is going forward; when an *Iago* is meditating
Revenge, and Mischief; tho' Art and Nature may be equally
strong in the Actor, the Spectator is shy of his Applause, lest he
should, in some sort, be look'd upon as an Aider or an Abettor
of the Wickedness in view; and therefore rather chuses to rob
the Actor of the Praise he may merit, than give it him in a Character, which he would have you see his Silence modestly dis-
10   courages. From the same fond Principle, many Actors have made
it a Point to be seen in Parts sometimes, even flatly written, only
because they stood in the favourable Light of Honour and
Virtue.

I have formerly known an Actress carry this Theatrical Pru-
dery to such a height, that she was, very near, keeping herself
chaste by it: Her Fondness for Virtue on the Stage, she began to
think, might perswade the World, that it had made an Impression on her private Life; and the Appearances of it actually
went so far, that, in an Epilogue to an obscure Play, the Pro-
20   fits of which were given to her, and wherein she acted a Part
of impregnable Chastity, she bespoke the Favour of the Ladies,
by a Protestation, that in Honour of their Goodness and Virtue,
she would dedicate her unblemish'd Life to their Example. Part
of this Vestal Vow, I remember, was contain'd in the following
Verse:

> *Study to live the Character I play.*

But alas! how weak are the strongest Works of Art, when Nature besieges it! for though this good Creature so far held out
her Distaste to Mankind, that they could never reduce her to
30   marry any one of 'em; yet we must own she grew, like *Caesar,*
greater by her Fall! Her first heroick Motive, to a Surrender,
was to save the Life of a Lover, who, in his Despair, had vow'd
to destroy himself, with which Act of Mercy (in a jealous Dis-

4.   pious Offspring ... Grand-children] Baker (I, 50-51) notes of Christopher Bullock that "in the Year 1717 he married a natural daughter of that great performer Mr. Wilks, by Mrs. Rogers the actress" (cf. Chetwood, *Lives*, p. 112).

pute once, in my hearing) she was provok'd to reproach him in
these very Words; *Villain! did not I save your Life?* The generous Lover, in return to that first tender Obligation, gave Life
to her First-born, and that pious Offspring has, since, rais'd to her
Memory, several innocent Grand-children.

 So that, as we see, it is not the Hood, that makes the Monk,
nor the Veil the Vestal; I am apt to think, that if the Personal
Morals of an Actor, were to be weighed by his Appearance on
the Stage, the Advantage and Favour (if any were due to either
10 side) might rather incline to the Traitor, than the Heroe, to the
Sempronius, than the *Cato;* or to the *Syphax,* than the *Juba:*
Because no Man can naturally desire to cover his Honesty with a
wicked Appearance; but an ill Man might possibly incline to cover his Guilt with the Appearance of Virtue, which was the Case
of the frail Fair One, now mentioned. But be this Question decided as it may, *Sandford* always appeared to me the honester
Man, in proportion to the Spirit wherewith he expos'd the wicked,
and immoral Characters he acted: For had his Heart been un-
sound, or tainted with the least Guilt of them, his Conscience
20 must, in spite of him, in any too near a Resemblance of himself, have been a Check upon the Vivacity of his Action. *Sandford,* therefore, might be said to have contributed his equal
Share, with teh foremost Actors, to the true and laudable Use of
the Stage: And in this Light too, of being so frequently the Object of common Distaste, we may honestly style him a Theatrical
Matryr, to Poetical Justice: For in making Vice odious, or Virtue
amiable, where does the Merit differ? To hate the one, or love
the other, are but leading Steps to the same Temple of Fame,
tho' at different Portals.

30 This Actor, in his manner of Speaking, varied very much from
those I have already mentioned. His Voice had an acute and
piercing Tone, which struck every Syllable of his Words distinctly upon the Ear. He had likewise a peculiar Skill in his Look
of marking out to an Audience whatever he judg'd worth their

9.	*Richard the Third* (with such Alterations …)] See note on p. 74.

23.	*Sanford … Lincoln's-Inn Fields*] Cibber's *Richard the Third* was presented at Drury Lane c. December 1700.

24.	King *William*'s License] This is the license from the king issued through the Lord Chamberlain's office (25 March 1695) to Betterton, Mrs. Barry, Mrs. Bracegirdle *et al.* which destroyed the monopoly created in 1682 (Hotson, pp. 294-95).

more than ordinary Notice. When he deliver'd a Command,
he would sometimes give it more Force, by seeming to slight
the Ornament of Harmony. In *Dryden's* Plays of Rhime, he
as little as possible glutted the Ear with the Jingle of it, rather
chusing, when the Sense would permit him, to lose it, than to
value it.

    Had *Sandford* liv'd in Shakespear's Time, I am confident his
Judgment must have chose him, above all other Actors, to have
play'd his *Richard the Third:* I leave his Person out of the
Question, which, tho' naturally made for it, yet that would have
been the least part of his Recommendation; *Sandford* had
stronger Claims to it; he had sometimes an uncouth Stateliness
in his Motion, a harsh and sullen Pride of Speech, a meditating
Brow, a stern Aspect, occasionally changing into an almost ludicrous Triumph over all Goodness and Virtue: From thence
falling into the most asswasive Gentleness, and soothing Candour
of a designing Heart. These, I say, must have preferr'd him
to it; these would have been Colours so essentially shining in
that Character, that it will be no Dispraise to that great Author,
to say, *Sandford* must have shewn as many masterly Strokes
in it (had he ever acted it) as are visible in the Writing it.

    When I first brought *Richard the Third* (with such Altera-
tions as I thought not improper) to the Stage, *Sandford* was engag'd in the Company then acting under King *William's* Licence in *Lincoln's-Inn Fields;* otherwise you cannot but suppose
my Interest must have offer'd him that Part. What encourag'd
me, therefore, to attempt it myself at the *Theatre-Royal,* was,
that I imagin'd I knew how *Sandford* would have spoken every
Line of it: If therefore, in any Part of it, I succeeded, let the
Merit be given to him: And how far I succeeded in that Light,
those only can be Judges who remember him. In order, therefore, to give you a nearer Idea of *Sandford,* you must give me
leave (compell'd as I am to be vain) to tell you, that the late
Sir *John Vanbrugh,* who was an Admirer of *Sandford,* after he

84

had seen me act it, assur'd me, That he never knew any one
Actor so particularly profit by antoher, as I had done by *Sand-*
ford in *Richard the Third: You have,* said he, *his very Look,*
Gesture, Gait, Speech, and every Motion of him, and have bor-
row'd them all, only to serve you in that Character. If therefore
Sir *John Vanbrugh's* Observation was just, they who remember me in *Richard the Third,* may have a nearer Conception of *Sandford,* than from all the critical Account I can give
of him.

10   I come now th those other Men Actors, who, at this time,
were equally famous in the lower Life of Comedy. But I find
myself more at a loss to give you them, in their true and proper Light, than Those I have already set before you. Why the
Tragedian warms us into Joy, or Admiration, or sets our Eyes
on flow with Pity, we can easily explain to another's Apprehension: But it may sometimes puzzle the gravest Spectator to
account for that familiar Violence of Laughter, that shall seize
him, at some particular Strokes of a true Comedian. How then
shall I describe what a better Judge migght not be able to ex-
20   press? The Rules to please the Fancy cannot so easily be laid
down, as those that ought to govern the Judgment. The Decency too, that must be observ'd in Tragedy, reduces, by the
manner of speaking it, oen Actor to be much more like another, than they can or need be suppos'd to be in Comedy: There
the Laws of Action give them such free, and almost unlimited
Liberties, to play and wanton with Nature, that the Voice,
Look, and Gesture of a Comedian may be as various, as
the Manners and Faces of the whole Mankind are different
from one another. These are the Difficulties I lie under.
30   Where I want Words, therefore, to describe what I may commend, I can only hope you will give credit to my Opinion:
And this Credit I shall most stand in need of, when I tell
you, that

11.   *Nokes*] James Nokes (or Noke), mentioned by Downes (*Roscius*, ed. Summers, p. 18) as being, with his elder brother Robert, from whom he should be distinguished, in Rhodes' company acting in "the *Cockpit* in *Drury Lane*" in 1659. Lowe (I, 141) states that Robert died c. 1673. For Leigh and Underhill, see Biographical Appendix.

29.   The Characters he particularly shone in] *Sir Martin Mar-all* [sic] (1667), *The Spanish Friar* (1679-80) and *Amphytrion or The Two Socia's* (1690) by John Dryden; *The Comical Revenge*, or, *Love in a Tub* (1664) by Sir George Etherege; *The Amorous Widow, or, The Wanton Wife* by Thomas Betterton (c. 1670); and *The Soldier's Fortune* (1679-80) by Thomas Otway.

Summers (ed., Downes, *Roscius*, pp. 151-54) lists in addition, some of the female roles for which he was famous; he played Gioseppe against his brother's Menanthe in *The Slighted Maid* (by Sir Robert Stapylton), the Nurse in Nevil Payne's *The Fatal Jealousie* (August, 1672), Lavinia's Nurse in Otway's *Caius Marius*—these two roles gained him the nickname "Nurse Nokes"—and Lady Beardly in D'Urfey's *The Virtuous Wife*. His death was announced September 9, 1696 (Hotson, p. 290); he left a fortune of £1500.

Nokes was an Actor of a quite different Genius from any I
have ever read, heard of, or seen, since or before his Time; and
yet his general Excellence may be comprehended in one Article, *viz.* a plain and palpable Simplicity of Nature, which was
so utterly his own, that he was often as unaccountably diverting
in his common Speech, as on the Stage. I saw him once, giving an Account of some Table-talk, to another Actor behind
the Scenes, which, a Man of Quality accidentally listening to,
was so deceiv'd by his Manner, that he ask'd him, if that was
10 a new Play, he was rehearsing? It seems almost amazing, that
this Simplicity, so easy to *Nokes*, should never be caught by any
one of his Successors. *Leigh* and *Underhill* have been well co-
pied, though not equall'd by others. But not all the mimical
Skill of *Estcourt* (fam'd as he was for it) thought he had often
seen *Nokes*, could scarce give us an Idea of him. After this,
perhaps it will be saying less of him, when I own, that though I
have still the Sound of every Line he spoke, in my Ear, (which
us'd not to be thought a bad one) yet I have often try'd, by my
self, but in vain, to reach the least distant Likeness of the *Vis*
20 *Comica* of *Nokes*. Though this may seem little to his Praise,
it may be negatively saying a good deal to it, because I have never seen any one Actor, except himself, whom I could not, at
least, so far imitate, as to give you a more than tolerable Notion
of his Manner. But *Nokes* was so singular a Species, and was
so form'd by Nature, for the Stage, that I question if (beyond
the trouble of getting Words by Heart) it ever cost him an
Hour's Labour to arrive at that high Reputation he had, and
deserved.

The Characters he particularly shone in, were Sir *Martin*
30 *Marr-al, Gomez* in the *Spanish Friar,* Sir *Nicholas Cully* in *Love*
in a Tub, *Barnaby Brittle* in the *Wanton Wife,* Sir *Davy Dunce*
in the *Soldier's Fortune, Sofia* in *Amphytrion,* &c &c. &c. To
tell you how he acted them, is beyond the reach of Criticism:
But, to tell you what Effect his Action had upon the Spectator,

is not impossible: This then is all you will expect from me, and
from hence I must leave you to guess at him.

He scarce ever made his first Entrance in a Play, but he was
received with an involuntary Applause, not of Hands only, for
those may be, and have often been partially prostituted, and be-
spoken; but by a General Laughter, which the very Sight of
him provok'd, and Nature cou'd not resist; yet the louder the
Laugh, the graver was his Look upon it; and sure, the ridiculous
Solemnity of his Features were enough to have set a whole Bench
of Bishops into a Titter, cou'd he have been honour'd (may it
be no Offence to suppose it) with such grave, and right reverend
Auditors. In the ludicrous Distresses, which by the Laws of
Comedy, Folly is often involv'd in; he sunk into such a mixture
of piteous Pusillanimity, and a Consternation so rufully ridiculous and inconsolable, that when he had shook you, to a Fatigue
of Laughter, it became a moot point, whether you ought not to
have pity'd him. When he debated any matter by himself, he
would shut up his Mouth with a dumb studious Powt, and roll
his full Eye, into such a vacant Amazement, such a palpable
Ignorance of what to think of it, that his silent Perplexity (which
would sometimes hold him several Minutes) gave your Imagination as full Content, as the most absurd thing he could say upon it. In the Character of Sir *Martin Marr-all,* who is always
committing Blunders to the Prejudice of his own Interest, when
he had brought himself to a Dilemma in his Affairs, by vainly
proceeding upon his own Head, and was, afterwards afraid to
look his governing Servant, and Counsellor in the Face; what a
copious, and distressful Harangue have I seen him make, with
his Looks (while the House has been in one continued Roar, for
several Minutes) before he could prevail with his Courage to speak
a Word to him! Then might you have, at once, read in his
Face *Vexation*---- that his own Measures, which he had piqued
himself upon, had fail'd. *Envy*--- of his Servant's superior Wit---
Distress--- to retrieve, the Occasion he had lost. *Shame*--- to con-

21. *His Life was Laughter* ... Actor] Cf. *Julius Caesar*, V, v, 73-75.

24. *Leigh*] Leigh died in December 1692 (Hotson, p. 290).

fess his Folly; and yet a sullen Desire, to be reconcil'd, and better advis'd, for the future! What Tragedy ever shew'd us such
a Tumult of Passions, rising, at once, in one Bosom! or what
buskin'd Hero standing under the Load of them, could have
more effectually, mov'd his Spectators, by the most pathetick
Speech, than poor miserable *Nokes* did, by this silent Eloquence,
and piteous Plight of his Features?

     His Person was of the middle size, his Voice clear, and audi-
ble; his natural Countenance grave, and sober; but the Moment
20 he spoke, the settled Seriousness of his Features was utterly discharg'd, and a dry, drolling, or laughing Levity took such full
Possession of him, that I can only refer the Idea of him to your
Imagination. In some of his low Characters, that became it,
he had a shuffling Shamble in his Gait, with so contented an
Ignorance in hsi Aspect, and an aukward Absurdity in his Gesture, that had you not known him, you could not have believ'd,
that naturally he could have had a Grain of common Sense. In
a Word, I am tempted to sum up the Character of *Nokes,* as a
Comedian, in a Parodie of what *Shakespear's Mark Antony* says
30 of *Brutus,* as a Hero.

        His Life was Laughter, and the Ludicrous
        So mixt, in him, that Nature might stand up,
        And say to all the World——— This was an Actor.

     Leigh was of the mercurial kind, and though not so strict an
Observer of Nature, yet never so wanton in his Performance, as
to be wholly out of her Sight. In Humour, he lov'd to take a
full Career, but was careful enough to stop short, when just upon the Precipice: He had great Variety, in his manner, and was
famous in very different Characters: In the canting, grave Hy-
30 pocirsy of the *Spanish* Frair, he stretcht the Veil of Piety so
thinly over him, that in every Look, Word, and Motion, you
saw a palpable, wicked Slyness shine through it——— Here he kept
his Vivacity demurely confin'd, till the pretended Duty of his

21. the Villain] *The Villain* (1662), a tragedy by Thomas Porter.

22. Sir *Solomon Single*] *Sir Salomon* [later known as *Sir Salomon Single*], *or, The Cautious Coxcomb* (c. 1669) by John Caryll. Baker, II, 345, notes that it is almost a direct translation of *L'Ecole des femmes* of Moliere.

23. *Soldier's Fortune*] *The Souldier's Fortune* (1680) by Thomas Otway.

23. *Squire of Alsatia*] *The Squire of Alsatia* (1688) by Thomas Shadwell.

27. Rest of Excellence] 'Rest' here has a technical meaning from tennis: it means a 'rally.' Cibber uses the word in *The Careless Husband*, IV, 1:

> *Lady Betty*: Nay, my Lord, there's no standing against two of you.

> *Lord Foppington*: No, Faith, that's odds at Tennis, my Lord: Not but if your Ladyship pleases, I'll endeavour to keep your Back hand a little: Tho' upon my Soul you may safely set me up at the Line: For, knock me down, if ever I saw a Rest of Wit better play'd ...
> [Lowe, I, 148]

Function demanded it; and then he exerted it, with a cholerick
sacerdotal Insolence. But the Frair is a Character of such glaring Vice, and so strongly drawn, that a very indifferent Actor
cannot but hit upon the broad Jests, that are remarkable, in
every Scene of it. Though I have never yet seen any one, that
has fill'd them with half the Truth, and Spirit of *Leigh*——
Leigh rais'd the Character as much above the Poet's Imagination
as the Character has sometimes rais'd other Actors above themselves! and I do not doubt, but the Poet's Knowledge of *Leigh's*
10 Genius help'd him to many a pleasant Stroke of Nature, which
without that Knowledge never might have enter'd into his Conception. *Leigh* was so eminent in this Character, that the late
Earl of *Dorset* (who was equally an Admirer, and a Judge
Theatrical Merit) had a whole Length of him, in the Friar's
Habit, drawn by *Kneller:* The whole Portrait is highly painted
and extremely like him. But no wonder *Leigh* arriv'd to such
Fame, in what was so completely written for him; when Characters that would made the Reader yawn, in the Closet, have
by the Strength of his Action, been lifted into the lowdest Laugh-
20 ter, on the Stage. Of this kind was the Scrivener's great boobily
Son in the *Villain; Ralph,* a stupid, staring, Under-servant, in
Sir *Solomon Single.* Quite opposite of those were Sir *Jolly Jum-
ble,* in the *Soldier's Fortune,* and his old *Belfond* in the *Squire* of
Alsatia. In Sir *Jolly* he was all Life, and laughing Humour
and when *Nokes* acted with him in the same Play, they return'd
the Ball so dexterously upon one another, that every Scene between them, seem'd but one continued Rest of Excellence——But
alas! when those Actors were gone, that Comedy, and many
others, for the same Reason, were rarely known to stand upon
30 their own Legs; by seeing no more of *Leigh* or *Nokes* in them
the Characters were quite sunk, and alter'd. In his Sir *William
Belfond, Leigh* shew'd a more spirited Variety, than ever I saw
any Actor, in any one Character come up to: The Poet, 'tis
true, had here, exactly chalk'd for him, the Out-lines of Na-

11.   *Penkethman*] *Comparison*, ed. Wells (p. 106), speaks of Penkethman as "the flower of *Bartholomew*-Fair, and Idol of the Rabble. A fellow that overdoes everything, and spoils many a Part with his own stuff." Wells notes (p. 189) that after about 1700, Penkethman, along with other actors, had earned extra money by performing at the fair.

19.   the *Fond Husband*] *A Fond Husband, or, The Plotting Sisters* (1677) by Thomas D'Urfey.

20.   *City Politicks*] *City Politiques* (January 1683) by John Crowne.

23.   the *Prophetess*] *The Prophetess, or, The History of Dioclesian* (June 1690) by Thomas Betterton; this is an alteration of a play by Fletcher which some authorities attribute to Dryden (Nicoll, I, 406-407).

23.   Sir *Courtly Nice*] *Sir Courtly Nice*, or *It Cannot Be* (May 1685) by John Crowne.

34.   *Imitation*] This is perhaps a slur at Pope's *Imitations of Horace*.

ture; but the high Colouring, the strong Lights and Shades of
Humour, that envliven'd the whole, and struck our Admiration,
with Surprize and Delight, were wholly owing to the Actor. The
easy Reader might, perhaps, have been pleas'd with the Author
without discomposing a Feature; but the Spectator must have
heartily held his Sides, or the Actor would have heartily made
them ach for it.

    Now, though I observ'd before, that *Nokes* never was tole-
rably touch'd by any of his Successors; yet, in this Character, I
must own, I have seen *Leigh* extremely well imitated, by my late
facetious Friend *Penkethman,* who though far short of what was
inimitable, in the Original, yet as to the general Resemblance,
was a very valuable Copy of him: And, as I know *Penkethman*
cannot yet be out of your Memory, I have chose to mention
him here, to give you the nearest Idea I can, of the Excellence
of *Leigh* in that particular Light: For *Leigh* had many masterly
Variations, which the other cou'd not, nor ever pretended to
reach; particularly in the Dotage, and Follies of extreme old
Age, in the Characters of *Fumble* in the *Fond Husband,* and
the Toothless Lawyer, in the *City Politicks;* both which Plays
liv'd only by the extraordinary Performance of *Nokes* and *Leigh.*

    There were two other Characrers, of the farcical kind, *Geta*
in the *Prophetess,* and *Crack* in Sir *Courtly Nice,* which as they
are less confin'd to Nature, the Imitation of them was less difficult to *Penkethman;* who, to say the Truth, delighted more in
the whimsical, than the natural; therefore, when I say he sometimes resembled *Leigh,* I reserve this Distinction, on his Master's
side; that the pleasant Extravagancies of *Leigh* were all the
Flowers of his own Fancy, while the less fertile Brain of my
Friend was contented to make use of the Stock his Predecessor
had left him. What I have said, therefore, is not to detract from
honest *Pinky's* Merit, but to do Justice to his Predecessor--- And
though, 'tis true, we as seldom see a good Actor, as a great Poet
arise from the bare *Imitation* of another's Genius; yet, if this

1. 14 I have chose] I have chosen 2nd ed. <u>Chose</u> as past part. was
      current in the eighteenth century (<u>OED</u>).

20.   *Emperor* of the *Moon*] *The Emperor of the Moon*, a farce by Aphra Behn, first
       played c. March 1687. Lowe (I, 151 n.) quotes an advertisement in *The Daily*
       Courant of 18 September 1702 stating that "At the desire of some Persons of
       Quality ... will be presented a Comedy, call'd *The Emperor of the Moon*. wherein
       Mr. *Penkethman* acts the part of *Harlequin* without a Masque, for the Entertainment
       of an *African* Prince lately arrived here."

27.   Shame of the Character] Satire and criticism of pantomime were commonplace in
       the earlier eighteenth century; Fielding also viewed these forms of entertainment as
       nonsense, satirizing them in *The Author's Farce* (1730) and in *Tumble-Down Dick*
       (1736) (see Nicoll, I, 254-58).

be a general Rule, *Penkethman* was the nearest to an Exception
from it; for with those, who never knew *Leigh*, he migh very
well have pass'd for a more than common Original. Yet again,
as my Partiality for *Penkethman* ought not to lead me from
Truth, I must beg leave (though out of its Place) to tell you
fairly what was the best of him, that the Superiority of *Leigh*
may stand in its due Light---- *Penkethman* had certainly, from
Nature, a great deal of comic Power about him; but his Judgment was, by no means equal to it; for he would make frequent
Deviations into the Whimsies of an *Harlequin*. By the way, (let
me digress a little farther) whatever Allowances are made for the
License of that Character, I mean of an *Harlequin,* whatever
Pretences may be urg'd, from the Practice of the ancient Comedy, for it's being play'd in a Mask, resembling no Part of the
human Species; I am apt to think, the best Excuse a modern
Actor can plead for his continuing it, is that the low, senseless,
and monstrous things he says, and does in it, no theatrical Assurance could get through, with a bare Face: Let me give you
an Instance of even *Penkethman's* being out of Countenance for
want of it: When he first play'd *Harlequin* in the *Emperor* of
the *Moon,* several Gentlemen (who inadvertently judg'd by the
Rules of Nature) fancy'd that a great deal of the Drollery, and
Spirit of his Grimace was lost, by his wearing that useless, unmeaning Masque of a black Cat, and therefore insisted, taht the enxt
time of his acting that Part, he should play without it: Their
Desire was accordingly comply'd with--- but, alas! in vain----
Penkethman could not take to himself the Shame of the Character without being conceal'd--- he was no more *Harlequin*---
his Humour was quite disconcerted! his Conscience could not,
with the same *Effronterie* declare against Nature, without the
Cover of that unchangning Face, which he was sure would never blush for it! no! it was quite another Case! without that
Armour his Courage could not come up to the bold Strokes,
that were necessary to get the better of common Sense. Now

5. *Harlequin Sauvage*] Baker (II, 21): "*Art and Nature.* C[omedy] by the Rev. Mr. Miller ... Acted at Drury Lane, 1738. The principal scenes in this play are founded on the *Arlequin Sauvage* of M. De l'Isle, and *Le Flateur* of Rousseau; but it met with no success." Nicoll (II, 203-204) cites it as an early instance of the theme of a noble savage in a comedy of sensibility. Lowe (I, 152 n.) states that Theophilus Cibber played Harlequin and that the failure of the piece was due to the hostility of the Templars to Miller for his supposed previous insult to them in his farce of *The Coffee House.*

24. *Odso*! I believe I *am* a *little wrong here*!] Davies (*Dram. Misc.*, III, 89-90) tells of how Penkethman, playing opposite Wilks in *The Recruiting Officer* by Farquhar, broke character to exchange remarks with the audience; at first he was applauded for the novelty, but later he was hissed. He regretted his violation of propriety and responded as Cibber quotes him.

if this Circumstance will justify the Modesty of *Penkethman,* it
cannot but throw a wholesome contempt on the low Merit of an
Harlequin. But how farther necessary the Masque is to that Fool's
Coat, we have lately had a stronger Proof, in the Favour, that
the *Harlequin Sauvage* met with, at *Paris,* and the ill Fate that
follow'd the same *Sauvage,* when he pull'd off his Masque in
London. So that it seems, what was Wit from an *Harlequin,* was
something too extravagant from a human Creature. If therefore *Penkethman,* in Characters drawn from Nature, might some-
10 times launch out into a few gamesome Liberties, which would
not have been excus'd from a more correct Comedian; yet, in
his manner of taking them, he always seem'd to me, in a kind
of Consciousness of the Hazard he was running, as if he fairly
confess'd, that what he did was only, as well as he *could* do---
That he was willing to take his Chance for Success, but if he
did not meet with it, a Rebuke should break no Squares; he
would mend it another time, and would take wahtever pleas'd
his Judges to think of him, in good part; and I have often
thought, that a good deal of the Favour he met with, was
20 owing to this seeming humble way of waving all Pretences to
Merit, but what the Town would please to allow him. What
confirms me in this Opinion is, that when it has been his ill
Fortune to meet with a *Disgraccia,* I have known him say a-
part to himself, yet loud enough to be heard--- *Odso!* I believe
I *am a little wrong here!* which once was so well receiv'd, by the
Audience, that they turn'd their Reproof into Applause.

Now, the Judgment of *Leigh* always guarded the happier
Sallies of his Fancy, from the least Hazard of Disapprobation:
he seem'd not to court, but to attack your Applause, and always
30 came off victorious; nor did his highest Assurance amount to
any more, than that just Confidence, without which the commendable Spirit of every good Actor must be abated; and of
this Spirit *Leigh* was a most perfect Master. He was much admir'd by King *Charles,* who us'd to distinguish him, when spoke

1. 7 an Harlequin] a Harlequin 2nd ed.

15.   the *Committee*] *The Committee* (1662) by Sir Robert Howard.

26.   *Epsome Wells*] *Epsom-Wells* (1672) by Thomas Shadwell.

of, by the Title of *his Actor:* Which however makes me imagine,
that in his Exile that Prince might have receiv'd his first Impression of good Actors from the *French* Stage; for *Leigh* had more
of that farcical Vivacity than *Nokes;* but *Nokes* was never languid by his more strict Adherence to Nature, and as far as my
Judgment is worth taking, if their intrinsick Merit could be
justly weigh'd, *Nokes* must have had the better in the Balance.
Upon the unfortunate Death of *Monfort, Leigh* fell ill of a Fever, and dy'd in a Week after him, in *December* 1692.

10   *Underhill* was a correct, and natural Comedian, his particular
Excellence was in Characters, that may be called Still-life, I
mean the stiff, the heavy, and the stupid; to these he gave the
exactest, and most expressive Colours, and in some of them,
look'd as if it were not in the Power of human Passions to alter
a Feature of him. In the solemn Formality of *Obadiah* in the
Committee, and in the boobily heaviness of *Lolpoop* in the *Squire
of Alsatia,* he seem'd the immoveable Log he stood for! a Countenance of Wood could not be more fixt than his, when the
Blockhead of a Character required it: His Face was full and

20 long; from his Crown to the end of his Nose, was the shorter
half of it, so that the Disproportion of his lower Features, when
soberly compos'd, with an unwandering Eye hanging over them,
threw him into the most lumpish, moping Mortal, that ever
made Beholders merry! not but, at other times, he could be
wakened into Spirit equally ridiculous---- In the course, rustick
Humour of Justice *Clodpate,* in *Epsome Wells,* he was a delightful Brute! and in the blunt Vivacity of Sir *Sampson,* in *Love* for
Love, he shew'd all that true perverse Spirit, that is commonly
seen in much Wit, and ill Nature. This Character is one of

30 those few so well written, with so much Wit and Humour, that
an Actor must be the grossest Dunce, that does not appear with
an unusual Life in it: But it will still shew as great a Proportion of Skill, to come near *Underhill* in the acting it, which
(not to undervalue those who soon came after him) I have not

1. 10 <u>Underhill</u>] <u>Underhil</u> 2nd ed.

2. *Tatler*] No. 20, 26 May 1709 and No. 22, 31 May 1709. Davies (*Dram. Misc.*, III, 139-40) notes that Underhill retired about 1703, but played occasionally until his death several years later; Lowe dates his retirement early in 1707 (I, 155-56).

10. Patent granted to Sir *Richard Steele*] For Cibber's account of these proceedings see Chapter XIV and XV of the *Apology*; a license was issued to Wilks, Dogget, Booth, and Cibber, with Steele replacing Collier, on 18 October 1714.

23. *Powel*] George Powel was known as a moderately competent actor (cf. *The Spectator*, No. 40, 16 April 1711: "Having spoken of Mr. Powell as sometimes raising himself Applause from the ill Taste of an Audience; I must do him the justice to own, that he is excellently formed for a Tragoedian, and, when he pleases, deserves the admiration of the best Judges"; cf. Downes, *Roscius*, ed. Summers, pp. 278-79.

23. *Verbruggen*] The author of *The Laureat* (pp. 58-59) remarks at length on the injustice of Cibber's omitting John Verbruggen: "He was an Original, and had a Roughness in his Manner, and a negligent agreeable Wildness in his Action and his Mein, which became him well ... He continued some Years in high and merited Reputation, tho' when he appear'd on the Stage at first, for some time, he, as well as our Friend *Colley*, were commonly received with a hiss" (p. 58). He must have died shortly after 1707 (cf. Lowe's note, I, 157 and Well's note in *Comparison*, p. 189). Nicoll, I, 384-85, gives an account of a petition by Verbruggen who felt he was not receiving his due share of the profits of the Lincoln's Inn Fields company.

23. *Williams*] Joseph Williams joined the Duke's Men about 1673 (Bellchambers, p. 169, n.); Davies (*Dram. Misc.*, III, 206-7) says, "Williams was an actor of merit, but courted the bottle with more vigour than the profession of acting."

26. *Wilks* or *Dogget*] These actors and those mentioned after them are treated at length in later chapters.

yet seen. He was particularly admir'd too, for the Grave-digger
in *Hamlet*. The Author of the *Tatler* recommends him to the
Favour of the Town, upon that Play's being acted for his Benefit, wherein, after his Age had some Years oblig'd him to leave
the Stage, he came on again, for that Day, to perform his old
Part; but, alas! so worn, and disabled, as if himself was to have
lain in the Grave he was digging; when he could no more excite
Laughter, his Infirmities were dismiss'd with Pity: He dy'd soon
after, a super-annuated Pensioner, in the List of those who, were
10   supported by the joint Sharers, under the first Patent granted to
Sir *Richard Steele*.

The deep Impressions of these excellent Actors, which I receiv'd in my Youth, I am afraid, may have drawn me into the
common Foible of us old Fellows; which is, a Fondness, and
perhaps, a tedious Partiality for the Pleasures we have formerly
tasted, and think are now fallen off, because we can no longer
enjoy them. If therefore I lie under that Suspicion, tho' I have
related nothing incredible, or out of the reach of a good Judge's
Conception, I must appeal to those Few, who are about my
20   own Age, for the Truth and Likeness of these Theatrical Por-
traicts.

There were, at this time, several others in some degree of Favour with the publick, *Powel, Verbruggen, Williams, &c.* But
as I cannot think their best Improvements made them, in any wise,
equal to those I have spoke of, I ought not to range them in
the same Class. Neither were *Wilks,* or *Dogget,* yet come to
the Stage; nor was *Booth* initiated till about six Years after them;
or Mrs. *Oldfield* known, 'till the Year 1700. I must therefore
reserve the four last for their proper Period, andproceed to the
30   Actresses, that were famous with *Betterton,* at the latter end of
the last Century.

Mrs. *Barry* was then in possession of almost all the chief Parts
in Tragedy: With what Skill she gave Life to them, you will

1.   *Cleomenes*] *Cleomenes, the Spartan Heroe*, produced at Drury Lane, April 1692.

3.   *Mrs.* Barry … *seen on the Theatre*] Preface to *Cleomenes* (1692), *The Works of Dryden*, ed. Scott (Edinburgh, 1821), 2nd ed., VIII, 197.

29.   Mrs. *Oldfield*] For an account of Mrs. Oldfield, see *Apology*, Chap. IX.

judge from the Words of *Dryden,* in his Preface to *Cleomenes,*
where he says,

> Mrs. Barry, *always excellent, has in this Tragedy excell'd her-*
> *self, and gain'd a Reputation, beyond any Woman I have ever*
> *seen on the Theatre.*

I very perfectly remember her acting that Part; and however
unnecessary it may seem, to give my Judgment after *Dryden's,*
I cannot help saying, I do not only close with his Opinion, but
will venture to add, that (tho' *Dryden* has been dead these Thirty
Eight Years) the same Compliment, to this Hour, may be due
to her Excellence. And tho' she was then, not a little, past her
Youth, seh was not, till that time, fully arriv'd to her Maturity
of Power and Judgment: From whence I would observe, That
the short Life of Beauty, is not long enough to form a complete
Actress. In Men, the Delicacy of Person is not so absolutely necessary, nor the Decline of it so soon taken notice of. The
Fame Mrs. *Barry* arriv'd to, is a particular Proof of the Difficulty there is, in judging with Certainty, from their first Trials,
whether young People will ever make any great Figure on a
Theatre. There was, it seems, so little Hope of Mrs. *Barry,* at
her first setting out, that she was, at the end of the first Year,
discharg'd the Company, among others, that were thought to be
a useless Expence to it. I take it for granted that the Objection
to Mrs. *Barry,* at that time, must have been a defective Ear, or
some unskilful Dissonance, in her manner of pronouncing: But
where there is a proper Voice, and Person, with the Additon of
a good Understanding, Experience tells us, that such Defect is
not always invincible; of which, not only Mrs. *Barry,* but the
late Mrs. *Oldfield,* are eminent Instances. Mrs. *Oldfield* had been
a Year, in the Theatre-Royal, before she was observ'd to give
any tolerable Hope of her being an Actress; so unlike, to all
manner of Propriety, was her Speaking! How unaccountably,

17.   *Otway's Monimia* and *Belvidera*] The former is in *The Orphan; or, The Unhappy Marriage* (1680), the latter in *Venice Preserved: or, A Plot Discovered* (1682).

29.   *Cleopatra*] In Dryden's *All for Love, or, The World Well Lost*, first performed in 1677 with Mrs. Boutell as Cleopatra. Lowe notes (I, 161) that Mrs. Barry had not played Cleopatra when Dryden wrote this encomium.

30.   *Roxana*] In Nathaniel Lee's *The Rival Queens* (1677).

33.   annual Benefit-Play] There is some dispute about when the custom of benefits arose; however, a petition of the players, December 1694, involved a controversy over Mrs. Barry's right to collect the amount guaranteed to her in her benefit (see Nicoll, I, 369) and, in this, reference is made to a long-standing agreement between her and the company. Avery (I, xcvi), citing this passage, accepts Cibber's authority.

then, does a Genius for the Stage make its way towards Perfec-
tion? For, notwithstandig these equal Disadvantages, botyh these
Actresses, tho' of different Excellence, made themselves complete
Mistresses of their Art, by the Prevalence of their Understanding.
If this Observation may be of any use, to the Masters of future
Theatres, I shall not then have made it to no purpose.

Mrs. *Barry,* in Characters of Greatness, had a Presence of elevated Dignity, her Mien and Motion superb, and gracefully ma-
jestick; her Voice full, clear, and strong, so that no Violence of
Passion could be too much for her: And when Distress, or Tenderness possess'd her, she subsided into the Most affecting Melody,
and Softness. In the Art of exciting Pity, she had a power beyond all the Actresses I have yet seen, or what your Imagination
can conceive. Of the former of these two great Excellencies,
she gave the most delightful Proofs in almost all the Heroic
Plays of *Dryden* and *Lee;* and of the latter, in the softer Passions of *Otway's Monimia* and *Belvidera.* In Scenes of Anger,
Defiance, or Resentment, while she was impetuous, and terrible, she pour'd out the Sentiment with an enchanting Harmony;
and it was this particular Excellence, for which *Dryden* made
her the above-recited Compliment, upon her acting *Cassandra* in
his *Cleomenes.* But here, I am apt to think his Partiality for that
Character, may have tempted his Judgment to let it pass for
her Master-piece; when he could not but know, there were several other Characters in which her Action might have given her
a fairer Pretence to the Praise he has bestow'd on her, for *Cassandra;* for, in no Part of that, is there the least ground for Compassion, as in *Monimia;* nor equal cause for Admiration, as in
the nobler Love of *Cleopatra,* or the tempestuous Jealousy of
Roxana. 'Twas in these Lights, I thought Mrs. *Barry* shone
with a much brighter Excellence than in *Cassandra.* She was the
first Person whose Merit was distinguish'd, by the Indulgence of
having an annual Benefit-Play, which was granted to her alone,
if I mistake not, first in King *James's* time, and which became

7. *Ha, Ha! ... Dozens!*] Mrs. Barry died in late 1713, whereas Queen Anne had created the twelve Tory Peers in January 1712, contrary to Cibber's belief that both events took place at the same period. The Queen's action was regarded by Whigs as an abuse of the royal prerogative and continued to be a source of bitter recrimination between Whigs and Tories; Cibber here expresses his party sympathy in the mouth of Mrs. Barry (cf. Plumb, I, 177-78).

8. Mrs. *Betterton*] In December 1662 Thomas Betterton married Mary Saunderson who was then about twenty-five years old (Lowe, *Betterton*, p. 83).

18. ... she quitted the Stage] She retired about 1695 (Lowe, *Betterton*, p. 182).

21. *Mithridates*] *Mithridates, King of Pontus* (1677/78) by Nathaniel Lee.

24. Pension ... first half Year of it] Either the pension was not granted immediately—since she survived her husband by two years—or Cibber is referring to the fact that the pension was not paid on time, and arrears were due to her on her death (see Lowe, Betterton, p. 183).

26. Mrs. Leigh] Elinor Leigh, wife of Anthony Leigh, acted from about 1677 to 1707 (see Downes, *Roscius*, ed. Summers, p. 31 and note on p. 203); Hotson, p. 280 n., establishes that it was Elinor, not Elizabeth, who was married to Anthony Leigh.

31. the *Chances*] *The Chances*, a play by Fletcher of which the Acts IV and V were rewritten by the Duke of Buckingham shortly after its revival in 1661 (see Downes, *Roscius*, ed. Summers, p. 120).

not common to others, 'till the Division of this Company, after
the Death of King *William's* Queen *Mary.* This great Actress
dy'd of a Fever, towards the latter end of Queen *Anne;* the
Year I have forgot; but perhaps you will recollect it, by an Expression that fell from her in blank Verse, in her last Hours, when
she was delirious, *viz.*

> *Ha, ha! and so they make us Lords, by Dozens!*

Mrs. *Betterton,* tho' far advanc'd in Years, was so great a
Mistress of Nature, that even Mrs. *Barry,* who acted the Lady
Macbeth after her, could not in that Part, with all her superior
Strength, and Melody of Voice, throw out those quick and careless Strokes of Terror, from the Disorder of a guilty Mind, which
the other gave us, with a Facility in her Manner, that render'd
them at once tremendous, and delightful. Time could not impair her Skill, tho' he had brought her Person to decay. She was,
to the last, the Admiration of all true Judges of Nature, and
Lovers of *Shakespear,* in whose Plays she chiefly excell'd, and
without a Rival. When she quitted the Stage, several good Actresses were the better for her Instruction. She was a Woman of
an unblemish'd, and sober Life; and had the Honour to teach
Queen *Anne,* when Princess, the Part of *Semandra* in *Mithri-*
dates, which she acted at Court in King *Charles's* time. After
the Death of Mr. *Betterton,* her Husband, that Princess, when
Queen, order'd her a Pension for Life, but she liv'd not to receive more than the first half Year of it.

Mrs. *Leigh,* the Wife of *Leigh* already mention'd, had a very
droll way of dressing the pretty Foibles of superannuated Beauties.
She had, in her self, a good deal of Humour, and knew how to
infuse it into the affected Mothers, Aunts, and modest stale
Maids, that had miss'd their Market; of this sort were the Modish
Mother in the *Chances,* affecting to be politely commode, for her
own Daughter; the coquette Prude of an Aunt, in Sir *Courtly*
Nice, who prides herself in being chaste, and cruel, at Fifty;

11.　*King Arthur*] *King Arthur, or, The British Worthy* (1691) by John Dryden.

18.　(*Villers*) Duke of *Buckingham*] George Villiers, whose rewriting of *The Chances* is noted on p. 96.

32.　Mr. *Ashbury*] Summers notes (ed., Downes, *Roscius*, p. 222) that "the theatre in Smockalley had been closed during the troubles between King James II and the Prince of Orange, but was opened by Mr. Ashbury on March 23, 1691-92."

And the languishing Lady *Wishfort,* in *The Way of the World:*
In all these, with many others, she was extremely entertaining,
and painted, in a lively manner, the blind Side of Nature.

    Mrs. *Butler,* who had her Christian Name of *Charlotte* given
her by King *Charles,* was the Daughter of a decay'd Knight,
and had the Honour of that Prince's Recommendation to the
Theatre; a provident Restitution, giving to the Stage in kind,
what he had sometimes taken from it: The Publick, at least, was
oblig'd by it; for she prov'd not only a good Actress, but was al-
10 low'd, in those Days, to sing and dance to great Perfection. In
the Dramatick Opera's of *Dioclesian,* and that of *King Arthur,*
she was a capital, and admired Performer. In speaking too, she
had a sweet-ton'd Voice, which, with her naturally genteel Air,
and sensible Pronunciation, render'd her wholly Mistress of the
Amiable, in many serious Characters. In Parts of Humour too
she had a manner of blending her assuasive Softness, even with
the Gay, the Lively, and the Alluring. Of this she gave an a-
greeable Instance, in her Action of the (*Villers*) Duke of *Buckingham's* second *Constantia* in the *Chances.* In which, if I should
20 say, I have never seen her exceeded, I might still do no wrong
to the late Mrs. *Oldfield's* lively Performance of the same Character. Mr. *Oldfield's* Fame may spare Mrs. *Butler's* Action this
Compliment, without the least Diminution, or Dispute of her
Superiority, in Characters of more moment.

    Here I cannot help observing, when there was but one Theatre
in *London,* at what unequal Sallaries, compar'd to those of later
Days, the hired Actors were then held, by the absolute Authority of their frugal Masters, the Patentees; for Mrs. *Butler* had
then but Forty Shillings a Week, and could she have obtain'd an
30 Addition of Ten Shillings more (which was refus'd her) would
never have left their Service; but being offer'd her own Conditions, to go with Mr. *Ashbury* to *Dublin* (who was then raising a
Company of Actors for that Theatre, where there had been none
since the Revolution) her Disconent, here, prevail'd with her to

25.   *Abigail*] In *The Scornful Lady* (1616).

28.   *The Western Lass*] *The Bath: or The Western Lass* (1701).

33.   *Joan Trot*] Apparently, a female *John Trot*, i.e., a bumpkin; cf. Trot, John in *OED*.

accept of his Offer, and he found his Account in her Value.
Were not those Patentees most sagacious Oeconomists, that could
lay hold on so notable an Expedient, to lessen their Charge? How
gladly, in my Time of being a Sharer, would we have given four
times her income, to an Actress of equal Merit?

     Mrs. *Monfort,* whose second Marriage gave her the Name of
Verbruggen, was Mistress of more variety of Humour, than I
ever knew in any one Woman Actress. This variety too, was attended with an equal Vivacity, which made her excellent in Cha-
10   racters extremely different. As she was naturally a pleasant Mimick, she had the Skill to make that Talent useful on the Stage,
a Talent which may be surprising in a Conversation, and yet be
lost when brought to the Theatre, which was the Case of *Estcourt*
already mention'd: But where the Elocution is round, distinct,
voluble, and various, as Mrs. *Monfort's* was, the Mimick, there,
is a great Assistant to the Actor. Nothing, tho' ever so barren,
if within the Bounds of Nature, could be flat in her Hands.
She gave many heightening Touches to Characters but coldly
written, and often made an Author vain of his Work, that in it
20   self had but little merit. She was so fond of Humour, in what
low Part soever to be found, that she would make no scruple of
defacing her fair Form, to come heartily into it; for when she
was eminent in several desirable Characters of Wit, and Humour,
in higher Life, she would be, in as much Fancy, when descend-
ing into the antiquated *Abigail,* of *Fletcher,* as when triumphing
in all the Airs, and vain graces of a fine Lady; a Merit, that
few Actresses care for. In a Play of *D'urfey's,* now forgotten,
call'd, *The Western Lass,* which Part she acted, she transform'd
her whole Being, Body, Shape, Voice, Language, Look, and
30   Features, into almost another Animal; with a strong *Devonshire*
Dialect, a broad laughing Voice, a poking Head, round Shoulders, an unconceiving Eye, and the most be-diz'ning, dowdy
Dress, that ever covered the untrain'd Limbs of a *Joan Trot.* To
have seen her here, you would have thought it impossible the

7.   seeing her a Man] For a discussion of the custom of actresses taking men's parts, see Nicoll, II, 49-50.

13.   *Marriage-Alamode*] *Marriage A-la-Mode* (1672) by John Dryden.

same Creature could ever have been recovered, to what was
as easy to her, the Gay, the Lively, and the Desirable. Nor
was her Humour limited, to her Sex; for, while her Shape permitted, she was a more adroit pretty Fellow, than is usually seen
upon the Stage: Her easy Air, Action, Mien, and Gesture, quite
chang'd from the Quoif, to the Cock'd Hat, and Cavalier in fashion. People were so fond of seeing her a Man, that when the
Part of *Bays* in the *Rehearsal,* had, for some time, lain dormant,
she was desired to take it up, which I have seen her act with all
10   the true, coxcombly Spirit, and Humour, that the Sufficiency of
the Character required.

But what found most Employment for her whole various Excellence at once, was the Part of *Melantha,* in *Marriage-Ala-*
mode. Melantha is as finish'd an Impertinent, as ever flutter'd in
a Drawing-Room, and seems to contain the most compleat System of Female Foppery, that could possibly be crowded into
the tortur'd Form of a Fine Lady. Her Language, Dress, Motion, Manners, Soul, and Body, are in a continual Hurry to be
something more, than is necessary, or commendable. And tho'
20   I doubt it will be a vain Labour, to offer you a just likeness of
Mrs. *Monfort's* Action, yet the fantastick Impression is still so
strong in my Memory, that I cannot help saying something, tho'
fantastically, about it. The first ridiculous Airs that break from
her, are, upon a Gallant, never seen before, who delivers her a
Letter from her Father, recommending him to her good Graces,
as an honourable Lover. Here now, one would think she might
naturally shew a little of the Sexe's decent Reserve, though never
so slightly cover'd! No, SIr; not a Tittle of it; Modesty is the
Virtue of a poor-soul'd Country Gentlewoman; she is too much
30   a Court Lady, to be under so vulgar a Confusion; she reads the
Letter, therefore, with a careless, dropping Lip, and an erected
Brow, humming it hastily over, as if she were impatient to out-
go her Father's Commands, by making a complete Conquest of
him at once; and, that the Letter might not embarrass her At-

13.   in a Twinkling] This occurs in Act II, scene 1.

100

tack, crack! she crumbles it at once, into her Palm, and pours
upon him her whole Artillery of Airs, Eyes, and Motion; down
goes her dainty, diving Body, to the Ground, as if she were
sinking under the conscious Load of her own Attractions; then
lanches into a Flood of Fine Language, and Compliment, still
playhing her Chest forward in fifty Falls and Risings, like a Swan
upon waving Water; and, to complete her Impertinence, she is
so rapidly fond of her own Wit, that she will not give her Lover
leave to praise it: Silent assenting Bows, and vain Endeavours
10   to speak, are all the share of the Covnersation he is admitted to,
which, at last, he is relive'd from, by her Engagement to half a
Score Visits, which she *swims* from him to make, with a Promise
to return in a Twinkling.

If this Sketch has Colour enough to give you any near Conception of her, I then need only tell you, that throughout the
whole Character, her variety of Humour was every way proportionable; as, indeed, in most Parts, that she whought worth her
care, or that had the least Matter for her Fancy to work upon,
I may justly say, That no Actress, from her own Conception,
20   could have heighten'd them with more lively Strokes of Nature.

I come now to the last, and only living Person, of all those
whose Theatrical Characters I have promis'd you, Mrs. *Brace-*
girdle; who, I know, would rather pass her remaining Days
forgotten, as an Actress, than to have her Youth recollected in
the most favourable Light I am able to place it; yet, as she is
essentially necessary to my Theatrical History, and, as I only
bring her back to the Company of those, with whom she pass'd
the Spring and Summer of her Life, I hope it will excuse the Li-
30   berty I take, in commemorating the Delight which the Publick
receiv'd from her Appearance, while she was an Ornament to the
Theatre.

Mrs. *Bracegirdle* was now, but just blooming to her Maturity;
her Reputation, as an Actress, gradually rising with that of her

19.　Authors … two of them] Rowe and Congreve (Nicoll, I, 73).

Person; never any Woman was in such general Favour of her
Spectators, which, to the last Scene of her Dramatick Life, she
maintain'd, by not being unguarded in her private Character.
This Discretion contributed, not a little, to make her the *Cara,*
the Darling of the Theatre: *For it will be no extravagant thing*
to say, Scarce an Audience saw her, that were less than half of
them Lovers, without a suspected Favourite among them: And
tho' she might be said to have been the Universal Passion, and under the highest Temptations; her Constancy in resisting them,
serv'd but to increase the number of her Admirers: And this perhaps you will more easily believe, when I extend not my Encomiums on her Person, beyond a Sincerity that can be suspected;
for she had no greater Claim to Beauty, than what the most desirable *Brunette* might pretend to. But her Youth, and lively
Aspect, threw out such a Glow of Health, and Chearfulness,
that, on the Stage, few Spectators that were not past it, could
behold her without Desire. It was even a Fashion among the
Gay, and Young, to have a Taste or *Tendre* for Mrs. *Bracegirdle.*
She inspired the best Authors to write for her, and two of them
when they gave her a Lover, in a Play, seem'd palpably to plead
their own Passions, and make their private Court to her, in fictitious Characters. In all the chief Parts she acted, the Desirable
was so predominant, that no Judge could be cold enough to consider, from what other particular Excellence she became delightful. To speak critically of an Actress, that was extremely good,
were as hazardous, as to be positive in one's Opinion of the best
Opera Singer. People often judge by Comparison, where there
is no Similitude, in the Performance. So that, in this case, we
have only Taste to appeal to, and of Taste there can be no disputing. I shall therefore only say of Mrs. *Bracegirdle,* That the
most eminent Authors always chose her for their favourite Character, and shall leave that uncontestable Proof of her Merit to
its own Value. Yet let me say, there were two very different
Characters, in which she acquitted herself with uncommon Ap-

4. *Millamant*] In Congreve's *The Way of the World* (1700).

12. Year 1710] Her name no longer appears in the play bills after the season of 1706-1707; she appeared for the last time at Betterton's benefit in 1709 (Avery, I, 130, 154, *et passim*). This means that she retired at about thirty, a circumstance for which numerous accounts are given. *The Laureat* (p. 36) suggests that her retirement was due to Cibber himself giving Mrs. Oldfield roles which properly should have gone to Mrs. Bracegirdle in the years 1706-1707. Cibber probably did not, as the author mistakenly believed, have the authority at that time to make such a decision (cf. Lowe, I, 175). Mrs. Bracegirdle died in 1748.

26. *Baron*] Michel Boyron, called *Baron* (1653-1729), French comic actor and author, first of Moliere's troupe, afterwards of the Hotel de Bourgogne.

plause: If any thing could excuse that desperate Extravagance
of Love, that almost frantick Passion of *Lee's Alexander the
Great,* it must have been, when Mrs. *Bracegirdle* was his *Statira:* As when she acted *Millamant,* all the Faults, Follies, and
Affectation of that agreeable Tyrant, were venially melted down
into so many Charms, and Attractions of a conscious Beauty. In
other Characters, where Singing was a necessary Part of them,
her Voice and Action gave a Pleasure, which good Sense, in those
Days, was not asham'd to give Praise to.

10   She retir'd from the Stage in the Height of her Favour from
the Publick, when most of her Cotemporaries, whom she had
been bred up with, were declining, in the Year 1710, nor could
she be perswaded to return to it, under new Masters, upon the
most advantageous Terms, that were offer'd her; excepting one
Day, about a Year after, to assist her good Friend, Mr. *Betterton,*
when she play'd *Angelica,* in *Love for Love,* for his Beneift. She
has still the Happiness to retain her usual Chearfulness, and to be,
without the transitory Charm of Youth, agreeable.

If, in my Account of these memorable Actors, I have not de-
20   viated from Truth, which, in the least Article I am not conscious
of, may we not venture to say, They had not their Equals, at
any one Time, upon any one Theatre in *Europe?* Or, if we
confine the Comparison, to that of *France* alone, I believe no
other Stage can be much disparag'd, by being left out of the question; which cannot properly be decided, by the single Merit of
any one Actor; whether their *Baron,* or our *Betterton,* might
be the Superior, (take which Side you please) that Point reaches,
either way, but to a thirteenth part of what I contend for, *viz.*
That no State, at any one Period, could shew thirteen Actors,
30   standing all in equal Lights of Excellence, in their Profession:
And I am the bolder, in this Challenge, to any other Nation,
because no Theatre having so extended a variety of natural Characters, as the *English,* can have a Demand for Actors of such
various Capacities; why then, where they could not be equally

1. 21 may we not venture] may we may not venture 2nd ed.

wanted, should we suppose them, at any one time, to have
existed?

　　How imperfect soever this copious Account of them may be,
I am not without Hope, at least, it may in some degree shew,
what Talents are requisite to make Actors valuable: And if that
may any ways inform, or assist the Judgment of future Spectators, it may, as often, be of service to their publick Entertainments; for as their Hearers are, so will Actors be; worse, or
better, as the false, or true Taste applauds, or discommends
10　them. Hence only can our Theatres improve, or must de-
generate.

　　There is another Point, relating to the hard Condition of those
who write for the Stage, which I would recommend to the Consideration of their Hearers; which is, that the extreme Severity
with which they damn a bad Play, seems too terrible a Warning to those whose untried Genius might hereafter give them a
good one: Whereas it might be a Temptation, to a latent Author, to make the Experiment, could he be sure that, though not
approved, his Muse might, at least, be dismiss'd with Decency:
20　But the Vivacity of our modern Criticks is of late grown so riotous, that an unsuccessful Author has no more Mercy shewn him,
than a notorious Cheat, in a Pillory; every Fool, the lowest
Member of the Mob, becomes a Wit, and will have a sling at
him. They come now to a new Play, like Hounds to a Carcass,
and are all in a full Cry, sometimes for an Hour together, before the Curtain rises to throw it amongst them. Sure, those Gentlemen cannot but allow, that a Play condemn'd after a fair Hearing, falls with thrice the Ignominy, as when it is refus'd that
common Justice.

30　　But when their critical Interruptions grow so loud, and of so
long a continuance, that the Attention of quiet People (though
not so complete Criticks) is terrify'd, and the Skill of the Actors
quite disconcerted by the Tumult, the Play then seems rather to
fall by Assassins, than by a lawful Sentence. It is possible that

27. *Non ignara ... disco*] *Aeneid*, I, 620: "Not being without experience of misfortune myself, I know how to comfort the miseries of others."

29. *I learn ... like my own*] Dryden, *The First Book of the Aeneis*, line 891 (*Poetical Works*, ed. Noyes, p. 533).

such Auditors can receive Delight, or think it any Praise to them,
to prosecute so injurious, so unmanly a Treatment? And tho'
perhaps the Compassionate, on the other side (who know they
have as good a Right to clap, and support, as others have to
catcall, damn, and destroy,) may oppose this Oppression; their
Good-nature, alas! contributes little to the Redress; for in this
sort of Civil War, the unhappy Author, like a good Prince,
while his Subjects are at mortal Variance, is sure to be a Loser
by a Victory on either Side; for still the Commonwealth, his
10 Play, is, during the Conflict, torn to pieces. While this is the
Case, while the Theatre is so turbulent a Sea, and so infested
with Pirates, what Poetical Merchant, of any Substance, will
venture to trade in it? If these valiant Gentlemen pretend to be
Lovers of Plays, why will they deter Gentlemen, from giving
them such, as are fit for Gentlemen to see? In a word, this new
Race of Criticks seem to me, like the Lion-Whleps in the *Tower,*
who are so boisterously gamesome at their Meals, that they
dash down the Bowls of Milk, brought for their own Breakfast.
20   As a good Play is certainly the most rational, and the highest
Entertainment, that human Invention can produce, let that be
my Apology (if I need any) for having thus freely delivered my
Mind, in behalf of those Gentlemen, who, under such calami-
tous Hazards, may hereafter be reduc'd to write for the Stage;
whose Case I shall compassionate, from the same Motive, that
prevail'd on *Dido,* to assist the *Trojans* in Distress.

　　　Non ignara mali miseris succurrere disco.　　Virg.
Or, as *Dryden* has it,

　　　I learn to pity Woes so like my own.

30   If those particular Gentlemen have sometimes made me the
humbled Object of their Wit, and Humour, their Triumph at
least has done me this involuntary Service, that it has driven me

CHAPTER VI

14.   Theatrical Triumvirat] This refers to the period beginning in 1709 when Wilks,
       Dogget, and Cibber were in control of the theater (cf. Barker, pp. 76 ff.).

16.   the Patentees] These were at first (November 1682) Charles D'Avenant and
       Charles Killigrew; in 1687 Alexander D'Avenant bought the remaining shares of
       the D'avenant patent from his half brother Charles (Nicoll, I, 331-36; Hotson, pp.
       270-85). Cf. below for the actual facts of this transaction.

a Year or two sooner into a quiet Life, than otherwise, my own
want of Judgment might have led me to: I left the Stage, before my Strength left me; and tho' I came to it again, for some
few Days, a Year or two after; my Reception there not only
turn'd to my Account, but seem'd a fair Invitation, that I would
make my Visits more frequent: But, to give over a Winner, can
be no very imprudent Resolution.

C H A P. VI.

The Author's first Step upon the Stage. His Discouragements.
The best Actors in Europe, *ill us'd. A Revolution, in their Fa-*
vour. King William *grants them a Licence to act in* Lincoln's-Inn Fields. *The Author's Distress, in being thought a*
worse Actor, than a Poet. Reduc'd to write a Part for him-
self. His Success. More Remarks, upon Theatrical Action.
Some, upon himself.

HAVING given you the State of the Theatre, at my
first Admission to it; I am now drawing towards
the several Revolutions it suffer'd, in my own Time.
But (as you find by the setting out of my History)
that I always intended myself the Heroe of it, it
may be necessary to let you know me, in my Obscurity, as
well as in my higher Light, when I became one of the Theatrical Triumvirat.

The Patentees, who were now Masters of this united, and
only Company of Comedians, seem'd to make it a Rule, that no
young Persons, desirous to be Actors, should be admitted into
Pay under, at least, half a Year's Probation; wisely knowing,
that how early soever they might be approv'd of, there could be
no great fear of losing them, while they had, then, no other
Market to go to. But, alas! Pay was the least of my Concern;

10

20

Grimace / Have no such Prospects [of living well when the theater closes] from this hatchet Face."

25.   *Goodman*] The *Apology* (p. 57) mentioned Goodman along with Clark as a younger successor to the older actors—Mohun and Hart—who retired at the *Union*. Davies (*Dram. Misc.*, II, 240) states that Goodman, after a career as a highwayman for which he was pardoned by James II, was the kept lover of the Duchess of Cleveland; he was, "long before his death ... so happy in his finances, that he acted only occasionally, perhaps when his noble mistress wished to see him in a principal character." Evidently these are the circumstances at the time of Cibber's anecdote.

31.   *Monfort* reply'd] Cibber's debut, therefore, must have been before 9/10 December 1692, when Mountfort was murdered (Van Lennep, p. 411). Van Lennep suggests that Cibber played the role of the Chaplain on 9 February 1692 (p. 406).

4.   Salary of Ten Shillings *per* Week] Davies (*Dram. Misc.*, III, 445) quotes the following account of Cibber's first salary: "He was known only, for some years, by the name of Master Colley. After waiting impatiently a long time for the prompter's notice, by good fortune he obtained the honour of carrying a message on the stage, in some play, to Betterton. Whatever was the cause, Master Colley was so terrified, that the scene was disconcerted by him. Betterton asked, in some anger, who the young fellow was that had committed the blunder. Downs [the prompter] replied, 'Master Colley.'—'Master Colley! then forfeit him.'—'Why, sir.' said the prompter, 'he has no salary.'—'No!' said the old man' 'why then put him down ten shillings a week, and forfeit him 5 s.' " [Lowe].

10.   Insufficiency of my Voice] This, along with other references to the absolute differences between acting comedy and tragedy, supports the suggestion that heroic or tragic parts were intoned or chanted by seventeenth-century actors. A. C. Sprague ("Did Betterton Chant?" *Theatre Notebook*, I, 1947, pp. 54-55), relying on Cibber's description along with that of others, thinks that tragic actors may have done so, but finds the evidence "far short of proof."

12.   pale Complexion] Lowe, (I, 182 n.) suggests that since actors are known to have used make-up (quoting Pepys, 5 October 1667, on actresses) perhaps young actors playing juvenile roles were expected not to use it.

12.   Under these Disadvantages] The author of *The History of Aesopus, the Tragedian*, presumably also the author of *The Laureat* with which it is printed, describes Cibber this way (p. 103): "He was in Stature of the middle Size, his Complexion fair, inclinable to the Sandy, his Legs somewhat of the thickest, his Shape a little clumsy, not irregular, and his Voice rather shrill than loud or articulate, and crack'd extremely, when he endeavour'd to raise it. He was in his younger Days so lean, as to be known by the Name of Hatchet Face … " He then cites the Epilogue of Cibber's *The Lady's Last Stake* (1707), which states, "But I, whose Beauty only is

the Joy, and Privilege of every Day seeing Plays, for nothing, I
thought was a sufficient Consideration, for the best of my Services. So that it was no Pain to my Patience, that I waited full
three Quarters of a Year, before I was taken into a Salary of Ten
Shillings *per* Week; which, with the Assistance of Food, and
Raiment, at my Father's House, I then thought a most plentiful
Accession, and myself the happiest of Mortals.

    The first Thing that enters into the Head of a young Actor,
is that of being a Heroe: In this Ambition I was soon snubb'd,
by the Insufficiency of my Voice; to which might be added,
an uninform'd meagre Person (tho' then not ill made) with a dismal pale Complexion. Under these Disadvantages, I had but a
melancholy Prospect of ever playing a Lover, with Mrs. *Bracegirdle,* which I had flatter'd my Hopes, that my Youth might
one Day, have recommended me to. What was most promising
in me, then, was the Aptness of my Ear; for I was soon allow'd
to speak justly, tho' what was grave and serious, did not equally
become me. The first Part, therefore, in which I appeared,
with any glimpse of Success, was the Chaplain in the *Orphan*
of *Otway.* There is in this Character (of one Scene only) a decent Pleasantry, and Sense enough to shew an Audience, whether the Actor has any himself. Here was the first Applause I
ever receiv'd, which, you may be sure, made my Heart leap
with a higher Joy, than may be necessary to describe; and yet
my Transport was not then half so high, as at what *Goodman*
(who had now left the Stage) said of me, the next Day, in my
hearing. *Goodman* often came to a Rehearsal for Amusement,
and having sate out the *Orphan,* the Day before; in a Conversation with some of the principal Actors, enquir'd what new
young Fellow that was, whom he had seen in the Chaplain?
Upon which, *Monfort* reply'd, *That's he, behind you.* *Goodman*
then turning about, look'd earnestly at me, and, after some
Pause, clapping me on the Shoulder, rejoin'd, *If he does not
make a good Actor, I'll be d----'d!* The Surprize of being com-

17. Matrimony] Cibber married (6 May 1693) Katherine Shore, a pupil of Purcell's for singing and harpsichord, and daughter of Matthias Shore, the Sergeant Trumpeter to the King. Her father did not give his consent to the match and immediately spent the money intended for her dowry on a large houseboat on the Thames known as 'Shore's Folly.' He relented in 1696 and in his will left her one-third of his property (Barker, pp. 16-18).

21. maintain ... young Couple] Barker states (p. 18) that Katherine Cibber was compelled to go on the stage to help support them during this period; she appeared as late as 1697 (cf. Van Lennep, pp. 486, 87, and 502.).

31. *Double Dealer*] The premier was in October 1695; the royal performance of which Cibber speaks was given on Saturday, 13 January 1694 (Nicoll, I, 397).

mended, by one who had been himself so eminent, on the Stage,
and in so positive a manner, was more than I could support; in
a Word, it almost took away my Breath, and (laugh, if you
please) fairly drew Tears from my Eyes! And, tho' it may be as
ridiculous, as incredible, to tell you what a full Vanity, and Content, at that time possess'd me, I will still make it a Question,
whether *Alexander* himself, or *Charles the Twelfth* of *Sweden,*
when at the Head of their first victorious Armies, could feel a
greater Transport, in their Bosoms, than I did then in mine, when
10   but in the Rear of this Troop of Comedians. You see, to what
low Particulars I am forc'd to descend, to give you a true Resemblance of the early and lively Follies of my Mind. Let me
give you another Instance, of my Discretion, more desperate, than
that, of preferring the Stage, to any other Views of Life. One
might think, that the Madness of breaking, from the Advice,
and care of Parents, to turn Player, could not easily be exceeded: But what think you, Sir, of ---- Matrimony? which, before
I was Two-and-twenty, I actually committed, when I had but
Twenty Pounds a Year, which my Father had assur'd to me,
20   and Twenty Shillings a Week from my Theatrical Labours, to
maintain, as I then thought, the happiest young Couple, that
ever took a Leap in the Dark! If after this, to complete my Fortune, I turn'd Poet too, this last Folly, indeed, had something a
better Excuse---Necessity: Had it never been my Lot to have
come to the Stage, 'tis probable, I might never have been inclin'd,
or reduc'd to have wrote for it: But having once expos'd my
Person there, I thought it could be no additional Dishonour
to let my Parts, whatever they were, take their Fortune along
with it. ------ But, to return to the Progress I made as an
30   Actor.

  Queen *Mary* having commanded the *Double Dealer* to be acted,
Kynaston happen'd to be so ill, that he could not hope to be able
next Day to perform his Part of the Lord *Touchwood.* In this
Exigence, the Author, Mr. *Congreve,* advis'd that it might be

11. *But never were ... bright a Queen*] Lines 9-10 of Congreve's "Prologue to the Queen upon Her Majesty's coming to see the *Old Batchelour*," spoken by Mrs. Barry (*Works*, ed. Summers, IV, 36). The prologue to *The Double Dealer* was apparently spoken by Mrs. Bracegirdle (*ibid.*, II, 16).

29. Government of the united Patents] At this period management of the company had passed into the hands of Thomas D'Avenant and Charles, younger brother of Alexander Killigrew (Nicoll, I, 334-35).

108

given to me, if at so short a Warning I would undertake it. The
Flattery of being thus distinguish'd by so celebrated an Author,
and the Honour to act before a Queen, you may be sure, made
me blind to whatever Difficulties might attend it. I accepted the
Part, and was ready in it before I slept; next Day the Queen was
present at the Play, and was receiv'd with a new Prologue from
the Author, spoken by Mrs. *Barry,* humbly acknowledging the
great Honour done to the Stage, and to his Play in particular:
Two Lines of it, which though I have not since read, I still re-
10 member.

> *But never were in* Rome, *nor* Athens *seen,*
> *So fair a Circle, or so bright a Queen.*

After the Play, Mr. *Congreve* made me the Compliment of saying, that I had not only answer'd, but had exceed his Expectations, and that he would shew me he was sincere, by his saying
more of me to the Masters---- He was as good as his Word, and
the next Pay-day, I found my Sallary, of fifteen, was then advanc'd to twenty Shillings a Week. But alas! this favourable
Opinion of Mr. *Congreve,* made no farther Impression upon the
20 Judgment of my good Masters; it only serv'd to heighten my
own Vanity; but could not recommend me to any new Trials
of my Capacity; not a Step farther could I get, 'till the Company was again divided; when the Desertion of the best Actors
left a clear Stage, for younger Champions to mount, and shew
their best Pretensions to favour. But it is now time to enter upon those Facts, that immediately preceded this remarkable Revolution of the Theatre.

You have seen how compleat a Set of Actors were under the
Government of the united Patents in 1690; if their Gains were
30 not extraordinary, what shall we impute it to, but some extraordinary ill Management? I was then too young to be in their Secrets, and therefore can only observe upon what I saw, and have
since thought visibly wrong.

theater. Here begins the intensification of woes described by Cibber (Hotson, pp. 284-93).

29.   bringing younger Actors forward] Cf. Nicoll, I, 334-36; Hotson, pp. 293-95.

1. *Prophetess*, and King *Arthur*] *The Prophetess, or, The History of Dioclesian* (June 1690) and *King Arthur* (May 1691) by Dryden both had music by Henry Purcell (Downes, *Roscius*, ed. Summers, p. 42 and pp. 246-47 n.; Nicoll, I, 406-407).

5. large Debt] The company was £800 in debt in February 1692 (Hotson, p. 290).

6. Court of Chancery ... weary] Certain of the stockholders (sharers) brought suit in 1704 for their due share of the profits of the company, complaining that the managers had defrauded them. Rich, the lawyer who controlled the company at the time (see below) paid no dividends to sharers and no rent on the Dorset Garden Theatre from 1695-1704, claiming that debts absorbed all profits (Hotson, pp. 300-302).

8. every Branch ... had been sacrific'd] Cf. Nicoll, I, 334; and Hotson, pp. 287 ff.

18. *Nokes, Monfort,* and *Leigh*] Mountfort and Leigh died in December 1692; Nokes died in September 1696 (Hotson, p. 290).

20. the Building grew weaker] Cibber fails to mention two important factors in the disintegration of the united company at this time. First, Alexander D'Avenant had been carrying on elaborate swindling operations, made possible largely by the credit he gained through the general belief that he owned the D'Avenant patent. Among other outrages, he had borrowed £600 to £800 from Mrs. Barry (from a summary of a *Petition of the Players*, c. December 1694, Nicoll, I, 369). When exposed, these brought on a flood of suits; the culprit escaped arrest by fleeing to the Canary Islands. In December of the same year, Christopher Rich, a lawyer, and Sir Thomas Skipwith, a courtier, disclosed that they had paid £2000 of the £2400 cost of buying the D'Avenant patent for Alexander from Charles. Since Alexander's flight, his claims were void; therefore, they announced, Rich, "an old snarling Lawyer Master and Sovereign; a waspish, ignorant, pettifogger in Law and Poetry." (*Comparison*, ed. Wells, p. 11), was assuming the management of the

Though the Success of the *Prophetess,* and King *Arthur* (two
dramatic Opera's, in which the Patentees had embark'd all their
Hopes) was, in Appearance, very great, yet their whole Receipts
did not so far ballance their Expence, as to keep them out of a
large Debt, which it was publickly known was, about this time,
contracted, and which found work for the Court of Chancery
for about twnty Years following, till one side of the Cause grew
weary. But this was not all that was wrong; every Branch of
the Theatrical Trade had been sacrific'd, to the necessary fitting
10   out those tall Ships of Burthen, that were to bring home the
Indies. Plays of course were neglected, Actors held cheap, and
slightly dress'd, while Singers, and Dancers were better paid, and
embroider'd. These Measures, of course, created Murmurings,
on one side, and ill Humour and Contempt on the other. When
it became necessary therefore to lessen the Charge, a Resolution
was taken to begin with the Sallaries of the Actors; and what
seem'd to make this Resolution more necessary at this time, was
the Loss of *Nokes, Monfort,* and *Leigh,* who all dy'd about the
same Year: No wonder then, if when these great Pillars were
20   at once remov'd, the Building grew weaker, and the Audiences
very much abated. Now in this Distress, what more natural Remedy could be found, than to incite and encourage (tho' with
some Hazard) the Industry of the surviving Actors? But the Patentees, it seems, thought the surer way was to bring down their
Pay, in proportion to the Fall of their Audiences. To make this Project more feasible, they propos'd to begin at the Head of 'em,
rightly judging, that if the Principals acquiesc'd, their Inferiors
would murmur in vain. To bring this about with a better Grace,
they under Pretence of bringing younger Actors forward, order'd
30   several of *Betterton's,* and Mrs. *Barry's* chief Parts to be given
to young *Powel,* and Mrs. *Bracegirdle.* In this they committed
two palpable Errors; for while the best Actors are in Health, and
still on the Stage, the Publick is always apt to be out of Humour, when those of a lower Class pretend to stand in their

1. 14 on one side] one on side 2nd ed.
1. 27 Principals acquiesc'd] acquese'd 2nd ed.

23.   a sort of Association, to stand, or fall together] Cf. *Petition of the Players* (Nicoll, I, 368 ff.; also 334 ff. for a general account).

29.   During these Contentions] Cibber here does not provide an accurate picture of what occurred; the actors had endured Rich's and Skipwith's management for a year (from December 1693 to December 1694) when Betterton laid a description of grievances with a request for redress before the Lord Chamberlain signed by himself, Underhill, Kynaston, Bowen, Bowman, Williams, Dogget, Bright, Sanford, Mrs. Barry, Mrs. Bracegirdle, Mrs. Verbruggen, Mrs. Bowman, Mrs. Betterton, and Mrs. "Ellenor" Leigh (Hotson, p. 294; see Nicoll, I, 368 ff. for the articles of grievance and a summary of the answer). The patentees denied the charges and demands and responded with countercharges, giving no satisfaction.

31.   many other Grievances] Some of these were that Skipwith and Rich, by concealing their ownership of the shares and the patent, had given Alexander D'Avenant credit which he used to cheat them; that the £100 due each sharing actor at his retirement had not been paid duly; that the actors had not received their share of the "aftermoney"—the fees paid for seeing the last two acts; Mrs. Barry's benefit money had not been paid, etc. See Nicoll, I, 368 ff.

Places; or admitting, at this time, they might have been accepted, this Project might very probably have lessen'd, but could
not possibly mend an Audience; and was a sure Loss of that
Time, in studying, which might have been better employ'd in
giving the Auditor Variety, the only Temptation to a pall'd Appetite; and Variety is only to be given by Industry: But Industry will always be lame, when the Actor has Reason to be
discontented. This the Patentees did not consider, or pretended
not to value, while they thought their Power secure, and uncon-
10   troulable: But farther, their first Project did not succeed; for
tho' the giddy Head of *Powel,* accepted the Parts of *Betterton;*
Mrs. *Bracegirdle* had a different way of thinking, and desir'd to
be excus'd, from those of Mrs. *Barry;* her good Sense was not
to be misled by the insidious Favour of the Patentees; she knew
the Stage was wide enough for her Success, without entring into
any such rash, and invidious Competition, with Mrs. *Barry,* and
therefore wholly refus'd acting any Part that properly belong'd
to her. But this Proceeding, however, was Warning enough to
make *Betterton* be upon his Guard, and to alarm others, with
20   Apprehensions of their own Safety, from the Design that was
laid against him: *Betterton,* upon this, drew into his Party most
of the valuable Actors, who to secure their Unity, enter'd with
him into a sort of Association, to stand, or fall together. All this
the Patentees for some time slighted, but when Matters drew towards a Crisis, they found it adviseable to take the same Measures, and accordingly open'd an Association on their part; both
which were severally sign'd, as the Interest or Inclination of either
Side led them.
        During these Contentions, which the impolitick Patentees ahd
30   rais'd against themselves (not only this I have mentioned, but
by many other Grievances, which my Memory retains not) the
Actors offer'd a Treaty of Peace; but their Masters imagining
no Consequence could shake the Right of their Authority, refus'd all Terms of Accommodation. In the mean time this Dis-

2.   before *Christmas*] Performances ceased on 22 December 1694 because of the illness of Queen Mary (see below).

25.   ... treating Actors had like to have ruin'd us] This refers to the secession of several actors in December 1714, caused, according to Cibber, by Wilks; see Chapter XV.

29.   The Patentees ... presum'd they might impose what Conditions] Cibber omits certain details in this and the parts following of his narrative. Betterton had seized on the leisure granted by the Queen's illness to consolidate his followers and to enlist support from the court (Hotson, p. 294). The Lord Chamberlain attempted to reconcile them on certain of the grievances (Nicoll, I, 335 n. 3 reprints the proposal from L.C. 7/3), but the actors refused; the Patentees continued to appeal to the Lord Chamberlain to exercise authority on the unreasonable actors who had meanwhile brought the Lord Chamberlain and Sir Robert Howard over to their side. Nicoll (I, 335-36 n. 4, from L.C. 7/3) cites their final protest: "Wee the Patentees of the Theatre's in Order to an amicable composure of matters, having severall times ... sent to Mr. Betterton & other Comedians in Combina[tion] with him, to meet us, they refused soe to doe ..."; this comes in March 1695 on their discovery that Betterton had begun to convert Lisle's Tennis Court into a theater (cf. below). King William—Mary had died on 28 December 1694—granted a license to Betterton, Mrs. Barry, Mrs. Bracegirdle, Bowman, Williams, Underhill, Dogget, Bowen, Mrs. Verbruggen, Mrs. Leigh and Bright on 25 March 1695 (L.C. 7/1, cited by Nicoll, I, 336; see Hotson, pp. 295-99).

sention was so prejudical to their daily Affairs, that I remember
it was allow'd by both Parties, that before *Christmas*, the Patent
had lost the getting of at least a thousand Pounds by it.

    My having been a Witness of this unnecessary Rupture, was
of great use to me, when many years after, I came to be a Manager my self. I laid it down as a settled Maxim, that no Company could flourish while the chief Actors, and the Undertakers
were at variance. I therefore made it a Point, while it was possible, upon tolerable Terms, to keep the valuable Actors in hu-
10 mour with their Station; and tho' I was as jealous of their Encroachments, as any of my Co-partners could be, I always guarded against the least Warmth, in my Expostulations with them;
not but at the same time they might see, I was perhaps more determin'd in the Question, than those that gave a loose to their
Resentment, and when they were cool, were as apt to recede. I
do not remember that I ever made a promise to any, that I did
not keep, and therefore was cautious how I made them. This
Coldness, though it might not please, at least left them nothing
to reproach me with; and if Temper, and fair Words could
20 prevent a Disobligation, I was sure never to give Offence or receive it. But as I was but one of three, I could not oblige others
to observe the same Conduct. However, by this means, I kept
many an unreasonable Discontent, from breaking out, and both
Sides found their Account in it.

    How a contemptuous and overbearing manner of treating
Actors had like to have ruin'd us, in our early Prosperity, shall
be shewn in its Place: If future Managers should chance to think
my way right, I suppose they will follows it; if not, when they
find what happen'd to the Patentees (who chose to disagree with
30 their People) perhaps they may think better of it.

    The Patentees then, who by their united Powers, had made
a Monopoly of the Stage, and consequently presum'd they might
impose what Conditions they pleas'd upon their People, did not
consider, that they were all this while endeavouring to enslave

10. Earl of *Dorset*] Charles Sackville (1638-1706), sixth Earl of Dorset; Lord
Chamberlain, 1689-97: Well known patron of the arts.

21. The Leavings of *Betterton*'s Interest] Sullen, in *A Comparison* (ed. Wells p. 7)
says, "… in my Opinion, 'twas strange that the general defection of the old Actors
which left *Drury-Lane*, and the fondness which the better sort shew'd for 'em at the
opening of their *New-house*, … had not quite destroy'd those few young ones that
remain'd behind. The disproportion was so great at parting, that 'twas almost
impossible, in *Drury-Lane*, to muster up a sufficient number to take in all the parts
of any Play; and of them so few were tolerable, that a Play must of necessity be
down'd that had not extraordinary favour from the Audience. No fewer than
Sixteen … went away; and with them the very beauty and vigour of the Stage; they
who were left behind being for the most part Learners, Boys and Girls a very
unequal match for them who revolted." The contest for good actors began:
Verbruggen and his wife had returned to the Theatre Royal and the Patentees on 10
April 1696 (from L.C. 7/3, summarized by Nicoll, I, 383); Cibber calls her Mrs.
Montfort below (p. 115), apparently forgetting that she had remarried. This context
led ultimately to the Lord Chamberlain's issuing commands on 16 April and 23 July
1695 that no actors would be permitted to change companies (from L.C. 7/1 and
7/3, reprinted by Nicoll, I, 338-39).

a Set of Actors, whom the Publick (more arbitrary than themselves) were inclin'd to support; nor did they reflect, that the
Spectator naturally wish'd, that the Actor, who gave him Delight,
might enjoy the Profits arising from his Labour, without regard
of what pretended Damage, or Injustice might fall upon his
Owners, whose personal Merit the Publick was not so well acquainted with. From this Consideration, then, several Persons
of the highest Distinction espous'd their Cause, and sometimes,
in the Circle, entertain'd the King with the State of the Theatre.

10   At length their Grievances were laid before the Earl of *Dorset,*
then Lord Chamberlain, who took the most effectual Method
for their Relief. The Learned of the Law were advis'd with, and
they gave their Opinion, that no Patent for acting Plays, & *c.*
could tie up the Hands of a succeeding Prince, from granting the
like Authority, where it might be thought proper to trust it. But
while this Affair was in Agitation, Queen *Mary* dy'd, which of
course occasion'd a Cessation of all publick Diversions. In this
melancholy Interim, *Betterton,* and his Adherents had more
Leisure to sollicit their Redress; and the Patentees now finding,

20   that the Party against them was gathering Strength, were reduc'd
to make sure of as good a Company, as the Leavings of *Betterton's* Interest could form; and these, you may be sure, would
not lose this Occasion of setting a Price upon their Merit, equal
to their own Opinion of it, which was but just double to what
they had before. *Powel,* and *Verbruggen,* who had then but
forty Shillings a Week, were now rais'd each of them to four
Pounds and others in proportion: As for my self, I was then
too insignificant to be taken into their Councils, and consequently stood among those of little Importance, like Cattle in a

30   Market, to be sold to the first Bidder. But the Patentees seeming in the greater Distress for Actors, condescended to purchase
me. Thus, without any farther Merit, than that of being a
scarce Commodity, I was advanc'd to thirty Shillings a Week:
Yet our Company was so far from being full, that our Com-

2.   *Johnson and Bullock*] Cibber appears to be the only authority for this statement; Bellchambers (p. 202) suggests that Johnson came from an itinerant company. Possibly this is true also of Bullock (Nicoll, I, 384, summarizes the contract from L.C. 7/3 in which Skipwith promises Bullock 20s. a week).

5.   Audience of the *King*] See note, p. 111.

16.   *Easter-Monday* in *April*] Easter fell on 24 March in 1695; they opened one week later, on Monday, 1 April (cf. Hotson, p. 311 n.).

manders were forc'd to beat up for Voluntiers, in several distant
Counties; it was this Occasion that first brought *Johnson* and
Bullock to the service of the Theatre-Royal.

Forces being thus rais'd, and the War declared on both Sides,
Betterton, and his Chiefs had the Honour of an Audience of the
King, who consider'd them as the only Subjects, whom he had
not yet deliver'd from arbitrary Power; and graciously dismiss'd
them, with an Assurance of Relief, and Support---Accordingly
a select number of them were impower'd by his Royal Licence
10   to act in a separate Theatre, for themselves. This great Point
being obtain'd, many People of Quality came into a voluntary
Subscription of twenty, and some of forty Guineas a-piece, for
the erecting a Theatre within the Walls of the Tennis-Court, in
Lincolns-Inn-Fields. But as it requir'd Time to fit it up,
it gave the Patentees more Leisure to muster their Forces, who
notwithstanding were not able to take the Field till the *Easter-
Monday* in *April* following. Their first Attempt was a reviv'd
Play, call'd *Abdelazar,* or the *Moor's Revenge,* poorly written,
by Mrs. *Behn.* The House was very full, but whether it was the
20   Play, or the Actors, that were not approv'd, the next Day's Audience sunk to nothing. However, we were assur'd, that let
the Audiences be never so low, our Masters would make good
all Deficiences, and so indeed they did, 'till towards the End
of the Season, when Dues to Ballance came too thick upon 'em.
But that I may go gradually on with my own Fortune, I must
take this Occasion to let you know, by the following Circumstance, how very low my Capacity, as an Actor, was then rated:
It was thought necessary, at our Opening, that the Town shou'd
be address'd in a new Prologue; but to our great Distress, among
30   several, that were offer'd, not one was judg'd fit to be spoken.
This I thought a favourable Occasion, to do my self some remarkable Service, if I should have the good Fortune, to produce
one that might be accepted. The next (memorable) Day my
Muse brought forth her first Fruit that was ever made publick;

1. 12-13 for the erecting] for erecting 2nd ed.

16. one of the Patentees ... knew no difference ...] "No doubt, Rich," (Lowe, I, 196).

28. *Love* for *Love*] This opened on 30 April 1695 (Downes, *Roscius*, ed. Summers, pp. 43-44) and ran "13 Days Successively." Hotson (p. 299) gives the date as 29 April. (Cf. *Comparison*, ed. Wells, pp. 10, 38 and n.; also, Downes, *ibid.*, p. 44; Van Lennep, pp. 445 ff.)

how good, or bad imports not; my Prologue was accepted, and
resolv'd on to be spoken. This Point being gain'd, I began to
stand upon Terms, you will say, not unreasonable; which were,
that if I might speak it my self, I would expect no farther Reward for my Labour: This was judg'd as bad as having no Prologue at all! You may imagine how hard I thought it, that
they durst not trust my poor poetical Brat, to my own Care.
But since I found it was to be given into other Hands, I insisted
that two Guineas should be the price of my parting with it;
10   which with a Sigh I receiv'd, and *Powel* spoke the Prologue:
But every Line, that was applauded, went sorely to my Heart,
when I reflected, that the same Praise might have been given to
my own speaking it; nor could the Success of the Author compensate the Distress of the Actor. However, in the End, it
serv'd, in some sort, to mend our People's Opinion of me; and
whatever the Criticks might think of it, one of the Patentees
(who, it is true, knew no difference between *Dryden* and *D'ursey*)
said, upon the Success of it, that insooth! I was an ingenious
young Man. This sober Compliment (though I could have no
20   Reason to be vain upon it) I thought was a fair Promise to my
being in favour. But to Matters of more Moment: Now let us
reconnoitre the Enemy.

        After we had stolen some few Days March upon them, the
Forces of *Betterton* came up with us in terrible Order: In about
three Weeks following, the new Theatre was open'd against us,
with a veteran Company, and a new Train of Artillery; or in
plainer *English,* the old Actors, in *Lincolns-Inn-Fields* began,
with a new Comedy of Mr. *Congreve's,* call'd *Love* for *Love;*
which ran on with such extraordinary Success, that they had
30   seldom occasion to act any other Play, 'till the End of the Season. This valuable Play had a narrow Escape, from falling into the Hands of the Patentees; for before the Division of the
Company, it had been read, and accepted of at the Theatre-
Royal: But while the Articles of Agreement for it were prepar-

---

1. 13 my own speaking it] my own speaking 2nd ed.

10. *Dryden*, in King *Charles*'s Time] Dryden had agreed in 1668 to write three plays each year in return for one and a quarter shares of stock in the King's Men (see Nicoll, I, 328-29).

15. Mr. *Congreve*, whatever Impediment] After *Love for Love* (1695) Betterton's company produced *The Mourning Bride* in February 1697 and *The Way of the World* in March 1700 (Nicoll, I, 398).

27. Mrs. *Monfort*] See note on p. 112.

ing, the Rupture, in the Theatrical State, was so far advanc'd,
that the Author took Time to pause, before he sign'd them;
when finding that all Hopes of Accommodation were impracticable, he thought it adviseable, to let it take its Fortune, with
those Actors for whom he had first intended the Parts.

Mr. *Congreve* was then in such high Reputation, as an Author, that besides his Profits, from this Play, they offer'd him a
whole Share with them, which he accepted; in Consideration of
which he oblig'd himself, if his Health permitted, to give them
10   one new Play every Year. *Dryden,* in King *Charles's* Time, had
the same Share, with the King's Company; but he bound himself to give them two Plays every Season. This you may imagine he could not hold long, and I am apt to think, he might
have serv'd them better, with one in a Year, not so hastily written. Mr. *Congreve,* whatever Impediment he met with, was three
Years before, in pursuance to his Agreement, he produc'd the
Mourning Bride; and if I mistake not, the Interval had been
much the same, when he gave them the *Way of the World.* But
it came out the stronger, for the Time it cost him, and to their
20   better Support, when they sorely wanted it: For though they
went on with Success for a Year or two, and even, when their
Affairs were declining, stood in much higher Estimation of the
Publick, than their Opponents; yet, in the End, both Sides were
great Sufferers by their Separation; the natural Consequence of
two Houses, which I have already mention'd in a former Chapter.

The first Error this new Colony of Actors fell into, was their
inconsiderately parting with *Williams,* and Mrs. *Monfort,* upon
a too nice (not to say severe) Punctilio; in not allowing them to
be equal Sharers with the rest; which before they had acted one
30   Play, occasion'd their Return to the Service of the Patentees. As
I have call'd this an Error, I ought to give my Reasons for it.
Though the Industry of *Williams* was not equal to his Capacity;
for he lov'd his Bottle better than his Business; and though
Mrs. *Monfort* was only excellent in Comedy, yet their Merit

10. *Abate the Wonder ... one tempted Eve*] Congreve, Prologue to *Love for Love*, 11. 20-22: "Forbear your wonder ..."

31. *Shakespear* was defac'd ... *Hamlet*, and *Othello*, ... *Brutus* and *Cassius*] Cibber's memory may be playing him false here; in the list of plays attended by Lady Morley at the Theatre Royal in the years 1696-1700 (printed by Hotson, pp. 377-78), the only Shakespeare plays listed are *Timon of Athens, The Tempest*, and *King Lear*. Furthermore, in *A Comparison* (p. 10) Ramble says, "And by this time [of the schism] the Town, not being able to furnish out two good Audiences every Day; chang'd their Inclinations for the two Houses, as they found 'emselves inclin'd to Comedy or Tragedy: If they desir'd a Tragedy, they went to *Lincolns-Inn-Fields*; if a Comedy, they flockt to *Drury-Lane*; which was the reason that several Days but one House Acted; but by this variety of Humour in the Town, they shared pretty equally the Profit." Cibber's testimony therefore accords neither with this far from exhaustive evidence, nor with a popular booklet much closer (1702) to the events than his own; yet it is difficult to believe that the highly circumstantial account which he gives below of the production of *Hamlet* is entirely his invention. His claims may represent a back-handed boasting. Van Lennep (pp. 439 ff.) gives no support to Cibber's listing of plays, but cites this section of the *Apology* as reliable; until further evidence becomes available, no final judgment can be made.

was too great, almost on any Scruples, to be added to the Enemy; and, at worst, they were certainly much more above those
they would have rank'd them with, than they could possibly
be under those, they were not admitted to be equal to. Of this
Fact there is a poetical Record, in the Prologue to *Love for
Love,* where the Author speaking of the, then, happy State of
the Stage, observes, that if, in Paradise, when two only were
there, they both fell; the Surprize was less, if from so numerous a Body as theirs, there had been any Deserters.

> *Abate the Wonder, and the Fault forgive,*
>
> *If, in our larger Family, we grieve*
>
> *One falling* Adam, *and one tempted* Eve.

These Lines alluded to the Revolt of the Persons above mention'd.

Notwithstanding the Acquisition of these two Actors, who
were of more Importance, than any of those, to whose Assistance
they came, the Affairs of the Patentees were still, in a very creeping Condition; they were now, too late, convinc'd of their Error, in having provok'd their People to this Civil War, of the
Theatre! quite chang'd, and dismal, now, was the Prospect before them! their Houses thin, and the Town crowding into a
new one! Actors at double Sallaries, and not half the usual Audiences, to pay them! and all this brought upon them, by those,
whom their full Security had contemn'd, and who were now in
a fair way of making their Fortunes, upon the ruin'd Interest of
their Oppressors.

Here, tho' at this time, my Fortune depended on the Success
of the Patentees, I cannot help, in regard to Truth, remembering the rude, and riotous Havock we made of all the late
dramatic Honours of the Theatre! all became at once the Spoil
of Ignorance, and Self-conceit! *Shakespear* was defac'd, and tortur'd in every signal Character---- *Hamlet,* and *Othello,* lost in
one Hour all their good Sense, their Dignity, and Fame. *Brutus*

and *Cassius* became noisy Blusterers, with bold unmeaning Eyes,
mistaken Sentiments, and turgid Elocution! Nothing, sure,
could more painfully regret a judicious Spectator, than to see,
at our first setting out, with what rude Confidence, those Habits, which Actors of real Merit had left behind them, were
worn by giddy Pretenders that so vulgarly disgrac'd them! Not
young Lawyers in hir'd Robes, and Plumes, at a Masquerade,
could be less, what they would seem, or more aukwardly per-
sonate the Characters they belong'd to. If, in all these Acts of
10   wanton Waste, these Insults, upon injur'd Nature, you observe,
I have not yet charg'd one of them upon my self; it is not
from an imaginary Vanity, that I could have avoided them; but
that I was rather safe, by being too low, at that time, to be admitted even to my Chance of falling into the same eminent Errors: So that as none of those great Parts ever fell to my Share,
I could not be accountable for the Execution of them: Nor indeed could I get one good Part of any kind, 'till many Months
after; unless it were of that sort, which no body else car'd for,
or would venture to expose themselves in. The first unintended
20   Favour, therefore, of a Part of any Value, Necessity threw upon
me, on the following Occasion.

As it has been always judg'd their natural Interest, where there
are two Theatres, to do one another as much Mischief as they
can; you may imagine it could not be long, before this hostile
Policy shew'd itself, in Action. It happen'd, upon our having
Information on a *Saturday* Morning, that the *Tuesday* after,
Hamlet was intended to be acted at the other House, where it
had not yet been seen; our merry menaging Actors (for they were
now in a manner left to govern themselves) resolv'd, at any rate,
30   to steal a March upon the Enemy, and take Possession of the
same Play the Day before them: Accordingly, *Hamlet* was given
out that Night, to be acted with us on *Monday*. The Notice of
this sudden Enterprize, soon reach'd the other House, who, in
my Opinion, too much regarded it; for they shorten'd their first

23. *Old Batchelor*] Congreve's first play, in 1693. It would have been acted by the major figures of the company at that time, who had moved to Lincoln's Inn Fields. The only performance of it attended by Lady Morley (Hotson, p. 379) is dated 25 March 1701. Van Lennep (p. 446) suggests that these events took place in late May 1695.

26. *Nemine contradicente*] "No one disagreeing."

30. *in petto*] "In reserve."

Orders, and resolv'd that *Hamlet* should to *Hamlet* be oppos'd,
on the same Day; whereas, had they given notice in their Bills,
that the same Play would have been acted by them the Day after,
the Town would have been in no doubt, which House they
should have reserv'd themselves for; ours must certainly have
been empty, and theirs, with more Honour, have been crowded:
Experience, many Years after, in like Cases, has convinc'd me,
that this would have been the more laudable Conduct. But be
that as it may; when, in their *Monday's* Bills, it was seen that
10   *Hamlet* was up against us, our Consternation was terrible, to find
that so hopeful a Project was frustrated. In this Distress, *Powell,*
who was our commanding Officer, and whose enterprising Head
wanted nothing but Skill to carry him thro' the most desperate Attempts; for, like others of his Cast, he had murder'd
many a Hero, only to get into his Cloaths. This *Powell,* I say,
immediately call'd a Council of War; where the Question was,
Whether he should fairly face the Enemy, or make a Retreat, to
some other Play of more probable Safety? It was soon resolv'd
that to act *Hamlet* against *Hamlet*, would be certainly throwing
20   away the Play, and disgracing themselves to little or no Audience; to conclude, *Powell,* who was vain enough to envy
Betterton, as his Rival, propos'd to change Plays with them,
and that, as they had given out the *Old Batchelor,* and had
chang'd it for *Hamlet*, against us; we should give up our *Ham-*
let, and turn the *Old Batchelor* upon them. This Motion was
agreed to, *Nemine contradicente;* but upon Enquiry, it was
found, taht there were not two Persons among them, who had
ever acted in that Play: But that Objection, it seems, (though all
the Parts were to be study'd in six Hours) was soon got over;
30   *Powell* had an Equivalent, *in petto,* that would balance any De-
ficiency on that Score; which was, that he would play the *Old*
Batchelor himself, and mimick *Betterton,* throughout the whole
Part. This happy Thought was approv'd with Delight, and
Applause, as whatever can be suppos'd to ridicule Merit, gene-

rally gives Joy to those that want it: Accordingly, the Bills were
chang'd, and at the bottom inserted,

The Part of the Old Batchelor, *to be perform'd in Imitation*
of the Original.

Printed Books of the Play were sent for in haste, and every Actor had one, to pick out of it the Part he had chosen: Thus,
while they were each of them chewing the Morsel, they had
most mind to, some one happening to cast his Eye over the
Dramatis Personae, found that the main Matter was still forgot,

10 that no body had yet been thought of for the Part of Alderman *Fondlewife.* Here we were all a-ground agen! nor was it
to be conceiv'd who could make the least tolerable Shift with it.
This Character had been so admirably acted by *Dogget,* that
though it is only seen in the Fourth Act, it may be no Dispraise
to the Play, to say, it probably ow'd the greatest Part of its Success to his Performance. But, as the Case was now desperate,
any Resource was better than none. Somebody must swallow
the bitter Pill, or the Play must die. At last it was recollected,
that I had been heard to say, in my wild way of talking, what

20 a vast mind I had to play *Nykin,* by which Name the Character
was more frequently call'd. Notwithstanding they were thus
distress'd about the Disposal of this Part, most of 'em shook their
Heads, at my being mention'd for it; yet *Powell,* who was resolv'd, at all Hazards, to fall upon *Betterton,* and having no
concern for what might become of any one, that serv'd his Ends
or Purpose, order'd me to be sent for; and, as he naturally
lov'd to set other People wrong, honestly said, before I came,
If the Fool has a ming to blow himself up, at once, let us ev'n
give him a clear Stage for it. Accordingly, the Part was put in-

30 to my Hands, between Eleven and Twelve that Morning, which
I durst not refuse, because others were as much straitned in time,
for Study, as myself. But I had this casual Advantage of most
of them; that having so constantly observ'd *Dogget's* Perfor-

mance, I wnated but little Trouble, to make me perfect in the
Words; so that when it came to my turn to rehearse, while
others read their Parts, from their Books, I had put mine in my
Pocket, and went thro' the first Scene without it; and though I
was more abash'd to rehearse so remarkable a Part before the
Actors (which is natural to most young People) than to act before an Audience, yet some of the better-natur'd encourag'd me
so far, as to say, they did not think I should make an ill Figure
in it: To conclude, the Curiosity to see *Betterton* mimick'd,
10   drew us a pretty good Audience, and *Powell* (as far as Applause
is a Proof of it) was allow'd to have burlesqu'd him very well.
As I have question'd the certain Value of Applause, I hope I may
venture, with less Vanity, to say how particular a Share I had of
it, in the same Play. At my first Appearance, one might have
imagin'd, by the various Murmurs of the Audience, that they
were in doubt whether *Dogget* himself were not return'd, or that
they could not conceive what strange Face it could be, that so
nearly resembled him; for I had laid the Tint of Forty Years,
more than my real Age, upon my Features, and, to the most
20   minute placing of a Hair, was dress'd exactly like him: When
I sopke, the Surprize was still greater, as if I had not only borrow'd his Cloaths, but his Voice too. But tho' that was the least
difficult Part of him, to be imitated, they seem'd to allow, I had
so much of him, in every other Requisite, that my Applause was,
perhaps, more than proportionable: For, whether I had done so
much, where so little was expected, or that the Generosity of
my Hearers were more than ususally zealous, upon so unexpected
an Occasion, or from what other Motive such Favour might be
pour'd upon me, I cannot say; but, in plain and honest Truth,
30   upon my going off from the first Scene, a much better Actor
might have been proud of the Applause, that follow'd me; after one loud *Plaudit* was ended, and sunk into a general Whisper,
that seem'd still to continue their private Approbation, it reviv'd
to a second, and again to a third, still louder than the former.

11.   *That was not in my Way ...*] His view appears not to have changed, for Davies

(*Dram. Misc.*, II, 469-71) notes that "Cibber had two passions, which constantly

exposed him to severe censure, and sometimes the highest ridicule: his writing

tragedy, and acting tragic characters. In both he persisted to the last ... The truth

is, Cibber, was endured, in ...tragic parts, on account of his general merit in

comedy ... [he] persisted so obstinately in acting parts in tragedy, that at last the

public grew out of patience, and fairly hissed him off the stage."

33.   *Quicquid agunt homines*] Juvenal, I, 85-86:

> "quidquid agunt homines, votum timor ira voluptas
> Gaudia discursus, nostris est farrago libelli."
>
> "Whatever men do, their vows, fears, angers, pleasures,
> Joys, and goings to and fro shall form my motley subject."

If, to all this, I add, that *Dogget* himself was, in the Pit, at
the same time, it would be too rank Affectation, if I should not
confess, that, to see him there a Witness of my Reception, was,
to me, as consummate a Triumph, as the Heart of Vanity could
be indulg'd with. But whatever Vanity I might set upon my
self, from this unexpected Success, I found that was no Rule to
other People's Judgment of me. There were few or no Parts,
of the same kind, to be had; nor could they conceive, from
what I had done in this, what other sort of Characters I could
10   be fit for. If I sollicited for any thing of a different Nature, I
was answer'd, *That was not in my Way.* And what *was* in my
Way, it seems, was not, as yet, resolv'd upon. And though I
reply'd, *That I thought any thing, naturally written, ought to be
in every one's Way that pretended to be an Actor;* this was look'd
upon as a vain, impracticable Conceit of my own. Yet it is a
Conceipt, that, in forty Years farther Experience, I have not
yet given up; I still think, that a Painter, who can draw but
one sort of Object, or an Actor that shines, but in one Light,
can neither of them boast of that ample Genius, which is ne-
20   cessary to form a thorough Master of his Art: For tho' Genius
may have a particular Inclination, yet a good History-Painter,
or a good Actor, will, without being at a loss, give you, upon
Demand, a proper Likeness of whatever Nature produces. If
he cannot do this, he is only an Actor, as the Shoemaker was
allow'd a limited Judge of *Appelles's* Painting; but *not beyond
his Last.* Now, tho' to do any one thing well, may have more
Merit, than we often meet with; and may be enough, to procure a Man the Name of a good Actor, from the Publick; yet,
in my Opinion, it is but still the Name without the Substance.
30   If his Talent is in such narrow bounds, that he dares not step
out of them, to look upon the Singularities of Mankind, and
cannot catch them, in whatever Form they present themselves;
if he is not Master of the *Quicquid agunt homines, &c.* in any
Shape, that Human Nature is fit to be seen in; if he cannot

11. 1-2   at the same time] at the same 2nd ed.

1. 34   Shape, that Human Nature] Shape, Human Nature 2nd ed.

15.   *Jovial Crew*] *The Jovial Crew, or, The Merry Beggar* (1641) a comedy by Richard Brome.

change himself into several distinct Persons, so as to vary his
whole Tone of Voice, his Motion, his Look, and Gesture, whether in high, or lower Life, and, at the same time, keep close
of those Variation, without leaving the Character they singly belong to; if his best Skill, falls short of this Capacity, what Pretence have we to call him a complete Master of his Art? And
tho' I do not insist, that he ought always to shew himself, in
these various Lights, yet, before we compliment him with that
Title, he ought, at least, by some few Proofs, to let us see, that
10 he has them all, in his Power. If I am ask'd, who, ever, arriv'd at this imaginary Excellence, I confess, the Instances are
very few; but I will venture to name *Monfort*, as one of them,
whose Theatrical Character I have given, in my last Chapter:
For, in his Youth, he had acted Low Humour, with great Success, even down to *Tallboy* in the *Jovial Crew;* and when he
was in great Esteem, as a Tragedian, he was, in Comedy, the
most complete Gentleman that I ever saw upon the Stage. Let
me add too, that *Betterton,* in his declining Age, was as eminent, in Sir *John Falstaff,* as in the Vigour of it, in his
20 *Othello.*

    While I thus measure the Value of an Actor, by the Variety
of Shapes he is able to throw himself into, you may naturally
suspect, that I am all this while, leading my own Theatrical
Character into your Favour: Why, really, to speak as an honest
Man, I cannot wholly deny it: But in this, I shall endeavour
to be no farther partial to myself, than known Facts will make
me; from the good, or bad Evidence of which, your better
Judgment will condemn, or acquit me. And to shew you, that
I will conceal no Truth, that is against me, I frankly own, that
30 had I been always left, to my own choice of Characters, I am
doubtful whether I might ever have deserv'd an equal Share of
that Estimation, which the Publick seem'd to have held me in:
Nor am I sure, that it was not Vanity in me, often to have
suspected, that I was kept out of the Parts, I had most mind to,

23. *Love's Last Shift*] Ernest Bernbaum (*The Drama of Sensibility*, pp. 10, 17) regards this as the first sentimental comedy; whether this importance may be attached to it or not, it was new in the sense that it operated largely within the amoral conventions of Restoration comedy in the first four acts, after which its hero enacted a highly improbable "last shift," that is, conversion, which won it praise for its morals: "The first comedy, acted since the Restoration, in which were preserved purity of manners and decency of language, with a due respect to the honour of the marriage-bed, was Colley Cibber's *Love's last* [sic] *Shift*" (Davies, *Dram. Misc.*, III, 436). Davies continued (III, 438-439): " ... the audience were particularly charmed with the great scene, in the last act, where the ill-treated and abandoned wife reveals herself to her surprised and admiring husband. The joy of unexpected reconcilement, from Loveless's remorse and repentance, spread such an uncommon rapture and pleasure in the audience, that never were spectators more happy in easing their minds by uncommon and repeated plaudits. The honest tears, shed by the audience at this interview, conveyed a strong reproach to our licentious poets, and was to Cibber the highest mark of honour."

by the Jealousy, or Prejudice of my Cotemporaries; some Instances
of which, I could give you, were they not too slight, to be remember'd: In the mean time, be pleas'd to observe, how slowly,
in my younger Days, my Good-fortune came forward.

My early Success in the *Old Batchelor,* of which I have given
so full an Account, having open'd no farther way to my Advancement, was enough, perhaps, to have made a young Fellow
of more Modesty despair; but being of a Temper not easily dis-
hearten'd, I resolv'd to leave nothing unattempted, that might
10 shew me, in some new Rank of Distinction. Having then no
other Resource, I was at last reduc'd to write a Character for
myself; but as that was not finish'd till about a Year after, I
could not, in the Interim, procure any one Part, that gave me
the least Inclination to act it; and consequently, such as I got,
I perform'd with a proportionable Negligence. But this Misfortune, if it were one, you are not to wonder at; for the same
Fate attended me, more, or less, to the last Days of my remaining on the Stage. What Defect in me, this may have been owing to, I have not yet had Sense enough to find out, but I soon
20 found out as good a thing, which was, never to be mortify'd at
it: Though I am afraid this seeming Philosophy was rather owing to my Inclination to Pleasure, than Business. But to my
Point. The next Year I produc'd the Comedy of *Love's last
Shift;* yet the Difficulty of getting it to the Stage, was not easily surmounted; for, at that time, as little was expected from
me, as an Author, as had been from my Pretensions to be an
Actor. However, Mr. *Southern,* the Author of *Oroonoko,* having had the Patience to hear me read it, to him, happened to
like it so well, that he immediately recommended it to the Pa-
30 tentees, and it was accordingly acted in *January 1695.* In this
Play, I gave myself the Part of Sir *Novelty,* which was thought,
a good Portrait of the Foppery then in fashion. Here too,
Mr. *Southern,* though he had approv'd my Play, came into the
common Diffidence of me, as an Actor: For, when on the first

25. *it was not my own*] "So little was hoped from the genius of Cibber, that the critics reproached him with stealing his play ..." (Davies, *Dram. Misc.*, III, 437). Cibber tried to answer these accusations, but apparently the notion that he stole his works recurred: Dr. Johnson later felt the need to defend him and "said there was no reason to believe the *Careless Husband* was not written by himself" (Boswell, II, 127).

Day of it, I was standing, myself, to prompt the *Prologue,* he
took me by the Hand, and said, *Young Man! I pronounce thy*
Play a good one; I will answer for its Success, if thou dost not
spoil it by thy own Action. Though this might be a fair *Salvo,*
for his favourable Judgment of the Play; yet if it were his real
Opinion of me, as an Actor, I had the good Fortune to deceive him: I succeeded so well, in both, that People seem'd at
a Loss, which they should give the Preference to. But (now let
me shew a little more Vanity, and my Apology for it, shall
10 come after) the Compliment which my Lord *Dorset* (then Lord
Chamberlain) made me upon it, is, I own, what I had rather
not suppress, *viz. That it was the best, First Play, that any Au-*
thor in his Memory, had produc'd; and that for a young Fellow,
to shew himself such an Actor, and such a Writer, in one Day,
was something extraordinary. But as this noble Lord has been
celebrated for his Good-nature, I am contented, that as much of
this Compliment should be suppos'd to exceed my Deserts, as
may be imagin'd to have been heighten'd, by his generous Inclination to encourage a young Beginner. If this Excuse cannot
20 soften the Vanity of telling a Truth so much, in my own Favour, I must lie, at the Mercy of my Reader. But there was
a still higher Compliment pass'd upon me, which I may publish
without Vanity, because it was not a design'd one, and apparently came from my Enemies, *viz.* That, to their certain Knowledge *it was not my own:* This Report is taken notice of in my
Dedication to the Play. If they spoke Truth, if they knew
what other Person in really belong'd to, I will, at least allow them
true to their Trust; for above forty Years have since past, and
they have not yet reveal'd the Secret.
30   The new Light, in which the Character of Sir *Novelty* had
shewn me, one might have thought, were enough, to have dissipated the Doubts, of what I might now, be possibly good for.
But to whatever Chance, my Ill-fortune was due; whether I
had still, but little Merit, or that the Menagers, if I had any,

6.   by writing his *Relapse*] *The Relapse, or, Virtue in Danger* was first performed at Drury Lane in November 1696. Cibber's standing in his company was firmly established by his performance as Lord Foppington. (See Introduction on Cibber's acting of fops.) Pope, in a note on the *Dunciad* (B), I, 167, remarked that Foppington's wig was brought on in a sedan chair.

24.   the *Provok'd Wife*] *The Provok'd Wife*, first performed at Lincoln's Inn Fields by the rival company in May 1697; see below for correction of Cibber's chronology.

were not competent Judges of it; or whether I was not generally elbow'd, by other Actors (which I am most inclin'd to think
the true Cause) when any fresh Parts were to be dispos'd of,
not one Part of any consequence was I preferr'd to, 'till the
Year following: Then, indeed, from Sir *John Vanbrugh's* favourable Opinion of me, I began, with others, to have a better
of myself: For he not only did me Honour, as an Author,
by writing his *Relapse*, as a Sequel, or Second Part, to *Love's
last Shift;* but as an Actor too, by preferring me, to the chief
10 Character in his own Play; (which from Sir *Novelty*) he had en-
nobled by the Style of Baron of *Foppington*. This Play (the *Relapse*) from its new, and easy Turn of Wit, had great Success,
and gave me, as a Comedian, a second Flight of Reputation
along with it.

As the Matter I write must be very flat, or impertinent, to
those, who have not Taste, or Concern for the Stage; and may
to those, who delight in it too, be equally tedious, when I talk of
no body but myself; I shall endeavour to relieve your Patience,
by a Word or two more of this Gentleman, so far as he lent his
20 Pen to the Support of the Theatre.

Though the *Relapse* was the first Play this agreeable Author
produc'd, yet it was not, it seems, the first he had written; for
he had at that time, by him, (more than) all the Scenes, that
were acted of the *Provok'd Wife;* but being then doubtful,
whether he should ever trust them to the Stage, he thought no
more of it: But after the Success of the *Relapse*, he was more
strongly importun'd, than able, to refuse it to the Publick. Why
the last written Play was first acted, and for what Reason they
were given to different Stages, what follows, will explain.

30 In his first Step, into publick Life, when he was but an En-
sign, and had a Heart above his Income, he happen'd somewhere, at his Winter-Quarters, upon a very slender Acquaintance
with Sir *Thomas Skipwith*, to receive a particular Obligation
from him, which he had not forgot at the Time I am speaking

12.   Lord *Hallifax*] Charles Montagu (1661-1715), only Earl of Halifax of the first

        creation, was an amateur poet, and generous patron of poets and the drama (cf.

        Loftis, *Politics*, pp. 41-42, 47); Pope, who did not admire him, modelled his *Bufo*

        in part on Halifax (*Epistle to Dr. Arbuthnot*, lines 231-48).

23.   *Aesop*] This comedy in two parts was performed at Drury Lane: Part I, c.

        December 1696, and Part II, c. March 1697; hence it is clear that Cibber was

        confused about the order of Vanbrugh's services to his friends. That he gave *The

        Provok'd Wife* to Betterton must indicate impatience with the Drury Lane company

        (Nicoll, I, 244, 436).

34.   Wisdom, in a Person deform'd] Aesop in the play cannot be justly characterized as

        wise; Nicoll (I, 244) states that he "proves a very objectionable and cynical

        personage in his stage existence." Cibber apparently takes the aphoristic mode of

        speech to show great wisdom.

of: When Sir *Thomas's* Interest, in the Theatrical Patent (for he
had a large Share in it, though he little concern'd himself in the
Conduct of it) was rising but very slowly, he thought, that to
give it a Lift, by a new Comedy, if it succeeded, might be the
handsomest Return he could make to those his former Favours;
and having observ'd, that in *Love's last Shift,* most of the Actors had acquitted themselves, beyond what was expected of
them; he took a sudden Hint from what he lik'd, in that Play,
and in less than three Months, in the beginning of *April* following, brought us the *Relapse* finish'd; but the Season being then
too far advanc'd, it was not acted 'till the succeeding Winter.
Upon the Success of the *Relapse,* the late Lord *Hallifax,* who
was a great Favourer of *Betterton's* Company, having formerly,
by way of Family-Amusement, heard the *Provok'd Wife* read to
him, in its looser Sheets, engag'd Sir *John Vanbrugh* to revise
it, and give it to the Theatre in *Lincolns-Inn Fields.* This was
a Request not to be refus'd to so eminent a Patron of the Muses,
as the Lord *Hallifax,* who was equally a Friend and Admirer of
Sir *John* himself. Nor was Sir *Thomas Skipwith,* in the least dis-
obliged, by so reasonable a Compliance: After which, Sir *John*
was agen at liberty, to repeat his Civilities to his Friend,
Sir *Thomas;* and about the same time, or not long after, gave
us the Comedy of *Aesop;* for his Inclination always led him to
serve Sir *Thomas.* Besides, our Company, about this time, began to be look'd upon, in another Light; the late Contempt we
had lain under, was now wearing off, and from the Success of
two or three new Plays, our Actors, by being Originals in a few
good Parts, where they had not the Disadvantage of Comparison
against them, sometimes found new Favour, in those old Plays,
where others had exceeded them.

Of this Good-fortune, perhaps, I had more than my Share,
from the two very different, chief Characters, I had succeeded
in; for I was equally approv'd in *Aesop,* as the Lord *Foppington,*
allowing the Difference, to be no less, than as Wisdom, in a Per-

son deform'd, may be less entertaining to the general Taste, than
Folly and Foppery, finely drest: For the Character that delivers Precepts of Wisdom, is, in some sort, severe upon the Auditor, by shewing him one wiser than himself. But when Folly
is his Object, he applauds himself, for being wiser than the coxcomb he laughs at: And who is not more pleas'd with an Occasion to commend, than accuse himself?

     Though, to write much, in a little time, is no Excuse for wri-
ing ill; yet Sir *John Vanbrugh's* Pen, is not to be a little ad-
10 mir'd, for its Spirit, Ease, and Readiness, in producing Plays so
fast, upon the Neck of one another; for, notwithstanding this
quick Dispatch, there is a clear and lively Simplicity in his Wit,
that neither wants the Ornament of Learning, nor has the least
Smell of the Lamp in it. As the Face of a fine Woman, with
only her Locks loose, about her, may be then in its greatest Beauty; such were his Productions, only adorn'd by Nature. There
is something so catching to the Ear, so easy to the Memory, in
all he writ, that it has been observ'd, by all the Actors of my
Time, that the Style of no Author whatsoever, gave their Me-
20 mory less trouble, than that of Sir *John Vanbrugh;* which I
myself, who have been charg'd with several of his strongest
Characters, can confirm by a pleasing Experience. And indeed
his Wit, and Humour, was so little laboured, that his most entertaining Scenes seem'd to be no more, than his common Conversation committed to Paper. Here, I confess my Judgment at
a Loss, whether, in this, I give him more, or less, than his due
Praise? For may it not be more laudable, to raise an Estate
(whether in Wealth, or Fame) by Pains, and honest Industry
than to be born to it? Yet, if his Scenes really were, as to me
30 they always seem'd, delightful, are they not, thus, expeditious-
ly written, the more surprising? let the Wit, and Merit of them,
then, be weigh'd by wiser Criticks, than I pretend to be: But
no wonder, while his Conceptions were so full of Life, and Humour, his Muse should be sometimes too warm, to wait the slow

5.   *Congreve* justly said of it] Barker (p. 28) supposes that this was said privately to

Cibber.

128

Pace of Judgment, or to endure the Drudgery, of forming a
regular Fable to them: Yet we see the *Relapse*, however imperfect, in the Conduct, by the mere Force of its agreeable Wit,
ran away with the Hearts of its Hearers; while *Love's last Shift*,
which (as Mr. *Congreve* justly said of it) had only in it, a great
many things, that were *like* Wit, that in reality were *not* Wit.
And what is still less pardonable (as I say of it myself) has a great
deal of Puerility, and frothy Stage-Language in it, yet by the
mere moral Delight receiv'd from its Fable, it has been, with
10   the other, in a continued, and equal Possession of the Stage, for
more than forty Years.

As I have already promis'd you, to refer your Judgment of me,
as an Actor, rather to known Facts, than my own Opinion,
(which, I could not be sure, would keep clear of Self-partiality) I
must a little farther risque my being tedious, to be as good as my
Word. I have elsewhere allow'd, that my want of a strong and
full Voice, soon cut short my Hopes of making any valuable Figure, in Tragedy; and I have been many Years since, convinced,
that whatever Opinion I might have of my own Judgment, or
20   Capacity to amend the palpable Errors, that I saw our Tragedians, most in favour, commit; yet the Auditors, who would
have been sensible of any such Amendments (could I have made
them) were so very few, that my best Endeavour would have
been but an unavailing Labour, or, what is yet worse, might
have appeared both to our Actors, and to many Auditors, the
vain Mistake of my own Self-Conceit: For so strong, so very
near indispensible, is that one Article of Voice, in the forming a
good Tragedian, that an Actor may want any other Qualification
whatsoever, and yet have a better Chance for Applause, than he
30   will ever have, with all the Skill, in the World, if his Voice is
not equal to it. Mistake me not; I say, for *Applause* only -----
but Applause does not always stay for, nor always follow intrinsick Merit; Applause will frequently open, like a young Hound,
upon a wrong Scent; and the Majority of Auditors, you know,

are generally compos'd of Babblers, that are profuse of their
Voices, before there is any thing on foot, that calls for them:
Not but, I grant, to lead, or mislead the Many, will always
stand in some Rank of a necessary Merit; yet when I say a
good Tragedian, I mean one, in Opinion of whose *real* Merit,
the best Judges would agree.

    Having so far given up my Pretensions to the Buskin, I ought
now to account for my having been, notwithstanding, so often
seen, in some particular Characters in Tragedy, as *Fago, Wolsey,*
10 *Syphax, Richard* the *Third,* & c. If, in any of this kind I have
succeeded, perhaps it has been a Merit dearly purchas'd; for,
from the Delight I seem'd to take in my performing them, half
my Auditors have been persuaded, that a great Share of the
Wickedness of them, must have been in my own Nature: If this
is true, as true I fear (I had almost said hope) it is, I look upon
it rather as a Praise, than Censure of my Performance. Aversion
there is an involuntary Commendation, where we are only hated,
for being like the thing, we *ought* to be like; a sort of Praise
however, which few Actors beside my self could endure: Had it
20 been equal to the usual Praise given to Vertue, my Cotemporaries would have thought themselves injur'd, if I had pretended
to any Share of it: So that you see, it has been, as much the
Dislike others had to them, as Choice, that has thrown me sometimes into these Characters. But it may be farther observ'd, that
in the Characters I have nam'd, where there is so much close
meditated Mischief, Deceit, Pride, Insolence, or Cruelty, they
cannot have the least Cast, or Proser of the Amiable in them;
consequently, there can be no great Demand for that harmonious
Sound, or pleasing, round Melody of Voice, which in the softer
30 Sentiments of Love, the Wailings of distressful Vertue, or in the
Throws and Swellings of Honour, and Ambition, may be needful to recommend them to our Pity, or Admiration: So that
again my want of that requisite Voice might less disqualify me for
the vicious, than the virtuous Character. This too may have been

1. 22 to any Share] to an Share 2nd ed.

130

a more favourable Reason for my having been chosen for them ---
a yet farther Consideration, that inclin'd me to them, was that
they are generally better written, thicker sown, with sensible
Reflections, and come by so much nearer to common Life, and
Nature, than Characters of Admiration, as Vice is more the
Practice of Mankind than Virtue: Nor could I sometimes help
smiling, at those dainty Actors, that were too squeamish to swallow them! as if they were one Jot the better Men, for acting a
good Man well, or another Man the worse, for doing equal

10 Justice to a bad one! 'Tis not, sure, *what* we act, but *how* we
act what is allotted us, that speaks our intrinsick Value! as in
real Life, the wise Man, or the Fool, be he Prince, or Peasant,
will, in either State, be equally the Fool, or the wise Man--- but
alas! in personated Life, this is no Rule to the Vulgar! they are
apt to think all before them real, and rate the Actor according
to his borrow'd Vice, or Virtue.

If then I had always too careless a Concern for false, or vulgar Applause, I ought not to complain, if I have had less of it,
than others of my Time, or not less of it, than I desir'd: Yet

20 I will venture to say, that from the common, weak Appetite of
false Applause, many Actors have run into more Errors, and Absurdities, than their greatest Ignorance could otherwise have
committed: If this Charge is true, it will lie chiefly upon the
better Judgment of the Spectator to reform it.

But not to make too great a Merit of my avoiding this common Road to Applause, perhaps I was vain enough to think, I
had more ways, than one, to come at it. That, in the Variety
of Characters I acted, the Chances to win it, were the strogner
on my Side--- That, if the Multitude were not in a Roar, to see

30 me, in *Cardinal Wolsey,* I could be sure of them in Alderman
Fondlewife. If they hated me in *Iago,* in Sir *Fopling* they took
me for a fine Gentleman; if they were silent at *Syphax,* no *Italian* Eunuch was more applauded than when I sung in Sir *Courtly.*
If the Morals of *Aesop* were too grave for them, Justice *Shallow*

CHAPTER VII

18.   now in 1693] Actually 1695.

was as simple, and as merry an old Rake, as the wisest of our
young ones could wish me. And though the Terror and Detestation rais'd by King *Richard*, might be too severe a Delight for
them, yet the more gentle and modern Vanities of a Poet *Bays*,
or the well-bred Vices of a Lord *Foppington*, were not at all,
more than their merry Hearts, or nicer Morals could bear.

  These few Instances out of fifty more I could give you, may
serve to explain, what sort of Merit, I at most pretended to;
which was, that I supply'd, with Variety, whatever I might want
of that particular Skill, wherein others went before me. How
this Variety was executed (for by that only is its value to be
rated) you who have so often been my Spectator, are the proper
Judge: If you pronounce my Performance to have been defective, I am condemn'd by my own Evidence; if you acquit me,
these Out-lines may serve for a Sketch of my Theatrical Character.

C H A P. VII.

The State of the Stage continued. The Occasion of Wilks's *com-*
mencing Actor. His Success. Facts relating to his Theatrical
Talent. Actors more or less esteem'd from their private Cha-
racters.

THE *Lincolns-Inn-Fields* Company were, now in
1693, a Common-wealth, like that of *Holland*, divided from the Tyranny of *Spain*: But the Similitude goes very little farther; short was the Duration of the Theatrical Power! for though Success
pour'd in so fast upon them, at their first Opening, that every
thing seem'd to support it self; yet Experience, in a Year or two
show'd them, that they had never been worse govern'd, than
when they govern'd themselves! many of them began to make

deserting the Theatre Royal, and by October 1700 he had signed a contract with Lincoln's Inn Fields (Nicoll, I, 338-40); cf. Cibber's account below.

34.   costly Trains and Plumes of Tragedy] After complaining of the immense plumes worn by heroes (cited above, Chapter IV, 67) Addison remarks (*Spectator*, No. 42, 18 April 1711) " ... a Princess generally receives her Grandeur from those additional encumbrances that fall into her Tail: I mean the broad sweeping Train that follows her in all her Motions, and finds constant Employment for a Boy who stands behind her to open and spread it to advantage."

3. several ... wanted to govern] The license given to Betterton's group had in fact established no authority in the company; Betterton exercised leadership, but as Cibber says, there appears to have been little harmony (witness the movements of Verbruggen and Dogget, cf. Nicoll, I, 339 n. 2 *et passim*). Detailed orders were given by the Lord Chamberlain for the financial affairs of the company (from L.C. 7/1 and 7/3, reprinted by Nicoll, I, 361-62) but it was found necessary on 11 November 1706 to appoint Betterton sole manager (from L.C. 7/1 and 7/3, reprinted by Nicoll, I, 340).

16. *Caesar Borgia*] *Caesar Borgia: the Son of Pope Alexander the Sixt*h (first played c. September 1679); it was revived in 1696 at the time of the first performance of *The Relapse November* (1696).

17. Lord *Foppington*] See Introduction on Cibber as a fop. There is a portrait by Giuseppe Grisoni (1699-1769) of Cibber in this role in the Garrick Club (Ellis Waterhouse, *Painting in Britain: 1530-1790*, p. 155). It was his success in this part that persuaded the patentees to allow him other important roles (cf. Barker, p.32).

19. pay Fiddles, and Candles] Music was used in many plays not designated operas (cf. Nicoll, I, 61-62); the stage was entirely lit by large rings of candles over the proscenium, and by footlights (Nicoll, I, 81-82).

33. *Dogget ... came over to us at the Theatre-Royal*] Dogget appears to have been unsettled; in November 1693 he had mutinied along with Bower against Rich, but Betterton and others calmed him; in April 1696 he made an agreement to abandon the Lincoln's Inn Fields company for the Theatre-Royal, and by 26 October 1696 he had done so. There exists a curious order from the Lord Chamberlain on this date (from L.C. 7/1, printed by Nicoll, I, 339 n.) in which Verbruggen is ordered to fulfil his obligations to the patentees, but Dogget is left explicitly free of his contract with Lincoln's Inn Fields. He was arrested 27 November 1697 for

132

their particular Interest more their Point, than that of the general: and though some Deference might be had to the Measures,
and Advice of *Betterton*, several of them wanted to govern, in
their Turn; and were often out of Humour, that their Opinion
was not equally regarded--- But have we not seen the same Infirmity in Senates? The Tragedians seem'd to think their Rank
as much above the Comedians, as in the Characters they severally acted; when the first were in their Finery, the latter were
impatient, at the Expence; and look'd upon it, as rather laid
10 out, upon the real, than the fictitious Person of the Actor; nay,
I have known, in our own Company, this ridiculous sort of Regret carry'd so far, that the Tragedian has thought himself injur'd, when the *Comedian* pretended to wear a fine Coat! I remember *Powel*, upon surveying my first Dress, in the *Relapse,*
was out of all temper, and reproach'd our Master in very rude
Terms, that he had not so good a Suit to play *Caesar Borgia* in!
tho' he knew, at the same time, my Lord *Foppington* fill'd the
House, when his bouncing *Borgia* would do little more than
pay Fiddles, and Candles to it: And though a Character of Va-
20 nity, might be suppos'd more expensive in Dress, than possibly
one of Ambition; yet the high Heart of this heroical Actor
could not bear, that a Comedian should ever pretend to be as
well dress'd as himself. Thus again on the contrary, when *Bet-*
terton propos'd to set off a Tragedy, the Comedians were sure
to murmur at the Charge of it: And the late Reputation which
Dogget had acquir'd, from acting his *Ben*, in *Love* for *Love,*
made him a more declar'd Male-content on such Occasions; he
over-valu'd Comedy for its being nearer to Nature, than Tragedy; which is allow'd to say many fine things, that Nature ne-
30 ver spoke, in the same Words; and supposing his Opinion were
just, yet he should have consider'd, that the Publick had a Taste,
as well as himself, which, in Policy, he ought to have comply'd with. *Dogget* however could not, with Patience, look
upon the costly Trains and Plumes of Tragedy, in which know-

18.   I remember him three times ... unemploy'd] Lowe (I, 230) notes that Dogget did

        not appear on any theatrical rosters from "1698 to 1700, both inclusive"; he did not

        appear during the season of 1706-1707, but after 10 January 1708 he was a

        member of the Drury Lane company (Avery, I, 154, 167). The third period may be

        that after Booth's promotion in 1713.

ing himself to be useless, he thought were all a vain Extravagance: And when he found his Singularity could no longer
oppose that Expence, he so obstinately adhered to his own Opinion, that he left the Society of his old Friends, and came over
to us at the *Theatre-Royal:* And yet this Actor always set up
for a Theatrical Patriot. This happen'd in the Winter following the first Division of the (only) Company. He came time
enough to the *Theatre-Royal*, to act the Part of *Lory,* in the
Relapse, an arch Valet, quite after the *French* cast, pert, and fa-
10 miliar. But it suited so ill with *Dogget's* dry, and closely-natural manner of acting, that upon the second Day he desir'd it
might be dispos'd of to another; which the Author complying
with, gave it to *Penkethman;* who though, in other Lights,
much his Inferior, yet this Part he seem'd better to become.
Dogget was so immoveable in his Opinion of whatever he thought
was right, or wrong, that he could never be easy, under any
kind of Theatrical Government; and was generally so warm, in
pursuit of his Interest, that he often out-ran it; I remember
him three times, for some Years, unemploy'd in any Theatre,
20 from his not being able to bear, in common with others, the
disagreeable Accidents, that in such Societies are unavoidable.
But whatever Pretences he had form'd for this first deserting,
from *Lincolns-Inn-Fields*, I always thought his best Reason for
it, was, that he look'd upon it as a sinking Ship; not only from
the melancholy Abatement of their Profits, but likewise from
the Neglect, and Disorder in their Government: He plainly
saw, that their extraordinary Success at first, had made them
too confident of its Duration, and from thence had slacken'd
their Industry--- by which he observ'd, at the same time, the
30 old House, where there was scarce any other Merit than Industry,
began to flourish. And indeed they seem'd not enough to consider, that the Appetite of the Publick, like that of a fine Gentleman, could only be kept warm, by Variety; that let their
Merit be never so high, yet the Taste of a Town was not al-

16. Never to pay their People] Rich may have been appropriating the profits for himself at this time—he paid no dividends to the sharers and no rent on the Dorset Garden Theatre—but he also reinvested large amounts of money in scenery and other spectacular equipment in order to attract audiences who were increasingly difficult to draw (cf. Barker, pp. 54-57, and Hotson, pp. 299-300).

22. the other House ... making the like scanty Payments] Lowe (I, 222) points out that Cibber acknowledged in the Preface to *Woman's Wit, or, The Lady in Fashion* (1697) that he had belonged to the Lincoln's Inn Fields company: "... during the time of my writing the two first Acts, I was entertain'd in the New Theatre .... In the middle of my Writing the Third Act, not liking my Station there, I return'd again to the Theatre-Royal."

34. Our Master] Christopher Rich.

ways constant, nor infallible: That it was dangerous to hold
their Rivals in too much Contempt; for they found, that a
young industrious Company were soon a Match, for the best
Actors, when too securely negligent: And negligent they certainly
were, and fondly fancy'd, that had each of their different Schemes
been follow'd, their Audiences would not so suddenly have fallen
off.

But alas! the Vanity of applauded Actors, when they are not
crowded to, as they may have been, makes them naturally im-
10 pute the Change to any Cause, rather than the true one, Satiety:
They are mighty loath, to think a Town, once so fond of them,
could ever be tired; and yet, at one time, or other, more or
less, thin Houses have been the certain Fate of the most prosperous Actors, ever since I remember the Stage! But against this
Evil, the provident Patentees had found out a Relief, which the
new House were not yet Masters of, *viz.* Never to pay their
People, when the Mony did not come in; nor then neither, but
in such Proportions, as suited their Conveniency. I my self was
one of the many, who for six acting Weeks together, never re-
20 ceiv'd one Day's Pay; and for some Years after, seldom had
above half our nominal Sallaries: But to the best of my Memory, the Finances of the other House, held it not above one
Season more, before they were reduc'd to the same Expedient
of making the like scanty Payments.

Such was the Distress, and Fortune of both these Companies,
since their Division, from the *Theatre-Royal;* either working at
half Wages, or by alternate Successes, intercepting the Bread from
one another's Mouths; irreconcileable Enemies, yet without Hope
of Relief, from a Victory on either side; sometimes both Parties
30 reduc'd, and yet each supporting their Spirits, by seeing the other
under the same Calamity.

During this State of the Stage, it was, that the lowest Expedient was made use of, to ingratiate our Company, in the Publick Favour: Our Master, who had some time practis'd the Law,

16.   This riotous Privilege ... most disgraceful Nusance] From the Restoration,
       footmen had been admitted into the topmost gallery after the fourth act. These were
       sent ahead by their masters to hold places for them before the play began, when
       they went into the stair wells until admitted to seats. (Dryden's "Epilogue on the
       Union of the Two Companies" in 1682 mentions their noisiness.) In 1697 Rich
       began to admit them from the beginning of the play, the withdrawal of which
       privilege led to a riot 19 February 1737 (cf. Nicoll, II, 12; Dudden, I, 39 ff.).

24.   admitted behind our Scenes, for Money] It was possible to gain admission to the
       "tyring-room" for chat with actresses (Nicoll, I, 13, 14). Chetwood (p. 235),
       speaking of Wilks', Cibber's and Swiney's years as managers, says "their Green-
       Rooms [retiring rooms] were free from Indencies of every Kind, and might justly
       be compared to the most elegant Drawing Rooms . . . . No Fops or Coxcombs
       ever shew'd their Monkey Trickes there; but if they chanc'd to thrust in, were aw'd
       into Respect."

and therefore lov'd a Storm, better than fair Weather (for it was
his own Conduct chiefly, that had brought the Patent into these
Dangers) took nothing so much to Heart, as that Partiality,
wherewith he imagin'd the People of Quality had preferr'd the
Actors of the other House, to those of his own: To ballance
this Misfortune, he was resolv'd, at least, to be well with their
Domesticks, and therefore cunningly open'd the upper Gallery to
them *gratis:* For before this time no Footman was ever admitted,
or had presum'd to come into it, till after the fourth Act was
10   ended: This additional Privilege (the greatest Plague that ever
Play-house had to complain of) he conceiv'd would not only incline them, to give us a good Word, in the respective Families they
belong'd to, but would naturally incite them, to come all hands
aloft, in the Crack of our Applauses: And indeed it so far succeeded, that it often thunder'd from the full Gallery above, while
our thin Pit, and Boxes below, were in the utmost Serenity. This
riotous Privilege, so craftily given, and which from Custom, was
at last ripen'd into Right, became the most disgraceful Nusance,
that ever depreciated the Theatre. How often have the most
20   polite Audiences, in the most affecting Scenes of the best Pays,
been distrub'd and insulted, by the Noise and Clamour of these
savage Spectators? From the same narrow way of thinking too,
were so many ordinary People, and unlick'd Cubs of Condition,
admitted behind our Scenes, for Money, and sometimes without
it: The Plagues, and Inconveniences of which Custom, we found
so intollerable, when we afterwards had the Stage in our Hands,
that at the Hazard of our Lives, we were forc'd to get rid of
them; and our only Expedient was, by refusing Money from
all Persons, without distinction, at the Stage Door; by this means
30   we preserv'd to our selves the Right and Liberty of chusing our
own Company there: And by a strict Observance of this Order,
we brought what had been before debas'd into all the Licenses
of a Lobby, into the Decencies of a Drawing-Room.

1. in the Year 1696, *Wilks*] Chetwood (p. 234) gives 1692 as the date; Lowe (I, 235)

    gives 1698, noting that his name did not appear on the bills until that date (cf. Van

    Lennep, pp. 501, 514, 517). The author of *The Laureat* (p. 43) claims to have seen

    Wilks at his first performance in this play, which was revived in 1698, confirming

    Lowe's date.

12. the Battle of the *Boyn*] 11 July 1690.

About the distressful Time I was speaking of, in the Year
1696, *Wilks,* who now had been five Years in great Esteem on
the *Dublin* Theatre, return'd to that of *Drury-Lane;* in which
last he had first set out, and had continued to act some small
Parts, for one Winter only. The considerable Figure which he
so lately made upon the Stage in *London,* makes me imagine
that a particular Account of his first commencing Actor may
not be unacceptable, to the Curious; I shall, therefore, give it
them, as I had it, from his own Mouth.

10   In King *James's* Reign he had been some time employ'd in
the Secretary's Office in *Ireland* (his native Country) and remain'd
in it, till after the Battle of the *Boyn,* which completed the Revolution. Upon that happy, and unexpected Deliverance, the
People of *Dublin,* among the various Expressions of their Joy,
had a Mind to have a Play; but the Actors being dispers'd, during the War, some private Persons agreed, in the best manner
they were able, to give one, to the Publick, *gratis,* at the *Theatre.*
The Play was *Othello,* in which *Wilks* acted the *Moor;* and the
Applause he receiv'd in it, warm'd him to so strong an Inclina-
20 tion for the Stage, that he immediately prefer'd it to all his
other Views in Life: For he quitted his Post, and with the first
fair Occasion came over, to try his Fortune, in the (then only)
Company of Actors in *London.* The Person, who supply'd his
Post, in *Dublin,* he told me, rais'd to himself, from thence, a
Fortune of fifty thousand Pounds. Here you have a much
stronger Instance of an extravagant Passion for the Stage, than
that, which I have elsewhere shewn in my self; I only quitted
my *Hopes* of being preferr'd to the like Post, for it; but *Wilks*
quitted his actual *Possession,* for the imaginary Happiness, which
30 the Life of an Actor presented to him. And, though possibly,
we might both have better'd our Fortunes, in a more honourable
Station, yet whether better Fortunes might have equally gratify'd
our Vanity (the universal Passion of Mankind) may admit of a
Question.

Upon his being formerly receiv'd into the *Theatre-Royal* (which
was in the Winter after I had been initiated) his Station there
was much upon the same Class, with my own; our Parts were
generally of an equal Insignificancy, not of consequence enough
to give either a Preference: But *Wilks* being more impatient of
his low Condition, than I was, (and, indeed, the Company was
then so well stock'd with good Actors, that there was very little
hope of getting forward) laid hold of a more expeditious way
for his Advancement, and return'd agen to *Dublin*, with Mr. *Ash-*
10 *bury*, the Patentee of that Theatre, to act in his new Company
there: There went with him, at the same time, Mrs. *Butler*,
whose Character I have already given, and *Estcourt*, who had
not appear'd upon any Stage, and was yet only known as an excellent Mimick: *Wilks* having no Competitor in *Dublin*, was
immediately preferr'd to whatever Parts his Inclination led him,
and his early Reputation on that Stage, as soon rais'd, in him,
an Ambition to shew himself on a better. And I have heard him
say (in Raillery of the Vanity, which young Actors are liable to)
that when the News of *Monfort's* Death came to *Ireland*, he
20 from that time thought his Fortune was made, and took a Resolution to return a second time to *England*, with the first Opportunity; but as his Engagements to the Stage, where he was, were
too strong to be suddenly broke from, he return'd not to the
Theatre-Royal, 'till the Year 1696.
  Upon his first Arrival, *Powel*, who was now in possession of
all the chief Parts of *Monfort*, and the only Actor that stood in
Wilks's way; in seeming Civility, offer'd him his choice of
whatever he thought fit, to make his first Appearance in; tho',
in reality, the Favour was intended to hurt him. But *Wilks*
30 rightly judg'd it more modest, to accept only of a Part of
Powel's, and which *Monfort* had never acted, that of *Palamede*
in *Dryden's Marriage Alamode*. Here too, he had the Advantage of having the Ball play'd into his Hand, by the inimitable Mrs. *Monfort*, who was then his *Melantha* in the same Play:

1. 13 upon any Stage] on any Stage 2nd ed.

to fight the Heroic *George Powel*, as well as one or two others, who were piqued at this being so highly encouraged by the Town."

33.   walk'd off ... *Lincoln's-Inn Fields*] Powell was with the Lincoln's Inn Fields company from 1700 until the season of 1703-1704; he received a benefit 17 June 1704 (Avery, I, 3-69 *passim*).

Whatever Fame *Wilks* had brought with him, from *Ireland,* he
as yet appear'd but a very raw Actor, to what he was afterwards
allow'd to be: His Faults however, I shall rather leave to the
Judgments of those, who then may remember him, than to
take upon me the disagreeable Office of being particular upon
them, farther than by saying, that in this Part of *Palamede,* he
was short of *Powel,* and miss'd a good deal of the loose Humour of the Character, which the other more happily hit. But
however, he was young, erect, of a pleasing Aspect, and,
10   in the whole, gave the Town, and the Stage, sufficient Hopes
of him. I ought to make some Allowances too, for the Restraint he must naturally have been under, from his first Appearance upon a new Stage. But from that he soon recovered,
and grew daily, more in Favour not only of the Town, but likewise of the Patentee, whom *Powel,* before *Wilks's* Arrival, had
treated, in almost what manner he pleas'd.

   Upon this visible Success of *Wilks,* the pretended Contempt,
which *Powel* had held him in, began to sour into an open
Jealousy; he, now, plainly saw, he was a formidable Rival,
20   and (which more hurt him) saw too, that other People saw it;
and therefore found it high time, to oppose, and be troublesome to him. But *Wilks* happening to be as jealous of his
Fame, as the other, you may imagine such clashing Candidates
could not be long without a Rupture: In short, a Challenge, I
very well remember, came from *Powel,* when he was hot-
headed; but the next Morning he was cool enough, to let it
end, in favour of *Wilks.* Yet however the Magnanimity, on
either Part, might subside, the Animosity was as deep in the
Heart, as ever, tho' it was not afterwards so openly avow'd:
30   For when *Powel* found that intimidating would not carry his
Point; but that *Wilks,* when provok'd, would really give Battle, he (*Powel*) grew so out of Humour, that he cock'd his Hat,
and in his Passion walk'd off, to the Service of the Company, in
Lincoln's-Inn Fields. But there, finding more Competitors, and

that he made a worse Figure among them, than in the Company he came from, he staid but one Winter with them, before
he return'd to his old Quarters, in *Drury-Lane*; where, after
these unsuccessful Pushes of his Ambition, he, at last became a
Martyr to Negligence, and quietly submitted to the Advantages,
and Superiority, which (during his late Desertion) *Wilks* had more
easily got over him.

      However trifling these Theatrical Anecdotes may seem, to a
sensible Reader, yet, as the different Conduct of these rival Ac-
10   tors may be of use, to others of the same Profession, and from
thence may contribute to the Pleasure of the Publick; let that
be my Excuse, for pursuing them. I must, therefore, let it be
known, that though, in Voice, and Ear, Nature had been more
kind to *Powel*, yet he so often lost the Value of them, by an
unheedful Confidence, that the constant wakeful Care, and Decency, of *Wilks,* left the other far behind, in the publick
Esteem, and Approbation. Nor was his Memory less tenacious
than that of *Wilks*; but *Powel* put too much Trust in it, and
idly deferr'd the Studying of his Parts, as School-boys do their
20   Exercise, to the last Day; which commonly brings them out
proportionably defective. But *Wilks* never lost an Hour of precious Time, and was, in all his Parts, perfect, to such an Ex-
actitude, that I question, if in forty Years, he ever five times
chang'd or misplac'd an Article, in any one of them. To be
Master of this uncommon Diligence, is adding, to the Gift of
Nature, all that is in an Actor's Power; and this Duty of Studying perfect, whatever Actor is remiss in, he will proportionably find, that Nature may have been kind to him, in vain: For
though *Powel* had an Assurance, that cover'd this Neglect much
30   better, than a Man of more Modesty might have done; yet with
all his Intrepidity, very often the Diffidence, and Concern for
what he was to *say*, made him lose the Look of what he was to
be: While, therefore, *Powel* presided, his idle Example made
this Fault so common to others, that I cannot but confess, in the

15. *Cato ... Painful Praeeminence!*} Addison, *Cato*, III, v, 23. Cf. Pope, *Essay on Man*, IV, 267, where the phrase is applied to Bolingbroke.

27. Indignity to his Memory] *The Laureat* (p. 45): "I have known him lay a Wager, and win it, that he would repeat the part of *Truewitt* in the *Silent Woman* ... without misplacing a single word, or missing an (*and*) or an (*or*)."

general Infection, I had my Share of it; nor was my too critical
Excuse for it, a good one, *viz.* That scarce one Part, in five,
that fell to my Lot, was worth the labour. But to shew Respect
to an Audience, is worth the best Actor's Labour, and, his Business considered, he must be a very impudent one, that comes before them, with a conscious Negligence of what he is about.
But *Wilks* was never known, to make any of these venial Distinctions; nor however barren his Part might be, could bear even
the Self-Reproach of favouring his Memory: And I have been

10   astonished, to see him swallow a Volume of Froth, and Insipi-
dity, in a new Play, that we were sure could not live above three
Days, tho' favoured, and recommended to the Stage, by some
good person of Quality. Upon such Occasions, in compassion
to his fruitless Toil, and Labour, I have sometimes cry'd out
with *Cato* ------ *Painful Praeeminence!* So insupportable, in my
Sense, was the Task, when the bare Praise, of not having been
negligent, was sure to be the only Reward of it. But so indefatigable was the Diligence of *Wilks*, that he seem'd to love it, as
a good Man does Virtue, for its own sake; of which the follow-

20   ing Instance will give you an extraordianry Proof.

In some new Comedy, he happen'd to complain of a crabbed
Speech in his Part, which, he said, gave him more trouble to
study, than all the rest of it had done; upon which, he apply'd to the Author, either to soften, or shorten it. The Author, that he might make the matter quite easy to him, fairly
cut it all out. But when he got home, from the Rehearsal,
Wilks thought it such an Indignity to his Memory, that any thing
should be thought too hard for it, that he actually made himself
perfect in that Speech, though he knew it was never to be made

30   use of. From this singular Act of Supererogation, you may
judge, how indefatigable the Labour of his Memory must have
been, when his Profit, and Honour, were more concern'd to make
use of it.

7.   *Ammon*] In *The Rival Queens, or the Death of Alexander the Great* (1676/77) by
      Nathaniel Lee.

7.   *Dorimant*] In *The Man of Mode*, or, *Sir Fopling Flutter* (1675/76) by Sir George
      Etherege.

19.   the *Beggars Opera*] *The Beggar's Opera* by John Gay, first performance on 27
      January 1728.

25.   *Love in a Riddle*] *Love in a Riddle: a Pastoral* (January 1729). The success of
      The Beggar's Opera established for a time a rage for ballad-operas, from which
      Cibber was not alone in trying to profit (cf. Nicoll, II, 237 ff. and n.). His attitude
      toward Gay's play must in part be a weak justification of his having turned it down
      when it was offered to Drury Lane. See Introduction, pp. xxi-xxii.

But besides this indispensable Quality of Diligence, *Wilks* had
the Advantage of a sober Character, in private Life, which *Powel*
not having the least Regard to, labour'd under the unhappy Disfavour, not to say, Contempt, of the Publick, to whom his licentious Courses were no Secret: Even when he did well, that
natural Prejudice pursu'd him; neither the Heroe, nor the Gentleman; the young *Ammon,* nor the *Dorimant,* could conceal,
from the conscious Spectator, the True *George Powel.* And this
sort of Disesteem, or Favour, every Actor, will feel, and more,
10 or less, have his Share of, as he *has,* or has *not,* a due Regard to
his private Life, and Reputation. Nay, even false Reprots shall
affect him, and become the Cause, or Pretence at least, of under-
valuing, or treating him injuriously. Let me give a known Instance of it, and, at the same time, a Justification of myself,
from an Imputation, that was laid upon me, not many Years, before I quitted the Theatre, of which you will see the Consequence.

     After the vast Success of that new Species of Dramatick Poetry,
the *Beggars Opera:* The Year following, I was so stupid, as to
20 attempt something of the same Kind, upon a quite different
Foundation, that of recommending Virtue, and Innocence; which
I ignorantly thought, might not have a less Pretence to Favour,
than setting Greatness, and Authority, in a contemptible, and the
most vulgar Vice, and Wickedness, in an amiable Light. But
behold how fondly I was mistaken! *Love in a Riddle* (for so my
new-fangled Performance was call'd) was as vilely damn'd, and
hooted at, as so vain a Presumption, in the idle Cause of Virtue, could deserve. Yet this is not what I complain of; I will
allow my Poetry, to have been as much below the other, as Taste,
30 or Criticism, can sink it: I will grant likewise, that the applauded Author of the *Beggars Opera* (whom I knew to be honest
good-natur'd Man, and who, when he had descended to write
more like one in the Cause of Virtue, had been as unfortunate,
as others of that Class;) I will grant, I say, that in his *Beggar's*

1. 15 not many Years] many Years 2nd ed.
1. 19 to have been] to be 2nd ed.

4.   *Nos haec novimus esse nihil*] Martial, XIII, ii, 8: "I know these efforts are worth nothing."

7.   *Sejanus*] Cibber mistakes *Sejanus* for *Catiline His Conspiracy* (1611) which preceded *Bartholomew Fair* (1614). Jonson's note "To the Reader in Ordinary" prefixed to *Catiline* is sharply critical of the taste of the mob, as is the declaration read by the Bookholder in the Introduction to *Bartholomew Fair*. The relation between the plays suggested by Cibber is not mentioned, however (*Ben Jonson's Plays*, ed. Felix E. Schelling, Everyman's Library, II, 91, 180-82).

11.   *Cato ... succeeded*] *Cato* opened on 14 April 1713 and played twenty times until 9 May, only closing when Mrs. Oldfield's pregnancy became too advanced for her to continue (cf. Smithers, *Addison*, pp. 253-55); *The Beggar's Opera* had an enormous run, playing sixty-two times from its opening 29 January until 19 June 1728 (Avery, II, 956-81).

23.   Second Part to the *Beggars Opera* ...] The suppression of *Polly: an Opera, Being the Second Part of The Beggar's Opera* (1729) was almost certainly Walpole's act of revenge on Gay for the satire against his regime in *The Beggar's Opera*. It was published by subscription and this brought Gay £800, twice the amount he gained from *The Beggar's Opera* (Nicoll, II, 240-41). The opposition press appears to have prepared the hostile reception to *Love in a Riddle* (cf. Mist's Weekly, 7-14 September 1728; *The Daily Journal*, 22 October 1728; and *The Craftsman*, 7 January 1729; see also Barker, pp. 150-51). *The Laureat* (pp. 46-47) claims that the uproar began, on the first night, only when Cibber appeared as Philautos—a pastoral lover—and began to sing "not in a mimick, not in a false, but in [his] own real natural Voice."

142

Opera, he had more skilfully gratify'd the Publick Taste, than
all the brightest Authors that ever writ before him; and I have
sometimes thought, from the Modesty of his Motto, *Nos' haec no-*
vimus esse nihil, that he gave them that Performance, as a Satyr
upon the Depravity of their Judgment (as *Ben. Johnson,* of old,
was said to have given his *Bartholomew-Fair,* in Ridicule of the
vulgar Taste, which had dislik'd his *Sejanus*) and that, by artfully
seducing them, to be the Champions of the Immoralities he himself detested, he should be amply reveng'd on their former Seve-
10 rity, and Ignorance. This were indeed a Triumph! which, even
the Author of *Cato,* might have envy'd! *Cato,* 'tis true, succeeded, but reach'd not, by full forty Days, the Progress, and Applauses, of the *Beggars Opera.* Will it, however, admit of a
Question, which of the two Compositions a good Writer,
would rather wish to have been the Author of? Yet, on the other
side, must we not allow, that to have taken a whole Nation,
High, and Low, into a general Applause, has shewn a Power in
Poetry, which, tho' often attempted in the same kind, none but
this one Author, could ever yet arrive at? By what Rule, then,
20 are we to judge of our true National Taste? But, to keep a little closer to my Point,

The same Author, the next Year, had, according to the Laws
of the Land, transported his Heroe to the *West-Indies,* in a Second Part to the *Beggars Opera;* but so it happen'd, to the Surprize of the publick, this Second Part was forbid to come upon
the Stage! Various were the Speculations, upon this Act of Power:
Some thought that the Author, others that the Town, was hardly dealt with; a third sort, who perhaps had envy'd him the
Success of his First Part, affirm'd, when it was printed, that
30 whatever the Intention might be, the Fact was in his Favour,
that he had been a greater Gainer, by Subscriptions to his copy,
than he could have been by a bare Theatrical Presentation. Whether any Part of these Opinions were true, I am not concerne'd
to determine, or consider. But how they affected me, I am go-

ing to tell you. Soon after this Prohibition, my Performance was
to come upon the Stage, at a time, when many People were out
of Humour, at the late Disappointment, and seem'd willing to
lay hold of any Pretence of making a Reprizal. Great Umbrage
was taken, that I was permitted, to have the whole Town to my
self, by this absolute Forbiddance of what, they had more mind
to have been entertain'd with. And, some few Days before my
Bawble was acted, I was inform'd, that a strong Party would be
made against it: This Report I slighted, as not conceiving why
10   it should be true; and when I was afterwards told, what was the
pretended Provocation of this Party, I slighted it, still more, as
having less Reason to suppose, any Persons could believe me capable (had I had the Power) of giving such a Provocation. The
Report, it seems, that had run against me, was this: That, to
make way for the Success of my own Play, I had privately found
means, or made Interest, that the Second Part of the *Beggars
Opera,* might be suppress'd. What an involuntary Compliment
did the Reporters of this Falshood make me? to suppose me of
Consideration enough, to influence a great Officer of State, to
20   gratify the Spleen, or Envy, of a Comedian, so far, as to rob the
Publick of an innocent Diversion (if it were such) that none,
but that cunning Comedian, might be suffered to give it them.
This is so very gross a Supposition, that it needs only its own
senseless Face, to confound it; let that along, then, be my Defence against it. But against blind Malice, and staring Inhumanity, whatever is upon the Stage, has no Defence! There, they
knew, I stood helpless, and expos'd, to whatever they might
please to load, or asperse me with. I had not considered, poor
Devil! that, from the Security of a full Pit, Dunces, might be
30   Criticks, Cowards valiant, and 'Prentices Gentlemen! Whether
any such were concern'd in the Murder of my Play, I am not
certain; for I never endeavour'd, to discover any one of its Assassins; I cannot afford them a milder Name, from their unmanly manner of destroying it. Had it been heard, they might

8. stepping forward ... told them] Avery (II, 1007) cites the *Universal Spectator*, 11 January 1729 on this performance (8 January) confirming Cibber's claim.

144

have left me nothing to say to them: 'Tis true, it faintly held
up its wounded Head, a second Day, and would have spoke for
Mercy, but was not suffer'd. Not even the Presence of a Royal
Heir apparent, could protect it. But then I was reduc'd to be
serious with them; their Clamour, then, became an Insolence,
which I thought it my Duty, by the Sacrifice of any Interest of
my own, to put an end to. I therefore quitted the Actor, for
the Author, and, stepping forward to the Pit, told them, *That*
since I found they were not inclin'd, that this Play should go for-
10   *ward, I gave them my Word, that after this Night, it should ne-*
ver be acted agen: But that, in the mean time, I hop'd, they
would consider, in whose Presence they were, and for that Reason,
at least, would suspend what farther Marks of their Displeasure,
they might imagine I had deserved. At this there was a dead Silence; and, after some little Pause, a few civiliz'd Hands, signify'd their Approbation. When the Play went on, I observ'd
about a Dozen Persons, of no extraordinary Appearance, sullenly walk'd out of the Pit. After which, every Scene of it, while
uninterrupted, met with more Applause, than my best Hopes had
20   expected. But it came too late: Peace to its *Manes!* I had
given my Word it should fall, and I kept it, by giving out another Play, for the next Day, though I knew the Boxes were all
lett, for the same again. Such, then, was the Treatment I met
with: How much of it, the Errors of the Play might deserve,
I refer to the Judgment of those, who may have Curiosity, and
idle Time enough to read it. But if I had no occasion to complain of the Reception it met with, from its *quieted* Audience,
sure it can be no great Vanity, to impute its Disgraces chiefly, to
that severe Resentment, which a groundless Report of me had
30   inflam'd: Yet those Disgraces have left me something to boast
of, an Honour preferable, even to the Applause of my Enemies:
A noble Lord came behind the Scenes, and told me, from the
Box, where he was in waiting, *That what I said, to quiet the*
Audience, was extremely well taken there; and that I had been

21. the *Maid's Tragedy*] *The Maid's Tragedy* (1610/11?) by Beaumont and Fletcher,

II, i, c. 350.

commended for it, in a very obliging manner. Now, though this
was the only Tumult, that I have known to have been so effectually appeas'd, these fifty years, by any thing that could be said
to an Audience, in the same Humour, I will not take any great
Merit to myself upon it; because when, like me, you will but
humbly submit to their doing you all the Mischief they can, they
will, at any time, be satisfy'd.

    I have mention'd this particular Fact, to inforce what I before
observ'd, That the private Character of an Actor, will always,
10 more or less, affect his Publick Performance. And if I suffer'd
so much, from the bare *Suspicion* of my having been guilty of
a base Action; what should not an Actor expect, that is hardy
enough, to think his whole private Character of no consequence?
I could offer many more, tho' less severe Instances, of the same
Nature. I have seen the most tender Sentiment of Love, in Tragedy, create Laughter, instead of Compassion, when it ahs been
applicable to the real Engagements of the Person, that utter'd
it. I have known good Parts thrown up, from an humble Consciousness, that something in them, might put an Audience in
20 mind of --- what was rather wish'd might be forgotten: Those
remarkable Words of *Evadne,* in the *Maid's Tragedy* ------------
A Maidenhead, Amintor, at my years? --- have sometimes been
a much stronger Jest, for being a true one. But these are Reproaches, which, in all Nations, the Theatre must have been us'd
to, unless we could suppose Actors something more, than Human
Creatures, void of Faults, or Frailties. 'Tis a Misfortune, at least,
not limited to the *English* Stage. I have seen the better-bred Audience, in *Paris,* made merry, even with a modest Expression,
when it has come from the Mouth of an Actress, whose private
30 Character it seem'd not to belong to. The Apprehension of these
kind of Fleers, from the Witlings of a Pit, has been carry'd so
far, in our own Country, that a late valuable Actress (who was
conscious her Beauty was not her greatest Merit) desired the
Warmth of some Lines might be abated, when they have made

13. The Patentee] This sketch of Christopher Rich accords with most of the evidence (cf. Barker, pp. 54-78; Nicoll, I, 331-42; Hotson, pp. 285-310).

her too remarkably handsome: But in this Discretion she was
alone, few others were afraid of undeserving the finest things,
that could be said, to them. But to consider this Matter seriously, I cannot but think, at a Play, a sensible Auditor would
contribute all he could, to his being well deceiv'd, and not suffer
his Imagination, so far to wander, from the well-acted Character before him, as to gratify a frivolous Spleen, by Mocks, or
personal Sneers, on the Performer, at the Expence of his better
Entertainment. But I must now take up *Wilks,* and *Powel,*
10   again, where I left them.

  Though the Contention for Superiority, between them, seem'd
about this time, to end in favour of the former, yet the Distress
of the Patentee (in having his Servant his Master, as *Powel* had
lately been) was not much reliev'd by the Victory; he had only
chang'd the Man, but not the Malady: For *Wilks,* by being in
Possession of so many good Parts, fell into the common Error of
most Actors, that of over-rating their Merit, or never thinking
it is so thoroughly consider'd, as it ought to be; which generally makes them proportionably troublesome to the Master; who,
20   they might consider, only pays them, to profit by them. The
Patentee therefore, found it as difficult to satisfy the continual
Demands of *Wilks*, as it was dangerous to refuse them; very
few were made, that were not granted, and as few were granted,
as were not grudg'd him: Not but our good Master, was as sly
a Tyrant, as ever was at the head of a Theatre; for he gave
the Actors more Liberty, and fewer Days Pay, than any of his
Predecessors: He would laugh with them over a Bottle, and bite
them, in their Bargains: He kept them poor, that they might
not be able to rebel; and sometimes merry, that they might not
30   think of it: All their Articles of Agreement had a Clause in
them, that he was sure to creep out at, *viz.* Their respective
Sallaries, were to be paid, in such manner, and proportion, as
others of the same Company were paid; which in effect, made
them all, when he pleas'd, but limited Sharers of Loss, and him-

16.   he was reduc'd even to take my Opinion ...] Cibber had signed a contract with Rich on 29 October 1696, giving Rich the right to all his future plays (from L.C. 7/3, printed by Nicoll, I, 381). Barker (pp. 57-61) traces Cibber's growing influence with Rich: by November 1704 he had become a general assistant in management and the highest paid actor in the company.

self sole Proprietor of Profits; and this Loss, or Profit, they only
had such verbal Accounts of, as he thought proper to give them.
'Tis true, he woudl sometimes advance them Money (but not
more, than he knew at most could be due to them) upon their
Bonds; upon which, whenever they were mutinous, he would
threaten to sue them. This was the Net we danc'd in for several
Years: But no Wonder we were Dupes, while our Master was a
Lawyer. This Grievance, however, *Wilks* was resolv'd for himself, at least, to remedy at any rate; and grew daily more in-
10   tractable, for every Day his Redress was delay'd. Here our Master found himself under a Difficulty, he knew not well how to
get out of: For as he was a close subtle Man, he seldom made
use of a Confident, in his Schemes of Government: But here
the old Expedient of Delay, would stand him in no longer stead;
Wilks must instantly be comply'd with, or *Powel* come again into Power! In a Word, he was push'd so home, that he was reduc'd even to take my Opinion into his Assistance: For he knew
I was a Rival to neither of them; perhaps too, he had fancy'd,
that from the Success of my first Play, I might know as much
20   of the Stage, and what made an Actor valuable, as either of
them: He saw too, that tho' they had each of them five good
Parts to my one; yet the Applause which in my few, I had met
with, was given me by better Judges, than, as yet, had approv'd
of the best They had done. They generally measured the goodness of a Part, by the Quantity, or Length of it: I thought
none bad for being short, that were closely-natural; nor any the
better, for being long, without that valuable Quality. But, in
this, I doubt, as to their Interest, they judg'd better, than my
self; for I have generally observ'd, that those, who do a great
30   deal not ill, have been preferr'd to those, who do but little,
though never so masterly. And therefore I allow, that while
there were so few good parts, and as few good Judges of them,
it ought to have been no Wonder to me, that, as an Actor, I
was less valued, by the Master, or the common People, than ei-

1.24   best They had done] best they done 2nd ed. The capitalization of the pronoun in the 1st ed. may give emphasis
to a contrast, so I have retained it.

2.   Master's personal Inclination, than any Actor of the male Sex] Rich was thought of
      as a philanderer; cf. *Comparison*, ed. Wells, p. 12: "... he knows not how to
      govern one Province in his Dominion, but that of Signing, Sealing, and something
      else, that shall be nameless" [Lowe].

ther of them: All the Advantage I had of them, was, that by
not being troublesome, I had more of our Master's personal Inclination, than any Actor of the male Sex; and so much of it,
that I was almost the only one, whom at that time, he us'd to
take into his Parties of Pleasure; very often *tete a tete,* and sometimes, in a *Partie quarree.* These then were the Qualifications,
however good, or bad, to which may be imputed our Master's
having made Choice of me, to assist him, in the Difficulty, under which he now labour'd. He was himself sometimes inclin'd
10   to set up *Powel* again, as a Check upon the over-bearing Temper
of *Wilks*: Tho' to say Truth, he lik'd neither of them; but was
still under a Necessity, that one of them should preside; tho'
he scarce knew which of the two Evils to chuse. This Question,
when I happen'd to be alone with him, was often debated in our
Evening Conversation; nor indeed, did I find it an easy matter
to know which Party I ought to recommend to his Election. I
knew they were neither of them Well-wishers to me, as in common they were Enemies to most Actors, in proportion to the
Merit, that seem'd to be rising, in them. But as I had the Pro-
20   sperity of the Stage more at Heart, than any other Consideration,
I could not be long undetermin'd, in my Opinion, and therefore
gave it to our Master, at once, in Favour of *Wilks*. I, with all
the Force I could muster, insisted, "That if *Powel* were pre-
"ferr'd, the ill Example of his Negligence, and abandon'd Cha-
"racter (whatever his Merit on the Stage might be) would re-
"duce our Company to Contempt, and Beggary; observing at
"the same time, in how much better Order our Affairs went
"forward, since *Wilks* came among us, of which I recounted
"several Instances, that are not so necessary to tire my Reader
30   "with. All this, though he allow'd to be true; yet *Powel*, he
"said, was a better Actor than *Wilks*, when he minded his Bu-
"siness (that is to say, when he was, what he seldom was, sober)
"But *Powel*, it seems, had a still greater Merit to him, which
"was, (as he observ'd) that when Affairs were in his Hands, he

19. *Wilks* became first Minister] The contract was signed on 9 October 1704, making him the highest paid actor only until 9 November when Cibber's contract (see above) was signed. In effect, Cibber wielded as much power as Wilks, though less conspicuously (Barker, pp. 60-61).

"had kept the Actors quiet, without one Day's Pay, for six
"Weeks together, and it was not every body could do that;
"for you see, said he, *Wilks* will never be easy, unless I give
"him his whole Pay, when others have it not, and what an
"Injustice would that be to the rest, if I were to comply with
"him? How do I know, but then they may be all, in a Mu-
"tiny, and *mayhap* (that was his Expression) with *Powel* at the
"Head of 'em?" By this Specimen of our Debate, it may be
judg'd, under how particular, and merry a Government, the
10 Theatre then labour'd. To conclude, this Matter ended in a
Resolution, to sign a new Agreement, with *Wilks*, which entitled him, to his full Pay of four Pounds a Week, without any
conditional Deductions. How far soever my Advice might have
contributed to our Master's settling his Affairs upon this Foot,
I never durst make the least Merit of it to *Wilks*, well knowing
that his great Heart would have taken it as a mortal Affront,
had I (tho' never so distantly) hinted, that his Demands had
needed any Assistance, but the Justice of them. From this Time,
then, *Wilks* became first Minister, or Bustle-master-general of the
20 Company. He, now, seem'd to take new Delight, in keeping
the Actors close to their Business; and got every Play reviv'd
with Care, in which he had acted the chief Part in *Dublin*.
'Tis true, this might be done with a particular View of setting
off himself to advantage; but if, at the same time, it serv'd the
Company, he ought not to want our Commendation: Now,
tho' my own Conduct, neither had the Appearance of his Merit, nor the Reward that follow'd his Industry; I cannot help
observing, that it shew'd me, to the best of my Power, a more
cordial Common-wealth's Man: His first Views, in serving him-
30 self, made his Service to the whole but an incidental Merit;
whereas, by my prosecuting the Means, to make him easy, in
his Pay, unknown to him, or without asking any Favour for my
self, at the same time, I gave a more unquestionable Proof of
my preferring the Publick, to my private Interest: From the

12. Sir *John Daw ... Truewit*] In Jonson's *Epicoene, or, The Silent Woman* (c. 1609).

24. Delight of his Life ... Joy of mine] The author of *The Laureat* (p. 48) says of this, "If Wilks was now alive to hear thee prate thus, Mr. Bayes, I would not give one Half-penny for thy Ears; but if he were alive, thou durst not for thy Ears rattle on in this affected *Matchiavilian* Stile." Davies (*Dram. Misc.*, III, 485, 488), noting Cibber's and Dogget's dislike of Wilks, says, "I shall not take the evidence of two such partial and interested men against so honest and steady a character, in the maintenance of everything that was decent, just, and generous ... However Cibber might be disliked by the players, it is certain that Wilks was esteemed and respected by them." The acrimony in Cibber's description developed during the years of their association as actor-managers (cf. below).

same Principle I never murmur'd at whatever little Parts fell to
my Share, and tho' I knew it would not recommend me to the
Favour of the common People, I often submitted to play wicked
Characters, rather than they should be worse done by weaker
Actors than my self: But perhaps, in all this Patience under my
Situation, I supported my Spirits, by a conscious Vanity: For I
fancy'd I had more Reason to value my self, upon being sometimes the Confident, and Companion of our Master, than *Wilks*
had, in all the more publick Favours he had extorted from him.

10   I imagin'd too, there was sometimes as much Skill to be shewn,
in a short Part, as in the most volumninous, which he generally
made choice of; that even coxcombly Follies of a Sir *John
Daw*, might as well distinguish the Capacity of an Actor, as all
the dry Enterprizes, and busy Conduct of a *Truewit*. Nor could
I have any Reason to repine at the Superiority he enjoy'd, when
I consider'd at how dear a Rate it was purchas'd, at the continual Expence of a restless Jealousy, and fretful Impatience----
These were the Passions, that, in the height of his Success,
kept him lean to his last Hour, while what I wanted in Rank,

20   or Glory, was amply made up to me, in Ease and Chearfulness.
But let not this Observation either lessen his Merity, or lift up my
own; since our different Tempers were not, in our Choice, but
equally natural, to both of us. To be employ'd on the Stage
was the Delight of his Life; to be justly excus'd from it, was
the Joy of mine: I lov'd Ease, and he Pre-eminence: In that,
he might be more commendable. Tho' he often disturb'd me,
he seldom could do it, without more disordering himself: In
our Disputes, his Warmth could less bear Truth, than I could
support manifest Injuries: He would hazard our Undoing, to

30   gratify his Passions, tho' otherwise an honest Man; and I rather
chose to give up my Reason, or not see my Wrong, than ruin
our Community by an equal Rashness. By this opposite Conduct, our Accounts at the End of our Labours, stood thus:
While he liv'd, he was the elder Man, when he dy'd, he was

26. *Mills* with making ... larger sallary] Nicoll (II, 287) cites a contract dated 30 March 1709 (from L.C. 7/3) giving Mills a salary of £100 in addition to a benefit in March.

not so old as I am: He never left the Stage, till he left the
World: I never so well enjoy'd the World, as when I left the
Stage: He dy'd in Possession of his Wishes; and I, by having
had a less cholerick Ambition, am still tasting mine, in Health,
and Liberty. But, as he in a great measure wore out the Or-
gans of Life, in his incessant Labours, to gratify the Publick,
the many whom he gave Pleasure to, will always owe his Memory a favourable Report--- Some Facts, that will vouch for the
Truth of this Account, will be found in the Sequel of these
10   Memoirs. If I have spoke with more Freedom of his quondam
Competitor *Powel*, let my good Intentions to future Actors, in
shewing what will so much concern them to avoid, be my Excuse for it: For though *Powel* had from Nature, much more
than *Wilks;* in Voice, and Ear, in Elocution, in Tragedy, and
Humour in Comedy, greatly the Advantage of him; yet, as I
have observ'd, from the Neglect, and Abuse of those valuable
Gifts, he suffer'd *Wilks,* to be of thrice the Service to our Society. Let me give another Instance of the Reward, and Favour, which in a Theatre, Diligence, and Sobriety seldom fail
20   of: *Mills* the elder grew into the Friendship of *Wilks,* with
not a great deal more, than those useful Qualities to recommend
him: He was an honest, quiet, careful Man, of as few Faults,
as Excellencies, and *Wilks* rather chose him for his second, in
many Plays, than an Actor of perhaps greater Skill, that was
not so labouriously diligent. And from this constant Assiduity,
Mills with making to himself a Friend in *Wilks,* was advanc'd
to a larger Sallary, than any Man-Actor had enjoy'd, during my
time, on the Stage. I have yet to offer a more happy Recommendation of Temperance, which a late celebrated Actor was
30   warn'd into, by the mis-conduct of *Powel*. About the Year,
that *Wilks* return'd from *Dublin, Booth,* who had commenc'd
Actor, upon that Theatre, came over to the Company, in *Lincolns-Inn-Fields:* He was, then, but an Under-graduate of the
Buskin, and as he told me himself, had been for some time too

frank a Lover of the Bottle; but having had the Happiness to
observe, into what Contempt, and Distresses *Powel* had plung'd
himself by the same Vice, he was so struck with the Terror of
his Example, that he fix'd a Resolution (which from that time,
to the end of his Days, he strictly observ'd) of utterly reforming
it; an uncommon Act of Philosophy in a young Man! of which
in his Fame, and Fortune, he afterwards enjoy'd the Reward
and Benefit. These Observations I have not meerly thrown to-
together as a Moralist, but to prove, that the briskest loose Liver,
10   or intemperate Man (though Morality were out of the Question)
can never arrive at the necessary Excellencies of a good, or useful Actor.

C H A P. VIII.

The Patentee of Drury-Lane *wiser than his Actors. His parti-*
cular Management. The Author continues to write Plays. Why.
The best dramatick Poets censur'd, by J. Collier, *in his* Short
View of the Stage. *It has a good Effect. The Master of the*
Revels, from that time, cautious, in his licensing new Plays.
A Complaint against him. His Authority founded upon Custom
only. The late Law for fixing that Authority, in a proper Per-
son, consider'd.

THOUGH the Master of our Theatre had no Conception himself of Theatrical Merit, either in Authors, or Actors; yet his Judgment was govern'd
by a saving Rule, in both: He look'd into his Receipts for the Value of a Play, and from common
Fame he judg'd of his Actors. But by whatever Rule he was
govern'd, while he had prudently reserv'd to himself a Power of
20   not paying them more than their Merit could get, he could not
be much deceiv'd by their being over, or under-valued. In a

16. *Funeral* or *Grief Alamode*] *The Funeral; Or, Grief A-la-mode* by Richard Steele, first performed c. December 1701.

22. above Fifteen Years Service] Cibber is speaking of the duration of Rich's control: from December 1693 until 1707.

32. some dy'd ... equal number ... were alive] His children living in 1733 were Charlotte, Theophilus, Anne, Elizabeth, and Catharine; his plays being performed regularly in 1733 were *Richard III, Love Makes a Man, She Would and She Would Not, The Careless Husband, The Double Gallant, Hob, or the Country Wake* [disputed], *The Provok'd Husband, Damon and Phillida, Love's Last Shift;* Scouten, throughout volumes I, II, lists the performances of these plays at this period and later.

Word, he had, with great Skill, inverted the Constitution of the
Stage, and quite chang'd the Channel of Profits arising from it:
Formerly (when there was but one Company) the Proprietors
punctually paid the Actors, their appointed Sallaries, and took to
themselves only the clear Profits: But our wiser Proprietor, took
first out of every Day's Receipts, Two Shillings in the Pound to
himself; and left their Sallaries to be paid, only, as the less, or
greater Deficiencies of Acting (according to his own Accounts)
would permit. What seem'd most extraordinary in these Mea-
10   sures, was, that at the same time, he had persuaded us to be
contented with our Condition, upon his assuring us, That as fast
as Mony would come in, we should all be paid our Arrears:
And, that we might not have it always in our Power to say he
had never intended it keep his Word; I remember, in a few
Years after this Time, he once paid us Nine Days, in one Week:
This happen'd, when the *Funeral,* or *Grief Alamode* was first
acted, with more than expected Success. Whether this well-tim'd
Bounty was only allow'd us, to save Appearances, I will not say;
but if that was his real Motive for it, it was too costly a Frolick
20   to be repeated, and was at least, the only Grimace of its Kind he
vouchsafed us; we never having received one Day more of those
Arrears in above Fifteen Years Service.

While the Actors were in this Condition, I think I may very
well be excus'd, in my presuming to write Plays; which I was
forc'd to do, for the Support of my increasing Family, my precarious Income, as an Actor, being then too scanty, to supply it,
with even the Necessaries of Life.

It may be observable too, that my Muse, and my Spouse, were
equally prolifick; that the one was seldom the Mother of a Child,
30   but, in the same Year, the other made me the Father of a Play:
I think we had about a Dozen of each sort between us; of both
which Kinds, some dy'd in their Infancy, and near an equal
number of each were alive, when I quitted the Theatre. But it
is no wonder, when a Muse is only call'd upon, by Family-Duty,

7. so bad was my Second] *Woman's Wit:* or *The Lady in Fashion*, performed c. January 1697 (Van Lennep, p. 472).

9. Two Volumes ... publish'd in *Quarto*] They contain *Love's Last Shift, Richard III, Love Makes a Man, She Would and She Would Not, The Careless Husband, The Lady's Last Stake, The Rival Fools, Ximena, The Non-Juror,* and *The Refusal.* He published these by subscription, which Davies (*Dram. Misc.,* III, 507) says "produced him a considerable sum of money."

25. *prodesse,* as *delectare*] Horace, *Ars Poetica,* 333: "Aut prodesse volunt aut delectare poetae"; "Poets wish either to profit or to please."

26. *Utile dulci*] Horace, *Ars Poetica,* 343: "Omne tulit punctum qui miscuit utile dulci'; "He has gained every vote who has mixed the instructive with the agreeable.

she should not always rejoice, in the Fruit of her Labour. To
this Necessity of Writing, then, I attribute the Defects of my second Play, which coming out too hastily, the Year after my first,
turn'd to very little Account. But having got as much, by my
First, as I ought to have expected, from the Success of them
Both, I had no great Reason to complain: Not but, I confess,
so bad was my Second, that I do not chuse to tell you the Name
of it; and, that it might be peaceably forgotten, I have not given
it a Place, in the Two Volumes of those I publish'd in *Quarto,*
in the Year 1721. And whenever I took upon me, to make
some dormant Play of an old Author, to the best of my Judgment, fitter for the Stage, it was, honestly, not to be idle, that
set me to work; as a good Housewife will mend old Linnen,
when she has not better Employment. But when I was more
warmly engag'd, by a Subject entirely new, I only thought it a
good Subject, when it seem'd worthy of an abler Pen, than my
own, and might prove as useful to the Hearer, as profitable, to
myself: Therefore, whatever any of my Productions, might want
of Skill, Learning, Wit, or Humour; or however unqualify'd I
might be, to instruct others, who so ill govern'd my self: Yet such
Plays (entirely my own) were not wanting, at least, in what our
most admired Writers seem'd to neglect, and without which, I
cannot allow the most taking Play, to be intrinsically Good, or
to be a Work, upon which a Man of Sense and Probity should
value himself: I mean, when they do not, as well *prodesse,* as *de-*
lectare, give Profit, with Delight. The *Utile dulci* was, of old,
equally the Point; and has always been my Aim, however wide
of the Mark, I may have shot my Arrow. It has often given
me Amazement, that our best Authors of that Time, could
think the Wit, and Spirit of their Scenes, could be an Excuse
for making the Looseness of them publick. The many Instances
of their Talents so abus'd, are too glaring, to need a closer Comment, and are sometimes too gross to be recited. If then, to
have avoided this Imputation, or rather to have had the Interest,

persons began to prefer the more sheltered boxes. The gallery above, like the pit, was occupied by the lesser sort:

> ... methinks some Vizard Masque I see,
> Cast out her lure from the mid Gallery:
> About her all the flutt'ring Sparks are rang'd;

> (Dryden, "Epilogue," 11-13, ed. Gardner, p. 131)

Footmen occupied the upper gallery when there was one.

17. it [wearing Masks] had been abolish'd] Davies (*Dram. Misc.*, III, 388-89) states that the disturbances caused by masked prostitutes began to discourage attendance: "at length, after this nuisance had been endured for near forty years, an accidental dispute, concerning one Mrs. Fawkes, which ended in a duel, produced an entire prohibition of women's wearing masks in the playhouse (I suppose, by order of the Lord Chamberlain) about the 5th of Queen Anne." Nicoll (I, 14, n.) cites an edict to the same effect in 1704.

20. The *London Cuckolds*] *The London Cuckolds* by Edward Ravenscroft, first performed in November 1681; there are records of its being performed before royalty 22 November 1681, again on 22 November 1682, with the Queen and maids of honor present, and again on 14 December 1682 (cf. Nicoll, I, 349).

25. *Pilgrim*] The first twenty-four lines of the Epilogue to Fletcher's *The Pilgrim*. The "Parson" is Jeremy Collier; 'Miss' had come to mean 'prostitute.'

3.   Libertines ... these grave Laws] These opinions are commonplaces on the morality of the theaters and were in the air before and long after Jeremy Collier's attacks on the stage. Cibber later discusses the role of Richard Steele in the reform of the theater (see Loftis, *Steele*, Part I, for this; for a complete account see Krutch, *Comedy and Conscience*; Sister Rose Anthony, *The Jeremy Collier Controversy*). The importance of *Love's Last Shift* in the turn toward sentimentalism and middle-class morality has been noted.

14.   in Masks] Pepys notes the fashion of ladies wearing masks (e.g. on June 12, 1663, at a performance of *The Committee* by Sir Robert Howard): "when the House began to fill ... [Lady Mary Cromwell] put on her vizard, and so kept it on all the play; which is of late become a great fashion among the ladies, which hides their whole face." Later the wearing of a mask became the sign of a prostitute and the name "vizard mask" a euphemism.

15.   the Pit, the Side-Boxes, and Gallery] The pit, in the Restoration theater, was by custom separated into two categories of audience: those who came to the theater to hear and see the play occupied the middle portion:

> Here's good accomodation in the Pit;
> The Grave demurely in the midst may Sit.
> And so the hot Burgundian on the Side
> Ply Vizard Masque, and o're the Benches stride:
> Here are convenient upper Boxes too,
> For those that make the most triumphant show,
> All that Keep Coaches must not Sit below.
> There Gallants, You betwixt the Acts retire,
> And at dull Plays have something to admire ...

> (Dryden, *Prologue for The Women*, when They Acted at the Old Theatre in Lincoln's Inn Fields, 11-19, ed. Gardner, p. 41)

In "Fop's Corner," probably near the edge of the proscenium, the gallants and rowdies sat to criticize and jeer, applaud or fight (there were a number of quarrels which ended in serious injuries or death for the contestants, Hotson, pp. 304-306). Although at first every sort sat there, beginning in the late 1660's higher ranking

and Honour of Virtue, always in view, can give Merit, to a
Play; I am contented, that my Readers should think such Merit,
the All, that mine have to boast of. Libertiness, of mere Wit,
and Pleasure, may laugh at these grave Laws, that would limit a
lively Genius; but every sensible honest Man, conscious of their
Truth, and Use, will give these Ralliers Smile for Smile, and
shew a due Contempt, for their Merriment.

   But while our Authors took these extraordinary Liberties with
their Wit, I remember, the Ladies were then observ'd, to be de-
10 cently afraid of venturing bare-fac'd to a new Comedy, 'till they
had been assur'd they might do it, without the Risque of an Insult, to their Modesty; or, if their Curiosity were too strong, for
their Patience, they took care, at least, to save Appearances, and
rarely came upon the first Days of Acting, but in Masks (then
daily worn, and admitted, in the Pit, the Side-Boxes, and Gallery)
which Custom, however, had so many ill Consequences attending
it, that it has been abolish'd these many Years.

   These Immoralities of the Stage, had, by an avow'd Indulgence, been creeping into it, ever since King *Charles* his Time:
20 Nothing that was loose, could then be too low for it: The *London Cuckolds*, the most rank Play that ever succeeded, was then in
the highest Court-Favour. In this almost general Corruption,
Dryden, whose Plays were more fam'd for their Wit, than their
Chastity, led the way, which he fairly confesses, and endeavours
to excuse in his Epilogue to the *Pilgrim*, reviv'd in 1700, for his
Benefit, in his declining Age, and Fortune. The following Lines
of it, will make good my Observation.

        Perhaps the Parson stretch'd a Point too far,
        When, with our Theatres, he wag'd a War.
30   *He tells you, that this very moral Age*
        Receiv'd the first Infection from the Stage.
        But sure, a banish'd Court, with Lewdness fraught,
        The Seeds of open Vice returning brought.

24. Sir *John Vanbrugh* ... in some Favour with him] Cibber and Vanbrugh had been in association through *Love's Last Shift* and *The Relapse*. This benefit was probably given on 29 April 1700 with Dryden's *Secular Masque* added (cf. Gardner, ed., Dryden's *Prologues and Epilogues*, pp. 335-40). Dryden died on 1 May 1700.

> *Thus lodg'd (as Vice by great Example thrives)*
> *If first debauch'd the Daughters, and the Wives.*
> *London, a fruitful Soil, yet never bore*
> *So plentiful a Crop of Horns before.*
> *The Poets, who must live by Courts, or starve,*
> *Were proud, so good a Government to serve;*
> *And mixing with Buffoons, and Pimps profane,*
> *Tainted the Stage, for some small Snip of Gain:*
> *For they, like Harlots under Bawds profest,*
> *Took all th' ungodly Pains, and got the least.*
> *Thus did the thriving Malady prevail,*
> *The Court, it's Head, the Poets but the Tail.*
> *The Sin was of our Native Growth, 'tis true,*
> *The Scandal of the Sin was wholly new.*
> *Misses there were but modestly conceal'd;*
> Whitehall *the naked* Venus *first reveal'd.*
> *Where standing, as at* Cyprus, *in her Shrine,*
> *The Strumpet was ador'd with Rites Divine, &c.*

This Epilogue, and the Prologue, to the same Play, written by
Dryden, I spoke myself, which not being usually done by the same
Person, I have a mind, while I think of it, to let you know on
what Occasion they both fell to my Share, and how other
Actors were affected by it.

Sir *John Vanbrugh,* who had given some light Touches of
his Pen to the *Pilgrim,* to assist the Benefit-Day of *Dryden,* had
the Disposal of the Parts; and I being then, as an Actor, in
some Favour with him, he read the Play first, with me along,
and was pleas'd to offer me my choice of what I might like best
for myself, in it. But as the chief Characters were not (according to my Taste) the most shining, it was no great Self-denial in
me, that I desired, he would first take care of those, who were
more difficult to be pleas'd; I therefore only chose, for my self,
two short incidental Parts, that of the *Shuttering Cook,* and the

33.   after the Death of *Betterton*] Actually his retirement.

Mad Englishman; in which homely Characters, I saw more Matter for Delight, than those that might have a better Pretence to
the Amiable: And when the Play came to be acted, I was not
deceiv'd, in my Choice. Sir *John*, upon my being contented
with so little a Share in the Entertainment, gave me the Epilogue
to make up my Mess, which being written so much above the
Strain of common Authors, I confess, I was not a little pleas'd
with. And *Dryden*, upon his hearing me repeat it, to him,
made me a further Compliment of trusting me with the Pro-
10 logue. This so particular Distinction, was look'd upon, by the
Actors, as something too extraordinary. But no one was so impatiently ruffled at it, as *Wilks*, who seldom chose soft Words,
when he spoke of any thing he did not like. The most gentle
thing he said of it was, That he did not understand such Treatment; that, for his part, he look'd upon it, as an Affront to all
the rest of the Company, that there should be but One, out of
the Whole, judg'd fit to speak either a prologue, or an Epilogue.
To quiet him, I offer'd to decline either in his Favour, or both,
if it were equally easy to the Author: But he was too much con-
20 cern'd, to accept of an Offer, that had been made to another, in
preference to himself; and which he seem'd to think his best way
of resenting, was to contemn. But from that time, however, he
was resolv'd, to the best of his Power, never to let the first Offer
of a Prologue escape him: Which little Ambition, sometimes,
made him pay too dear, for his Success; the Flatness of the
many miserable Prologues, that by this means fell to his Lot,
seem'd wofully unequal, to the few good ones, he might have reason to triumph in.

I have given you this Fact, only as a Sample of those frequent
30 Rubs, and Impediments I met with, when any Step was made
to my being distinguish'd as an Actor; and from this Incident
too, you may partly see what occasion'd so many Prologues, after the Death of *Betterton*, to fall into the Hands of one Speaker:
But it is not every Successor, to a vacant Post, that brings into

1.9 further] farther 2nd ed.

29.   *View of the Stage] A Short View of the Immorality and Profaneness of the English
Stage: together with the sense of Antiquity upon this Argument,* published in 1698,
threw into focus the growing resentment against a stage tradition which, having
evolved for an exclusively aristocratic audience, continued to mock middle-class
mores while looking increasingly to that class for support. Collier, a non-juring
clergyman, had acquired some notoriety in 1696 for having attended to the scaffold
Sir John Friend and Sir William Parkyns, who had attempted to assassinate King
William (cf. below; DNB, article Jeremy Collier). Cibber, in the passage
following, allies himself with the moderate reformers led by Richard Steele.

it, the Talents equal to those of a Predecessor. To speak a good
Prologue well, is, in my Opinion, one of the hardest Parts, and
strongest Proofs of sound Elocution; of which, I confess, I never thought, that any of the several who attempted it, shew'd
themselves, by far, equal Masters to *Betterton*. *Betterton*, in the
Delivery of a good Prologue, had a natural Gravity, that gave
Strength to good Sense; a temper'd Spirit, that gave Life to Wit;
and a dry Reserve, in his Smile, that threw Ridicule into its
brightest Colours; of these Qualities, in the speaking of a Pro-
10 logue, *Booth* only had the first, but attain'd not to the other two:
Wilks had Spirit, but gave too loose a Rein to it, and it was sel-
dom he could speak a grave and weighty Verse, harmoniously:
His Accents were frequently too sharp, and violent, which sometimes occasion'd his eagerly cutting off half the Sound of Sylla-
bles, that ought to have been gently melted into the Melody of
Metre. In Verses of Humour too, he would sometimes carry the
Mimickry farther than the Hint would bear, even to a trifling
Light, as if himself were pleas'd to see it so glittering. In the
Truth of this Criticism, I have been confirm'd by those, whose
20 Judgment I dare more confidently rely on, than my own. *Wilks*
had many Excellencies; but if we leave Prologue-speaking out
of the Number, he will still have enough to have made him a
valuable Actor. And I only make this Exception from them, to
caution others from imitating, what, in his Time, they might
have too implicitly admired. But I have a Word or two more to
say concerning the Immoralities of the Stage. Our Theatrical
Writers were not only accus'd of Immorality, but Prophaneness;
many flagrant Instances of which were collected, and publish'd
by a Non-juring Clergyman, *Jeremy Collier,* in his *View of the*
30 *Stage, &c.* about the Year 1697. However just his Charge
against the Authors, that then wrote for it, might be, I cannot
but think his Sentence, against the Stage itself, is unequal; Reformation, he thinks, too mild a Treatment for it, and is therefore for laying his Ax to the Root of it. If this were to be a

2. Pulpit … seditious and corrupted Teacher] The non-juring clergy.

14. *Old Batchelor*] Congreve's reply to Collier, *Amendments of Mr. Collier's false and imperfect Citations, etc. from the Old Batchelor, Double Dealer. By the Author of those plays* (1698), is characterized by Davies (*Dram. Misc.*, III, 401) as containing "some wit, a good deal of learning, many unwilling concessions, and no small share of disingenuity. Congreve's pride was hurt by Collier's attack on plays which all the world had admired and commended; and no hypocrite showed more rancor and resentment, when unmasked, than this author, so greatly celebrated for sweetness of temper and elegance of manners." Vanbrugh's defense was *A Short Vindication of the Relapse and the Provok'd Wife from immorality and profaneness* by the author (1698). These were not the last words of Collier or the two dramatists.

19. My first Play] Davies gives Cibber credit (*Dram. Misc.*, III, 436) for producing "the first comedy, acted since the Restoration, in which were preserved purity of manners and decency of language …"

32. a very wholesom Effect, upon those, who write after this Time] Collier's attack served as a point of reference for future critics of the theater (cf. Loftis, *Steele*, pp. 13 ff.). Nicoll (II, 125) contradicts the claim that the attack immediately brought on the reformation (see also J. W. Krutch, "Government Attempts to Regulate the Stage after the Jeremy Collier Controversy," *PMLA*, XXXVIII, March, 1923, 153-74; and *Comedy and Conscience after the Restoration*, pp. 166-91).

Rule of Judgment, for Offences of the same Nature, what might
become the Pulpit, where many a seditious and corrupted
Teacher, has been known, to cover the most pernicious Doctrine
with the Mask of Religion? This puts me in mind of what the
noted *Jo.Hains,* the Comedian, a Fellow of a wicked Wit, said
upon this Occasion; who being ask'd, What could transport
Mr. *Collier* into so blind a Zeal, for a general Suppression of the
Stage, when only some particular Authors had abus'd it; whereas the Stage, he could not but know, was generally allow'd,
when rightly conducted, to be a delightful Method of mending
our Morals? *For that Reason,* (reply'd *Hains:*) Collier *is, by
Profession, a Moral-mender himself, and two of Trade, you know,
can never agree.*

The Authors of the *Old Batchelor,* and of the *Relapse,* were
those, whom *Collier* most labour'd to convict of Immorality; to
which they severally publish'd their Reply. The first seem'd too
much hurt, to be able to defend himself; and the other felt him
so little, that his Wit only laugh'd at his Lashes.

My first Play, of the *Fool in Fashion,* too, being then in a
course of Success; perhaps for that Reason, only, this severe Author thought himself oblig'd to attack it; in which, I hope, he
has shewn more Zeal, than Justice. His greatest Charge against
it is, That is sometimes uses the Word, *Faith!* as an Oath, in
the Dialogue: But if *Faith* may as well signify our given Word,
or Credit, as our Religious Belief, why might not his Charity have
taken it, in the less criminal Sense? Nevertheless, Mr. *Collier's*
Book, was, upon the whole, thought so laudable a Work, that
King *William,* soon after it was publish'd, granted him a *Nolo
prosequi,* when he stood answerable to the Law, for his having
absolv'd two Criminals, just before they were executed for High-
Treason. And it must be farther granted, that his calling our
Dramatick Writers to this strict Account, had a very wholesome
Effect, upon those, who writ after this Time. They were, now,
a great deal more upon their Guard; Indecencies were no longer

3. Master of the Revels] An office under the Lord Chamberlain held by Charles Killigrew (1655-1725) from 1680 until his death (*DNB*). The first act of *Richard III* in Cibber's version (1700) contains the murder of *Henry VI* from the last play of Shakespeare's Henry VI cycle: he was unable to perform the whole until 1710 (there is a possibility that it was played entire in April 1704: see Barker, pp. 34-39).

32. The Patent granted ... to Sir *Richard Steele*] This interpretation of the rights accompanying the patent was allowed to prevail only as long as the Duke of Shrewsbury, whom the managers also defied, was Lord Chamberlain; after the Duke of Newcastle succeeded to that post (13 April 1717) the dispute became bitter and ended with the revocation of the patent (cf. Loftis, *Steele*, pp. 39 ff. and pp. 124 ff.).

Wit; and, by degrees, the Fair Sex came again to fill the Boxes,
on the first Day of a new Comedy, without Fear or Censure.
But the Master of the Revels, who then, licens'd all Plays, for
the Stage, assisted this Reformation, with a more zealous Severity,
than ever. He would strike out whole Scenes of a vicious, or
immoral Character, tho' it were visibly shewn to be reform'd, or
punish'd. A severe Instance of this Kind falling upon my self,
may be an Excuse for my relating it. When *Richard the Third*
(as I alter'd it from *Shakespear*) came from his Hands, to the
10 Stage, he expung'd the whole First Act, without sparing a Line
of it. This extraordinary Stroke of a *Sic volo*, occasioned my
applying to him, for the small Indulgence of a Speech, or two,
that the other four Acts might limp on, with a little less Absurdity. No, he had not Leisure to consider what might be separately inoffensive. He had an Objection to the whole Act, and
the Reason he gave for it was, that the Distresses of King *Henry
the Sixth,* who is kill'd by *Richard* in the first Act, would put
weak People too much in mind of King *James*, then living in
France; a notable Proof of his Zeal for the Government! Those
20 who have read, either the Play, or the History, I dare say, will
think he strain'd hard for the Parallel. In a word, we were forc'd,
for some few Years, to let the Play take its Fate, with only four
Acts divided into five; by the Loss of so considerable a Limb,
may one not modestly suppose, it was robb'd of, at least, a fifth
part of that Favour, it afterwards met with? For tho' this first
Act was at last recovered, and made the Play whole agen; yet
the Relief came too late, to repay me for the Pains I had taken
in it. Nor did I ever hear that this zealous Severity of the
Master of the Revels, was afterwards thought justifiable. But my
30 Good-fortune, in process of Time, gave me an Opportunity to
talk with my Oppressor, in my Turn.

  The Patent granted by his late majesty, King *George I.* to
Sir *Richard Steele,* and his Assigns, of which I was one, made
us sole Judges of what Plays might be proper for the Stage,

1.32 his late Majesty] his Majesty 2nd ed.
1.32 King <u>George</u> I.] King <u>George</u> the First 2nd ed.

24.   the Law lately pass'd] The *Stage Licensing Ac*t of 1737.

34.   Theatre … erected in *Goodman's-Fields*] It was set up by Thomas Odell and opened 31 October 1729 (F. T. Wood, "Goodman's Fields Theatre," *Modern Language Review*, XXV, 1930, 443-56; Nicoll, II, 429-30).

without submitting them, to the Approbation, or License of any
other particular Person. Notwithstanding which, the Master of
the Revels demanded his Fee of Forty Shillings, upon our acting
a new One, tho' we had spar'd him the Trouble of perusing it.
This occasion'd my being deputed to him, to enquire into the
Right of his Demand, and to make an amicable End of our Dispute. I confess, I did not dislike the Office; and told him, according to my Instructions, That I came not to defend, even our
own Right, in prejudice to his; that if our Patent, had inadver-
10   tently superseded the Grant of any former Power, or Warrant,
whereon he might ground his Pretensions, we would not insist
upon our Broad Seal, but would readily answer his Demands upon
sight of such his Warrant, any thing in our Patent to the contrary
notwithstanding. This I had reason to think he could not do;
and, when I found he made no direct Reply to my Question, I
repeated it with greater Civilities, and offers of Compliance, 'till
I was forc'd in the end to conclude, with telling him, That as
his Pretensions were not back'd with any visible Instrument of
Right, and as his strongest Plea was Custom, we could not so far
20   extend our Complaisance, as to continue his Fees upon so slender
a Claim to them: And from that Time, neither our Plays,
or his Fees, gave either of us any farther trouble. In this Negotiation, I am the bolder to think Justice was on our Side, because
the Law lately pass'd, by which the Power of Licensing Plays,
&c. is given to a proper Person, is a strong Presumption, that
no Law had ever given that Power to any such Person before.

My having mentioned this Law, which so immediately affected the Stage, inclines me to throw out a few Observations upon it: But I must first lead you gradually thro' the Facts, and
30   natural Causes, that made such a Law necessary.

Although it had been taken for granted, from Time immemo-
rial, that no Company of Comedians, could act Plays, &c. without the Royal License, or Protection of some legal Authority; a
Theatre was, notwithstanding, erected in *Goodman's-Fields,*

4. Lord-Mayor ... petition'd the Crown] This was effected on 28 April 1730 (Nicoll, II, 284 and 429-30).

11. It happened that the Purchasers of the Patent] Cibber's account of these extremely complex proceedings is disingenuous (for a more accurate account, see Barker, 167 ff., and Davies, *Dram. Misc.*, III, 474). In brief, Cibber sold his share in the patent for 3,000 guineas to John Highmore and John Ellys in March 1733, Booth having already sold one-half of his to Highmore for £2500 (Lowe, I, 283, asserts the other half went to Giffard). Therefore, Theophilus Cibber was deprived of authority in the theater. He responded by organizing the actors to demand higher pay, and claiming possession of the theater (to which he held the lease). All this had no effect, so they began giving plays without a patent. (Davies accuses C. Cibber of attempting to use his prestige to obtain a patent for Theophilus, but says that the Lord Chamberlain refused when he saw the dishonesty of soliciting a second patent to devalue the one just sold.) Without players, Highmore was unable to provide satisfactory performances, so he went to court to silence the rebellious players; after a technically flawed action, he managed to have John Harper arrested just before a performance as Falstaff in *Henry IV*. When the case was tried, Harper was freed. Theophilus occupied Drury Lane, and Highmore was so entirely discredited that he sold his share of the patent to John Fleetwood in 1734 and left the theater.

about seven Years ago, where Plays, without any such License,
were acted for some time, unmolested, and with Impunity. After a Year or two, this Playhouse was thought a Nusance too near
the City: Upon which the Lord-Mayor, and Aldermen, petition'd the Crown to suppress it: What Steps were taken, in favour of that Petition, I know not, but common Fame seem'd to
allow from what had, or had not been done in it, that acting
Plays in the said Theatre was not evidently unlawful. However,
this Question of Acting without a License, a little time after,
10   came to a nearer Decision in *Westminster-Hall;* the Occasion of
bringing it thither was this: It happened that the Purchasers of
the Patent, to whom Mr. *Booth* and Myself had sold our Shares,
were at variance with the Comedians, that were then left to their
Government, and the Variance ended, in the chief of those Comedians deserting, and setting up for themselves in the little
House in the *Hay-Market,* in 1733, by which Desertion the Patentees were very much distressed, and considerable Losers. Their
Affairs being in this desperate Condition, they were advis'd, to
put the Act of the Twelfth of Queen *Anne,* against Vagabonds,
20   in force, against these Deserters, then acting in the *Hay-Market*
without License. Accordingly, one of their chief Performers was
taken from the Stage, by a Justice of Peace his Warrant, and
committed to *Bridewell* as one within Penalty of the said Act.
When the Legality of this Commitment was disputed in *Westminster-Hall,* by all I could observe, from the learned Pleadings
on both Sides (for I had the Curiosity to hear them) it did not
appear to me, that the Comedian, so committed, was within the
Description of the said Act, he being a House-keeper, and having
a Vote for the *Westminister* Members of Parliament. He was dis-
30   charged accordingly, and conducted through the Hall, with the
Congratulations of the Crowds that attended, and wish'd well to
his Cause.

     The Issue of this Trial threw me, at that time, into a very
odd Reflexion, *viz.* That if acting Plays, without License, did

27.   *Fleetwood*] Cf. p. 162, n. It was Theophilus Cibber who exacted very generous terms from Fleetwood at this point (Barker, p. 173), and led his players back into Drury Lane 12 March 1734.

3. three late Menaging Actors] Cibber, Booth, and Wilks (before 1713 Booth had been a hired actor and Dogget had been an actor-manager. See Barker, 90-96).

10. Sir *John Vanbrugh*, and Mr. *Congreve*] They were appointed to manage Lincoln's Inn Fields after Betterton's retirement in 1705. Congreve withdrew soon after (before the end of 1705 according to John C. Hodges, *William Congreve the Man: A Biography from New Sources*, New York, 1941, p. 77); but Vanbrugh first built the Haymarket Theatre; although its acoustics were poor for a legitimate stage, they proved to be effective for opera. The first performance—*The Loves of Ergasto* given by a troop of inferior Italian singers on 9 April 1705 (Downes, ed. Summers, p. 48; Avery, I, 91)—was a disastrous failure, and the fortunes of the company declined so swiftly that after three months Vanbrugh petitioned the Lord Chamberlain to unify the companies.

15. three Actors] He is speaking of himself, Wilks, and Dogget.

17. new Place, and a *Sine-cure*] Owen Swiney, whose relations with Cibber and the company are discussed below, was paid a stipend of £600 both for the use of the Haymarket theater for which he held the lease and to keep him from any active share of the management. William Collier exchanged theaters with Swiney in April 1712, and the former afterwards received a total payment of £700, leaving the management to Dogget, Wilks, and Cibber. Richard Steele later displaced Collier; this is discussed below in the *Apology*, pp. 252 ff., and by Barker, pp. 86-88.

21. Sir *Francis Wronghead*] In *The Provok'd Husband, or, A Journey to London*, by Vanbrugh and Cibber, a country squire who has come seeking a place at court, tells his nephew of introducing himself to a great man and asking a favor:

> Sir *Francis*, says my Lord, pray what Sort of place
> may you ha' turned your Thoughts upon? My Lord,
> says I, Beggars must not be Chusers; but any
> Place, says I, about a thousand a Year ...
>
> (IV, i) [Lowe]

not make the Performers Vagabonds, unless they wandered from
their Habitations so to do, how particular was the Case of Us
three late Menaging Actors, at the *Theatre-Royal*, who in twenty
Years before had paid, upon an Averidge, at least Twenty Thousand Pounds, to be protected (as Actors) from a Law, that has
not since appeared to be against us. Now, whether we might
certainly have acted without any License at all, I shall not pretend to determine; but this I have, of my own Knowledge, to
say, That in Queen *Anne's* Reign, the Stage was in such Confu-
10 sion, and its Affairs in such Distress, that Sir *John Vanbrugh,* and
Mr. *Congreve,* after they had held it about one Year, threw up
the Menagement of it, as an unprofitable Post, after which, a
License for Acting was not thought worth any Gentleman's asking for, and almost seem'd to go a begging, till some time after,
by the Care, Application, and Industry of three Actors, it
became so prosperous, and the Profits so considerable, that it created a new Place, and a *Sine-cure* of a Thousand Pounds a Year,
which the Labour of those Actors constantly paid, to such Persons
as had from time to time, Merit or Interest enough, to get their
20 Names inserted as Fourth Menagers in a License with them, for
acting Plays, &c. a Preferment, that many a Sir *Francis Wronghead* would have jump'd at. But to go on with my Story. This
Endeavour of the Patentees, to suppress the Comedians acting in
the *Hay-Market,* proving ineffectual, and no Hopes of a Re-
union then appearing, the Remains of the Company left in *Drury-
Lane,* were reduced to a very Low Condition. At this time a
third Purchaser, *Charles Fleetwood,* Esq; stept in; who judging
the best Time to buy was, when the Stock was at the lowest Price,
struck up a Bargain at once, for Five Parts in Six of the Patent;
30 and, at the same time, gave the revolted Comedians their own
Terms to return, and come under his Government in *Drury-
Lane,* where they now continue to act, at very ample Sallaries,
as I am informed, in 1738. But (as I have observ'd) the late
Cause of the prosecuted Comedian having gone so strongly in

and he thought it preferable to feed by nonsense than to starve by sense." Cibber resented them because he found himself repeatedly satirized in them, and because they were often extremely successful.

19. *Aude aliquid ... esse aliquis*] Juvenal, Satire I, 73-74: "If you want to be anybody nowadays, you must commit some crime that merits narrow Gyara or jail."

25. *Herculean* Satyrist ... *Drawcansir* in Wit] These became Fielding's pseudonyms: *Captain Hercules Vinegar* was used in *The Champion* which began publication 15 November 1739. Drawcansir was the blustering hero in *The Rehearsal*; sthe name had been applied to critics and satirists, but Fielding after Cibber's application of it to him here used 'Sir Alexander Drawcansir, Knight, Censor of Great Britain,' as his *nom de plume* for *The Covent Garden Journal*, first published 4 January 1752 (cf. Dudden, I, 886-87).

28. writing up to an Act of Parliament to demolish it] Fielding's dramatic satires, especially *Pasquin* and *The Historical Register*, no doubt led to Walpole's determination to control the theaters, but it was a lost play by an unknown author, *The Golden Rump*, which served, because of its extreme scurrility, as leverage for Walpole to force the Stage Licensing Act through Parliament. Horace Walpole believed, as Cibber evidently did, that Fielding had written the piece (*Memoirs of the Reign of King George the Second*, ed. Lord Holland, 2nd ed., London, 1847, I, 13-14 n.). The author of *TC*, in which Fielding may have had a hand, suggests that the play was written at Walpole's instigation and given to Giffard, manager by this time of Lincoln's Inn Fields. Giffard was instructed to present the piece to Walpole with a show of indignation; in return he was promised a separate patent. By this device, Walpole was furnished with a play attacking the royal family as much as himself, so that in righteous wrath he could force the Act through (*TC*, pp. 93-94; cf. Loftis, *Politics*, 139-42).

3.   a broken Wit] I.e. Fielding, a return blow for many Cibber had received, e.g. the characterization of Cibber as "Ground-Ivy" in *The Historical Register for 1736*.

3.   collect a fourth company] There were five companies acting in London in 1729 when Fielding presented himself as a dramatist (cf. *Apology*, p. 165): 1) Drury Lane, 2) The Haymarket for opera, directed by Heidegger and Handel, 3) the redecorated theater in Lincoln's Inn Fields which was still managed by John Rich, son of Christopher, where the specialty was pantomime, light musical entertainments and much overshadowed orthodox plays, 4) the Little Theatre in the Haymarket opened in 1726 by French comedians, and hence known as the French House, where farce, vaudeville, and burlesque were given, 5) the theater in Goodman's Fields managed by Henry Giffard (cf. Nicoll, II, 271-72, 429-30; and Dudden, I, 33-38). Fielding's first play to be presented after *Love in Several Masques* (Drury Lane, 16 February 1728) was *The Temple Beau* at Goodman's Fields, 26 January 1730, which Cibber had insultingly refused. In the period following he wrote prolifically but seems to have had nothing to do with organizing a company, until the winter of 1735, when, unable to get *Pasquin* produced by John Rich in his new theater in Covent Garden, he took the Little Theatre in the Haymarket and organized 'The Great Mogul's Company of English Comedians'; under these circumstances he took up the thread of political satire on 5 March 1736 with a production of *Pasquin* (Dudden, I, 46 ff. and 170).

4.   acted Plays in the *Hay-Market*] When *The Author's Farce; and the Pleasures of the Town* was complete, Goodman's Fields was involved in the difficulties mentioned on p. 162, so Fielding gave it to the Little, or French, Theatre in the Haymarket, not, as Cibber supposed, the Vanbrugh building occupied by the opera. It was first performed 30 March 1730 (Dudden, I, 49).

10.   Pieces of an extraordinary Kind] These were extravagant, broad, satirical plays; according to Dudden (I, 49), "As an artist ... he had little admiration for these flimsy performances; but he was an impecunious author, struggling to earn a living,

his Favour, and the House in *Goodman's-Fields* too, continuing
to act with as little Authority, unmolested; these so tollerated
companies gave Encouragement to a broken Wit, to collect a
fourth Company, who, for some time acted Plays in the *Hay-
Market,* which House the united *Drury-Lane* Comedians had
lately quitted: This enterprising Person, I say (whom I do not
chuse to name, unless it could be to his Advantage, or that it
were of Importance) had Sense enough to know, that the best
Plays, with bad Actors, would turn but to a very poor Account;
10 and therefore found it necessary to give the Publick some Pieces
of an extraordinary Kind, the Poetry of which he conceiv'd
ought to be so strong, that the greatest Dunce of an Actor could
not spoil it: He knew too, that as he was in haste to get Mony,
it would take up less Time to be intrepidly abusive, than decently entertaining; that, to draw the Mob after him, he must
rake the Channel, and pelt their Superiors; that, to shew himself somebody, he must come up to *Juvenal's* Advice, and stand
the Consequence:

    Aude aliquid brevibus Gyaris, et carcere dignum
20   *Si vis esse aliquis ----*   Juv.Sat.I.

Such then, was the mettlesome Modesty he set out with; upon
this Principle he produc'd several frank, and free Farces, that
seem'd to knock all Distinctions of Mankind on the Head: Religion, Laws, Government, Priests, Judges, and Ministers, were
all laid flat, at the Feet of this *Herculean* Satyrist! This *Drawcansir* in Wit, that spared neither Friend nor Foe! who, to make
his Poetical Fame immortal, like another *Erostratus,* set Fire to
his Stage, by writing up to an Act of Parliament to demolish it.
I shall not give the particular Strokes of his Ingenuity a Chance
30 to be remembred, by reciting them; it may be enough to say, in
general Terms, they were so openly flagrant, that the Wisdom of
the Legislature thought it high time, to take a proper Notice of
them.

1. 13 get Mony] get Money 2nd ed.

10.   uncommon Eloquence was employ'd against it] The Earl of Chesterfield was an
        important opponent of the Act (Loftis, *Politics*, pp. 143 ff.). For a discussion of
        the Act, see Loftis, *ibid.*, pp. 128 ff.; and Dudden, I, 189 ff. Loftis maintains that
        Cibber's defense of the Act (below), in spite of his bias, places the law more firmly
        in its historical context than any other contemporary defense. Whereas Chesterfield
        (and Samuel Johnson later in his ironic *Complete Vindication of the Licensers of
        the Stage in 1739*) merely defended 'liberty' as a principle in isolation, Cibber
        argues with an eye focused on the theater's actual history. Loftis concludes,
        however, that in general the Act was extremely damaging to the English drama.

16.   to an Attack, upon the Liberty of the Press] In addition to Johnson and
        Chesterfield, the poet James Thomson attacked it as such in a preface to an edition
        of the *Areopagitica* (January 1738).

30.   *Collier*, in his *Defense*] *A Defense of the Short View of the profaneness and
        immorality of the English Stage, etc. Being a reply to Mr. Congreve's
        Amendments, etc. and to the Vindication of the author of the Relapse*, by Jeremy
        Collier, M.A. (London, Keble, 1699).

Having now shewn, by what means there came to be four
Theatres, besides a fifth for Operas, in *London*, all open at the
same time, and that while they were so numerous, it was evident some of them must have starv'd, unless they fed upon the
Trash and Filth of Buffoonery, and Licentiousness; I now
come, as I promis'd, to speak of that necessary Law, which
has reduced their Number, and prevents the Repetition of
such Abuses, in those that remain open, for the Publick Recreation.

10   While this Law was in Debate, a lively Spirit, and uncommon Eloquence was employ'd against it. It was urg'd, That
one of the greatest Goods we can enjoy, is *Liberty*. (This we
may grant to be an incontestable Truth, without its being the
least Objection to this Law.) it was said too, That to bring
the Stage under the Restraint of a Licenser, was leading the
way to an Attack, upon the Liberty of the Press. This a-
mounts but to a Jealousy at best, which I hope, and believe
all honest *Englishmen* have as much Reason to think a groundless, as to fear, it is a just Jealousy: For the Stage, and the
20   Press, I shall endeavour to shew, are very different Weapons
to wound with. If a great Man could be no more injured, by
being personally ridicul'd, or made contemptible, in a Play, than
by the same Matter only printed, and read against him, in a
Pamphlet, or the strongest Verse; then indeed the Stage, and
the Press might pretend, to be upon an equal Foot of Liberty:
But when the wide Difference between these two Liberties
comes to be explain'd, and consider'd, I dare say we shall
find the Injuries from one, capable of being ten times more
severe, and formidable, than from the other: Let us see, at
30   least, if the Case will not be vastly alter'd. Read what Mr. *Collier,* in his *Defence* of his *Short View of the Stage &c.* Page 25,
says to this Point; he sets this Difference, in a clear Light. These
are his Words:

7. *Segnius ... fidelibus*] Horace, *Ars Poetica*, 180-81: "Things which enter through the ear stir up the feelings more slowly than those which are submitted to the faithful eyes."

11. The Life of an Actor] Up to this point Cibber's quotation is largely accurate—though he omits several articles—but in this passage his change is tendentious: Collier, p. 26, says "The Life of the *Action* [italics mine] fortifies the Object."

17. is often made one for his Life] Collier, p. 26, "made one for his Lifetime."

"The Satyr of a Comedian, and another Poet have a different
"effect upon Reputation: A Character of Disadvantage, upon
"the Stage, makes a stronger Impression, than elsewhere: Read-
"ing is but Hearing at second-hand; now Hearing, at best, is
"a more languid Conveyance, than Sight. For as *Horace* ob-
"serves,

> *Segnius irritant animum, demissa per aurem,*
> *Quam quae sunt oculis subjecta fidelibus.*

"The Eye is much more affecting, and strikes deeper into the
10 "Memory, than the Ear: Besides, upon the Stage, both the
"Senses are in Conjunction. The Life of the Actor fortifies the
"Object, and awakens the Mind to take hold of it--- Thus a
"dramatic Abuse is rivetted, in the Audience; a Jest is im-
"prov'd into Argument, and Rallying grows up into Reason:
"Thus a Character of Scandal becomes almost indelible; a Man
"goes for a Blockhead, upon *Content*, and he that is made a
"Fool in a Play, is often made one for his Life. 'Tis true, he
"passes for such only among the prejudic'd, and unthinking;
"but these are no inconsiderable Division of Mankind. For these
20 "Reasons, I humbly conceive, the Stage stands in need of a great
"deal of Discipline, and Restraint: To give them an unlimited
"Range, is in effect to make them Masters of all moral Di-
"stinctions, and to lay Honour and Religion, at their Mercy.
"To shew Greatness ridiculous, is the way to lose the Use, and
"abate the Value of the Quality. Things made little in jest,
"will soon be so in earnest; for Laughing, and Esteem, are sel-
"dom bestow'd on the same Object."

If this was Truth, and Reason (as sure it was) forty Years ago;
will it not carry the same Conviction with it to these Days, when
30 there came to be a much stronger Call for a Reformation of the
Stage, than when this Author wrote against it, or perhaps than
was ever known, since the *English* Stage had a Being? And
now let us ask another Question! Does not the general Opinion

6. Wound that Guiscard gave to the late Lord Oxford] On 8 March 1711 Robert
   Harley (1661-1724), afterwards Earl of Oxford and Mortimer, was stabbed with a
   penknife by the Abbe de la Bourlie, known as the Marquis de Guiscard, who was
   under investigation by a committee of the House of Lords for treasonable
   correspondence with the French (Plumb, I, 170; *DNB* article Robert Harley).

8. later Minister] A reference to Walpole and opposition attacks; Cibber felt Fielding's
   and other opposition attacks on Walpole keenly, not only because he was associated
   as Poet Laureate with the court party, but also because the commonplace analogy
   between court and stage meant that he, as 'the master of a playhouse' (as in
   Eurydice Hiss'd, 1737) became the overt object of their thrusts. Often the Laureate
   and later Theophilus (as in *The Historical Register*) also stood for Walpole (Loftis,
   Politics, p. 135). The "Harlequin" mentioned below appears in *Pasquin* (March
   1736).

of Mankind suppose, that the Honour, and Reputation of a Minister is, or ought to be, as dear to him, as his Life? Yet when
the Law, in Queen *Anne's* Time, had made even an unsuccessful Attempt upon the Life of a Minister, capital, could any
Reason be found, that the Fame, and Honour of his Character
should not be under equal Protection? Was the Wound that
Guiscard gave to the late Lord *Oxford,* when a Minister, a greater
Injury, than the Theatrical Insult which was offer'd to a later
Minister, in a more valuable Part, his Character? Was it not as
10   high time, then, to take this dangerous Weapon of mimical Insolence, and Defamation out of the Hands of a mad Poet, as to
wrest the Knife from the lifted Hand of a Murderer? And is
not that Law of a milder Nature, which *prevents* a Crime, than
that which *punishes* it, after it is committed? May not one think
it amazing, that the Liberty of defaming lawful Power and Dignity, should have been so eloquently contended for? or especially that this Liberty ought to triumph in a Theatre, where the
most able, the most innocent, and most upright Person, must
himself be, while the Wound is given, defenceless? How long
20   must a Man so injur'd, lie bleeding, before the Pain and Anguish
of his Fame (if it suffers wrongfully) can be dispell'd? or say, he
has deserv'd Reproof, and publick Accusation, yet the Weight
and Greatness of his Office, never can deserve it from a publick
Stage, where the lowest Malice by sawcy Parallels, and abusive
Inuendoes, may do every thing but name him: But alas! Liberty is so tender, so chaste a Virgin, that, it seems, not to suffer
her to do irreparable Injuries, with Impunity, is a Violation of
her! It cannot sure be a principle of Liberty, that would turn
the Stage into a Court of Enquiry, that would let the partial
30   Applauses of a vulgar Audience give Sentence upon the Conduct
of Authority, and put Impeachments into the Mouth of a *Har-*
lequin? Will not every impartial Man think, that Malice, Envy,
Faction, or Mis-rule, might have too much Advantage over lawful Power, if the Range of such a Stage-liberty were unlimit-

1.   26   not to suffer] not suffer 1st ed.
1.   33   or Mis-rule] and Mis-rule 2nd ed.

ed, and insisted on to be enroll'd among the glorious Rights of
an *English* Subject?

I remember much such another ancient Liberty, which many
of the good People of *England* were once extreamly fond of; I
mean that of throwing Squibs, and crackers, at all Spectators
without distinction, upon a Lord-Mayor's Day; but about forty
Years ago a certain Nobleman happening to have one of his
Eyes burnt out by this mischievous Merriment, it occasion'd a
penal Law, to prevent those Sorts of Jests, from being laugh'd
10 at for the future: Yet I have never heard, that the most zealous
Patriot ever thought such a Law was the least Restraint upon
our Liberty.

If I am ask'd, why I am so voluntary a Champion for the
Honour of this Law, that has limited the Number of Play-
Houses, and which now can no longer concern me, as a Proses-
sor of the Stage? I reply, that it being a Law, so nearly relating to the Theatre, it seems not at all foreign to my History,
to have taken notice of it; and as I have farther promis'd, to
give the Publick a true Portrait of my Mind, I ought fairly to
20 let them see how far I am, or am not a Blockhead, when I pretend to talk of serious Matters, that may be judg'd so far above
my Capacity: Nor will it in the least discompose me, whether
my Observations are contemn'd, or applauded. A Blockhead is
not always an unhappy Fellow, and if the World will not flatter
us, we can flatter our selves; perhaps too it will be as difficult
to convince us, we are in the wrong, as that you wiser Gentlemen are one Tittle the better for you Knowledge. It is yet a
Question, with me, whether we weak Heads have not as much
Pleasure too, in giving our shallow Reason a little Exercise, as
30 those clearer Brains have, that are allow'd to dive into the deepest
Doubts and Mysteries; to reflect, or form a Judgment upon remarkable things *past*, is as delightful to me, as it is to the gravest Politician to penetrate into what is *present,* or to enter, into
Speculations upon what is, or is not likely to come. Why are

6.   *this Restraint upon the Stage*] This is Cibber's paraphrase of a line of argument in Chesterfield's speech against the Act. (For the speech see M. Maty, ed., *Chesterfield's Miscellanious Works*, 1777, ii, 229-41).

Histories written, if all Men are not to judge of them? Therefore, if my Reader has no more to do, than I have, I have a
Chance for his being as willing to have a little more upon the
same Subject, as I am to give it him.

  When direct Arguments against this Bill were found too weak,
Recourse was had to dissuasive ones: It was said, that *this Restraint upon the Stage, would not remedy the Evil complain'd of:
That a Play refus'd to be licens'd, would still be printed, with
double Advantage, when it should be insinuated, that it was re-
10 fus'd, for some Strokes of Wit, &c. and would be more likely,
then, to have its Effect, among the People.* However natural this
Consequence may seem, I doubt it will be very difficult, to give
a *printed* Satyr, or Libel, half the Force, or Credit of an *acted*
one. The most artful, or notorious Lye, or strain'd Allusion
that ever slander'd a great Man, may be read, by some People,
with a Smile of Contempt, or at worst, it can impose but on
one Person, at once: But when the Words of the same plausible Stuff, shall be repeated on a Theatre, the Wit of it among
a Crowd of Hearers, is liable to be over-valu'd, and may unite,
20 and warm a whole Body of the Malicious, or Ignorant, into a
Plaudit; nay, the partial Claps of only *twenty* ill-minded Persons, among several hundreds of silent Hearers, shall, and often
have been, mistaken for a general Approbation, and frequently
draw into their Party the Indifferent, or Inapprehensive, who
rather, than be thought not to understand the Conceit, will
laugh, with the Laughers, and join in the Triumph! But alas!
the *quiet* Reader of the same ingenious Matter, can only like
for *himself*; and the Poison has a much slower Operation, upon
the Body of a People, when it is so retail'd out, than when sold
30 to a full Audience by wholesale. The *single* Reader too may
happen to be a sensible, or unprejudic'd Person; and then the
merry Dose meeting with the Antidote of a sound Judgment,
perhaps may have no Operation at all: With such a one, the
Wit of the most ingenious Satyr, will only, by its intrinsick

Truth, or Value, gain upon his Approbation; or if it be worth
an Answer, a printed Falshood, may possibly be confounded by
printed Proofs against it. But against Contempt, and Scandal
heighten'd, and colour'd by the Skill of an *Actor*, ludicrously
infusing it into a Multitude, there is no immediate Defence to
be made, or equal Reparation to be had for it; for it would
be but a poor Satisfaction, at last, after lying long patient, under
the Injury, that Time only is to shew (which would probably
be the Case) that the Author of it was a desperate Indigent, that

10   did it for Bread. How much less dangerous, or offensive, then,
is the *written*, than the *acted* Scandal? The Impression the Comedian gives to it, is a kind of double Stamp upon the Poet's
Paper, that raises it to ten times the intrinsick Value. Might
we not strengthen this Argument too, even by the Eloquence,
that seem'd to have oppos'd this Law?   I will say for my self, at
least, that when I came to read the printed Arguments against
it, I could scarce believe they were the same, that had amaz'd,
and rais'd such Admiration, in me, when they had the Advantage of a lively Elocution, and of that Grace and Spirit, which

20   gave Strength and Lustre to them, in the Delivery!

Upon the whole; if the Stage ought ever to have been reform'd; if to place a Power *somewhere* of restraining its Immoralities, was not inconsistent, with the Liberties of a civiliz'd
People (neither of which, sure any moral Man of Sense can dispute) might it not have shewn a Spirit too poorly prejudic'd,
to have rejected so rational a Law, only because, the Honour,
and Office of a Minister might happen, in some small Measure,
to be protected by it.

But however little Weight there may be, in the Observations
30   I have made upon it, I shall for my own Part always think
them just; unless I should live to see (which I do not expect)
some future Set of upright Ministers use their utmost Endeavours to repeal it.

3. so many could honestly subsist, on what was fit to be seen] The closing of all
    unlicensed theaters meant, not finer quality of theatrical entertainment, but
    narrowing of opportunity for new plays to be produced. The patentees exploited
    their monopolies for money, and one of them, John Rich of Covent Garden, was
    interested only in pantomime. In general the Act had an effect contrary to Cibber's
    hope. Since the law's ruinous effects should have been evident to him by the time
    of the writing of the *Apology*, his reasoning again seems disingenuous (see Loftis,
    Politics, pp. 151-53).

And now, we have seen the Consequence of what many People are apt to contend for, Variety of Play-houses! How was it
possible so many could honestly subsist, on what was fit to be
seen? Their extraordinary Number, of Course, reduc'd them to
live upon the Gratification of such Hearers, as they knew would
be best pleas'd with public Offence; and public Offence, of
what kind soever, will always be a good Reason for making
Laws, to restrain it.

     To conclude, let us now consider this Law, in a quite dif-
ferent Light; let us leave the political Part of it quite out of
the Question; what Advantage could either the Spectators of
Plays, or the Masters of Play-houses have gain'd, by its having
never been made? How could the same Stock of Plays supply
four Theatres, which (without such additional Entertainments,
as a Nation of common Sense ought to be asham'd of) could
not well support two? Satiety must have been the natural Consequence, of the same Plays being twice as often repeated, as
now they need be; and Satiety puts an end to all Tastes, that
the Mind of Man can delight in. Had therefore, this Law been
made seven Years ago, I should not have parted with my Share
in the Patent, under a thousand Pounds more, than I receiv'd
for it— So that as far as I am able to judge, both the Public,
as Spectators, and the Patentees, as Undertakers, are, or might
be, in a way of being better entertain'd, and more considerable
Gainers by it.

     I now return to the State of the Stage, where I left it, about
the Year 1697, from whence this Pursuit of its Immoralities,
has led me farther, than I first design'd to have follow'd it.

C H A P. IX.

A small Apology, for writing on. The different State of the two
Companies. Wilks *invited over from* Dublin. Estcourt, *from*
the same Stage, the Winter following. Mrs. Oldfield's *first*
Admission to the Theatre-Royal. *Her Character. The Great*
Theatre in the Hay-Market *built, for* Betterton's *Company. It*
answers not their Expectation. Some Observations upon it.
A Theatrical State Secret.

I NOW begin to doubt, that the *Gayetè du Coeur,*
in which I first undertook this Work, may have
drawn me, into a more laborious Amusement, than
I shall know how to away with: For though I cannot say, I have yet jaded my Vanity, it is not impossible but, by this time, the most candid of my Readers may
want a little Breath; especially, when they consider, that all this
Load, I have heap'd upon their Patience, contains but seven
Years of the forty three I pass'd upon the stage; the History of
10   which Period I have enjoyn'd my self to transmit to the Judgment (or Oblivion) of Posterity. However, even my Dulness will
find somebody to do it right; if my Reader is an ill-natur'd one,
he will be as much pleas'd to find me a Dunce in my old Age,
as possibly he may have been, to prove me a brisk Blockhead,
in my Youth: But if he has no Gall to gratify, and would (for
his simple Amusement) as well know, how the Play-houses went
on forty Years ago, as how they do now, I will honestly tell
him the rest of my Story, as well as I can. Lest therefore, the
frequent Digressions, that have broken in, upon it, may have en-
20   tangled his Memory, I must beg leave, just to throw together
the Heads of what I have already given him, that he may again
recover the Clue of my Discourse.

1. the Year 1660 to 1684] The same error as before: 1682.

12. *Estcourt . . . added a fourth Line*] Estcourt is cast as the Gravedigger on the playbill, so he must have doubled as the speaker of the Prologue. This was the first performance under the union, 15 January 1707/8.

16. *For Us, and for our Tragedy . . .*] *Hamlet*, III, ii, 159-61:

> For us, and for our tragedy
> Here stooping to your clemency
> We beg your hearing patiently.

Let him, then, remember, from the Year 1660 to 1684, the
various Fortune of the (then) King's, and Duke's, two famous
Companies; their being reduc'd to one united; the distinct Cha-
racters I have given of thirteen Actors, which in the Year 1690
were the most famous, then, remaining of them; the Cause of
their being again divided in 1695, and the Consequences of that
Division, 'till 1697; from whence I shall lead them to our Se-
cond Union in------Hold! let me see----ay, it was in that me-
morable Year, when the two Kingdoms of England and Scotland
10 were made one. And I remember a Particular, that confirms
me I am right in my Chronology; for the Play of *Hamlet* being
acted soon after, *Estcourt*, who then took upon him to say any
thing, added a fourth Line to *Shakespear's* Prologue to the Play,
in that Play, which originally consisted but of three, but *Est-*
court made it run thus:

> For Us, and for our Tragedy,
> Thus stooping to your Clemency,
> [This being a Year of Unity,]
> We beg your Hearing patiently.

20 This new Chronological Line coming unexpectedly upon the Audience, was receiv'd with Applause, tho' several grave Faces look'd
a little out of Humour at it. However, by this Fact, it is plain
our Theatrical Union happen'd in 1707. But to speak of it, in its
Place, I must go a little back again.

From 1697, to this Union, both Companies went on, without any memorable Change in their Affairs, unless it were that
Betterton's People (however good in their Kind) were most of
them too far advanc'd in Years to mend; and tho' we, in Drury-
Lane, were too young to be excellent, we were not too old to
30 be better. But what will not Satiety depreciate? For though I
must own, and avow, that in our highest Prosperity, I always
thought we were greatly their Inferiors; yet, by our good Fortune
of being seen in quite new Lights, which several new-written Plays

1.23 happen'd in 1707] happen'd in 1708 1st ed.

3. *Oroonoko*] *Oroonoko* by Thomas Southerne, first performed at Drury Lane, December 1695.

5. shew'd themselves in a new Style of Acting] Cibber is referring to the new 'sentimental drama' itself more than to a style of acting, except insofar as the dramatic form imposed a style suitable for dealing seriously with some sort of moral problem (see Nicoll, I, 263-67).

8. *Hildebrand Horden*] Baker (I, 244) adds that he had been on the stage (in 1696) for about seven years, and that his death was judged to have been caused by "an accidental *rencontre*." Hotson (pp. 304-306) documents a number of violent deaths during the period. *The London News Letter*, 20 May 1696: "On *Monday* Capt *Burges* who Kill'd Mr. *Fane*, and was found guilty of Manslaughter at the *Old Baily*, kill'd Mr. *Harding* a Comedian in a Quarrel at the *Rose* Tavern in [Covent] Garden, and is taken into custody."

9. *Rose-Tavern*] The Rose Tavern was close to the Drury Lane Theatre: in *A Comparison Between the Two Stages* (ed. Wells, pp. 75-76) Sullen and Ramble go there, and Ramble exclaims on entering, "Defend us! what a hurry of Sin is in this House!" Sullen: "Drunkenness, which is the proper Iniquity of a Tavern, is here the most excusable Sin; so many other Sins overrun it, 'tis hardly seen in the Crowd." They go on to note that the room is full of prostitutes and rakes. Pepys mentions it many times as a meeting place for Doll Lane and as a place to eat before the theater (e.g., 9 May 1668).

10. Colonel *Burgess*] Charged with the death of Hildebrand Horden, he escaped and lived in Venice until he received the King's pardon on 30 November 1697 (Luttrell, IV, 81).

21. Return of *Wilks*] In Chapter VII, 136, Cibber mentions that Wilks had attempted unsuccessfully to return to London at Mountfort's death in 1694.

24. *Escourt*] Estcourt's first performance of *The Spanish Fryar, or, The Double Discovery* by Dryden on an English stage took place at the Theatre Royal on 18 October 1704 (Avery, I, 78); it should be remembered that Leigh had died some ten years before Estcourt's imitation.

had shewn us in, we now began to make a considerable Stand
against them. One good new Play, to a rising Company, is of
inconceivable Value. In *Oroonok,* (and why may I not name another, tho' it be my own?) in *Love's last Shift,* and in the Sequel
of it, the *Relapse;* several of our People shew'd themselves in a
new Style of Acting, in which Nature had not as yet been seen.
I cannot here forget a Misfortune that befel our Society, about
this time, by the Loss of a young Actor, *Hildrebrand Horden,*
who was kill'd at the Bar of the *Rose-Tavern,* in a frivolous, rash,
10 accidental Quarrel; for which a late Resident at *Venice,* Colonel
Burgess, and several other Persons of Distinction, took their Trials
and were acquitted. This young Man had almost every natural
Gift, that could promise an excellent Actor; he had besides, a
good deal of Table-wit, and Humour, with and handsom Person,
and was every Day rising into publick Favour. Before he was bury'd, it was observable, that two or three Days together, several
of the Fair Sex, well dress'd came in Masks (then frequently
worn) and some in their own Coaches, to visit this Theatrical Heroe, in his Shrowd. He was the elder Son of Dr. *Horden,* Mi-
20 nister of *Twickenham,* in *Middlesex.* But this Misfortune was
soon repair'd, by the Return of *Wilks,* from *Dublin* (who upon
this young Man's Death, was sent for over) and liv'd long enough
among us to enjoy that Approbation, from which the other was
so unhappily cut off. The Winter following, *Estcourt,* the famous Mimick, of whom I have already spoken, had the same Invitation from *Ireland,* where he had commenc'd Actor: His first
Part here, at the *Theatre-Royal,* was the *Spanish Friar,* in which,
tho' he had remembered every Look, and Motion of the late *Tony
Leigh,* so far as to put the Spectator very much in mind of him;
30 yet is was visible through the whole, notwithstanding his Exactness in the Out-lines, the true Spirit, that was to fill up the Figure, was not the same, but unskilfully dawb'd on, like a Child's
Painting upon the Face of a *Metzo-tinto:* It was too plain to the
judicious, that the Conception was not his own, but imprinted

7. *Mrs. Oldfield* . . . almost a Mute] "Curll, in his *Life of Mrs. Oldfield*, says that the only part she played, previous to appearing as Alinda, was Candiope in *Secret Love*" (Lowe, I, 305). This was presumably the production in which Cibber recited both Prologue and Epilogue (see Chapter VIII, 156-57). The author of *Comparison* (ed. Wells, p. 106) says of Mrs. Oldfield in 1702 or earlier that she "ought to be swept off the stage with the Filth and Dust." (cf. *James Thomson, Letters and Documents*, ed. McKillop, 1958, pp. 7 ff.). Cf. Pope, *Sober Advice From Horace*, lines 1-6; she also appears in Pope's *Epistle to Cobham* as the woman vain to the last:

> "Odious! in woollen! 'twould a Saint provoke,
> (Were the last words that poor Narcissa spoke)
> ....
> "One would not, sure, be frightful when one's dead —
> "And—Betty—give this Cheek a little Red."
> (lines 242-43; 246-47)

(Davies [*Dram. Misc.*, III, 464] suggests that Betty was Mrs. Saunders.)

26. Mrs. *Verbruggen*, by reason of her last Sickness] Davies (*Dram. Misc.*, III, 421): "This admirable comic actress died in childbed, 1703."

in his Memory, by another, of whom he only presented a dead
Likeness. But these were Defects, not so obvious to common
Spectators; no wonder, therefore, if by his being much sought
after, in private Companies, he met with a sort of Indulgence,
not to say Partiality, for what he sometimes did upon the
Stage.

   In the Year 1699, Mrs. *Oldfield* was first taken into the House,
where she remain'd about a Twelvemonth almost a Mute, and
unheeded, 'till Sir *John Vanbrugh*, who first recommended her,
10 gave her the Part of *Alinda*, in the *Pilgrim* revis'd. This gentle
Character, happily became that want of Confidence, which is inseparable from young Beginners, who without it, seldom arrive
to any Excellence: Notwithstanding, I own I was, then, so far
deceiv'd in my Opinion of her, that I thought, she had little
more than her Person, that appear'd necessary to the forming a
good Actress; for she set out with so extraordinary a Diffidence,
that it kept her too despondingly down, to a formal, plain (not
to say) flat manner of speaking. Nor could the silver Tone of
her Voice, 'till after some time, incline my Ear to any Hope, in
20 her favour. But Publick Approbation is the warm Weather of a
Theatrical Plant, which will soon bring it forward, to whatever
Perfection Nature has design'd it. However Mrs. *Oldfield* (perhaps for want of fresh Parts) seem'd to come but slowly forward,
'till the Year 1703. Our Company, that Summer, acted at the
Bath, during the Residence of Queen *Anne* at that Place. At
this time it happen'd, that Mrs. *Verbruggen*, by reason of her last
Sickness (of which she some few Months after, dy'd) was left in
London; and though most of her Parts were, of course to be
dispos'd of, yet so earnest was the Female Scramble for them,
30 that only one of them fell to the Share of Mrs. *Oldfield*, that of
Leonora, in Sir *Courtly Nice*; a Character of good plain Sense,
but not over elegantly written. It was in this Part Mrs. *Oldfield*
surpris'd me into an Opinion of her having all the innate Powers of
a good Actress, though they were yet, but in the Bloom of what

26. *Careless Husband* . . . Fate upon the Stage] It was first performed on 7 December 1704, played nine times during the first fortnight, six times later in the season, and remained one of the most popular comedies in the English repertory for a century (Barker, 52-53). It came to be regarded as Cibber's one claim to greatness; even Pope in *Imitations of Horace, Epistles* II, i, 91-94, acknowledges its merits (see Introduction, pp. xxxv ff.).

they promis'd. Before she had acted this Part, I had so cold an
Expectation from her Abilities, that she could scarce prevail with
me, to rehearse with her the Scenes, she was chiefly concern'd in,
with Sir *Courtly*, which I then acted. However, we ran
them over, with a mutual Inadvertency of one another. I seem'd
careless, as concluding, that any Assistance I could give her,
would be to little, or no purpose; and she mutter'd out her
Words in a sort of misty manner, at my low Opinion of her.
But when the Play came to be acted, she had a just Occasion to
10 triumph over the Error of my Judgment, by the (almost) Amazement, that her unexpected Performance awak'd me to; so forward, and sudden a Step into Nature, I had never seen; and
what made her Performances more valuable, was, that I knew it
all proceeded from her own Understanding, untaught, and unas-
sisted by any one more experienc'd Actor. Perhaps it may not
be unacceptable, if I enlarge a little more upon the Theatrical
Character of so memorable an Actress.

  Though this Part of *Leonora*, in itself, was of so little value,
that when she grew more into Esteem, it was one of the several
20 she gave away, to inferior Actresses; yet it was the first (as I have
observ'd) that corrected my Judgment of her, and confirm'd me,
in a strong Belief, that she could not fail, in very little time, of
being what she was afterwards allow'd to be, the foremost Ornament of our Theatre. Upon this unexpected Sally, then, of the
Power, and Disposition, of so unforeseen an Actress, it was, that
which I had written the Summer before, and had thrown aside,
in despair of having Justice done to the Character of Lady *Betty
Modish*, by any one Woman, then among us; Mrs. *Verbruggen*
being now in a very declining state of Health, and Mrs. *Bracegirdle* out of my Reach, and engag'd in another Company: But,
as I have said, Mrs. *Oldfield* having thrown out such new Prof-
fers of a Genius, I was no longer at a loss for Support; my
Doubts were dispell'd, and I had now a new Call to finish it:

1.13 what made] what what made 2nd ed.
1.19 when she grew more into] when she more into 2nd ed.

17. *Bath, November* 11, 1738] After his retirement from the stage Cibber spent much of his time at fashionable watering places (Barker, p. 239). He wrote verses to "Beau" Nash, Arbiter Elegantiarum at Bath, and these drew a sharp epigram from Pope which begins, "O Nash! more blest in ev'ry other things, / But in thy Poet wretched as a King!" (Pope, *Poems*, VI, 360-61).

32. *Lady Townly*] Mrs. Oldfield played Lady Townly in *The Provok'd Husband*, 10 January 1728, but later was the original Sophonisba in James Thomson's adaptation of Lee's play, 28 February 1730 (Scouten, I, 40). She died 23 October 1730 and was buried in Westminster Abbey, though because she had had two illegitimate children by two 'protectors' she was not permitted a monument there (Dudden, I, 22). It was of Mrs. Oldfield's performance in *The Provok'd Husband* that Cibber, in the preface to the first edition, made his widely ridiculed remark, "She outdid her usual out-doing"; he went on to praise her ability as a comic actress and her 'naturalness.' For an account of the first performance, see Avery, II, 954.

Accordingly, the *Careless Husband* took its Fate upon the Stage
the Winter following, in 1704. Whatever favourable Reception,
this Comedy has met with from the Publick; it would be unjust
in me, not to place a large Share of it to the Account of
Mrs. *Oldfield*; not only from the uncommon Excellence of her
Action; but even from her personal manner of Conversing. There
are many Sentiments in the Character of Lady *Betty Modish*, that
I may almost say, were originally her own, or only dress'd with
a little more Care, than when they negligently fell, from her
lively Humour: Had her Birth plac'd her in a higher Rank of
Life, she had certainly appear'd, in reality, what in this Play
she only, excellently, acted, an agreeably gay Woman of Quality, a little too conscious of her natural Attractions. I have often
seen her, in private Societies, where Women of the best Rank
might have borrow'd some part of her Behavior, without the
least Diminution of their Sense, or Dignity. And this very Morning, where I am now writing at the *Bath*, *November* 11, 1738,
the same Words were said of her, by a Lady of Condition, whose
better Judgment of her Personal Merit, in that Light, has em-
bolden'd me to repeat them. After her Success, in this Character
of higher Life; all that Nature had given her of the Actress,
seem'd to have risen to its full Perfection: But the Variety of her
Power could not be known, 'till she was seen, in variety of Characters; which, as fast as they fell to her, she equally excell'd in.
Authors had much more, from her Performance, than they had
reason to hope for, from what they had written for her; and none
had less than another, but as their Genius in the Parts they allotted her, was more or less elevated.

In the Wearing of her Person, she was particularly fortunate;
her Figure was always improving, to her Thirty-fixth Year; but
her Excellence in acting was never at a stand: And the last new
Character she shone in (*Lady Townly*) was a Proof that she was
still able to do more, if more could have been done for *her*. She
had one Mark of good Sense, rarely known, in any Actor of ei-

30. *Ubi plura . . . maculis*] Horace, *Ars Poetica*, 351-52: "Verum ubi plura nitent in carmine, non ego paucis / Offendor maculis": "Where more [beauties] shine in a poem, I will not be offended with a few blemishes."

ther Sex, but herself. I have observ'd several, with promising Dispositions, very desirous of Instruction at their first setting out;
but no sooner had they found their least Account, in it, than they
were, as desirous of being left to their own Capacity, which they,
then, thought would be disgrac'd, by their seeming to want any
farther Assistance. But this was not Mrs. *Oldfield's* way of thinking; for to the last Year of her Life, she never undertook any Part
she lik'd, without being importunately desirous of having all the
Helps in it, that another could possibly give her. By knowing
10 so much herself, she found how much more there was of Nature
yet needful to be known. Yet it was a hard matter to give her
any Hint, that she was not able to take, or improve. With all
this Merit, she was tractable, and less presuming, in her Station,
than several, that had not half her Pretensions to be troublesome:
But she lost nothing by her easy Conduct; she had every thing she
ask'd, which she took care should be always reasonable, because
she hated as much to be *grudg'd*, as *deny'd* a Civility. Upon her
extraordinary Action in the *Provok'd Husband*, the Menagers made
her a Present of Fifty Guineas more than her Agreement, which
20 never was more than a Verbal one; for they knew she was above
deserting them, to engage upon any other Stage, and she was
conscious, they would never think it their Interest, to give her
cause of Complaint. In the last two Months of her Illness, when
she was no longer able to assist them, she declin'd receiving her
Sallary, tho' by her Agreement, she was entitled to it. Upon
the whole, she was, to the last Scene she acted, the Delight of her
Spectators: Why then may we not close her Character, with
the same Indulgence with which *Horace* speaks of a commendable Poem:

30
        Ubi plura nitent----non ego paucis
        Offender maculis-------

        Where in the whole, such various Beauties shine,
        'Twere idle, upon Errors, refine.

2. Preface to the *Provok'd Husband*] See Appendix B.

30. Theatre; . . . small, and poorly fitted up] Their theater, the old Lisle's Tennis Court, was about 75 feet by 30 feet (for a complete history, plan and description, see Hotson, pp. 120-27).

What more might be said of her as an Actress, may be found
in the Preface to the *Provok'd Husband*, to which I refer the
Reader.

   With the Acquisition, then, of so advanc'd a Comedian as
Mrs. *Oldfield*, and the Addition of one so much in Favour as
Wilks, and by the visible Improvement of our other Actors, as
Penkethman, *Johnson*, *Bullock*, and I think I may venture to
name myself in the Number (but, in what Rank, I leave to the
Judgment of those who have been my Spectators) the Reputation
10 of our Company began to get around; Mrs. *Oldfield*, and *Wilks*,
by their frequently playing against one another, in our best Comedies, very happily supported that Humour, and Vivacity,
which is so peculiar to our *English* Stage. The *French*, our only
modern Competitors, seldom give us their Lovers, in such various
Lights: In their Comedies (however lively a People they are by
nature) their Lovers are generally constant, simple Sighers, both of
a Mind, and equally distress'd, about the Difficulties of their coming together; which naturally makes their conversation so serious,
that they are seldom good Company to their Auditors: and tho' I
20 allow them many other Beauties, of which we are too negligent;
yet our Variety of Humour has Excellencies that all their valuable
Observance of Rules have never yet attain'd to. By these Advantages, then, we began to have an equal Share of the politer sort
of Spectators, who, for several Years, could not allow our Company to stand in any comparison, with the other. But Theatrical Favour, like Publick Commerce, will sometimes deceive the
best Judgments, by an unaccountable change of its Channel; the
best Commodities are not always known to meet with the best
Markets. To this Decline of the Old Company, many Acci-
30 dents might contribute; as the too distant Situation of their Theatre; or their want of a better, for it was not, then, in the condition it now is; but small, and poorly fitted up, within the
Walls of a Tennis *Quaree* Court, which is of the lesser sort.
Booth, who was then a young Actor, among them, has often

1.10 and *Wilks*] and Mr. *Wilks*   2nd ed.

Companys have been forc'd for their Subsistance to bring on the Stage Dancers on the Ropes, Tumblers, Vaulters, Ladder dancers etc. . . and thereby debas'd the Theatre, and almost levell'd it with Bartholomew ffaire." Rich made a practice of hiring the most famous entertainers from the capitals of Europe; Barker (pp. 55-58) cites enthusiastic reports of them in contemporary newspapers.

27. Mr. *Rowe*, thus complains in his Prologue] This is from the Epilogue to *The Ambitious Stepmother*, Rowe's first produced play (c. December 1700 at Lincoln's Inn Fields). Date of premiere unknown (Avery, I, 5).

1. Difficulties *Betterton* . . . labour'd under] For an account of Betterton at this period, see Lowe, *Betterton*, pp. 75-146.

7. inactive Negligence] David Crawford in the preface to his play, *Courtship-a-la-Mode*, explains why he first offered the play to Betterton's company, then withdrew it and gave it to Drury Lane: "It was enter'd in the other House, where Mr. *Betterton* did me all the Justice I could indeed reasonably hope for. But that example he gave, was not it seems to be follow'd by the whole company, since 'tis known that Mr. *Bowman* (I mention his name to keep the reflection from the other sharers) kept the first character of my play six weeks, and they cou'd hardly read six lines on't. How far that way of management makes of late for the interest and honour of that House, is easie to be judg'd. Some who valu'd their reputations more, were indeed rarely or never absent. To these I gave my thanks; but finding that six or seven people cou'd not perform what was design'd for fifteen, I was oblig'd to remove it after so many sham rehearsals, and in two days it got footing upon the other stage. Where 'twas immediately cast to the best advantage, and plaid in less than twenty days" (quoted by Lowe, *Betterton*, p. 157.)

15. have recourse to foreign Novelties] Downes, *Roscius*, ed. Summers, p. 46: "In the space of Ten Years past, Mr. *Betterton* to gratify the desire and Fancies of the Nobility and Gentry; procur'd from Abroad the best Dancers and Singers [he repeats Cibber's list of dancers and adds] *Margarita Delpine, Maria Gallia* and divers others; who being Exorbitantly Expensive, produc'd small Profit to him and his Company, but vast Gain to themselves; Madame *Delpine* since her Arrival in *England*, by Modest Computation; having got by the Stage and Gentry, above 10000 Guinease." Delpine and Gallia were singers. *Comparison* (ed. Wells, p. 29) cites the popularity of Balon as "an evident sign of the degeneracy of our Plays."

24. their exhibiting these Novelties . . .] Betterton petitioned against Rich's Company's use of these forms of attractions (printed in Nicoll, I, 340, A.): ". . . the Two Companies have by their bidding against each other for Singers, Dancers etc. . . . rais'd the Prices so high that both are impoverisht by it, and most of their Profits cary'd away by Foreigners . . . both

told me of the Difficulties *Betterton*, then, labour'd under, and
complain'd of: How impracticable he found it, to keep their
Body to that common Order, which was necessary for their Support; of their relying too much upon their intrinsick Merit; and
though but few of them were young, even when they first became their own Masters, yet they were all now, ten Years older,
and consequently more liable to fall into an inactive Negligence,
or were only separately diligent, for themselves, in the sole Regard of their Benefit-Plays; which several of their Principals
10 knew, at worst, would raise them Contributions, that would
more than tolerably subsist them, for the current Year. But as
these were too precarious Expedients, to be always depended upon, and brought in nothing, to the general Support of the Numbers, who were at Sallaries under them; they were reduc'd to
have recourse to foreign Novelties; *L'Abbee'*, *Balon*, and Mademoiselle *Subligny*, three of the, then, most famous Dancers of
the *French* Opera, were at several times, brought over at extraordinary Rates, to revive that sickly Appetite, which plain Sense,
and Nature had satiated. But alas! there was no recovering to
20 a sound Constitution, by those mere costly Cordials; the Novelty of a Dance, was but of a short Duration, and perhaps hurtful, in its consequence; for it made a Play, without a Dance,
less endur'd, than it had been before, when such Dancing was
not to be had. But perhaps, their exhibiting these Novelties,
might be owing to the Success we had met with, in our more barbarous introducing of *French* Mimicks, and Tumblers the Year
before; of which Mr. *Rowe*, thus complains in his Prologue to
one of his first Plays:

> *Must* Shakespear, Fletcher, *and laborious* Ben,
30 > *Be left for* Scaramouch, *and* Harlequin?

While the Crowd, therefore, so fluctuated, from one House, to
another, as their Eyes were more, or less regaled, than their Ears,
it could not be a Question much in Debate, which had the bet-

22. Sir *Harry Wildair*] In *The Constant Couple*, or *A Trip to the Jubilee* (first performed at Drury Lane, November 1699) and its sequel *Sir Harry Wildair* (c. April 1701) by George Farquhar; dates of premieres unknown (Avery, I, 10).

ter Actors; the Merit of either, seem'd to be of little moment;
and the Complaint in the foregoing Lines, tho' it might be just,
for a time, could not be a just one for ever; because the best Play
that ever was writ, may tire by being too often repeated, a Misfortune naturally attending the Obligation, to play every Day;
not that whenever such Satiety commences, it will be any Proof
of the Play's being a bad one, or of its being ill acted. In a
word, Satiety is, seldom, enough consider'd, by either Criticks,
Spectators, or Actors, as the true, not to say just, Cause of de-
10 clining Audiences, to the most rational Entertainments: And tho'
I cannot say, I ever saw a good new Play, not attended with
due Encouragement, yet to keep a Theatre daily open, without
sometimes giving the Publick a bad old one, is more than, I
doubt, the Wit of human Writers, or Excellence of Actors, will
ever be able to accomplish. And, as both Authors, and Comedians, may have often succeeded, where a sound Judgment would
have condemn'd them, it might puzzle the nicest Critick living,
to prove in what sort of Excellence, the true Value of either consisted: For, if their Merit were to be measur'd by the full Houses,
20 they may have brought; if the Judgment of the Crowd were infallible; I am afraid we shall be reduc'd to allow, that the *Beg-*
gars Opera was the best-written Play, and Sir *Harry Wildair* (as
Wilks play'd it) was the best acted Part, that ever our *English*
Theatre had to boast of. That Critick indeed, must be rigid, to
a Folly, that would deny either of them, their due Praise, when
they severally drew such Numbers after them; all their Hearers
could not be mistaken, and yet, if they were all, in the right,
what sort of Fame will remain to those celebrated Authors, and
Actors, that had so long, and deservedly been admired, before
30 these were in Being. The only Distinction I shall make between
them is, That to write, or act, like the Authors, or Actors, of
the latter end of the last entury, I am of Opinion, will be found
a far better Pretence to Success, than to imitate these who have
been so crowded to, in the beginning of this. All I would in-

16. *The Little Whig*] This was Anne Churchill (1688-1716), daughter of the then Earl of Marlborough, and wife of Charles Spencer (1674-1722), third Earl of Sunderland, second member of the Junto. She was noted for her devotion to the Whig party (cf. Letters of Horace Walpole, ed. Toynbee, XIII, 412). The "Thirty Persons of Quality" were largely members of the Whig Kit Cat Club (Loftis, *Politics*, pp. 39-41; also see Robert J. Allen, "The Kit-Cat Club and the Theatre," *Review of English Studies*, VII, 1931, 56-61). "Mr. Percy Fitzgerald (*New History*, I, 328) states that it was said that workmen, on 19th March, 1825, found a stone with the inscription: 'April 18th, 1704. This cornerstone of the Queen's Theatre was laid by his Grace Charles Duke of Somerset,'" (Lowe, I, 320 n.). The theater burned 17 June 1788.

19. In the Year 1706] It was 9 April 1705 (Hotson, p. 309).

fer from this Explanation, is, that though we had, then, the
better Audiences, and might have more of the young World on
our Side; yet this was no sure Proof, that the other Company
were not, in the Truth of Action, greatly our Superiors. These
elder Actors, then, besides the Disadvantages I have mention'd,
having only the fewer, true Judges to admire them, naturally
wanted the Support of the Crowd, whose Taste was to be pleas'd
at a cheaper Rate, and with coarser Fare. To recover them
therefore, to their due Estimation, a new Project was form'd of
10 building them a stately Theatre, in the *Hay-Market*, by Sir *John
Vanbrugh*, for which he rais'd a Subscription of thirty Persons
of Quality, at one hundred Pounds each, in Consideration where-
of every Subscriber, for his own Life, was to be admitted, to
whatever Entertainments should be publickly perform'd there,
without farther Payment for his Entrance. Of this Theatre, I
saw the first Stone laid, on which was inscrib'd *The little Whig*,
in Honour to a Lady of extraordinary Beauty, then the celebrated Toast, the Pride of that Party.

In the Year 1706, when this House was finish'd, *Betterton*,
20 and his Co-partners dissolv'd their own Agreement, and threw
themselves under the Direction of Sir *John Vanbrugh*, and
Mr. *Congreve*; imagining, perhaps, that the Conduct of two
such eminent Authors, might give a more prosperous Turn to
their Condition; that the Plays, it would, now, be their Interest, to write for them, would soon recover the Town to a true
Taste, and be an Advantage, that no other Company could
hope for; that in the Interim till such Plays could be written,
the Grandeur of their House, as it was a new Spectacle, might
allure the Crowd to support them: But if these were their Views
30 we shall see, that their Dependence upon them, was too sanguine.
As to their Prospect of new Plays, I doubt it was not enough
consider'd, that good ones were Plants of a slow Growth; and
though, Sir *John Vanbrugh* had a very quick Pen, yet Mr. *Congreve* was too judicious a Writer, to let any thing come hastily

29. Those costly Spaces] Grosvenor, Hanover, and Cavendish Squares mentioned above were developed as fashionable residential areas in the first half of the eighteenth century (John Summerson, *Architecture in Britain: 1530 to 1830*, London, Penguin, 1953, pp. 230-235).

out of his Hands: As to their other Dependence, the House,
they had not yet discover'd, that almost every proper Quality,
and Convenience of a good Theatre had been sacrific'd, or neglected, to shew the Spectator a vast, triumphal Piece of Architecture! And that the best Play, for the Reasons I am going to
offer, could not but be under greater Disadvantages, and be less
capable of delighting the Auditor, here, then it could have been
in the plain Theatre they come from. For what could their vast
Columns, their gilded Cornices, their immoderate high Roofs
10 avail, when scarce one Word in ten, could be distinctly heard
in it? Nor had it, then, the Form, it now stands in, which
Necessity, two or three Years after reduc'd it to: At the first
opening it, the flat Cieling, that is now over the Orchestra, was
then a Semi-oval Arch, that sprung fifteen Feet higher from above
the Cornice: The Cieling over the Pit too, was still more rais'd,
being one level Line from the highest back part of the upper
Gallery, to the Front of the Stage: The Front-boxes were a
continued Semicircle, to the bare Walls of the House on each
Side: This extraordinary, and superfluous Space occasion'd such
20 an Undulation, from the Voice of every Actor, that generally
what they said sounded like the Gabbling of so many People,
in the lofty Isles in a Cathedral--- The Tone of a Trumpet, or
the Swell of an Eunuch's holding Note, 'tis true, might be
sweeten'd by it; but the articulate Sounds of a speaking Voice
were drown'd, by the hollow Reverberations of one Word upon another. To this Inconvenience, why may we not add that
of its Situation; for at that time it had not the Advantage of
almost a large City, which has since been built, in its Neigh-
bourhood: Those costly Spaces of *Hanover*, *Grosvenor*, and *Ca-*
30 *vendish* Squares, with the many, and great adjacent Streets about
them, were then all but so many green Fields of Pasture, from
whence they could draw little, or no Sustenance, unless it were
that of a Milk-Diet. The City, the Inns of Court, and the
middle Part of the Town, which were the most constant Sup-

1.13 Cieling] Ceiling 2nd ed. Both spellings were acceptable in mid-
               eighteenth century (OED).
1.15 Cieling] Ceiling 2nd ed.

2. Coach-hire is often too hard a Tax, upon the Pit, and Gallery] These sections of the theater
   were the least expensive; in the pit sat the critics and middle-class playgoers where seats cost
   2s. 6d.; in the first and second galleries sat common-folk and servants, where seats cost
   respectively 1s. 6d. and 1s. Boxes cost 4s. (Dudden, I, 39; Lowe, *Betterton*, p. 18).

port of a Theatre, and chiefly to be rely'd on, were now too
far, out of the Reach of an easy Walk; and Coach-hire is often too hard a Tax, upon the Pit, and Gallery. But from the
vast Increase of the Buildings I have mention'd, the Situation of
that Theatre has since that Time receiv'd considerable Advantages; a new World of People of Condition are nearer to it,
than formerly, and I am of Opinion, that if the auditory Part
were a little more reduc'd to the Model of that in *Drury-Lane*,
an excellent Company of Actors would, now, find a better Ac-
10 count in it, than in any other House in this populous City: Let
me not be mistaken, I say, an excellent Company, and such as
might be able to do Justice to the best of Plays, and throw out
those latent Beauties in them, which only excellent Actors can
discover, and give Life to. If such a Company were now there,
they would meet with quite different Set of Auditors, than
other Theatres have lately been us'd to: Polite Hearers would
be content with polite Entertainments; and I remember the time,
when Plays, without the Aid of Farce, or Pantomine, were as
decently attended as Opera's, or private Assemblies, where a noisy
20 Sloven would have past his time as uneasily, in a Front-box, as
in a Drawing-room; when a Hat upon a Man's Head there
would have been look'd upon, as a sure Mark of a Brute, or a
Booby: But of all this I have seen too, the Reverse, where in
the Presence of Ladies, at a Play, common Civility has been
set at defiance, and the Privilege of being a rude Clown, even
to a Nusance, has, in a manner been demanded, as one of the
Rights of *English* Liberty: Now, though I grant, that Liberty
is so precious a Jewel, that we ought not to suffer the least Ray
of its Lustre, to be diminish'd; yet methinks the Liberty of
30 seeing a Play, in quiet, has as laudable a Claim to Protection,
as the Privilege of not suffering you to do it, has to Impunity.
But since we are so happy, as not to have a certain Power among
us, which, in another Country is call'd the *Police*, let us rather
bear this Insult, than buy its Remedy at too dear a Rate; and

32. *Confederacy*] First performed early the next season, 30 October 1705 (Avery, I, 105); it was taken from *Les Bourgeoises a la Mode*.

7. *Italian* Opera began first to steal into *England*] Italian opera was introduced into England only in the early years of the eighteenth century, although Italian singers had appeared in the latter years of the previous century—the Margarita Delpine mentioned by Downes (quoted above) whose real name was Francesca Margherita de l'Epine, came to London in 1692 and is said to have been "the first Italian vocalist of marked distinction who sang in England" (Summers, ed., Downes, *Roscius*, p. 261 n.). The first Italian opera, prepared for by greater frequency of music, singing, and dancing on the legitimate stage between 1700 and 1704, was *Arsinoe, Queen of Cyprus*; this was an old play by Tomaso Stanzani, originally with music by Petronio Franceschini, first produced in Bologna in 1677. Adapted to English by Pierre Antoine Motteux, Nicolino Haym, and Charles Dieuport, it was first presented 16 January 1705 and was extremely successful, with fourteen performances in its first season, seventeen in 1705/06 (Nicoll, II, 226; Summers, Downes, *Roscius*, p. 261-62; Avery, I, 85).

13. first *Italian* Performer . . . Valentini] This singer remained in England for a number of years after 1707 (Nicoll, II, 278, 285).

19. *Turnus* in *Camilla*] This opera with music by Buononcini and libretto by Silvio Stampaglia, translated by Northman and Motteux, was performed 30 March 1706 (Avery, I, 121; Nicoll, II, 227-28, gives 29 March). Cibber therefore has confused the chronology; first came *Arsinoe* at Drury Lane, then the opera called by Cibber *The Triumph of Love* (see below) but properly known as *The Loves of Ergasto* at the opening of the Haymarket on 24 April 1705 (Avery, I, 92); then *Camilla* the year following at Drury Lane (Nicoll, II, 226-27; Downes, *Roscius,* ed. Summers, p. 262).

27. a translated Opera . . . not having in it, the Charms of *Camilla*] See above. *The Loves of Ergasto: A Pastoral* supposedly by Giacomo Greber, the husband of the singer de l'Epine mentioned above, was "perform'd by a new Set of Singers, Arriv'd from *Italy*: (the worst that e'er came from thence) for it last but 5 Days, and they being lik'd but indifferently by the Gentry; they in a little time marcht back to their own country," (Downes, *Roscius*, ed. Summers, p. 48).

let it be the Punishment of such wrong-headed Savages, that they
never will, or can know the true Value of that Liberty, which
they so stupidly abuse: Such vulgar Minds possess their Liberty,
in profligate Husbands do fine Wives, only to disgrace them.
In a Word, when Liberty boils over, such is the Scum of it. But
to our new erected Theatre.

Not long before this time, the *Italian* Opera began first to
steal into *England*; but in as rude a Disguise, and unlike it self,
as possible; in a lame, hobling Translation, into our own Lan-
10 guage, with false Quantities, or metre out of Measure, to its
original Notes, sung by our own unskilful Voices, with Graces
misapply'd to almost every Sentiment, and with Action, lifeless
and unmeaning, through every Character The first *Italian*
Performer, that made any distinguish'd Figure in it, was *Valen-*
tini, a true sensible Singer, at that time, but of a Throat too
weak, to sustain those melodious Warblings, for which the fairer
Sex have since idoliz'd his Successors. However, this Defect
was so well supply'd by his Action, that his Hearers bore with
the Absurdity of his Singing his first Part of *Turnus* in *Camilla*,
20 all in *Italian*, while every other Character was sung and recited
to him in *English*. This I have mention'd to shew not only
our Tramontane Taste, but that the crowded Audiences, which
follow'd it to *Drury-Lane*, might be another Occasion of their
growing thinner in *Lincolns-Inn-Fields*.

To strike in, therefore, with this prevailing Novelty, Sir *John*
Vanbrugh and Mr. *Congreve*, open'd their new *Hay-Market*
Theatre, with a translated Opera, to *Italian* Musick, call'd the
Triumph of Love, but this not having in it, the Charms of *Ca-*
milla, either from the Inequality of the Musick, or Voices, had
30 but a cold Reception, being perform'd but three Days, and those
not crowded. Immediately, upon the Failure of this *Opera*,
Sir *John Vanbrugh* produc'd his Comedy call'd the *Confederacy*,
taken (but greatly improv'd) from the *Bourgeois* 'a la mode of
Dancour: Though the Fate of this Play was something better,

16. the *Cuckold in Conceit*] First performed 22 March 1707 though never printed. The three plays in the same season were *Squire Trelooby* on 30 March 1704 of which only the last act was new; *The Mistake*, from Moliere's *Le Depit Amoureux* on 27 December 1705; and *The Confederacy*, taken from Dancourt's *Les Bourgeoises a la Mode* on 30 October 1705 (Avery, I, *passim*; Nicoll, II, 151-52).

yet I thought, it was not equal to its Merit: For it is written
with an uncommon Vein of Wit and Humour; which confirms
me, in my former Observation, that the difficulty of hearing
distinctly in that, then wide Theatre, was no small Impediment
to the Applause, that might have follow'd the same Actors in it,
upon any other Stage; and indeed every Play acted there, before the House was alter'd, seem'd to suffer, from the same Inconvenience: In a Word, the Prospect of Profits, from this
Theatre was so very barren, that Mr. *Congreve*, in a few Months
10 gave up his Share, and Interest in the Government of it, wholly
to Sir *John Vanbrugh*. But Sir *John* being sole Proprietor of
the House, was at all Events, oblig'd to do his utmost to support it. As he had a happier Talent of throwing the *English*
Spirit, into his Translation of *French* Plays, than any former Author, who had borrow'd from them, he, in the same Season, gave
the Publick three more of that kind, call'd the *Cuckold in Conceit*; from the *Cocu imaginaire* of *Moliere*; *Squire Trelooby*, from
his *Monsieur de Pourceaugnac*, and the *Mistake*, from the *D'epit
Amoureux* of the same Author. Yet all these, however well
20 executed, came to the Ear in the same undistinguish'd Utterance, by which almost all their Plays had equally suffer'd: For
what few could plainly hear, it was not likely a great many
could applaud.

   It must farther be consider'd too, that this Company were,
not now, what they had been, when they first revolted from
the Patentees in *Drury-Lane*, and became their own Masters,
in *Lincolns-Inn-Fields*. Several of them, excellent, in their different Talents, were now dead; as *Smith*, *Kynaston*, *Sandford*,
and *Leigh*: Mrs. *Betterton*, and *Underhill* being, at this time,
30 also superannuated Pensioners, whose Places were generally but
ill supply'd: Nor could it be expected that *Betterton* himself, at
past seventy, could retain his former Force, and Spirit; though
he was yet far distant from any Competitor. Thus then were
these Remains of the best Set of Actors, that I believe were ever

1.29 *Underhill*] *Underhil* 2nd ed.

3. nothing but a Union] Cf. Barker, pp. 62-63. For an account of this lawsuit and another parallel to it, see Hotson, pp. 300-302, 306-307.

18. struck the Tipstaff blind] That is, Rich was bribing the bailiff not to present him with a summons.

25. this close Master . . . had no Inclination to a Union] Barker contradicts this, reasoning that Rich's refusal at the time of Vanbrugh's suggestion was merely intended as a delaying action until he could organize, with Swiney, a second company to take over the Haymarket on his own terms (pp. 62-64). It appears that Rich had been in touch with Owen Swiney during the negotiations with Vanbrugh (the summer of 1706).

known, at once, in *England*, by Time, Death, and the Satiety
of their Hearers mould'ring to decay.

It was now, the Town-talk, that nothing but a Union of
the two Companies could recover the Stage, to its former Reputation, which Opinion was certainly true: One would have
thought too, that the Patentee of *Drury-Lane* could not have
fail'd to close with it, he being, then, on the prosperous Side
of the Question, having no Relief to ask for himself, and little
more to do in the matter, than to consider what he might safely
10 grant: But it seems this was not his way of counting; he had
other Persons, who had great Claims to Shares, in the Profits of
this Stage, which Profits, by a Union, he foresaw would be too
visible to be doubted of, and might raise up a new Spirit, in
those Adventurers, to revive their Suits at Law with him; for
he had led them a Chace in Chancery several Years, and when
they had driven him, into a Contempt of that Court, he con-
jur'd up a Spirit, in the Shape of Six and eight Pence a-day,
that constantly struck the Tipstaff blind, whenever he came
near him: He knew the intrinsick Value of Delay, and was
20 resolv'd to stick to it, as the surest way to give the Plantiffs
enough on't. And by this Expedient our good Master had
long walk'd about, at his Leisure, cool, and contented, as a Fox,
when the Hounds were drawn off, and gone home from him.
But whether I am right, or not, in my Conjectures, certain it is
that this close Master of *Drury-Lane*, had no Inclination to a
Union, as will appear by the Sequel.

Sir *John Vanbrugh* knew too, that to make a Union worth
his while, he must not seem too hasty for it; he therefore found
himself under a Necessity, in the mean time of letting his whole
30 Theatrical Farm to some industrious Tenant, that might put
it into better Condition. This is that Crisis, as I observ'd,
in the Eight Chapter, when the Royal License, for acting
Plays, &c. was judg'd of so little Value, as not to have one
Suitor for it. At this time then, the Master of *Drury-Lane*

happen'd to have a sort of primier Agent in his Stage-Affairs,
that seem'd in Appearance as much to govern the Master, as the
Master himself did to govern his Actors: But this Person was
under no Stipulation, or Sallary, for the Service he render'd; but
had gradually wrought himself into the Master's extraordinary
Confidence, and Trust, from an habitual Intimacy, a cheerful
Humour, and an indefatigable Zeal for his Interest. If I should
farther say, that this Person has been well known in almost every
Metropolis, in *Europe*; that few private Men have, with so lit-
10 tle Reproach, run through more various Turns of Fortune; that,
on the wrong side of Three-score, he has yet the open Spirit of
a hale young Fellow of five and twenty; that though he still
chuses to speak what he thinks, to his best Friends, with an un-
disguis'd Freedom, he is, notwithstanding acceptable to many
Persons of the first Rank, and Condition; that any one of them
(provided he likes them) may now send him, for their Service, to
Constantinople, at half a Day's Warning; that Time has, not
yet, been able to make a visible Change, in any Part of him,
but the Colour of his Hair, from a fierce coal-black, to that of
20 a milder milk-white: When I have taken this Liberty with him,
methinks it cannot be taking a much greater, if I at once
should tell you, that this Person was Mr. *Owen Swiney*, and that
it was to him Sir *John Vanbrugh*, in this Exigence of his Theatrical Affairs, made an Offer of his Actors, under such Agreements of Sallary, as might be made with them; and of his
House, Cloaths, and Scenes, with the Queen's License to employ
them, upon Payment of only the casual Rent of five Pounds,
upon every acting Day, and not to exceed *700 l.* in the Year.
Of this Proposal, Mr. *Swiney* desir'd a Day, or two to consider;
30 for however he might like it, he would not meddle in any sort,
without the Consent, and Approbation of his Friend, and Patron, the Master of *Drury-Lane*. Having given the Reasons
why this Patentee was averse to a Union, it may now seem less
a Wonder, why he immediately consented that *Swiney* should

11. he took the *Hay-Market* Theatre] This agreement was signed 14 August 1706 (Barker, p. 63). Downes (*Roscius*, ed. Summers, p. 50) gives a parallel account of these events; he regarded it as a reunion of the two acting companies, noting, however, that only Betterton and Underhill had been acting since 1662.

16. he chiefly depended upon his Singers, and Dancers] During the season of 1706/07, Drury Lane.

22. *Wilks, Estcourt . . .*] Estcourt appears to have remained with Rich for this season (Lowe, I, 332 n.). Barker (p. 66) says that Norris, Bullock, and Johnson joined Swiney; Congreve remarks (in a letter to Joseph Keally, 10 September 1706, *Works*, ed. Summers, I, 80), "The playhouses have undergone another revolution; and Swiney, with Wilks, Mrs. Oldfield, Pinkethman, Bullock, and Dickey [Henry Norris], are come over to the Hay-Market. Vanbrugh resigns his authority to Swiney, which occasioned the revolt. Mr. Rich complains and rails like Volpone counterplotted by Mosca. My Lord Chamberlain approves and ratifies the desertion; and the design is to have plays only at the Hay-Market, and opera only at Covent Garden. I think the design right to restore acting; but the houses are misapplied, which time may change."

27. a Gentleman's House in *Gloucestershire*] This was Henry Brett, who had married the former Countess of Macclesfield, alleged mother of Savage (Boswell, I, 108 n.).

30. a Letter from *Swiney*] This letter, received 5 October 1706, was in the possession of Grove who provides a summary of it in his *Dictionary of Music and Musicians*, article Swiney; cf. Barker, pp. 64-65. Primarily, the letter reveals an intimacy between Cibber and Swiney and a common distrust of Rich.

take the *Hay-Market* House, &c. and continue that Company to
act against him; but the real Truth was, that he had a mind both
Companies should be clandestinely under one, and the same Interest; and yet in so loose a manner, that he might declare his
Verbal Agreement with *Swiney* good, or null, and void, as he
might best find his Account in either. What flatter'd him, that
he had this wholesom Project, and *Swiney* to execute it, both in
his Power, was, that at this time, *Swiney* happen'd to stand in
his Books, Debtor to Cash, upwards of Two Hundred Pounds:
10 But here, we shall find, he over-rated his Security. However,
Swiney as yet follow'd his Orders; he took the *Hay-Market* Theatre, and had farther, the private Consent of the Patentee, to
take such of his Actors from *Drury-Lane*, as either from Inclination, or Discontent, might be willing to come over to him,
in the *Hay-Market*. The only one he made an Exception of,
was myself: For tho' he chiefly depended upon his Singers, and
Dancers, he said, it would be necessary to keep some one tolerable Actor with him, that might enable him to set those Machines a going. Under this Limitation, of not entertaining me,
20 *Swiney* seem'd to acquiesce, 'till after he had open'd, with the so
recruited Company, in the *Hay-Market*: the Actors that came
to him from *Drury-Lane*, were *Wilks*, *Estcourt*, *Mills*, *Keen*,
Johnson, *Bullock*, Mrs. *Oldfield*, Mrs. *Rogers*, and some few
others of less note: But I must here let you know, that this Project was form'd, and put in Execution, all in very few Days, in
the Summer-Season, when no Theatre was open. To all which
I was entirely a Stranger, being at this time at a Gentleman's
House in *Gloucestershire*, scribbling, if I mistake not, the *Wife's
Resentment*.
30   The first World I heard of this Transaction, was by a Letter
from *Swiney*, inviting me to make One in the *Hay-Market*
Company, whom he hop'd I could not but now think the stronger
Party. But, I confess, I was not a little alarm'd, at this Revo-
lution: For I consider'd, that I knew of no visible Fund to sup-

1.22 *Estcourt*] *Estcoart* 1st ed.

port these Actors, but their own Industry; that all his Recruits
from *Drury-Lane* would want new Cloathing; and that the
warmest Industry would be always labouring up Hill, under so
necessary an Expence, so bad a Situation, and so inconvenient a
Theatre. I was always of opinion too, that in changing Sides,
in most Conditions, there generally were discovered more unforeseen Inconveniences, than visible Advantages; and that at
worst, there would always some sort of Merit remain with Fidelity, tho' unsuccessful. Upon these Considerations, I was only
10 thankful for the Offers made me, from the *Hay-Market*, without accepting them; and soon after came to Town towards the
usual time of their beginning to act, to offer my Service to our
old Master. but I found our Company so thinn'd, that it was
almost impracticable, to bring any one tolerable Play upon the
Stage. When I ask'd him, where were his Actors, and in what
manner he intended to proceed? he reply'd, *Don't you trouble
yourself, come along, and I'll shew you.* He then led me about
all the By-places in the House, and shew'd me fifty little Back-
doors, dark Closets, and narrow Passages, in Alterations and
20 Contrivances of which kind he had busied his Head, most part
of the Vacation, for he was scarce ever, without some notable
Joyner, or a Bricklayer extraordinary, in pay, for twenty Years.
And there are so many odd obscure Places about a Theatre, that
his Genius in Nook-building was never out of Employment; nor
could the most vain-headed Author, be more deaf to an Interruption in reciting his Works, than our wise Master was, while
entertaining me with the Improvements he had made in his in-
visible Architecture; all which, without thinking any one Part
of it necessary; tho' I seem'd to approve, I could not help, now
30 and then, breaking in, upon his Delight, with the impertinent
Question of---*But, Master, where are your Actors?* But it seems
I had taken a wrong time for this sort of Enquiry; his Head was
full of Matters of more moment (and, as you find) I was to
come another time for an Answer: a very hopeful condition

I found myself in, under the conduct of so profound a Ver-
tuoso, and so considerate a Master! But, to speak of him seriously, and to account for this Disregard to his Actors, his Notion was, that Singing, and Dancing, or any sort of Exotick Entertainments, would make an ordinary Company of Actors too
hard, for the best Set, who had only plain Plays to subsist on.
Now, tho' I am afraid too much might be said, in favour of this
Opinion, yet I thought he laid more Stress upon that sort of
Merit, than it would bear; as I therefore found myself of so lit-
10 tle Value with him, I could not help setting a little more upon
myself, and was resolv'd to come to a short Explanation with
him. I told him, I came to serve him, at a time, when many
of his best Actors had deserted him; that he might now have
the Refusal of me; but I could not afford to carry the Compliment so far, as to lessen my Income by it; that I therefore expected, either my casual Pay to be advanced, or the Payment
of my former Sallary made certain, for, as many Days, as we
had acted the Year before.---No, he was not willing to alter his
former Method; but I might chuse whatever Parts I had a mind
20 to act, of theirs who had left him. When I found him, as I
thought, so insensible, or impregnable, I look'd gravely in his
Face, and told him---He knew upon what Terms, I was willing
to serve him; and took my leave. By this time, the *Hay-Market*
Company had begun acting, to Audiences something better than
usual, and were all paid their full Sallaries, a Blessing they had
not felt, in some Years, in either House before. Upon this Success, *Swiney* press'd the Patentee to execute the Articles they had
as yet only verbally agreed on, which were in Substance, That
Swiney should take the *Hay-Market* House in his own Name,
30 and have what Actors he thought necessary from *Drury-Lane*,
and after all Payments punctually made, the Profits should be
equally divided between these two Undertakers. But soft, and
fair! Rashness was a Fault, that had never yet been imputed to
the Patentee; certain Payments were Methods he had not of a

16. to act with *Swiney*] Swiney's company began to act at the Haymarket 15 October 1706, and
Cibber made his first appearance on 7 November as Lord Foppington (Avery, I, 130, 131).
Rich attempted to avenge himself at first by a series of individual suits against the deserting
actors, of which Barker gives some account (p. 66).

long, long time been us'd to; that Point still wanted time for
Consideration. But *Swiney* was as hasty, as the other was slow,
and was resolv'd to know what he had to trust to, before they
parted; and to keep him the closer, to his Bargain, he stood upon his Right of having *Me* added to that Company, if I was willing to come into it. But this was a Point as absolutely refus'd
on one side, as insisted on, on the other. In this Contest, high
Words were exchang'd on both sides, 'till, in the end, this their
last private Meeting came to an open Rupture: But before it was
10 publickly known, *Swiney*, by fairly letting me into the whole
Transaction, took effectual means to secure me in his Interest.
When the Mystery of the Patentee's Indifference to me was un-
folded, and that his slighting me, was owing, to the Security he
rely'd on, of *Swiney's* not daring to engage me, I could have no
further Debate with myself, which side of the Question I should
adhere to. To conclude, I agree, in two Words, to act with
Swiney; and from this time, every Change that happen'd in the
Theatrical Government, was a nearer Step to that twenty Years
of Prosperity, which Actors, under the Menagement of Actors,
20 not long afterwards, enjoy'd. What was the immediate Consequence of this last Desertion from *Drury-Lane*, shall be the Subject of another Chapter.

CHAPTER X

1. Conduct of the Patentee, in refusing so fair an Opportunity] Rich's loss of the Haymarket was not really due to his refusing the opportunity (cf. above and Barker, pp. 63-66) but to his underestimating the docility of Swiney, Cibber, *et. al.*

7. compell'd the same Patentee, to receive both Companies] Cf. below, Chapter XI, 212 ff.

15. Plays, by this means began to recover . . . former Esteem] From the beginning of his management, Swiney made clear his opposition to Rich's theatrical policies; in the playbills of *The Spanish Friar* which opened the season at the Haymarket on 15 October 1706, Swiney advertised it *"Without Singing or Dancing"* (Avery, I, 130), to which Rich, in the *Daily Courant*, 23 October 1706, responded by saying in his notice for *The Recruiting Officer* to be given the following day, "by the *deserted company* of comedians of the Theatre Royal . . . In which *they pray* there may be *singing by Mrs. Tofts* in English and Italian. *And some dancing"* (Barker, p. 64). The prosperity of the Haymarket company was short-lived even though the actors and repertory were excellent.

C H A P. X.

The recruited Actors, in the Hay-Market, *encourag'd by a Sub-*
scription. Drury-Lane, *under a particular Menagement. The*
Power of a Lord-Chamberlain, over the Theatres, consider'd.
How it had been formerly exercis'd. A Digression to Tragick
Authors.

HAVING shewn the particular Conduct of the Patentee, in refusing so fair an Opportunity of secu-
ring to himself both Companies, under his sole
Power, and Interest; I shall now lead the Reader,
after a short View of what pass'd in this new Establishment of the *Hay-Market* Theatre, to the Accidents, that the
Year following, compell'd the same Patentee, to receive both Companies, united, into the *Drury-Lane* Theatre, notwithstanding
his Disinclination to it.

10   It may now, be imagin'd, that such a Detachment of Actors, from *Drury-Lane,* could not but give a new Spirit to those
in the *Hay-Market*; not only by enabling them to act each others
Plays to better Advantage; but by an emulous Industry, which
had lain too long inactive among them, and without which they
plainly saw, they could not be sure of Subsistance. Plays, by this
means began to recover a good Share of their former Esteem, and
Favour; and the Profits of them, in about a Month, enabled
our new Menager to discharge his Debt (of something more than
Two Hundred Pounds) to his old Friend, the Patentee; who had
20   now left him, and his Troop, in trust, to fight their own Battles.
The greatest Inconvenience they still labour'd under, was the
immoderate Wideness of their House; in which, as I have observ'd, the Difficulty of Hearing, may be said to have bury'd half

4. *Strategem . . .*] *The Beaux' Stratagem*, by George Farquhar, first played 8 March 1707; *The Lady's Last Stake*, or, *The Wife's Resentment*, by Cibber, first performed on 13 December 1707; *The Double Gallant*, or, *The Sick Lady's Cure*, pieced together cy Cibber from Burnaby's *The Reformed Wife* and *The Lady's Visiting Day*, and Mrs. Centlivre's *Love at a Venture*, first performed 1 November 1707 (Genest, II, 388-89).

9. *Double Gallant* has had a Place, every Winter . . . these Thirty Years . . .] It was not played apparently in 1709, 1710, 1711, or 1712, but every other season through 1749 (Avery, *passim*; Scouten, *passim*).

11. As I was only the Compiler] Barker (p. 262) lists it as published as "*A Comedy* Written by Mr. Cibber" in quarto, advertised in the *Daily Courant* 8 November 1707. Rich, in order to embarrass Cibber, gave *The Reformed Wife* 3 November 1707; the fact that it had already been revived on 31 October may suggest that Rich knew about Cibber's intentions, or may be coincidence. In the prologue Cibber acknowledged that he owed debts, but did not state the extent of them:

> For tho' from former *Scenes* some hints he draws.
> The Ground-Plots wholly chang'd from what it was:
> Not but he hopes you'll find enough that's new,
> In Plot, in Persons, Wit, and Humour too:
> Yet what's not his, he owns in other's Right,
> Nor toils he now for Fame, but your Delight.

His preface "To the Reader" was also intended to minimize his claims to originality.

23. Lord *Hallifax ...*] Loftis (*Politics*, pp. 41-42) attributes Whig sponsorship of drama largely to Halifax (cf. *Apology*, p. 182 and n.); he cites Joseph Spence on this project: "The paper was all in Lord Hallifax's hand writing [giving Pope as his source of information] of a subscription of four hundred guineas for the encouragement of good comedies, and was dated 1709" (*Anecdotes*, ed. Singer, p. 338). The date Cibber gives below (1707) is the correct one.

the Auditors Entertainment. This Defect seem'd evident, from
the much better Reception several new Plays (first acted there)
met with when they afterwards came to be play'd by the same
Actors, in *Drury-Lane*: of this Number were the *Stratagem*,
and the *Wife's Resentment*; to which I may add, the *Double*
10 *Gallant*. This last, was a Play made up of what little was tolerable, in two, or three others, that had no Success, and were
laid aside, as so much Poetical Lumber; but by collecting and
adapting the best Parts of 'em all, into one Play, the *Double*
Gallant has had a Place, every Winter, amongst the Publick
Entertainments, these Thirty Years. As I was only the Compi-
ler of this Piece, I did not publish it in my own Name; but as
my having but a Hand in it, could not be long a Secret, I have
been often treated as a Plagiary on that Account: Not that I think
I have any Right to complain, of whatever would detract from
the Merit of that sort of Labour; yet, a Cobler may be allow'd
to be useful, though he is not famous: And I hope a Man is not
blameable for doing a little Good, tho' he cannot do as much as
another? But so it is———Two penny Criticks must live, as well as
20 Eighteenpenny Authors!

While the Stage was thus recovering its former Strength, a
more honourable Mark of Favour was shewn to it, than it was
every known before, or since, to have receiv'd. The, then, Lord
Hallifax, was not only the Patron of the Men of Genius of this
Time, but had likewise a generous Concern for the Reputation,
and Prosperity of the Theatre, from whence the most elegant
Dramatick Labours of the Learned, he knew, had often shone
in their brightest Lustre. A Proposal therefore was drawn up
and address'd to that Noble Lord for his Approbation, and As-
30 sistance, to raise a publick Subscription for Reviving Three Plays
of the best Authors, with the full Strength of the Company;
every Subscriber to have Three Tickets, for the first Day of each
Play, for his single Payment of Three Guineas. This Subscription his Lordship so zealously encourag'd, that from his Recom-

1.19 must live] mustlive 1st ed.

in *The Rival Fools*, where Bullock sitting on the shoulders of Penkethman—who had made a specialty of ass-epilogues—taunted his mount who returned the wit. Miss Wiley finds two occasions when an elephant is said to have appeared on stage: "An Epilogue spoken by Mr. Pinkeman [sic], upon the back of an Elephant" (*The Third Volume consisting of Poems on Divers Subjects*, by the author of the *London Spy*, 1706, pp. 347-50 [cited by Wiley, p. 201 n.]); and also an occasion when Spillor, similarly mounted, delivered an epilogue (Wiley, p. 200). Avery (I, 66) reprints an advertisement for Pinkeman's [sic: presumably Penkethman's] Booth at the Brookfield Market-Place: "He [Penkethman] speaks an Epilogue upon an Elephant between Nine and Ten Foot high, arriv'd from Guinea, led upon the Stage by six Blacks.

2. *Julius Caesar . . . Maiden Queen*] *Julius Caesar* played 14 January 1707: "For the Encouragement of the Comedians Acting in the Haymarket, and to enable them to keep the Diversion of Plays under a separate Interest from the Opera. By Subscription. The Boxes to be open'd to the Pit, and none to be admitted but by the Subscription Tickets. First Gallery 2 5. Upper Gallery 1 5." It played the following day "As it was perform'd by Subscription" but at raised prices (Avery, I, 137). *A King and No King* played under the same terms 21 January, but without being repreated (ibid., p. 138). Cibber's reworking of *Marriage a la mode* and *The Maiden Queen* was called *Marriage a la Mode*, or, *The Comical Lovers* and was acted under both names.

12. By the Aid of this Subscription] As Cibber's complaints below show, this assistance did not remedy the cause of the company's troubles, which were due to the great success of Rich's operas and stage shows (cf. Barker, pp. 99 ff.).

17. the Patentee of *Drury-Lane* went on in his usual Method] The extraordinary salaries of singers apparently were paid no less grudgingly than those of actors: Mrs. Tofts, the singer, was under contract from 5 January 1705 for a year, and continued accordingly until Rich claimed a part of £60 given her by the nobility. When she objected and everyone sided with her in the matter, Rich began to harrass her, forcing her to sing so often that she lost her voice, then deducting any missed performances from the money due her at the end of the season. This and many other abuses which she lists finally led her to appeal to the Lord Chamberlain, to whom she described Rich as "a Man unfitt to deale with for his ill Manners & Management of them which are in his Power." One may therefore conclude that the large salaries he contracted to pay singers were dearly won if at all. (The documents from L.C. 7/3 are printed by Nicoll, II, 290-91).

33. . . . an extraordinary large Elephant] Autrey Nell Wiley (*Rare Prologues and Epilogues: 1642-1700*, London, n.d., pp. 196-203 *et passim*) discusses the use of animals on the stage. Doggett's speaking the epilogue to D'Urfey's *Don Quixote* (Part I, 1694) in Dorset Garden while mounted on an ass had begun a rage for mounted epilogues. Cibber burlesqued the fad

mendation chiefly, in a very little time, it was compleated. The
Plays were *Julius Caesar of Shakespear*; the *King and no King* of
Fletcher; and the Comic Scenes of *Dryden's Marriage 'a la mode*,
and of his *Maiden Queen* put together, for it was judg'd, that as
these comic Episodes were utterly independent of the serious
Scenes, they were originally written to, they might on this Occasion be as well Episodes either to the other, and so make up
five livelier Acts between them: At least the Project so well succeeded, that those comic Parts have never since been replac'd,
10 but were continu'd to be jointly acted, as one Play, several Years
after.

By the Aid of this Subscription, which happen'd in 1707, and
by the additional Strength, and Industry of this Company, not
only the Actors, (several of which were handsomely advanc'd, in
their Sallaries) were duly paid, but the Menager himself too, at
the Foot of his Account stood a considerable Gainer.

At the same time, the Patentee of *Drury-Lane* went on in his
usual Method of paying extraordinary Prices to Singers, Dancers
and other exotick Performers, which were as constantly deducted
20 out of the sinking Sallaries of his Actors: 'Tis true, his Actors,
perhaps, might not deserve much more, than he gave them;
yet, by what I have related, it is plain he chose not to be troubled,
with such, as visibly had deserv'd more: For it seems he had not
purchas'd his Share of the Patent, to mend the Stage, but to
make Mony of it: And to say Truth, his Sense of every thing
to be shewn there, was much upon a Level, with the Taste of
the Multitude, whose Opinion, and whose Mony weigh'd with
him full as much, as that of the best Judges. His Point was to
please the Majority, who, could more easily comprehend any
30 thing they *saw*, than the daintiest things, that could be said to
them. But in this Notion he kept no medium; for in my Memory, he carry'd it so far, that he was (some few Years before
this time) actually dealing for an extraordinary large Elephant,
at a certain Sum, for every Day he might think fit to shew the

2. in the Theatre (then standing in Dorset-Garden] Hotson, who gives a full description of the theater (pp. 233-36) with a drawing facing p. 234, notes (pp. 308-309) that it was used with sharply decreasing frequency in the years 1702-1704; it was demolished June 1709 (Nicoll, II, 271).

tractable Genius of that vast quiet Creature, in any Play, or
Farce, in the Theatre (then standing) in *Dorset-Garden*. But
from the Jealousy, which so formidable a Rival had rais'd in his
Dancers, and by his Bricklayer's assuring him, that if the Walls
were to be open'd wide enough for its Entrance, it might en-
danger the Fall of the House, he gave up his Project, and with
it, so hopeful a Prospect of making the Receipts of the Stage run
higher than all the Wit, and Force of the best Writers had ever
yet rais'd them to.

10   About the same time of his being under this Disappointment,
he put in Practice another Project of as new, though not of so
bold a Nature; which was his introducing a Set of Rope-dancers,
into the same Theatre; for the first Day of whose Performance,
he had given out some Play, in which, I had a material Part:
But I was hardy enough to go into the Pit, and acquainted the
Spectators near me, that I hop'd, they would not think it a
Mark of my Disrespect to them, if I declin'd acting upon any
Stage, that was brought to so low a Disgrace, as ours was like to
be by that Day's Entertainment. My Excuse was so well taken,
20 that I never after found any ill Consequences, or heard of the
least Disapprobation of it: And the whole Body of Actors too,
protesting against such an Abuse of their Profession, our cautious
Master was too much alarm'd, and intimidated to repeat it.

After what I have said, it will be no Wonder, that all due
Regards to the original Use, and Institution of the Stage should
be utterly lost, or neglected: Nor was the Conduct of this Menager easily to be alter'd, while he had found the Secret of
making Mony, out of Disorder and Confusion: For however
strange it may seem, I have often observ'd him inclin'd to be
30 cheerful, in the Distresses of his Theatrical Affairs, and equally
reserv'd and pensive, when they went smoothly forward with a
visible Profit. Upon a Run of good Audiences, he was more
frightened to be thought a Gainer, which might make him accountable to others, than he was dejected with bad Houses, which

1.15 acquainted] acquaint 2nd ed.

4. adjusted by a Master in Chancery] Hotson discusses three suits against him: that of Sir
   Edward Smith (pp. 300-302) to collect interest on shares, which came to nothing; that of
   Charles Killigrew (p. 306) to recover control of the Drury Lane theater, which also was
   unsuccessful; and that of Lady Morley (pp. 306-307) in which her claim was balanced by a
   reasonable counterclaim. Nicoll (II, Appendix B, 274 ff.) prints the texts or summaries from
   L.C. 7/3; 5/157, p. 287; 5/160, p. 104 of numerous complaints and countercomplaints
   involving Rich.

at worst, he knew would make others accountable to him: And
as, upon a moderate Computation, it cannot be suppos'd, that
the contested Accounts of a twenty Years Wear, and Tear, in a
Play-house, could be fairly adjusted by a Master in Chancery,
under four-score Years more, it will be no Surprize, that by the
Neglect, or rather the Discretion of other Proprietors, in not
throwing away good Money after bad, this Hero of a Menager
who alone supported the War, should in time so fortify himself
by Delay, and so tire his Enemies, that he became sole Monarch
10 of his Theatrical Empire, and left the quiet Possession of it, to
his Successors.

If these Facts seem too trivial for the Attention of a sensible
Reader, let it be consider'd, that they are not chosen Fictions,
to *entertain*, but Truths necessary to *inform* him, under what
low Shifts, and Disgraces, what Disorders and Revolutions the
Stage labour'd, before it could recover that Strength, and Reputation, wherewith it began to flourish, towards the latter End
of Queen *Anne's* Reign; and which it continu'd to enjoy, for a
Course of twenty Years following. But let us resume our Ac-
20 count of the new Settlement, in the *Hay-Market*.

It may be natural Question, why the Actors, whom *Swiney*
brought over to his Undertaking, in *Hay-Market*, would
tie themselves down to limited Sallaries? for though he, as their
Menager was oblig'd to make them certain Payments, it was not
certain that the Receipts would enable him to do it; and since
their own Industry was the only visible Fund they had to depend
upon, why would they not, for that Reason, insist upon their
being Sharers as well of possible Profits, as Losses? How far in
this Point, they acted right, or wrong, will appear from the
30 following State of their Case.

It must first be consider'd, that this Scheme of their Desertion,
was all concerted, and put in execution in a Week's Time, which
short Warning might make them overlook that Circumstance,
and the sudden Prospect of being deliver'd from having seldom

13. the Power of a Lord Chamberlain] For a discussion of the relations of the Lords Chamberlain with the theater, see Loftis, *Politics*, pp. 20-21, 44-50, *et passim*; and Loftis, *Steele, passim*. Avery (I, xxxix-xliii) states that his power derived from the legal fiction that actors were servants of the Crown with immunity from arrest except by warrant from the Lord Chamberlain. The issue was not clarified until the passage of the Licensing Act of 1737.

more, than half their Pay, was a Contentment that had bound-
ed all their farther Views. Besides, as there could be no room
to doubt of their receiving their full Pay, previous to any Profits, that might be reap'd by their Labour, and as they had no
great Reason to apprehend those Profits could exceed their re
spective Sallaries, so far as to make them repine at them, they
might think it but reasonable to let the Chance of any extraordinary Gain be on the Side of their Leader, and Director.
But farther, as this Scheme had the Approbation of the Court,
10 these Actors, in reality, had it not, in their Power to alter any
Part of it: And what induc'd the Court to encourage it, was,
that by having the Theatre, and its Menager more immediately
dependent on the Power of the Lord Chamberlain, it was not
doubted but the Stage would be recover'd into such a Reputation, as might now do Honour, to that absolute Command,
which the Court, or its Officers seem'd always fond of having
over it.

Here, to set the Constitution of the Stage in a clearer Light,
it may not be amiss, to look back a little on the Power of a
20 Lord Chamberlain, which, as may have been observ'd, in all
Changes of the Theatrical Government, has been the main Spring
without which no Scheme, of what kind soever, could be set in
Motion. My Intent is not to enquire how far, by Law, this
Power has been limited, or extended; but meerly as an Historian, to relate Facts, to gratify the Curious, and then leave them
to their own Reflections: This, too, I am the more inclin'd to,
because there is no one Circumstance, which has affected the
Stage, wherein so many Spectators, from those of the highest
Rank, to the Vulgar, have seem'd more positively knowing, or
30 less inform'd in.

Though in all the Letters Patent, for acting Plays, &c. since
King *Charles* the *First's* Time, there has been no mention of the
Lord Chamberlain, or of any Subordination to his Command,
or Authority---yet it was still taken for granted, that no Letters

27. *Maid's Tragedy*] According to Downes (*Roscius*, ed. Summers, p. 5) it was among the

"stock" of pre-Restoration plays; Pepys saw it as early as 16 May 1661, but thought it "too

sad and melancholy," and recorded seeing it several times more (18 May 1668, the last time).

Langbaine (p. 59) says of it, "This Play was often Acted at the King's Theatre since the

Restauration; but somewhat in it displeasing King *Charles* the Second, it was for some time

forbid coming on the Stage, till Mr. Waller Reviving it, and wholly altering the last Act [it]

appeared again publickly." He gives the date of the revival (p. 146) as 1690.

Patent, by the bare Omission of such a great Officer's Name,
could have superseded, or taken out of his Hands, that Power,
which Time out of Mind, he always had exercis'd over the
Theatre. The common Opinions then abroad were, that if the
Profession of Actors was unlawful, it was not in the Power of
the Crown to license it; and, if it were not unlawful, it ought
to be free, and independent, as other Professions; and that a
Patent to exercise it, was only an honorary Favour; from the
Crown, to give it a better Grace of Recommendation to the
10 Publick. But as the Truth of this Question seem'd to be wrapt
in a great deal of Obscurity, in the old Laws made in former
Reigns, relating to Players, &c. it may be no Wonder, that the
best Companies of Actors should be desirous of taking Shelter
under the visible Power of a Lord Chamberlain, who they knew
had, at his Pleasure, favour'd, and protected, or born hard upon
them: But be all this as it may, a Lord Chamberlain (from
whencesoever his Power might be deriv'd) had, till of later
Years, had always an implicit Obedience paid to it: I shall now
give some few Instances, in what manner it was exercis'd.
20   What appear'd to be most reasonably, under his Cognizance
was the licensing, or refusing new Plays, or striking out what
might be thought offensive, in them: Which Province had been,
for many Years, assign'd to his inferior Officer, the Master of the
Revels; yet was not this License irrevocable; for several Plays,
though acted, by that Permission, had been silenc'd afterwards.
The first Instance of this kind, that common Fame has delivered
down to us, is that of the *Maid's Tragedy of Beaumont* and
Fletcher, which was forbid in King *Charles* the *Second's* time,
by an Order from the Lord Chamberlain. For what Reason this
30 Interdiction was laid upon it, the Politicks of those Days, have
only left us to guess. Some said, that the killing of the King,
in that Play, while the tragical Death of King *Charles* the *First*,
was then so fresh, in People's Memory, was an Object too hor-
ribly impious, for a publick Entertainment. What makes this

20. *Lucius Junius Brutus*] *Lucius Junius Brutus, Father of his Country* first presented 8 December 1680, prohibited 11 December 1680, after three performances (Van Lennep, pp. 292-3).

24. a Prologue . . . to the *Prophetess*] This prologue along with the 1690 edition of the play was immediately suppressed, and apparently only a few copies survived. When finally reprinted by John Oldmixon in *The Muses Mercury: or, the Monthly Miscellany* (a Whig publication) in 1707, the editor attributed the suppression to Shadwell's vengeful insistence to the Secretary of State that it had a 'double meaning' and reflected on the Revolution of 1688 (Shadwell believed his own plays were kept off the stage by Dryden). The offending lines were probably these:

> Never content with what you had before,
> But true to Change, right English Men all o'er,
> New Honour calls you hence, and all your Care
> Is to provide the horrid Pomp of War.
> (19-22)

(*Dryden, Prologues and Epilogues*, ed. Gardner, pp. 156-57 and n., 314-15).

30. The Tragedy of *Mary* Queen of *Scotland*] *The Island Queens: Or, The Death of Mary, Queen of Scotland*, by John Banks, was published in 1684, "only in Defense of the Author and the Play, against some mistaken Censures, occasion'd by its being prohibited the Stage." It was altered and given at Drury Lane at raised prices, "by reason of the extraordinary Charge in the Decoration of it," 6 March 1704, as *The Albion Queens: or The Death of Mary Queen of Scotland* (Nicoll, I, 389; Avery, I, 60).

Conjecture seem to have some Foundation, is that the celebrated
Waller, in Compliment to that Court, alter'd the last Act of
this Play (which is printed at the End of his Works) and gave
it a new Catastrophe, wherein the Life of the King is loyally
sav'd, and the Lady's Matter made up, with a less terrible Reparation. Others have given out, that a repenting Mistress, in a
romantick Revenge of her Dishonour, killing the King, in the
very Bed he expected her to come into, was shewing a too dangerous Example to other *Evadnes*, then shining at Court, in the
10 same Rank of royal Distinction; who, if ever their Consciences
should have run equally mad, might have had frequent Opportunities of putting the Expiation of their Frailty, into the like
Execution. But this I doubt is too deep a Speculation, or too
ludicrous a Reason, to be rely'd on; it being well known, that
the Ladies, then in favour, were not so nice, in their Notions,
as to think their Preferment their Dishonour, or their Lover a
Tyrant: Besides, that easy Monarch lov'd his Roses, without
Thorns; nor do we hear, that he much chose, to be himself
the first Gatherer of them.

20   The *Lucius Junius Brutus* of *Nat. Lee*, was, in the same
Reign, silenc'd after the third Day of acting it; it being objected that the Plan, and Sentiments of it had too badly vindicated, and might enflame Republican Principles.

A Prologue (by *Dryden*) to the *Prophetess*, was forbid by the
Lord *Dorset*, after the first Day of its being spoken. This happen'd when King *William* was prosecuting the War, in *Ireland*.
It must be confess'd that this Prologue had some familiar, me-
taphorical Sneers, at the Revolution itself; and as the Poetry of
it was good, the Offence of it was less pardonable.

30   The Tragedy of *Mary* Queen of *Scotland*, had been offer'd to
the Stage twenty Years before it was acted: But from the profound Penetration of the Master of the Revels, who saw political Spectres in it, that never appear'd in the Presentation, it had
lain, so long upon the Hands of the Author; who had at last,

20. *Bays* in the *Rehearsal ... What the Devil*] *The Rehearsal*, II, i.

33. the Author last mention'd] John Banks: *The Unhappy Favorite, or the Earl of Essex* (Drury

    Lane c. September 1681); *Vertue Betray'd: or, Anna Bullen* (Drury Lane, c. 1682); both of

    them were revived several times (cf. Nicoll, I, 384). Baker (II, 391) says of *Virtue Betrayed*,

    "This play met with great success at its first representation, more particularly becoming a

    favorite with the fair sex. In short, it has that kind of merit which the most of this author's

    pieces possess, viz. a happiness in the choice of its story, and a pathetical manner of

    conducting the plot, which seldom fails of engaging the hearts, and drawing tears from the

    eyes of the audience, even in spight of the greatest deficiency both of poetry and nature in the

    language." Dryden wrote a prologue and epilogue for *The Unhappy Favorite* (*The Poetry of

    Dryden*, ed. Noyes, Cambridge, Mass., n.d., pp. 107-108).

the good Fortune to prevail with a Nobleman, to favour his Petition to Queen *Anne*, for Permission to have it acted: The Queen
had the Goodness to refer the Merit of his Play, to the Opinion
of that noble Person, although he was not her Majesty's Lord
Chamberlain; upon whose Report of its being, every way, an
innocent Piece, it was soon after acted with Success.

 Reader, by your Leave---I will but just speak a Word, or two
to any Author, that has not yet writ one Line of his next Play,
and then I will come to my Point again---What I would say to
10 him, is that---Sir, before you set Pen to Paper, think well, and
principally of your Design, or chief Action, towards which
every Line you write ought to be drawn, as to its Centre: If we
can say of your finest Sentiments, This, or That might be left
out, without maiming the Story you would tell us, depend upon
it, that fine thing is said in a wrong Place; and though you may
urge, that a bright Thought is not to be resisted, you will not
be able to deny, that those very fine Lines would be much finer,
if you could find a proper Occasion for them: Otherwise you
will be thought to take less Advice from *Aristotle, or* Horace,
20 than from Poet *Bays* in the *Rehearsal*, who very smartly says---
What the Devil is the Plot good for, but to bring in fine things?
Compliment the Taste of your Hearers, as much as you please
with them, provided they belong to your Subject, but don't like
a dainty Preacher, who has his Eye more upon this World, than
the next, leave your Text for them. When your Fable is good,
every Part of it will cost you much less Labour, to keep your
Narration alive, than you will be forced to bestow upon those
elegant Discourses, that are not absolutely conducive to your
Catastrophe, or main Purpose: Scenes of that kind, shew but
30 at best, the unprofitable, or injudicious Spirit of a Genius. It is
but a melancholy Commendation of a fine Thought, to say,
when we have heard it, *Well! but what's all this to the Purpose?*
Take therefore, in some part, Example by the Author last mention'd! There are three Plays of his, The *Earl of Essex, Anna*

Bullen, and *Mary Queen* of *Scots,* which tho' they are all written
in the most barren, barbarous Stile, that was ever able to keep
Possession of the Stage, have all interested the Hearts of his Auditors. To what then could this Success be owing, but to the
intrinsick, and naked Value of the well-conducted Tales, he has
simply told us? There is something so happy in the Disposition
of all his Fables; all his chief Characters are thrown into such
natural Circumstances of Distress, that their Misery, or Affliction
wants very little Assistance from the Ornaments of Stile, or Words
10 to speak them. When a skillful Actor is so situated, his bare
plaintive Tone of Voice, the Cast of Sorrow from his Eye, his
slowly graceful Gesture, his humble Sighs of Resignation under
his Calamities: All these, I say, are sometimes without a Tongue,
equal to the strongest Eloquence. At such a time, the attentive
Auditor supplies from his own Heart, whatever the Poet's Language may fall short of, in Expression, and melts himself into
every Pang of Humanity, which the like Misfortunes in real Life
could have inspir'd.

After what I have observ'd, whenever I see a Tragedy defective
20 in its Fable, let there be never so many fine Lines in it; I hope
I shall be forgiven, if I impute that Defect, to the Idleness, the
weak Judgment, or barren Invention of the Author.

If I should be ask'd, why I have not always, my self, follow'd the Rules I would impose upon others; I can only answer,
that whenever I have not, I lie equally open to the same critical
Censure. But having often observ'd a better than ordinary Stile
thrown away, upon the loose, and wandering Scenes of an ill-
chosen Story, I imagin'd these Observations might convince some
future Author, of how great Advantage a Fable well plann'd
30 must be to a Man of any tolerable Genius.

All this, I own, is leading my Reader out of the way; but
if he has as much Time upon his Hands, as I have, (provided
we are neither of us tir'd) it may be equally to the Purpose,
what he reads or what I write of. But as I have no Objection

1.7 chief Characters] chie fCharacters 1st ed.

10. no Actor ... should presume to go] This order was given 16 April 1695 and confirmed 25 July 1696 in a second decree (from L.C. 7/1 and 7/3, printed by Nicoll, I, 338, n.). The former forbids members of the newly formed Lincoln's Inn Fields company to desert; the latter generally forbids desertion from either company. The original license to Betterton's company had regulated the movement of its actors (from L.C. 7/1 and 7/3, printed by Nicoll, I, 361-63) and the order against actors' leaving either company was reissued 27 May 1697 (L.C. 5/152, p. 15, cited by Nicoll, I, 340).

19. *Powel*] Cibber's chronology is confused; George Powell spent three seasons with Betterton's company, from 1702-1704; he appears then in the Lord Chamberlain's records requesting, with the endorsement of the Lord Chamberlain, release from Rich (from L.C. 7/3 and L.C. 5/154, p. 119, p. 124, summarized by Nicoll, II, 287); Rich granted it 7 April 1705. On 14 November (as Lowe summarizes, II, 19) he refused to act his part at the Haymarket (which had opened under Congreve and Vanbrugh 9 April 1705) so that the audience had to be dismissed; he also tried to raise a mutiny among the actors; for these offenses he was ordered arrested and confined at the Porter's Lodge. As a result of his recalcitrance at the Haymarket, an order forbidding Rich to hire him was issued 24 November 1705. He apparently remained suspended until 4 March 1707 when he delivered the prologue at a subscription performance of an opera, in defiance of the earlier order; this violation led to a silencing of Rich (from L.C. 5/154, p. 224, printed by Nicoll, II, 282).

Cibber implies that these events occurred at the period just after the formation of the rival Lincoln's Inn Fields company, but unless there is a parallel series of events between 1698 (when Wilks probably joined Drury Lane) and 1705, Cibber's account distorts the reasons for dealing severely with Powell.

to Method, when it is not troublesome, I return to my Subject.

About the middle of King *William's* Reign, an Order of

Hitherto we have seen no very unreasonable Instance of this
absolute Power of a Lord Chamberlain, though we were to admit, that no one knew of any real Law, or Construction of Law,
by which this Power was given him. I shall now offer some
Facts relating to it of a more extraordinary Nature, which I leave
my Reader to give a Name to.

About the middle of King *William's* Reign, an Order of
10 the Lord Chamberlain was, then, subsisting, that no Actor of
either Company, should presume to go from one, to the other,
without a Discharge from their respective Menagers, and the Permission of the Lord Chamberlain. Notwithstanding such Order,
Powel being uneasy, at the Favour, *Wilks*, was then rising into,
had without such Discharge, left the *Drury-Lane* Theatre, and
engag'd himself to that of *Lincolns-Inns-Fields*: But by what
follows, it will appear, that this Order was not so much intended, to do both of them *good*, as to do, that which the Court
chiefly favour'd (*Lincolns-Inn-Fields*) no harm. For when *Powel*
20 grew dissatisfy'd at his Station there too, he return'd to *Drury-
Lane* (as he had before gone from it) without a Discharge: But
halt a little! here, on this Side of the Question, the Order was
to stand, in force, and the same Offence against it now, was
not to be equally pass'd over. He was the next Day taken up
by a Messenger, and confin'd to the Porter's-Lodge, where, to
the best of my Remembrance, he remain'd about two Days;
when the Menagers of *Lincolns-Inn-Fields*, not thinking an Actor
of his loose Character worth their farther Trouble, gave him up;
though perhaps he was release'd, for some better Reason. Upon
30 this occasion, the next Day, behind the Scenes, at *Drury-Lane*,
a Person of great Quality, in my hearing, enquiring of *Powel*,
into the Nature of his Offence, after he had heard it, told him,
That if he had had Patience, or Spirit enough, to have staid in his

3. Another Time the same Actor, *Powel*] Listed as John Powell, a warrant was issued on 3 May 1698 to commit him prisoner in the Gatehouse "by the Right Hon. Mr. Secretary Vernon for breach of peace and 'for his Insolence in Affronting and drawing his Sword upon Collonell Stanhop and Mr. Davenant,' and whereas the patentees have admitted him again, a warrant is issued to suspend them from acting." (from L.C. 5/152, p. 80, quoted by Nicoll, I, 368). Lowe notes (II, 20) that the suspension was removed the day after this, but that on 19 May he was "forbidden to be received at either Drury Lane or Dorset Garden."

24. In the same King's Reign] Cibber supposed that both anecdotes of Powell deal with events in William's reign.

24. *Dogget ... Drury-Lane ... Articles drawn firm*] The contract (from L.C. 7/1 and 7/3, printed by Nicoll, I, 338-39 and n.) show that he should begin acting 10 October 1696, though he had planned the return on 3 April 1696. He was ordered arrested on 23 November 1697, but by October 1700 was engaged to play with Lincoln's Inn Fields (Nicoll, I, 339-40 and n.).

Confinement, till he had given him Notice of it, he would have
found him a handsomer way of coming out of it.

Another Time the same Actor, *Powel*, was provok'd at *Will's*
Coffee-house, in a Dispute about the Play-house Affairs, to strike
a Gentleman, whose Family had been sometimes Masters of it;
a Complaint of this Insolence was, in the Absence of the Lord
Chamberlain, immediately made to the Vice-Chamberlain, who
so highly resented it, that he thought himself bound in Honour, to carry his Power of redressing it, as far as it could pos-
10 sibly go: For *Powel* having a Part in the Play, that was acted
the Day after; the Vice-Chamberlain sent an Order to silence
the whole Company, for having suffer'd *Powel* to appear upon
the Stage, before he had made that Gentleman Satisfaction, although the Masters of the Theatre had had no Notice of *Powel's*
Misbehaviour: However, this Order was obey'd, and remain'd
in force for two or three Days, till the same Authority was
pleas'd, or advis'd, to revoke it. From the Measures this injur'd
Gentleman took for his Redress, it may be judg'd how far it
was taken for granted, that a Lord Chamberlain had an absolute
20 Power over the Theatre.

I shall now give an Instance of an Actor, who had the Resolution to stand upon the Defence of his Liberty, against the
same Authority, and was reliev'd by it.

In the same King's Reign, *Dogget*, who though, from a severe
Exactness in his Nature, he could be seldom long easy in any
Theatre, where Irregularity, not to say Injustice, too often prevail'd, yet in the private Conduct of his Affairs, he was a pru-
dent, honest Man. He therefore took an unusual Care, when
he return'd to act under the Patent, in *Drury-Lane*, to have
30 his Articles drawn firm and binding: But having some Reason
to think the Patentee had not dealt fairly with him, he quitted
the Stage, and would act no more, rather chusing to lose his
whatever unsatisfy'd, Demands, than go through the chargeable,

20. Lord Chief Justice Holt] Sir John Holt (1642-1710). Lord Chief Justice of the King's Bench 1689-1710. Known for strict views of treason and seditious libel.

and tedious Course of the Law to recover it. But the Pantentee,
who (from other People's Judgment) knew the Value of him,
and who wanted too, to have him sooner back, than the Law
could possibly bring him, thought the surer way would be, to
desire a shorter Redress from the Authority of the Lord Chamberlain. Accordingly upon his Complaint, a Messenger was immediately dispatch'd to *Norwich*, where *Dogget* then was, to bring
him up, in Custody: But doughty *Dogget*, who had Mony in
his Pocket, and the Cause of Liberty at his Heart, was not, in
10 the least intimidated, by this formidable Summons. He was observ'd to obey it, with a particular Chearfulness, entertaining his
fellow Traveller, the Messenger, all the way in the Coach (for he
had protested against riding) with as much Humour, as a Man
of his Business might be capable of tasting. And as he found
his Charges were to be defray'd, he, at every Inn, call'd for the
best Dainties the Country could afford, or a pretended weak Appetite could digest. At this Rate they jollily roll'd on, more with
the Air of a Jaunt, than a Journey, or a Party of Pleasure, than
of a poor Devil in durance. Upon his Arrival in Town, he im-
20 mediately apply'd to the Lord Chief Justice *Holt*, for his *Habeas
Corpus*. As his Case was something particular, that eminent,
and learned Minister of the Law took a particular Notice of it:
For *Dogget* was not only discharg'd, but the Process of his Confinement (according to common Fame) had a Censure pass'd upon it, in Court, which I doubt, I am not Lawyer enough to
repeat! To conclude, the officious Agents in this Affair finding
that, in *Dogget*, they had mistaken their Man, were mollify'd
into milder Proceedings, and (as he afterwards told me) whisper'd
something, in his Ear, that took away *Dogget's* farther Uneasi-
30 ness about it.

By these Instances we see how naturally Power only founded
on Custom, is apt, where the Law is silent, to run into Excesses,
and while it laudably pretends to govern others, how hard it is
to govern itself. But since the Law has lately open'd its Mouth,

and has said plainly, that some Part of this Power to govern the
Theatre shall be, and is plac'd in a proper Person; and as it is
evident, that the Power of that white Staff, ever since it has been
in the noble Hand, that now holds it, has been us'd with the
utmost Lenity, I would beg Leave of the murmuring Multitude,
who frequent the Theatre, to offer them a simple Question or
two, *viz.* Pray Gentlemen, how came you, or rather your Fore-
fathers never to be mutinous, upon any of the occasional Facts
I have related? And why have you been so often tumultuous,
10 upon a Law's being made, that only confirms a less Power, than
was formerly exercis'd, without any Law to support it? You
cannot sure, say, such Discontent is either just, or natural, unless
you allow it a Maxim in your Politicks, that Power exercis'd
without Law, is a less Grievance, than the same Power exercis'd
according to law!

　　Having thus given the clearest View I was able, of the usual
Regard paid to the Power of a Lord Chamberlain, the Reader
will more easily conceive, what Influence, and Operation that
Power must naturally have, in all Theatrical Revolutions; and
20 particularly in the complete Re-union of both Companies, which
happen'd in the Year following.

CHAP. XI.

Some Chimaerical Thoughts of making the Stage useful: Some, to
its Reputation. The Patent unprofitable, to all the Proprietors,
but one. A fourth Part of it given away to Colonel Brett. *A*
Digression to his Memory. The two Companies of Actors re-
united, by his Interest, and Menagement. The first Direction
of Opera's only, given to Mr. Swiney.

FROM the Time, that the Company of Actors, in
the *Hay-Market,* was recruited with those from
Drury-Lane, and came into the Hands of their
new Director, *Swiney,* the Theatre, for three or four
Years following, suffer'd so many Convulsions, and
was thrown every other Winter under such different Interests,
and Menagement, before it came to a firm and lasting Settlement, that I am doubtful, if the most candid Reader will have
Patience, to go through a full, and fair Account of it: And yet
10   I would fain flatter my self, that those, who are not too wise,
to frequent the Theatre (or have Wit enough to distinguish what
sort of Sights there, either do Honour, or Disgrace to it) may
think their national Diversion no contemptible Subject, for a
more able Historian, than I pretend to be: If I have any particular Qualification, for the Task, more than another, it is that I
have been an ocular Witness of the several Facts, that are to fill
up the rest of my Volume; and am, perhaps, the only Person
living (however unworthy) from whom the same Materials can
be collected; but let them come from whom they may, whe-
20   ther, at best, they will be worth reading; perhaps a Judgment
may be better form'd after a patient Perusal of the following Digression.

18. — *Si quid ... si non* —] Horace, *Epistles*, I, vi, 68-69: "If you know anything better than these [maxims], candidly impart it; if not, ..."

30. *Cato* was first acted] At Drury Lane, 14 April 1713. Cibber's allusions to the first night of Cato (cf. Chapter XIV) would lead one to believe that his sympathies had been Whig all along; however, Loftis (*Politics*, p. 56 n.) cites evidence that he may have performed services for the Tories as a pamphleteer c. 1710. That Addison's play was written to serve the cause of the Whig party likewise is untenable. Loftis (*Politics*, pp. 57 ff.) discusses the ambiguity of its political meaning and suggests that Addison "can scarcely be acquitted, if not of a certain amount of double dealing, then of an extreme degree of caution to avoid giving offence." See Introduction, p. xxi, and p. 276 n.

In whatever cold Esteem, the Stage may be, among the wise
and powerful; it is not so much a Reproach, to those, who
contentedly enjoy it in its lowest Condition, as that Condition
of it, is to those, who (though they cannot but know, to how
valuable a publick Use, a Theatre, well establish'd, might be
rais'd) yet in so many civiliz'd Nations, have neglected it. This
perhaps will be call'd thinking my own wiser, than all the wise
Heads, in *Europe*. But I hope a more humble Sense will be
given to it; at least I only mean, that if so many Govern-
10 ments have their Reasons, for their Disregard of their Theatres, those Reasons may be deeper, than my Capacity has yet
been able to dive into: If therefore my simple Opinion is a
wrong one, let the Singularity of it expose me: And though I
am only building a Theatre in the Air, it is there, however, at
so little Expence, and in so much better a Taste, than any I have
yet seen, that I cannot help saying of it, as a wiser Man did (it
may be) upon a wiser Occasion:

    ----*Si quid novisti rectius istis,*
    Candidus imperti; si non----

Hor.

20 Give me leave to play, with my Project, in Fancy.

I say then, that as I allow nothing is more liable to debase,
and corrupt the Minds of a People, than a licentious Theatre;
so under a just, and proper Establishment, it were possible to
make it, as apparently the School of Manners, and of Virtue.
Were I to collect all the Arguments, that might be given for my
Opinion, or to inforce it by exemplary Proofs, it might swell
this short Digression to a Volume; I shall therefore trust the Va-
lidity of what I have laid down, to a single Fact, that may be
still fresh, in the Memory of many living Spectators. When the
30 Tragedy of *Cato* was first acted, let us call to mind the noble
Spirit of Patriotism, which that Play then infus'd into the Breast
of a free People, that crowded to it; with what affecting Force,
was that most elevated of Human Virtues recommended? Even

8. and join in their equal Applauses of it] Cf. Johnson's version in the *Life of Addison*: "The Whigs applauded every line in which liberty was mentioned, as a satire on the Tories; and the Tories echoed every clap to show that the satire was unfelt" [Lowe].

the false Pretenders to it felt an unwilling Conviction, and made
it a Point of Honour to be foremost, in their Approbation; and
this too at a time, when the fermented Nation had their different Views of Government. Yet the sublime Sentiments of Liberty, in that venerable Character, rais'd, in every sensible Hearer
such conscious Admiration, such compell'd Assent to the Conduct of a suffering Virtue, as even *demanded* two almost irreconcilable Parties to embrace, and join in their Applauses of
it. Now, not to take from the Merit of the Writer, had that
10 Play never come to the Stage, how much of this valuable Effect
of it must have been lost? It then could have had no more immediate weight with the Publick, than our poring upon the
many ancient Authors, through whose Works the same Sentiments have been, perhaps, less profitably dispers'd, tho' amongst
Millions of Readers; but by bringing such Sentiments to the
Theatre, and into Action, what a superior Lustre did they shine
with? There, *Cato* breath'd again, in Life; and tho' he perish'd
in the Cause of Liberty, his Virtue was victorious, and left the
Triumph of it in the Heart of every melting Spectator. If Ef-
20 fects, like these are laudable; if the Representation of such
Plays can carry Conviction with so much Pleasure, to the Un-
derstanding, have they not vastly the Advantage of any other
Human Helps to Eloquence? What equal Method can be found
to lead, or stimulate the Mind, to a quicker Sense of Truth, and
Virtue, or warm a People into the Love, and Practice of such
Principles, as might be at once a Defence, and Honour to their
Country? In what Shape could we listen to Virtue with equal
Delight, or Appetite of Instruction? The Mind of Man is naturally free, and when he is compell'd, or menac'd into any Opi-
30 nion that he does not readily conceive, he is more apt to doubt
the Truth of it, than when his Capacity is led by Delight, into
Evidence and Reason. To preserve a Theatre in this Strength,
and Purity of Morals, is, I grant, what the wisest Nations, have
not been able to perpetuate, or to transmit long to their Poste-

12. Holy Policy ... Sacred History] Cibber may have in mind plays like Racine's *Athalie* and *Esther*, or the form of religious theater utilized in Jesuit schools. Actors were not permitted Christian burial by the Roman Catholic Church in France until the Council of Soissons, 1849 (*Grande Larousse encyclopedique*, article Comedien).

21. Religious Inhumanity short of that famous Painter's] Possibly an apocryphal anecdote about Caravaggio famed both for his realistic style of painting and the violence of his temper. Cibber gives his source (below) as "common Fame."

30. Hundred Thousand Pounds ... Tragedy of *Sophocles*] Neither Lowe nor the present editor can find the source of this.

rity: But this Difficulty will rather heighten, than take from the
Honour of the Theatre: The greatest Empires have decay'd, for
want of proper Heads to guide them, and the Ruins of them
sometimes have been the Subject of Theatres, that could not be,
themselves exempt, from as various Revolutions: Yet may not the
most natural Inference from all this be, That the Talents requisite to form good Actors, great Writers, and true Judges, were
like those of wise and memorable Ministers, as well the Gifts of
Fortune, as of Nature, and not always to be found, in all Climes
10 or Ages.   Or can there be a stronger modern Evidence of the
Value of Dramatick Performances, than that in many Countries,
where the Papal Religion prevails, the Holy Policy (though it allows not to an Actor Christian Burial) is so conscious of the Use-
fulness of his Art, that it will frequently take in the Assistance
of the Theatre, to give even Sacred History, in a Tragedy, a Recommendation to the more pathetick Regard of their People.
How can such Principles, in the Face of the World, refuse the
Bones of a Wretch the lowest Benefit of Christian Charity, after having admitted his Profession (for which they deprive him
20 of that Charity) to serve the solemn Purposes of Religion? How
far then is this Religious Inhumanity short of that famous Painter's,
who, to make his *Crucifix* a Master-piece of Nature, stabb'd the
innocent Hireling, from whose Body he drew it; and having
heighten'd the holy Portrait, with his last Agonies of Life, then
sent it to be the consecreated Ornament of an Altar? Though
we have only the Authority of common Fame, for this Story,
yet be it true, or false, the Comparison will still be just.   Or let
me ask another Question more humanly political.

   How came the *Athenians* to lay out an Hundred Thousand
30 Pounds, upon the Decorations of one single Tragedy of *Sopho-*
cles? Not sure, as it was merely a Spectacle for Idleness, or
Vacancy of Thought to gape at, but because it was the most rational, most instructive, and delightful Composition, that human Wit had yet arriv'd at; and consequently the most worthy

2. whether the *Sophocles*] The author of *The Laureat* (p. 65) derides Cibber's ambiguous grammar, taking it to indicate he thought "the *Sophocles*" was the name of a play.

9. *Caviare to the Multitude*] *Hamlet*, II, ii, c. 457: "caviar to the general."

9. Honest *John Trott*] OED: "a man of slow or uncultured intellect, a bumpkin, a clown."

to be the Entertainment of a wise, and warlike Nation: And
it may be still a Question, whether the *Sophocles* inspir'd this Publick Spirit, or this Publick Spirit inspir'd the *Sophocles*?

But alas! as the Power of giving, or receiving such Inspira-
tions, from either of these Causes, seems pretty well at an End;
now I have shot my Bolt, I shall descend to talk more like a
Man of the Age, I live in: For, indeed, what is all this to a
common *English* Reader? Why truly, as *Shakespear* terms it----
Caviare to the Multitude! Honest *John Trott* will tell you, that
10 if he were to believe what I have said of the *Athenians*, he is
at most, but astonish'd at it; but that if the twentieth Part of
the Sum I have mention'd were to be apply'd, out of our Publick Money, to the Setting off the best Tragedy, the nicest
Noddle in the Nation could produce, it would probably raise the
Passions higher in those that did *Not* like it, than in those that
did; it might as likely meet with an Insurrection, as the Applause of the People, and so, mayhap, be fitter for the Subject
of a Tragedy, than for a Publick Fund to support it.----Truly,
Mr. *Trott*, I cannot but own, that I am very much of your Opi-
20 nion: I am only concern'd, that the Theatre has not a better
Pretence to the Care and further Consideration of those Governments, where it is tolerated; but as what I have said will not probably do it any great Harm, I hope I have not put you out of
Patience, by throwing a few good Wishes after an old Acquaintance.

To conclude this Disgression. If, for the Support of the Stage,
what is generally shewn there, must be lower'd to the Taste of
common Spectators; or if it is inconsistent with Liberty, to mend
that vulgar Taste, by making the Multitude less merry there; or
30 by abolishing every low, and senseless Jollity, in which the Understanding can have no Share; whenever, I say, such is the
State of the Stage, it will be as often liable, to unanswerable
Censure, and manifest Disgraces. Yet there *was* a Time, not
yet, out of many People's Memory, when it subsisted upon its

13. Sir *Thomas Skipwith* ... equal Share] Skipwith claimed three-fifths of the patent when suing Brett for the return of the patent in 1708/1709 (Hotson gives the complete text of the bill of complaint and Brett's reply on pp. 386-97). Rich had claimed in 1693 to have paid £400 of the original £2400 purchase price of Charles D'Avenant's shares (Hotson, p. 293). Rich later bought, in addition, Alexander D'Avenant's lesser share (Nicoll, I, 333). These questions are immensely complicated by the distinction between ownership of the patents which conferred control, and interest or shares in the profits of the company. The Union in 1682 had brought the two original patents together, with Charles Killigrew claiming three-twentieths of the profits and the right to joint control, but he did not exercise this right at all times (Hotson, pp. 289 ff. For a list of the minor sharers and how the profits should be divided, see Hotson, p. 301). In any case, Skipwith owned controlling interest.

15. actually made a Present of his entire Interest] Skipwith's share was formally 'sold' for 10 shillings (at least according to Brett: cf. Hotson, p. 393).

19. Colonel Brett] Colonel Henry Brett (d. 1724) known primarily for having married the divorced wife of the Earl of Macclesfield.

34. Gentleman of the Law ... happening to be a Guest there] Brett, in his answer to Skipwith's petition, says, "Humphrey Brent Esquire being all that time att this Defend[ant's] house att Sandiwell (there not being any Attorney or Agent in the neighborehood proper for that purpose did prepare an Instrument or Deed of Assignm[ent] bearing date the 6th day of October ..." (Hotson, p. 393).

own rational Labours; when even Success attended an Attempt to
reduce it to Decency; and when Actors themselves were hardy
enough to hazard their Interest, in pursuit of so dangerous a
Reformation. And this Crisis, I am myself as impatient, as any
tir'd Reader can be, to arrive at. I shall therefore endeavour to
lead him the shortest way to it. But as I am a little jealous of
the badness of the Road, I must reserve to myself the Liberty
of calling upon any Matter, in my Way, for a little Refreshment
to whatever Company may have the Curiosity, or Goodness, to
10 go along with me.

When the sole menaging Patentee at *Drury-Lane*, for several
Years could never be persuaded or driven to any Account with
the Adventurers; Sir *Thomas Skipwith* (who, if I am rightly inform'd, had an equal Share with him) grew so weary of the Affair, that he actually made a Present of his entire Interest in it,
upon the following Occasion.

Sir *Thomas* happen'd, in the Summer preceding the Re-union
of the Companies, to make a Visit to an intimate Friend of his,
Colonel *Brett*, of *Sandywell*, in *Gloucestershire*; where the Plea-
20 santness of the Place, and the agreeable manner of passing his
Time there, had rais'd him to such a Gallantry of Heart, that,
in return to the Civilities of his Friend the Colonel, he made
him an Offer of his whole Right in the Patent; but not to over-
rate the Value of his Present, told him, he himself had made
nothing of it, these ten Years: But the Colonel (he said) being
a greater Favourite of the People in Power, and (as he believ'd)
among the Actors too, than himself was, might think of some
Scheme, to turn it to Advantage, and in that Light, if he lik'd
it, it was at his Service. After a great deal of Raillery on both
30 sides, of what Sir *Thomas* had *not* made of it, and the particular Advantages the Colonel was likely to make of it; they came
to a laughing Resolution, That an Instrument should be drawn the
next Morning, of an absolute Conveyance of the Premises. A
Gentleman of the Law, well known to them both, happening to

be

3. sign'd, seal'd, and deliver'd] Dated 6 October 1707.

7. the Success of *Swiney*] Swiney's Haymarket company at this period was prostrate (Barker, p. 73); the failure of Cibber's new play, *The Lady's Last Stake* (13, 17, 19 December 1707; 28 February 1707/8) completed the destruction of the company.

14. this Gentleman was the first] Cibber had been Brett's guest during the Rich-Swiney negotiations (cf. above, p. 189).

26. Whatever Failings he might have to others] Cibber may be alluding to scandal attached to Brett through his marriage to Anne Mason, divorced wife of the Earl of Macclesfield, (cf. *DNB*, article Henry Brett; Johnson, *Life of Savage*) or to a belief repeated by Boswell (I, 108-109) that he was "free in his gallantry with his lady's maid." It is important to understand that Brett introduced Cibber into fashionable society in London, and that without his sponsorship, the actor would never have come to know enough about this life to represent it on stage. Boswell's note therefore, is not surprising: "Colley Cibber, I am informed, had so high an opinion of her taste and judgement as to genteel life and manners, that he submitted every scene of his *Careless Husband* to Mrs. Brett's revisal and correction."

be a Guest there, at the same time, the next Day produc'd the
Deed, according to his Instructions, in the Presence of whom, and
of others, it was sign'd, seal'd, and deliver'd, to the Purposes
therein contain'd.

This Transaction may be another Instance (as I have elsewhere
observ'd) at how low a Value, the Interest, in a Theatrical License were then held; tho' it was visible, from the Success
of *Swiney* in that very Year, that with tolerable Menagement,
they could, at no time have fail'd of being a profitable Pur-
10 chase.

The next Thing to be consider'd was, what the Colonel
should do with his new Theatrical Commission, which, in another's Possession, had been of so little Importance. Here it may
be necessary to premise, that this Gentleman was the first of any
Consideration, since my coming to the Stage, with whom I had
contracted a Personal Intimacy; which might be the Reason,
why, in this Debate, my Opinion had some weight with him:
Of this Intimacy too, I am the more tempted to talk, from the
natural Pleasure of calling back, in Age, the Pursuits, and hap-
20 py Ardours of Youth long past, which, like the Ideas of a delightful Spring, in a Winter's Rumination, are sometimes equal to
the former Enjoyment of them. I shall therefore, rather chuse,
in this Place to gratify myself, than my Reader, by setting the
fairest Side of this Gentleman in view, and by indulging a little
conscious Vanity, in shewing how early in Life, I fell into the
Possession of so agreeable a Companion: Whatever Failings he
might have to others, he had none to me; nor was he, where
he had them, without his valuable Qualities to balance or soften
them. Let, then, what was not, to be commended in him, rest
30 with his Ashes, never to be rak'd into: But the friendly Favours
I receiv'd from him, while living, give me still a Pleasure, in
paying this only Mite of an Acknowledgment, in my Power, to
his Memory. And if my taking this Liberty, may find Pardon
from several of his fair Relations, still living, for whom I profess

21. *Green Room*] This was a room built behind the stage as a place of resort for the actors and persons interested in their company. It replaced the 'settle' (cf. Davies, *Dram. Misc.*, III, 489).

29. fair full-bottom'd Perriwig ... wore in my first Play] The date of the play was January 1696. As for the style of periwigs admired by Brett, Davies notes (*Dram. Misc.*, III, 83-85) that the fashion for them did not die out among actors until about 1720 and that Wilks, Booth, and Cibber, when full-dressed, wore them; he adds that though Booth did not approve the fashion, "he and Wilks bestowed forty guineas each on the exorbitant thatching of their heads."

the utmost Respect, it will give me but little Concern, tho' my
critical Readers should think it all Impertinence.

This Gentleman then, *Henry*, was the eldest Son of *Henry
Brett*, Esq; of *Cowley*, in *Gloucestershire*, who coming early to
his Estate of about Two Thousand a Year, by the usual Negli-
gences of young Heirs, had, before this his eldest son came of
age, sunk it to about half that Value, and that not wholly free
from Incumbrances. Mr. *Brett*, whom I am speaking of, had
his Education, and I might say ended it, at the University of
10 *Oxford*; for tho' he was settled some time after at the *Temple*, he
so little followed the Law there, that his Neglect of it, made the
Law (like some of his fair and frail Admirers) very often follow
him. As he had an uncommon Share of Social Wit, and a handsome Person, with a sanguine Bloom in his Complexion, no wonder they persuaded him, that he might have a better Chance of
Fortune, by throwing such Accomplishments, into the gayer
World, than by shutting them up, in a Study. The first View,
that fires the Head of a young Gentleman of this modish Ambition, just broke loose, from Business, is to cut a Figure (as they
20 call it) in a Side-box, at the Play, from whence their next Step
is, to the *Green Room* behind the Scenes, sometimes their *Non
ultra*. Hither, at last then, in this hopeful Quest of his Fortune, came this Gentleman-Errant, not doubting but the fickle
Dame, while he was thus qualify'd to receive her, might be
tempted to fall into his Lap. And though, possibly, the Charms
of our Theatrical Nymphs might have their Share, in drawing
him thither; yet in my Observation, the most visible Cause of
his first coming, was a more sincere Passion he had conceiv'd for
a fair full-bottom'd Perriwig, which I then wore in my first Play
30 of the *Fool in Fashion*, in the Year 1695. For it is to be noted,
that, the *Beaux* of those Days, were a quite different Cast,
from the modern Stamp, and had more of the Stateliness of the
Peacock in their Mien, than (which now seems to be their highest
Emulation) the pert Air of a Lapwing. Now whatever Con-

1.6 his eldest Son] his eldst Son 1st ed.

tempt Philosophers may have, for a fine Perriwig; my Friend,
who was not to despise the World, but to live in it, knew very
well, that so material an Article of Dress, upon the Head of a
Man of Sense, if it became him, could never fail of drawing to
him a more partial Regard, and Benevolence, than could possibly
be hop'd for, in an ill-made one. This perhaps may soften the
grave Censure, which so youthful a Purchase might otherwise,
have laid upon him: In a word, he made his Attack upon this
Perriwig, as your young Fellows generally do upon a Lady of
10 Pleasure; first, by a few, familiar Praises of her Person, and
then, a civil Enquiry, into the Price of it. But upon his observing me a little surpriz'd at the Levity of his Question, about
a Fop's Perriwig, he began to railly himself, with so much Wit,
and Humour, upon the Folly of his Fondness for it, that he struck
me, with an equal Desire of granting any thing, in my Power,
to oblige so facetious a Customer. This singular Beginning of
our Conversation, and the mutual Laughs that ensued upon it,
ended in an Agreement, to finish our Bargain that Night, over a
Bottle
20   If it were possible, the Relation of the happy Indiscretions
which pass'd between us that Night, could give the tenth Part of
the Pleasure, I then receiv'd from them, I could still repeat
them with Delight: But as it may be doubtful, whether the Patience of a Reader may be quite so strong, as the Vanity of an
Author, I shall cut it short, by only saying, That single Bottle
was the Sire of many a jolly Dozen, that for some Years following, like orderly Children, whenever they were call'd for, came
into the same Company. Nor indeed, did I think from that time,
whenever he was to be had, any Evening could be agreeably en-
30 joy'd without him. But the long continuance of our Intimacy,
perhaps, may be thus accounted for.

He who can taste Wit in another, may, in some sort, be said
to have it himself: Now, as I always had, and (I bless myself
for the Folly) still have a quick Relish of whatever did, or can

give me Delight: This Gentleman could not but see the youthful Joy, I was generally rais'd to, whenever I had the Happiness of a *Téte a téte* with him; and it may be a moot Point,
whether Wit is not as often inspir'd, by a proper Attention, as
by the brightest Reply, to it. Therefore as he had Wit enough
for any two People, and I had Attention enough for any four,
there could not well be wanting a sociable Delight, on either
side. And tho' it may be true, that a Man of a handsom Person is apt to draw a partial Ear to every thing he says; yet this
10 Gentleman seldom said any thing, that might not have made a
Man of the plainest Person agreeable. Such a continual Desire
to please, it may be imagin'd, could not but, sometimes lead
him into a little venial Flattery, rather than not succeed in it.
And I, perhaps, might be one of those Flies, that was caught in
this Honey. As I was, then, a young successful Author, and
an Actor, in some unexpected Favour, whether deservedly, or
not, imports not; yet such Appearances, at least were plausible
Pretences enough, for an amicable Adulation to enlarge upon;
and the Sallies of it a less Vanity, than mine might not have
20 been able to resist. Whatever this Weakness on my side might
be, I was not alone in it; for I have heard a Gentleman of Condition say, who knew the World as well, as most Men, that live
in it, that let his Discretion be ever so much upon its guard, he
never fell into Mr. *Brett's* Company, without being loth to leave
it, or carrying away a better Opinion of himself, from it. If his
Conversation had this Effect among the Men; what must we
suppose to have been the Consequence, when he gave it, a yet
softer turn among the Fair Sex? Here now, a *French* Novellist
would tell you fifty pretty Lies of him; but as I chuse to be
30 tender of Secrets of that sort, I shall only borrow the good Breeding of that Language, and tell you, in a Word, that I knew several Instances of his being *un Homme a bonne Fortune.* But
though his frequent Successes might generally keep him, from the
usual Disquiets of a Lover, he knew this was a Life too liquorish

7. introduc'd him, where there was a Lady] Barker (p. 15) estimates her fortune at £12,000 to £25,000. He had apparently won her sympathy when being arrested outside her window (*DNB*, article Henry Brett). The events Cibber is describing took place in 1700 or shortly before.

to last; and therefore had Reflexion enough, to be govern'd by
the Advice of his Friends, to turn these his Advantages of Nature
to a better use.

Among the many Men of Condition, with whom, his Conversation had recommended him, to an Intimacy; Sir *Thomas Skipwith* had taken a particular Inclination to him; and as he had
the Advancement of his Fortune, at Heart, introduc'd him,
where there was a Lady, who had enough, in her Power, to
disencumber him of the World, and make him every way, easy,
10 for Life.

While he was in pursuit of this Affair, which no time was to
be lost in (for the Lady was to be in Town but for three Weeks)
I one Day found him idling behind the Scenes, before the Play
was begun. Upon sight of him, I took the usual Freedom he
allow'd me, to rate him roundly, for the Madness of not improving every Moment, in his Power, in what was of such consequence to him. Why are you not (said I) where you know
you only should be? If your Design should once get Wind, in
the Town, the Ill-will of your Enemies, or the Sincerity of the
20 Lady's Friends, may soon blow up your Hopes, which, in your
Circumstances of Life, cannot be long supported, by the bare
Appearance of a Gentleman.-----But it is impossible to proceed,
without some Apology, for the very familiar Circumstance, that
is to follow.-----Yet, as it might not be so trivial in its Effect, as
I fear it may be in the Narration, and is a Mark of that Intimacy, which is necessary should be known, had been between
us, I will honestly make bold with my Scruples, and let the
plain Truth of my Story take its Chance for Contempt, or Approbation.

30   After twenty Excuses, to clear himself of the Neglect, I had
so warmly charg'd him with, he concluded them, with telling
me, he had been out all the Morning, upon Business, and that
his Linnen was too much soil'd, to be seen in Company. Oh,
ho! said I, is that all? Come along with me, we will soon get

10. *Greenwich-Park*] *Greenwich-Park* by William Mountfort, first performed c. May 1691; Cibber played Reveller.

19. King William dy'd] 8 March 1702.

over that dainty Difficulty: Upon which I haul'd him, by the
Sleeve, into my Shifting-Room, he either staring, laughing, or
hanging back all the way. There, when I had lock'd him in,
I began to strip off my upper Cloaths, and bad him do the
same; still he either did not, or would not, seem to understand
me, and continuing his Laugh, cry'd, What! is the Puppy mad?
No, no, only positive, said I; for look you, in short, the Play
is ready to begin, and the Parts that you, and I, are to act to
Day, are not of equal consequence; mine of young *Reveller* (in
10 *Greenwich-Park*) is but a Rake; but whatever you may be, you
are not to appear so; therefore take my Shirt, and give me
yours; for depend upon't, stay here you shall not, and so go a
about your Business. To conclude, we fairly chang'd Linnen,
nor could his Mother's have wrap'd him up more fortunately;
for in about ten Days he marry'd the Lady. In a Year or two
after his Marriage, he was chosen a Member of the Parliament,
which was fitting, when King *William* dy'd. And, upon the
raising of some new Regiments, was made Lieutenant-Colonel,
to that of Sir *Charles Hotham*. But as his Ambition extended
20 not beyond the Bounds of a Park Wall, and a pleasant Retreat
in the Corner of it, which, with too much Expence he had just
finish'd, he, within another Year, had leave to resign his Company to a younger Brother.

This was the Figure, in Life, he made, when Sir *Thomas Skipwith* thought him the most proper Person, to oblige (if it could
be an Obligation) with the Present of his Interest in the Patent.
And from these Anecdotes of my Intimacy with him, it may be
less a Surprise, when he came to Town invested with this new
Theatrical Power, that I should be the first Person, to whom he
30 took any Notice of it. And notwithstanding he knew I was then
engag'd, in another Interest, at the *Hay-Market*, he desired we
might consider together, of the best Use he could make of it, assuring me, at the same time, he should think it of none to himself, unless it could in some Shape be turn'd to my Advantage.

This friendly Declaration, though it might be generous in him to
make, was not needful, to incline me, in whatever might be honestly in my Power, whether by Interest or Negotiation, to serve
him. My first Advice, therefore, was, That he should produce
his Deed to the other Menaging Patentee of *Drury-Lane*, and
demand immediate Entrance to a joint Possession of all Effects,
and Powers, to which that Deed had given him an equal Title.
After which, if he met with no Opposition, to this Demand (as
upon sight of it he did not) that he should be watchful against
10 any Contradiction, from his Collegue, in whatever he might
propose, in carrying on the Affair, but to let him see, that he
was determin'd in all his Measures. Yet to heighten that Resolution, with an Ease and Temper in his manner, as if he took it
for granted, there could be no Opposition made, to whatever he
had a mind to. For that this Method, added to his natural Talent of Persuading, would imperceptibly lead his Collegue, into
a Reliance on his superior Understanding, That however little
he car'd for Business, he should give himself the Air at least, of
Enquiry into what *had* been done, that what he intended to do,
20 might be thought more considerable, and be the readier comply'd with: For if he once suffer'd his Collegue to seem wiser
than himself, there would be no end of his perplexing him with
absurd, and dilatory Measures; direct, and plain Dealing being
a Quality his natural Diffidence would never suffer him to be
Master of; of which, his not complying with his Verbal Agreement with *Swiney*, when the *Hay-Market* House was taken for
both their Uses, was an Evidence. And though some People
thought it Depth, and Policy in him, to keep things often in
Confusion, it was ever my Opinion they over-rated his Skill, and
30 that, in reality his Parts were too weak, for his Post, in which
he had always acted, to the best of his Knowledge. That his
late Collegue, Sir *Thomas Skipworth*, had trusted too much to his
Capacity, for this sort of Business; and was treated by him accordingly, without ever receiving any Profits from it, for several

Years: Insomuch that when he found his Interest in such desperate Hands, he thought the best thing he could do with it was
(as he saw) to give it away. Therefore if he (Mr. *Brett*) could
once fix himself, as I had advis'd, upon a different Foot with
this, hitherto untractable Menager, the Business would soon run
through whatever Channel, he might have a mind to lead it.
And though I allow'd the greatest Difficulty he would meet with,
would be in getting his Consent to a Union of the two Companies, which was the only Scheme, that could raise the Patent to
10 its former Value, and which, I knew, this close Menager would
secretly lay all possible Rubs in the way to; yet it was visible,
there was a way of reducing him to Compliance: For though,
it was true his Caution would never part with a Straw, by way
of Concession, yet to a high Hand, he would give up any thing,
provided he was suffer'd to keep his Title to it: If his Hat were
taken from his Head, in the Street, he would make no farther
Resistance, than to say, *I am not willing to part with it.* Much
less would he have the Resolution, openly to oppose any just Measures, when he should find one, who with an equal Right, to
20 his, and with a known Interest to bring them about, was resolv'd
to go through with them.

Now though I knew my Friend was as thoroughly acquainted
with this Patentee's Temper, as myself, yet I thought it not amiss
to quicken and support his Resolution, by confirming to him,
the little Trouble he would meet with, in pursuit of the Union
I had advis'd him to; for it must be known, that on our side,
Trouble was a sort of Physick we did not much care to take:
But as the Fatigue of this Affair was likely to be lower'd by a
good deal of Entertainment, and Humour, which would natu-
30 rally engage him, in his dealing with so exotick a Partner; I
knew that this softening the Business, into a Diversion, would lessen every Difficulty, that lay in our way to it.

However copiously I may have indulg'd my self in this Com-
memoration of a Gentleman, with whom I had pass'd so many

5. union of the two Companies … in 1708] As in Chapter IX, Cibber considers 15 January 1707/8 to be in the same year as May 1707.

23. *Dedication* of the *Wife's Resentment*] *The Lady's Last Stake, or, the Wife's Resentment*, published in 1707.

of my younger Days, with Pleasure, yet the Reader may by this
Insight into his Character, and by that of the other Patentee,
be better able to judge of the secret Springs, that gave Motion
to, or obstructed so considerable an Event, as that of the Re-
union of the two Companies of Actors in 1708. In Histories
of more weight, for what of such Particulars, we are often deceiv'd in the true Causes of Facts, that most concern us, to be let
into; which sometimes makes us ascribe to Policy, or false Appearances of Wisdom, what perhaps, in reality, was the mere Ef-
10 fect of Chance, or Humour.

Immediately after Mr. *Brett* was admitted as a joint Patentee,
he made use of the Intimacy he had with the Vice-Chamberlain
to assist his Scheme of this intended Union, in which he so far
prevail'd, that it was soon after left to the particular Care of the
same Vice-Chamberlain, to give him all the Aid, and Power,
necessary to the bringing what he desired, to Perfection. The
Scheme was, to have but one Theatre for Plays, and another
for Operas, under separate Interests. And this the generality of
Spectators, as well as the most approv'd Actors, had been some-
20 time calling for, as the only Expedient to recover the Credit of
the Stage, and the valuable Interest of its Menagers.

As the Condition of the Comedians at this time, is taken notice of in my *Dedication* of the *Wife's Resentment*, to the Marquis (now Duke) of *Kent*, and then Lord-Chamberlain, which
was publish'd above thirty Years ago, when I had no thought of
ever troubling the World, with this Theatrical History, I see no
Reason, why it may not pass, as a Voucher of the Facts I am now
speaking of; I shall therefore give them, in the very Light I then
saw them. After some Acknowledgment for his Lordship's Pro-
30 tection of our (*Hay-Market*) Theatre, it is further said ---

" The Stage has, for many Years, 'till of late, groan'd under
" the greatest Discouragements, which have been very much, if
" not wholly owing to the Mismenagement of those, that have
" aukwardly govern'd it. Great Sums have been ventur'd upon

" empty Projects, and Hopes of immoderate Gains; and when
" those Hopes have fail'd, the Loss has been tyrannically deducted
" out of the Actors Sallary. And if your Lordship had not re-
" deem'd them---*This is meant of our being suffer'd to come over*
" *to* Swiney---they were very near being wholly laid aside, or,
" at least, the Use of their Labour was to be swallow'd up, in the
" pretended Merit of Singing, and Dancing."

What follows, relates to the Difficulties in dealing with the then
impracticable Menager, *viz.*

10 "---And though your Lordship's Tenderness of oppressing, is
" so very just, that you have rather staid to convince a Man of
" your good Intentions to him, than to do him even a Service
" against his Will; yet since your Lordship has so happily begun
" the Establishment of the separate Diversions, we live in hope,
" that the same Justice, and Resolution, will still persuade you,
" to go as successfully through with it. But while any Man is
" suffer'd to confound the Industry, and Use of them, by acting
" publickly, in opposition, to your Lordship's equal Intentions,
" under a false, and intricate Pretence of not being able to com-
20 " ply with them; the Town is likely to be more entertain'd with
" the private Dissensions, than the publick Performance of either,
" and the Actors, in a perpetual Fear, and Necessity of petition-
" ing your Lordship every Season, for new Relief."

Such was the State of the Stage, immediately preceding the
time of Mr. *Brett's* being admitted a joint Patentee, who, as he
saw, with clearer Eyes, what was its evident Interest, left no
proper Measures unattempted, to make this, so long despair'd-of,
Union practicable. The most apparent Difficulty to be got over,
in this Affair, was, what could be done for *Swiney*, in consider-
30 ation of his being oblig'd to give up those Actors, whom the
Power and Choice of the Lord-Chamberlain, had the Year before, set him at the Head of, and by whose Menagement, those
Actors had found themselves, in a prosperous Condition. But an
Accident, at this time, happily contributed, to make that Mat-

1.5 laid aside] laid asider 1st ed.

5. the famous Signior *Cavaliero Nicolini*] This singer's name was Nicolino Grimaldi, but he
was known both as Signor Nicolini and as Signor Grimaldi; having been given the order of
Saint Mark by the Doge of Venice, he used the title *Cavaliero*. He came to England to sing in
Pyrrhus and Demetrius, translated by Swiney from the libretto *Pirro e Demetrio* by Adriono
Morselli, music by Alessandro Scarlatti altered by Haym, first performed at the Haymarket 14
December 1708 (David Ewen, *Encyclopedia of Opera*, 1955, article Nicolini. For an account
of the emergence of the opera sung in Italian, see Nicoll, II, 228 ff.). His arrival was not so
decisive in the history of Italian opera in England as Cibber claims; furthermore, this division
of the functions in the two theaters had already taken place on 31 December 1707, and Brett
had resigned as manager-reformer of Drury Lane on 31 March 1708 in favor of Wilks,
Estcourt, and Cibber.

ter Easy. the Inclination of our People of Quality for foreign
Operas, had now reach'd the Ears of *Italy*, and the Credit of
their Taste had drawn over from thence, without any more particular Invitation, one of their capital Singers, the famous Signior *Cavaliero Nicolini*: From whose Arrival, and the Impatience of the Town, to hear him, it was concluded, that Operas
being, now, so completely provided, could not fail of Success;
and that, by making *Swiney* sole Director of them, the Profits
must be an ample Compensation, for his Resignation of the Ac-
10 tors. This Matter being thus adjusted, by *Swiney's* Acceptance
of the Opera only to be perform'd at the *Hay-Market* House; the
Actors were all order'd to return to *Drury-Lane*, there to remain
(under the Patentees) her Majesty's only Company of Comedians.

CHAPTER XII

8. various Heresies in Taste] Referring to the conflicts between English, Italian, and English-adaptations-of-Italian opera which rivalled one another in the first years of the century (see Nicoll, II, 225 ff.).

13. first Opera that appear'd] Actually the first opera to be produced under the new arrangement was *Thomyris, Queen of Scythia* (13 January 1708); the receipts were £193 17 s. 6d. (Avery, I, 163).

C H A P. XII.

A short view of the Opera, when first divided from the Comedy.
   Plays recover their Credit. The old Patentee uneasy at their
   Success. Why. The Occasion of Colonel Brett's *throwing up his*
   Share in the Patent. The Consequences of it. Anecdotes of
   Goodman *the Actor. The Rate of favourite Actors, in his*
   Time. The Patentees, by endeavouring to reduce their Price,
   lose them all a second time. The principal Comedians return to
   the Hay-Market *in Shares with* Swiney. *They alter that*
   Theatre. The original and present Form of the Theatre in
   Drury-Lane, *compar'd. Operas fall off. The Occasion of it.*
   Farther Observations upon them. The Patentee dispossess'd of
   Drury-Lane *Theatre. Mr.* Collier, *with a New License, heads*
   the Remains of that Company.

PLAYS, and Operas, being thus establish'd, upon separate Interests, they were now left, to make the
best of their way, into Favour, by their different
Merit. Although the Opera is not a Plant of our
Native Growth, nor what our plainer Appetites are
fond of, and is of so delicate a Nature, that without excessive
Charge, it cannot live long among us; especially while the nicest
Connoisseurs in Musick fall into such various Heresies in Taste,
every Sect pretending to be the true one: Yet, as it is call'd a
10   Theatrical Entertainment, and by its Alliance, or Neutrality, has
more or less affected our Domestick Theatre, a short View of its
Progress may be allow'd a Place in our History.

   After this new Regulation, the first Opera that appear'd, was
Pyrrhus. Subscriptions, at that time were not extended, as of
late, to the whole Season, but were limited to the first Six Days
only of a new Opera. The chief Performers, in this, were

1. *Nicolini, Valentini* and Mrs. *Tofts*] Nicolini was not hired until the season of 1709-10 (Avery, I, 198). Valentino Urbani was first listed in the cast of *Camilla* at Drury Lane on 8 March 1707 (Avery, I, 142; cf. Nicoll, II, 391; and Downes, *Roscius*, ed. Summers, p. 262); Mrs. Tofts sang in English against his Italian. She had joined the Drury Lane company in the season of 1704-1705 (Avery, I, 75-76). For a thorough account of the management of opera at this period, see Avery, I, lxx ff.

10. *Farinelli*] Carlo Broschi Farinelli, a *castrato*, was brought to England in 1734 by the English *dilettanti* in opposition to Handel. "His singing excited almost frenzied admiration; after one of his arias the exclamation was heard, 'One God, one Farinelli.' ... He had a plain, rather piglike face, and an extremely clumsy person, which he gorgeously arrayed in satins and diamonds. But, thanks to his voice, he was adored by the ladies. Hogarth included a portrait of him in the scene of the Countess's levee in 'Marriage a la Mode' (Plate IV)." He was paid enormous sums of money for his performances (Dudden, I, 197-208).

15. 115th Tatler] 3 January 1710.

28. *Senesino*] A *castrato*, born Francesco Bernardi, came to London in 1720, when he appeared in Buononcini's *Astarto*; for the next fifteen years he was exceedingly popular, singing the principal roles in several Handel operas. He quarrelled with Handel in 1733 and, after singing for a rival company for a period, returned to Italy in 1735 (David Ewen, *Encyclopedia of the Opera*, 1955, article Senesino). Nicoll (II, 286) prints an order of 14 May 1719 to "Mr. Hendel" to "engage Senezino as soon as possible ... for as many years as may be." Nicolini's "second visit" came also in 1720, when he was reported to have been paid £1,100 (Avery, I, lxx).

34. Losses by Operas ... to the End of the Year 1738] This is possibly an allusion to Handel's bankruptcy in 1737 (cf. Pope, *Dunciad* (B), IV, 45-70) and to the noble sponsors of the fashion. The losses Cibber speaks of were in part due to the serious competition given opera by ballad operas following the success of *The Beggar's Opera* in 1728.

Nicolini, Valentini, and Mrs. *Tofts;* and for the inferior Parts, the
best that were then to be found. Whatever Praises may have
been given to the most famous Voices, that have been heard
since *Nicolini;* upon the whole, I cannot but come into the
Opinion, that still prevails among several Persons of Condition,
who are able to give a Reason for their liking, that no Singer,
since his Time, has so justly, and gracefully acquitted himself,
in whatever Character he appear'd, as *Nicolini.* At most, the
Difference between him, and the greatest Favourite of the Ladies,
10 *Farinelli,* amounted but to this, that he might sometimes more
exquisitely surprize us, but *Nicolini* (by pleasing the Eye, as well
as the Ear) fill'd us with a more various, and *rational* Delight.
Whether in this Excellence, he has since had any Competitor,
perhaps, will be better judg'd, by what the Critical Censor of
Great Britain says of him in his 115th *Tatler, viz.*

  " *Nicolini* sets off the Character he bears in an Opera, by his
  " Action, as much as he does the Words of it, by his Voice;
  " much that a deaf Man might go along with him in the Sense
20 " of it. There is scarce a beautiful Posture, in an old Statue,
  " which he does not plant himself in, as the different Circum-
  " stances of the Story give occasion for it---- He performs the
  " most ordinary Action, in a manner suitable to the Greatness
  " of his Character, and shews the Prince, even in the giving of
  " a Letter, or dispatching of a Message, &c.

  His Voice at this first Time of being among us, (for he made
us a second Visit when it was impair'd) had all that strong, clear,
Sweetness of Tone, so lately admir'd in *Senesino.* A blind Man
could scarce have distinguish'd them; but in Volubility of Throat,
30 the former had much the Superiority. This so excellent Performer's Agreement was Eight Hundred Guineas for the Year,
which is but an eighth Part more, than half the Sum, that has
since been given to several, that could never totally surpass him:
The Consequence of which is, that the Losses by Operas, for

8. was then not an Adept in it]. This statement, as it appeared in the first edition, was the most remarkable verbal blunder in the *Apology* (if it was not a printer's error). Fielding (in *The Champion*, 22 April 1740) derided it at length: "This Word *adept* our great *Master* hath tortured and wrested to signify a *Tyro* or *Novice*, being directly contrary to the Sense in which it hath been hitherto used." On Mrs. Tofts, see also p. 225; she became insane in 1709 (see *The Tatler*, No. 20, 26 May 1709 for a notice of her), and died in 1756 in Venice; she had been known, in England, for her avarice (cf. *Wentworth Papers*, 17 March 1709, p. 66).

several Seasons, to the End of the Year 1738, have been so great,
that those Gentlemen of Quality, who last undertook the Direction of them, found it ridiculous any longer to entertain the
Publick, at so extravagant an Expence, while no one particular
Person thought himself oblig'd by it.

Mrs. *Tofts*, who took her first Grounds of Musick here in her
own Country, before the *Italian* Taste had so highly prevail'd,
was then not an Adept in it: Yet, whatever Defect the fashion-
ably Skilful might find in her manner, she had, in the general
10 Sense of her Spectators, Charms that few of the most learned
Singers ever arrive at. The Beauty of her fine proportion'd Figure, and the exquisitely sweet, silver Tone of her Voice, with
that peculiar, rapid Swiftness of her Throat, were Perfections
not to be imitated by Art, or Labour. *Valentini* I have already
mention'd, therefore need only say farther of him, that though
he was every way inferior to *Nicolini*, yet as he had the Advantage of giving us our first Impression of a good Opera Singer,
he had still his Admirers, and was of great Service, in being so
skilful a Second to his Superior.

20   Three such excellent Performers, in the same kind of Entertainment at once, *England* till this Time had never seen: Without any farther Comparison, then, with the much dearer bought,
who have succeeded them; their Novelty, at least, was a Charm
that drew vast Audiences of the fine World after them. *Swiney*
their sole Director was prosperous, and in one Winter, a Gainer
by them, of a moderate younger Brother's Fortune. But as
Musick, by so profuse a Dispensation of her Beauties, could not
always supply our dainty Appetites, with equal Variety, nor for
ever please us with the same Objects; the Opera, after one lux-
30 urious Season, like the fine Wife a roving Husband, began to
lose its Charms, and every Day discovered to our Satiety, Imperfections, which our former Fondness had been blind to: But
of this I shall observe more in its Place; in the mean time, let
us enquire into the Productions of our native Theatre.

1.8 then not an Adept in it] then but an Adept in it 1st ed.

30. He plainly saw, that as this disagreeable Prosperty ...] Cibber's memory of the dates is inaccurate. Brett assigned his rights to Wilks, Estcourt, and Cibber on 31 March 1708. This should not be taken as evidence of Brett's withdrawal from management of the theater as Barker (pp. 74 ff., following Percy Fitzgerald, *New History of the English Stage*, I, 263; II, 443-46) supposes; Lowe's suggestion (II, 56) that it was one of his earlier acts of authority as a manager, can be supported by Brett's own testimony (Loftis, *Politics*, p. 48, also states erroneously that Brett withdrew altogether shortly after entering the management). In his deposition (dated 17 February 1709) in response to Skipwith's suit for the return of the patent, he states (spelling modernized):

> —And this defendant says that since the execution of the said deed or grant to him he hath concerned himself in the management of the affairs relating to the said playhouse and premises, and hath bestowed much time and been at considerable charge and very great expense in bringing the same into a better posture and into a considerable improvement and greater advantage than the same have hitherto been unless this defendant be obstructed in his good design by the complainant and this unnecessary and ... vexacious suit.
>
> (printed by Hotson, p. 395)

From this, one may suppose Brett to have been actively engaged in the management of the theater at the time of Skipwith's suit—February 1709—over a year after deputizing the actors.

It may easily be conceiv'd, that by this entire Re-union of the
two Companies, Plays must generally have been perform'd, to a
more than usual Advantage, and Exactness: For now every chief
Actor, according to his particular Capacity, piqued himself upon rectifying those Errors, which during their divided State, were
almost unavoidable. Such a Choice of Actors added a Richness
to every good Play, as it was, then, serv'd up, to the publick
Entertainment: The common People crowded to them, with a
more joyous Expectation, and those of the higher Taste return'd
10 to them, as to old Acquaintances, with new Desires, after a long
Absence. In a Word, all Parties seem'd better pleas'd, but he,
who one might imagine had most Reason to be so, the (lately)
sole menaging Patentee. he, indeed saw his Power daily moul-
d'ring from his own Hands, into those of Mr. *Brett*; whose Gen-
tlemanly manner of making every one'd Business easy to him,
threw their old Master under a Disregard, which he had not
been us'd to, nor could with all his happy Change of Affairs,
support. Although this grave Theatrical Minister, of whom I
have been oblig'd to make such frequent mention, had acquired
20 the Reputation of a most profound Politician, by being often   .
incomprehensible, yet I am not sure, that his Conduct at this
Juncture, gave us not an evident Proof, that he was, like other
frail Mortals, more a Slave to his Passions, than his Interest;
for no Creature ever seem'd more fond of Power, that so little
knew how to use it, to his Profit and Reputation; otherwise he
could not possibly have been so discontented, in his secure,
and prosperous State of the Theatre, as to resolve, at all Hazards,
to destroy it. We shall now see what infallible Measures he took,
to bring this laudable Scheme to Perfection.
30   He plainly saw, that as this disagreeable Prosperity was chiefly
owing to the Conduct of Mr. *Brett* weary of his Charge:
recovering the Stage to its former Confusion, but by finding
some effectual Means to make Mr. *Brett* weary of his Charge:
The most probable he could, for the present, think of, in this

1. to call in the Adventurers] Lowe (II, 58) reprints the following names of the signers of a petition against the silencing of Rich in 1709; they presumably were adventurers, though possibly additional influential names were secured: Lord Guilford; Lord John Harvey; Dame Alice Brownlow; Mrs. Shadwell; Sir Edward Smith, Bart; George Sayer; Charles Killigrew; Christopher Rich; Charles D'Avenant; John Metcalf; Thomas Goodall; Ashburnham Toll; Ashburnham Frowd; William East; Richard Middlemore; Robert Gower; and William Collier. A number of these appear in a lawsuit against Rich in 1704 (see Hotson, pp. 300-301).

23. an unexpected Dispute between him, and Sir *Thomas Skipwith*] See the note above and the text and notes on pp. 212-13.

Distress, was to call in the Adventurers (whom for many Years,
by his Defence in Law, he had keep out) now to take care of
their visibly improving Interests. This fair Appearance of Equity,
being known to be his own Proposal, he rightly guess'd would
incline these Adventurers to form a Majority of Votes on his
Side, in all Theatrical Questions; and consequently become a
Check upon the Power of Mr. *Brett*, who had so visibly alienated the Hearts of his Theatrical Subjects, and now began to
govern without him. When the Adventurers, therefore, were
10 re-admitted to their old Government; after having recommended himself to them, by proposing to make some small Dividend
of the Profits (though he did not design that Jest should be repeated) he took care that the Creditors of the Patent, who were,
then, no inconsiderable body, should carry off the every Weeks
clear Profits, in proportion to their several Dues and Demands.
This Conduct, so speciously just, he had Hopes would let
Mr. *Brett* see, that his Share, in the Patent, was not so valuable
an Acquisition as, perhaps, he might think it; and probably
might make a Man of his Turn to Pleasure, soon weary of the
20 little Profit, and great Plague it gave him. Now, though these
might be all notable Expedients, yet I cannot say they would
have wholly contributed to Mr. *Brett's* quitting his Post, had not
a Matter of much stronger Moment, an unexpected dispute between him, and Sir *Thomas Skipwith*, prevail'd with him to lay
it down: For in the midst of this flourishing State of the Patent, Mr. *Brett* was surpriz'd with a Subpoena into Chancery,
from Sir *Thomas Skipwith*, who alledg'd, in his Bill, that the
Conveyance he had made of his Interest, in the Patent, to
Mr. *Brett*, was only intended in Trust. (Whatever the Intent
30 might be, the Deed it self, which I then read, made no mention of any Trust whatever.) But Whether Mr. *Brett*, as Sir *Thomas* farther asserted, had previously, or after the Deed was sign'd,
given his Word of Honour, that if he should ever make the Stage
turn to any Account, or Profit, he would certainly restore it:

ll. 18-19 probably might make a Man] probably make a Man 2nd ed.

That indeed, I can say nothing to; but be the Deed valid, or
void, the Facts that apparently follow'd were, that tho' Mr. *Brett*,
in his answer to this Bill, absolutely deny'd his receiving this
Assignment, either in Trust, or upon any limited Condition, of
what kind soever; yet he made no farther Defence, in the Cause.
But since he found Sir *Thomas* had thought fit, on any Account
to sue for the Restitution of it; and Mr. *Brett* being himself
conscious, that, as the World knew, he had paid no consideration for it; his keeping it might be misconstrued, or not favour-
10 ably spoken of; or perhaps finding, tho' the Profits were great,
they were constantly swallow'd up (as has been observ'd) by the
previous Satisfaction of old Debts, he grew so tir'd of the Plague,
and Trouble, the whole Affair had given him, and was likely still
to engage him in, that in a few Weeks after, he withdrew himself, from all Concern with the Theatre, and quietly left Sir
Thomas to find his better Account in it. And thus stood this un-
decided Right, till upon the Demise of Sir *Thomas*, Mr. *Brett*
being allow'd the Charges he had been at, in his Attendance,
and Prosecution of the Union, reconvey'd this Share of the Pa-
20 tent to Sir *George Skipwith*, the Son, and Heir of Sir *Thomas*.

Our Politician, the old Patentee, having thus fortunately got
rid of Mr. *Brett*, who had so rashly brought the Patent once
more to be a profitable Tenure, was now again at liberty, to
chuse rather to lose all, than not to have it all to himself.

I have, elsewhere, observ'd, that nothing can so effectually
secure the Strength, or contribute to the Prosperity of a good
Company, as the Directors of it having always, as near as possible, an amicable Understanding, with three or four of their
best Actors, whose good, or ill-will, must naturally make a wide
30 Difference, in their profitable, or useless manner of serving them:
While the Principal are kept reasonably easy, the lower Class
can never be troublesome, without hurting themselves: But when
a valuable Actor is hardly treated, the Master must be a very

15. Answer I made to one of the Adventurers] Rich was apparently governing through a committee at this time.

29. against Sir *John Fenwick*, in the Assassination-Plot] Goodman was involved in the Jacobite plot to assassinate William III, but turned King's evidence at the trial of Peter Cook, Esq. (9-13 May 1696) to escape the gallows; he had left the country before that of Fenwick which began 6 November 1696, probably bribed to do so either by Lady Fenwick, or one of the other plotters (Downes, *Roscius*, ed. Summers, pp. 83-84). His indirect evidence helped convict Fenwick. For an account of the plot and Goodman's part in it, see *DNB* article Sir John Fenwick. See also David Ogg, *England in the Reigns of James II and William III*, pp. 426-27.

cunning Man, that finds his Account in it. We shall now see
how far Experience will verify this Observation.

The Patentees thinking themselves secure, in being restor'd
to their former absolute Power, over this, now, only Company,
chose rather to govern it by the Reverse of the Method I have
recommended: For tho' the daily Charge of their united Company amounted not, by a good deal, to what either of the two
Companies, now in *Drury-Lane*, or *Covent-Garden*, singly, arises;
they notwithstanding fell into their former Politicks, of thinking
10 every Shilling taken from a hir'd Actor, so much clear Gain to
the Proprietor: Many of their People, therefore, were actually,
if not injudiciously, reduc'd in their Pay, and others given to understand, the same Fate was design'd them, of which last Number I, my self, was one, which occurs to my Memory, by the
Answer I made to one of the Adventurers; who, in Justification of their intended Proceeding, told me, that my Sallary,
tho' it should be less, than it was, by ten Shillings a Week,
would still be more than ever *Goodman* had, who was a better
Actor, than I could pretend to be: To which I reply'd, This
20 may be true, but then you know, Sir, it is as true, that *Goodman* was forc'd to go upon the High-way for a Livelihood. As
this was a known Fact of *Goodman*, my mentioning it, on that
Occasion, I believe, was of Service to me; at least my Sallary
was not reduc'd after it. To say a Word or two more of *Goodman,* so celebrated an Actor, in his Time, perhaps may set the
Conduct of the Patentees in a clearer Light. Tho' *Goodman*
had left the Stage, before I came to it, I had some slight Acquaintance with him. About the Time of his being expected to
be an Evidence against Sir *John Fenwick*, in the Assassination-
30 Plot, in 1696, I happen'd to meet him at Dinner, at Sir *Thomas
Skipwith's*, who as he was an agreeable Companion himself, liked
Goodman for the same Quality. Here it was, that *Goodman*, without Disguise, or sparing himself, fell into a laughing Account of

3. defacing ... *Monmouth's* Picture] James Scott (1649-1685), Duke of Monmouth, natural son of Charles II and Lucy Walter, was deprived of his Chancellorship by royal injunction in April 1682, and his portrait burned. Cibber's version implies that the destruction was illicit, but it in fact appears to have been an official act, not likely to have been punished (*DNB*, article James Scott).

34. *Clytus,* or *Alexander*] Clitus "the Black" had saved Alexander the Great's life at Guanicus; he was killed by Alexander during a drinking brawl for praising the simplicity and heroism of Philip of Macedon. Nathaniel Lee dramatized the conflict in *The Rival Queens*, IV, ii.

several loose Passages of *his* younger Life; as his being expell'd
the University of *Cambridge*, for being one of the hot-headed
Sparks, who were concern'd in the cutting, and defacing the
Duke of *Monmouth's* Picture, then Chancellor of that Place. But
this Disgrace, it seems, had not disqualify'd him for the Stage;
which, like the Sea-Service, refuses no Man, for his Morals, that
is able-body'd: There, as an Actor, he soon grew into a different Reputation; but whatever his Merit might be, the Pay of
a hired Hero, in those Days, was so very low, that he was forc'd,
10 it seems, to take the Air (as he call'd it) and borrow what Mony
the first Man he met, had about him. But this being his first
Exploit of that kind, which the Scantiness of his Theatrical Fortune had reduc'd him to, King *James* was prevail'd upon, to
pardon him: Which *Goodman* said, was doing him so particular an Honour, that no Man could wonder, if his Acknowledgment had carry'd him, a little farther, than ordinary, into the
Interest of that Prince: But as he had, lately, been out of Luck,
in backing his old Master, he had now no way to get home
the Life he was out, upon his account, but by being under the
20 same Obligations to King *William*.

Another Anecdote of him, tho' not quite so dishonourably
enterprizing, which I had from his own Mouth, at a different
time, will equally shew, to what low Shifts in Life, the poor
Provision for good Actors, under the early Government of the
Patent, reduc'd them. In the younger Days of their Heroism,
Captain *Griffin,* and *Goodman,* were confin'd by their moderate
Sallaries, to the Oeconomy of lying together, in the same Bed,
and having but one whole Shirt between them: One of them
being under the Obligation of a Rendezvous, with a fair Lady,
30 insisted upon his wearing it, out of his Turn, which occasion'd
so high a Dispute, that the Combat was immediately demanded,
and accordingly their Pretensions to it, were decided by a fair
Tilt upon the Spot, in the Room, where they lay: But whether
Clytus, or *Alexander* was oblig'd to see no Company, till a worse

could be wash'd for him, seems not to be a material Point, in
their History, or to my Purpose.

By this Rate of *Goodman*, who, till the Time of his quitting
the Stage, never had more, than what is call'd forty Shillings a
Week, it may be judg'd, how cheap the Labour of Actors had
been formerly; and the Pantentees thought it a Folly to continue
the higher Price, (which their Divisions had since rais'd them
to) now there was but one Market for them; but alas! they had
forgot their former fatal Mistake of squabbling with their Actors,
10 in 1695; nor did they make any Allowance for the Changes
and Operations of Time, or enough consider the Interest the
Actors had in the Lord Chamberlain, on whose Protection they
might always rely, and whose Decrees had been less restrain'd
by Precedent, than those of a Lord Chancellor.

In this mistaken View of their Interest, the Patentees, by treating their Actors as Enemies, really made them so: And when
once the Masters of a hired Company think not their Actors
Hearts as necessary, as their Hands, they cannot be said to have
agreed for above half the Work, they are able to do in a Day:
20 Or, if an unexpected Success should, notwithstanding, make the
Profits, in any gross Disproportion, greater, than the Wages;
the Wages will always have something worse, than a Murmur,
at the Head of them, that will not only measure the Merit of
the Actor, by the Gains of the Proprietor, but will never naturally be quiet, till every Scheme of getting into Property has
been try'd, to make the Servant his own Master: And this, as
far as Experience can make me judge, will always be, in either
of these Cases, the State of our *English* Theatre. What Truth
there may be, in this Observation, we are now coming to a
30 Proof of.

To enumerate all the particular Acts of Power, in which the
Patentees daily bore hard, upon this, now only Company of
Actors, might be as tedious, as unnecessary; I shall therefore
come, at once, to their most material Grievance, upon which

10. *Indulto*] "In Spain, a duty, tax, or custom, paid to the King for all goods imported" (Lowe, II, 66).

they grounded their Complaint to the Lord-Chamberlain, who
in the Year following, 1709, took effectual Measures for their
Relief.

The Patentees observing that the Benefit-Plays of the Actors,
towards the latter end of the Season, brought the most crowded
Audiences in the Year; began to think their own Interests too
much neglected, by these partial Favours of the Town, to their
Actors; and therefore judg'd, it would not be impolitick, in
such wholesom annual Profits, to have a Fellow-feeling with
10 them. Accordingly, an *Indulto* was laid of one Third, out
of the Profits of every Benefit, for the proper Use, and Behoof
of the Patent. But, that a clear Judgment may be form'd of
the Equity, or Hardship of this Imposition, it will be necessary to
shew from whence, and from what Causes, the Actors Claim to
Benefits originally proceeded.

During the Reign of King *Charles*, an Actor's Benefit had never been heard of. The first Indulgence of this Kind, was
given to Mrs. *Barry* (as has been formerly observed) in King
James's Time, in consideration of the extraordinary Applause,
20 that had followed her Performance: But there this Favour rested,
to her alone, 'till after the Division of the only Company in
1695, at which time the Patentees were soon reduc'd to pay
their Actors, half in good Words, and half in ready Mony. In
this precarious Condition, some particular Actors (however binding their Agreements might be) were too poor, or too wise to
go to Law with a Lawyer; and therefore rather chose to com-
pound their Arrears, for their being admitted to the Chance of
having them made up, by the Profits of a Benefit Play. This
Expedient had this Consequence; That the Patentees tho' their
30 daily Audiences, might, and did sometimes mend, still kept the
short Subsistance of their Actors, at a stand, and grew more
steady in their Resolution so to keep them, as they found them
less apt to mutiny, while their Hopes of being clear'd off, by a

31. Whereupon the Patentees were warn'd at their Peril] Contracts between Swiney and the actors had been arranged with the consent of the Lord Chamberlain as a part of the plot to free them from Rich (Nicoll, II, 286-87, reprints and summarizes a number of them). The sequence of events must have been the following: Rich's enforcement of his *indulto*; the working out and formulation of an agreement with Swiney during February and March 1709; Mrs. Oldfield's complaint to the Lord Chamberlain 4 March 1709 (Nicoll, II, 291), about Rich's deductions from her benefit; the signing of a contract 10 March 1709 (Barker, pp. 76-77; also see below, p. 235); the issue by the Lord Chamberlain of an order dated 30 April 1709 to pay actors their full benefit due them from the previous winter less no more than £40 (Nicoll, II, 282), an order which ignored the evasions set forth by Rich and several adventurers (see the case of Mrs. Oldfield: Nicoll, II, 391); finally the Lord Chamberlain's order of 6 June 1709 definitively silencing Rich "for contempt," i.e., for ignoring the earlier order (Nicoll, II, 282).

Benefit, were depending. In a Year, or two, these Benefits grew
so advantageous, that they became, at last, the chief Article, in
every Actor's Agreement.

Now though the Agreements of these united Actors, I am
speaking of in 1708, were as yet, only Verbal; yet that made
no difference in the honest Obligation, to keep them: But, as
Honour at that time happen'd to have but a loose hold of their
Consciences, the Patentees rather chose to give it the slip, and
went on with their Work without it. No actor, therefore, could
10 have his Benefit fix'd, 'till he had first sign'd a Paper, signifying
his voluntary Acceptance of it, upon the, above, Conditions, any
Claims from Custom, the the contrary notwithstanding. Several
at first refus'd to sign this Paper; upon which the next in Rank
were offer'd on the same Conditions, to come before the Refu-
surs; this smart Expedient got some few of the fearful the Preference to their Seniors; who at last, seeing the time was too
short for a present Remedy, and that they must either come into the Boat, or lose their Tide, were forc'd to comply, with
what, they, as yet, silently, resented as the severest Injury. In
20 this situation, therefore, they chose to let the principal Benefits
be over, that their Grievances might swell into some bulk, before they made any Application for Redress to the Lord-Chamberlain; who, upon hearing their general Complaint, order'd
the Patentees to shew cause, why their Benefits had been diminish'd one Third, contrary to the common Usage? The Patentees pleaded the sign'd Agreement, and the Actors Receipts of
the other two Thirds, in full Satisfaction. But these were prov'd
to have been exacted from them, by the Methods already mentioned. They notwithstanding insist upon them as lawful. But
30 as Law, and Equity do not always agree, they were look'd upon
as unjust, and arbitrary. Whereupon the Patentees were warn'd
at their Peril, to refuse the Actors full Satisfaction. But here it
was thought necessary, that Judgment should be for some time

16. As to the two celebrated Actresses] Mrs. Bracegirdle retired in February 1707. Mrs. Barry is listed among the actresses through 1709-10, but in these last two seasons she appears to have acted very rarely. She moved from Drury Lane to the Haymarket with the company for her last season (Avery, I, 176, 198).

20. *Booth* ... declin'd ...] Lowe (II, 70) suggests that Booth remained behind largely because of Wilks' "unfair partiality for John Mills," and refers to Chapter XVI below.

respited, 'till the Actors, who had leave so to do, could form a
Body strong enough to make the Inclination of the Lord-Chamberlain to relieve them, practicable.

Accordingly *Swiney* (who was then sole Director of the Opera
only) had Permission to enter into a private Treaty, with such
of the united Actors in *Drury-Lane*, as might be thought fit to
head a Company, under their own Management, and to be Sharers with him in the *Hay-Market*. The Actors chosen for this
Charge, were *Wilks*, *Dogget*, Mrs. *Oldfield*, and Myself. But,
10 before I proceed, lest it should seem surprizing, that neither *Bet-*
terton, Mrs. *Barry*, Mrs. *Bracegirdle*, or *Booth*, were Parties in
this Treaty; it must be observ'd, that *Betterton* was now Seventy-
three, and rather chose, with the Infirmities of Age upon him,
to rely on such Sallary, as might be appointed him, than to involve himself, in the Cares, and Hurry, that must unavoidably
attend the Regulation of a new Company. As to the two celebrated Actresses I have named, this has been my first proper Occasion of making it known, that they had both quitted the
Stage the Year before this Transaction was thought of. And
20 *Booth*, as yet, wa scarce out of his Minority as an Actor, or only in the Promise of that Reputation, which in about four or
five Years after, he happily arriv'd at. However, at this Juncture, he was not so far overlook'd, as not to be offer'd a valuable Addition to his Sallary: But this he declin'd, being, while
the Patentees were under this Distress, as much, if not more, in
favour, with their chief Manager, as a Schematist, than as an
Actor: And indeed he appear'd, to my Judgment, more inclin'd to risque his Fortune in *Drury-Lane*, where he should
have no Rival in Parts, or Power, than on any Terms to em-
30 bark in the *Hay-Market*; where he was sure to meet with Opponents in both. However this his Separation from our Interest,
when our All was at stake, afterwards kept his Advancement,
to a Share with us, in our more successful Days, longer postpon'd,
than otherwise it probably might have been.

8. Mrs. *Oldfield* receiv'd it rather as a Favour] Her contract was for thirteen years, a benefit in February, and 10 June to 10 September to be free (Nicoll, II, 286).

16. When a sufficient number of Actors were engag'd] In addition to the actors signing the agreement on 10 March, Swiney contracted with Mrs. Mary Porter (24 May), Benjamin Husband (10 May), William Bullock (4 April), William Pinkethman (30 April), Benjamin Johnson (11 April), John Mills (30 March) to act for him; most of these contracts begin 1 July 1709. Others were signed after Rich was silenced (Nicoll, II, 286-87).

30. The Actor who particularly solicited their Cause] Barker (p. 77) believes that this was almost certainly Cibber himself.

When Mrs. *Oldfield* was nominated as a joint Sharer, in our
new Agreement to me made with *Swiney*; *Dogget*, who had no
Objection to her Merit, insisted that our Affairs could never be
upon a secure Foundation, if there was more, than one Sex admitted to the Management of them. He therefore hop'd, that
if we offer'd Mrs. *Oldfield* a *Carte Blanche*, instead of a Share,
she would not think herself slighted. This was instantly agreed
to, and Mrs. *Oldfield* receiv'd it rather as a Favour, than a Dif-
obligation: Her Demands therefore were Two Hundred Pounds
10 a Year certain, and a Benefit clear of all Charges; which were
readily sign'd to. Her Easiness on this Occasion, some Years after, when our Establishment was in Prosperity, made us, with
less Reluctancy, advance her Two Hundred Pounds, to Three
Hundred Guineas *per Annum*, with her usual Benefit, which upon
an Average for several Years at least, doubled that Sum.

When a sufficient number of Actors were engag'd, under our
Confederacy with *Swiney*, it was then judg'd a proper time, for
the Lord-Chamberlain's Power, to operate, which, by lying a-
above a Month dormant, had so far recover'd the Patentees, from
20 any Apprehensions of what might fall upon them, from their
late Usurpations on the Benefits of the Actors, that they began
to set their Marks, upon those who had distinguish'd themselves,
in the Application for Redress. Several little Disgraces were put
upon them; particularly in the Disposal of Parts, in Plays to be
reviv'd, and as visible a Partiality was shewn in the Promotion
of those in their Interest, though their Endeavours to serve them
could be of no extraordinary use. How often does History shew
us, in the same State of Courts, the same Politicks have been
practis'd? Al this while, the other Party were passively silent;
30 'till one Day, the Actor who particularly solicited their Cause,
at the Lord-Chamberlain's Office, being shewn there the Order
sign'd, for absolutely silencing the Patentees, and ready to be
serv'd, flew back with the News to his Companions, then at a
Rehearsal, in which he had been wanted; when being call'd to

18. *Read o'er that! and now ...*] *King Henry VIII*, III, ii, 201-203: "Read o'er this;/ And after, this: and then to breakfast with/ What appetite you have [sic]."

24. The Authority of the Patent now no longer subsisting] Barker adds (pp. 77-78): "Some time apparently elapsed before Rich fully realized the significance of the order. In June he did nothing to contest its legality, though he made several half-hearted attempts to annoy the managers of the new Haymarket company. In the name of his treasurer, Zachary Boggs, he issued a statement defending the *indulto*, and at the same time he revived old breach-of-contract suits against several of the deserting actors. But during the summer he made plans to reopen Drury Lane; indeed he actually went so far as to advertise *The Recruiting Officer* for September 6, when he was peremptorily told by the Lord Chamberlain that he must not presume to act until he had further orders from the Queen" (cf. below, p. 239).

28. Instance of the Authority of a Lord-Chamberlain] Rich was in the process of appealing to the Queen in Council against the authority of the Lord Chamberlain to control a patent theater when Collier was able to take over Drury Lane (Barker, p. 78).

his Part, and something hastily question'd by the Patentee, for
his Neglect of Business: This Actor, I say, with an erected
Look, and a Theatrical Spirit, at once threw off the Mask, and
roundly told him------Sir, *I have now no more Business Here,*
than you have; in half an Hour, you will neither have Actors to
command, nor Authority, to employ them.----The Patentee, who
though he could not readily comprehend his mysterious manner
of Speaking, had just a Glimpse of Terror enough from the
Words, to soften his Reproof into a cold formal Declaration,
10 That *if he would not do his Work, he should not be paid.*----But
now, to complete the Catastrophe of these Theatrical Commotions, enters the Messenger, with the Order of Silence in his
Hand, whom the same Actor officiously introduc'd, telling the
Patentee, that the Gentleman wanted to speak with him, from
the Lord-Chamberlain. When the Messenger had delivered the
Order, the Actor throwing his Head over his Shoulder, towards
the Patentee, in the manner of *Shakespear's Harry the Eighth* to
Cardinal *Wolsey,* cry'd----*Read o'er that! and now---to Break-*
fast, with what Appetite you may. Though these Words might be
20 spoken, in too vindictive, and insulting a manner, to be commended; yet from the Fulness of a Heart injuriously treated,
and now reliev'd by that instant Occasion, why might they not
be pardon'd?

The Authority of the Patent now no longer subsisting, all the
confederated Actors immediately walk'd out of the House, to
which they never return'd, 'till they become themselves the Te-
nants, and Masters of it.

Here again, we see an higher Instance of the Authority of a
Lord-Chamberlain, than any of those I have elsewhere mention-
30 ed: From whence that Power might be deriv'd, as I have already said, I am not Lawyer enough to know; however it is
evident that a Lawyer obey'd it, though to his Cost; which
might incline one, to think, that the Law was not clearly against
it: Be that as it may, since the Law has lately made it no longer

22. the 193d *Tatler* ... *Downs* the Prompter] This famous letter, in fact a political allegory, was published by Steele 4 July 1710; authorship has not been certainly determined; George W. Aitken, ed. *Tatler*, III, 407, discusses possible authorship and the effect its publication had on Steele, quoting Swift's *Journal to Stella*, 22 October 1710: "He [Steele] has lost his place of Gazeteer, three hundred pounds a year, for writing a *Tatler*, some months ago against Mr. Harley ..." It is difficult to say whether Cibber could really have believed the letter to have been written by the author of the *Roscius Anglicanus* or whether he is being uncommonly subtle.

a Question, let us drop the Enquiry, and proceed to the Facts,
which follow'd this Order, that silenc'd the Patent.

   From this last injudicious Disagreement of the Patentees with
their principal Actors, and from what they had suffered on the
same Occasion, in the Division of their only Company in 1695,
might we not imagine there wa something of Infatuation, in
their Management? For though I allow Actors, in general,
when they are too much indulg'd, or govern'd by an unsteady
Head, to be as unruly a Multitude as Power can be plagued
10 with; yet there is a Medium, which, if cautiously observed by
a candid use of Power, making them always know, without
feeling their Superior, neither suffering their Encroachments, nor
invading their Rights, with an immoveable Adherence to the
accepted Laws, they are to walk by; such a Regulation, I say,
has never fail'd, in my Observation, to have made them a tractable, and profitable Society. If the Government of a well-
establish'd Theatre were to be compar'd to that of a Nation;
there is no one Act of Policy, or Misconduct in the one, or the
other, in which the Manager might not, in some parallel Case
20 (laugh, if you please) be equally applauded, or condemned with
the Statesman. Perhaps this will not be found so wild a Conceit, if you look into the 193d *Tatler*, Vol. 4. where the Affairs of the State, and those of the very Stage, which I am now
treating of, are, in a Letter of *Downs* the Prompter, compar'd, and with a great deal of Wit, and Humour, set upon an
equal Foot of Policy. The Letter is suppos'd to have been written, in the last Change of the Ministry in Queen *Anne's* Time.
I will therefore venture, upon the Authority of that Author's
Imagination, to carry the Comparison as high, as it can possi-
30 bly go, and say, That as I remember one of our Princes, in
the last Century, to have lost his Crown, by too arbitrary a Use
of his Power, though he knew how fatal the same Measures
had been to his unhappy Father before him; why should we
wonder, that the same Passions taking Possession of Men, in lower

4. During the Vacation] See note on page 237.

33. the new-built Theatre in *Lincoln's Inn Fields* was open'd] It opened 18 December 1714 (Nicoll mistakenly says 18 November). This was in fact only an extensive remodeling of the old theater under the supervision of the architect Edward Shepherd; it was used by Rich until the construction of the Covent Garden theater in 1732, thereafer by Fielding, 1735-37 (Nicoll, II, 271-72). Cf. Avery, I, 334.

Life, by an equally impolitick Usage of their Theatrical Subjects, should have involved the Patentees, in proportionable Calamities.

During the Vacation, which immediately follow'd the Silence
of the Patent, both Parties were at leisure to form their Schemes
for the Winter: For the Patentee would still hold out, notwithstanding his being so miserably maim'd, or over-match'd: He
had no more Regard to Blows, than a blind Cock of the Game;
he might be beaten, but would never yield, the Patent was still
10 in his Possession, and the Broad-Seal to it visibly as fresh as ever:
Besides, he had yet some Actors in his Service, at a much
cheaper Rate than those who had left him, the Sallaries of which
last now they would not work for him, he was not oblig'd to
pay. In this way of thinking, he still kept together such, as
had not been invited over to the *Hay-Market*, or had been in-
fluenc'd by *Booth*, to follow his Fortune in *Drury-Lane*.

By the Patentee's keeping these Remains of his broken Forces
together, it is plain , that he imagin'd this Order of Silence, like
others of the same Kind, would be recall'd of course, after a
20 reasonable time of Obedience had been paid to it: But it seems
he had rely'd too much upon former Precedents: nor had his
Politicks yet div'd, into the Secret, that the Court Power, with
which the Patent had been so long, and often at variance, had
now a mind to take the publick Diversions more absolutely into
their own Hands: Not that I have any stronger Reasons for this
Conjecture, than that the Patent, never after this Order of Silence, got leave to play during the Queen's Reign. But upon
the Accession of his late Majesty, Power having then a different Aspect, the Patent found no Difficulty in being permitted to
30 exercise its former Authority for acting Plays, &c. which, however from this time of their lying still, in 1709, did not happen 'till 1714, and which the old Patentee never liv'd to see:
For he dy'd about six Weeks before the new-built Theatre in
Lincoln's-Inn Fields was open'd, where the first Play acted was

1. under the Management of his Heirs] Tese were John and Christopher Mosier Rich; the former became important in theatrical affairs, the latter is heard little of (cf. Loftis, *Politics*, pp. 63-64).

10. the original Model of that in *Drury-Lane*] For a descrption of the old theater, see Hotson, pp. 233 ff. Allardyce Nicoll, in *The Development of the Theatre* (New York, 1927), pp. 163-64, reproduces Wren's drawings of this theater; these (especially Fig. 194) make Cibber's later comments clear.

the *Recruiting Officer*, under the Management of his Heirs, and
Successors. But of that Theatre, it is not yet time to give any
further Account.

   The first Point resolv'd on, by the Comedians now re-
established in the *Hay-Market*, was to alter the Auditory Part
of their Theatre; the Inconveniences of which have been fully
enlarg'd upon in a former Chapter. What embarrass'd them
most in this Design, was, their want of Time to do it in a more
complete manner, than it now remains in, otherwise they had
10 brought it, to the original Model of that in *Drury-Lane*, only
in a larger Proportion, as the wider Walls of it would require;
as there are not many Spectators, who may remember what Form
the *Drury-Lane* Theatre stood in, about forty Years ago, before
the old Patentee, to make it hold more Mony, took it in his Head
to alter it, it were but Justice to lay the original Figure, which
Sir *Christopher Wren* first gave it, and the Alterations of it, now
standing, in a fair Light; that equal Spectators may see, if they
were at their choice, which of the Structures would incline them
to a Preference. But in this Appeal, I only speak to such Spec-
20 tators as allow a good Play, well acted, to be the most valuable
Entertainment of the Stage. Whether such Plays (leaving the
Skill of the dead, or living Actors equally out of the Question)
have been more, or less, recommended in their Presentation, by
either of these different Forms of that Theatre, is our present
Matter of Enquiry.

   It must be obvserv'd then, that the Area, or Platform of the
old Stage, projected about four Foot forwarder, in a Semi-oval
Figure, parallel to the Benches of the Pit; and that the former,
lower Doors of Entrance for the Actors, were brought down be-
30 tween the two foremost (and then only) Pilasters; in the Place of
which Doors, now the two Stage-Boxes are fixt. That where the
Doors of Entrance now are, there formerly stood two additional
Side-Wings, in front to a ful Set of Scenes, which had then almost a double Effect, in their Loftiness, and Magnificence.

By this original Form, the usual Station of the Actors, in almost every Scene, was advanc'd at least ten Foot nearer to the
Audience, than they now can be; because, not only from
the Stage's being shorten'd, in front, but likewise from the additional Interposition of those Stage-Boxes, the Actors (in respect to
the Spectators, that fill them) are kept so much more backward
from the main Audience, than they us'd to be: But when the
Actors were in Possession of that forwarder Space, to advance
upon, the Voice was then more in the Centre of the House, so
10 that the most distant Ear had scarce the least Doubt, or Difficulty in hearing what fell from the weakest Utterance: All Objects were thus drawn nearer to the Sense; every painted Scene
was stronger; every Grand Scene and Dance more extended;
every rich, or fine-coloured Habit had a more lively Lustre:
Nor was the minutest Motion of a Feature (properly changing
with the Passion, or Humour it suited) ever lost, as they frequently must be in the Obscurity of too great a Distance: And
how valuable an Advantage the Facility of hearing distinctly, is
to every well-acted Scene, every common Spectator is a Judge.
20 A Voice scarce rais'd above the Tone of a Whisper, either in
Tenderness, Resignation, innocent Distress, or Jealousy, suppress'd, often have as much concern with the Heart, as the most
clamorous Passions; and when on any of these Occasions, such
affecting Speeches are plainly heard, or lost, how wide is the
Difference, from the great or little Satisfaction receiv'd from
them? To all this a Master of a Company may say, I now receive Ten Pounds more, than could have been taken formerly,
in every full House! Not unlikely. But might not his House
be oftner ful, if the Auditors were oftener pleas'd? Might not
30 every bad House too, by a Possibility of being made every Day
better, add as much to one side of his Account, as it could take
from the other? If what I have said, carries any Truth in it,
why might not the original Form of this Theatre be restor'd?
But let this Digression avail what it may, the Actors now re-

10. There was now no other Theatre open against them] The Haymarket opened 15 September 1709, and the Drury Lane did not reopen until 23 November; it had attempted to open 6 September, but was forced to dismiss the audience (Avery, I, 198-99).

15. the great Expense ... of the Opera] *Camilla* was given 20 October and four times thereafter that season; *Thomyris*, 17 November, and seven times thereafter; a new opera, *Almahide*, 10 January 1710, and fourteen times thereafter; *Hydespes*, 23 March 1710, and eleven times thereafter; it is clear, therefore, that, expenses notwithstanding, repeated performances were possible.

turn'd to the *Hay-Market*, as I have observ'd, wanted nothing
but length of time to have govern'd their Alteration of that
Theatre, by this original Model of *Drury-Lane*, which I have
recommended. As their time therefore was short, they made
their best use of it; they did something to it: They contracted
its Wideness, by three Ranges of Boxes on each Side, and brought
down its enormous high Cieling, within so proportionable a
Compass, that it effectually cured those hollow Undulations of the
Voice formerly complain'd of. The Remedy had its Effect; their
10 Audiences exceeded their Expectation. There was now no other
Theatre open against them; they had the Town to themselves;
they were their own Masters, and the Profits of their Industry
came into their own Pockets.

 Yet with all this fair Weather, the Season of their uninterrupted Prosperity was not yet arriv'd; for the great Expence, and
thinner Audiences of the Opera (of which they then were equally
Directors) was a constant Draw-back upon their Gains, yet not
so far, but that their Income this Year, was better than in their
late Station, at *Drury-Lane*. But by the short Experience we
20 had then had of Operas; by the high Reputation they seem'd
to have been arriv'd at, the Year before; by their Power of
drawing the whole Body of Nobility, as by Enchantment, to their
Solemnities; by that Prodigality of Expence, at which they were
so willing to support them; and from the late extraordinary
Profits *Swiney* had made of them; what Mountains did we not
hope from this Mole-hill? But alas! the fairy Vision was vanish'd,
this bridal Beauty was grown familiar to the general Taste, and
Satiety began to make Excuses for its want of Appetite: Or
what is still stranger, its late Admirers now as much valued their
30 Judgment, in being able to find out the Faults of the Performers, as they had before, in discovering their Excellencies. The
Truth is, that this kind of Entertainment being so entirely sensual, it had no Possibility of getting the better of our Reason,
but by its Novelty; and that Novelty could never be supported

1.1 wanted nothing] wanting nothing 2nd ed.
1.7 Cieling] Ceiling 2nd ed.
1.29 stranger] stronger 1st ed.

7. Charms Sufficient to make that Crown sit easy] Farinelli (1705-82) was able, by the therapeutic powers of his singing, to persuade the extremely melancholy Philip V (1683-1746) of Spain to resume his responsibilities of kingship. He was retained in this service for ten years, until the death of the king, being paid 50,000 francs per year to sing the same four arias nightly. He became a favorite of Ferdinand VI (1713-1759) also, with power superior to that of any minister, but was exiled by Charles III (1716-1788) in 1759, though his salary continued (*Grove's Dictionary of Music and Musicians*, article Farinelli).

25. *Faustina* and *Cuzzoni*] Faustina Bordoni (1700-1781) made her London debut on 5 May 1726, but remained there only two seasons because of her rivalry with Francesca Cuzzoni (1700-1770) who had first appeared in London on 12 January 1723. Partisans of each were so disruptive of a rival's performance that the managers of the opera offered a lower salary to Cuzzoni than to Faustina. The former, unwilling to accept less than her rival, left England, but returned from 1734-36. Handel exploited both their voices and their competitiveness; Gay satirized their rivalry in *The Beggar's Opera* (II, ii). For the program of a Concert given 16 April 1729 in which both sang, see Avery, II, 1026.

but by an annual Change of the best Voices, which like the
finest Flowers, bloom but for a Season, and when that is over,
are only dead Nose-gays. From this Natural Cause, we have
seen within these two Years, even *Farinelli* singing to an Audience of five and thirty Pounds; and yet, if common Fame
may be credited, the same Voice, so neglected in one Country,
has in another had Charms sufficient to make that Crown fit
easy, on the Head of a Monarch, which the Jealousy of Politicians (who had their Views, in his keeping it) fear'd without some
10 such extraordinary Amusement, his Satiety of Empire might
tempt him, a second time, to resign.

　　There is too, in the very Species of an *Italian* Singer, such an
innate, fantastical Pride, and Caprice, that the Government of
them (here at least) is almost impracticable. The Distemper, as
we were not sufficiently warn'd, or appriz'd of, threw our musical Affairs into Perplexities, we knew not easily how to get out
of. There is scarce a sensible Auditor, in the Kingdom, that has
not, since that Time, had Occasion to laugh at the several Instances of it: But what is still more ridiculous, these costly Ca-
20 nary-Birds have sometimes infested the whole Body of our dignified Lovers of Musick, with the same childish Animosities:
Ladies have been known to decline their Visits, upon account of
their being of a different musical Party. *Ceasar*, and *Pompey*
made not a warmer Division, in the *Roman* Republick, than
those Heroines, their Country Women, the *Faustina* and *Cuzzoni* blew up in our Common-wealth, of Academical Musick,
by their implacable Pretensions to Superiority! And while this
Greatness of Soul is their unalterable Virtue, it will never be
practicable to make two capital Singers of the same Sex, do as
30 they should do, in one Opera, at the same Time! no, not tho'
England were to double the Sums it has already thrown after
them: For even in their own Country, where an extraordinary
Occasion, has called a greater Number of their best, to sing together, the Mischief they have made has been proportionable;

21. *Suis et ipsa Roma viribus ruit.*] Horace, *Epode*, XVI, 2: "Rome herself is wrecked by her own powers."

26. something of this kind ... has generally embarrass'd ... Operas] He has in mind the repeated rivalries of opera companies, perhaps especially those in the 1730's which damaged Handel badly.

an Instance of which, if I am rightly inform'd, happen'd at
Parma, where upon the Celebration of the Marriage of that
Duke, a Collection was made of the most eminent Voices, that
Expence, or Interest could Purchase, to give as complete an
Opera, as the whole vocal Power of *Italy* could form. But
when it came to the Proof of this musical Project, behold!
what woeful Work they made of it! Every Performer would
be a *Ceasar*, or nothing; their several Pretensions to Preference
were not to be limited within the Laws of Harmony; they
10 would all chuse their own Songs, but not more to set off themselves, than to oppose, or deprive another of an Occasion to
shine: Yet any one would sing a bad Song, provided no body
else had a good one, till at last, they were thrown together like
so many feather'd Warriors, for a Battle-royal, in a Cock-pit,
where every one was oblig'd to kill another, to save himself!
What Pity it was these froward Misses, and Masters of Musick
had not been engag'd to entertain the Court of some King of
Morocco, that could have known a good Opera, from a bad one!
with how much Ease would such a Director have brought them
20 to better Order? But alas! as it has been said of greater Things,

Suis et ipsa Roma viribus ruit.   Hor.

Imperial *Rome* fell, by the too great Strength of its own Citi-
zens! So fell this mighty Opera, ruin'd by the too great Excel-
lency of its Singers! For, upon the whole, it prov'd to be as
barbarously bad, as if Malice it self had compos'd it.

Now though something of this kind, equally provoking, has
generally embarrass'd the State of Operas, these thirty Years; yet
it was the Misfortune of the menaging Actors, at the *Hay-
Market*, to have felt the first Effects of it: The Honour of the
30 Singer, and the Interest of the Undertaker were so often at Variance, that the latter began to have but a bad Bargain of it. But
not to impute more to the Caprice of those Performers, than was
really true, there were two different Accidents, that drew Num-

3. Trial of Doctor *Sacheverel*] Doctor Henry Sacheverel (1674-1724), a clergyman whose sympathies were strongly with the Stuarts, had preached on Guy Fawkes Day a fierce anti-Whig sermon in which he denied the right to resist a king under any circumstances, i.e., the whole legal basis of the Revolution of 1688; in order not to lose face, the Whig ministry attempted to impeach him, but in the course of a long and elaborately staged trial (Wren altered Westminster Hall for it, and the Queen had a box built for her) the government was profoundly embarrassed, especially by the very light punishment, which caused widespread rejoicing (cf. Burnet, II, 538-46; Plumb, I, 146-50). The trial opened 27 February 1710 and lasted longer than three weeks.

7. *William Collier*, Esq.] Collier, a Tory, was taking advantage of the deflation of Whig power, as shown by the Sacheverel trial; he also held a minor part of the patent.

20. the Interest of the joint Landlords] The theater belonged to the Duke of Bedford who leased it to renters, who then leased it to the patentees (Barker, p. 82).

26. the Means of getting into Possession.] Aitken, Tatler, II, 336, quotes a deposition of Collier's dated 8 January 1710 describing his technique: "On or about the 22nd of November, it being a day of public rejoicing, he ordered a bonfire to be made before the play-house door, and gave the actors money to drink your Majesty's heatlh ... and ... he came that evening to the playhouse and showed the players Sir John Stanley's letter, and told them they might act as soon as they pleased, for that he had the Queen's leave to employ them. Upon which the players themselves and some soldiers got into the playhouse, and the next day performed a play, but not the play that was given out, for Rich had carried away the clothes." The play advertised was *Aureng-Zebe*; Avery (I, 202) makes no mention of a substitution.

bers from our Audiences, before the Season was ended; which
were another Company permitted to act in *Drury-Lane*, and
the long Trial of Doctor *Sacheverel*, in *Westminster-Hall*: By
the way, it must be observ'd, that this Company was not under
the Direction of the Patent (which continued still silenc'd) but
was set up by a third Interest, with a License from Court. The
Person to whom this new License was granted, was *William
Collier*, Esq; a Lawyer of an enterprizing Head, and a jovial
Heart; what sort of Favour he was in, with the People, then
10 in Power, may be judg'd, from his being often admitted to partake with them those detach'd Hours of Life, when Business
was to give way to Pleasure: But this was not all his Merit, he
was, at the same time, a Member of Parliament for *Truro* in
Cornwall, and we cannot suppose a Person so qualified could be
refus'd such a Trifle, as a License to head a broken Company
of Actors. This sagacious Lawyer, then, who had a Lawyer to
deal with, observing that his Antagonist kept Possession of a
Theatre, without making use of it, and for which he was not
oblig'd to pay Rent, unless he actually *did* use it, wisely con-
20 ceiv'd it might be the Interest of the joint Landlords, since their
Tenement was in so precarious a Condition, to grant a Lease to
one, who had an undisputed Authority, to be liable, by acting
Plays in it, to pay the Rent of it; especially when he tempted
them with an Offer of raising it from three, to four Pounds *per
Diem*. His Project succeeded, the Lease was sign'd; but the
Means of getting into Possession were to be left to his own Cost,
and Discretion. This took him up but little Time, he immediately laid Siege to it, with a sufficient Number of Forces, whether lawless, or lawful, I forget, but they were such as oblig'd
30 the old Governor to give it up; who, notwithstanding had got
Intelligence of his Approaches, and Design, time enough to
carry off every thing, that was worth moving, except a great
Number of old Scenes, and new Actors, that could not easily
follow him.

1. a ludicrous Account] *The Tatler*, No. 99, 26 November 1709. The account by Steele, calling Rich *Divito*, makes the assault into a mock-epic. The only additional information it contains is this: "The neighboring inhabitants report, that the refuse of Divito's followers marched off the night before disguised in magnificence; door-keepers came out clad like cardinals, and scene drawers like heathen gods. Divito himself was wrapped up in one of his black clouds, and left to the enemy nothing but an empty stage, full of trap-doors, known only to himself and his adherents." These leavings were later the subject of a suit. Barker (p. 83) quotes the Chancery record listing the scenes left behind.

18. *The fair Quaker of Deal*] This comedy, by Charles Shadwell, had been offered to Cibber, c. 1707, but as the author states in the Preface, Cibber "took care to beat down the value of it so much as to offer the author to alter it, fit to appear on the stage, on condition he might have half the profits of the third day and the dedication entire, that is as much as to say that it might pass for one of his, according to custom. The author not agreeing to this reasonable proposal, it lay in his hands till the beginning of this winter, when Mr. Booth read it and liked it, and persuaded the author that with little alteration 'twould please the town" (Preface to the edition of 1710, p. 84). The play was first performed 25 February 1710, and overlapped the trial, being repeated that season on 28 February, 2, 4, 6, 13, 18 and 25 March; Cibber fails to note that Collier had withdrawn from active management of the theater by this time, because of the poor prospects of returns on his investment, and had given over the contracts of seven of his principal actors. The success of the play, therefore, was the occasion of his reasserting his rights and placing the theater under the management of Aaron Hill (Barker, pp. 84-84). See Chapter XIII, 245 ff., for Cibber's account of this. Avery (I, 202) states that Hill had been manager since 22 November 1709.

A ludicrous Account of this Transaction, under fictitious
Names, may be found in the 99th *Tatler*, Vol. 2. which this
Explanation may now render more intelligible, to the Readers of
that agreeable Author.

This other new License being now in Possession of the *Drury-
Lane* Theatre; those Actors, whom the Patentee, ever since the
Order of Silence, had retain'd in a State of Inaction, all to a
Man came over to the Service of *Collier*. Of these, *Booth* was
then the chief. The Merit of the rest had as yet made no con-
10 siderable Appearance, and as the Patentee had not left a Rag of
their Cloathing behind him, they were but poorly equip'd for a
publick Review; consequently at their first Opening, they were
very little able to annoy us. But during the Trial of *Sacheverel*,
our Audiences were extremely weaken'd, by the better Rank of
People's daily attending it: While, at the same time, the lower
Sort, who were not equally admitted to that grand Spectacle,
as eagerly crowded into *Drury-Lane*, to a new Comedy, called
The fair Quaker of Deal. This Play, having some low Strokes
of natural Humour in it, was rightly calculated, for the Capa-
20 city of the Actors, who play'd it, and to the Taste of the Multitude, who were now, more dispos'd, and at leisure to see it:
But the most happy Incident, in its Fortune, was the Charm of
the fair Quaker, which was acted by Miss *Santlow*, (afterwards
Mrs. *Booth*) whose Person was then in the full Bloom of what
Beauty she might pretend to: Before this, she had only been admired as the most excellent Dancer, which, perhaps, might not
a little contribute to the favourable Reception, she now met
with as an Actress, in this Character, which so happily suited
her Figure, and Capacity: The gentle Softness of her Voice, the
30 compos'd Innocence of her Aspect, the Modesty of her Dress,
the reserv'd Decency of her Gesture, and the Simplicity of the
Sentiments, that naturally fell from her, made her seem the
amiable Maid she represented: In a Word, not the enthusiastick
Maid of *Orleans*, was more serviceable of old, to the *French*

Army, when the *English* had distress'd them, than this fair Quaker was, at the Head of that Dramatick Attempt, upon which
the Support of their weak Society depended.

But when the Trial, I have mention'd, and the Run of this
Play was over, the Tide of the Town beginning to turn again
in our Favour, *Collier* was reduc'd to give his Theatrical Affairs
a different Scheme; which advanc'd the Stage another Step towards that Settlement, which, in my Time, was of the longest
Duration.

C H A P. XIII

The Patentee, having now no Actors, rebuilds the new Theatre in
Lincolns-Inn-Fields. *A Guess at his Reasons for it. More*
Changes, in the State of the Stage. The Beginning of its better
Days, under the Triumvirate *of Actors. A Sketch of their*
governing Characters.

10   AS coarse Mothers may have comely Children; so
            Anarchy has been the Parent of many a good Go-
            vernment; and by a Parity of possible Consequences
            we shall find, that from the frequent Convulsions of
            the Stage, arose, at last, its longest Settlement, and
Prosperity; which many of my Readers (or if I should happen
to have but few of them, many of my Spectators, at least) who,
I hope, have not yet liv'd half their Time, will be able to remember.

        Though the Patent had been often under Distresses, it had
20   never felt any Blow, equal to this unrevoked Order of Silence;
        which it is not easy to conceive could have fallen upon any other
        Person's Conduct, than that of the old Patentee: For if he was
        conscious, of his being under the Subjection of that Power,

l. 3   the Support] TheS upport 1st ed.

7. preserv'd to his Heirs the Property of the Patent] The elder Rich had received permission from George I to reopen Lincoln's Inn Fields, but died before he could exercise the privilege, leaving the theater and patent to his sons John and Christopher Mosier (Loftis, *Politics*, p. 64, and Avery, I, xxxii-xxxiv).

which had silenc'd him, why would he incur the Danger of a
Suspension, by his so obstinate, and impolitick Treatment of
his Actors? If he thought such Power over him illegal, how
came he to obey it now, more than before, when he slighted a
former Order, that injoin'd him to give his Actors their Benefits,
on their usual Conditions? But to do him Justice, the same
Obstinacy, that involv'd him, in these Difficulties, at last, preserv'd to his Heirs the Property of the Patent, in its full Force,
and Value; yet to suppose that he foresaw a milder use of Power,
10 in some future Prince's Reign, might be more favourable to him,
is begging at best but a cold Question. But whether he knew
that this broken Condition of the Patent would not make his
troublesome Friends, the Adventurers, fly from it, as from a
falling House, seems not so difficult a Question. However, let
the Reader form his own Judgment of them, from the Facts,
that follow'd: It must therefore by observ'd, that the Adventurers seldom came near the House, but when there was some
visible Appearance of a Dividend: But I could never hear, that
upon an ill Run of Audiences, they had ever returned, or
20 brought in a single Shilling, to make good the Deficiencies of
their daily Receipts. Therefore, as the Patentee, in Possession,
had alone, for several Years, supported, and stood against this
Uncertainty of Fortune, it may be imagin'd, that his Accounts
were under so voluminous a Perplexity, that few of those Adventurers would have leisure, or Capacity enough to unravel
them: And as they had formerly thrown away their Time, and
Mony at Law, in a fruitless Enquiry into them, they now seem'd
to have intirely given up their Right and Interest: And, according to my best Information, notwithstanding the subsequent
30 Gains of the Patent have been sometimes extraordinary, the
farther Demands, or Claims of Rights, of the Adventurers
have lain dormant, above these five and twenty Years.

Having shewn by what means *Collier* had dispossess'd this Patentee, not only of the *Drury-Lane* House, but likewise of those

previous season at the Haymarket, and, second, that the welfare of the opera be promoted, possibly by a subsidy of around £500; Wilks, Cibber, and Dogget wished to have a license in their names giving them complete control of the drama and possession of the Drury Lane Theatre if a lease could be procured (summarized by Barker, pp. 84-85, from BM, Add. MSS. 38, 607). These proceedings led to a tentative agreement on 4 November and the issue of a license to Swiney, Wilks, Cibber, and Dogget for the management of a "Company of Comedians" (L.C. 5/155, p. 44, Nicoll documents, II, 275) at the Haymarket. The first arrangement was that both opera and players should share this one theater, plays being given Mondays, Tuesdays, Thursdays, and Fridays, operas being given by Collier and his singers on Wednesdays and Saturdays, a situation not entirely satisfactory to the actors (see *Apology*, below, and Barker, p. 85; from PRO, C.8, 621/30 and BM Add. MS. 38, 607). It was only on 20 November 1710 that the arrangement Cibber describes was finally arrived at; by then Cibber had secured a three-year lease of Drury Lane, to which the actors and properties were to move, leaving the Haymarket to Collier and the singers. The acting company was to pay the rent of Drury Lane, though Collier retained possession of the lease; the acting company also was to pay £200 per year toward the rent of the Haymarket, considered by Swiney and Vanbrugh as rent for the properties which had been removed from the Haymarket to Drury Lane (summarized by Barker, pp. 85-86, from Add. Ms. 20, 736; L.C. 7/3; C.8 621/30).

10. Lease, ... since Betterton's Company had first left it] It is conceivable that he had leased the house in 1705, as Nicoll (II, 429), following Cibber, states. But in Barker's (pp. 99-100) more plausible and better documented version, Rich rented the Lincoln's Inn Fields from Messrs. Porcino and Sniff c. August 1709; he began to remodel it only after Drury Lane was taken from him, largely because of his natural delight in building. His reasons for rebuilding the theater are not so mysterious as Cibber suggests; during the latter period of Queen Anne's life it was not uncommon for those who were able to represent themselves as persecuted by the Tories to expect restitution in the event that the Whigs succeeded in establishing the House of Hanover on the throne (cf. Plumb, I, 185 ff.; for a discussion of the alliance between Whigs and the theater, and of Tory suspiciousness toward it, see Loftis, *Politics*, Chapter III).

24. which he naturally took Delight in] Cf. Chapter IX, p. 190.

25. Theatrical Forces of *Collier*] Cibber is being elliptical here; the management of the theater, after the success of *The Fair Quaker of Deal*, had been turned over to Aaron Hill (cf. p. 246 n.) as Collier's representative. The actors resented Hill and their disputes finally led to an open revolt; the Lord Chamberlain sent an order dated 14 June 1710 to punish the five leaders for refusing to obey Hill and because "they did also lately in a riotous manner break open the Doors of the Play house, beating and abusing the s[aid] Mr. Hill and w[ith] their Swords drawn threatning his life ..." (from L.C. 5/155, p. 11, printed by Nicoll, II, 292). They apparently went so far as to stab Hill's brother and to attempt to return to the services of Rich, against all of which Collier was powerless since he had no lease on the playhouse and no contracts with the actors. This is the background of negotiations beginning on 2 September 1710 with Swiney which Cibber describes in the passage following (cf. Barker, p. 84).

32. giving up the *Drury-Lane* ... to *Swiney* ... *Collier* ... *Hay-Market*] Cibber here and in the account following omits a number of relevant facts: from the negotiations which had begun in September 1710 Collier wished to emerge with a company of actors and a theater, which would bring him an income; Swiney wished, first, that his partners share the debts of the

few Actors, which he had kept, for some time unemploy'd in
it; we are now led to consider another Project of the same Patentee, which, if we are to judge of it by the Event, as shewn
him more a Wise, than a Weak Man; which I confess, at the
time he put it in Execution, seem'd not so clear a Point: For
notwithstanding he now saw the Authority, and Power of his
Patent was superseded, or was at best but precarious, and that he
had not one Actor left, in his Service; yet under all these Di-
lemmas, and Distresses, he resolv'd upon rebuilding the New
10 Theatre in *Lincoln's-Inn Fields*, of which he had taken a Lease,
at a low Rent, ever since *Betterton's* Company had first left it.
This Conduct seem'd too deep for my Comprehension! What are
we to think of his taking this Lease, in the height of his Prosperity, when he could have no Occasion for it? Was he a Pro-
phet? Could he then foresee, he should, one time or other, be
turn'd out of *Drury-Lane?* Or did his mere Appetite of Architecture urge him to build a House, while he could not be
sure, he should ever have leave to make use of it? But of all
this, we may think as we please; whatever was his Motive, he,
20 at his own Expence, in this Interval of his having nothing else
to do, rebuilt that Theatre from the Ground, as it is now standing. As for the Order of Silence, he seem'd little concern'd at it,
while it gave him so much uninterrupted Leisure to supervise a
Work, which he naturally took Delight in.

After this Defeat of the Patentee, the Theatrical Forces of
Collier in *Drury-Lane*, notwithstanding their having drawn the
Multitude after them, for about three Weeks, during the Trial
of *Sacheverel*, had made but an indifferent Campaign, at the
end of the Season. *Collier*, at least, found so little Account in it,
30 that it oblig'd him to push his Court-Interest (which, wherever
the Stage was concern'd, was not inconsiderable) to support him
in another Scheme; which was, that in consideration of his giving up the *Drury-Lane*, Cloaths, Scenes, and Actors, to *Swiney*,
and his joint Shareers, in the *Hay-Market*, he (*Collier*) might be

1.3 to judge of it by the Event] to judge of by the Event 1st ed.

21. every *Wednesday*, whereon an Opera could be perform'd ...] After their removal to Drury Lane, the actors were permitted to give plays on Saturdays, and since the opera had not been ready to perform, they had performed on Wednesdays and Saturdays during 4-18 November (Barker, p. 86 n.; also Avery, I, 235-36).

put into an equal Possession of the *Hay-Market* Theatre, with
all the Singers, &c. and be made sole Director of the Opera.
Accordingly, by Permission of the Lord-Chamberlain, a Treaty
was enter'd into, and in a few Days ratified by all Parties, con-
formable to the said Preliminaries. This was that happy Crisis of
Theatrical Liberty, which the labouring Comedians had long
sigh'd for; and which, for above twenty Years following, was so
memorably fortunate to them.

 However, there were two hard Articles, in this Treaty, which
10 though it might be Policy in the Actors to comply with, yet the
Imposition of them seem'd little less despotick, than a Tax upon
the Poor, when a Government did not want it.

 The first of these Articles was, That whereas the sole License
for acting Plays, was presum'd to be a more profitable Authority,
than that for acting Operas only; that therefore Two Hundred
Pounds a Year should be paid to *Collier*, while Master of the
Opera, by the Comedians; to whom a Verbal Assurance was
given by the *Plenipo's* on the Court-side, that while such Payment subsisted, no other Company should be permitted to act.
20 Plays, against them, within the Liberties, &c. The other Article was, That on every *Wednesday*, whereon an Opera could be
perform'd, the Plays should, *toties quoties*, be silent at *Drury-
Lane*, to give the Opera a fairer Chance, for a full House.

 This last Article, however partial, in the Intention, was in its
Effect, of great Advantage to the sharing Actors: For in all publick Entertainments, a Day's Abstinence naturally increases the
Appetite to them: Our every *Thursday's* Audience, therefore,
was visibly the better, by thus making the Day before it a Fast.
But as this was not a Favour design'd us, this Prohibition of a
30 Day, methinks, deserves a little farther Notice, because it evidently took a sixth Part of their Income, from all the hired
Actors, who were only paid, in proportion to the Number of
acting Days. This extraordinary Regard to Operas, was in effect making the Day-labouring Actors the principle Subscribers to

3. tho' I was one ... who profited] Cibber, as a manager, drew his income from the total profits; and since he believed that one acting day less did not significantly decrease these, the regulation merely meant lower costs.

29. Bridge at *Westminster*] The building of Westminster Bridge, violently opposed by the Corporation of London, was authorized by an Act of Parliament in 1736; work began in 1738 but was not completed until 1750. The "Noble Commissioner" [see p. 252] was Henry Herbert (1693-1751), ninth Earl of Pembroke, who laid the first stone in 1739 and the last in 1750 (*DNB*, article Henry Herbert).

them, and the shutting out People from the Play every Wednesday, *many murmured at, as an Abridgment of their usual Liberty. And tho' I was one of those, who profited by that Order, it ought not to bribe me, into a Concealment of what was
then said and thought of it. I remember a Nobleman of the
first Rank, then in a high Post, and not out of Court-Favour,
said openly behind the Scenes*————It was shameful to take part of
the Actors Bread from them to support the silly Diversion of People of Quality. *But alas! what was all this Grievance, when*
20 weighed against the Qualifications of so grave, and stanch a Se-
nator, as Collier? Such visible Merit, it seems, was to be made
easy, tho' at the Expence of the*————I had almost said, Honour *of
the Court, whose gracious Intention for the Theatrical Common-
wealth, might have shone with thrice the Lustre, if such a paltry Price had not been paid for it. But as the Government of
the Stage, is but that of the World in Miniature, we ought not
to have wondered, that* Collier *had Interest enough to quarter
the Weakness of the Opera, upon the Strength of the Comedy.
General good Intentions are not always practicable to a Perfec-*
20 *tion. The most necessary Law can hardly pass, but a Tenderness to some private Interest, shall often hang such Exceptions
upon particular Clauses, 'till at last it comes out lame, and lifeless, with the Loss of half its Force, Purpose, and Dignity. As
for instance; how many fruitless Motions have been made in
Parliaments, to moderate the enormous Exactions, in the Practice of the Law? And what sort of Justice must that be call'd,
which, when a Man has not a mind to pay you a Debt of Ten
Pounds, it shall cost you Fifty, before you can get it? How long
too, has the Publick been labouring for a Bridge at Westminster?*
30 But the Wonder, that it was not built a Hundred Years ago ceases,
when we are told, That the Fear of making one End of *London*,
as rich, as the other, has been, so long, an Obstruction to it: And
tho' it might seem a still greater Wonder, when a new Law for
building one had at last got over that Apprehension, that it

18. *Collier* being thus possess'd of his Musical Government] Cibber apparently has confused this with the season before when Collier had farmed the Drury Lane company to Hill (cf. pp. 246 n. and 249 n.). Barker's account based on the documents of these affairs (pp. 86-88: C.7 668/31; Add. MS. 38, 607; C.8 621/30, C.11 6/44 and 2342/26) does not indicate that Hill had any part in the management of the opera during the season of 1710-11. Cibber's admission (below) of an imperfect memory of the cause of Hill's leaving strengthens the supposition that he has confused these highly involved affairs.

should meet with any farther Delay; yet Experience has shewn
us, that the Structure of this useful Ornament to our Metropolis
has been so clogg'd by private Jobs, that were to be pick'd out
of the Undertaking, and the Progress of the Work so disconcerted by a tedious Contention of Private Interests, and Endeavours to impose upon the Publick abominable Bargains, that a
whole Year was lost, before a single Stone could be laid to its
Foundation. But Posterity will owe its Praises, to the Zeal, and
Resolution of a truly Noble Commissioner, whose distinguish'd
10 Impatience has broke thro' those narrow Artifices, those false and
frivolous Objections, that delay'd it, and has already began to
raise, above the Tide, that future Monument of his Publick
Spirit.

How far all this may be allow'd applicable to the State of the
Stage, is not of so great Importance, nor so much my Concern,
as that what is observ'd upon it should always remain a memorable Truth, to the Honour of that Nobleman. But now I go
on: *Collier* being thus possess'd of his Musical Government,
thought his best way would be to farm it out to a Gentleman,
20 *Aaron Hill*, Esq; (who, he had reason to suppose, knew something more of Theatrical Matters, than himself) at a Rent, if I
mistake not, of Six Hundred Pounds *per Annum*: But before
the Season was ended (upon what occasion, if I could remember, it might not be material to say) took it into his Hands a-
gain: But all his Skill, and Interest, could not raise the Direction
of the Opera, to so good a Post, as he thought due to a Person of his Consideration: He therefore, the Year following,
enter'd upon another high-handed Scheme, which, 'till the Demise of the Queen, turn'd to his better Account.
30   After the Comedians were in Possession of *Drury-Lane*, from
whence, during my time upon the Stage, they never departed;
their Swarm of Audiences exceeded all that had been seen, in
thirty Years before; which, however, I do not impute so much
to the Excellence of their Acting, as to their indefatigable In-

rent of the Haymarket, which he kept for himself (Barker, p. 87, based on C.11 1175/59; he notes the difference between his account and Cibber's without calling Cibber's incorrect).

33. *Swiney* ... Opera ... Winter following 1711] Correctly, the winter of 1712-13, when he produced two new Handel operas, *Teseo,* and *Pastor Fido* (Barker, p. 87).

34. he was driven] Barker (p. 88) notes that Cibber and Swiney had renewed their friendship when Swiney returned to England in the mid 1730's; Cibber acted in a benefit for him on 26 February 1735.

7. *Collier*, then, like a true liquorish Courtier] It is difficult to say whether Cibber is falsifying

his account here and below for the sake of his revived friendship with Swiney (see Barker,

pp. 87-88), or whether he actually cannot remember. However that may be, the facts are that

shortly after the settlement of 4 November 1710, Cibber, Wilks, and Dogget set about to

exclude Swiney from any part of the management of the theater (see the documents regulating

the playhouses at this period, printed by Nicoll, II, 278-81; they are from L.C. 5/155, p. 3;

L.C. 7/3; L.C. 5/155, p. 159), reduced his salary to one-fourth of the profits, refused to share

the debts of the previous season, and ordered their treasurer not to make any payments

without the signatures of their manager (this regulation, L.C. 7/31, is printed by Nicoll, II,

280-81). When Swiney appealed to the Lord Chamberlain, they likewise presented their case

to him, asking that the articles of agreement of 10 March 1709—linking Swiney, and the three

actor-managers—be cancelled, an act which would definitively release them from the debts of

the season of 1709/10. They also asked that they be permitted to give Swiney a fixed annual

income, excluding him entirely from authority as a manager. On 12 January 1710/11 he sued

in Chancery; the decision rendered 19 May 1711 cancelled the 1709 agreement, fixed

Swiney's stipend at £600 per year, and left the settlement of the losses of the 1709 season to

arbitration which continued until spring of 1712 (this is taken from Barker, pp. 86-87, who

According to Barker (*idem.*) it was Swiney who approached Collier soon after the

arbitration had been completed. After making inquiries of Doggett and receiving

encouragement from him, Collier agreed to the exchange of theaters in April 1712. Swiney

moved to the Haymarket to give operas (see his license L.C. 7/3 and L.C. 5/155, p. 160,

printed by Nicoll, II, 284); and the three actors and Collier occupied Drury Lane, where they

were licensed for comedy. Collier then bargained for and received a reduction of £100 on the

dustry, and good Management; for as I have often said, I never
thought, in the general, that we stood in any Place of Comparison with the eminent Actors before us; perhaps too, by there
being now an End of the frequent Divisions, and Disorders, that
had from time to time broke in upon, and frustrated their Labours, not a little might be contributed to their Success.

    Collier, then, like a true liquorish Courtier, observing the Pro-
sperity of a Theatre, which he, the Year before had parted with
for a worse, began to meditate an Exchange of Theatrical Posts
10 *Swiney*, who had visibly very fair Pretensions to that he
was in, by his being first chosen, by the Court, to regulate, and
rescue the Stage from the Disorders it had suffer'd, under its
former Menagers: Yet *Collier* knew that sort of Merit could
stand in no Competition, with his being a Member of Parliament: He therefore had Recourse to his Court-Interest (where
meer Will, and Pleasure, at that time, was the only Law, that
dispos'd of all Theatrical Rights) to oblige *Swiney* to let him be
off, from his bad Bargain, for a better. To this, it may be
imagin'd *Swiney* demurr'd, and as he had Reason, strongly re-
20 monstrated against it: But as *Collier* has listed his Conscience
under the Command of Interest, he kept it to strict Duty, and
was immoveable; insomuch that Sir *John Vanbrugh*, who was
a Friend to *Swiney*, and who by his Intimacy with the People
in Power, better knew the Motive of their Actions, advis'd
Swiney rather to accept of the Change, than by a Non-com-
pliance to hazard his being excluded from any Post, or Concern
in either of the Theatres: To conclude, it was not long before
Collier had procured a new License for acting Plays, &c. for himself, *Wilks, Dogget,* and *Cibber*, exclusive of *Swiney*, who by
30 this new Regulation was reduc'd to his *Hobson's* Choice of the
Opera.

    Swiney being thus transferr'd to the Opera, in the sinking Con-
dition *Collier* had left it, found the Receipts of it, in the Winter
following 1711, so far short of the Expences, that he was driven

17. likewise insisted, upon a Moiety ... in Aid of the Operas] The actors interpreted the £200 rent for the properties carried from the Haymarket as a subsidy for the opera. The warrant to Swiney dated 17 April 1712 (L.C. 7/3 and L.C. 5/155, p. 160, printed by Nicoll, II, 284) suggests that although the £200 of the earlier contract (20 November 1711) had been "towards the Rent of the Theatre in the Hay Market," the reduced amount of £100 was directly "for the better Support of the expenses of the Opera."

to attend his Fortune in some more favourable Climate, where
he remain'd twenty Years an Exile, from his Friends, and Country; tho' there has been scarce an *English* Gentleman, who in
his *Tour* of *France,* or *Italy,* has not renew'd, or created an Acquaintance with him. As this is a Circumstance, that many People may have forgot, I cannot remember it, without that Regard, and Concern it deserves from all that know him: Yet it
is some Mitigation of his Misfortune, 'that since his Return to
England, his grey Hairs, and cheerful Disposition have still found
10 a general Welcome among his foreign, and former domestick Acquaintance.

   Collier being now, first-commission'd Menager with the Comedians, drove them too, to the last Inch of a hard Bargain (the
natural Consequence of all Treaties between Power, and Necessity) He not only demanded six hundred a Year, neat Mony, the
Price at which he had farm'd out his Opera, and to make the
Business a *sine Cure* to him; but likewise insisted, upon a Moiety
of the two hundred, that had been levied upon us the Year before, in Aid of the Operas; in all *700 l.* These large, and am-
20 ple Conditions, considering in what Hands we were, we resolv'd
to swallow without wry Faces; rather chusing to run any Hazard, than contend with a formidable Power, against which we
had no Remedy: But so it happen'd, that Fortune took better
Care of our Interest, than we ourselves had like to have done:
For had *Collier* accepted of our first Offer, of an equal Share
with us, he had got three hundred Pounds a Year more, by
complying with it, than by the Sum he imposed upon us; our
Shares being never less, than a thousand annually, to each of us,
till the End of the Queen's Reign, in 1714. After which *Collier's*
30 Commission was superseded; his Theatrical Post, upon the Accession of his late Majesty, being given to Sir *Richard Steele.*

   From these various Revolutions, in the Government of the
Theatre, all owing to the Patentees mistaken Principle of increasing their Profits, by too far enslaving their People, and keeping

18. I am not unwilling it should be twice taken notice of.] Cf. Chapter VIII, p. 163.

26. only acting Managers, under the Queen's License] L.C. 5/155, p. 157, dated 17 April 1712. The license is granted in the same terms as that to Swiney, Dogget, Wilks, and Cibber (printed by Nicoll, II, 275-76), which stated that the company was "allow'd and Established by Our Royall License under the direction of the Chamberlain of Our Household for the time being ..."

down the Price of good Actors (and I could almost insist, that
giving large Sallaries to bad Ones, could not have had a worse
Consequence) I say, when it is consider'd, that the Authority for
acting Plays, &c. was thought of so little worth, that (as has
been observ'd) Sir *Thomas Skipwith* gave away his Share of it, and
the Adventurers had fled from it; that Mr. *Congreve*, at another
time, had voluntarily resign'd it; and Sir *John Vanbrugh* (merely
to get the Rent of his new House paid) had, by Leave of the
Court, farm'd out his License, to *Swiney*, who not without some
10 Hesitation had ventur'd upon it; let me say again, out of this
low Condition of the Theatre, was it now owing to the Industry
of three, or four Comedians, that a new Place was now created
for the Crown to give away, without any Expence attending it,
well worth the Acceptance of any Gentleman, whose Merit, or
Services had no higher Claim to Preferment, and which *Collier*,
and Sir *Richard Steele*, in the two last Reigns, successively enjoy'd? Though, I believe, I may have said something like this,
in a former Chapter, I am not unwilling it should be twice taken
notice of.

20   We are now come to that firm Establishment of the Theatre,
which except the Admittance of *Booth* into a Share, and *Dogget's*
retiring from it, met with no Change, or Alteration, for above
twenty Years after.

    Collier, as has been said, having accepted of a certain Ap-
pointment of seven hundred *per Annum*; *Wilks, Dogget,* and
Myself were now the only acting Menagers, under the Queen's
License; which being a Grant, but during Pleasure, oblig'd us
to a Conduct that might not undeserve that Favour. At this
Time we were All in the Vigour of our Capacities as Actors; and
30 our Prosperity enabled us, to pay, at least, double the Sallaries,
to what the same Actors had usually receiv'd, or could have
hoped for under the Government of the Patentees. *Dogget*, who
was naturally an Oeconomist, kept our Expences, and Accounts
to the best of his Power, within regulated Bounds, and Modera-

tion. *Wilks*, who had a stronger Passion, for Glory, than Lucre,
was a little apt to be lavish, in what was not always as necessary
for the Profit, as the Honour of the Theatre: For Example, at
the Beginning of almost every Season, he would order two, or three
Suits to be made, or refresh'd, for Actors of moderate Consequences, that his having constantly a new one for himself, might
seem less particular, tho' he had, as yet, no new Part for it.
This expeditious Care of doing us good, without waiting for our
Consent to it, *Dogget* always look'd upon, with the Eye of a
10 Man, in Pain: But I, who hated Pain, (tho' I as little liked the
Favour, as *Dogget* himself) rather chose to laugh at the Circumstance, than complain of what I knew was not to be cured, but
by a Remedy, worse than the Evil. Upon these Occasions, therefore, whenever I saw him, and his Followers so prettily dress'd
out, for an old Play, I only commended his Fancy; or at most
but whisper'd him not to give himself so much Trouble, about
others, upon whose Performance it would but be thrown away:
To which, with a smiling Air of Triumph, over my want of
Penetration, he has reply'd---Why, now, that was what I really
20 did it for! to shew others, that I love to take Care of them, as
well as of myself. Thus whenever he made himself easy, he had
not the least Conception, let the Expence be what it would,
that we could possibly dislike it. And from the same Principle,
provided a thinner Audience were liberal of their Applause, he
gave himself little Concern about the Receipt of it. As in these
different Tempers of my Brother-Menagers, there might be
equally something right, and wrong, it was equally my Business
to keep well with them both: And tho' of the two, I was rather inclin'd to *Dogget's* way of thinking, yet I was always un-
30 der the disagreeable Restraint of not letting *Wilks* see it: Therefore, when in any material Point of Menagement, they were
ready to come to a Rupture, I found it adviseable to think neither of them, absolutely in the wrong; but by giving to one as
much of the Right, in his Opinion this way, as I took from the

8. we never had Creditor that had Occasion to come twice for his Bill] This practice was regulated by agreement (L.C. 7/3, printed by Nicoll, II, 280-81).

other in that; their Differences were sometimes soft'ned into
Concessions, that I have Reason to think prevented many ill
Consequences, in our Affairs, that otherwise might have attended
them. But this was always to be done with a very gentle Hand;
for as Wilks *was apt to be easily hurt, by Opposition, so when
he felt it he was as apt to be insupportable. However, there
were some Points, in which we were always unanimous. In the
twenty Years, while we were our own Directors, we never had
a Creditor that had Occasion to come twice for his Bill; every*
10 Monday *Morning discharged us of all Demands, before we took
a Shilling for our own Use. And from this Time, we neither
ask'd any Actor, nor were desired by them, to sign any written
Agreement (to the best of my Memory) whatsoever: The Rate
of their respective Sallaries were only enter'd in our daily Pay-
Roll; which plain Record ever one look'd upon, as good as
City-Security: For where an honest Meaning is mutual, the mutual Confidence will be Bond enough, in Conscience, on both
sides: But that I may not ascribe more to our Conduct than was
really its Due, I ought to give Fortune her Share of the Com-*
20 mendation; *for had not our Success exceeded our Expectation, it
might not have been in our Power, so throughly to have observ'd
those laudable Rules of Oeconomy, Justice, and Lenity, which
so happily supported us: But the Severities, and Oppression we
had suffer'd under our former Masters, made us incapable of imposing them upon others; which gave our whole Society the
cheerful Looks of a rescued People. But notwithstanding this
general Cause of Content, it was not above a Year or two before the Imperfection of human Nature began to shew itself in
contrary Symptoms. The Merit of the Hazards which the Me-*
30 nagers *had run, and the Difficulties they had combated, in
bringing to Perfection, that Revolution, by which they had all
so amply profited, in the Amendment of their general Income,
began now to be forgotten; their Acknowledgments, and thankful Promises of Fidelity, were no more repeated, or scarce*

21. The only Actor ... advanc'd to a Share with us, was certainly *Booth*] The opposition Cibber refers to was Booth's service to Collier in 1709 (cf. above, p. 246). See Chapter XIV for the circumstances of Booth's elevation to the role of manager. *The Laureat* (p. 76) accuses the actor-managers of excluding Booth in order not to distribute their profits to a fourth person.

thought obligatory: Ease and Plenty, by an habitual Enjoyment,
had lost their Novelty, and the Largeness of their Sallaries, seem'd
rather lessen'd than advanc'd, by the extraordinary Gains of the
Undertakers; for that is the Scale, in which the hired Actor will
always weigh his Performance; but whatever Reason there may
seem to be, in his Case, yet as he is frequently apt to throw a
little Self-partiality into the Balance, that Consideration may a
good deal alter the Justness of it. While the Actors, therefore,
had this way of thinking, happy was it, for the Menagers, that
10 their united Interest was so inseparably the same, and that their
Skill and Power in Acting, stood in a Rank so far above the
rest, that if the whole Body of private Men had deserted them,
it would yet have been an easier Matter, for the Menagers to
have pick'd up Recruits, than for the Deserters to have found
proper Officers to head them. Here, then, in this Distinction
lay our Security: Our being Actors ourselves, was an Advantage
to our Government, which all former Menagers, who were only
idle Gentlemen, wanted: Nor was our Establishment easily to be
broken, while our Health, and Limbs enabled us, to be Joint-
20 labourers in the Work we were Masters of.

The only Actor, who, in the Opinion of the Publick, seem'd
to have had a Pretence of being advanc'd to a Share with us,
was certainly Booth: But when it is consider'd, how strongly he
had oppos'd the Measures, that had made us Menagers, by set-
ing himself (as has been observ'd) at the Head of an opposite
Interest, he could not as yet, have much to complain of: Beside, if the Court had thought him, now, an equal Object of
Favour, it could not have been in our Power, to have oppos'd
his Preferment: This I mention, not to take from his Merit, but
30 to shew, from what Cause it was not, as yet, better provided for.
Therefore, it may be no Vanity to say, our having at that Time,
no visible Competitors on the Stage, was the only Interest, that
rais'd us to be the Menagers of it.

28. *Hoc est ... priore frui.*] Martial, X, 23, 7: "He lives twice who can find delight in life gone past."

But here, let me rest a while, and since, at my time of Day,
our best Possessions are but Ease, and Quiet, I must be content, if
I will have Sallies of Pleasure, to take up with those only, that
are to be found in Imagination. When I look back, therefore,
on the Storms of the Stage, we had been toss'd in; when I consider, that various Vicissitude of Hopes and Fears, we had for
twenty Years struggled with, and found our selves, at last, thus
safely set on Shore, to enjoy the Produce of our own Labours;
and to have rais'd those Labours by our Skill, and Industry, to
10 a much fairer Profit, than our Task-masters, by all their severe,
and griping Government had ever reap'd from them, a good-
natured Reader, that is not offended at the Comparison of great
things, and small, will allow was a Triumph, in proportion,
equal to those, that have attended the most heroick Enterprizes
for Liberty! What Transport could the first Brutus feel, upon
his Expulsion of the Tarquins, greater than that which now danc'd
in the Heart of a poor Actor, who from an injur'd Labourer,
unpaid his Hire, had made himself, without Guilt, a legal Menager of his own Fortune? Let the Grave, and Great contemn,
20 or yawn at these low Conceits, but let me be happy, in the Enjoyment of them! To this Hour my Memory runs o'er that
pleasing Prospect of Life past, with little less Delight, than when
I was first, in the real Possession of it. This is the natural
Temper of my Mind, which my Acquaintance are frequently
Witnesses of: And as this, was all the Ambition, Providence had
made my obscure Condition capable of, I am thankful, that
Means were given me to enjoy the Fruits of it.

————————Hoc est
Vivere b'is, vit^a posse priore frui.

30 Something like the Meaning of this, the less learned Reader may
find in my Title Page.

C H A P. XIV.

The Stage, in its highest Prosperity. The Menagers not without
Errors. Of what Kind. Cato *first acted. What brought it*
to the Stage. The Company go to Oxford. *Their Success, and*
different Auditors there. Booth *made a Sharer.* Dogget *ob-*
jects to him. Quits the Stage upon his Admittance. That not
his true Reason. What was. Dogget's *Theatrical Character.*

NOtwithstanding the Menaging Actors were, now,
in a happier Situation, than their utmost Pretensions
could have expected; yet it is not to be suppos'd,
but wiser Men might have mended it. As we could
not all govern our selves, there were Seasons, when
we were not all fit to govern others. Our Passions, and our Interest drew not always the same way. *Self,* had a great Sway in
our Debates: We had our Partialities; our Prejudices; our Fa-
vourites of less Merit; and our Jealousies of those who came too
near us; Frailties, which Societies of higher Consideration,
while they are compos'd of Men, will not always be free from.
To have been constantly capable of Unanimity, had been a
Blessing too great for our Station: One Mind, among three People, were to have had three Masters, to one Servant; but when
that one Servant is called three different ways, at the same time,
whose Business is to be done first? For my own Part, I was
forced, almost all my Life, to give up my Share of him. And
if I could, by Art, or Persuasion, hinder others from making,
what I thought, a wrong use of their Power, it was the all, and
utmost I desired. Yet whatever might be our Personal Errors,
I shall think I have no Right to speak of them farther, than
where the Publick Entertainment was affected by them. If there-

6. Noble Person … threaten my Work, with a Supplement] Neither Bellchambers nor Lowe
   suggests who this might have been; it is conceivable it was the Earl of Chesterfield, the Duke
   of Richmond, or the Duke of Grafton, with all of whom Cibber was friendly at this period (c.
   1738-39), (see Barker, p. 240). *The Laureat* (p. 77) expresses doubts of his existence.

fore, among so many, some particular Actors were remarkable
in any part of their private Lives, that might sometimes make
the World merry without Doors; I hope my laughing Friends
will excuse me, if I do not so far comply, with their Desires, or
Curiosity, as to give them a Place, in my History. I can only
recommend such Anecdotes to the Amusement, of a Noble Person, who (in case I conceal them) does me the flattering Honour, to threaten my Work, with a Supplement. 'Tis enough
for me, that such Actors had their Merits, to the Public: Let
10 those recite their Imperfections, who are themselves without
them: It is my Misfortune not to have that Qualification. Let
us see, then (whatever was amiss in it) how our Administration
went forward.

   When we were first invested, with this Power; the Joy of
our so unexpectedly coming into it, kept us, for some time, in
Amity, and Good-humour, with on another: And the Pleasure
of reforming the many false Measures, Absurdities, and Abuses,
that like Weeds, had suck'd up the due Nourishment from the
Fruits of the Theatre, gave us, as yet, no leisure, for private
20 Dissentions. Our daily Receipts exceeded our Imagination:
And we seldom met, as a Board, to settle our weekly Accounts,
without the Satisfaction of Joint-Heirs, just in Possession of an
unexpected Estate, that had been distantly intail'd upon them.
Such a sudden change of our Condition, it may be imagined,
could not but throw out of us a new Spirit, in almost every
Play we appear'd in: Nor did we ever sink into that common
Negligence, which is apt to follow Good-fortune: Industry, we
knew, was the Life of our Business; that it not only conceal'd
Faults, but was the equal Value to greater Talents without it;
30 which the Decadence once of **Betterton's** Company in **Lincoln's-
Inn Fields**, had lately shewn us a Proof of.

   This then was that happy Period, when both Actors and Menagers were in their highest Enjoyment of general Content,
and Prosperity. Now it was that the politer World too, by

3. the Stage, under a due Regulation] This opinion had been common currency at the time about which Cibber is writing; Addison, *Spectator* (no. 93, 16 June 1711), makes almost exactly this comment, and this section of the *Apology* reflects the language of that paper.

11. Tragedy of *Cato* ... first acted in 1712] First acted 14 April 1713. See pp. 73-74, 208-209 and 267 ff. and notes for Cibber's other comments on this play (for a complete account, see Smithers, *Addison*, pp. 251 ff. and Loftis, *Politics*, pp. 57 ff.).

27. from the *Dublin* Theatre two uncelebrated Actors] *The Laureat* (p. 78) identifies these as Elrington and Griffith and adds, "*Elrington* was an actor of some Merit, the other not considerable." Lowe (II, 121) suggests that Cibber really was thinking of Elrington and Evans, noting that both of these played important roles in the season of 1714-15, whereas Griffith did little. Both of the former had benefits, whereas Griffith had none; their separate benefits (Elrington, 19 March; Evans, 28 March: Avery, I, 348-49) do not fit Cibber's story, however. The rosters printed by Avery (I, 308, 328, 368) show that these three actors appeared only for the single season. Elrington reappears at Lincoln's Inn Fields 1716-17, and at Drury Lane 1718-19; Evans was at Lincoln's Inn Fields in 1718-19. Apparently they moved between Dublin and London fairly indifferently.

their decent Attention, their sensible Taste, and their generous
Encouragements to Authors, and Actors, once more saw, that
the Stage, under a due Regulation, was capable of being what
the wisest Ages thought it might be, The most rational Scheme,
that Human Wit could form, to dissipate, with Innocence, the
Cares of Life; to allure even the Turbulent, or Ill-disposed
from worse Meditations, and to give the leisure Hours of Business,
and Virtue, an instructive Recreation.

If this grave Assertion is less recommended, by falling from
10 the Pen of a Comedian; I must appeal, for the truth of it, to
the Tragedy of Cato, which was first acted in 1712. I submit
to the Judgment of those, who were then the sensible Spectators of it, if the Success, and Merit of that Play, was not an
Evidence of every Article of that Value, which I have given to
a decent Theatre? But (as I was observing) it could not be expected the Summer-Days, I am speaking of, could be the constant Weather of the Year; we had our clouded Hours, as well
as our sun-shine, and were not always in the same Good-Humour
with one another: Fire, Air, and Water, could not be more
20 vexatiously opposite, than the different Tempers of the Three
Menagers, though they might equally have their useful, as well
as their destructive Qualities. How variously these Elements,
in our several Dispositions, operated, may be judg'd from the
following single Instance, as well as from a thousand others; which,
if they were all to be told, might possibly make my Reader wish
I had forgot them.

Much about this time, then, there came over from the Dublin
Theatre two uncelebrated Actors, to pick up a few Pence among
us, in the Winter, as Wilks had a Year, or two before, done on
30 their side the Water, in the Summer. But it was not so clear to
Dogget, and myself, that it was in their Power, to do us the
same Service in Drury-Lane, as Wilks might have done them,
in Dublin. However, Wilks was so much a Man of Honour,
that he scorn'd to be outdone in the least Point of it, let the

----

1.11 submit] submi 1st ed.

3. *Wilks* so order'd it] If this is accurate, Wilks had violated the regulations agreed upon, "That no Actor, Officer, or Servant be discharg'd taken down, or rais'd without the consents, & hands of all the Three [managers]" (printed by Nicoll, II, 280-81, from L.C. 7/3).

32. the extraordinary Labour of *Wilks* … at least twice to *Dogget*'s once] "Genest's record gives Wilks about one hundred and fifty different characters, Dogget only about sixty," (Lowe, II, 123 n.).

Cost be what it would, to his Fellow-Menagers, who had no
particular Accounts of Honour open with them. To acquit
himself therefore with a better Grace, *Wilks* so order'd it, that
his *Hibernian* Friends were got upon our Stage, before any other
Menager had well heard of their Arrival. This so generous Dispatch of their Affair, gave *Wilks* a very good Chance of con-
vincing his Friends, that Himself was sole Master of the Masters
of the Company. Here now, the different Elements in our
Tempers began to work with us. While *Wilks* was only ani-
10 mated by a grateful Hospitality to his Friends, *Dogget* was ruffled into a Storm, and look'd upon this Generosity, as so much
Insult, and Injustice upon himself, and the Fraternity. During
this Disorder, I stood by, a seeming quiet Passenger, and, since
talking to the Winds, I knew could be to no great Purpose,
(whatever Weakness it might be call'd) could not help smiling, to
observe with what officious Ease, and Delight, *Wilks* was treating his Friends at our Expence, who were scarce acquainted with
them: For, it seems, all this was to end in their having a Benefit-Play, in the Height of the Season, for the unprofitable
20 Service they had done us, without our Consent, or Desire to employ them. Upon this *Dogget* bounc'd, and grew almost as
untractable as *Wilks* himself. Here, again, I was forc'd to clap
my Patience to the Helm, to weather this difficult Point between
them: Applying myself therefore to the Person, I imagin'd was
most likely to hear me, I desired *Dogget*, "to consider, that I
" must naturally, be as much hurt, by this vain, and over-bear-
" ing Behaviour of *Wilks*, as he could be; and that tho' it was
" true, these Actors, had no Pretence, to the Favour design'd
" them; yet we could not say they had done us any farther
" Harm, than letting the Town see, the Parts they had been
" shewn in, had been better done by those, to whom they pro-
" perly belong'd: Yet as we had greatly profited, by the ex-
" traordinary Labour of *Wilks*, who acted long Parts almost
" every Day, and at least twice to *Dogget's* once, and that I

14. could not be sure even of the Charge] That is, of the deduction from benefit receipts for expenses of the theater.

17. give them the Ready-mony taken …] That is, the money paid at the entrance to the theater and the additional sums collected for the variously priced galleries, pit, and boxes later; it was the custom for actors having a benefit to go about personally to sell tickets to their friends and admirers (on this practice, see *Joseph Andrews*, III, 3; see also Dudden, I, 42-43).

" granted it might not be so much his Consideration of our
" common Interest, as his Fondness for Applause, that set him
" to work; yet even that Vanity, if he supposed it such, had
" its Merit to us; and as we had found our Account in it, it
" would be Folly upon a Punctilio, to tempt the Rashness of a
" Man, who was capable to undo all he had done, by any Act
" of Extravagance, that might fly, into his Head: That admit-
" ting this Benefit might be some little Loss to us, yet to break
" with him upon it, could not but be ten times of worse conse-
10 " quence, than our over-looking his disagreeable manner of ma-
" king the Demand upon us.

    Tho', I found this had made *Dogget* drop the Severity of
his Features, yet he endeavour'd still to seem uneasy, by his start-
ing a new Objection, which was, That we could not be sure
even of the Charge, they were to pay for it: For *Wilks*, said
he, you know will go any Lengths, to make it a good Day, to
them, and may whisper the Door-keepers, to give them the
Ready-mony taken, and return the Account, in such Tickets only, as these Actors, have not themselves dispos'd of. To make
20 this easy too, I gave him my Word, to be answerable for the
Charge, myself. Upon this he acceded, and accordingly they
had the Benefit-Play. But so it happen'd (whether as *Dogget*
had suspected, or not, I cannot say) the Ready-Mony receiv'd
fell Ten Pounds short of the Sum, they had agreed to pay for
it. Upon the *Saturday* following, (the Day on which we constantly made up our Accounts) I went early to the Office, and
inquired, if the Ten Pounds had yet been paid in; but not hearing that one Shilling of it had found its way thither, I immediately supply'd the Sum out of my own Pocket, and directed the
30 Treasurer to charge it receiv'd from me, in the deficient Receipt of the Benefit-Day. Here, now, it might be imagined,
all this silly Matter was accommodated, and that no one could
so properly say, he was aggrieved, as myself: But let us observe what the Consequence says ----why, the Effect of my in-

solent interposing, honesty prov'd to be this: That the Party
most oblig'd, was the most offended; and the Offence was imputed to me, who had been Ten Pounds out of Pocket, to be
able to commit it: For when *Wilks* found, in the Account, how
spitefully the Ten Pounds had been paid in, he took me aside into the adjacent Stone-Passage, and with some Warmth ask'd me,
What I meant by pretending to pay in this Ten Pounds? and
that, for his part, he did not understand such Treatment. To
which I reply'd, That tho' I was amazed, at his thinking him-
10 self ill-treated, I would give him a plain, justifiable Answer.---
That I had given my Word to *Dogget*, the charge of the Benefit should be fully paid, and since his Friends had neglected it,
I found myself bound to make it good. Upon which he told
me, I was mistaken, if I thought, he did not see into the bottom of all This---That *Dogget*, and I, were always endeavouring to thwart, and make him uneasy; but he was able to stand
upon his own Legs, and we should find he would not be us'd
so: That he took this Payment of the Ten Pounds, as an Insult upon him, and a Slight to his Friends; but rather than suf-
20 fer it, he would tear the whole Business to pieces: That I knew
it was in his Power to do it; and if he could not do a civil
thing to a Friend, without all this senseless Rout about it, he
could be receiv'd in *Ireland* upon his own Terms, and could as
easily mend a Company there, as he had done here: That if he
were gone, *Dogget* and I would not be able to keep the Doors
open a Week, and, by G---, he would not be a Drudge for nothing. As I knew all this was but the Foam of the high Value
he had set upon himself, I thought it not amiss, to seem a little
silently concern'd, for the helpless Condition, to which his Re-
30 sentment of the Injury I have related, was going to reduce us:
For I knew I had a Friend in his Heart, that, if I gave him a
little time to cool, would soon bring him to Reason: The sweet
Morsel of a Thousand Pounds a Year, was not to be met with
at every Table, and might tempt a nicer Palate than his own,

32. *Impiger ... acer*] *Ars Poetica*, 121: "Indefatigable, wrathful, inexorable, fierce," speaking of an heroic character like Achilles.

to swallow it, when he was not out of Humour. This I knew
would always be of weight with him, when the best Arguments
I could use, would be of none. I therefore gave him no farther
Provocation, than by gravely telling him, We all had it in our
Power to do one another a Mischief; but I believ'd none of us
much cared to hurt ourselves; that if he was not of my Opinion, it would not be in my Power, to hinder whatever new
Scheme, he might resolve upon; that *London* would always have
a Playhouse, and I should have some Chance in it, tho' it might
10 not be so good as it had been; that he might be sure, if I had
thought my paying in the Ten Pounds could have been so ill receiv'd; I should have been glad to have sav'd it. Upon this he
seem'd to mutter something to himself, and walk'd off, as if he
had a mind to be alone. I took the Occasion, and return'd to
Dogget, to finish our Accounts. In about six Minutes *Wilks*
came in, to us; not in the best Humour, it may be imagin'd;
yet not in so ill a one, but that he took his Share of the Ten
Pounds, without shewing the least Contempt of it; which, had
he been proud enough to have refus'd, or to have paid in him-
20 self, I might have thought, he intended to make good his Me-
naces, and that the Injury I had done him would never have
been forgiven; but, it seems we had different ways of thinking.

Of this kind, more or less delightful, was the Life I led, with
this impatient Man, for full twenty Years. *Dogget*, as we shall
find, could not hold it so long; but as he had more Mony than
I, he had not occasion for so much Philosophy. And thus were
our Theatrical Affairs frequently disconcerted, by this irascible
Commander, this *Achilles* of our Confederacy; who, I may be
30 bold to say, came very little short of the Spirit *Horace* gives to
that Hero in his———

   Impiger, iracundus, inexorabilis, acer.

This, then, is one of those Personal Anecdotes of our Variances,

12. In 1703, nine Years before it was acted] Addison had begun *Cato* while at Oxford, before 1699, and had continued to work on it during his tour of the continent, from which he did not return until 1704, when it is likely that Cibber saw it. He did not complete the fifth act until shortly before its production. One should note that, in contrast to Cibber's and Steele's enthusiasm, both Dryden and Pope had judged the play undramatic (Smithers, *Addison*, pp. 250-52).

34. at a time when three Days a Week …} Benefits for actors were forbidden before the first of March by order of the Lord Chamberlain (L.C. 5/55, p. 159, dated 17 April 1712, printed by Nicoll, II, 281). By 14 April 1713, several actors had already had their benefits, and during the run of *Cato* Johnson, Keene, and Mrs. Bicknell had theirs on Monday nights; after its close, 9 May, several benefits each week were given (Avery, I, 296-305).

which, as our publick Performances were affected by it, could
not with regard to Truth, and Justice, be omitted.

From this time, to the Year 1712, my Memory (from which
Repository alone, every Article of what I write is collected) has
nothing worth mentioning, 'till the first acting of the Tragedy of
Cato. As to the Play itself, it might be enough to say, That the
Author, and the Actors had their different Hopes of Fame, and
Profit, amply answer'd by the Performance; but as its Success
was attended with remarkable Consequences, it may not be amiss
to trace it, from its several Years Concealment, in the Closet, to
the Stage.

In 1703, nine Years before it was acted, I had the Pleasure of
reading the first four Acts (which was all of it then written)
privately with Sir *Richard Steele:* It may be needless, to say it
was impossible to lay them out of my Hand, 'till I had gone
thro' them; or to dwell upon the Delight, his Friendship to the
Author receiv'd, upon my being so warmly pleas'd with them:
But my Satisfaction was as highly disappointed, when he told
me, Whatever Spirit Mr. *Addison* had shewn, in his writing it,
he doubted, he would never have Courage enough, to let his
Cato stand the Consure of the *English* Audience; that it had only been the Amusement of his leisure Hours in *Italy,* and was
never intended, for the Stage. This Poetical Diffidence Sir *Richard* himself spoke of with some Concern, and in the Transport
of his Imagination, could not help saying, *Good God! what a
Part would* Betterton *make of* Cato! But this was seven Years
before *Betterton* died, and when *Booth* (who afterwards made his
Fortune by acting it) was in his Theatrical Minority. In the
latter end of Queen *Anne's* Reign, when our National Politics
had changed Hands; the Friends of Mr. *Addison,* then thought
it a proper time to animate the Publick with the Sentiments of
Cato; in a word, their Importunities were too warm, to be resisted; and it was no sooner finish'd, than hurried to the Stage,
in *April* 1712, at a time when three Days a Week were usually

6. It was therefore ... for a Month] It was given twenty times in this season, on Tuesdays, Thursdays, Friday, and Saturdays, Wednesdays being opera days; the last performance was Saturday, 9 May, possibly ending because of Mrs. Oldfield's advanced pregnancy (Avery, I, 299-301; Smithers, *Addison*, p. 255).

8. Author had made us a Present] That is, of the profits of the third night, which traditionally belonged to the author.

23. *Whig* Principles ... had Sense enough] It was the Tory Lord Harley who set this pattern of response for his party (Smithers, *Addison*, p. 255).

28. one Day ... collected fifty Guineas] This was done by Bolingbroke. The Whigs later collected a purse also (Smithers, *Addison*, p. 256).

30. *Opposition to a perpetual Dictator*] An allusion to the Whig Duke of Marlborough who, before his fall, had expressed a wish to be made Captain General for life; though Addison had originally intended to dedicate the play to an unidentified person, probably Sarah, wife of the Duke, he eventually published it without a dedication in order to hold to his neutrality in the face of party rivalry (Smithers, *Addison*, p. 256).

31. What was insinuated, by any Part of these Words] The sentence was widely admired for its pointedness: Cibber cannot have failed to understand its "insinuations" (see Smithers, *Addison*, p. 256).

appointed for the Benefit Plays of particular Actors: But a Work
of that critical Importance, was to make its way, through all
private Considerations; nor could it possibly give place to a
Custom, which the Breach of could very little prejudice the Benefits, that on so unavoidable an Occasion, were (in part, tho'
not wholly) postpon'd; it was therefore (*Mondays* excepted) acted
every Day for a Month, to constantly crowded Houses. As the
Author had made us a Present of whatever Profits he might have
claim'd from it, we thought our selves oblig'd, to spare no Cost,
10   in the proper Decorations of it. Its coming so late in the Season,
to the Stage, prov'd of particular Advantage, to the sharing
Actors; because the Harvest of our annual Gains was generally
over, before the middle of *March*; many select Audiences being
then, usually reserv'd, in favour to the Benefits of private Actors;
which fixt Engagements naturally abated the Receipts of the Days,
before and after them: But this unexpected After-crop of *Cato*,
largely supplied to us, those Deficiencies; and was almost equal
to two fruitful Seasons, in the same Year; at the Close of which,
the three menaging Actors found themselves, each a Gainer of
20   thirteen hundred, and fifty Pounds: But to return to the first
Reception of this Play from the Publick.

  Although *Cato* seems plainly written upon what are called
Whig Principles; yet the *Torys* of that time had Sense enough
not to take it, as the least Reflection, upon their Administration; but on the contrary, they seem'd to brandish, and vaunt
their approbation of every Sentiment in favour of Liberty, which
by a publick Act of their Generosity, was carried so high, that
one Day, while the Play was acting, they collected fifty Guineas
in the Boxes, and made a Present of them to *Booth*, with this
30   Compliment-----*For his honest Opposition to a perpetual Dictator;
and his dying so bravely, in the Cause of Liberty:* What was insinuated, by any Part of these Words, is not my Affair; but so
publick a Reward had the Appearance of a laudable Spirit, which
only such a Play, as *Cato*, could have inspired; nor could *Booth*

3. The Favour he stood in, with a certain Nobleman] Theophilus Cibber's *Life of Barton Booth, Esq.* (pp. 6-7) asserts that Booth had been acquainted with Lord Bolingbroke from before 1710, and that it was his influence at court (Bolingbroke was Secretary of State in 1713) that secured for Booth a share in the company. Loftis (*Politics*, p. 61) adds that as early as 16 December 1712 Booth had appealed to Lord Lansdowne (the letter is BM, Add. MS, 38607, p. 9, and printed in part by Barker, p. 92) for support with the Vice-Chamberlain; Chetwood (pp. 92-93) relates that during this period just before he was made a sharer, "... great Interest was made against him by the other *Patentees*; who, to prevent his soliciting his Patrons at Court, then at *Windsor*, gave out Plays every Night, where Mr. *Booth* had a principal Part. Notwithstanding this Step, he had a Chariot and Six of a Nobleman's waiting for him at the End of every Play, that whipt him the Twenty Miles in three Hours, and brought him back to the Business of the Theatre the next Night."

19. Menagers ... make the same Present to *Booth*] Loftis (*Politics*, p. 58) interprets this as an attempt to placate Booth to prevent his pursuing his claims to an equal share of the company's profits. See below for Cibber's view of the act.

be blam'd, if upon so particular a Distinction of his Merit, he
began himself to set more Value upon it: How far he might
carry it, in making use of the Favour he stood in, with a certain Nobleman, then in Power, at Court, was not difficult to
penetrate; and indeed, ought always to have been expected by
the menaging Actors: For which of them (making the Case
every way his own) could with such Advantages, have contented
himself, in the humble Station of an hired Actor? But let us see
how the Menagers stood severally affected, upon this Occasion.

Dogget, who, expected, though he fear'd not, the Attempt of
what after happen'd, imagin'd he had thought of an Expedient
to prevent it: And to cover his Design with all the Art of a
Statesman, he insinuated to us (for he was a staunch *Whig*) that
this Present of fifty Guineas, was a sort of a *Tory* Triumph,
which they had no Pretence to; and that for his Part, he could
not bear, that so redoubted a Champion for Liberty, as *Cato*,
should be bought off, to the Cause of a contrary Party: He
therefore, in the seeming Zeal of his Heart, proposed, that the
Menagers themselves should make the same Present to *Booth*,
which had been made him, from the Boxes, the Day before.
This, he said, would recommend the Equality, and liberal Spirit
of our Menagement, to the Town, and might be a Means, to
secure *Booth* more firmly in our Interest; it never having been
known, that the Skill of the best Actor had receiv'd so round a
Reward, or Gratuity, in one Day, before. *Wilks*, who wanted
nothing but Abilities to be as cunning, as *Dogget*, was so charm'd
with the Proposal, that he long'd, that Moment, to make *Booth*
the Present, with his own Hands; and though he knew he had
no Right to do it, without my Consent, had not Patience to ask
it; upon which I turn'd to *Dogget*, with a cold Smile, and told
him, that if *Booth* could be purchas'd at so cheap a Rate, it
would be one of the best Proofs of his Oeconomy, we had ever
been beholden to: I therefore desired we might have a little Patience; that our doing it too hastily might be only making sure

1.29 had not Patience] had no Patience 2nd ed.

of an Occasion, to throw the fifty Guineas away; for if we should
be oblig'd to do better for him, we could never expect, that
Booth would think himself bound, in Honour, to refund them.
This seem'd so absurd an Argument to *Wilks*, that he began with
his usual Freedom of Speech, to treat it, as a pitiful Evasion of
their intended Generosity: But *Dogget*, who was not so wide of
my Meaning, clapping his Hand upon mine, said, with an Air
of Security, O! don't trouble yourself! there must be two Words
to that Bargain; let me alone, to menage that Matter. *Wilks*,
10   upon this dark Discourse, grew uneasy, as if there were some Secret between us, that he was to be left out of. Therefore to
avoid the Shock of his Intemperance, I was reduc'd to tell him,
that it was my Opinion, that *Booth* would never be made easy,
by any thing we could do for him, till he had a Share, in the
Profits, and Menagement; and that, as he did not want Friends
to assist him, whatever his Merit might be before, every one
would think, since his acting of *Cato*, he had now enough to
back his Pretensions to it. To which *Dogget* reply'd, that no-
body could think his Merit was slighted, by so handsome a Pre-
20   sent, as fifty Guineas; and that for his farther Pretensions, whatever the License might avail, our Property of House, Scenes,
and Cloaths were our own, and not in the Power of the Crown
to dispose of. To conclude, my Objections, that the Mony
would be only thrown away, &c. were over-rul'd, and the same
Night *Booth* had the fifty Guineas, which he receiv'd with a
Thankfulness, that made *Wilks*, and *Dogget* perfectly easy; insomuch that they seem'd, for some time to triumph in their
Conduct, and often endeavour'd to laugh my Jealousy out of
Countenance: But in the following Winter, the Game happen'd
30   to take a different Turn; and then, if it had been a laughing
Matter, I had as strong an Occasion to smile at their former Se-
curity. But before I make an End of this Matter, I cannot pass
over the good Fortune of the Company, that follow'd us, to the
Act at *Oxford*, which was held in the intervening Summer:

3. *Cavalier,* and *Round-head*] Cibber's equation of these parties has some justification, especially on the points of the attitudes toward Church and Civil government (see Humphreys, *The Augustan World,* pp. 103 ff.).

6. Date of several Prologues written by *Dryden*] The so-called Oxford prologues and epilogues (Nos. XXXV, XXXVI, XXXIX, XL, LVIII, LIX, LXI, and LXIII in Gardner's edition, of which the first three were spoken by Hart) were written for performances at Oxford between 1673 and 1681.

7. more frequently held, than in later Reigns] These "Acts" were given in 1661 and commonly thereafter. The two companies competed for the right to perform there, though after the union in 1682 they came again only in 1686 and 1693 (see Montagu Summers, *Playhouse of Pepys,* pp. 125 ff.).

13. King *James* ... had the Honour of it] The performance of 1686; Summers (*Playhouse of Pepys,* p. 131) quotes a dating of the performance of *The Committee* by Sir Robert Howard—without his source—as "acted about the 16th July once or twice," and confirms Cibber's account (below).

18. *Obadiah Walker*] Obadiah Walker (1616-1699) was Master of University College, Oxford from 1676 until his removal after the Revolution of 1688. His Roman Catholicism was of long standing and not, as Cibber's anecdote suggests, a political expedient. He was widely unpopular for his open practice of his religion after the accession of James. He spent the last years of his life in extreme poverty, and was temporarily imprisoned (*DNB,* article Obadiah Walker).

29. *Upon my Shoule ... Shange*] The spelling represents Teague's Irish accent.

Perhaps too, a short View of the Stage, in that different Situation, may not be unacceptable to the Curious.

After the Restoration of King *Charles*, before the *Cavalier*, and
Round-head Parties, under their new Denomination of *Whig*, and
Tory, began again to be politically troublesome, publick Acts at
Oxford (as I find by the Date of several Prologues written by
Dryden, for *Hart* on those Occasions) had been more frequently
held, than in later Reigns. Whether the same Party-Dissentions
may have occasion'd the Discontinuance of them, is a Speculation, not necessary to be enter'd into. But these Academical Ju-
bilees have usually been look'd upon as a kind of congratulatory
Compliment, to the Accession of every new Prince, to the
Throne, and generally, as such have attended them. King *James*,
notwithstanding his Religion, had the Honour of it; at which
the Players, as usual, assisted. This I have only mention'd, to
give the Reader a Theatrical Anecdote of a Liberty, which *Tony*
Leigh the Comedian took with the Character of the well known
Obadiah Walker, then Head of *University College*, who, in that
Prince's Reign, had turn'd *Roman Catholick*: The Circumstance
is this.

In the latter End of the Comedy call'd the *Committee, Leigh,*
who acted the Part of *Teague*, hauling in *Obadiah*, with an
Halter about his Neck, whom, according to his written Part,
he was to threaten to hang, for no better Reason than his refusing to drink the King's Health, (but here *Leigh*) to justify
his Purpose, with a stronger Provocation, put himself into a
more, than ordinary Heat, with his Captive *Obadiah*, which
having heightened his Master's Curiosity, to know what *Oba-*
diah had done to deserve such Usage, *Leigh*, folding his Arms,
with a ridiculous Stare of Astonishment, reply'd-----*Upon my*
Shoule, he has shange his Religion. As the Merit of this Jest lay
chiefly in the Auditors sudden Application of it, to the *Oba-*
diah of *Oxford*, it was receiv'd with all the Triumph of Applause, which the Zeal of a different Religion could inspire. But

1.18 *College*] *Colledge* 1st ed.

4. our own Affairs there, in 1712] Actually 1713. The performance of 23 June was announced as "positively the last time of Acting till Winter, the Company being obliged to go immediately to Oxford" (Avery, I, 305).

27. *Oxford* ... the different Taste of Plays there] It should be noted that Dryden, in the Oxford prologues and epilogues, also contrasted the tastes of London unfavorably with those of Oxford (e.g., *LIX*) but he also wrote c. 1673 to Lord Rochester (C. E. Ward, ed., *The Letters of John Dryden*, p. 10) after referring to a satire by Etherege, "Because I deale not in Satyre, I have sent Your Lordship a prologue and epilogue which I made for our players when they went down to Oxford [Nos. XXXV and XXXVI in Gardner]. I heare, since they have succeeded; And by the event your Lordship will judge how easy 'tis to passe any thing upon an University; and how grosse flattery the learned will endure."

Leigh was given to understand, that the King was highly displeas'd at it, inasmuch, as it had shewn him, that the University was in a Temper to make a Jest of his Proselyte. But to return to the Conduct of our own Affairs there, in 1712.

 It had been a custom for the Comedians, while at *Oxford*,
to act twice a Day; the first Play ending every Morning, before
the College Hours of dining, and the other never to break into
the Time of shutting their Gates in the Evening. This extraordinary Labour gave all the hired Actors a Title to double Pay,

10 which, at the Act, in King *William's* Time, I had myself accordingly receiv'd there. But the present Menagers considering, that
by acting only once a Day, their Spirits might be fresher for
every single Performance, and that by this Means, they might
be able to fill up the Term of their Residence, without the Repetition of their best, and strongest Plays; and as their Theatre
was contriv'd to hold a full third more, than the usual form of
it had done, one House well fill'd, might answer the Profits of
two but moderately taken up: Being enabled too, by their late
Success, at *London*, to make the Journey pleasant, and profit-

20 able, to the rest of their Society, they resolv'd to continue to
them, their double Pay, notwithstanding this new Abatement of
half of their Labour. This Conduct of the Menagers more than
answer'd their Intention, which was rather to get nothing themselves, than not let their Fraternity be the better for the Expedition. Thus they laid an Obligation, upon their Company, and
were themselves considerably, though unexpected, Gainers by it.
But my chief Reason for bringing the Reader to *Oxford*, was to
shew the different Taste of Plays there, from that which prevail'd at *London*. A great deal of that false, flashy Wit, and

30 forc'd Humour, which had been the Delight of our Metropo-
litan Multitude, was only rated there at its bare, intrinsick Value; Applause was not to be purchas'd there, but by the true
Sterling, the *Sal Atticum* of a Genius; unless where the Skill
of the Actor pass'd it upon them, with some extraordinary Strokes

1. *Shakespear,* and *Johnson* had, there, a sort of classical Authority] Dryden had also attributed

   to Oxford a preference for these writers:

   > With joy we bring what our dead Authors writ,
   > And beg from you the value of their Wit.
   > That *Shakespeare's, Fletcher's*, and great
   >   *Johnson's* claim
   > May be Renew'd from those, who gave them fame.
   > None of our living Poets dare appear,
   > For Muses so severe are worshipt here
   > That conscious of their Faults they shun the Eye,
   > And as Prophane, from Sacred places fly ...
   >   (Dryden, *Prologues and Epilogues*, ed. Gardner,
   >   XXXIX, lines 19-26)

17. The only distinguish'd Merit, allow'd to any modern Writer ...] Addison had won popularity

    at predominantly Tory Oxford by his lack of partisan spirit in *The Spectator* (Smithers,

    Addison, pp. 258-59).

28. The same Crowds continued for three Days together] Avery (I, 305) prints the company's

    notice of 23 June 1713 that "This is positively the last time of Acting till Winter, the Company

    being obliged to go immediately to Oxford." For the Oxford repertory, however, he cites

    Cibber.

of Nature. *Shakespear*, and *Johnson* had, there, a sort of classical Authority; for whose masterly Scenes they seem'd to have as
implicit a Reverence, as formerly, for the Ethicks of *Aristotle*;
and were as incapable of allowing Moderns to be their Competitors, as of changing their Academical Habits for gaudy Colours,
or Embroidery. Whatever Merit, therefore, some few of our
more politely-written Comedies might pretend to, they had not
the same Effect upon the Imagination there, nor were receiv'd
with that extraordinary Applause, they had met with, from the
People of Mode, and Pleasure, in *London*; whose vain Accomplishments did not dislike themselves, in the Glass, that was held
to them: The elegant Follies of higher Life, were not, at *Oxford*,
among their Acquaintance, and consequently might not be so
good Company, to a learned Audience, as Nature, in her plain
Dress, and unornamented, in her Pursuits and Inclinations, seem'd
to be.

The only distinguish'd Merit, allow'd to any modern Writer,
was to the Author of *Cato*, which Play being the Flower of a
Plant, rais'd in that learned Garden, (for there Mr. *Addison* had
his Education) what Favour may we not suppose was due to
him, from an Audience of Brethren, who from that local Relation to him, might naturally have a warmer Pleasure, in their
Benevolence to his Fame? But not to give more Weight to this
imaginary Circumstance, than it may bear, the Fact was, that
on our first Day of acting it, our House was, in a manner, invested; and Entrance demanded by twelve a Clock at Noon, and
before one, it was not wide enough for many, who came too
late for Places. the same Crowds continued for three Days together, (an uncommon Curiosity in that Place) and the Death of
Cato triumph'd over the Injuries of *Caesar*, everywhere. To conclude, our Reception at *Oxford*, whatever our Merit might be,
exceeded our Expectation. At our taking Leave, we had the
Thanks of the Vice-Chancellor, for the Decency, and Order, observ'd by our whole Society; an Honour which had not always

1. Act, in King *William's* Time, I remember some Pranks] Probably that of 1693 (for an account of the Act at Oxford, see Montagu Summers, *Playhouse of Pepys*, pp. 124-32).

been paid, upon the same Occasions; for at the Act, in King
William's Time, I remember some Pranks of a different Nature
had been complain'd of. Our Receipts had not only enabled us
(as I have obser'd) to double the Pay of every Actor, but to
afford out of them, towards the Repair of St. *Mary's* Church,
the Contribution of fifty Pounds: Besides which, each of the
three Menagers had to his respective Share, clear of all Charges,
one hundred and fifty more, for his one and twenty Day's Labour; which being added to his thirteen hundred, and fifty,
shared in the Winter preceding, amounted, in the whole, to
fifteen hundred; the greatest Sum ever known to have been
shared, in one Year, to that time: And to the Honour of our
Auditors, here, and elsewhere be it spoken, all this was rais'd,
without the Aid of those barbarous Entertainments, with which,
some few Years after (upon the Re-establishment of two contending Companies) we were forc'd to disgrace the Stage, to support it.

This, therefore, is that remarkable Period, when the Stage,
during my Time upon it, was the least reproachable: And it
may be worth the publick Observation (if any thing I have said
of it can be so) that *One* Stage may, as I have prov'd it has
done, very laudably support it self, but such Spectacles only, as
are fit to delight a sensible People; but the equal Prosperity of
Two Stages has always been of a very short Duration. If therefore the Publick should ever recover, into the true Taste of that
Time, and stick to it; the Stage must come into it, or *starve*;
as whenever the general Taste is vulgar, the Stage must come
down to it, to *live*-----But I ask Pardon of the Multitude, who,
in all Regulations of the Stage, may expect, to be a little indulg'd, in what they like: If therefore they *will* have a May-
pole, why, the Players must *give* them a May-pole; but I only
speak, in case they should keep an old Custom of changing their
Minds; and by their Privilege of being in the *wrong*, should
take a Fancy, by way of Variety, of being in the *right*---Then,

1.14 Entertainments] Entertaiments 1st ed.

4. *Booth* was at full Leisure, to sollicit his Admission] See p. 269 n. The new license was issued 11 November 1713 (L.C. 5/155, p. 261, Nicoll, II, 276) to Collier Wilks, Cibber, Dogget, and Booth.

in such a Case, what I have said may appear to have been no
intended Design, against their Liberty of judging, for themselves.

 After our Return, from *Oxford, Booth* was at full Leisure, to
sollicit his Admission, to a Share, in the Menagement; in which
he succeeded, about the Beginning of the following Winter: Accordingly a new License (recalling all former Licenses) was issued,
wherein *Booth's* Name was added, to those of the other Menagers. But still, there was a Difficulty, in his Qualification, to
10 be adjusted; what Consideration he should allow, for an equal
Title to our Stock of Cloaths, Scenes, &c. without which, the
License was of no more use, than the Stock was without the
License; or, at least, if there were any Difference, the former
Menagers seem'd to have the Advantage, in it; the Stock being
intirely theirs, and three Parts in four of the License; for *Collier,*
though now but a fifth Menager, still insisted on his former Appointment of 700 *l.* a Year; which, in Equity ought certainly
to have been proportinably abated: But Court-Favour was not
always measur'd by *that* Yard; *Collier's* Matter was soon out of
20 the Question; his Pretensions were too visible, to be contested;
but the Affair of *Booth* was not so clear a Point: The Lord
Chamberlain, therefore, only recommended it, to be adjusted,
among ourselves; which, to say the Truth, at that Time, was a
greater Indulgence than I expected. Let us see, then, how this
critical Case was handled.

 Wilks was of Opinion, that to set a good round Value upon
our Stocks, was the only way, to come near an Equivalent, for the
Diminution of our Shares, which the Admission of *Booth* must
occasion: But *Dogget* insisted, that he had no Mind to dispose
30 of any Part of his Property, and therefore would set no Price
upon it at all. Though I allow'd, that Both these Opinions
might be grounded, on a good deal of Equity, yet I was not
sure that either of them was practicable; and therefore told them,
that when they could Both agree, which of them could be made

8. a Secretary of State ... Protection] For Lord Bolingbroke, cf. p. 269 n.; Cibber's implication that Booth's Tory alliances alone enabled him to be named in the license bypasses a fact embarrassing to the Whig Poet Laureate, that he also had had affiliations with the Tory party during their administration (Loftis, *Politics*, pp. 56 n. and 83). See also p. 208 n.

so, they might rely on my Consent, in any Shape.   In the mean
time, I desired they would consider, that as our License subsisted only during Pleasure, we could not pretend, that the Queen
might not recall, or alter it: But that to speak out, without
mincing the Matter on either Side, the Truth was plainly this.
That *Booth* had a manifest Merit, as an Actor; and as he was
not supposed to be a *Whig*, it was as evident, that a good deal
for that Reason, a Secretary of State had taken him into his Protection, which I was afraid the weak Pretence of our invaded
10   Property, would not be able to contend with: That his having
signaliz'd himself, in the Character of *Cato* (whose Principles
the *Tories* had affected to have taken, into their own Possession)
was a very popular Pretence of making him free of the Stage,
by advancing him, to the Profits of it.   And, as we had seen,
that the Stage was frequently treated, as if it was not suppos'd,
to have any Property at all; this Favour intended to *Booth* was
thought a right Occasion, to avow that Opinion, by disposing
of its Property, at Pleasure: But be that, as it might, I own'd
it was not so much my Apprehensions of what the *Court* might
20   do, that sway'd me, into an Accommodation with *Booth*, as what
the *Town*, (in whose Favour he now apparently stood) might
think *ought* to be done: That, there might be more danger in
contesting their arbitrary Will, and Pleasure, than in disputing
this less terrible Strain of the Prerogative.   That if *Booth* were
only impos'd upon us, from his Merit to the Court, we were
then, in the Condition of other Subjects: Then, indeed, Law,
right, and Possession, might have a tolerable Tug, for our
Property: But as the Town would always look upon his Merit
to *them*, in a stronger Light, and be Judges of it themselves, it
30   would be a weak, and idle Endeavour, in us, not to sail with
the Stream, when we might possibly make a Merit of our cheer-
fully admitting him: That though his former Opposition to our
Interest, might, between Man and Man, a good deal justify our
not making an earlier Friend of him; yet that was a Disobliga-

tion, out of the Town's Regard, and consequently would be of
no weight, against so approv'd an Actor's being preferr'd. But
all this, notwithstanding, if they could both agree, in a different
Opinion, I would, at the Hazard of any Consequence, be guided by it.

Here, now, will be shewn another Instance of our different
Tempers: *Dogget* (who in all Matters, that concern'd our common Weal, and Interest, little regarded our Opinion, and even
to an Obstinacy, walked by his own) look'd only out of Humour,
at what I had said, and without thinking himself oblid'd to give any
Reason for it, declar'd, he would maintain his Property. *Wilks*,
(who, upon the same Occasions, was as remarkably ductile, as
when his Superiority on the Stage, was in question, he was assuming, and intractable, said, for his Part, provided our Business of acting was not interrupted, he did not care what we did:
But, in short, he was for playing on, come what would of it.
This last Part of his Declaration I did not dislike, and therefore
I desir'd, we might all enter into an immediate Treaty with
Booth, upon the Terms of his Admission. *Dogget* still sullenly
reply'd, that he had no Occasion, to enter into any Treaty.
Wilks then, to soften him, propos'd, that, if I liked it, *Dogget*
might undertake it himself. I agreed. No! he would not be
concern'd in it. I then offer'd the same Truth to *Wilks*, if *Dogget* approv'd of it. *Wilks* said, he was not good at making of
Bargains, but if I was willing, he would rather leave it to me.
Dogget, at this, rose up, and said, we might both do as we
pleas'd, but that nothing but the Law, should make him part
with his Property---and so went out of the Room. After which
he never came among us more, either as an Actor, or Menager.

By his having, in this abrupt manner, abdicated his Post, in
our Government; what he left of it, naturally desolv'd, upon
Wilks, and myself. However, this did not so much distress our
Affair, as I have Reason to believe *Dogget* thought it would:
For though, by our Indentures tripartite, we could not dispose

8. *Booth* made no Objection … allow us Six Hundred Pounds] Barker's more complete version
(p. 93) throws considerable light on Cibber's tendency to show himself in a kindly,
peacemaking role; at the point where Dogget was proving intractable, "They [Cibber and
Wilks] … drew up 'An Humble Remonstrance' to the Lord Chamberlain in which they valued
their stock at £5350 (£3600 for the stock of Drury Lane, £1400 for the open stock at the
Haymarket, and £350 which they had paid to Swiney); obviously hinting that Booth would
have to pay some £1200 or £1300 [P.R.O., C.11 6/44]. The Lord Chamberlain was
extremely angry, and ignoring the humble remonstrance, immediately made terms of his own.
He appraised the stock, fixed the value of a fourth share at £600, and told the managers that if
they did not admit Booth without farther delay, he would inform the Queen of their
disobedience and have their names struck from the license [L.C. 7/3]." Barker adds (p. 94)
that Cibber and Wilks then attempted to stop payment of Collier's share and of the £100
supplement to the opera (by now going to Vanbrugh, not Swiney). In the former they failed
utterly; in the latter they succeeded (based upon L.C. 7/3 and 5.156; Vanbrugh, *Works*, ed.
Dobree and Webb, IV, 57-58).

of his Property, without his Consent: Yet those Indentures
could not oblige us to fast, because he had no Appetite; and
if the Mill did not grind, we could have no Bread: We therefore determin'd, at any Hazard, to keep our Business still going,
and that our safest way would be, to make the best Bargain we
could with *Booth;* one Article of which was to be, That *Booth*
should stand equally answerable with us, to *Dogget,* for the
Consequence: To which *Booth* made no Objection, and the rest
of his Agreement, was to allow us Six Hundred Pounds for his
10 Share, in our Property, which was to be paid by such Sums as
should arise from half his Profits of Acting, 'till the whole was
discharg'd: Yet so cautious were we in this Affair, that this
Agreement was only Verbal on our Part, tho' written, and sign'd
by *Booth,* as what intirely contented him: However, Bond and
Judgment, could not have made it more secure, to him; for he
had his Share, and was able to discharge the Incumbrance upon
it, by his Income of that Year only. Let us see what *Dogget* did
in this Affair, after he had left us.

Might it not be imagin'd, that *Wilks,* and Myself, by having
20 made this Matter easy to *Booth,* should have deserv'd the Approbation at least, if not the Favour of the Court, that had exerted so much Power to prefer him? But shall I be believed, when
I affirm, that *Dogget,* who had so strongly oppos'd the Court,
in his Admission to a Share, was very near getting the better of
us both, upon that Account, and for some time appeared to
have more Favour there, than either of us? Let me tell out my
Story, and then think what you please of it.

Dogget, who was equally oblig'd, with us, to act, upon the
Stage, as to assist, in the Menagement of it, tho' he had refus'd
30 to do either, still demanded of us his whole Share of the Profits, without considering what Part of them *Booth* might pretend
to, from our late Concessions. After many fruitless Endeavours
to bring him back, to us; *Booth* join'd with us, in making him
an Offer of half a Share, if he had a mind totally to quit the

8. as an invincible *Whig* ... defense of his Property] The doctrine of the sacredness of property had developed out of the Revolution of 1688 and was generally more loudly proclaimed by Whigs. See A.R. Humphreys, *The Augustan World*, pp. 52-59.

26. The Vice-Chamberlain] "The Right Hon. Thomas Coke" [Lowe, II, 146].

Stage, and make it a *Sine cure*. No! he wanted the Whole,
and to sit still himself, while we (if we pleased) might work for
him, or let it alone, and none of us all, neither he, nor we, be
the better for it. What we imagin'd encourag'd him to hold us
at this short Defiance, was, that he had laid up enough to live
upon, without the Stage (for he was one of those close Oeconomists, whom Prodigals call a Miser) and therefore partly from
an Inclination, as an invincible *Whig*, to signalize himself in defence of his Property, and as much presuming that our Necessi-
10   ties would oblige us to come to his own Terms, he was determin'd (even against the Opinion of his Friends) to make no
other Peace, with us. But not being able, by this inflexible
Perseverance, to have his wicked Will of us, he was resolv'd to
go to the Fountain-head of his own Distress, and try, if from
thence, he could turn the Current against us. He appeal'd to
the Vice-Chamberlain, to whose Direction, the adjusting of all
these Theatrical Difficulties, was then committed: But there, I
dare say, the Reader does not expect he should meet with much
Favour: However, be that, as it may; for whether any regard
20   was had, to his having some Thousands, in his Pocket; or that
he was consider'd, as a Man, who would, or could make more
Noise, in the Matter, than Courtiers might care for: Or what
Charms, Spells, or Conjurations he might make use of, is all
Darkness to me; yet so it was, he one way or other, play'd his
Part so well, that, in a few Days after, we received an Order,
from the Vice-Chamberlain, positively commanding us, to pay
Dogget his whole Share, notwithstanding, we had complain'd
before of his having withdrawn himself from acting on the Stage,
and from the Menagement of it. This I thought was a dainty
30   Distinction, indeed! that *Dogget's* Defiance of the Commands in
favour of *Booth*, should be rewarded with so ample a *Sine cure*;
and that we, for our Obedience, should be condemn'd to dig
in the Mine, to pay it him! This bitter Pill, I confess, was
more than I could down with, and therefore soon determin'd, at

31. *Dogget* ... preferred a Bill in *Chancery*] The following complicated events, which began in

December 1714, are accounted for in Appendix C.

all Events, never to take it. But, as I had a Man in Power to
deal with, it was not my business to speak *out* to him, or to set
forth our Treatment, in its proper Colours. My only Doubt was,
Whether I could bring *Wilks* into the same Sentiments (for he
never car'd to litigate any thing, that did not affect his Figure
upon the Stage.) But I had the good Fortune to lay our Condition, in so precarious, and disagreeable a Light to him, if we
submitted to this Order, that he fir'd, before I could get thro'
half the Consequences of it; and I began now to find it more
10 difficult, to keep him within bounds, than I had before to alarm
him. I then propos'd to him this Expedient: That we should
draw up a Remonstrance, neither seeming to refuse, or comply
with this Order; but to start such Objections, and perplexing
Difficulties, that should make the whole impracticable: That
under such Distractions, as this would raise in our Affairs, we
could not be answerable to keep open our Doors, which consequently would destroy the Fruit of the Favour lately granted to
Booth, as well as of This intended to *Dogget* himself. To this
Remonstrance we receiv'd an Answer in Writing, which varied
20 something, in the Measures, to accommodate Matters with *Dog-*
get. This was all I desired, when I found the Style of *Sic ju-*
beo was alter'd, when this formidable Power began to *parley* with
us, we knew there could not be much, to be fear'd, from it:
For I would have remonstrated, 'till I had died, rather than have
yielded to the roughest, or smoothest Persuasion, that could inti-
midate, or deceive us. By this Conduct, we made the Affair
at last, too troublesome for the Ease of a Courtier to go thro'
with. For when it was consider'd, that the principal Point, the
Admission of *Booth* was got over, *Dogget* was fairly left to the
30 Law, for Relief.

Upon this Disappointment, *Dogget* accordingly preferred a Bill
in *Chancery* against us. *Wilks*, who hated all Business, but that
of entertaining the Publick, left the Conduct of our Cause to
me; in which we had, at our first setting out, this Advantage

of *Dogget*, that we had three Pockets to support our Expence,
where he had but One. My first Direction to our Solictor was
to use all possible Delay, that the Law would admit of; a Direction, that Lawyers seldom neglect; by this means we hung up
our Plaintiff about two Years, in *Chancery*, 'till we were at full
Leisure to come to a Hearing before the Lord-Chancellor *Cooper*;
which did not happen 'till after the Accession of his late Majesty.
The Issue of it was this. *Dogget* had about fourteen Days allow'd him to make his Election, whether he would return to act,
as usual: But he declaring, by his Counsel, That he rather
chose to quit the Stage, he was decreed Six Hundred Pounds for
his Share, in our Property, with *15 per Cent*. Interest, from the
Date of the last License: Upon the Receipt of which, both Parties were to sign General-Releases, and severally to pay their
own Costs. By this Decree, *Dogget*, when his Lawyer's Bill was
paid, scarce got one Year's Purchase, of what we had offered
him without Law, which (as he survived but seven Years after it)
would have been an Annuity of Five Hundred Pounds, and a *Sine
cure* for Life.

Tho' there are many Persons living, who know every Article of
these Facts, to be true: Yet it will be found, that the strongest
of them, was not the strongest Occasion of *Dogget's* quitting the
Stage. If therefore the Reader should not have Curiosity enough
to know, how the Publick came, to be depriv'd of so valuable
an Actor, let him consider, that he is not oblig'd to go through
the rest of this Chapter, which I fairly tell him before-hand,
will only be fill'd up with a few idle Anecdotes, leading to that
Discovery.

After our Law-suit was ended, *Dogget*, for some few Years,
could scarce bear the Sight of *Wilks*, or myself; tho' (as shall be
shewn) for different Reasons: Yet it was his Misfortune to meet
with us almost every Day. *Button's* Coffee-house, so celebrated
in the *Tatlers*, for the Good-Company, that came there, was at
this time, in its highest Request. *Addison, Steele, Pope*, and se-

veral other Gentlemen of different Merit, then made it their constant *Rendezvous*. Nor could *Dogget* decline the agreeable Conversation there, tho' he was daily sure to find *Wilks*, or myself,
in the same Place, to sour his Share of it: For as *Wilks*, and
He were differently proud; the one rejoycing in a captious, over
bearing, valiant Pride; and the other, in a stiff, sullen, Purse-
Pride, it may be easily conceiv'd, when two such Tempers met,
how agreeable the Sight of one was to the other. And as *Dogget*
knew, I had been the chief Conductor of our Defence, against
10   his Law-suit, which had hurt him more, for the Loss he had
sustain'd, in his Reputation of understanding Business, which he
valued himself upon, than his Disappointment had, of getting
so little by it; it was no wonder if I was intirely out of his good
Graces, which I confess, I was inclin'd, upon any reasonable
Terms, to have recover'd; he being of all my Theatrical Brethren, the Man I had most delighted in: For when he was not
in a Fit of Wisdom, or not over-concern'd about his Interest,
he had a great deal of entertaining Humour: I therefore, notwithstanding his Reserve, always left the Door open to our for-
20   mer Intimacy, if he were inclin'd to come into it. I never
fail'd to give him my Hat, and, *Your Servant*, wherever I met
him; neither of which he would ever return, for above a Year
after; but I still persisted, in my usual Salutation, without observing, whether it was civilly receiv'd, or not. This ridiculous
Silence between two Comedians, that had so lately liv'd in a
constant course of Raillery, with one another, was often smil'd
at, by our Acquaintance, who frequented the same Coffee-house:
And one of them carried his Jest upon it so far, that when I
was at some distance from Town, he wrote me a formal Ac-
30   count, that *Dogget* was actually dead. After the first Surprize,
his Letter gave me, was over, I began to consider, that this coming from a droll Friend to both of us, might possibly be written,
to extract some Merriment out of my real Belief of it: In this
I was not unwilling to gratify him, and return'd an Answer, as
l.9 the chief Conductor] the Conductor 2nd ed.
l.16 Man I had most] Man I most 2nd ed.

if I had taken the Truth of his News for granted; and was not
a little pleas'd, that I had so fair an Opportunity of speaking
my Mind freely of *Dogget,* which I did, in some Favour of his
Character; I excus'd his Faults, and was just to his Merit. His
Law-suit with us, I only imputed to his having naturally deceiv'd himself in the Justice of his Cause. What I most complain'd of was, his irreconcilable Disaffection to me, upon it
whom he could not reasonably blame, for standing in my own
Defence; that not to endure me, after it, was a Reflexion upon
his Sense, when all our Acquaintance had been Witnesses of our
former Intimacy; which my Behavior in his Life-time, had
plainly shewn him, I had a mind to renew. But since he was
now gone (however great a Churl he was to me) I was sorry my
Correspondent had lost him.

  This Part of my Letter, I was sure, if *Dogget's* Eyes were still
open, would be shewn to him; if not, I had only writ it to no
purpose. But about a Month after, when I came to Town, I
had some little Reason to imagine it had the Effect I wish'd from
it: For one Day sitting over-against him, at the same Coffee-
house, where we often mixt at the same Table, tho' we never exchang'd a single Syllable, he graciously extended his Hand, for
a Pinch of my Snuff: As this seem'd, from him, a sort of breaking the Ice of his Temper, I took courage upon it, to break Silence on my side, and ask'd him how he lik'd it? To which,
with a slow Hesitation, naturally assisted by the Action of his
taking the Snuff, he reply'd---*Umh! the best*---*Umh!*---*I have
tasted a great while!*---If the Reader, who may possibly think
all this extremely trifling, will consider, that Trifles sometimes
shew Characters in as strong a Light, as Facts of more serious
Importance, I am in hopes he may allow, that my Matter
less needs an Excuse, than the Excuse itself does; if not, I must
stand condemn'd at the end of my Story.-------But let me
go on.

After a few Days of these coy, Lady-like Compliances, on
his side, we grew into a more conversable Temper: At last, I
took a proper Occasion, and desired he would be so frank with
me, as to let me know, what was his real Dislike, or Motive,
that made him throw up so good an Income, as his Share
with us annually brought him in? For tho' by our Admission
of *Booth*, it might not probably amount to so much by a Hundred, or two a Year, as formerly; yet the Remainder was too
considerable, to be quarrel'd with, and was likely to continue

10   more, than the best Actors before us, had ever got, by the Stage.
And farther, to encourage him to be open, I told him, If I had
done any thing, that had particularly disoblig'd him, I was ready, if he could put me in the way, to make him any amends
in my Power; if not, I desired he would be so just to himself,
as to let me know the real Truth, without Reserve: But Reserve he could not, from his natural Temper, easily shake off.
All he said came from him, by half Sentences, and *Innuendos*,
as---No, he had not taken any thing particularly ill----for his
Part, he was very easy, as he was; but where others were to dis-

20   pose of his Property as they pleased---if you had stood it out,
as I did, *Booth* might have paid a better Price for it.---You were
too much afraid of the Court---but that's all over.---There were
other things in the Playhouse.---No Man of Spirit.---In short,
to be always pester'd, and provok'd by a trifling Wasp---a---
vain---shallow!---A Man would sooner beg his Bread, than
bear it.-----(Here it was easy to understand him: I therefore ask'd

30   him, what he had to bear, that I had not my Share of?) No!
it was not the same thing, he said.---You can play with a Bear,
or let him alone, and do what he would; but I could not let
him lay his Paws upon me, without being hurt; you did not
feel him, as I did.---And for a Man to be cutting of Throats,
upon every Trifle, at my time of Day!---If I had been as co-
vetous, as he thought me, may be I might have born it, as well
as you---but I would not be a Lord of the Treasury, if such a
Temper, as *Wilks's*, were to be at the Head of it.---

Here, then, the whole Secret was out. The rest of our Conversation was but explaining upon it. In a Word, the painful Behavior of *Wilks* had hurt him so sorely, that the Affair of
Booth was look'd upon, as much a Relief, as a Grievance, in giving him so plausible a Pretence to get rid of us all, with a better
Grace.

    Booth too, in a little time, had his Share of the same Uneasi-
ness, and often complain'd of it to me: Yet as we neither of us
could, then, afford to pay *Dogget's* Price, for our Remedy; all
we could do, was to avoid every Occasion, in our Power, of in-
flaming the Distemper: So that we both agreed, tho' *Wilk's* Nature was not to be chang'd, it was a less Evil to live with him,
than without him.

    Tho' I had often suspected, from what I had felt myself, that
the Temper of *Wilks* was *Dogget's* real Quarrel, to the Stage; yet
I could never thoroughly believe it, 'till I had it from his own
Mouth. And I, then, thought the Concern he had shewn at it
was a good deal inconsistent with that Understanding, which was
generally allow'd him. When I give my Reasons for it, perhaps
the Reader will not have a better Opinion of my own: Be that,
as it may, I cannot help wondering, that he, who was so much
more capable of Reflexion, than *Wilks*, could sacrifice so valuable an Income, to his Impatience of another's natural Frailty!
And tho' my Stoical way of thinking may be no Rule, for a wiser Man's Opinion; yet if it should happen to be right, the Reader may make his Use of it. Why then should we not always
consider, that the Rashness of Abuse is but the false Reason of a
weak Man? and that offensive Terms are only us'd, to supply the
want of Strength in Argument? Which, as to the common Practice of the sober World, we do not find, every Man, in Business,
is oblig'd to resent, with a military Sense of Honour: Or if he
should, would not the Conclusion amount to this? Because another wants Sense, and Manners, I am oblig'd to be a Madman?
For such every Man is, more, or less, while the Passion of An-

ger is in Possession of him. And what less can we call that
proud Man, who would put another out of the World, only for
putting him out of humour? If Accounts of the Tongue were
always to be made up with the Sword, all the Wisemen in the
World might be brought in Debtors, to Blockheads. And when
Honour pretends, to be Witness, Judge, and Executioner, in its
own Cause, if Honour were a Man, would it be an Untruth, to
say Honour is a very impudent Fellow? But in *Dogget's* Case,
it may be ask'd, How was he to behave himself? Were passio-
nate Insults, to be born, for Years together? To these Questions,
I can only answer with two, or three more, Was he to punish
himself, because another was in the wrong? How many sensible
Husbands endure the teizing Tongue of a froward Wife, only
because she is the weaker Vessel? And why should not a weak
Man have the same Indulgence? Daily Experience will tell us,
that the fretful Temper of a Friend, like the Personal Beauty of
a fine Lady, by Use, and Cohabitation, may be brought down,
to give us neither Pain, nor Pleasure. Such, at least, and no
more, was the Distress I found myself in, upon the same Provocations, which I generally return'd with humming an Air to my
self; or if the Storm grew very high, it might, perhaps, sometimes ruffle me enough to sing a little out of Tune. Thus
too (if I had any ill Nature to gratify) I often saw the unruly
Passion of the Aggressor's Mind punish itself, by a restless Disorder of the Body.

What inclines me, therefore, to think the Conduct of *Dogget*
was as rash, as the Provocations he complain'd of is, that in
some time after he had left us, he plainly discover'd he had re-
pented it. His Acquaintance observ'd to us, that he sent many a
long Look after his Share, in the still prosperous State of the
Stage: But, as his Heart was too high to declare (what we saw too)
his shy Inclination to return, he made us no direct Overtures.
Nor, indeed, did we care (tho' he was a golden Actor) to pay too
dear for him: For as most of his Parts had been pretty well sup-

3. Benefit of Mrs. *Porter*, in the *Wanton Wife*] *The Amourous Widow*, or, *The Wanton Wife* (c. 1670), by Thomas Betterton; the performance was on 18 March 1717, in which Dogget played Barnaby Brittle, a part normally taken by Cibber (e.g., 23 October 1716).

10. their Desire of seeing him oftner] Dogget's willingness may also have been due to a special request of George I (Victor, *Memoirs of the Late Barton Booth, Esq.*, p. 8).

15. he never return'd to the Stage] Dogget did return on 25 March 1717 to play Ben in *Love for Love* and on 1 April 1717 to play Hob in his own *Country Wake*, to assist in benefits for Mrs. Santlow and Mrs. Bicknell (Avery, I, 442, 444).

ply'd, he could not, now, be of his former Value, to us. However to shew the Town, at least, that he had not forsworn the
Stage, he, one Day, condescended, to play for the Benefit of
Mrs. *Porter*, in the *Wanton Wife*, at which he knew his late Majesty was to be present. Now (tho' I speak it not of my own
Knowledge) yet it was not likely Mrs. *Porter* would have ask'd that
Favour of him, without some previous Hint, that it would be
granted. His coming among us, for that Day only, had a strong
appearance of his laying it in our way, to make him Proposals,
10 or that he hoped the Court, or Town, might intimate to us, their
Desire of seeing him oftner: But as he acted only to do a particular Favour, the Menagers ow'd him no Compliment for it, beyond
common Civilities. And, as that might not be all he propos'd by
it, his farther Views (if he had any) came to nothing. For after
this Attempt, he never return'd to the Stage.

　　To speak of him, as an Actor: He was the most an Original,
and the strictest Observer of Nature, of all his Contemporaries. He
borrow'd from none of them: His Manner was his own: He was
a Pattern to others, whose greatest Merit was, that they had some-
20 times tolerably imitated him. In dressing a Character to the
greatest Exactness, he was remarkably skillful; the least Article
of whatever Habit he wore, seem'd in some degree to speak and
mark the different Humour he presented; a necessary Care in a
Comedian, in which many have been too remiss, or ignorant. He
could be extreamly ridiculous, without stepping into the least Im-
propriety, to make him so. His greatest Success was in Characters
of lower Life, which he improv'd, from the Delight he took, in
his Observations of that Kind, in the real World. In Songs, and
particular Dances too, of Humour, he had no Competitor. *Con-*
30 *greve* was a great Admirer of him, and found his Account, in
the Characters he expressly wrote for him. In those of *Fondle-*
wife, in his *Old Batchelor;* and *Ben* in *Love for Love*, no Author,
and Actor could be more oblig'd to their mutual masterly Performances. He was very acceptable to several Persons of high

23. *Take him* for *All* ...] *Hamlet*, I, ii, 187-88: "He was a man, take him for all in all./ I shall not look upon his like again."

Rank, and Taste: Tho' he seldom car'd to be the Comedian, but among his more intimate Acquaintance.

And now, let me ask the World a Question. When Men have any valuable Qualities, why are the generality of our modern Wits so fond of exposing their Failings only, which the wisest of Mankind will never wholly be free from? Is it of more use to the Publick, to know their Errors, than their Perfections? Why is the Account of Life to be so unequally stated? Tho' a Man may be sometimes Debtor to Sense, or Morality, is it not doing him
10 Wrong, not to let the World see, at the same time, how far he may be Creditor to both? Are Defects and Disproportions, to be the only labour'd Features in a Portrait? But perhaps such Authors may know how to please the World better than I do, and may naturally suppose, that what is delightful to themselves, may not be disagreeable to others. For my own part, I confess myself a little touch'd in Conscience, at what I have, just now, observ'd to the Disadvantage of my other Brother-Menager.

If therefore, in discovering the true Casues of the Publick's losing so valuable an Actor, as *Dogget*, I have been oblig'd to shew
20 the Temper of *Wilks*, in its natural Complexion, ought I not, in amends, and balance of his Imperfections, to say at the same time of him, That if he was not the most correct, or judicious, yet (as *Hamlet* says of the King his Father) *Take him for All, in All,* &c. he was certainly the most diligent, most laborious, and most useful Actor, that I have seen upon the Stage, in Fifty Years.

CHAPTER XV

3. on the first of *August*] 1714.

10. they knew the Pension ... must still be paid to somebody] Cibber sees the position as having been assimilated into the complex structure of royal patronage, where it had small chance of being allowed to lapse no matter how irrational it was, as long as it could serve to repay or build political obligations (see Plumb, I, 72 ff.).

16. Sir *Richard Steele* ... Zeal for the House of Hanover] Steele was knighted only in April 1715. For an account of his political service, see Loftis, *Steele*, Part One. The most important services he had performed for the Hanoverian, as distinguished from the Whig cause, was the publication of the fifty-six numbers of the first volume of *The Englishman* (6 October 1713 to 11 February 1714) almost all of which defended the Hanoverian succession.

17. expell'd the House of Commons] Two pamphlets signed by Steele, *The Crisis* and *The Importance of Dunkirk Consider'd*, both attacking the Tories for their policies toward France, led to Steele's expulsion 18 March 1714. The government's intention in attacking Steele had been to divert debate from the issue of the succession, for at this time Bolingbroke was attempting to persuade James Stuart to convert to Protestantism; Walpole, as spokesman for the Whigs and Steele's defender, maintained that the attack on Steele was an attack on protestant succession (Plumb, I, 189-91; for Steele's political tracts, see *Tracts and Pamphlets by Richard Steele*, ed. Rae Blanchard, Baltimore, 1944).

20. Favour, in which he now stood, at Court] Steele had been offered the patent c. December 1712 by the Tory Lord Lansdowne, who had been made Comptroller of the Household the June before, probably to secure Steele's powers as a journalist for Tory use, or at least to forestall his opposition (Loftis, *Steele*, pp. 25-33; Cibber alluded to such offers in the dedicatory epistle of *Ximena*, addressed to Steele, in 1719). It is, therefore, significant that Cibber should omit to mention it at this point; to acknowledge his past friendship with Steele would not accord with his attitude toward him in the late 1730's.

C H A P. XV.

Sir Richard Steele *succeeds* Collier, *in the Theatre-Royal.* Lincolns-
Inn-Fields *House rebuilt. The Patent restored. Eight Actors
at once desert, from the King's Company. Why. A new Patent
obtain'd, by Sir* Richard Steele, *and assign'd in Shares, to the
menaging Actors of* Drury-Lane. *Of modern Pantomimes.
The Rise of them. Vanity invincible, and asham'd. The* Non-
juror *acted. The Author, not forgiven; and rewarded for it.*

UPON the Death of the Queen, Plays (as they always had been on the like Occasions) were silenc'd
for six Weeks. But this happening on the first of
August, in the long Vacation of the Theatre, the
Observance of that Ceremony, which at another
Juncture would have fallen like wet Weather upon their Harvest,
did them now no particular Damage. Their License however
being of course to be renewed, that Vacation gave the Menagers
Time to cast about, for the better Alteration of it: And since
10   they knew the Pension of seven hundred a Year, which had been
levied upon them for *Collier,* must still be paid to somebody,
they imagin'd the Merit of a *Whig* might now have as good a
Chance for getting into it, as that of a *Tory* had for being continued in it: Having no Obligations, therefore, to *Collier,* who
had made the last Penny of them; they applied themselves to
Sir *Richard Steele,* who had distinguished himself, by his Zeal
for the House of *Hanover,* and had been expell'd the House of
Commons, for carrying it (as was judg'd at a certain Crisis) into
a Reproach of the Government. This we knew was his Preten-
20   sion to that Favour, in which he now stood, at Court: We knew
too, the Obligations the Stage had to his Writings, there being

l. 14   in it:] in it? 1st ed.

12. supporting the Stage, in that Reputation] Steele's importance in the reform of the stage after Collier's attack, notably in his essays in *The Tatler* and his own plays, made his association in the management natural and easily accomplished (for an account of his role in reform, see Loftis, *Steele*, pp. 13-25).

29. apply'd himself to the Duke of *Marlborough*] The Duke was obliged to Steele who had published a tract, *The Englishman's Thanks to the Duke of Marlborough* on 4 January 1712, five days after the Duke had been deprived of all offices by Queen Anne. The license was granted without delay, 18 October 1714 (Loftis, *Steele*, p. 11).

32. *Collier* we heard no more of] Not so. He sued immediately to have the company ejected from Drury Lane to which he held the lease. The manager started a counter-suit in Chancery, and Barker supposes that Collier did not pursue the action because he could not afford the expense (P.R.O., C.11 1175/59; Chancery Decrees and Orders, 1714 B, p. 258; 1718 B, pp. 292, 347, cited by Barker, p. 102).

scarce a Comedian of Merit, in our whole Company, whom his
Tatlers had not made better, by his publick Recommendation of
them. And many Days had our House been particularly fill'd,
by the Influence, and Credit of his Pen. Obligations of this
kind from a Gentleman, with whom they all had the Pleasure
of a personal Intimacy, the Menagers thought could not be more
justly return'd, than by shewing him some warm Instance of
their Desire, to have him, at the Head of them. We therefore
beg'd him to use his Interst, for the Renewal of our License,
10 and that he would do us the Honour of getting our Names to
stand with His, in the same Commission. This, we told him,
would put it still farther into his Power of supporting the Stage,
in that Reputation, to which his Lucubrations had already so
much contributed; and that therefore we thought no Man had
better Pretences to partake of its Success.

Though it may be no Addition to the favourable Part of this
Gentleman's Character, to say with what Pleasure he receiv'd this
Mark of our Inclination to him, yet my Vanity longs to tell you,
that it surpriz'd him into an Acknowledgement, that People, who
20 are shy of Obligations, are cautious of confessing. His Spirits
took such a lively Turn upon it, that had we been all his own
Sons, no unexpected Act of filial Duty could have more endear'd
us to him.

It must be observ'd, then, that as *Collier* had no Share, in any
Part of our Property, no Difficulties, from that Quarter, could
obstruct this Proposal. And the usual Time of our beginning
to act for the Winter-Season, now drawing near, we press'd him
not to lose any Time in his Sollicitation of this new License.
Accordingly Sir *Richard*, apply'd himself to the Duke of *Mal-*
30 *borough*, the Hero of his Heart, who, upon the first mention of
it, obtain'd it of his Majesty, for Sir *Richard*, and the former
Menagers, who were Actors. *Collier* we heard no more of.

The Court, and Town, being crowded very early, in the
Winter-Season, upon the critical Turn of Affairs, so much ex-

4. About this Time the Patentee] Barker (p. 100) states that it was rather Rich's son John who applied for permission to form a company (citing P.R.O. C.11, 2346/4).

13. he prevail'd with Mr. Craggs the younger] James Craggs (1686-1721) succeeded Addison as Secretary of State.

29. we had been forced to dismiss an Audience] At the first performance of Ambrose Phillips' *The Distrest Mother*, 17 March 1712, partisans of Mrs. Rogers, who had been expected to play the leading role, Andromache, rioted because Mrs. Oldfield had been given the part instead (Egerton, *Life of Mrs. Anne Oldfield*, quoted by Avery, I, 271-72).

pected from the *Hanover* Succession, the Theatre had its particular Share of that general Blessing, by a more than ordinary
Concourse of Spectators.

About this Time the Patentee, having very near finish'd his
House, in *Lincolns-Inn-Fields*, began to think of forming a new
Company; and in the mean Time, found it necessary to apply
for Leave to employ them. By the weak Defence he had always
made against the several Attacks upon his Interest, and former
Government of the Theatre, it might be a Question, if his House
10 had been ready, in the Queen's Time, whether he would, then,
have had the Spirit to ask, or Interest enough to obtain Leave to
use it: But in the following Reign, as it did not appear he had
done any thing to forfeit the Right of his Patent, he prevail'd
with Mr. *Craggs* the younger, (afterwards Secretary of State) to
lay his Case before the King, which he did in so effectual a manner, that (as Mr. *Craggs* himself told me) his Majesty was pleas'd
to say upon it, "That he remember'd, when he had been in
" *England* before, in King *Charles* his Time, there had been
" Two Theatres in *London*; and as the Patent seem'd to be a
20 " lawful Grant, he saw no Reason, why Two Play-houses might
" not be continued."

The Suspension of the Patent being thus taken off, the
younger Multitude seem'd to call aloud for two Play-houses!
Many desired another, from the common Notion, that *Two* would
alway create Emulation, in the Actors (An Opinion, which I
have consider'd in a former Chapter.) Others too, were as eager
for them, from the natural Ill-will that follows the Fortunate,
or Prosperous, in any Undertaking. Of this low Malevolence we
had, now and then, had remarkable Instances; we had been
30 forced to dismiss an Audience of a hundred and fifty Pounds,
from a Disturbance spirited up, by obscure People, who never
gave any better Reason for it, than that it was their Fancy, to
support the idle Complaint of one rival Actress, against another,
in their several Pretensions to the chief Part in a new Tragedy.

16. Mist's Journal ... censure our Menagement] Mist did not begin his pursuit of Cibber until after *The Non-Juror*, in 1717 (Barker, p. 125).

34. gratify the little Spleen of our Enemies by wincing ...] Cibber did grow angry enough, when in 1720 Dennis attacked him along with Steele, to advertise in the *Daily Post*, "Ten Pounds will be paid by Mr. *Cibber*, of the Theatre Royal, to any person who shall (by a legal proof) discover the Author of a Pamphlet, intituled, 'The Characters and Conduct of Sir John Edgar, etc.'" (quoted by Lowe, II, 168).

But as this Tumult seem'd only to be the Wantonness of *English*
Liberty, I shall not presume to lay any farther Censure upon it.

　　Now, nothwithstanding this publick Desire of re-establishing
two Houses; and though I have allow'd the former Actors greatly our superiors; and the Menagers I am speaking of, not to have
been without their private Errors. Yet, under all these Disadvantages, it is certain, the Stage, for twenty Years before this
time, had never been in so flourishing a Condition: And it was
10 as evident to all sensible Spectators, that this Prosperity could be
only owing to that better Order, and closer Industry, now daily
observ'd; and which had formerly been neglected by our Predecessors. But that I may not impose upon the Reader a Merit,
which was not generally allow'd us, I ought honestly to let him
know, that about this time, the publick Papers, particuarly
Mist's Journal, took upon them very often to censure our Menagement, with the same Freedom, and Severity, as if we had
been so many Ministers of State: But so it happen'd, that these
unfortuante Reformers of the World, these self-appointed *Censors*
20 hardly ever hit upon what was really wrong, in us; but taking
up Facts upon Trust, or Hear-say, piled up many a pompous
Paragraph, that they had ingeniously conceiv'd was sufficient to
demolish our Administration, or at least, to make us very uneasy
in it; which, indeed, had so far its Effect, that my equally-in-
jur'd Brethren *Wilks*, and *Booth*, often complain'd to me of these
disagreeable Aspersions, and propos'd, that some publick Answer
might be made to them, which I always oppos'd, by perhaps,
too secure a Contempt of what such Writers could do to hurt
us; and my Reason for it was, that I knew but of one way to
30 silence Authors of that Stamp; which was, to grow insignificant,
and good for nothing, and then we should hear no more of
them: But while we continued in the Prosperity of pleasing
others, and were not conscious of having deserv'd what they said
of us, why should we gratify the little Spleen of our Enemies,

17. *Lincolns-Inn-Field*s was ready to be open'd] It opened 18 December 1714 with *The Recruiting Officer*, to which were added *entr'acte* entertainments (Barker, p. 101).

19. postpone many of our best Plays] Avery (I, 334 ff.) gives no indication of what these postponements might have been; the bills at this time do not list casts, probably a reflection of turmoil in the company.

30. The Chief of these Deserters] Both William Bullock and Christopher Bullock, Griffin, Keene, Pack, Mrs. Knight, and Mrs. Rogers left Drury Lane (Avery, I, 328); perhaps also those mentioned by Davies (*Dram. Misc.*, III, 485-86): "When Quin, Walker, and Ryan left Drury-lane theatre, it was not from a dislike to Wilks, but from an offer of advanced salary, with the possession of the capital parts. Ryan chose 5 1. per week, at Lincoln's-inn-fields, with the part of Hamlet, in preference to Laertes, in the same play, and 50s. at Drury-lane … The mean subterfuge of Cibber, to cloke his spleen to Wilks by the Suffrage of others is visible." Steele applied to the Lord Chamberlain to force the deserters to return, got no satisfaction, then attempted to sue them, and finally prepared a direct petition to the King—though it is not known whether he presented it. Loftis sees in this episode the beginning of the long series of conflicts with the Lord Chamberlain (*Steele*, p. 43). Avery (I, 334) cites a threat in *The Weekly Packet*, 18 December, to the deserters "to return to their Colours, upon Pain of not exercising their Lungs anywhere."

by wincing at it, or give them fresh Opportunities to dine upon
any Reply they might make to our publickly taking Notice of
them? And though Silence might, in some Cases, be a sign of
Guilt, or Error confess'd, our Accusers were so low, in their Credit and Sense, that the Content we gave the Publick, almost
every Day, from the Stage, ought to be our only Answer to
them.

However (as I have observ'd) we made many Blots, which
these unskilful Gamesters never hit: But the Fidelity of an Hi-
10 storian, cannot be excus'd the Omission of any Truth, which
might make for the other Side of the Question. I shall therefore confess a Fact, which, if a happy Accident had not inter-
vened, had brought our Affairs, into a very tottering Condition.
This too, is that Fact, which in a former Chapter, I promis'd
to set forth as a Sea-Mark of Danger, to future Menagers, in their
Theatrical Course of Government.

When the new-built Theatre, in *Lincolns-Inn Fields* was ready
to be open'd, seven or eight Actors, in one Day, deserted from
us, to the Service of the Enemy, which oblig'd us to postpone
20 many of our best Plays, for want to some inferior Part in them,
which these Deserters had been used to fill: But the Indulgence
of the Royal Family, who then frequently honour'd us, by their
Presence, was pleas'd to accept of whatever could be hastily got
ready for their Entertainment. And though this critical good
Fortune prevented, in some measure, our Audiences falling so
low, as otherwise they might have done, yet it was not sufficient to keep us in our former Prosperity: For that Year, our
Profits amounted not to above a third Part of our usual Dividends; though in the following Year we intirely recover'd them.
30 The Chief of these Deserters were *Keene, Bullock, Pack, Leigh,*
Son of the famous *Tony Leigh,* and others of less note. 'Tis
true, they none of them had more than a negative Merit, in
being only able to do us more Harm by their leaving us, without Notice, than they could do us Good, by remaining with us:

11. the greatest Grievance they had, in our Company] Cibber himself was heartily disliked by his actors; Davies (*Dram. Misc.*, III, 489-91), describing the 'settle' or gathering place of actors and their associates, remarks, "Cibber seldom came amongst the *settlers*; tyrants fear, as they know they are feared." See also Barker, pp. 111 ff. and Davies, *Dram. Misc.*, III, 472 ff. for a further account of Cibber's unpopularity.

21. that short Run of Favour, which is apt to follow Novelty] The Drury Lane company attempted to imply that their rivals were tainted with the elder Rich's Jacobitism (see Loftis, *Politics*, p. 65). The Drury Lane company had made £1700 profits in the autumn before the opening of Lincoln's Inn Fields, only £820 for the rest of the season (P.R.O., C 33/335 contains the master's report of 17 December 1716 on Doggett's withdrawal; it is cited by Loftis, *Steele*, p. 42). Apparently the Drury Lane company only recovered fully as a result of the production of *The Non-Juror* in December 1717, by which time Lincoln's Inn Fields was deserted (Barker, p. 109).

For though the best of them could not support a Play, the
worst of them, by their Absence, could maim it; as the Loss of
the least Pin, in a Watch, may obstruct its Motion. But to
come to the true Cause of their Desertion: After my having dif-
cover'd the (long unknown) Occasion that drove *Dogget* from the
Stage, before his settled Inclination to leave it; it will be less
incredible, that these Actors, upon the first Opportunity to relieve themselves, should all, in one Day, have left us from the
same Cause of Uneasiness. For, in a little time after, upon not
10 finding their Expectations answer'd, in *Lincolns-Inn-Fields*, some
of them, who seem'd to answer for the rest, told me, the greatest Grievance they had, in our Company, was the shocking
Temper of *Wilks*, who, upon every, almost no Occasion, let
loose the unlimited Language of Passion upon them, in such a
manner as their Patience was not longer able to support. This,
indeed, was what we could not justify! This was a Secret, that
might have made a wholesome Paragraph, in a critical News-
Paper! But as it was our good Fortune, that it came not to the
Ears of our Enemies, the Town was not entertaine'd, with their
20 publick Remarks upon it.

After this new Theatre had enjoy'd that short Run of Favour,
which is apt to follow Novelty; their Audiences began to flag:
But whatever good Opinion we had of our own Merit, we had
not so good a one of the Multitude, as to depend too much upon the Delicacy of their Taste: We knew too, that this Company being so much nearer to the City, than we were, would in-
tercept many an honest Customer, that might not know a good
Market, from a bad one; and that the thinnest of their Audiences, must be always taking something from the Measure of
30 our Profits. All these Disadvantages, with many others, we
were forced to lay before Sir *Richard Steele*, and farther to re-
monstrate to him, that as he now stood in *Collier's* Place, his
Pension of *700 l.* was liable to the same Conditions, that *Collier*
had receiv'd it upon; which were, that it should be only pay-

2. this Pension was to be liquidated] Note that even so his share was approximately £630 for the season (see note above).

13. before the Effects of his Good-nature ... Distresses] Conflict between Steele and the managers largely centers upon his attempts to claim income during his suspension from the governorship of Drury Lane in 1720. The episode is extremely complex, the battles over the matter ranging over many years; for a complete account, see Loftis, *Steele*, pp. 213-18 *et passim.*.

26. Reason to grieve ... one Lord-Chamberlain] Of the three Lords Chamberlain Cibber had directly or indirectly to deal with, the Dukes of Shrewsbury and Bolton were tolerant of his insolence, possibly as a result of vagueness in the question of the prerogatives of his office, but the Duke of Newcastle, who became Lord Chamberlain on 13 April 1717, wished to exercise full authority over the theaters (Loftis, *Steele*, pp. 43-44, 123 ff.) and this led to a bitter struggle directed toward Steele who maintained that the Lord Chamberlain had no power to interfere with the patent theater. Cibber had directed his insolence only to the Master of the Revels, somehow—illegitimately—dissociating him from his superior (Loftis, *Steele*, pp. 48-49). Barker (p. 103) quotes a letter of 22 January 1715 (L.C. 7/3) from Cibber to the Lord Chamberlain refusing bluntly to obey his order to pay Vanbrugh the £100 due to the opera. He had previously refused the Master of the Revel's licensing fee for a new play when the latter could not show evidence of authority to demand it (Loftis, *Steele*, pp. 48-49).

30. *Insolence* of *Office*] *Hamlet*, III, i, 73.

able during our being the only Company permitted to act, but
in case another should be set up against us, that then this Pension was to be liquidated into an equal Share with us; and
which we now hoped he would be contented with. While we
were offering to proceed, Sir *Richard* stopt us short, by assuring
us, that as he came among us, by our own Invitation, he should
always think himself oblig'd, to come into any Measures, for our
Ease, and Service: That to be a Burthen to our Industry, would
be more disagreeable to him, than it could be to us; and as he
10 had always taken a Delight, in his Endeavours for our Prosperity, he should be still ready on our own Terms, to continue
them. Every one who knew Sir *Richard Steele*, in his Prosperity (before the Effects of his Good-nature had brought him to
Distresses) knew that this was his manner of dealing with his
Friends, in Business: Another Instance of the same nature will
immediately fall in my way.

When we propos'd to put this Agreement, into Writing, he
desired us not to hurry ouselves; for that he was advis'd, upon
the late Desertion of our Actors, to get our License (which only
20 subsisted during Pleasure) enlarg'd into a more ample, and dura-
ble Authority, and which he said he had reason to think would
be more easily obtain'd, if we were willing, that a Patent for the
same purpose might be granted to Him only, for his Life, and
three Years after, which he would then assign over to us. This
was a Propsect beyond our Hopes; and what we had long wish'd
for; for tho' I cannot say, we had ever Reason to grieve at the
Personal Severities, or Behaviour, of any one Lord-Chamberlain,
in my Time, yet the several Officers, under them, who had not
the Hearts of Noblemen, often treated us (to use *Shakespear's*
30 Expression) with all the *Insolence of Office*, that narrow Minds are
apt to be elated with; but a Patent, we knew, would free us
from so abject a State of Dependency. Accordingly, we desired
Sir *Richard* to lose no time; he was immediately promis'd it: In
the Interim, we sounded the Inclination of the Actors remaining

9. the Patent ... pass'd the Great Seal] The decision to apply for a patent was taken probably in December 1714 or early January 1715; it was the Attorney and Solicitor General, Northey and Lechmere, who insisted upon the consent of the managers for the patent (for a full account of these proceedings, see Loftis, *Steele*, pp. 44-45).

13. We receiv'd the Patent *January* 19, 1718] 19 January 1715. In it are granted no extraordinary powers, but the right to perform operas as well as plays is conferred, as distinct from the earlier license which forbade them; Dogget's name is included (Loftis, *Steele*, pp. 95 ff.; the patent and other documents discussed here are reprinted on pp. 243-45).

14. Burrowbridge in Yorkshire, where he was ... elected Member] He was elected in February 1715 upon nomination by the Duke of Newcastle, an evidence of good relations between them at this period (Loftis, *Steele*, p. 123).

17. his Assignment to us of equal Shares] See Steele's account of these procedures in *The Theatre*, No. VIII (26 January 1720) in which he pleads for redress of grievances to Newcastle.

33. *Collier*, by insisting ... Three Hundred Pounds] Cibber means that while Collier drew only £700, the sharing managers made about £1000.

with us; who had all Sense enough to know, that the Credit
and Reputation we stood in, with the Town, could not but be a
better Security for their Sallaries, than the Promise of any other
Stage, put into Bonds, could make good to them.   In a few
Days after, Sir *Richard* told us, that his Majesty being apprised
that others had a joint Power with him, in the License, it was
expected, we should, under our Hands, signify, that his Petition
for a Patent was preferr'd, by the Consent of us all.   Such an Acknowledgement was immediately sign'd, and the Patent there-
10 upon pass'd the Great Seal; for which I remember the Lord-
Chancellor *Cooper*, in Compliments to Sir *Richard*, would receive
no Fee.

   We receiv'd the Patent *January 19, 1718*, and (Sir *Richard*
being oblig'd the next Morning to set out for *Burrowbridge* in
Yorkshire, where he was soon after elected Member for the new
Parliament) we were forc'd that very Night, to draw up in a
hurry ('till our Counsel might more advisably perfect it) his Assignment to us of equal Shares, in the Patent, with farther Conditions of Partnership: But here I ought to take Shame to myself,
20 and at the same time to give this second Instance of the Equity
and Honour of Sir *Richard*: For this Assignment (which I had
myself the hasty Penning of) was so worded, that it gave Sir *Richard* as equal a Title to our Property, as it had given us to his
Authority in the Patent: But Sir *Richard*, notwithstanding, when
he return'd to Town, took no Advantage of the Mistake, and
consented in our second Agreement, to pay us Twelve Hundred
Pounds, to be equally intitled to our Property, which at his
Death, we were oblig'd to repay (as we afterwards did) to his
Executors: and which, in case any of us had died before him,
30 the Survivors were equally oblig'd to have paid to the Executors
of such deceased Person, upon the same Account.   But Sir *Ri-
chard's* Moderation with us, was rewarded with the Reverse of
Collier's Stiffness: *Collier*, by insisting on his Pension, lost Three
Hundred Pounds a Year; and Sir *Richard*, by his accepting a

11.8-9 Acknowledgement] Acknowledment 1st ed.

6. *Dryden's All for Love*] Revived 3 December 1718; the company had instituted the policy of expensive productions much earlier, in 1716, advertising Rowe's *Tamerlane* (5 November) and *The Man of Mode* (22 November) as "new dressed" (Avery, I, 420, 422; Barker, p. 109). The next year in response to the sumptuous decorations of Lincoln's Inn Fields, they had delayed opening their season; Lowe (II, 175 n.) quotes this notice in *The Daily Courant*, 6 October 1715: "His Majesty's Company of Comedians give Notice that the Middle of next Week they will begin to act Plays, every day, as usual; they being oblig'd to lye still so long, to finish the New Decorations of the House." This production occasioned the postponement of Dennis' *Invader of his Country* (cf. *The Theatre*, ed. Nichols, p. 544, cited by Lowe, II, 176; see also *The Works of John Dennis*, ed. Hooker, II, 162-65).

24. to have our Tenement survey'd by Sir *Thomas Hewit*] A report by Hewett (reprinted by Lowe, II, 177, from John Nichols' edition of Steele's *The Theatre*, London, 1791, p. 470) shows that Cibber is mistaken about the time, for he dates his examination 21 January 1721.

Share in lieu of it, was, one Year with another, as much a
Gainer.

The Grant of this Patent having assur'd us of a competent
Term, to be relied on, we were now emboldened, to lay out
larger Sums, in the Decorations of our Plays: Upon the Revival
of *Dryden's All for Love*, the Habits of that Tragedy amounted
to an Expence of near Six Hundred Pounds; a Sum unheard of
for many Years before, on the like Occasions. But we thought
such extraordinary Marks of our Acknowledgment were due to
10 the Favours, which the Publick were now, again pouring in upon us. About this time we were so much in fashion, and follow'd, that our Enemies (who they were, it would not be fair to
guess, for we never knew them) made their Push of a good round
Lye upon us, to terrify those Auditors, from our Support, whom
they could not mislead by thei private Arts, or publick Invec-
tives. A current Report, that the Walls, and Roof of our House,
were liable to fall, had got such ground in the Town, that on a
sudden, we found our Audiences unusually decreas'd by it:
Wilks was immediately for denouncing War, and Vengeance on
20 the Author of this Falshood, and for offering a Reward, to
whoever could discover him. But it was thought more necessary
first to disprove the Falshood, and then to pay what compliments might be thought adivseable to the Author. Accordingly an Order from the King was obtain'd, to have our Tenement survey'd by Sir *Thomas Hewit*, then the proper Officer;
whose Report of its being in a safe, and sound Condition, and
sign'd by him, was publish'd in every News-Paper. This had so
immediate an Effect, that our Spectators, whose Apprehensions had lately kept them absent, now made up our Losses, by
30 returning to us, with a fresh Inclination, and in greater Numbers.

When it was first publickly known, that the New Theatre
would be open'd against us; I cannot help going a little back to
remember the Concern that my Brother-Menagers express'd at

1.25 *Hewit*] *Hewet*   2nd ed.

3. shutting them out, from behind our Scenes] An order to this effect was issued 13 November 1711 (L.C. 5/155, p. 125, printed by Nicoll, II, 282); orders of this sort had been issued before.

what might be the Consequences of it. They imagin'd, that
now, all those who wish'd Ill to us, adn particularly a great Party, who had been disoblig'd, by our shutting them out, from behind our Scenes, even to the Refusal of their Mony, would now
exert themselves, in any partial, or extravagant Measures, that
might either hurt us, or support our Competitors: These too
were some of those farther Reasons, which had discourag'd them,
from running the hazard of continuing to Sir *Richard Steele* the
same Pension, which had been paid to *Collier*. Upon all which
10 I observed to them, that for my own Part, I had not the same
Apprehensions; but that I foresaw as many good, as bad Consequences from two Houses: That tho' the Novelty might possibly at first abate a little of our Profits; yet if we slacken'd not
our Industry, that Loss would be amply balanc'd, by an equal
Increase of our Ease, and Quiet: That those turbulent Spirits
which were always molesting us, would now have other Employment: That the question'd Merit of our Acting would now
stand in a clearer Light, when others were faintly compared to
us: That tho' Faults might be found, with the best Actors,
20 that ever were, yet the egregious Defects, that would appear in
others, would now be the effectual means to make our Superiority shine, if we had any Pretence to it: And that what some
People hoped might ruin us, would in the end reduce them to
give up the Dispute, and reconcile them to those who could best
entertain them.

In every Article of this Opinion, they afterwards found I had
not been deceiv'd; and the Truth of it may be so well remember'd by many living Spectators, that it would be too frivolous
and needless a Boast, to give it any farther Observation.

30 But, in what I have said, I would not be understood to be an
Advocate, for two Playhouses: For we shall soon find that two
Sets of Actors, tolerated in the same Place, have constantly
ended in the Corruption of the Theatre; of which the auxiliary
Entertainments, that have so barbarously supply'd the Defects of

17. the Fable of *Mars* and *Venus*] *The Loves of Mars and Venus* by John Weaver, 2 March 1717. Baker (II, 204) characterizes it as a "Dramatic Entertainment of Dancing, attempted in imitation of the Pantomimes of the ancient Greek and Romans." The company had already presented musical afterpieces during the preceding autumn (Barker, p. 104).

weak Action, have for some Years past, been a flagrant Instance; it may not therefore, be here improper to shew how our
childish Pantomimes first came to take so gross a Possession of
the Stage.

I have upon several Occasions already observ'd, that when one
Company is too hard for another, the lower, in Reputation, has
always been forc'd to exhibit some new-fangled Foppery, to draw
the Multitude after them: Of these Expedients, Singing and
Dancing had formerly been the most effectual; but, at the Time
10 I am speaking of, our *English* Musick had been so discountenanc'd, since the Taste of *Italian* Operas prevail'd, that it was
to no purpose, to pretend to it. Dancing therefore was, now,
the only Weight in the opposite Scale, and as the New Theatre
sometimes found their Account in it, it could not be safe for us,
wholly to neglect it. To give even Dancing therefore some Improvement, and to make it something more than Motion without Meaning, the Fable of *Mars* and *Venus*, was form'd into a
connected Presentation of Dances in Character, wherein the Passions were so happily express'd, and the whole Story so intelligi-
20 bly told, by a mute Narration of Gesture only, that even thinking Spectators allow'd it both a pleasing, and a rational Entertainment; tho', at the same time, from our Distrust of its Reception, we durst not venture to decorate it, with any extraordinary Expence of Scenes, or Habits; but upon the Success of
this Attempt, it was rightly concluded, that if a visible Expence
in both, were added to something of the same Nature, it could
not fail of drawing the Town proportionably after it. From this
original Hint then (but ever way unequal to it) sprung forth the
Succession of monstrous Medlies, that have so long infested the
30 Stage, and which arose upon one another alternately, at both
Houses outvying, in Expence, like contending Bribes on both
sides at an Election, to secure a Majority of the Multitude. But
so it is, Truth may complain, and Merit murmur with what
Justice it may, the Few will never be a Match for the Many,

3. dishonour their Understanding] Cf. Pope's description of pantomimes and Cibber's part in them in *The Dunciad* (A), Book III, 11. 226 ff. Cibber reiterated his disdain for pantomime and denied also that he had been "Dunce enough to mount a Machine" (Cibber, *Letter*, p. 37).

unless Authority should think fit to interpose, and put down these
Poetical Drams, these Gin-shops of the Stage, that intoxicate its
Auditors, and dishonour their Understanding, with a Levity, for
which I want a Name.

    If I am ask'd (after my condemning these Fooleries, myself)
how I came to assent, or continue my Share of Expence to them?
I have no better Excuse for my Error, than confessing it. I did
it against my Conscience! and had not virtue enough to starve,
by opposing a Multitude, that would have been too hard for

10 me. Now let me ask an odd Question: Had *Harry the Fourth*
of *France* a better Excuse, for changing his Religion? I was
still in my Heart, as much as he could be, on the side of Truth
and Sense, but with this difference, that I had their leave to
quit them, when they could not support me: For what Equivalent could I have found for my falling a Martyr to them?
How far the Heroe, or the Comedian, was in the wrong, let
the Clergy, and the Criticks decide. Necessity will be as good
a Plea for the one, as the other. But let the Question go which
way it will, *Harry* IV. has been always allow'd a Great Man:

20 And what I want of his Grandeur, you see by the Inference,
Nature has amply supply'd to me, in Vanity; a Pleasure which
neither the Pertness of Wit, or the Gravity of Wisdom, will ever
persuade me to part with. And why is there not as much Honesty in owning, as in concealing it? For though to hide it may
be Wisdom, to be without it is impossible; and where is the
Merit of keeping a Secret, which every Body is let into? To
say we have no Vanity then, is shewing a great deal of it; as
to say we *have* a great deal, cannot be shewing so much: And
tho', there may be Art, in a Man's accusing himself, even then

30 it will be more pardonable, than Self-commendation. Do we
not find, that even good Actions have their Share of it? that it
is as inseperable, from our Being, as our Nakedness? And tho'
it may be equally decent to cover it, yet the wisest Man can no
more be without it, than the weakest can believe he was born,

1.28 to say] to save 1st ed.

in his Cloaths. If then what we say of ourselves be true, and
not prejudicial to others, to be called vain upon it, is no more a
Reproach, than to be called a brown, or a fair Man. Vanity is
of all Complexions; 'tis the growth of every Clime, and Capacity; Authors of all Ages have had a Tincture of it; and yet
you read *Horace, Montaign,* and Sir *William Temple,* with Pleasure. Nor am I sure, if it were curable by Precept, that Mankind would be mended by it! Could Vanity be eradicated, from
our nature, I am afraid, that the Reward of most human Vir-
10 tues, would not be found, in this World! And happy is he,
who has no greater Sin to asnwer for, in the next!

But what is all this to the Theatrical Follies I was talking of?
Perhaps not a great deal; but it is to my Purpose; for though I
am an Historian, I do not write to the Wise, and Learned only; I hope to have Readers of no more Judgment, than some
of my *quondam* Auditors; and I am afraid they will be as hardly contented, with dry Matters of Fact, as with a plain Play,
without Entertainments: This Rhapsody, therefore, has been
thrown in, as a Dance between the Acts, to make up for the
20 Dullness of what would have been by itself only proper. But I
now come to my Story again.

Notwithstanding, then, this our Compliance with the vulgar
Taste; we generally made use of these Pantomimes, but as
Crutches to our weakest Plays: Nor were we so lost to all Sense
of what was valuable, as to dishonour our best Authors, in such
bad Company: We had still a due Respect to several select
Plays, that were able to be their own Support; and in which
we found our constant Account, without painting, and patching
them out, like Prostitutes, with these Follies, in fashion: If
30 therefore we were not so strictly chaste, in the other part of our
Conduct, let the Error of it stand among the silly Consequences
of Two Stages. Could the Interest of both Companies have
been united, in one only Theatre; I had been one of the Few,
that would have us'd my utmost Endeavour of never admitting

14. About this time *Jacobitism*] That is, the Scottish Rebellion under the Old Pretender in 1715.

27. *Nonjuror*] Produced at Drury Lane on 6 December 1717. Cibber used the translation by Matthew Medbourne in making his adaptation (see Dudley H. Miles, "The Original of the *Non-Juror*," *PMLA*, xxiii, 1915, 195-214). Non-jurors were those clergymen of the Church of England who, as a matter of conscience, would not take the oath of allegiance to the supplanters of James II. Cibber's identification of them with Roman Catholic subversion and extremists of the Tory party was slanderous. Pope's enmity certainly was strongly reinforced by the play if not actually originated by it (cf. Barker, pp. 106-109, 203 ff.; Ault, pp. 298-315).

to the Stage any spectacle, that ought not to have been seen
there; the Errors of my own Plays, which I could not see, excepted. And though probably, the Majority of Spectators would
not have been so well pleas'd with a Theatre so regulated; yet
Sense, and Reason cannot lose their intrinsick Value, because
the Giddy, and the Ignorant, and blind and deaf, or numerous;
and I cannot help saying, it is a Reproach to a sensible People,
to let Folly so publickly govern their Pleasures.

    While I am making this grave Declaration of what I *would*
10 have done, had One only Stage been continued; to obtain an
easier Belief of my Sincerity, I ought to put my Reader in mind
of what I *did* do, even after Two Companies were again establish'd.

    About this Time *Jacobitism* had lately exerted itself, by the
most unprovoked Rebellion, that our Histories have handed down
to us, since the *Norman* Conquest: I therefore thought that to
set the Authors, and Principles of that desperate Folly in a fair
Light, by allowing the mistaken Consciences of some their best
Excuse, and by making the artful Pretenders to Conscience, as
20 ridiculous, as they were ungratefully wicked, was a Subject fit
for the honest Satire of Comedy, and what might, if it succeeded, do Honour to the Stage, by shewing the valuable Use of it.
And considering what Numbers, at that time, might come to it,
as prejudic'd Spectators, it may be allow'd that the Undertaking
was not less hazardous, than laudable.

    To give Life, therefore, to this Design, I borrow'd the *Tar-
tuffe* of *Moliere*, and turn'd him, into a modern *Nonjuror*: Upon
the Hypocricy of the *French* Character, I ingrafted a stronger
Wickedness, that of an *English* Popish Priest, lurking under the
30 Doctrine of our own Church, to raise his Fortune, upon the
Ruin of a worthy Gentleman, whom his dissembled Sanctity
had seduc'd into the treasonable Cause of a *Roman Catholick*
Out-law. How this Design, in teh Play, was executed, I refer
to the Readers of it; it cannot be mended, by any critical Re-

3. acted eighteen Days running] From 6-21 December 1717, omitting Sundays, and then at intervals.

17. Mr. *Mist,* whose *Weekly Journal* ...] Nathaniel Mist, known to be a Jacobite, was responsible (in an indefinable way) for the newspaper known successively as *The Weekly Journal, Mist's,* or *Fog's Journal*; it ran about twenty years. For an account of his pursuit of Cibber, see Barker, pp. 125 ff.

20. *Minheer Keiber*] The Teutonic sound of this form of address suggested a link between Cibber (whose father was Danish) and the heavily German court which Mist abhorred.

marks, I can make, in its favour: Let it speak for it self. All
the Reason I had to think it no bad Performance, was, that it
was acted eighteen Days running, and that the Party, that were
hurt by it (as I have been told) have not been the smallest Number of my back Friends ever since. But happy was it for this
Play, that the very Subject was its Protection; a few Smiles of
silent Contempt were the utmost Disgrace, that on the first Day
of its Appearance it was thought safe to throw upon it; as the
Satire was chiefly employ'd on the Enemies of the Government,
10 they were not so hardy, as to own themselves such, by any
higher Disapprobation, or Resentment. But as it was then probable I might write again, they knew it would not be long before they might with more Security give a Loose to their Spleen,
and make up Accounts with me. And to do them Justice, in
every Play I afterwards produced, they paid me the Balance, to
a Tittle. But to none was I more beholden, than that celebrated
Author Mr. *Mist*, whose *Weekly Journal*, for about fifteen Years
following scarce ever fail'd of passing some of his Party Compliments upon me: The State, and the Stage were his frequent
20 Parallels, and the Minister, and *Minheer Keiber* the Menager,
were as constantly droll'd upon: Now, for my own Part, though
I could never persuade my Wit to have an open Account with
him (for as he had no Effects of his own, I did not think myself oblig'd to answer his Bills) Notwithstanding, I will be so
charitable to his real *Manes*, and to the Ashes of his Paper, as
to mention one particular Civility, he paid to my Memory, after
he thought he had ingeniously kill'd me. Soon after the *Non-
juror* had receiv'd the Favour of the Town, I read, in one of
his Journals, the following short Paragraph, *viz. Yesterday died*
30 Mr. Colley Cibber, *late Comedian of the Theatre-Royal, notorious
for writing the* Nonjuror. The Compliment, in the latter part,
I confess, I did not dislike, because it came from so impartial a
Judge: and it really so happen'd, that the former part of it was
very near being true; for I had that very Day just crawled out,

4. the Play of the *Orphan*] This must have been 23 March 1717, for which the cast was not announced. On 2 February Cibber is listed for the Chaplain (Avery, II, 434, 442). Cibber had last been listed 1 March so he must have been ill between 1 and 23 March.

24. the *Provok'd Husband*] 10 January 1728. Avery (II, 954) quotes parallel accounts of the first night.

after having been some Weeks laid up by a Fever: However,
I saw no use, in being thought to be thoroughly dead, before
my Time, and therefore had a mind to see, whether the Town
cared to have me alive again: So the Play of the *Orphan* being
to be acted that Day, I quietly stole myself into the Part of the
Chaplain, which I had not been seen in, for many Years before.
The Surprize of the Audience at my unexpected Appearance on
the very Day, I had been dead in the News, and the Paleness of
my Looks, seem'd to make it a Doubt, whether I was not the
10 Ghost, of my real Self departed: But when I spoke, their Wonder eas'd itself by an Applause; which convinc'd me, they were
then satisfied, that my Friend *Mist* had told a *Fib* of me. Now,
if simply to have shewn myself in broad Life, and about my
Business, after he had *notoriously* reported me dead, can be called
a Reply, it was the only one, which his Paper, while alive, ever
drew from me. How far I may be vain, then, in supposing
that this Play brought me into the Disfavour of so many Wits,
and valiant Auditors, as afterwards appear'd against me, let those
who may think it worth their Notice, judge. In the meantime,
20 till I can find a better Excuse for their, sometimes particular,
Treatment of me, I cannot easily give up my Suspicion: And if
I add a more remarkable Fact, that afterwards confirm'd me in
it, perhaps it may incline others to join in my Opinion.

On the first Day of the *Provok'd Husband*, ten Years after the
Nonjuror had appear'd; a powerful Party, not having the Fear
of publick Offence, or private Injury before their Eyes, appear'd
most impetuously concern'd for the Demolition of it; in which
they so far succeeded, that for some Time I gave it up for lost;
and to follow their Blows, in the publick Papers of the next
30 Day, it was attack'd, and triumph'd over, as a dead, and damn'd
Piece; a swinging Criticism was made upon it, in general invective Terms, for they disdain'd to trouble the World with Particulars; their Sentence, it seems, was Proof enough of its de-
serving the Fate it had met with. But this damn'd Play was,

notwithstanding, acted twenty-eight Nights together, and left
off, at a Receipt of upwards of a hundred and forty Pounds,
which happen'd to be more, than in fifty Years before, could be
then said, of any one Play whatsoever.

Now, if such notable Behavior could break out upon so successful a Play (which too, upon the Share Sir *John Vanbrugh*
had in it, I will venture to call a good one) what shall we impute it to? Why may not I plainly say, it was not the Play, but
Me, who had a Hand in it, they did not like? And for what
10 Reason? if they were not asham'd of it, why did not they publish it? No! the Reason had publish'd itself, I was the Author
of the *Nonjuror*! but, perhaps, of all Authors, I ought not to
make this sort of Complaint, because I have Reason to think
that that particular Offence has made me more honourable
Friends than Enemies; the latter of which I am not unwilling
should know (however unequal the Merit may be to the Reward)
that Part of the Bread I now eat, was given me, for having writ
the *Nonjuror*.

And yet I cannot but lament with many quiet Spectators, the
20 helpless Misfortune, that has so many Years attended the Stage!
That no Law has had Force enough to give it absolute Protection! for till we can civilize its Auditors, the Authors, that write
for it, will seldom have a greater Call to it, than Necessity; and
how unlikely is the Imagination of the Needy, to inform, or delight the many, in Affluence? or how often does Necessity make
many unhappy Gentlemen turn Authors, in spite of Nature?

What a Blessing, therefore, is it! what an enjoy'd Deliverance! after a Wretch has been driven by Fortune, to stand so
many wanton Buffets of unmanly Fierceness, to find himself at
30 last, quietly lifted above the Reach of them!

But let not this Reflection fall upon my Auditors, without
Distinction; for though Candour, and Benevolence, are silent
Virtues, they are as visible, as the most vociferous Ill-nature; and
I confess, the Publick has given me more frequent Reason to be
thankful, than to complain.

CHAPTER XVI

13. tedious Time of our Tranquility] The period of which Cibber chooses to omit a detailed
account is best filled by Barker, pp. 99 ff.

C H A P. XVI.

The Author steps out of his Way. Pleads his Theatrical Cause,
in Chancery. Carries it. Plays acted at Hampton-Court.
Theatrical Anecdotes in former Reigns. Ministers, and Mena-
gers always censur'd. The Difficulty of supplying the Stage,
with good Actors, consider'd. Courtiers, and Comedians govern'd
by the same Passions. Examples of both. The Author quits the
Stage. Why.

HAVING brought the Government of the Stage
through such various Changes, and Revolutions, to
this settled State, in which it continued to almost
the Time of my leaving it; it cannot be suppos'd,
that a Period of so much Quiet, and so long a
Train of Success, (though happy for those, who enjoy'd it) can
afford such Matter of Surprize, or Amusement, as might arise,
from Times of more Distress, and Disorder. A quiet Time, in
History, like a Calm, in a Voyage, leave us, but in an indolent
10   Station: To talk of our Affairs, when they were no longer
ruffled, by Misfortunes, would be a Picture without Shade, a
flat Performance, at best. As I might, therefore, throw all that
tedious Time of our Tranquillity, into one Chasm, in my History,
and cut my Way short, at once, to my last Exit, from the Stage,
I shall, at least, fill it up with such Matter only, as I have a
Mind should be known, how few soever may have Patience to
read it: Yet, as I despair not of some Readers, who may be
most awake, when they think others have most occasion to
sleep; who may be more pleas'd to find me languid, than live-
20   ly, or in the wrong, than in the right; why should I scruple
(when it is so easy a Matter too) to gratify their particular Taste,

7. pleading his own Theatrical Cause, in a Court of *Chancery*] The lawsuit between Steele and Cibber was initiated 4 September 1725 (for a discussion of the suit, see Loftis, *Steele*, pp. 57-64).

13. with a Man ... in an agreeable Amity] In the years from 1719, when Cibber had been suspended (19 December 1719 until 28 January 1720) through the difficulties of Steele's quarrels with the Lord Chamberlain, then the Duke of Newcastle, there had been friction between the managers and Steele (for an account of this period see Loftis, *Steele*, pp. 118 ff. and Barker, pp. 111 ff.).

22. Sir *Richard*'s totally absenting himself] The actor's deposition of 11 January 1726, in a countersuit to Steele's mentioned above, accused Steele of having totally neglected the affairs of the theater after 28 January 1720.

27. expected to make the Business a *sine Cure*] Loftis cites evidence that Steele may have regarded his position in the theater, even during his first five years of association there, as having no duties. The managers took the position that Steele had recognized his obligations to them during that period and had fulfilled them adequately (Loftis, *Steele*, pp. 55-61).

29. to charge our selves at a Sallary] That is, £5 per day. This deduction, unknown to Steele, began on 28 January 1720. He appears to have agreed to a reduction of the amount ordered paid him after his release from his suspension 2 May 1721; reports of the amount vary from £1200 to £1400. The managers argued that they had lost heavily in the South Sea Bubble and that he had not carried his share of responsibility during this time from January until May (Loftis, *Steele*, pp. 56, 214-15).

by venturing upon any Error, that I like, or the Weakness of
my Judgment misleads me to commit? I think too, I have a
very good Chance, for my Success, in this passive Ambition, by
shewing myself in a Light, I have not been seen in.

By your Leave then, Gentlemen! let the Scene open, and, at
once, discover your Comedian, at the Bar! There you will find
him a Defendant, and pleading his own Theatrical Cause, in a
Court of *Chancery*: But, as I chuse, to have a Chance of pleasing others, as well as of indulging you, Gentlemen; I must first
10 beg leave, to open my Case to them; after which, my whole
Speech, upon that Occasion, shall be at your Mercy.

In all the Transactions of Life, there cannot be a more painful Circumstance, than a Dispute at Law, with a Man, with
whom we have long liv'd, in an agreeable Amity: But when
Sir *Richard Steele*, to get himself out of Difficulties, was oblig'd
to throw his Affairs, into the Hands of Lawyers, and Trustees,
that Consideration, then, would be of no weight: The Friend,
or the Gentleman, had no more to do in the Matter! Thus,
while Sir *Richard* no longer acted, from himself, it may be no
20 Wonder, if a Flaw was found in our Conduct, for the Law to
make Work with. It must be observ'd then, that about two,
or three Years, before this Suit was commenc'd, upon Sir *Richard's*
totally absenting himself, from all Care, and Menagement of the
Stage (which by our Articles of Partnership he was equally, and
jointly oblig'd with us, to attend) we were reduc'd to let him
know, that we could not go on, at that Rate; but that if he
expected to make the business a *sine Cure*, we had as much Reason to expect a Consideration for our extraordinary Care of it;
and that during his Absence, we therefore intended to charge
30 our selves at a Sallary of 1 *l*. I3 s. 4 *d* every acting Day (unless
he could shew us Cause, to the contrary) for our Menagement:
To which, in his compos'd manner, he only answer'd; That
to be sure, we knew what was fitter to be done, than he did;
that he had always taken a Delight, in making us easy, and

5. an Attendance, which he was now grown weary of] After his suspension, Steele's health was poor (Loftis, *Steele*, p. 56).

17. before the late Sir *Joseph Jekyll* ... in the Year 1726] The hearing was held 7 February 1728. Loftis (*Steele*, p. 229) cites PRO C 38/394 and Aitken, *Life*, II, 316-17. Sir Joseph Jekyll (1663-1738) was an ardent Whig who was noted for his probity and willingness to vote against his party when he felt bound by conscience to do so; cf. Pope, *Epilogue to the Satires, Dialogue* I, lines 37-40 and n.

had no Reason to doubt of our doing him Justice. Now whether, under this easy Stile of Approbation, he conceal'd any Dislike of our Resolution, I cannot say. But, if I may speak my
private Opinion, I really believe, from his natural Negligence of
his Affairs, he was glad, at any rate, to be excus'd an Attendance, which he was now grown weary of. But whether I am
deceiv'd, or right in my Opinion, the Fact was truly this, that
he never once, directly, nor indirectly, complain'd, or objected
to our being paid the above-mention'd daily Sum, in near three
10 Years together; and yet still continued to absent himself from
us, and our Affairs. But notwithstanding, he had seen, and done
all this with his Eyes open; his Lawyer thoughts here was still a
fair Field, for a Battle, in Chancery, in which, though his Client
might be beaten, he was sure his Bill must be paid for it: Accordingly, to work with us he went. But not to be so long, as
the Lawyers were in bringing this Cause to an Issue, I shall, at
once, let you know, that it came to a hearing, before the late
Sir *Joseph Jekyll*, then Master of the Rolls, in the Year 1726.
Now, as the chief Point, in dispute, was of what Kind, or Im-
20 portance, the Business of a Menager was, or in what it principally consisted; it could not be suppos'd, that the most learned
Council could be so well appris'd of the Nature of it, as one,
who had himself gone through the Care, and Fatigue of it. I
was therefore encourag'd by our Council, to speak to that particular Head myself; which I confess I was glad he suffer'd me
to undertake; but when I tell you, that two of the learned
Council against us, came, afterwards, to be successively Lord
Chancellors, it sets my Presumption in a Light, that I still tremble to shew it in: But however, not to assume more Merit, from
30 its Success, than was really its Due, I ought fairly to let you
know, that I was not so hardy, as to deliver my Pleading without Notes, in my Hand, of the Heads I intended to enlarge upon; for though I thought I could conquer my Fear, I could not
be so sure of my Memory: But when it came to the critical

23. the Words of the Assignment] The managers, in their deposition (PRO C 11/2416/49, cited by Loftis, *Steele*, p. 58), had made this same assertion. 'The Assignment' was the distribution of the rights of the patent; cf. Chapter XV. Steele had not been expected to perform the same functions as the others, but to write plays and to help in matters of publicity (Loftis, *Steele*, pp. 213-15).

Moment, the Dread, and Apprehension of what I had undertaken, so disconcerted my Courage, that though I had been us'd
to talk to above Fifty Thousand different People every Winter,
for upwards of Thirty Years together; an involuntary, and un-
affected Proof of my Confusion, fell from my Eyes; and, as I
found myself quite out of my Element, I seem'd rather gasping
for Life, than in a condition to cope with the eminent Orators,
against me. But however, I soon found, from the favourable
Attention of my Hearers, that my Diffidence had done me no
10 Disservice: And as the Truth, I was to speak to, needed no
Ornament of Words, I delivered it, in the plain manner following, *viz.*

In this Cause, Sir, I humbly conceive, there are but two
Points, that admit of any material Dispute. The first is, Whether Sir *Richard Steele*, is as much oblig'd to do the Duty, and
Business of a Menager, as either *Wilks, Booth,* or *Cibber*: And
the second is, Whether, by Sir *Richard's* totally withdrawing
himself from the Business of a Menager, the Defendants are justifiable, in charging to each of themselves the 1 *l.* I3 s. 4 *d. per*
20 *Diem,* for their particular Pains, and Care, in carrying on the
whole Affairs of the Stage, without any Assistance from Sir *Richard Steele.*

As to the First, if I don't mistake the Words of the Assignment, there is a Clause in it, that says, All Matters relating to
the Government, or Menagement of the Theatre, shall be concluded by a Majority of Voices. Now I presume, Sir, there is
no room left to alledge, that Sir *Richard* was ever refus'd his
Voice, though in above three Years, he never desired, to give it:
And I believe there will be as little room to say, that he could
30 have a Voice, if he were not a Menager. But, Sir, his being a
Menager is so self-evident, that it seems amazing how he could
conceive, that he was to take the Profits, and Advantages of a
Menager, without doing the Duty of it. And I will be bold
to say, Sir, that his Assignment of the Patent, to *Wilks, Booth,*

1.31 it seems] it is 2nd ed.

16. Sir *Richard* ... was often in want of Mony] Loftis comments, "He was grossly irresponsible in financial affairs—the multitudinous contemporary allusions to his prodigality and incapacity for practical business leave no doubt that he was a trying man to his creditors" (*Steele*, pp. 91-98, *et passim*). In 1716 he was forced to mortgage his share of the patent; creditors claimed his considerable income from the company, possibly, as Cibber suggests, before it was actually due. These difficulties, Loftis concludes, contributed to his neglect of his duties as manager.

29. He made an Assignment of his Share] A reference to Steele's preparations in 1724 for retirement and payment of his debts with his income from the theater; David Scurlock, a relation of his wife's, was named his trustee and was authorized to examine the account books of Drury Lane. The managers, in resisting the transference of his share of the patent, based their case on an agreement of 19 September 1721, which stated that no one of the partners would sell his share without consent from all the others. Steele had ignored this in making his assignment to Scurlock on 3 June 1724; and since the earlier agreement had not been registered until after the transfer was registered, it was not held legally binding (Loftis, *Steele*, pp. 224-25).

and *Cibber*, in no one Part of it, by the severest Construction in
the World, can be wrested to throw the heavy Burthen of the
Menagement only upon their Shoulders. Nor does it appear,
Sir, that either in his Bill, or in his Answer to our Cross-Bill, he
has offer'd, any Hint, or Glimpse of a Reason, for his withdrawing from the Menagement, at all; or so much as pretend,
from the Time complained of, that he ever took the least part
of his Share of it. Now, Sir, however unaccountable this Conduct of Sir *Richard* may seem, we will still allow, that he had
10 some Cause for it; but whether or no, that Cause, was a reasonable one, your Honour will the better judge, if I may be indulg'd
in the Liberty of explaining it.

Sir, the Case, in plain Truth and Reality, stands thus: Sir *Ri-*
chard, though no Man alive can write better of Oeconomy than
himself, yet, perhaps, he is above the Drudgery of practising it:
Sir *Richard*, then, was often in want of Mony; and while we
were in Friendship with him, we often assisted his Occasions:
But those Compliances had so unfortunate an Effect, that they
only heightened his Importunity, to borrow more, and the more
20 we lent, the less he minded us, or shew'd any Concern for our
Welfare. Upon this, Sir, we stopt our Hands, at once, and peremptorily refus'd to advance another Shilling, 'till by the Balance of our Accounts, it became due to him. And this Treatment (though we hope, not in the least unjustifiable) we have
reason to believe so ruffled his Temper, that he at once, was as
short with us, as we had been with him; for from that Day he
never more came near us: Nay, Sir, he not only continued to
neglect, what he *should* have done, but actually did what he
ought *not* to have done: He made an Assignment of his Share
30 without our Consent, in a manifest Breach of our Agreement:
For, Sir, we did not lay that Restriction upon ourselves, for no
Reason: We knew, before-hand, what trouble, and Inconvenience it would be, to unravel, and expose our Accounts to
Strangers, who if they were to do us no hurt, by divulging our

1.21 Upon this, Sir,] Upon this, Si, 1st ed.

Secrets, we were sure could do us no good, by keeping them.
If Sir *Richard* had had our common Interest at heart, he would
have been as warm in it, as we were, and as tender of hurting
it: But supposing his assigning his Share to others, may have
done us no great Injury, it is at least, a shrewd Proof, that he
did not care whether it did us any, or no. And if the Clause
was not strong enough to restrain him from it, in Law, there
was enough in it, to have restrain'd him, in Honour, from breaking it. But take it, in its best Light, it shews him as remiss a
10 Menager, in our Affairs, as he naturally was in his own. Suppose, Sir, we had all been as careless as himself, which I can't
find he has any more Right to be, than we have, must not our
whole Affair have fallen to Ruin? And may we not, by a pa-
rity of Reason suppose, that by his Neglect a fourth Part of it
does fall to Ruin? But, Sir, there is a particular Reason to believe, that, from our want of Sir *Richard*, more, than a fourth
Part *does* suffer by it: His Rank, and Figure, in the World,
while he gave us the Assistance of them, were of extraordinary
Service to us: He had an easier Access, and a more regarded
20 Audience at Court, than our low Station of Life could pretend
to, when our Interest wanted (as it often did) a particular Soli-
citation there. But since we have been depriv'd of him, the very End, the very Consideration of his Share in our Profits, is
not perform'd on his Part. And will Sir *Richard*, then, make
us no Compensation, for so valuable a Loss, in our Interests, and
so palpable an Addition to our Labour? I am afraid, Sir, if we
were all to be as indolent, in the Menaging-Part, as Sir *Richard*
presumes he has a Right to be; our Patent would soon run us,
as many Hundreds, in Debt, as he has had (and still seems wil-
30 ling to have) his Share of, for doing of nothing.

Sir, our next Point, in question, is whether *Wilks, Booth,*
and *Cibber,* are justifiable, in charging the *1 1. I3 s. 4 d. per*
diem, for their extraordinary Menagement, in the Absence of
Sir *Richard Steele*. I doubt, Sir, it will be hard to come to the

1.29 as he has had] as he had 2nd ed.

2. necessary Business, and Duty of a Menager] Steele, in his suit in 1725, denied having
   promised to attend meetings or to instruct young actors, but the actor-managers insisted in
   their cross-action that he had accepted specific duties and had performed them until January
   1720 (PRO, C 11/2416/49, cited by Loftis, *Steele*, pp. 57-59).

Solution of this Point, unless we may be a little indulg'd, in setting forth, what is the daily, and necessary Business, and Duty
of a Menager. But, Sir, we will endeavour to be as short, as
the Circumstances will admit of.

Sir, by our Books, it is apparent, that the Menagers have under their Care, no less than One Hundred, and Forty Persons, in
constant, daily Pay: And among such Numbers, it will be no
wonder, if a great many of them are unskilful, idle, and sometimes untractable; all which Tempers are to be led, or driven,
10 watch'd, and restrain'd by the continual Skill, Care, and Patience of the Menagers. Every Menager, is oblig'd, in his turn,
to attend two, or three Hours every Morning, at the Rehearsal
of Plays, and other Entertainments for the Stage, or else every
Rehearsal would be but a rude Meeting of Mirth and Jollity.
The same Attendance, is as necessary at every Play, during the
time of its publick Action, in which one, or more of us, have
constantly been punctual, whether we have had any part, in the
Play, then acted, or not. A Menager ought to be at the Reading of every new Play, when it is first offer'd to the Stage, tho'
20 there are seldom one of those Plays in twenty, which upon
hearing, proves to be fit for it, and upon such Occasions the
Attendance must be allow'd, to be as painfully tedious, as the
getting rid of the Authors of such Plays, must be disagreeable,
and difficult. Besides this, Sir, a Menager is to order all new
Cloaths, to assist in the Fancy, and Propriety of them, to limit
the Expence, and to withstand the unreasonable Importunities of
some, that are apt to think themselves injur'd, if they are not
finer than their Fellows. A Menager, is to direct and oversee
the Painters, Machinists, Musicians, Singers, and Dancers; to
30 have an Eye upon the Door-keepers, Under-Servants, and Officers,
that without such care, are too often apt to defraud us, or neglect
their Duty.

And all this, Sir, and more, much more, which we hope will
be needless to trouble you with, have we done every Day, with-

6. confessing, in the Dedication of a Play] This was the dedication to Steele of *Ximena*: or, *The Heroic Daughter*, dated 29 September 1719.

out the least Assistance from Sir *Richard*, even at times when
the Concern, and Labour of our Parts, upon the Stage, have
made it very difficult, and irksome to go thro' with it.

In this Place, Sir, it may be worth observing, that Sir *Richard*, in his Answer to our Cross-Bill, seems to value himself
upon *Cibber's* confessing, in the Dedication of a Play, which he
made to Sir *Richard*, that he (Sir *Richard*) had done the Stage
very considerable Service, by leading the Town to our Plays,
and filling our Houses, by the Force and Influence of his *Tat-*
10 *lers*. But Sir *Richard* forgets, that those *Tatlers* were written in
the late Queen's Reign, long before he was admitted to a Share
in the Playhouse: And in truth, Sir, it was our real Sense of
those Obligations, and Sir *Richard's* assuring us they should be
continued, that first and chiefly inclin'd us to invite him to share
the Profits of our Labours, upon such farther Conditions, as in
his Assignment of the Patent to us, are specified. And, Sir, as
Cibber's publick Acknowledgment of those Favours is at the
same time an equal Proof of Sir *Richard's Power* to continue
them; so Sir, we hope, it carries an equal Probability, that
20 without his Promise to *use* that Power, he would never have been
thought on, much less have been invited by us, into a Joint-
Menagement of the Stage, and into a Share of the Profits:
And indeed what Pretence could he have form'd, for asking a
Patent from the Crown, had he been possess'd of no eminent
Qualities, but in common with other Men? But, Sir, all these
Advantages, all these Hopes, nay Certainties of greater Profits,
from those great Qualities, have we been utterly depriv'd of by
the wilful, and unexpected Neglect of Sir *Richard*. But we
find, Sir, it is a common thing, in the Practice of Mankind, to
30 justify one Error, by committing another: For Sir *Richard* has
not only refus'd us the extraordinary Assistance, which he is able
and bound to give us; but on the contrary, to our great Expence, and loss of Time, now calls us to account, in this Honourable court, for the Wrong we have done him, in not doing

2. He has not writ Plays for us, for *Nothing*] Steele acknowledged making £329/5s. from his benefits on *The Conscious Lovers*, first performed 7 November 1722, in addition to his share of the profits (PRO, c11/2416/49, cited by Loftis, *Steele*, p. 194).

5. in writing that Play, he had more Assistance from one of the Menagers] Steele thanked Cibber in the preface to the play for his alterations and for directing the rehearsals. Later he claimed that Cibber's changes were damaging. It is possible that the subplot was added because Cibber thought the play too serious (Barker, p. 115).

13. they have all of them been able to do … as profitable a thing] Steele estimated the company's income from the play to have been £2,536/3/6 (PRO, C 11/2416/49, cited by Loftis, *Steele*, p. 193); it ran eighteen days and possibly might have run longer (*St. James's Journal*, 8 December 1722, cited by Loftis, *Steele*, p. 193). The pantomime representation of the coronation of Ann Boleyn in Act IV of *Henry VIII*, drawing on interest in the coronation of George II, was first performed 26 October 1727. After a panic on the first night caused by a false alarm of fire (Avery, II, 940), the coronation proved enormously successful and the show was extended to include "The Ceremony of the Champion in Westminster Hall." In the *First Epistle of the Second Book of Horace Imitated*, Pope satirizes the use of historical armor which the players borrowed from the Tower:

> The Play stands still; damn action and discourse,
> Back fly the scenes, and enter foot and horse;
> Pageants on pageants, in long order drawn,
> Peers, Heralds, Bishops, Ermin, Gold, and Lawn;
> The Champion too! and, to complete the jest,
> Old Edward's Armour beams on Cibber's breast!
> (314-19)

These pageants, later detached from the play and acted as afterpieces, were performed about seventy times before the end of the season (Barker, pp. 140-41).

his Business of a Menager, for nothing. But, Sir, Sir *Richard* has
not met with such Treatment from us: He has not writ Plays
for us, for *Nothing*, we paid him very well, and in an extraordinary manner, for his late Comedy of the *Conscious Lovers*:
And though, in writing that Play, he had more Assistance from
one of the Menagers, than becomes me to enlarge upon, of
which Evidence has been given upon Oath, by several of our
Actors; yet, Sir, he was allow'd the full, and particular Profits
of that Play, as an Author, which amounted to Three Hundred
10 Pounds, besides about Three Hundred more, which he receiv'd
as a Joint-Sharer of the general Profits, that arose from it. Now,
Sir, though the Menagers are not all of them able to write Plays,
yet they have all of them been able to do (I won't say, as good,
but at least) as profitable a thing. They have invented, and
adorn'd a Spectacle, that for forty Days together has brought
more Mony, to the House, than the best Play that ever was writ.
The Spectacle I mean, Sir, is that of the Coronation-Ceremony
of *Anna Bullen*: And though we allow a good Play to be the
more laudable Performance, yet, Sir, in the profitable Part of
20 it, there is no Comparison. If therefore, our Spectacle brought
in as much, or more Mony, than Sir *Richard's* Comedy, what
is there, on his side but Usage, that intitles him, to be paid for
one, more, than we are, for t'other? But then, Sir, if he is so
profitably distinguish'd for his Play, if we yield him up the Preference, and pay him, for his extraordinary Composition, and
take nothing for our own, tho' it turn'd out more to our common Profit; sure, Sir, while we do such extraordinary Duty, as
Menagers, and while he neglects his Share of that Duty, he cannot grudge us the moderate Demand we make for our separate
30 Labour?

     To conclude, Sir, if by our constant Attendance, our Care,
our Anxiety (not to mention the disagreeable Contests, we sometimes meet with, both within, and without Doors, in the Menagement of our Theatre) we have not only sav'd the whole

12. we were allow'd the Sums, in dispute] Steele did manage finally to collect £1061/17/2 as his share of the back profits, though it went to Scurlock as his trustee; the court allowed the actor-managers their expenses and the extra compensation they claimed (Loftis, *Steele*, p. 229).

31. Great old Hall at *Hampton-Court*] Early in the century a rumor had circulated that a theater for the entertainment of royalty would be built at Hampton Court; it is possible that alterations were performed on the Great Hall in 1702 and 1715. The Drury Lane company did perform there on 23 September 1718 and six times thereafter. Their expenses of £374/1/8 were greater than at Drury Lane, and the King contributed £200 to make up the difference (Avery, I, xxxiv-xxxv).

from Ruin, which, if we had all follow'd Sir *Richard's* Example, could not have been avoided; I say, Sir, if we have still
made it so valuable an Income to him, without his giving us the
least Assistance for several Years past; we hope, Sir, that the poor
Labourers, that have done all this for Sir *Richard*, will not be
thought unworthy of their Hire.

How far our Affairs, being set in this particular Light, might
assist our Cause, may be of no great Importance to guess; but
the Issue of it was this: That Sir *Richard* not having made any
10 Objection, to what we had charg'd for Menagement, for three
Years together; and as our Proceedings had been all transacted,
in open Day, without any clandestine Intention of Fraud; we
were allow'd the Sums, in dispute, above-mention'd; and Sir *Richard* not being advis'd, to appeal to the Lord-Chancellor, both
Parties paid their own Costs, and thought it their mutual Interest,
to let this be the last of their Law-suits.

And now, gentle Reader, I ask Pardon, for so long an Imposition on your Patience: For though I may have no ill Opinion
of this Matter myself; yet to you, I can very easily conceive it
20 may have been tedious. You are therefore, at your own Liberty
of charging the whole Impertinence of it, either to the Weakness of my Judgment, or the Strength of my Vanity; and I will
so far join in your Censure, that I farther confess, I have been so
impatient to give it you, that you have had it, out of its turn:
For, some Years, before this Suit was commenc'd, there were
other Facts, that ought to have had a Precedence in my History:
But that, I dare say, is an Oversight you will easily excuse, provided you afterwards find them worth reading. However, as to
that Point, I must take my chance, and shall therefore proceed
30 to speak of the Theatre, which was order'd by his late Majesty
to be erected in the Great old Hall at *Hampton-Court*; where
Plays were intended to have been acted twice a Week, during
the Summer-Season. But before the Theatre could be finish'd,
above half the Month of *September* being elaps'd, there were but

5. In former Reigns, Theatrical Entertainments at the Royal Palaces] For an account of Jacobean and Caroline Masques, see Allardyce Nicoll, *Stuart Masques and the Renaissance Stage* (1937); Percy Simpson and C. F. Bell, *Designs by Ingo Jones for Masques and Plays at Court* (Oxford, 1924).

10. the *Musaeum* of our greatest Master, and Patron of Arts] The Earl of Burlington, who published *The Designs of Inigo Jones*, in 1727. He was very important in forwarding English Palladian architecture; cf. Pope, "Epistle to Burlington," lines 191-204.

14. after the Restoration of *Charles* II. some Faint Attempts] For an account of Masques at this period, see Eleanore Boswell, *The Restoration Court Stage* (Cambridge, Mass., 1932), pp. 134 ff., *et passim*; she disputes Cibber's dating and argues that masques, if defined broadly, had been given earlier, almost certainly in 1670-71 (p. 138). She deals with *Calisto*, first performed in 1675, in great detail (pp. 175 ff.).

19. For what reason *Crown* was chosen] Boswell (*Restoration Court Stage*, p. 179) maintains the choice was due to Rochester, who at this time was feuding with Dryden. Dryden, as Poet Laureate, would ordinarily be expected to provide court entertainments. Rochester also wished to snub Settle, the other likely candidate, and decided on Crowne partly as a jest.

22. Offence the then Duke of *Buckingham ... Zimri*] *Absalom and Achitophel* was written in 1681, *Calisto* in 1675.

24. a Return, to his Grace's *Drawcansir*] Bayes, not Drawcansir, is the satiric model of Dryden in *The Rehearsal*; Cibber is correct, however, in suggesting that Dryden's *Zimri* provided a counterthrust at Buckingham (see *The Poetical Works of Dryden*, ed. George M. Noyes, pp. xxviii, xliii-xliv).

28. *Windsor ...* they acted in St. *George's* Hall] Boswell (*Restoration Court Stage*, pp. 59-62) provides details of the hall and the alterations made on it to permit performances by Scaramouche in 1674; it proved unsuitable for further performances and in 1683 other arrangements had to be made there. Cf. Leslie Hotson, pp. 12 ff.

seven Plays acted before the Court return'd to *London*. This
throwing open a Theatre, in a Royal Palace, seem'd to be reviving the Old *English* hospitable Grandeur, where the lowest
Rank of neighboring subjects might make themselves merry at
Court, without being laugh'd at themselves. In former Reigns,
Theatrical Entertainments at the Royal Palaces, had been perform'd at vast Expence, as appears by the Description of the
Decorations, in several of *Ben. Johnson's* Masques, in King *James,*
and *Charles the First's* time; many curious, and original Draughts
10 of which, by Sir *Inigo Jones*, I have seen, in the *Museum* of
our greatest Master, and Patron of Arts, and Architecture, whom
it would be a needless Liberty to name. But when our Civil
Wars ended in the Decadence of Monarchy, it was then an Honour to the Stage, to have fallen with it: Yet, after the Restoration of *Charles II.* some faint Attempts were made to revive
these Theatrical Spectacles at court; but I have met with no
Account of above one Masque acted there, by the Nobility;
which was that of *Calisto*, written by *Crown*, the Author of
Sir *Courtly Nice*. For what Reason *Crown* was chosen to that
20 Honour, rather than *Dryden*, who was then Poet-Laureat, and
out of all comparison his Superior, in Poetry, may seem surprizing: But if we consider the Offence which the then Duke of
Buckingham took at the Character of *Zimri*, in Dryden's *Absalom*, &c. (which might probably be a Return, to his Grace's
Drawcansir in the *Rehearsal*) we may suppose the Prejudice
and Recommendation of so illustrious a Pretender to Poetry,
might prevail, at Court, to give *Crown* this Preference. In the
same Reign, the King had his Comedians at *Windsor*, but upon a particular Establishment; for tho' they acted in St. *George's*
30 Hall, within the Royal Palace yet (as I have been inform'd by
an Eye-witness) they were permitted to take Mony at the Door,
of ever Spectator; whether this was an Indulgence, in Conscience, I cannot say; but it was a common Report among the
principle Actors, when I first came into the *Theatre-Royal*, in

1. due to the Company, from that Court] The acting companies did at times have trouble collecting for court performances, but there are numerous records of payments to acting companies (see Appendix D of Boswell's *Restoration Court Stage* and pp. 170-74).

8. old Solemn *Boman*, the late Actor of venerable Memory] Lowe (II, 211) notes that Boman (or Bowman), who died 23 March 1739 [this section of the *Apology* must have been written after that date], had acted for a period of about sixty-five years from 1673 until very near his death (cf. Davies, *Dram. Misc.*, I, 286; II, 100).

24. the reverend Historian of his *Own Time*] Bishop Burnet's anecdotal *History of His Own Time*: Vol. I *From the Restoration of King Charles II To the Settlement of King William and Queen Mary at the Revolution* ... (London: Printed for Thomas Ward, 1724). Vol. II appeared in 1734.

26. *indiscreetest ... in a Court]* Burnet, I, 263; the passage reads: "The Duke of *Buckingham* ... broke with [the Duchess of York] and studied to take the King from her by new amours: And because he thought a gaity of humour would take much with the King, he engaged him to entertain two players one after another, *Davies* and *Gwin* [sic]. The first did not keep her hold long: but Gwin, the indiscreetest and wildest creature that was ever in a Court, continued to the end of the King's life in great Favour, and was maintained at a vast expence [sic] ... She acted all persons in so lively a manner, and was such a constant diversion to the King, that even a new mistriss [sic] could not drive her away. But after all he had never treated her with the decencies of a mistriss [sic]."

1690, that there was then, due to the Company, from that Court,
about One Thousand Five Hundred Pounds, for Plays commanded, &c. and yet it was the general Complaint, in that
Prince's Reign, that he paid too much Ready-mony, for his
Pleasures: But these Assertions I only give, as I receiv'd them,
without being answerable, for their Reality. This Theatrical
Anecdote, however, puts me in mind of one of a more private
nature, which I had from old solemn *Boman*, the late Actor of
venerable Memory. *Boman*, then a Youth, and fam'd for his
10 Voice, was appointed to sing some Part, in a Concert of Musick
at the private Lodgings of Mrs. *Gwin*; at which were only present, the King, the Duke of *York*, and one, or two more, who
were usually admitted upon those detached Parties of Pleasure.
When the Performance was ended, the King express'd himself
highly pleas'd, and gave it extraordinary Commendations: Then,
Sir, said the Lady, to shew you don't speak like a Courtier, I
hope you will make the Performers a handsom Present: The
King said, he had no Mony about him, and ask'd the Duke if
he had any? To which the Duke reply'd, I believe, Sir, not
20 above a Guinea, or two. Upon which the laughing Lady, turning to the People about her, and making bold with the King's
common Expression, cry'd, *Od's Fish! What Company am I
got into!*

Whether the reverend Historian of his *Own Time*, among the
many other Reasons of the same Kind, he might have for sti-
ling this Fair One the *indescreetest, and wildest Creature, that
ever was in a Court,* might know This to be one of them, I
can't say: But if we consider her, in all the Disadvantages of
her Rank, and Education, she does not appear to have had any
30 criminal Errors more remarkable, than her Sex's Frailty to answer for: And, if the same Author, in his latter end of that
Prince's Life, seems to reproach his Memory, with too kind a
Concern for her Support, we may allow, that it becomes a Bishop
to have had no Eyes, or Taste for the frivolous Charms or play-

11. the same Author, in the same Page, 263,] Cibber refers to the first edition, actually pp. 263-64; the passage begins, "The King had another mistriss [sic], that was managed by Lord *Shaftsbury* [sic], who was the daughter of a Clergyman, *Roberts*, ..." The remainder of his quotation is accurate apart from variants of capitalization and spelling.

22. Mitred Historian] Gilbert Burnet, Bishop of Salisbury in 1689, was intimately involved in the political intrigues of the court in the last decades of the seventeenth century, and appears to have learned the "Personal Secrets" he recounts at first hand; for example, phrases like "The Duke of *Buckingham* told me" (I, 263) abound.

ful *Badinage* of the Kings' Mistress: Yet, if the common Fame
of her may be believ'd which in my Memory was not doubted,
she had less to be laid, to her Charge, than any other of those
Ladies, who were in the same State of Preferment: She never
meddled in Matters of serious Moment, or was the Tool of
working Politicians: Never broke into those amorous Infidelities,
which others, in that grave Author are accus'd of; but was as
visibly distinguish'd, by her particular Personal Inclination to the
King, as her Rivals were, by their Titles, and Grandeur. Give
10 me leave to carry (perhaps, the Partiality of) my Observation a
little farther. The same Author, in the same Page, 263, tells
us, that, " Another of the King's Mistresses, the Daughter of
" a Clergyman, Mrs. *Roberts,* in whom her first Education had so
" deep a Root, that tho' she fell into many scandalous Disorders,
" with very dismal Adventures in them all, yet a Principle of
" Religion was so deep laid in her, that tho' it did not restrain
" her, yet it kept alive in her, such a constant Horror of Sin, that
" she was never easy, in an ill course, and died with a great
" Sense of her former ill Life.
20   To all this let us give an implicit Credit: Here is the Account
of a frail Sinner made up, with a Reverend Witness! Yet I cannot but lament, that this Mitred Historian, who seems to know
more Personal Secrets, than any that ever writ before him, should
not have been as inquisitive after the last Hours of our other Fair
Offender, whose Repentance I have been unquestionably inform'd, appear'd in all the contrite Symptoms of a Christian Sincerity. If therefore you find I am so much concern'd to make
this favourable mention of the one, because she was a Sister of
the *Theatre,* why may not---But I dare not be so presumptuous,
30 so uncharitably bold, as to suppose the other was spoken better
of, merely because she was the Daughter of a *Clergyman.* Well,
and what then? What's all this idle Prate, you may say, to the
matter in hand? Why, I say your Question is a little too critical; and if you won't give an Author leave, now and then, to

embellish his Work, by a natural Reflexion, you are an ungentle
Reader. But I have done with my Digression, and return to
our Theatre at *Hampton-Court*, where I am not sure the Reader,
be he ever so wise, will meet with any thing more worth his
notice: However, if he happens to read, as I write, for want
of something better to do, he will go on; and perhaps, wonder
when I tell him, that.

    A Play presented at Court, or acted on a publick Stage, seem
to their different Auditors, a different Entertainment. Now hear
10 my Reason for it. In the common Theatre, the Guests are at
home, where the politer Forms of Good-breeding are not so nicely regarded: Every one there, falls to, and likes or finds fault,
according to his natural Taste, or Appetite. At Court, where
the Prince gives the Treat, and honours the Table with his own
Presence, the Audience is under the Restraint of a Circle, where
Laughter, or Applause, rais'd higher than a Whisper, would be
star'd at. At a publick Play the are both let loose, even 'till
the Actor is, sometimes, pleas'd with his not being able to be
heard, for the Clamour of them. But this coldness or Decency
20 of Attention, at Court, I observ'd had but a melancholy Effect,
upon the impatient Vanity of some of our Actors, who seem'd
inconsolable, when their flashy Endeavours to please had pass'd
unheeded: Their not considering where they were, quite disconcerted them; nor could they recover their Spirits, 'till from the
lowest Rank of the Audience, some gaping *John* or *Joan*, in
the fullness of their Hearts, roar'd out their Approbation: And
indeed, such a natural Instance of honest Simplicity, a Prince
himself, whose Indulgence knows where to make Allowances,
might reasonably smile at, and perhaps not think it the worst
30 part of his Entertainment. Yet it must be own'd, that an Audience may be as well too much reserv'd, as too profuse of their
Applause: For though, it is possible a *Betterton* would not have
been discourag'd, from throwing out an Excellence, or elated
into an Error, by his Auditors being too little, or too much

1.22 had pass'd] had pass 2nd ed.

18. In *Shakespear's Harry the Eighth*] The passage cited is Act I, ii, 102-8. The play was
    performed at Hampton Court, October 1718; the role of Wolsey was a specialty of Cibber's,
    upon which Davies comments (*Dram. Misc.*, I, 351), "Colley Cibber has been much praised
    for his assuming port, pride, and dignity in Wolsey; but his manner was not correspondent to
    the grandeur of the character." Later (I, 365) he records, "Wolsey's filching from his royal
    master the honour, of bestowing grace and pardon on the subject, appeared so gross and
    impudent a prevarication, that, when this play was acted before George I, at Hampton-Court,
    about the year 1717, the courtiers laughed so loudly at this ministerial craft, that his majesty,
    who was unacquainted with the English language, asked the lord-chamberlain the meaning of
    their mirth; upon being informed of it, the king joined in a laugh of approbation."

pleas'd, yet as Actors of his Judgment are Rarities; those of less
Judgment may sink into a Flatness, in their Performance, for
want of that Applause, which from the generality of Judges,
they might perhaps, have some Pretence to: And the Auditor,
when not seeming to feel what ought to affect him, may rob
himself of something more, that he might have had, by giving
the Actor his Due, who measures out his Power to please, according to Value he sets upon his Hearer's Taste, or Capacity.
But however, as we were not, here, itinerant Adventurers, and
10 had properly but one Royal Auditor to please; after that Honour was attain'd to, the rest of our Ambition had little to look
after: And that the King was often pleas'd, we were not only
assur'd, by those who had the Honour to be near him; but
could see it, from the frequent Satisfaction in his Looks at particular Scenes, and Passages: One Instance of which I am
tempted to relate, because it was at a Speech, that might more
naturally affect a Sovereign Prince, than any private Spectator.
In *Shakespear*'s *Harry the Eighth;* that King commands the
Cardinal to write circular Letters of Indeminity, into every Coun-
20 ty, where the Payment of certain heavy Taxes had been disputed: Upon which the Cardinal whispers the following Directions
to his Secretary *Cromwell*:

> -------- *A Word with you:*
> *Let there be Letters writ to every Shire,*
> *Of the King's Grace, and Pardon: The griev'd Commons*
> *Hardly conceive of me. Let it be nois'd,*
> *That through our Intercession, this Revokement,*
> *And Pardon comes. ---I shall anon advise you*
> *Farther, in the Proceeding ------*

30 The Solicitude of this Spiritual Minister, in filching from his
Master the Grace, and Merit of a good Action, and dressing up
himself in it, while himself had been Author of the Evil complain'd of, was so easy a Stroke of his Temporal Conscience,

8. his Majesty's particular Taste for it] George I saw *Henry VIII* 1 October 1718 and 6 April 1719 by command, and it possibly was scheduled for 20 April 1719 by command, but the king was unable to attend, so *All for Love* was performed instead (Avery, II, 507, 534, 536).

27. stated Fee, for a Play acted, at *Whitehall*] In the Restoration period, for performances at court and when both the king and queen were present at the Theatre Royal the fee appears to have been £20, but when only one of them was present at the theater the fee appears frequently to have been £10 (Nicoll, I, 343-52, lists the warrants for payment, and notes, pp. 8-9, that Charles was slow to pay).

That it seem'd to raise the King into something more than a
Smile, whenever that Play came before him: And I had a more
distinct Occasion, to observe this Effect; because my proper
Stand on the Stage, when I spoke the Lines, required me to be
near the Box, where the King usually sate. In a Word, this
Play is so true a Dramatick Chronicle of an old *English* Court,
and where the Character of *Harry the Eighth* is so exactly drawn,
even to a humorous Likeness, that it may be no wonder why his
Majesty's particular Taste for it, should have commanded it three
10 several times in one Winter.

This too calls to my Memory an extravagant Pleasantry of
Sir *Richard Steele*, who being ask'd by a grave Nobleman, after
the same Play had been presented at *Hampton-Court*, how the
King lik'd it; reply'd, *So terribly well, my Lord, that I was
afraid I should have lost all my Actors! For I was not sure, the
King would not keep them to fill the Posts at Court, that he saw
them so fit for in the Play.*

It may be imagin'd, that giving Plays to the People at such a
distince from *London*, could not but be attended with an extra-
20 ordinary Expence; and it was some Difficulty, when they were
first talk'd of, to bring them under a moderate Sum; I shall
therefore, in as few Words, as possible, give a Particular of
what Establishment they were then brought to, that in case the
same Entertainments, should at any time hereafter be call'd to the
same Place, future Courts may judge, how far the Precedent may
stand good, or need an Alteration.

Though the stated Fee, for a Play acted, at *Whitehall* had
been formerly, but Twenty Pounds; yet, as that hinder'd not the
Company's acting on the same Day, at the Publick Theatre,
30 that Sum was almost all clear Profits to them: But this Circumstance not being practicable, when they were commanded to
Hampton-Court, a new, and extraordinary Charge was unavoidable: The Menagers, therefore, not to inflame it, desired no

10. the Expense of every Play amounted to Fifty Pounds] That is, to a total of £374/1/8. The warrant for payment is dated 15 November 1718 (Lowe, II, 219).

33. Entertainment of the *Duke of Lorrain*] This visit occurred in 1730-31.

Consideration, for their own Labour, farther than the Honour of
being employ'd, in his Majesty's Commands; had, if the other
Actors might be allow'd, each their Days Pay, and travelling
Charges, they should hold themselves ready, to act any Play,
there, at a Day's Warning: And that the Trouble might be less,
by being divided, the Lord-Chamberlain was pleas'd to let us
know, that the Household-Musick, the Wax Lights, and a *Chaise-
Marine*, to carry our moving Wardrobe to every different Play,
should be under the Charge of the proper Officers. Notwith-
10 standing these Assistances, the Expence of every Play amounted
to Fifty Pounds: Which Account, when all was over, was not
only allow'd us, but his Majesty was graciously pleas'd to give
the Menagers Two Hundred Pounds more, for their particular
Performance, and Trouble, in only seven times acting. Which
last Sum, tho' it might not be too much, for a Sovereign Prince
to give, it was certainly more than our utmost Merit ought to
have hop'd for: And I confess, when I receiv'd the Order for
the Mony, from his Grace the Duke of *Newcastle*, then Lord-
Chamberlain, I was so surpris'd, that I imagin'd his Grace's Fa-
20 vour, or Recommendation of our Readiness, or Diligence, must
have contributed to so high a Consideration of it, and was offering my Acknowledgments, as I thought them due; but was
soon stopt short, by his Grace's Declaration, That we had no Obligations for it, but to the King himself, who had given it, from
no other Motive, than his own Bounty. Now whether we may
suppose that Cardinal *Wolsey* (as you see *Shakespear* has drawn him)
would silently have taken such low Acknowledgments to himself,
perhaps may be as little worth consideration, as my mentioning
this Circumstance has been necessary: But if it is due to the
30 Honour and Integrity of the (then) Lord-Chamberlain, I cannot
think it wholly impertinent.

Since that time, there has been but one Play given at *Hampton-Court*, which was for the Entertainment of the Duke of *Lor-*

20. *Justement, comme chez nous*!] "Precisely, the same as ourselves." No source located.

rain; and for which his present Majesty was pleas'd to order us
a Hundred Pounds.

The Reader may, now, plainly see, that I am ransacking my
Memory, for such remaining Scraps of Theatrical History, as
may not, perhaps, be worth his Notice: But if they are such as
tempt me to write them, why may I not hope, that in this wide
World, there may be many an idle Soul, no wiser than myself,
who may be equally tempted to read them?

I have so often had occasion to compare the State of the State
10 to the State of a Nation, that I yet feel a Reluctancy to drop
the Comparison, or speak of the one, without some Application
to the other. How many Reigns, then, do I remember, from
that of *Charles* the Second, through all which, there has been,
from one half of the People, or the other, a Succession of Clamour, against every different Ministry for the Time being? And
yet, let the Cause of this Clamour have been never so well
grounded, it is impossible, but that some of those Ministers must
have been wiser, and honester Men, than others: If this be true,
as true, I believe it is, why may I not then say, as some Fool
20 in a *French* Play does, upon a like Occasion---*Justement, comme
chez nous!* 'Twas exactly the same with our Menagement! let
us have done never so well, we could not please every body: All
I can say, in our Defence is, that though many good Judges,
might possible conceive how the State of the Stage might have
been mended, yet the best of them never pretended to remember the Time when it was better! or could shew us the way to
make their imaginary Amendments practicable.

For though I have often allow'd, that our best Merit, as Actors, was never equal to that of our Predecessors, yet I will ven-
30 ture to say, that in all its Branches, the Stage had never been under so just, so prosperous, and so settled a Regulation, for forty
Years before, as it was at the Time I am speaking of. The most
plausible Objection to our Administration, seem'd to be, that we

1. no Care to breed up young Actors] The old actor-managers retained control of the major roles in Drury Lane until death or retirement. The lack of excellent young actors, as a result, persisted until Garrick and his generation filled the gap. Cf. Barker, pp. 165 ff. and 201 ff.

took no Care to breed up young Actors, to succeed us; and
this was imputed as the greater Fault, because it was taken for
granted, that it was a Matter as easy as planting so many Cab-
bages: Now might not a Court be as well reproach'd, for not
breeding up a Succession of complete Ministers? And yet it is
evident, that if Providence, or Nature don't supply us with
both, the State, and the Stage will be but poorly supported. If
a Man of an ample Fortune, should take it into his Head, to
give a younger Son an extraordinary Allowance, in order to breed
10 him a great Poet, what might we suppose would be the Odds,
that his Trouble, and Mony would be all thrown away? Not
more, than it would be, against the Master of a Theatre, who
should say, this, or that young Man, I will take care shall be
an excellent Actor! Let it be our Excuse then, for that mistaken
Charge against us; that since there was no Garden, or Market,
where accomplish'd Actors grew, or were to be sold, we could
only pick them up, as we do Pebbles of Value, by Chance: We
may polish a thousand, before we find one, fit to make a Figure, in the Lid of a Snuff-Box. And how few soever we were
20 able to produce, it is no Proof, that we were not always in
search of them: Yet, at worst, it was allow'd, that our Defi-
ciency of Men Actors, was not so visible, as our Scarcity of
tollerable Women: But when it is consider'd, that the Life of
Youth and Beauty is too short for the bringing an Actress to
her Perfection; were I to mention too, the many frail fair Ones,
I remember, who, before they could arrive to their Theatrical
Maturity, were feloniously stolen from the Tree, it would rather
be thought our Misfortune, than our Fault, that we were not
better provided.
30   Even the Laws of a Nunnery, we find, are thought no sufficient Security against Temptations, without iron Grates, and
high Walls to inforce them; which the Architecture of a
Theatre will not so properly admit of: And yet, methinks

1.27 stolen] stoln 1st ed.

26. *Pierre*, in *Venice Preserv'd*] In a performance at the Haymarket Theatre, 9 May 1707,

Verbruggen played Pierre; in the next performance, the following season, 15 November

1707, Mills had the part (Avery, I, 147 and 150; also cf. above, Chapter XII). Davies (*Dram.

Misc.*, III, 252-53) discusses this circumstance, but supposes it to have occurred after Booth

had become a sharer; as he relates it (giving Victor as the source), Booth wished to take Mill's

role as Pierre, but Wilks grew angry and gave him his own role as Jaffeir instead. Even this

date is not accurate, for Wilks' name appears as Jaffeir for the last time on 16 January 1711,

though several subsequent performances list no casts, and Booth appears as Jaffeir 13 May

1713 (Avery, I, 240, 302). The conflict must have occurred, if at all, between these dates.

Beauty that has not those artificial Fortresses about it, that has
no Defence but its natural Virtue (which upon the Stage has
more than once been met with) makes a much more merito-
rious Figure, in Life, than that immur'd Virtue, which could
never be try'd. But alas! as the poor Stage, is but the Show-
glass to a Toy-shop, we must not wonder, if now and then,
some of the Bawbles should find a Purchaser.

However, as to say more, or less than Truth, are equally un-
faithful in an Historian; I cannot but own, that in the Govern-
10 ment of the Theatre, I have known many Instances, where the
Merit of promising Actors has not always been brought forward,
with the Regard, or Favour, it had a Claim to: And if I put
my Reader in mind, that in the early Part of this Work, I have
shewn, through what continued Difficulties, and Discouragements
I myself made my way up the Hill of Preferment; he may justly
call it, too strong a Glare of my Vanity: I am afraid he is in
the right; but I pretend not to be one of those chaste Authors,
that know how to write without it: When Truth is to be told
it may be as much Chance, as Choice, if it happens to turn out
20 in my favour: But to shew that this was true of others, as well
as myself, *Booth* shall be another Instance. In 1707, when
Swiney was the only Master of the Company in the *Hay-Market*;
Wilks, though he was, then, but an hired Actor himself, rather
chose to govern, and give Orders, than to receive them; and
was so jealous of *Booth*'s rising, that, with a high Hand, he
gave the Part of *Pierre*, in *Venice Preserv'd*, to *Mills* the elder,
who (not to undervalue him) was out of Sight, in the Pretensions
that *Booth*, then young, as he was, had to the same Part: And
this very Discouragement so strongly affected him, that not long
30 after, when several of us became Sharers with *Swiney*, *Booth* rather chose to risque his Fortune, with the old Patentee in *Drury-
Lane*, than come into our Interest, where he saw he was like to
meet with more of those Partialities. And yet again, *Booth* him-

5. How many white Staffs] The emblem of a member of the privy counsel.

23. *'Tis an ill Bird that* ...] Possibly a confused version of Thomas Heywood's "An ill winde that Bloweth no man to good" (*Proverbes*, Part II, Ch. VII); version with *bird* unknown.

self, when he came to be a Menager, would sometimes suffer
his Judgment to be blinded by his Inclination to Actors, whom
the Town seem'd to have but an indifferent Opinion of. This
again, inclines me to ask another of my odd Questions, *viz.* Have
we never seen the same Passions govern a Court! How many
white Staffs, and great Places do we find, in our Histories, have
been laid at the Feet of a Monarch, because they chose not to
give way to a Rival, in Power, or hold a second Place in his
Favour? How many *Whigs*, and *Tories* have chang'd their Parties,
10 when their good or bad Pretensions have met with a Check to
their higher Preferment?

Thus, we see, let the Degrees, the Rank of Men, be ever
so unequal, Nature throws out their Passions, from the same
Motives; 'tis not the Eminence, or Lowliness of either, that
when provok'd, more or less a reasonable creature than the other:
makes the one: when provok'd, more or less a reasonable creature than the other: The Courtier, and the Comedian, when
their Ambition is out of Humour, take just the same Measures
to right themselves.

If this familiar Stile of talking should, in the Nostrils of Gra-
20 vity, and Wisdom, smell a little too much of the Presumptuous,
or the Pragmatical, I will, at least, descend lower, in my Apology for it, by calling to my Assistance the old, humble Pro-
verb, *viz. 'Tis an ill Bird that,* &c. Why then should I debase
my Profession, by setting it in vulgar Lights, when I may shew
it to more favourable Advantages? And when I speak of our
Errors, why may I not extenuate them by illustrious Examples?
or by not allowing them greater, than the greatest Men have
been subject to? Or why, indeed, may I not suppose, that a sensible Reader will rather laugh, than look grave, at the Pomp of
30 my Parallels?

Now, as I am tied down to the Veracity of an Historian,
whose Facts cannot be supposed, like those in a Romance, to
be in the Choice of the Author, to make them more marvellous,

1.6 Staffs] Saffs 2nd ed.

26. Though *Wilks* had more Industry] Davies (*Dram. Misc.*, III, 255-56) makes a strangely
contradictory statement about Cibber's and Wilks' relations; after recounting the anecdote (cf.
Apology, p. 325 n.) of Booth's unsuccessful attempt to take the role of Pierre from Mills, he
says Booth suppressed his anger, because he "knew that Cibber would espouse the cause of
Wilks on all occasions; for, however Colley may complain, in his *Apology*, of Wilks's fire
and impetuosity, he, in general, was Cibber's great admirer; he supported him on all
occasions, where his own passion of interest did not interpose; nay, he deprived the
inoffensive Harry Carey of the liberty of the scenes, because he had, in common with others,
made merry with Cibber in a song, on his being appointed poet laureat, saying ... he was
surprised at his impertinence, in behaving so improperly to *a man of such great merit.*"
Davies then gives other evidence of Booth's dislike for Wilks. These anecdotes, even though
ostensibly in defense of Wilks, confirm Cibber's view that Wilks was extremely trying to
work with.

18. the Water-gruel Work of some insipid Author] Lowe (II, 226) quotes John Dennis'
advertisement to *The Invader of his Country:* "I am perfectly satisfied that any author who
brings a Play to *Drury Lane*, must, if 'tis a good one, he sacrificed to the Jealousie of this fine
Writer [Cibber], unless he either has a powerful Cabal, or unless he will flatter Mr. *Robert
Wilks*, and make him believe he is an excellent tragedian."

24. But the *Tempest* having done Wonders formerly] It had last played 10 July 1710 with
Elrington as Ferdinand; this revival took place 7 January 1712, "With new Scenes, Machines,
and all the Original Decorations proper to the Play," (Avery, I, 266) and it was performed
eleven times that season; the cast was never listed.

by Invention, if I should happen to sink into a little farther Insignificancy, let the simple Truth of what I have farther to say,
be my Excuse for it. I am oblig'd, therefore, to make the Experiment, by shewing you the Conduct of our Theatrical ministry in such Lights, as on various Occasions it appear'd in.

    Though *Wilks* had more Industry, and Application, than any
Actor I had ever known, yet we found it possible that those
necessary Qualities might sometimes be so misconducted, as not
only to make them useless, but hurtful to our Common-wealth;
10 for while he was impatient to be foremost, in every thing, he
frequently shock'd the honest Ambition of others, whose Measures might have been more serviceable, could his Jealousy have
given way to them. His own Regards for himself, therefore,
were, to avoid a disagreeable Dispute with him, too often comply'd with: But this leaving his Diligence, to his own Conduct,
made us, in some Instances, pay dearly for it: For Example; he
would take as much, or more Pains in forwarding to the Stage,
the Water-gruel Work of some insipid Author, that happen'd
rightly to make his Court to him, than he would for the best
20 Play, wherein it was not his Fortune to be chosen for the best
Character. So great was his Impatience to be employ'd, that I
scarce remember, in twnety Years, above one profitable Play,
we could get to be reviv'd, wherein he found he was to make
no considerable Figure, independent of him: But the *Tempest*
having done Wonders formerly, he could not form any Pretensions, to let it lie longer dormant: However, his Coldness to
it was so visible, that he took all Occasions to postpone, and
discourage its Progress, by frequently taking up the morning
Stage with something more in his Mind. Having been myself
30 particularly sollicitous for the reviving this Play, *Dogget* (for this
was before *Booth* came into the Mengagement) consented that the
extraordinary Decorations, and Habits, should be left to my Care,
and Direction, as the fittest Person, whose Temper could jossle

through the petulant Opposition, that he knew *Wilks* would be
always offering to it, because he had but a middling Part in it,
that of *Ferdinand*: Notwithstanding which, so it happen'd,
that the Success of it shew'd (not to take from the Merit of
Wilks) that it was possible to have good Audiences, without
his extraordinary Assistance. In the first six Days of acting it,
we paid all our constant, adn incidental Expence, and shar'd
each of us a hundred Pounds: The greatest Profit, that in so
little a Time had yet been known within my Memory! But, alas!
10 what was paltry Pelf, to Glory? That was the darling Passion
of *Wilks*'s Heart! and not to advance in it, was, to so jealous
an Ambition, a painful Retreat, a meer Shade to his Laurels!
and the common Benefit was but a poor Equivalent, to his want
of particular Applause! To conclude, not Prince *Lewis* of *Baden*,
though a Confederate General, with the Duke of *Malborough*,
was more inconsolable, upon the memorable Victory at *Blenheim*,
at which he was not present, than our Theatrical Hero was, to
see any Action prosperous, that he was not himself at the Head
of. If this then was an Infirmity in *Wilks*, why may not my
20 shewing the same Weakness in so great a Man, mollify the Imputation, and keep his Memory in Countenance?

   This laudable Appetite for Fame, in *Wilks*, was not, however,
to be fed, without that constant Labour, which only himself was
able to come up to: He therefore bethought him of the means,
to lessen the Fatigue, and at the same time, to heighten his Reputation; which was by giving up now, and then, a Part to
some raw Actor, who he was sure would disgrace it, and consequently put the Audience in mind of his superior Performance:
Among this sort of Indulgences to young Actors, he happen'd
30 once to make a Mistake, that set his Views in a clear Light. The
best Criticks, I believe, will allow, that in *Shakespear*'s *Macbeth*,
there are in the Part of *Macduff* two Scenes, the one of Terror,
in the second Act; and the other of Compassion, in the fourth,

9. This Part of *Macduff* ... he had given to one *Williams*] Lowe, II, 229: "Charles Williams was a young actor of great promise who died in 1731." It may have been this actor to whom Booth's role of Julio in *The Double Falsehood* was assigned when he became ill, 13 December 1727 (Avery, I, cxxxi, n.).

31. the same Hazard, by any farther Offer to resign it] Elrington played the part 27 November 1718. See *The Tatler*, No. 68, 15 September 1709, for a description of Wilks in this part.

equal to any that dramatick Poetry has produc'd: These Scenes
Wilks had acted with Success, tho' far short of that happier
Skill and Grace, which *Monfort* had formerly shewn, in them.
Such a Part, however, one might imagine would be one of the
last, a good Actor would chuse to part with: But *Wilks* was of
a different Opinion; for *Macbeth* was thrice as long, had more
great Scenes of Action, and bore the Name of the Play: Now,
to be a second in any Play, was what he did not much care for,
and had been seldom us'd to: This Part of *Macduff*, therefore,
10 he had given to one *Williams*, as yet no extraordinary, though
a promising Actor. *Williams*, in the Simplicity of his Heart,
immediately told *Booth*, what a Favour *Wilks* had done him.
Booth, as he had Reason, thought *Wilks* had here carried his
Indulgence, and his Authority, a little too far; for as *Booth* had
no better a Part, in the same Play, than that of *Banquo*, he found
himself too much disregarded, in letting so young an Actor take
Place of him: *Booth*, therefore, who knew the Value of *Macduff*, proposed to do it himself, and to give *Banquo* to *Williams*;
and to make him farther amends, offer'd him any other of his
20 Parts, that he thought might be of Service to him. *Williams*
was content with the Exchange, and thankful for the Promise.
This Scheme, indeed, (had it taken Effect) might have been an
Ease to *Wilks*, and possibly no Disadvantage to the Play; but
softly---That was not quite what we had a Mind to! No sooner
then, came this Proposal to *Wilks*, but off went the Masque,
and out came the Secret! For though *Wilks* wanted to be eas'd
of the Part, he did not desire to be *excell'd* in it; and as he
was not sure but that might be the case, if *Booth* were to act
it, he wisely retracted his own Project, took *Macduff* again to
30 himself, and while he liv'd, never had a Thought of running
the same Hazard, by any farther Offer to resign it.

Here, I confess, I am at a Loss for a Fact in History, to
which this can be a Parallel! To be weary of a Post, even to

a real Desire of resigning it; and yet to chuse, rather to
drudge on in it, than suffer it to be well supplied (though to
share in that Advantage) is a Delicacy of Ambition, that *Machiavil* himself has made no mention of: Or if in old *Rome*,
the Jealousy of any pretended Patriot, equally inclin'd to ab-
dicate his Office, may have come up to it; 'tis more than my
reading remembers.

As nothing can be more impertinent, than shewing too frequent a Fear, to be thought so, I will, without farther Apology,
10 rather risque that Imputation, than not tell you another Story
much to the same purpose, and of no more consequence than
my last. To make you understand it however, a little Preface will
be necessary.

If the Merit of an Actor (as it certainly does) consists more in
the Quality, than the Quantity of his Labour; the other Menagers had no visible Reason to think, this needless Ambition of
Wilks, in being so often, and sometimes so unnecessarily employ'd, gave him any Title to a Superiority; especially when our
Articles of Agreement, had allow'd us all to be equal. But what
20 are narrow Contracts to great Souls with growing Desires. *Wilks*
therefore, who thought himself lessen'd, in appealing to any
Judgment, but his own, plainly discovered, by his restless Behaviour (though he did not care to speak out) that he thought he
had a Right to some higher Consideration, for his Performance:
This was often *Booth*'s Opinion, as well as my own. It must be
farther observ'd, that he actually had a separate Allowance of
Fifty Pounds a Year, for writing our daily Play-Bills, for the
Printer: Which Province, to say the Truth, was the only one
we car'd to trust to his particular Intendance, or could find out
30 for a Pretence to distinguish him. But, to speak a plainer Truth,
this Pension, which was no part of our original Agreement, was
merely paid to keep him quiet, and not that we thought it due
to so insignificant a Charge, as what a Prompter had formerly

15. to revive the *Provok'd Wife*] 11 January 1726, advertised as "Revis'd by the Author."
    Regularly acted at Lincoln's Inn Fields, the most recent performance had been on 22 April
    1724; Drury Lane's most recent production had been in March 1706. The allusion is to
    Jeremy Collier's attacks which had taken special note of Vanbrugh; Davies (*Dram. Misc.*, III,
    456) gives Cibber credit for persuading Vanbrugh to make the changes.

24. he clapt the same Debauchee] Sir John Brute.

executed. This being really the Case, his frequent Complaints
of being a Drudge to the Company, grew something more, than
disagreeable to us: For we could not digest the Imposition of a
Man's setting himself to work, and then bringing in his own
Bill for it. *Booth*, therefore, who was less easy, than I was, to
see him so often setting a Merit upon this Quantity of his Labour, which neither could be our Interest, or his own, to lay
upon him; proposed to me, that we might remove this pretended Grievance, by reviving some Play, that might be likely to
10 live, and be easily acted, without *Wilks* having any Part in it.
About this time, an unexpected Occasion offer'd itself, to put our
Project, in practice: What follow'd our Attempt, will be all (if
any thing be) worth Observation, in my story.

In 1725, we were call'd upon, in a manner, that could not be
resisted, to revive the *Provok'd Wife*, a Comedy, which, while
we found our Account, in keeping the Stage clear of those loose
Liberties, it had formerly, too justly been charg'd with; we had
laid aside, for some Years. The Author, Sir *John Vanbrugh*,
who was conscious of what it had too much of, was prevail'd
20 upon, to substitute a new-written Scene in the Place of one, in
the fourth Act, where the Wantonness of his Wit, and Humour,
had (originally) made a Rake talk like a Rake, in the borrow'd
Habit of a Clergyman: To avoid which Offence, he clapt the
same Debauchee, into the Undress of a Woman of Quality:
Now the Character, and Profession of a Fine Lady, not being
so indelibly sacred as that of a Churchman; whatever Follies
he expos'd, in the Petticoat, kept him, at least clear of his former Prophaneness, and were now innocently ridiculous, to the
Spectator.
30   This Play being thus refitted for the Stage, was, as I have observed, call'd for, from Court, and by many of the Nobility.
Now, then, we thought was a proper time to come to an Explanation with *Wilks*: Accordingly, when the Actors were sum-

25. he could stand upon his own Bottom] Bottom: "That on which anything is built or rests; the foundation." *OED*

mon'd to hear the Play read, and receive their Parts; I address'd
myself to *Wilks*, before them all, and told him, That as the
Part of *Constant*, which he seem'd to chuse, was a Character
of less Action, than he generally appear'd in, we thought this
might be a good Occasion to ease himself, by giving it to another.---Here he look'd grave.---That the Love-Scenes of it were
rather serious, than gay, or humourous, and therefore might fit
very well upon *Booth*.---Down dropt his Brow, and furl'd were
his Features.---That if we were never to revive a tolerable Play,
10 without him, what would become of us, in case of his Indispo-
sition?---Here he pretended to stir the Fire.---That as he could
have no farther Advantage, or Advancement, in his Station to
hope for, his acting in this Play was but giving himself an unprofitable trouble, which neither *Booth*, or I, desired to impose
upon him.---Softly.---Now the Pill began to gripe him.---In a
Word, this provoking Civility, plung'd him into a Passion,
which he was no longer able to contain; out it came, with all
the Equipage of unlimited Language, that on such Occasions his
Displeasure usually set out with; but when his Reply was stript
20 of those Ornaments, it was plainly this: That he look'd upon
all I had said, as a concerted Design, not only to signalize our
selves, by laying him aside; but a Contrivance to draw him into
the Disfavour of the Nobility, by making it suppos'd his own
Choice, that he did not act in a Play so particularly ask'd for;
but we should find, he could stand upon his own Bottom, and
it was not all our little caballing should get our Ends of him:
To which I answer'd with some Warmth, That he was mistaken
in our Ends; for Those, Sir, said I, you have answer'd already,
by shewing the Company, you cannot bear to be left out of any
30 Play. Are not you ever Day complaining of your being over-
labour'd? And now, upon our first offering to ease you, you fly
into a Passion, and pretend to make that a greater Grievance,
than t'other: But, Sir, if your being In, or Out of the Play, is

a Hardship, you shall impose it upon yourself: The Part is in
your Hand, and to us, it is a Matter of Indifference now, whether you take it, or leave it. Upon this he threw down the Part
upon the Table, cross'd his Arms, and sate knocking his Heel,
upon the Floor, as seeming to threaten most, when he said least;
but when no body persuaded him to take it up again, *Booth,* not
chusing to push the matter too far, but rather to split the difference of our Dispute, said, That for his Part, he saw no such
great matter in acting every Day; for he believed it the whol-
10 somest Exercise in the World; it kept the Spirits in motion, and
always gave him a good Stomach. Tho' this was, in a manner,
giving up the Part to *Wilks,* yet it did not allow, he did us any
Favour in receiving it. Here, I observ'd Mrs. *Oldfield* began to
titter, behind her Fan: But *Wilks* being more intent, upon what
Booth had said, reply'd, Every one could best feel for himself
but he did not pretend to the Strength of a Pack-horse; therefore
if Mrs. *Oldfield* would chuse any body else to play with her, he
should be very glad to be excus'd: This throwing the Negative
upon Mrs. *Oldfield,* was, indeed, a sure way to save himself;
20 which I could not help taking notice of, by saying, It was making
but an ill Compliment, to the Company, to suppose, there was
but one Man in it, fit to play an ordinary Part with her. Here
Mrs. *Oldfield* got up, and turning me half round to come forward, said with her usual Frankness, Pooh! you are all a Parcel
of Fools, to make such a rout about nothing! Rightly judging,
that the Person, most out of humour, would not be more dif-
pleas'd at her calling us all, by the same Name. As she knew,
too, the best way of ending the Debate, would be to help the
Weak; she said, she hop'd Mr. *Wilks* would not so far mind
30 what had past, as to refuse his acting the Part, with her; for
though it might not be so good, as he had been us'd to; yet,
she believed, those who had bespoke the Play, would expect to
have it done to the best Advantage, and it would make but an

2. *Wilks* had the Part] He played Constant, Lady Brute's lover; Cibber, Sir John Brute; Booth, Razor; Mrs. Oldfield, Lady Brute (Avery, II, 850).

17. Not even *Betterton*] Cf. Chapter VII.

odd Story abroad, if it were known, there had been any Difficulty in that point among ourselves. To conclude, *Wilks* had the
Part, and we had all we wanted; which was an Occasion to let
him see, that the Accident, or Choice of one Menager's being
more employ'd than another, would never be allow'd a Pretence
for altering our Indentures, or his having an extraordinary
Consideration for it.

However disagreeable it might be, to have this unsociable Temper daily to deal with; yet I cannot but say, that from the same
10 impatient Spirit, that had so often hurt us, we still drew valuable
Advantages: For as *Wilks* seem'd to have no Joy, in Life, beyond his being distinguish'd on the Stage; we were not only
sure of his always doing his best, there, himself,; but of making others more careful, than without the Rod of so irascible a
Temper over them, they would have been. And I much question, if a more temperate, or better Usage of the hired Actors,
could have so effectually kept them to Order. No even *Betterton* (as we have seen) with all his good Sense, his great Fame,
and Experience, could, by being only a quiet Example of In-
20 dustry himself, save his Company from falling, while neither
Gentleness could govern, or the Consideration of their common
Interest reform them. Diligence, with much the inferior Skill,
or Capacity, will beat the best negligent Company, that ever
came upon a Stage. But when a certain dreaming Idleness, or
jolly Negligence of Rehearsals gets into a Body of the Ignorant,
and Incapable (which before *Wilks*) came into *Drury-Lane*,
when *Powell* was at the Head of them, was the Case of that
Company) then, I say, a sensible Spectator might have look'd
upon the fallen Stage, as *Portius* in the Play of *Cato*, does up-
30 on his ruin'd Country, and have lamented it, in (something near)
the same Exclamation, *viz.*

1. *O ye Immortal Bards*! ...] *Cato*, I, i:

> Ye Gods, what Havock does Ambition make
> Among your Works! ...

8. *And murder Plays* ...] "To Mr. Granville, on his Excellent Tragedy Call'd *Heroic Love*"

> And, in despair their empty pit to fill,
> Set up some foreign monster in a bill.
> Thus they job on, still tricking, never thriving,
> And murd'ring plays, which they miscall revising.

(*The Poetical Works of Dryden*, ed. Noyes, p. 734, lines 21-24.)

> -----*O ye Immortal Bards!*
> *What Havock do these Blockheads make among your Works!*
> *How are the boasted Labours of an Age,*
> *Defac'd, and tortur'd, by Ungracious Action?*

Of this wicked Doings, *Dryden* too complains in one of his Prologues, at that time, where speaking of such lewd Actors, he
closes a Couplet with the following Line, *viz.*

> *And murder Plays, which they miscall Reviving.*

The great Share, therefore, that *Wilks*, by his exemplary Dili-
10 gence, and Impatience of Neglect, in others, had in the Refor-
ation of this Evil, ought in Justice to be remember'd; and let
my own Vanity here take Shame, to itself, when I confess, That
had I had half his Application, I still think I might have shewn
myself twice the Actor, that in my highest State of Favour, I
appear'd to be. But, if I have any Excuse for that Neglect (a
Fault, which if I loved not Truth, I need not have mentioned)
it is that so much of my Attention was taken up in an incessant
Labour to guard against our private Animosities, and preserve a
Harmony, in our Menagement, that I hope, and believe, it
20 made ample Amends, for whatever Ommision, my Auditors
might sometimes know it cost me some pains to conceal. But
Nature takes care to bestow her Blessings, with a more equal Hand
than Fortune does, and is seldom known to heap too many upon
one Man: One tolerable Talent, in an Individual, is enough to
preserve him, from being good for nothing; and, if that was not
laid to my Charge, as an Actor, I have in this Light too, less to
complain of, than to be thankful for.

Before I conclude my History, it may be expected, I should
give some further View of these my last Contemporaries of the

29. *Wilks* ... certainly form'd his manner of Acting ... *Monfort*] Lowe (II, 241) notes that since Mountfort was killed in 1692, Wilks would have had to have seen him very early in his career.

31. *Haud passibus aequis*] "Not with equal steps"; *Aeneid*, II, 724: "Non passibus aequis."

Theatre, *Wilks,* and *Booth*, in their different acting Capacities.
If I were to paint them in the Colours they laid upon one another, their Talents would not be shewn with half the Commendation, I am inclin'd to bestow upon them, when they are left
to my own Opinion. But People of the same Profession, are
apt to see themselves, in their own clear Glass of Partiality, and
look upon their Equals through a Mist of Prejudice. It might
be imagin'd too, from the difference of their natural Tempers,
that *Wilks* should have been more blind, to the Excellencies of
10 *Booth*, than *Booth* was to those of *Wilks*; but it was not so:
Wilks would sometimes commend *Booth* to me; but when *Wilks*
excell'd, the other was silent: *Booth* seem'd to think nothing valuable, that was not tragically Great, or Marvellous: Let that
be as true, as it may; yet I have often thought, that from his
having no Taste of Humour himself, he might be too much inclin'd to depreciate the Acting of it in others. The very slight
Opinion, which in private conversation with me, he had of
Wilks's acting Sir *Harry Wildair*, was certainly more, than
could be justified; not only from the general Applause that was
20 against that Opinion (through Applause is not always infallible)
but from the visible Capacity which must be allow'd to an Actor, that could carry such slight Materials to such a height of
Approbation: For though the Character of *Wildair*, scarce in
any one Scene, will stand against a just Criticism; yet in the
Whole, there are so many gay, and false Colours of the fine
Gentleman, that nothing but a Vivacity in the Performance, proportionably extravagant, could have made them so happily glare,
upon a common Audience.

    Wilks, from his first setting out, certainly form'd his manner
30 of Acting, upon the Model of *Monfort*; as *Booth* did his, on
that of *Betterton*. But---*Haud passibus aequis:* I cannot say,
either of them came up to their Original. *Wilks* had not that
easy regulated Behavior, or the harmonious Elocution of the

9. greatest Praises given to *Virgil*] Quintilian, 10.1.86, quoting his teacher Domitius Afer, says, "Secundus est Vergilius, proprior tamen primo quam tertio"; "Vergil is second [to Homer] but nearer first than third."

One, nor *Booth* that conscious Aspect of Intelligence, nor requisite Variation of Voice, that made every Line the Other spoke
seem his own, natural, self-deliver'd Sentiment: Yet there is still
room for great Commendation of Both the first mentioned;
which will not be so much diminish'd, in my having said, they
were only excell'd by such Predecessors, as it will be rais'd, in
venturing to affirm, it will be a longer time, before any Successors will come near them. Thus one of the greatest Praises given
to *Virgil* is, That no Successor in Poetry came so near Him, as
10 He himself did to *Homer*.

　Tho' the Majority of Publick Auditors are but bad Judges of
Theatrical Action, and are often deceiv'd into their Approbation of what has no solid Pretence to it; yet, as there are no
other appointed Judges to appeal to, and as ever single Spectator has a Right to be one of them, their Sentence will be defini-
tive, and the Merit of an Actor must, in some degree, be weigh'd
by it: By this Law then, *Wilks* was pronounc'd an Excellent
Actor; which if the few true Judges did not allow him to be,
they were at least too candid to slight, or discourage him. *Booth*
20 and he were Actors so directly opposite in their Manner, that, if
either of them could have borrow'd a little of the other's Fault,
they would Both have been improv'd by it: If *Wilks* had sometimes too violent a Vivacity; *Booth* as often contented himself
with too grave a Dignity: The Latter seem'd too much to
heave up his Words, as the Other to dart them to the Ear, with
too quick, and sharp a Vehemence: Thus *Wilks* would too frequently break into the Time, and Measure of the Harmony, by
too many spirited Accents, in one Line; and *Booth*, by too solemn a Regard to Harmony, would as often lose the necessary
30 Spirit of it: So that (as I have observ'd) could we have sometimes rais'd the one, and sunk the other; they had both been
nearer to the Mark. Yet this could not be always objected to
them: They had their Intervals of unexceptionable Excellence,

4. highest Advancement, to his acting Cato] That is, his elevation to actor-manager.

33. *Wilks* act *Othello*, and *Booth* the *Earl of Essex*] Wilks first played Othello in England at a benefit for Cibber, who played Iago, on 22 June 1710; *The Tatler* (No. 187, 20 June 1710) notes the interest in seeing "Wilks play a part so very different from what he had ever before appeared in ..." No. 188, 22 June 1710 expresses an interest in contrasting Wilks and Cibber with Betterton and Sandford. Booth acted the part of Essex in Bank's *Unhappy Favorite* at Drury Lane 25 November 1709; it was a specialty of Wilks' (cf. *The Tatler*, No. 14, 12 May 1709, in which the play is damned and Wilks praised; see also *Apology*, pp. 201-2).

that more, than balanc'd their Errors. The Master-piece of
Booth was *Othello:* There, he was most in Character, and
seem'd not more to animate, or please himself, in it, than his
Spectators. 'Tis true he ow'd his last, and highest Advancement, to his acting *Cato:* But it was the Novelty, and critical
Appearance of that Character, that chiefly swell'd the Torrent
of his Applause: For let the Sentiments of a declaiming Patriot
have all the Sublimity, that Poetry can raise them to; let them
be deliver'd too, with the utmost Grace, and Dignity of Elocu-
10 tion, that can recommend them to the Auditor: Yet this is but
one Light, wherein the Excellence of an Actor can shine: But
in *Othello* we may see him, in the Variety of Nature: There the
Actor is carried through the different Accidents of domestick,
Happiness, and Misery, occasionally torn, and tortur'd by the
most distracting Passion, that can raise Terror, or Compassion,
in the Spectator. Such are the Characters, that a Master Actor
would delight in; and therefore in *Othello*, I may safely aver,
that *Booth* shew'd himself thrice the Actor, that he could in *Cato.*
And yet his Merit in acting *Cato* need not be diminish'd by this
20 Comparison.

   Wilks often regretted, that in Tragedy, he had not the full,
and strong Voice of *Booth* to command, and grace his Periods
with: But *Booth* us'd to say, That if his Ear had been equal
to it, *Wilks* had Voice enough to have shewn himself a much
better Tragedian. Now though there might be some Truth in
this; yet these two Actors were of so mixt a Merit, that even,
in Tragedy, the Superiority was not always on the same
side: In Sorrow, Tenderness, or Resignation, *Wilks* plainly had
the Advantage, and seem'd more pathetically to feel, look, and
30 express his Calamity: But, in the more turbulent Transports of
the Heart, *Booth* again bore the Palm, and left all Competitors
behind him. A Fact perhaps will set this Difference, in a
clearer Light. I have formerly seen *Wilks* act *Othello*, and

1.31 and left all] and all 2nd ed.

11. Reception *Wilks* met with in *Hamlet*] Cf. Chapter IV on Betterton and Wilks.

Booth the *Earl of Essex*, in which they both miscarried: Neither the exclamatory Rage, or Jealousy of the one, or the plaintive Distresses of the other, were happily executed, or became either of them; tho' in the contrary Characters, they were both excellent.

When an Actor Becomes, and naturally Looks the Character
he stands in, I have often observ'd it to have had as fortunate
an Effect, and as much recommended him to the Approbation
of the common Auditors, as the most correct, or judicious Ut-
10 terance of the Sentiments: This was strongly visible, in the favourable Reception *Wilks* met with in *Hamlet*, where I own
the Half of what he spoke, was as painful to my Ear, as every
Line, that came from *Betterton* was charming; And yet it
is not impossible, could they have come to a Poll, but
Wilks might have had a Majority of Admirers: However,
such a Division had been no Proof, that the Praeeminence
had not still remain'd in *Betterton*; and if I should add, that
Booth too, was behind *Betterton* in *Othello*, it would be saying no more, than *Booth* himself had Judgment, and Can-
20 dour enough to know, and confess. And if both he, and
Wilks, are allow'd, in the two above-mention'd Characters, a second Place, to so great a Master, as *Betterton*, it will be a Rank
of Praise, that the best Actors, since my Time, might have been
proud of.

I am now come towards the End of that Time, through which
our Affairs had long gone forward in a settled course of Prosperity. From the visible Errors of former Menagements, we
had, at last, found the necessary Means to bring our private
Laws, and Orders, into the general Observance, and Approba-
30 tion of our Society: Diligence, and Neglect, were under an
equal Eye; the one never fail'd of its Reward, and the other,
by being very rarely excus'd, was less frequently committed.
You are now to consider us in our height of Favour, and so

30. *Corelli*, at *Rome*] Archangelo Corelli (1653-1713), Italian violinist and composer; his patron was Cardinal Pietro Ottoboni.

much in fashion, with the Politer part of the Town, that
our House, every *Saturday*, seem'd to be the appointed As-
embly of the First Ladies of Quality: Of this too, the
common Spectators were so well apprized, that for twenty
Years successively, on that Day, we scarce ever fail'd of a
crowded Audience; for which Occasion we particularly reserv'd our best Plays, acted in the best manner we could give
them.

Among our many necessary Reformations; what not a little
10 preserv'd to us the Regard of our Auditors, was the Decency
of our clear Stage; from whence we had now, for many Years
shut out those idle Gentlemen, who seem'd more delighted to
be pretty Objects themselves, than capable of any Pleasure,
from the Play: Who took their daily Stands, where they
might best elbow the Actor, and come in for their Share of
the Auditor's Attention. In many a labour'd Scene of the
warmest Humour, and of the most affecting Passion, have I
seen the best Actors disconcerted, while these buzzing Mus-
catos have been fluttering round their Eyes, and Ears. How
20 was it possible an Actor, so embarrass'd, should keep his
Impatience, from entering into that different Temper which
his personated Character might requre him, to be Master of?

Future Actors may perhaps wish I would set this Grievance,
in a stronger Light; and, to say the truth, where Auditors
are ill-bred, it cannot well be expected, that Actors should
be polite. Let me therefore shew, how far an Artist in any
Science is apt to be hurt by any sort of Inattention to his Performance.

30 While the famous *Corelli*, at *Rome*, was playing some Musical Composition of his own, to a select Company in the private Apartment of his Patron-Cardinal, he observed, in the
height of his Harmony, his Eminence was engaging, in a de-

14. At the Tragedy of *Zaire*] By Voltaire (1732) inspired by *Othello*.

15. the celebrated Mademoiselle *Gossin*] Jeanne Catherine Gaussin, d. 1767, celebrated actress of the *Comedie francaise*, 1731-63, the original Zaire (Lowe, II, 248).

tach'd Conversation; upon which he suddenly stopt short, and
gently laid down his Instrument: The Cardinal, surpriz'd at
the unexpted Cessation, ask'd him, if a String was broke?
To which, *Corelli*, in an honest Conscience of what was due
to his Musick, reply'd, No, Sir, I was only afraid I interrupted Business. His Eminence, who knew that a Genius
could never shew itself to Advantage, where it had not its
proper Regards, took this Reproof in good part, and broke
off his conversation, to hear the whole *Concerto* play'd over
10 again.

Another Story will let us see, what Effect a mistaken Offence of this Kind had upon the *French* Theatre; which was
told me by a Gentleman of the long Robe, then at *Paris*,
and who was himself the innocent Author of it. At the Tragedy of *Zaire*; while the celebrated Mademoiselle *Gossin* was
delivering a Soliloquy, this Gentleman was seized with a
sudden Fit of Coughing, which gave the Actress some Surprize,
and Interruption; and his Fit increasing, she was forced
to stand silent so long, that it drew the Eyes of the uneasy
20 Audience upon him; when a *French* Gentleman leaning forward to him, ask'd him, If this Actress had given him any
particular Offence, that he took so publick an Occasion to resent it? The *English* Gentleman, in the utmost Surprize, assur'd him, So far from it, that he was a particular Admirer of her Performance; that his Malady was his real Misfortune, and if he apprehended any Return of it, he would
rather quit his Seat, than disoblige either the Actress, or the
Audience.

This publick Decency in their Theatre, I have myself seen
30 carried so far, that a Gentleman in their *second Loge*, or
Middle-Gallery, being observ'd to sit forward himself, while a
Lady sate behind him, a loud Number of Voices call'd out
to him, from the Pit, *Place a la Dame! Place a la Dame!* When

1.7 Advantage] Advanrage 1st ed.
1.33 *Place a la Dame! Place a la Dame!*] Place a Dame! Place a Dame! 1st
       ed.

31. *invita Minerva*] "Against the will of Minerva."

the Person so offending, either not apprehending the Meaning of the Clamour, or possibly being some *John Trott*,
who fear'd no man alive, the Noise was continued for several Minutes; nor were the Actors, though ready on the
Stage, suffer'd to begin the Play, till this unbred Person
was laugh'd out of his Seat, and had placed the Lady before
him.

Whether this Politeness, observ'd at Plays, may be owing
to their Clime, their Complexiion, or their Government, is
10 of no great Consequnce; but, if it is to be acquired, methinks it is a pity our accomplish'd Countrymen, who every
Year, import so much of this Nation's gawdy Garniture,
should not, in this long course of our Commerce with them,
have brought over a little of their Theatrical Good-breeding
too.

I have been the more copious upon this Head, that it might
be judged, how much it stood us upon, to have got rid of those
improper Spectators, I have been speaking of: For whatever
Regard we might draw by keeping them, at a Distance, from
20 our Stage, I had observ'd, while they were admitted behind
our Scenes, we but too often shew'd them the wrong Side of
our Tapestry; and that many a tollerable Actor was the
less valued, when it was known, what ordinary Stuff he was
made of.

Among the many more disagreeable Distresses, that are almost unavoidable, in the Government of a Theatre, those we
so often met with from the Persecution of bad Authors, were
what we could never intirely get rid of. But let us state both
our Cases, and then see, where the Justice of the Complaint
30 lies. 'Tis true, when an ingenious Indigent, had taken, perhaps, a whole Summer's Pains, *invitâ Minervâ*, to heap up
a Pile of Poetry, into the Likeness of a Play, and found, at
last, the gay Promise of his Winter's Support, was rejected,

15. when Actors pretended to be Judges of Authors] See Introduction, pp. xv-xxx, on Cibber's treatment of playwrights.

and abortive, a Man almost ought to be a Poet himself, to
be justly sensible of his Distress! Then, indeed, great Allowances ought to be made for the severe Reflections, he might
naturally throw upon those pragmatical Actors, who had no
Sense, or Taste of good Writing. And yet, if his Relief was
only to be had, by his imposing a bad Play upon a good Set
of Actors, methinks the Charity that first looks at home, has
as good an Excuse for its Coldness, as the unhappy Object of it,
had a Plea for his being reliev'd, at their Expence. But im-
10 mediate Want was not always confess'd their Motive for Writing; Fame, Honour, and *Parnassian* Glory had sometimes
taken a romantick Turn in their Heads; and then they gave
themselves the Air of talking to us, in a higher Strain------
Gentlemen were not to be so treated! the Stage was like to be
finely govern'd, when Actors pretended to be Judges of Authors, &c. But dear Gentlemen! if they were good Actors,
why not? How should they have been able to act, or rise to
any Excellence, if you suppos'd them not to feel, or understand what you offer'd them? Would you have reduc'd them,
20 to the meer Mimickry of Parrots, and Monkies, that can only
prate, and play a great many pretty Tricks, without Reflection? Or how are you sure, your Friend, the infallible Judge,
to whom you read your fine Piece, might be sincere in the
Praises he gave it? Or, indeed, might not you have thought
the best Judge a bad one, if he had disliked it? Consider too,
how possible it might be, that a Man of Sense would not care
to tell you a Truth, he was sure you would not believe! And,
if neither *Dryden, Congreve, Steele, Addison*, nor *Farqubar*, (if
you please) ever made any Complaint of their Incapacity to
30 judge, why is the World to believe the Slights you have met
with from them, are either undeserv'd, or particular? Indeed!
indeed, I am not conscious that we ever did you, or any of
your Fraternity the least Injustice! Yet this was not all we had

4. *cout que cout*] "Cost what it may."

6. the Actors were, perhaps, abus'd in a Preface] Cibber is objecting to a general practice of blaming actors for the failure of plays.

16. *became the Mouth of a Man*] *The Man of Mode*: or *Sir Fopling Flutter* (1676) by Sir George Etherege, III, iii: Mrs. Loveit, "Oh, that sound, that sound becomes the mouth of a man of quality!"

to struggle with; to supersede our Right of rejecting, the Recommendation, or rather Imposition of some great Persons (whom
it was not Prudence to disoblige) sometimes came in, with a
high Hand, to support their Pretensions; and then, *cout que
cout* acted it must be! So when the short Life of this wonderful
Nothing was over, the Actors were, perhaps, abus'd in a Preface, for obstructing the Success of it, and the Town publickly
damn'd us, for our private Civility.

I cannot part, with these fine Gentlemen Authors, without
10 mentioning a ridiculous *Disgraccia*, that befell one of them, many
Years ago: This solemn Bard, who, like *Bayes*, only writ for
Fame, and Reputation; on the second Day's publick Triumph
of his Muse, marching in a stately full-bottom'd Perriwig into
the Lobby of the House, with a Lady of Condition in his
Hand, when raising his Voice to the Sir *Fopling* Sound, that
became the Mouth of a Man of Quality, and calling out---Hey!
Box-keeper, where is my Lady such-a-one's Servant, was unfortunately answer'd, by honest *John Trott*, (which then happen'd
to be the Box-keeper's real Name) Sir, we have dismiss'd, there
20 was not Company enough to pay Candles. In which mortal
Astonishment, it may be sufficient to leave him. And yet had
the Actors refus'd this Play, what Resentment might have been
thought too severe for them?

Thus was our Administration often censured for Accidents,
which were not in our Power to prevent: A possible Case, in
the wisest Governments. If therefore some Plays have been preferr'd to the Stage, that were never fit to have been seen there,
let this be our best Excuse for it. And yet, if the Merit of our
rejecting the many bad Plays, that press'd hard upon us, were
30 weigh'd against the few, that were thus imposed upon us, our
Conduct, in general, might have more Amendments of the Stage
to boast of, than Errors to answer for. But it is now Time to
drop the Curtain.

8. Mrs. *Porter* ... was lost to us] The accident occurred in 1731, but she returned to the stage after Cibber's retirement in 1733 (Lowe, II, 254); Scouten shows her not to have been on any roster of actresses during the seasons of 1731-32 and 1734-35; she was listed in all other seasons from 1729-35 (I, *passim*).

11. Death of *Wilks*] 27 September 1732.

30. an Inclination ... to purchase the whole Power of the Patent] The death of Steele in 1729 meant that his patent would expire three years later; the managers, therefore, applied for a new patent in their own names, and it passed the Great Seal in April 1732. Booth sold his share of it for £2500 to John Highmore in July 1732. Wilks retired later the same year, and Cibber retired from the management, assigning his share of the patent to his son Theophilus on 29 October 1732. In 1733 he sold his share, without consulting Theophilus, for 3000 guineas (Barker, pp. 167-70; see his account of these involved negotiations).

During our four last Years, there happen'd so very little unlike what has been said before, that I shall conclude with
barely mentioning those unavoidable Accidents, that drew on
our Dissolution. The first, that for some Years had led the way
to greater, was the continued ill State of Health, that render'd
Booth incapable of appearing on the Stage. The next was the
Death of Mrs. *Oldfield*, which happen'd on the 23d of *October*,
1730. About the same Time too Mrs. *Porter*, then in her
highest Reputation for Tragedy, was lost to us, by the Misfor-
10 tune of a dislocated Limb, from the overturning of a *Chaise*.
And our last Stroke was the Death of *Wilks*, in *September*, the
Year following, 1731.

Notwithstanding such irreparable Losses; whether, when these
favourite Actors, were no more to be had, their Successors
might not be better born with, than they could possibly have
hop'd, while the former were in being; or that the generality
of Spectators, from their want of Taste, were easier to be
pleas'd, than the few that knew better: Or that, at worst, our
Actors were still preferable to any other Company, of the seve-
20 ral, then subsisting: Or to whatever Cause it might be imputed, our Audiences were far less abated, than our Apprehensions had suggested. So that, though it began to grow late
in Life with me; having still Health, and Strength enough,
to have been as useful on the Stage, as ever, I was under no
visible Necessity of quitting it: But so it happen'ed that our surviving Fraternity having got some chimaerical, and as I thought,
unjust Notions into their Heads, which though I knew they
were without much Difficulty to be surmounted; I chose not,
at my time of Day, to enter into new Contentions; and, as
30 I found an Inclination in some of them, to purchase the
whole Power of the Patent into their own Hands; I did my
best, while I staid with them, to make it worth their while
to come up to my Price; and then patiently fold out my

3. What Commotions the Stage fell into the Year following] For an account of this era, see

Barker, pp. 165 ff.; Avery, "Introduction"; Scouten, "Introduction."

Share, to the first Bidder, wishing the Crew, I had left in the
Vessel, a good Voyage.

What Commotions the Stage fell into the Year following,
or from what Provocations, the greatest Part of the Actors
revolted, and set up for themselves, in the little House, in
the *Hay-Market*, lies not within the Promise of my Title-
Page to relate: Or as it might set some Persons living, in a
Light, they possibly might not chuse to be seen in, I will
rather be thankful, for the involuntary Favour they have done
10 me, than trouble the Publick, with private Complaints of
fancied, or real Injuries.

APPENDICES

APPENDIX A

Pope in the Bagnio

From Cibber, *Letter*, pp. 46-49[1]

As to the latter charge, the whore, there indeed I doubt you will have the better of me; for I must own that I believe I know more of *your* whoring than you do of *mine*; because I don't recollect that I ever made you the least confidence of *my* amours, though I have been very near an eyewitness of *yours* ... [Pope] may remember then (or if he won't I will) when Button's Coffeehouse was in vogue, and so long ago as when he had not translated above two or three books of Homer; there was a late young nobleman (as much his lord as mine) who had a good deal of wicked humor, and who, though he was fond of having wits in his company, was not so restrained by his conscience but that he loved to laugh at any merry mischief he could do them; this noble wag, I say, in his usual *gaiete de coeur,* with another gentleman still in being, one evening slyly seduced the celebrated Mr. Pope as a wit and myself as a laugher to a certain house of carnal recreation near the Haymarket, where his Lordship's frolic proposed was to slip his little Homer, as he called him, at a girl of the game, that he might see what sort of figure a man of his size, sobriety, and vigor (in verse) would make when the frail fire of love had got into him; in which he so far succeeded that the smirking damsel who served us tea happened to have charms sufficient to tempt the little tiny manhood of Mr. Pope into the next room with her: at which you may imagine his lordship was in as much joy at what might happen within, as our small friend could probably be in possession of it. But I (forgive me all ye mortified mortals whom his fell satire has since fallen upon) observing he had stayed as long as without hazard of his health he might, I,

---

[1]The capitalization of the original has not been followed.

Pricked to it by foolish honesty of love,

as Shakespeare says, without ceremony threw open the door upon him, where I found this little hasty hero, like a terrible tom-tit, pertly perching upon the mount of love! But such was my surprise, that I fairly laid hold of his heels and actually drew him down safe and sound from his danger. My lord, who stayed tittering without in hopes the sweet mischief he came for would soon have been completed, upon my giving an account of the action within, began to curse and call me an hundred silly puppies for my impertinently spoiling the sport; to which with great gravity I replied, "Pray, my lord, consider what I have done was in regard to the honour of our nation! For would you have had so glorious a work as that of making Homer speak elegant English cut short by laying up our little gentleman of a malady which his thin body might never have been cured of? No, my lord, Homer would have been too serious a sacrifice to our evening merriment." Now as his Homer has since been so happily completed, who can say that the world may not have been obliged to the kindly care of Colley that so great a work ever came to perfection?

APPENDIX B

On Mrs. Oldfield's Acting

(from the preface of *The Provok'd Husband*; or, *A Journey to London*.
by Sir John Vanbrugh and Mr. Cibber. London, Printed for J. Watts,
1734)

But there is no doing Right to Mrs. Oldfield, without putting People in mind of what others, of

great Merit, have wanted to come near her—'Tis not enough to say she *Here Out-did* her usual

Excellence. I might therefore justly leave her to the constant Admiration of those Spectators, who

have the Pleasure of living while She is an Actress. But as this is not the only Time She has been

the Life of what I have given the Publick, so perhaps my saying a little more of so memorable an

Actress, may give this Play a Chance to be read, when the People of this Age shall be

Ancestors————May it therefore give Emulation to our Successors of the Stage, to know, That to

the ending of the Year 1727, a Co-temporary Comedian relates, that Mrs. *Oldfield* was, then, in

her highest Excellence of Action, happy in all the rarely-found Requisites, that meet in one Person

to compleat them for the Stage————She was in Stature just rising to that Height, where the

Graceful can only begin to shew it self; of a lively Aspect, and a Command in her Mien, that like

the principal Figure in the finest Paintings, first seizes, and longest delights the Eye of the

Spectator. Her Voice was sweet, strong, piercing, and melodious: her Pronunciation voluble,

distinct, and musical; and her Emphasis always placed where the Spirit of the Sense, in her

Periods, only demanded it. If She delighted more in the Higher Comick, than the Tragick Strain,

'twas because the last is too often written in a lofty Disregard of Nature. But in Characters of

modern practis'd Life, she found occasions to add the particular Air and Manner which

distinguish'd the different Humours she presented. Whereas in Tragedy, the Manner of Speaking

varies, as little, as the Blank Verse it is written in————She has one peculiar Happiness from

Nature, she Look'd and maintain'd the Agreeable at a time, when other Fine Women only raise

Admirers by their Understanding————The Spectator was always as much informed by her Eyes, as

her Elocution; for the Look is the only Proof that an Actor rightly conceives what he utters, there

being scarce an Instance, where the Eyes do their Part, that the Elocution is known to be faulty.

The Qualities she had *acquired*, were the *Genteel* and the *Elegant*. The one in her Air, and the other in her Dress, never had her Equal on the Stage; and the Ornaments she herself provided, (particularly in the Play) seem'd in all Respects the *Paraphernalia* of a Woman of Quality. And of that Sort were the Characters she chiefly excell'd in; but her natural good Sense, and lively Turn of Conversation made her Way so easy to Ladies of the highest Rank, that it is a less Wonder, if on the Stage she sometimes *was*, what might have become the finest Woman in real Life to have supported.

Theatre-Royal
Jan. 27   C. Cibber
1727/28

APPENDIX C

On Dogget's Contest with the Managers[1]

I   From *Mr. Cibber of Drury Lane*,
by Richard Hindry Barker, pp. 94-96

In the meantime Doggett's attitude remained unchanged [in the matter of admitting Booth to an equal share of the company]. He was a party neither to the humble remonstrance nor to the negotiations with Vanbrugh and Collier, and when the new license was brought to the theatre by Wilks, he refused to admit its authority. "I know there is such a license," he said, "but I will not look at it, or acknowledge it, or have anything directly or indirectly to do with it." In fact—after instructing the treasurer not to pay any bills without his consent—he dropped out of the company and announced that he would hence forth live on his investment. Wilks and Cibber wrote the Lord Chamberlain stating their grievances; Doggett did likewise; and soon there were discussions, meetings between legal advisers, and humble remonstances enough to stagger the whole force of the Royal Household. The Lord Chamberlain was bewildered. He ordered Wilks and Cibber to pay Doggett his share of the profits, ordered Doggett to return to the theatre, ordered the managers to meet and draw up a new set of rules and regulations. But in each case his orders were ignored, and in each case one party or the other drafted a humble remonstrance. [C.11 6/44 and 2342/26; L.C. 7/3; Add. Ms. 38, 607; *Apology*, Chapter XIV]

Quarrels in the theatre nearly always ended in the Court of Chancery, and the Doggett quarrel was no exception. On December 17, 1714, Doggett started an action; on March 5, 1715, his partners started a cross-action; and for two years the complicated case dragged on, principally, it seems, because Cibber, conducting the defense, arranged to protract it as long as possible. I knew, he says in the *Apology*, "we had at our first setting out this advantage of Doggett, that we

---

[1] These materials, though of small intrinsic interest, make clear in detail a struggle which Cibber passes over briefly. They are included because they tend to show how Cibber's sympathies at the time he was writing the *Apology* warped his presentation of events in the past.

had three pockets to support our expense where he had but one. My first direction to our solicitor was to use all possible delay that the law would admit of ..." [in the present edition, pp. 280-81].

At the hearing the Lord Chancellor decided that Doggett was entitled to a share of the profits [at the end of two years of delay]; but clearly the theatre had suffered by his absence and the other managers were also entitled to a special allowance for doing his share of the work. Figures were therefore compiled and computations made, and it was finally discovered, rather surprisingly, that Doggett was actually in debt to the company. The whole account was then for obvious reasons set aside and the other questions at issue were settled as simply as possible. The managers were to pay Doggett one third of the £600 given by Booth for the stock, less two thirds of the £233 which still remained in his possession. At the same time the Master in Chancery was to draw up articles of agreement for the regulation of the company—similar to the articles of March 10, 1709—and was to insert a special clause freeing Doggett from the obligation to act tragic parts. Within fourteen days Doggett was to sign the articles and return to the theatre. But if he refused to sign he was to be paid £600 for his interest in the stock and permanently excluded from the management [Chancery Decrees and Orders, 1715 A, pp. 180, 212; 1716 A, p. 226; Masters Reports, Vol. 335 (1716)].

Doggett apparently found the decision acceptable, for he returned to the stage on March 18, 1717. . . . But—possibly when the articles were drafted—he changed his mind: accepted the £600 and severed all connection with Drury Lane [after considering Cibber's version of this, and Victor's (in this edition, pp. 278-81, 286-87 and n.) Barker, in a note on p. 96, states " ... the Chancery records suggest that there was a connection between the court decision and Doggett's return to the stage"].

II   From *The Laureat*, pp. 80-81

Some Time before *Dogget abdicated his Post in the Government of the Stage (*as our wise Author has it) there was left in his Hand 200£ by his Brethren *Wilks* and *Cibber*, as a Deposit to defray any extraordinary incidental Charges; and it was agreed among them, that this Sum, nor any Part of it, should be disposed without the general Consent, without the joint Agreement of these three *Managers*. Now, upon *Dogget's* Separation, this Sum remain'd intire in his Hands; but, when upon this Occasion, *Wilks* and *Cibber* came to withdraw their Share of the 200£, the *Comedian* twisted his ridiculous Muscles, shook his Head, snuffed, and after some Pause, told them very gravely, That he could not deliver any Part of the Money; for that they knew very well, it was left in his Hands, not to be parted with, unless they *all three* consented: Now, says he, I am *one* of the *three*, and *I do not consent to part with this Money*, or with any Part of it. They stared, and desired he wou'd repeat his Words; for they thought, from the Particularity of his Answer, that they misunderstood him; And when they found he was in earnest, in this subtile and equable Distinction, in his own Favour, they told him, his Reasoning was so ridiculous, it hardly deserved an Answer; but that, if he thought it proper to expose himself, by consulting his Friends upon it, they wou'd wait a Day or two for his Resolution: And it was some Time, before he cou'd persuade himself, or be persuaded to pay them; and they were apprehensive they should be obliged to desire the Equity of the Lord *Chancellor* to interpose on this silly Occasion.

III   From R. W. Lowe's edition of the *Apology*, II, 148-49 n.

The dates regarding this quarrel with Dogget are very difficult to fix satisfactorily. In the collection of Mr. Francis Harvey of St. James's Street are some valuable letters by Dogget in connection with this matter. From these, and from Mr. Percy Fitzgerald's "New History" (i, 352-358), I have made up a list of dates, which, however I give with all reserve. We know from "The Laureat" that Dogget had some funds of the theatre in his hands when he ceased acting, and this fact makes a Petition by Cibber and Wilks, that he should account with them for money, intelligible. This is dated 16th January, 1714—it cannot be 1713, as Mr. Fitzgerald says, for Booth was not admitted then, and the quarrel had not arisen. Then follows a Petition from Cibber, Booth, and Wilks, dated 5th February, 1714, praying the Chamberlain to settle the dispute.

Petitions by Dogget bear date 17th April, 1714; and, I think, 14th June, 1714. Mr. Fitzgerald gives this latter date as 14th January, 1714, and certainly the date on the document itself is more like "jan" than "June"; but in the course of the Petition Dogget says that the season will end in a few days, which seems to fix June as the correct month. The season 1713-14 ended 18th June, 1714. Next comes a Petition that Dogget should be compelled to act if he was to draw his share of the profits, which is dated 3rd November, 1714. In this case we are on sure ground, for the Petition is preserved among the Lord Chamberlain's Papers. Another Petition by Dogget, in which he talks of his being forced into Westminster Hall to obtain his rights, is dated "Jan.ye 6 1714," that is, 1715. After this, legal action was no doubt commenced, as related by Cibber.

APPENDIX D

On Audiences in the Theater

From *An Apology for the Life of Mr. T. ... C. ..., Comedian*
(London, 1740) p. 27

But notwithstanding all I have said, and my Father before me, the Profession of a Player still continues, as by his Memoirs I find it has always done, to be held by many Gentlemen and People of Quality in no great Esteem; and many outragious Insults have been committed by Persons who would be thought Gentlemen, or Actors, whom they dar'd not have us'd so in any other Place but a Theatre. But these Insulters of *Audiences*, as well as *Players*, are not to be rul'd; there is no contending with them; they are all Patriots, Liberty and Property; Men who roar out to defend their *Magna Charta*, of doing what they will in a Theatre. This Usage of Players Mr. *Cibber* says, "keeps young People of Sense from coming on the Stage; they fear entering into a Society, whose Institution, if not abus'd, is an excellent School of Morality: But alas! as *Shakespeare* says:

> "Where's that Palace where into sometimes
> "Foul Things intrude not?"
> [cited in *Apology*, pp. 49-50]

And really the Abuse of the Stage by the Actors, be it as great as it will, by acting indiscreetly in their private Lives, it is not greater than the Abuse that those noisy Rioters make of it by their publick Disturbances: I cannot apprehend what rational Authority this *Society for the Reformation of Theatrical Manners* can plead, to call an Actor to an account on the Stage for what he has done off it: Would an Judge pay less Regard to a Counsellor's Argument at the Bar, because he may be an indiscreet, or even a bad Man at home?—But it is otherwise at our Theatric Bar of Judgment; our *Judges* are also *Jury*, and likewise Executioners; and though you appear there not as your own Person, they make you the *Culprit*, put you immediately on your Trial,—and *G--d send you a good Deliverance.*—But I may say what I will against these unjust, unlimited Insults, yet the Player who falls under such a Caprice of publick Displeasure, must be left *adrift, and ride out the Storm as well as he is able* [*Apology*, p. 57].

APPENDIX E

On Thomas Betterton's Acting

From *The Laureat*, pp. 30-32.

But at last both Companies united in 1684. And here he enters on the Character of *Betterton*, who was most certainly the compleatest Actor we ever could boast of; he had the largest Compass of Action; he could throw himself into many and quite opposite and different Shapes, from *Peircy* to *Falstaff*, from *Othello* to *Thercites*, from *Brutus* to *Sir Solomon Single*, &c. And here our *Apologist* talking of this great Actor in the Part of *Hamlet*, chuses to introduce his *Eulogium* on him, by his first Attack upon Mr. *Wilks*. *You have seen*, says he, *an* Hamlet, *who on the first appearance of his Father's Spirit, threw himself into strange Vociferations, expressing Rage and Fury; and he has been applauded.* Wilks play'd this part with great decency and Justness, and always with the general approbation of the Audience. If in some Places he wanted that Strength of Voice and Dignity of Aspect, that Mr. *Bayes* has seen in Betterton, this is only saying, that he had not his Person and Voice, that he was not *Betterton*; therefore here, I think, Sir, you went out of your Way, purely to make an invidious Reflection. Your Observation upon Mr. *Booth* too, (tho' it should be true) is not quite so tender a one as it ought to have been on a deceas'd Brother: you say, he sometimes *heavily dragg'd the Sentiment along like a dead Weight, with a long-ton'd Voice*, (he means drawling out his Words) *and absent Eye, as if they had fairly forgot what they were about.*

And here I submit my self to the Indulgence of my Reader for a short Digression: I have lately been told by a Gentleman who has frequently seen Mr. *Betterton* perform this Part of *Hamlet*, that he has observ'd his Countenance (which was naturally ruddy and sanguin) in this Scene of the fourth Act, where his Father's Ghost appears, thro' the violent and sudden Emotions of Amazement and Horror, turn instantly on the Sight of his Father's Spirit, as pale as his Neckcloath, when every Article of his Body seem'd to be affected with a Tremor inexpressible; so that, had his Father's Ghost actually risen before him; he could not have been seized with more real Agonies; and this was felt so strongly by the Audience, that the Blood seemed to shudder in their Veins likewise, and they in some Measure partook of the Astonishment and Horror, with which they saw this excellent Actor affected. And when *Hamlet* utters this line, upon the Ghost's leaving the Stage, (in Answer to his Mother's impatient Enquiry into the Occasion of his Disorder, and what he sees)—*See—where he goes—ev'n now—out at the Portal*: The whole Audience hath remain'd in a dead Silence for near a Minute, and then,——as if recovering all at once from their Astonishment, have joined as one Man, in a Thunder of universal Applause. And yet, the same Gentleman assured me, he has seen Mr. *Betterton*, more than once, play this Character to an Audience of twenty Pounds, or under.

APPENDIX F

Aaron Hill on Cibber as a Fop

From *The Prompter*, 19 November 1734[1]

As to his person, his shape was finely proportioned yet not graceful, easy but not striking. Though it was reported by his enemies that he wanted a soul, yet it was visible enough that he had one, because he carried it in his countenance; for his features were narrowly earnest, and attentively insignificant. There was a peeping pertness in his eye, which would have been spirit had his heart been warmed with humanity or his brain been stored with ideas. In his face was a contracted kind of passive yet protruded sharpness, like a pig half roasted; and a voice not unlike his own might have been borrowed from the same suffering animal while in a condition a little less desperate. With all these comic accomplishments of person, he had an air and a mind which completed the risible talent, insomuch that, when he represented a ridiculous humour, he had a mouth in every nerve and became eloquent without speaking. His attitudes were pointed and exquisite, and his expression was stronger than painting; he was beautifully absorbed by the character, and demanded and monopolized attention; his very extravagances were colored with propriety; and affectation sat so easy about him that it was in danger of appearing amiable.

---

[1]The capitalization and spelling of the original have not been followed.

APPENDIX G

Biographical Appendix

In the course of the *Apology* Cibber names a great many persons: it seems clearly unnecessary to identify the most famous—Dryden, Robert Walpole, or the Earl of Chesterfield. Lesser political, governmental, artistic, and ecclesiastical figures, who appear only fleetingly, I have identified in the explanatory notes (cf. Preface, p. vii) because the reader needs the information at hand in order to understand Cibber's point. For figures who reappear throughout the book, dates (when available) and minimal identification are provided in this appendix. Identifications of the most important figures in the *Apology* are brief, because Cibber's own account is cumulatively quite full. Of the very minor figures often little more is known than what he supplies. Because most of the dramatists are mentioned only as authors of plays, not as *personae* in the narrative, only brief identification has been provided. [Lowe reprinted Bellchambers' biographical notes, but the information contained in them was drawn on (especially the eighteenth-century works listed on pp. xiv-xvii). I have checked my information against the standard biographical references, viz., the *DNB*, and *Grove's Dictionary of Music and Musicians*.]

ASHBURY, Joseph (1638-1720). P. 97. In 1662 became Deputy Master of the Revels. In 1682 became Master of the Revels and a Patentee of the theater. An excellent actor best known for comic roles.

BARRY, Elizabeth (1658-1713). P. 59. Actress. Reared as charge of Lady D'Avenant, received good education, sponsored in her stage career by the Earl of Rochester, who was probably her lover. Showed little promise at first but became famous in comedy.

BEHN, Mrs. Afra (1640-1689). P. 113. English dramatist and novelist. Lived from childhood to 1658 in Surinam, West Indies. Wrote *Oroonoko* which was the basis of Southerne's tragedy. Wrote a series of comic plays for the stage, *The Rover* (1677), *Forc'd Marriage* (1671).

BETTERTON, Mrs. Mary Saunderson (died c. 1712). P. 59. Gave dramatic lessons to Queen Mary and Queen Anne and to the Duchess of Marlborough. Married Thomas Betterton c. 1662. Became insane after her husband's death in 1710.

BETTERTON, Thomas (1635?-1710). P. 52. Actor. Joined D'Avenant's company in 1661. One of the greatest and most influential actors of his period.

BOOTH, Barton (1681-1733). P. 3. Son of a Lancashire squire, instead of attending Cambridge, entered the theater in Ireland. Came to England at the turn of the century, became known as a tragic actor. The original Cato. Extremely popular with the aristocracy.

BRACEGIRDLE, Anne (1663-1748). P. 52. Actress. Noted for her upright character, she retired from the stage in 1707. Associated with Congreve's heroines.

BULLOCK, Christopher (1690?-1724). Actor and dramatist. Played the class of character for rival companies which Cibber played.

BULLOCK, William (1657?-1740?). P. 113. Actor. Father of Christopher.

BUTLER, Charlotte, P. 59 (active 1660-1692), actress and singer.

CIBBER, Caius Gabriel (1630-1700). P. 5. Sculptor, father of Colley. Born in Holstein, son of the King of Denmark's cabinet-maker. Studied modeling in Rome. Spent major portion of his career in England.

CIBBER, Theophilus (1703-1758). Wastrel son of Colley. Actor and playwright. Object of much satire. Drowned in the Irish Sea.

COLLIER, Jeremy (1650-1726). P. 158. Non-juring clergyman. Educated at Cambridge. Noted primarily for his severe attacks on the stage. Became an outlaw for absolving Sir John Friend and Sir William Parkyns, who had attempted to assassinate King William. Was consecrated non-juring bishop in 1713.

CROWNE, John (1640?-1703?). P. 316. Restoration dramatist. A favorite with Charles II. Most popular play, *Sir Courtly Nice* (1685).

DANCOURT, Florent (1662-1725). P. 185. French Dramatist. Wrote comedies of manners, of which the most famous are *Le Chevalier a la mode* and *Les Bourgeoises de qualite*.

D'AVENANT, Charles (1656-1714). Son of Sir William. Political economist. Appointed by James II licenser of plays. Inspector General of exports and imports.

D'AVENANT, Sir William (1606-1668). P. 53. Poet, dramatist, theatrical organizer. Produced operas despite Puritan prohibition (after 1656); because of services to Crown enormously influential in Restoration theater.

DOGGET or DOGGETT, Thomas (d. 1721). P. 93. Actor. Born in Dublin. First appeared in London in 1691 as Nincompoop in D'Urfey's *Love for Money*. Became actor-manager in 1709-10.

DOWNES, John (d. 1710). P. 238. Prompter for acting companies from 1662 until 1706. Wrote *Roscius Anglicanus, or An Historical Review of the Stage*, important source for Restoration theater.

D'URFEY, Thomas (1653-1723). P. 98. Famous as writer of occasional verse, songs, and a few plays.

ELRINGTON, Thomas (1688-1732). Actor. Rival of Cibber. Became Deputy Master of the Revels c. 1713.

ESTCOURT, Richard (1668-1712). P. 69. Actor and dramatist. Began career in Dublin. Later succeeded on London stage as comedian despite Cibber's low opinion of him.

FARINELLI, Carlo Broschi (1705-1782). P. 225. Italian *castrato*, most famous singer of his day. Went to England in 1734. Moved to Spain in 1737 where he wielded great influence on Philip V and Ferdinand VI. Exiled to Bologna with large income by Charles III.

FENWICK, Sir John (1645?-1697). P. 230. Conspirator against King William in 1689, pardoned. Planned another assassination, was caught, and beheaded 28 January 1696.

FLEETWOOD, Charles (? - ?). P. 163. Possibly a descendent of the English Parliamentarian general.

GOODMAN, Cardell (1649?-1699). P. 57. Actor and adventurer. A paramour of the Duchess of Cleveland, he was dismissed for having attempted to poison her children. When implicated in a plot to assassinate William III, he fled to France where he was supported by those against whom he had escaped testifying.

GRIFFIN, Captain Benjamin (1680-1740). P. 52. Actor and dramatist. Noted primarily for character parts.

GWYN, Eleanor (1650-1687). Actress and mistress to Charles II. Began career as orange vendor. Trained for stage by Charles Hart, a lover. Retired from stage in 1682.

HAINES, Joseph (d. 1701). P. 159. Dancer and actor, but most famous for prologues and epilogues delivered under strange conditions, as a madman or seated upon an ass.

HART, Charles (d. 1683). P. 55. Actor. First lover of Nell Gwyn.

HILL, Aaron (1685-1750). P. 252. Critic of stage, historian of the Ottoman Empire (1709), and projector. Unsuccessful playwright; author of the libretto of Handel's *Rinaldo*.

HORDEN, Hildebrand (d. 1696). P. 174. Actor. Played in original production of Cibber's *Love's Last Shift*. Killed in Brawl at the Rose Tavern, Covent Garden, by Colonel Burgess.

JOHNSON, Benjamin (1665?-1742). P. 179. Character actor. Assumed Dogget's roles at his retirement.

KEEN, Theophilus (d. 1719). P. 189. Actor from 1695-1719. Noted for 'majesty' (Lowe, II, 365).

KILLIGREW, Henry (1613-1700). P. 53. Dramatist. Patentee of Drury Lane Theatre.

KYNASTON, Edward (1640?-1706). P. 59. Actor, one of the last to play female roles. Later played male roles of lesser importance. Retired 1699.

LEE, Nathaniel (1653?-1692). P. 63. Dramatist. Wrote heroic plays in rhymed couplets (*Gloriana* and *Sophonisba*, 1676) and his most famous in blank verse, *The Rival Queens, or The Death of Alexander the Great*.

LEIGH, Anthony (d. 1692). P. 59. Comic actor, popular with Restoration court.

LEIGH, Mrs. Elinor. P. 59. Wife of Anthony Leigh. Actress of distinction.

LEIGH, Francis. P. 293. Son of Anthony Leigh. One of the actors who broke down the doors of Drury Lane on 14 June 1710 and who deserted Lincoln's Inn Fields in 1714. Ceased acting in 1719.

MILLS, John (d. 1736). P. 151. Actor. Noted for the large number of roles he played.

MIST, Nathaniel (d. 1737). P. 292. Printer. A Jacobite who published a newspaper under a series of titles, noted for its furious attacks on Hanoverian governments. For these he was arrested and punished severely a number of times.

MOHUN, Michael (1620?-1684). P. 57. Actor of great ability. One of the two major figures of the Restoration stage, along with Hart. Much admired by Dryden and Rochester.

MOUNTFORT, Mrs. Susanna. P. 59. See Susanne Verbruggen.

MOUNTFORT, William (1664?-1692). P. 52. Actor and dramatist. Unsuccessful in writing tragedy, succeeded in comedy, *Greenwich Park* (1691). Was stabbed by Captain Richard Hill on his own doorstep 9 December 1692.

NICOLINI (Nicolino GRIMALDI) (b. 1673?). P. 223. Italian male contralto. Important figure in development of taste for Italian opera in England in the first quarter of the eighteenth century. Retired to Venice.

NOKES, James (d. 1692?). P. 59. Popular Restoration comedian.

OLDFIELD, Anne (1683-1730). P. 3. Important actress.

OTWAY, Thomas (1652-1685). P. 95. Dramatist. Most important play, *Venice Preserved* (1681-82). Said to have been in love with Mrs. Barry, who refused his suit. Extremely popular in his own time.

PACK, George. P. 293. Actor and singer (career, 1700-1724).

PINKETHMAN or PENKETHMAN, William (d. 1725), P. 89. Actor. Noted for playing to the groundlings and departures from script.

PORTER, Mary (d. 1765). P. 287. Popular actress. Life free of scandal.

POWEL or POWELL, George (1658?-1714). P. 93. Actor and dramatist. Acting career from 1687 intermittently until his death. Known for disruptive drinking.

ROGERS, Mrs. (? - ?). P. 189. Nothing further is known of her.

ROWE, Nicholas (1674-1718). P. 180. Important dramatist, known for tragedies (*The Ambitious Stepmother*, 1700; *The Fair Penintent,* 1703). Edited Shakespeare in 1709. A Whig, named Poet Laureate by George I.

SANTLOW or SANTLOE, Hester (d. 1778). P. 246. Dancer and actress. Married Barton Booth, after she had been mistress of the Duke of Marlborough and Secretary Craggs.

SANDFORD, Samuel (d. 1705?). P. 59. Actor. Famous for villain roles.

SENESINO (Francesco BERNARDI) (1680?-1750). P. 225. Italian male mezzo-soprano. Associated with Handel, both in opera and in oratorio from c. 1720 to c. 1735. Retired to Sienna, his birthplace, a rich man.

SMITH (actor), (d. 1696). P. 49. Important Restoration actor.

SOUTHERNE, Thomas (1660-1746). P. 123. Dramatist. Friend of Dryden. *Oroonoko*, or *The Royal Slave* (1696), his most noted play, was extremely popular.

SUBLIGNY, Mlle. (d. 1736?). P. 180. French dancer, career from c. 1681-1705 (Lowe, I, 316).

SWINEY (MACSWINEY), Owen (1680-1754). P. 188. Impresario and theater manager. Instrumental in development of Italian opera in England.

TOFTS, Catherine (d. 1756). P. 225. Singer. First person of English birth to sing Italian opera in England. Sang important roles from 1704 until c. 1709 when she became insane. She was cured temporarily and married Mr. Joseph Smith, afterwards English consul at Venice, where her illness returned. She remained there until her death.

UNDERHILL, Cave (1634-1710). P. 59. Famous for comic roles from 1661 to c. 1695.

VALENTINI (Valentino URBANI). (? - ?). P. 185. Italian soprano *castrato*. Came to England c. 1707. Influential in raising prestige of Italian opera.

VERBRUGGEN, John (1668?-1707?). P. 93. Actor. Known for dissipated personal life and rough, but competent acting style.

VERBRUGGEN, Susanne (1667-1703). P. 175. Comedienne. Married William Mountfort in 1682. Married John Verbruggen in 1693 after Mountfort's murder the previous year. Finest actress of comic parts during the Restoration.

WILKS, Robert (1665?-1732). P. 3. Actor-manager.

WILLIAMS, Joseph (d. 1700). P. 93. Actor. On stage from c. 1673. Competent actor but undependable because of his heavy drinking.

A SELECTED BIBLIOGRAPHY

Aitken, George A. *The Life of Richard Steele*, 2 vols. (London, 1889).

Allen, Robert J. *The Clubs of Augustan London* (Cambridge, Mass., 1933).

An Apology for the Life of Mr. T... C..., Comedian (London: J. Mechell, 1740).

Ashley, Leonard R. N. "The Theatre Royal in Drury Lane, 1711-16, under Colley Cibber, Barton Booth, and Robert Wilks," (unpub. Doct. Diss., Princeton University, 1956 [Abstract in *DA*, 1957, XVII, 625]).

Ault, Norman. *New Light on Pope* (London, 1949).

Avery, E. L. "Cibber, King John and the Students of the Law," *MLN*, LIII (1938).

_____. "'The Craftsman' of July 2, 1737 and Cibber," *Washington State College Research Studies*, VII (1939).

_____. "Foreign Performers in the London Theatres in the Early Eighteenth Century," *Philological Quarterly*, XVI (1937).

Baker, David Erskine. *Biographia Dramatica*, or, *A Companion to the Playhouse*, 2 vols. (London, Printed for Messrs. Rivingtons, 1782).

Baker, Sheridan. "Political Allusion in Fielding's *Authors' Farce, Mock Doctor*, and *Tumbledown Dick*," PMLA, lxxvii (1962), 221-31.

Barker, Richard Hindry. *Mr. Cibber of Drury Lane* (New York, 1939).

[Betterton, Thomas]. *A History of the English Stage* (London, 1741).

A Blast upon Bays, or, *A New Lick at the Laureat*, 2nd ed. (London, Printed for T. Rabbins, 1742).

Bond, Richmond P. *English Burlesque Poetry 1700-1750* (Cambridge, 1932).

Boys, Richard C., ed. *Studies in the Literature of the Augustan Age* (Ann Arbor, 1952).

British Historical Portraits: A Selection from the National Portrait Gallery, with Biographical Notes (Cambridge, 1957).

Broadus, E. K. *The Laureateship: A Study of the Office of Poet Laureate in England* (Oxford, 1921).

Burnet, Gilbert. *History of His Own Time*, 2 vols. (London, 1724-34).

Carritt, C. F. *A Calendar of British Taste 1600-1800* (London, n.d.).

[Chetwood, William Rufus]. *The British Theatre*, containing *The Lives of the English Dramatic Poets* ... to which is prefixed a Short View of the Rise ... of the English Stage (Dublin, Printed for Peter Wilson, 1750).

_____. *A General History of the Stage* (London, Printed for W. Owen, 1749).

The Dramatic Works of Colley Cibber, Esq., 5 vols. (London, Printed for W. Feales, 1736).

Cibber, Colley. *The Egoist:* or, *Colley upon Cibber* (London, Printed by W. Lewis, 1743).

_____. *A Letter From Mr. Cibber to Mr. Pope, Inquiring into the Motives that Might Induce Him in His Satyrical Works, to be so frequently Fond of Mr. Cibber's Name* (London, 1742).

_____. *A Second Letter from Mr. Cibber to Mr. Pope* (London, Printed for A. Dodd, 1743).

Cibber, Theophilus. *The Lives and Characters of the most Eminent Actors and Actresses of Great Britain and Ireland*, Part I (London, Printed for R. Griffiths, 1753).

_____. *The Lives of the Poets of Great Britain and Ireland to the Time of Dean Swift,* 5 vols. (London, Printed for R. Griffiths, 1753).

Collier, Jeremy. *A Short View of the Immorality and Profaneness of the English Stage* (London, 1698).

A Comparison Between the Two Stages: A Late Restoration Book of the Theatre, ed. Staring B. Wells (Princeton, 1942).

The Complete Works of William Congreve, ed. Montague Summers, 4 vols. (London, 1923).

Davies, Thomas. *Dramatic Miscellanies*, consisting of Critical Observations on several Plays of Shakespeare, 3 vols. (London, printed for the Author, 1785).

_____. *Memoirs of the Life of David Garrick, Esq.*, 3rd ed., 2 vols. (London, Printed for the Author, 1781).

The Critical Works of John Dennis, ed. E. N. Hooker (Baltimore, 1939).

Dobree, Bonamy. *Alexander Pope* (London, 1949).

Downer, Alan S. "Nature to Advantage Dressed: eighteenth-century acting," *PMLA*, LVIII (1943), 1002-37.

Downes, John. *Roscius Anglicanus*, ed. Montague Summers (London, n.d.).

_____. *Roscius Anglicanus, or an Historical Review of the Stage*, with additions by Thomas Davies (London, Printed for the editor, 1789), printed in *The Literary Museum*; or, *A Selection of Scarce Old Tracts*, ed. F. G. Waldron (London, Printed for the editor, 1792).

The Letters of John Dryden, with Letters Addressed to him, ed. Charles E. Ward (Durham, N.C., 1942).

The Poetical Works of John Dryden, ed. G. R. Noyes (Cambridge, Mass., 1909).

The Prologues and Epilogues of John Dryden: a Critical Edition by William Bradford Gardner (New York, 1951).

The Works of John Dryden, ed. Sir Walter Scott, 2nd ed., 18 vols. (Edinburgh, 1821).

Dudden, F. Homes. *Henry Fielding: His Life, Works and Times*, 2 vols. (Oxford, 1952).

Egerton, William. *Faithful Memoirs of the Life, Amours and Performances of … Mrs. Anne Oldfield* (London, 1731).

Elledge, Scott, ed. *Eighteenth-Century Critical Essays*, 2 vols. (Ithaca, 1961).

Ewen, David. *Encyclopedia of Opera* (New York, 1955).

Faber, Harold. *Caius Gabriel Cibber* (Oxford, 1926).

Fielding, Henry. *The Adventures of Joseph Andrews*, ed. J. Paul DeCastro (London, 1929).

Foord, Archibald S. *His Majesty's Opposition: 1714-1830* (Oxford, 1964).

Gardner, William Bradford. "George Hickes and the Origin of the Bangorian Controverys," *SP*, XXXIX (1942), 65-78.

The Letters of David Garrick, ed. David M. Little and George M. Kahul, Associate Editor Phoebe deK. Wilson, 3 vols. (Cambridge, Mass., 1963).

Genest, John. *Some Account of the English Stage, from 1660-1830*, 10 vols. (Bath, 1832).

George, M. Dorothy. *English Political Caricature: A Study of Opinion and Propaganda to 1792* (Oxford, n.d.).

[Gildon, Charles]. *The Life of Mr. Thomas Betterton* (London, Printed for Robert Gosling, 1710).

Goldstein, Malcolm. *Pope and the Augustan Stage* (Stanford, 1958).

Halsband, Robert. *The Life of Lady Mary Wortley Montagu* (Oxford, 1956).

Hill, Aaron. *The Actor: or, A Treatise on the Art of Playing* (London, Printed for R. Griffiths, 1750).

Hotson, Leslie. *The Commonwealth and Restoration Stage* (Cambridge, Mass., 1928).

Humphreys, A. R. *The Augustan World* (New York, n.d.).

Jack, Ian. *Augustan Satire: Intention and Idiom in English Poetry 1660-1750* (Oxford, 1950).

The Poems of Samuel Johnson, ed. David Nichol Smith and Edward L. McAdam (Oxford, 1941).

Johnson, T. *The Tryal of Colley Cibber, Comedian, etc.* (London, Printed for the Author, 1740).

Kernan, Alvin. *The Cankered Muse* (New Haven, 1959).

Langbaine, Gerard. *The Lives and Characters of the English Dramatic Poets* (London, Printed for Tho. Leigh [1699]).

The Laureat: or, the Right Side of Colley Cibber, Esq. ... To which is added, The HISTORY of the Life, Manners and Writings of AESOPUS the Tragedian (London, Printed for J. Roberts, 1740).

Lehrer, Francis C. *The Literary Views of Colley Cibber,* Unpublished Doctoral Dissertation, University of Wisconsin, 1955 (Abstract in Summaries of Doctoral Dissertations, University of Wisconsin, 1956, XVI, 544-45).

Loftis, John. *The Politics of Drama in Augustan England* (Oxford, 1963).

_____. *Steele at Drury Lane* (Berkeley, 1952).

_____. "Steele and the Drury Lane Patent," *Modern Language Notes*, LXIV (1949), 19-21.

The London Stage: 1660-1800: Part 2, 1700-1729, ed. Emmett L. Avery (1960); Part 3, 1729-1747, ed. Arthur Scouten (1961), Carbondale, Ill.

Lowe, Robert W. *A Bibliographical Account of English Theatrical Literature* (London, 1888).

_____. *Thomas Betterton* (London, 1891).

Luttrell, Narcissus. *A Brief Historical Relation of State Affairs from September 1678 to April 1714*, 6 vols. (Oxford, 1857).

Neale, J. E. *Queen Elizabeth* (Garden City, N. Y. 1934).

Nicoll, Allardyce. *The Development of the Theatre* (New York, 1927).

_____. *A History of English Drama: 1660-1900*; Vol. I, *Restoration Drama*, 4th ed. (Cambridge, 1961); Vol. II, *Early Eighteenth Century Drama*, 3rd ed. (Cambridge, 1961).

Ogg, David. *England in the Reign of Charles II*, 2 vols. (Oxford, 1955).

_____. *England in the Reigns of James II and William III* (Oxford, 1955).

_____. *William III* (London, 1956).

[Oldys, William]. *The History of the English Stage, including the Lives, Characters and Amours of the Most Eminent Actors and Actresses with Instructions for Public Speaking* by Thomas Betterton (Boston, Printed for William S. and Henry Spear, 1814).

Peterson, William M. "Pope and Cibber: *The Non-Juror*," MLN, LXX (1955), 332-35.

_____. *Sir Robert Walpole: The King's Minister* (London, 1960).

_____. *Sir Robert Walpole: The Making of a Statesman* (London, 1956).

The Correspondence of Alexander Pope, ed. George Sherburn, 5 vols (Oxford, 1956).

The Twickenham Edition of the Poems of Alexander Pope, General Editor John Butt, 6 vols. (New Haven [1951-62]).

The Present State of the Stage in Great Britain and Ireland and the *Theatrical Characters of the Principal Performers* (London, Printed for Paul Vaillant, 1753).

Price, Martin. *To the Palace of Wisdom* (New York, 1964).

Rosenfeld, S. "The Wardrobe of Lincoln's Inn Fields and Covent Garden," *Theatre Notebook*, V (1951).

The Scribleriad. Being an Epistle to the Dunces. On Renewing their Attack upon Mr. Pope under their Leader the Laureat (1742).

Senior, Dorothy. *The Life and Times of Colley Cibber* (London, 1928).

Sherburn, George. "The Fortunes and Misfortunes of *Three Hours After Marriage*," Mod. Phil., XXIV (1926-27), 99 ff.

Smith, Dane F. *Plays about the Theatre in England from the Rehearsal in 1671 to the Licensing Act in 1737* (New York, 1936).

Smithers, Peter. *The Life of Joseph Addison* (Oxford, 1954).

The Spectator, ed. Gregory Smith, 4 vols. (London, n.d.).

Spence, Joseph. *Anecdotes, Observations and Characters of Books and Men*, ed. Samuel Weller Singer (London, 1820).

The Correspondence of Richard Steele, ed. Rae Blanchard (Oxford, 1941).

Steele, Richard. *Mr. Steele's Apology for Himself and His Writings* (London, 1714).

_____. *The Theatre*: 1720, ed. John Loftis (Oxford, 1962).

Sutherland, James. *Background for Queen Anne* (London, 1939).

_____. *English Satire* (Cambridge, 1958).

The Correspondence of Jonathan Swift, ed. Harold Williams, 3 vols. pub. (Oxford, 1963).

Swift's Poems, ed. Harold Williams (Oxford, 1958).

The Tatler, 4 vols. (London, 1797).

The Tatler, ed. George A. Aitken, 4 vols. (London, 1898).

Taylor, Houghton W. "Fielding upon Cibber," *MP*, XXIX (1931), 73-90.

_____. "Fielding and the Cibbers," *PQ*, I (1922), 278-89.

The Temple of Dullness With the Humours of Signor Capochio and Signora Dovinna (London, Printed for J. Watts, 1745).

Theatrical Records, or, *An Account of English Dramatic Authors and their Works* (London, Printed for R. and J. Dodsley, 1756).

Thomson, James. *Letters and Documents*, ed. A. D. McKillop (1958).

Tillotson, Geoffrey. *Augustan Studies* (London, 1961).

_____. *Essays in Criticism and Research* (Cambridge, 1942).

_____. *Pope and Human Nature* (Oxford, 1958).

Tucker, Susie I. "A Note on Colley Cibber's Name," *Notes and Queries*, VI (N.S.), 400.

Tupper, Fred S. "Colley and Caius Cibber," *MLN*, LV (1940), 393-96.

Turner, F. C. *James II* (London, 1948).

Universal Spectator, August 7, 14, 21, reprinted in *Gentleman's Magazine*, August 1742 and *London Magazine*, August 1742.

The Complete Works of Sir John Vanbrugh, ed. B. Dobree and G. Webb, 4 vols. (1927-28).

Victor, Benjamin. *The History of the Theatres of London and Dublin*, 2 vols (London, Printed for T. Davies, 1761); Vol. 3, *The History of the Theatres of London* (London, Printed for T. Becket, 1771).

Villiers, George, Duke of Buckingham. *The Rehearsal*, ed. Montague Summers (Stratford-upon-Avon, 1914).

The Letters of Horace Walpole, Fourth Earl of Oxford, ed. Paget Toynbee, 16 vols. (Oxford, 1903).

Wickham, Glynne. *Early English Stages: 1300-1660*, Part I, 2 vols. (London, 1963).

Wiley, Autry Nell, ed. *Rare Prologues and Epilogues: 1642-1700* (London, [1940]).

Wilson, John Harold. *Nell Gwyn: Royal Mistress* (New York, 1952).

Winton, Calhoun. *Captain Steele: The Early Career of Richard Steele* (Baltimore, 1964).

Wood, Frederick T. "A Letter of Colley Cibber," *Notes and Queries*, CXCI (1946), 15.

Wright, Austin. *Joseph Spence: A Critical Biography* (Chicago, 1950).

B

A Bibliographic Description of the
Editions of the *Apology* in 1740

A. *First Edition*:

TITLE: AN/ APOLOGY/ FOR THE/ LIFE/ OF/ Mr. COLLEY CIBBER, Comedian, / AND/ Late PATENTEE of the *Theatre-Royal./ With an Historical View of the* STAGE *during his* OWN TIME./ [Rule]/ WRITTEN BY HIMSELF./ [Rule]/ —*Hoc est/ Vivere bis, vitâ posse priore frui.* Mart. lib. 2./ *When Years no more of active Life retain,/ 'Tis Youth renew'd, to laugh 'em o'er again.* Anonym./ [Double rule]/ *LONDON:*/ Printed by JOHN WATTS for the AUTHOR./ [Half rule centered]/ M DCC XL.

Collation: Quarto. [portrait]; A^4, a^4, B-Z^4, Aa-Xx^4, Yy^1. pp. [portrait] + [1-16 unpaged] + [1]-346. 182 leaves.

Contents: [engraved portrait of Cibber]; [A] la title; [A] lb blank; A2a-[a]2a dedication; [a]2b blank; [a]3a-4b contents; B-Z^4, Aa-Xx^4, Yy^1 text.

Copy: Beinecke Rare Book and Manuscript Library.

Notes: Published 7 April 1740.

B. *Second Edition*:

TITLE: AN/ APOLOGY [In red]/ FOR THE/ LIFE/ OF/ *Mr*. COLLEY CIBBER, *Comedian,/* AND/ Late PATENTEE of the *Theatre-Royal./ With an Historical View of the* STAGE *during/ his* OWN TIME./ [Rule]/ WRITTEN BY HIMSELF. [In red]/ [Rule]/ —*Hoc est/ Vivere bis, vita posse priore frui.* Mart. lib. 2./ *When Years no more of active Life retain,/ 'Tis Youth renew'd, to laugh 'em o'er again.* Anonym./ [Rule]/ The SECOND EDITION./ [Double rule]/ *LONDON*: [In red]/ Printed by JOHN WATTS for the AUTHOR:/ And Sold by W. LEWIS in *Russell-Street,* near/ *Convent-Garden./* [Half rule centered]/ MDCCXL.

Collation: 8vo. A^8, a^4, B-Z^8, Aa-Hh^8, Ii^5. pp. [1-12 unpaged] + [1]-488 + [blank, unpaged]. 257 leaves.

Contents: [A]1a title; [A]1b blank; A2a-[A]8a dedication; [A]8b blank; a1a-a4a contents; a4b blank; B1a-Yy4b text; Yy5 a and b blank.

Copy: McCormick Library, Washington and Lee University.

Notes: This edition contains several revisions probably by Cibber himself (cf. preface to the present edition). In accidentals, however, it is inferior as a text to the first edition. Published 14 May 1740.

C. *The Dublin Edition*:

TITLE: AN/ APOLOGY / FOR THE/ LIFE/ OF/ Mr. COLLEY CIBBER, Comedian,/ AND/ Late PATENTEE of the *Theatre-Royal./ With an Historical View of the* STAGE *during his/* OWN TIME./ [Rule]/ WRITTEN BY HIMSELF./ [Rule]/ *—Hoc est/ Vivere bis, vita posse priore frui.* Mart. lib. 2./ *When Years no more of active Life retain,/ 'Tis Youth renew'd, to laugh 'em o'er again.* Anonym./ [Rule]/ The Fourth EDITION./ [Rule]/ *DUBLIN:/* Re-printed by and for GEORGE FAULKNER,/ [Half rule centered]/ M DCC XL.

Collation: 12 mo. [A]^6, B-Z^6, Aa-Gg^6, [blank, unpaged]^1.

Copy: British Museum.

Notes: This edition was apparently hastily and carelessly set from the first London edition; the corrections in the 2nd ed. do not appear in it. Although the claim "Fourth Edition" suggests that the publisher made an attempt to deceive, there is evidence (cf. preface) that Cibber knew of Faulkner's publication of a Dublin edition. It is sometimes mistakenly referred to as an 8vo.